Cured, Fermented and Smoked Foods
Proceedings of the Oxford Symposium on Food and Cookery 2010

Cured, Fermented and Smoked Foods

Proceedings of the Oxford Symposium on Food and Cookery 2010

Edited by Helen Saberi

Prospect Books
2011

First published in Great Britain in 2011 by Prospect Books, Allaleigh House, Blackawton, Totnes, Devon, TQ9 7DL.

ISBN 978-1-903018-85-9

The illustration on the front cover is of Delicacies from Siam, 1883: peas, sea cucumber and glutinous rice, from the National Museum of Ethnology, Leiden; courtesy of Linda Roodenburg.
The illustration on the back cover is of dried fermented bamboo shoots; taken from the paper by Caroline Rowe.

Design and typesetting in Gill Sans and Adobe Garamond by Tom Jaine and Oliver Pawley.
Printed and bound in Great Britain by Jellyfish Solutions.

Contents

7

Foreword

The 2010 Symposium got off to a merry start on a bright summer evening with welcome drinks in the college garden followed by the presentation by Raymond Blanc of the winners of the Young Chef's Grant, all of whom were already hard at work on the preparations for a stupendous Feast of Cockaigne under the supervision of Tim Kelsey, Head Chef of the College kitchen, and guest-chef Jeremy Lee of The Blueprint Cafe in London's docklands.

The Symposium began in earnest, as always, first thing Saturday morning with a plenary session and opening remarks from our retiring Chair Carolin Young, newly-elected Chair Paul Levy and co-Chair Claudia Roden, with myself, Elisabeth Luard, taking on the role of Director previously filled by Carolin Young who acted as both Chair and Director. Practical business was then followed by the presentation of the Sophie Coe Prize of £1500 to Zona Spray Starks for a remarkable paper on 'Drying and Fermenting in the Arctic: Dictating Women's Roles in Alaska's Inupiat Culture'. Ken Albala received a special commendation for 'Cooking as Research Methodology: Experiments in Renaissance Cuisine'. Symposiasts were then treated to a distinguished appetizer by anthropologist Sidney Mintz, 'The Absent Third: the Place of Fermentation in a Thinkable World Food System', setting the scene for discussion of a subject which, while not immediately obvious when reading the label on the frozen ready-meal, is still deeply embedded in every culinary tradition on the planet. After the coffee-break, symposiasts crowded back into the Lecture Theatre to hear Harold McGee present 'A Chemical Introduction to Cured, Fermented and Smoked Foods'.

After the coffee-break and a chance to inspect the bookstalls, the choice of papers in the Symposium's three venues included the stories of *bacalao*, Afro-American foodways and, courtesy of presenter Renée Valeri, an open-air tasting of *surströmming*, Sweden's famous fermented herrings, a preparation so explosively pungent that travellers are forbidden to carry a tin of it onto a plane. Other subjects discussed in the morning sessions included preserved sausages in the classical world, Roman fish sauces, fermented fish seasonings in Japan and the Mediterranean, fermented taro in Africa and, elsewhere, Korean *kimchi* and food preservation in central Asia and Siberia.

Lunch was an exquisitely fiery Sichuanese feast delivered by Soho's Bar Shu organized by Symposium Trustee Fuchsia Dunlop, just back from researching foodways in central China. Parallel sessions then continued through the afternoon with papers on unidentified fermented foods gathering dust in the Museum of Ethnology in the Netherlands, preserved food in art, Transylvanian charcoal bread, Jewish pickles and their travels from Eastern Europe to the wilds of Canada, dried and fermented foods and the role of women in the culture of the Inupiat nation, the smoke-cured and fermented milk of Kenya's Samburu, an anthropological study of the use of fermented root-starch, enset, in Ethiopia.

After the tea-break, symposiasts returned to the fray for a study of *tempeh* followed by stinking bean-curd and rotten vegetable-stalks as a delicacy in Shaoxing; alternative sessions tackled bacterial fermentation as an unacknowledged taste-enhancer in historical recipes, fermentation as a useful tool in contemporary food-preparation, sourdough fermentation from the viewpoint of the microbe, and elsewhere symposiasts were treated to the smoky story of American shad-planking, Italy's oil-preserved sausages transferred to Utica in New York and the creation of a smoked-meat tradition in Montreal.

Saturday evening got off to a flying start with Tourism Ireland's specially filmed interviews on the farm with the producers who contributed their expertise (and impeccable materials) to the grand Irish banquet presented by chef Páidric Óg Gallagher of Gallagher's Boxty House with the assistance of Máirtin Mac Con Iomaire, Pauline Danaher and Grace O'Sullivan. The evening was rounded off in her inimitable technicolour style by Alicia Rios' artistic entertainment, 'Pickled Messages for Future Symposiasts'.

Next morning, symposiasts assembled in plenary session to hear Cathy Kaufman, Chair of the American Friends of the Symposium, announce this year's winner of the Cherwell Scholarship: Lara Rabinovitch for her paper on *pastirma*, and listen to Ivan Day's Sunday scene-setter, 'Amnesia in the Smokehouse'. Everyone then made their way to a variety of parallel sessions: the choice included corned beef in Ireland, an archaeologist's view of salt-cured meat in soldiers' diet, and marmalade as medicine as well as preserve; elsewhere discussions revolved around the role of yoghurt in the Turkish kitchen, fermented foods in Nagaland and what and why is 'Boza, Innocuous and Less So'; others unravelled the secrets of ancient Jewish sausages, classical and modern olive-preservation in Greece and the folklore and preparation of Cyprus' cured ham, *hiromeri*.

After a quick coffee-break, fun and games continued with Charles Perry's playlet, 'Wurstenders', with costumes and interjections by the multi-talented Alicia Rios, followed by raffle-prizes and grand auction. But the day's honours undoubtedly go to Ove Fosså and Sven Fosså who, with the assistance of Terje Inderhaug and Pål Drønen, gathered together a consortium of Norwegian small-producers who delivered (via sailboat from Norway to Cardiff) a dramatic array of traditional Norwegian ingredients preserved, as the subject of the Symposium dictated, by salting, fermenting and smoking. The menu included very little that was familiar and much that was both unknown and delicious: mutton ham, smoked reindeer-tongue and several preparations based on wind-dried stockfish, along with unusual crispbreads and cheeses, the whole rounded off with soured cream and cloudberries, a raspberry-like berry native to the Arctic tundra with a flavour of smoky pine-needles.

Thereafter, replete with good food (not to mention miniature bottles of aquavit) symposiasts returned to the lecture theatre for a panel chaired by Harry West on 'Fermentation as a Co-evolutionary Force', 'Artisanship and Control as applied to Farmhouse Cheddar' and 'The Science and Savour of Dry-Fermented Sausages'. The Symposium concluded with an expression of deep gratitude from the whole Board of Trustees to our departing Chair, Carolin Young, followed by a show of hands on the choice of subject for 2013 which, in the event, turned out to be Food and Material Culture which, following on from 2012's Wrapped and Stuffed, gives plenty of time for thought.

Elisabeth Luard
Director, Oxford Symposium on Food & Cookery Trust

11

The Absent Third: The Place of Fermentation in a Thinkable World Food System

Sidney W. Mintz

If we mean by 'fresh', food unaltered by any means, neither cooked nor otherwise changed, then perhaps two-thirds of the world's food is altered before being eaten. The not-cooked but also not-fresh fraction includes foods preserved by drying, salting, smoking, immersion in an anaerobic medium such as sugar or oil, canning, fermentation, and so on. Fermentation alone has been estimated to typify at least one-third of total global food intake. Its relationships to the rest of what humans eat deserves careful study, particularly as populations grow and global food resources become increasingly critical.[1]

Man vs. animal

My subject is fermentation, but permit me to offer some preliminary general observations. For the larger part of the animal world, an unending struggle necessarily typifies the balance between food and hunger. The great nineteenth-century French observer of insect life, Jean-Henri Fabre (1823–1915), lets us see a curious aspect of that struggle up close when he describes the larva-laying behavior of the venomous hunting wasp, *Cerceris bupresticida*. Her species name comes from the manner in which she paralyzes her insect prey, a member of one of the species of the beetle *Buprestis*. Then she carefully lays her larvae close nearby, so that, as they grow, they are nourished by living tissue until they are ready to fly away.

But there is more to it than that. Fabre writes:

> A tiny drop of the venomous liquid accompanying the sting, [serves] as a kind of brine or pickle to preserve the meat on which the larva is to feed. But how immensely superior to our own pickling-processes is that of the hunting wasp *Cerceris*! We salt, or smoke, or tin foodstuffs which remain fit to eat, it is true, but which are very far from retaining the qualities which they possessed when fresh. Tins of sardines soaked in oil, Dutch smoked herrings, codfish reduced to hard slabs by the sun: which of these can compare with the same fish supplied to the cook, so to speak, all alive and kicking? In the case of [flesh] meat, things are even worse. Apart from salting and curing, we have nothing that can keep a piece of meat fit for consumption for even a fairly short period.[2]

Fabre was writing in the middle of the nineteenth century, before the wonders of modern food technology were born. But the fierce drama he depicts – the hunting wasp, securing and preserving fresh food for her yet unborn larvae – suggests how living creatures are obliged to struggle, to tilt in their favor the balance of food against hunger.

Culture

The behavior exhibited by mammals as varied as squirrels and wolves shows that many species instinctively collect and hide food for the future, when they can. Such behavior is genetically inscribed. But in the case of *Homo sapiens sapiens*, while there is doubtless a genetic past to the human struggle to store and preserve, it did not continue to be based upon instinctual messages. In the case of humans, food-preservation behavior depends upon the unique qualities of human intelligence. The emergence of a symbolic form of communication, when combined with the imaginative nature of human tool-making and tool-using, made our learning cumulative. Our species alone interposes an invented, constructed, symbolically transmitted technology between ourselves and nature.

Through our distinctive endowments, we humans became the creatures that bind time, piling up our knowledge by symbolically linking together past and present, accumulating incrementally the benefits of social learning. If we do not recognize that we remembering, symbol-using, tool-making humans make our own history, then we do not really understand the differences between a squirrel burying a walnut, and a human pickling a cucumber. The hard truth is that such analogies risk confusing two only superficially similar activities, since the behavioral differences between the organisms that exhibit them are unbridgeable.

Place and time are shorthand terms for the conditions that make it so difficult for other forms of life to defer the consumption of their food. Their limited means intensifies the fight to live and reproduce. The seasonal migrations of wild herds; the hibernation of hedgehogs, bears and bats; the food storage of the social insects – all of these genetically driven behaviors are ways by which other forms of life, through the agency of mutation and natural selection, evolve and come to terms with space and time. In their place we humans, as we became human, invented the means we use to annul seasonal (chronological/calendric) and spatial (geographic) differences to defeat – or anyway to moderate radically – the time-space grid that nature imposes upon life on earth.

Taste: a collateral benefit of preservation

Over time, humans developed a wide variety of ways to store and preserve food. Everywhere we know about, people have foods that they savor, and children in all of those societies learn to like what they will thereafter call 'good.' Learning about new foods and learning to like them is part of growing up. Whenever I make this point about cultural patterning, someone may want to qualify it because of the importance of individual differences. There always are individual differences. But individual variation does not qualify patterning; it is simply part of it. Everywhere some persons grow up without learning to like the foods their cohorts find delicious. These exceptions are of interest in their own right; they also bring the rule into sight.

Since nearly all foods require some kind of processing so that they will keep, they may have quite a different taste when they are eaten from the way they tasted before the processing – outcomes that usually differ from those achieved instinctively by the storage habits of other forms of life. In the human case, differences resulting from processing probably have been quite important to the play of taste, the nature of taste differences and preferences, and the additional variety that gradually became incorporated into cuisine.

Archeological and ethnographic evidence reveals that in most of the world, even under conditions that were inhibited by environmental difficulties and rudimentary technology, humans experimented tirelessly with food preservation. At times the foods they produced might have seemed disagreeable even to their producers. But how things look, taste or smell on first tasting is not a fair measure of how they may come to taste, after one has more time and experience with a particular food. Just as the first experimenters must have only learned through repetition to savor some of their own concoctions, so alien peoples can learn to relish foods that seem unappetizing at first. In the West, all of us had to learn on some first occasion, for example, to like olives and anchovies. Today we can add hot peppers, sushi, miso, jellyfish, and much else.

We have ample evidence that the techniques of preservation, much as with cooking, often led to agreeable results. Sun drying and salting of fish, for example, usually has the effect of intensifying what we refer to as the 'fishyness' of odor and taste. Those unacquainted with such delicacies can find them nearly intolerable the first time, but they may be a good deal more 'interesting' the second, and perhaps even eagerly awaited the third. The appeal of some tastes has certainly been demonstrated to 'grow' on us. We may notice that we perceive most such novel tastes as 'strong' – in odor, color or taste. Habituation often has a way of making the taste more 'ordinary' – think here of gradually learning to like the 'hot' capsicums or turmeric. At the same time, peer pressure, snobbishness, simple hunger and other motives may induce us to try something a second and then a third time. In those societies where alternatives are few, at least at some times of the year, there may also be more yielding standards of taste.

It is hard to imagine that any early experiment with preservation was aimed primarily at the creation of different tastes. But it turned out that preservation added variety as well as greater security to cuisine, and experiments in preservation led quite naturally to novel tastes. Preserved foods might come to be eaten during a later and different season, especially when other food was scarce. This could mean that the taste of certain preserved foods, once committed to memory, became beloved markers of pleasure, the calendar and the round of seasons. If once tied to family, co-operative labor, seasonal smells and the pleasure of the familiar – tastes that 'came back in season' each year – then they were like returning schools of fish or flocks of birds. Such associations are of a sort achingly absent in modern life, now that *everyone has everything all of the time* – pizza in all-night laundromats, sweets in every room in the house but one, and giant strawberries, which grow best near nuclear power plants. But I digress.

I have addressed elsewhere the fact that agrarian diets are often based upon some core complex carbohydrate, either cereal or tuber.[3] Such core foods are commonly bland in taste. The sharp tastes of many fermented foods can harmonize neatly with the core food by enhancing on the one hand the beloved familiarity of the core, even while, on the other, providing an appetizing taste-counterpoint to it.

The importance of preservation

Foods may be eaten raw, cooked or otherwise altered. They are parts of the total food supply that, for whatever reason, were not eaten when gathered, caught or cultivated, whether they were set aside when freshly harvested or gathered, or left uneaten after a meal. Usually they are altered in some manner so as not to become what is considered – a culturally specific adjective – 'rotten'. Many of today's preservation techniques, including even canning, are quite new. Some such as canning, freezing and – excuse the barbarism – cryovacking, are still not globally widespread. Some of us may even remember when canned goods might swell or explode on opening. The world still relies upon old preservation methods, in some instances, fatally.

It has been fashionable to think that peoples in less industrial, less 'modern' societies know more than we do about preserving foods. Indeed sometimes they do. But careful fieldwork also reveals that many protection and preservation techniques still in use are pathetically imperfect. Haitian peasants customarily hoist bundles of drying corn (*makòn*) high in the air, to hang over crossbars driven through the trunks of palm trees (*croké mayi*), in vain hopes of protecting their maize from rats, insects and birds. This inefficient procedure, however, owes mostly to a scarcity of means for building proper sheds or storage facilities. Similarly ineffective was the sun-drying of fish by Nigerian fishermen in the north-east of the country, whose catches would be shipped by rail to the coastal seaports of Nigeria and Ghana. By the time of their arrival, up to half the weight of the fish consisted of the insects with which they were infested. The lack of water- and insect-proof storage facilities for small-scale farmers and fishermen in the less developed countries has been the cause of terrible waste. In fact, throughout history, a powerful incentive for finding more effective preservation methods has been the grievous losses to farmers and fisher folk due to lack of means, climatic change, and insect and rodent depredation.

These losses have by no means ended in much of the world, and fermentation is not a complete answer to them. Yet fermented foods will surely have a critical role in the future of human food systems, particularly as population continues to rise, and the world's arable lands, forests and water resources continue to decline.

Preservation and the transition to settled life

Archeologists have contended that mastery of food preservation was crucial to the move from a hunting and gathering mode of life to stable settlement. Pioneering communities that were learning only gradually to subsist on farmed crops and animal husbandry must have been caught out, at times, by their declining commitment to the chase, and their incomplete adjustment to village life. All sorts of disasters – flood, drought, fire, frost – can ruin the harvest of a farmed crop. It was, as Miller and Wetterstrom write, '…new techniques of chemically transforming food'[4] that enabled Neolithic peoples to realize the advantages of having both farm crops and animals, and the gradual decline of the hunting adaptation. The first, and for many cultures still, the single most important technique for 'chemically transforming food' beyond simple cooking is fermentation.

There are other common forms of preservation: sun-drying; smoking; salting; total immersion in fat or a supersaturated liquid sugar. All are ways to preserve food, and they have been employed around the globe. The term 'curing' is also used to describe preservation but is not always precise. It can mean foods dried using the sun, or smoke, or salt, or chemicals such as sodium nitrite; or by some combination of different agents. Fermentation can also be combined with other kinds of preservation. Taken together, these skills become an immense catalogue of human skill. As they were perfected, they became a step forward in the mastery of environments, both meager and generous.

Fermentation
History

Fermentation is a natural process that occurs without human intervention. It was present in nature long before any humans were around. McGovern, one of its most zealous students, believes that fermentation was familiar to our hominid ancestors long before the appearance of *Homo sapiens*. Huang writes of the drunken monkeys of Huang Shan, famous for their knack of collecting flowers and fruits and stashing them in crevices until they fermented into an intoxicating drink.

Hard evidence for the stabilization of fermentation as a preservation technique for human food, in this case alcoholic beverages, is demonstrable from at least nine thousand years ago: as early as the seventh millennium before Christ or earlier, in the case of China, and by 6000 BC in the case of the Middle East.[5] McGovern's work in China suggests that alcoholic beverages were first made from fruit, rather than grain. Success led to more fermentation experiments in both of these regions, but particularly in China, as documented in the magnificent study of fermentation there by Huang.[6]

'Fermentation' is no single phenomenon, invention or event. McGovern[7] declares that primitive monocellular organisms may have been consuming simple sugars and excreting ethanol and carbon dioxide – that is, *fermented* substances – two *billion* years ago. He unravels for his readers a chronicle of creatures of all kinds feasting on the fermenting sugars of plants during the lengthy history of life itself. He suggests that human experiments with fermentation may be 100,000 years old.

Whatever the case, once fermentation did become of concern to humans, it must have been deliberately undertaken hundreds of times. Many fermented products are recent, and some are still little known in the West. They have been perfected at various places on the earth, from the tropics to the polar wastes. Enterprising humans, learning how to keep uneaten or slightly spoiled food for another day or longer, hit upon ways to preserve by fermentation. There is no doubt that some particularly useful or attractive such change might diffuse rapidly, as probably happened in Eurasia with the first leavened breads, and in east Asia with the fermentation of legumes. Yet many such inventions probably remained local, and may have served to accentuate differences relevant to social and political life. Concrete examples of this phenomenon abound in Steinkraus,[8] who thoroughly documents the widespread presence of fermentation, often in the hands of people in societies who must rely upon a severely limited technical inventory. His work and that of Dirar [9] on the Sudan let us see the humble familial, but enormously important level at which fermented foods were perfected and eventually standardized for whole communities, then even regions, spreading in time over wider areas. The remarkably wide diffusion of these skills, in Eurasia in particular, is convincing inferential evidence that fermentation skills were mastered very early by humans.

Micro-organisms

Food fermentation is primarily carried out by micro-organisms. It is the chemical means by which they capture the energy to continue living. Humans in their turn employ micro-organisms as one means to obtain *their* food. Fermentation under human control thus parallels crudely the ways that wind, water and other forces of nature have became appropriable and exploitable sources of energy.

The success of fermentation rested ultimately on the human impulse to bend the living world to its will, in this case by domestication. The domestication of the micro-organisms that do the fermentation for us was the achievement of unknown, anonymous persons. It happened unimaginably long ago, and we are fortunate if we can learn roughly when, and where, for any plant, animal or micro-organism. Obviously we lack the identity of a single such domesticator. For micro-organisms that humans came to know and to use, it is important to remark that they have short life-spans, a highly convenient characteristic for the would-be domesticator.

There is no consensus on the best definition of domestication. For animals, three changes are often said to measure its success: control of territorial movement; change and control of diet; and purposeful restructuring and control of sexual and reproductive behavior. All three of these kinds of control figure in human interaction with the molds, yeasts and bacteria used in fermentation. The history of that interaction clearly involved the cultivation of specific micro-organismic cultures *to ferment with,* which closely approaches what happened with domestication otherwise. I believe that there are no grounds for excluding the domestication of life forms successfully put to human ends, even though taxonomically they are neither plants nor animals.

The micro-organisms that play roles in fermentation are staggering in number, and taxonomists indicate that millions of species are yet to be classified, both among the Fungi and among the Bacteria, the particular kingdoms from which the micro-organisms used in food fermentation are drawn. It is notable that the Fungi, which include mushrooms and lichens as well as the molds and yeasts crucial to some fermentation, are considered by taxonomists to be more closely related to animals than they are to plants.

Fermenters in the so-called developed world are usually well acquainted with the specific micro-organisms they employ in order to produce fermented food of all kinds. And yet probably more than half of the world's food fermentation takes place in the *rest* of the world.

Steinkraus defines fermented foods as follows:

Fermented foods are substrates that are invaded or overgrown by edible micro-organisms whose enzymes, particularly amylases, proteases and lipases, hydrolyze the polysaccharides, proteins and lipids to non-toxic products with flavors, aromas and textures pleasant and attractive to the human consumer.

(1997: 311)

In other words, fermented foods are those invaded by micro-organisms whose enzymes change the composition of the food chemically by turning proteins and lipids and polysaccharides into non-toxic products whose flavors, odors and textures human consumers find pleasant and attractive.

To grasp fully the significance of fermentation for the global food future, we need also to see that chemical changes made possible by the action of the enzymes in the micro-organisms can enrich the substrate nutritively. Cronk provides a notable example:

In the Indonesian *take ketan*... rice starch is [first] hydrolyzed to maltose and glucose and [then] fermented to ethyl alcohol. The loss of starch solids results in a doubling of the protein-content (from about 8 to 16% in rice) on a dry solids basis.[10]

(Cronk et al., 1977)

However, the chemical consequences of what those micro-organisms do can also be negative. Steinkraus adds to his earlier definition the following important proviso:

If the products of enzyme activities have unpleasant odors or undesirable, unattractive flavors or the products are toxic or disease-producing the foods are described as spoiled.

(1997: 311)

There are two important points here. We learn that fermentation may be linked through the action of enzymes to the production of toxic materials. Moreover, we are told that what is defined as 'spoiled' or 'rotten' is not necessarily toxic, but may be only *perceived* as inedible. For instance, fermented bean curd, a fairly common Chinese product, is often experienced as rotten on first tasting, by foreign palates. The same might be said of a common Asian reaction to Roquefort cheese. Which is 'rotten' and which is 'fermented' and delicious depends on whether one has been raised to eat one or the other. Both are thought very tasty by some, but spoiled, inedible or worse by others. These two foods illuminate the power of culture and social learning in the shaping of taste patterns. That the same food may taste 'rotten' to some people and 'delicious' to others probably should not surprise us. But up close – by which I mean on *your* plate – culture-specific definitions of acceptable fare can weigh heavily upon us.

I noted that two different categories of micro-organism are employed by those who ferment: fungi and bacteria. In the first category are unicellular organisms used by humans to leaven bread (*Saccharomyces cerevisiae*); to ferment soybeans and rice (*Aspergillus oryzae*); and to ripen some cheeses (*Penicillium roquefortii*, and *Penicillium camemberti*). The Bacteria Kingdom includes species of *Lactobacillus, Lactococcus, Pediococcus,* and *Leucostonoc,* which are used to ferment milk products, and many of which are also used to ferment vegetables. These are just a few of the better-known micro-organisms used in commercial fermentations, and worldwide. Many are retained and re-used, from one batch of breads, wines, cheeses or preserved vegetables to the next.

Whether it be cheese, wine, bread or half-sour pickles – and even when processors may lack scientific knowledge of the world of micro-organisms – food-makers live in intimate relations with those particular creatures, invisible to the naked eye, that are involved in processing their products. Indeed, our growing consciousness as lay persons of the important roles of micro-organisms in food production was confirmed for me recently by the legislature of the great American state of Wisconsin which, on being asked to voted officially for a state microbe, wisely chose *Lactococcus lactis*, the bacterium that is used to make the Colby, Monterey Jack and cheddar cheeses there.

Categories of fermentation

But what 'fermentation' now means gives us eloquent proof that life is never simple. In a concise global overview of fermented foods by Steinkraus (1997), he sketches seven distinguishable but overlapping categories to describe the world's fermented foods. The categories are based on fermenting agent and food type, as follows:

i.   Those producing textured vegetable protein meat substitutes from legume/cereal mixtures. Examples are Indonesian *tempe* and *ontjom*.

ii. High salt/meat-flavored amino acid/peptide sauce and paste fermentations. Examples are Chinese soy sauce, Japanese *shoyu* and *miso*, and fish sauces such as Vietnamese *nuocmam*, etc.

iii. Lactic acid fermentations including sauerkraut, Korean *kimchi*; cucumber and other vegetables; lactic acid-fermented milks, yoghurts, Russian *kefir* and cheeses; yoghurt/ wheat mixtures such as Egyptian *kishk* and Greek *trahanas*; boiled rice mixtures with raw shrimp or fish, as in Philippine *balao balao;* and also sourdough bread, Indian *idli*, Ethiopian *enjera* and Sudanese *kisra*.

iv. Alcoholic fermentations include grape wines, Mexican *pulque*, honey wines, South American Indian *chicha* and beers, palm and jackfruit wines in India, sugar cane wines, Japanese *sake*, Indonesian *tape*, Chinese *lao-chao*, Thai rice wine.

v. Acetic acid fermentations include apple vinegar in the Philippines, tea fungus/ Kombucha in Europe, Manchuria, Indonesia, Japan and recently in the United States, and Philippine *nata de piña* and *nata de coco*.

vi. Alkaline fermentations include Nigerian *dawa dawa,* Ivory Coast *soumbara,* African *iru, ogiri*, Indian *kenim*a, Japanese *natto* and Thai *thua-nao*.

vii. Leavened breads include Western yeast and sourdough.

This overview is useful. But when we look at the fermenting agents, we see that many of them are not microbial (or at least not primarily microbial) as, for instance, the fish sauces in category ii. (Some microbial activity may be involved at later stages.)

So although the original meaning of fermentation referred particularly to the conversion of sugar into alcohol, a broadening of meaning has taken place over time and has led to some confusion. The term came to mean 'the conversion of substrates to products by the intervention of any external biological agent, especially microbes, or enzymes extracted from them' (Huang *in lit.*, 2011). The meaning was then further amplified when 'fermentation' came to cover products when no external agents were added, such as soy sauce, *miso*, and *nuoc mam*. In such cases, the cells of the substrate start to break down, the enzymes freed by the start of decomposition react with the cellular materials that are present, and we say the product is fermented.

The following discussion of fermentation types is greatly abridged, because adequate description would require too much space. Entirely omitted from systematic review in this paper are three of the largest, most diverse and most important categories – alcoholic beverages, breads, and cheeses – because even the sketchiest of descriptions would make this paper completely unwieldy. I will also omit discussion of the fermented fish dishes associated with northern Europe, such as *lutefisk* and *surströmming,* important though they are; most of us will have encountered them in one way or another. The fermented foods I do want to touch on fall into five food classes: dairy, cereals, vegetables, legumes, and meat. I will deal with them briefly in that order.

Dairy

Fermented milk products such as *yogurt, kumiss, kefir, laban, kaeshk* and all cheeses depend for their continuous production upon a tradition of dairying. Milk-producing animals, whether cows – which Americans always think of first – goats, sheep, camels, donkeys, water buffaloes, reindeer or yaks, have all been bred to give milk copiously, when compared to their wild ancestors. In most cases they have been bred for many millennia. In the modern world, fermented milk drinkers mostly depend upon cows, sheep, goats, water buffaloes and camels; but reindeer, yaks, donkeys and other animals produce milk, drunk fresh or fermented by humans. Nutritionists and physicians claim that the bacilli of *Lactococcus bulgaricus* and other strains of *Lactococcus* provide protection by lowering the pH in the gut and acidifying digested foods. Milk, and to a much lesser extent, cheeses are treasured by pastoral peoples across North Africa and interior mainland Asia including India. In India, soured milk is especially highly valued and consumed in the millions of gallons annually. Such old habits merit much more study. Yet so far as I have been able to tell, anthropological work on fermentation and fermented products is still almost nonexistent.

Pastoralists were not big meat eaters anywhere, so much as users of sour milk, yoghurts and cheese. This may seem startling, but brief reflection makes it more understandable. People with herds value the herds and their products; eating meat usually only marks occasions of importance. Among the pastoralists of southern Iran, for example, sour milk and curds are eaten daily, if possible. Surplus curds are customarily reduced to hard pellets the size and shape of golf balls (*kaeshk*), in which form they can be preserved for months. Meat is only eaten rarely. The Bantu-speaking pastoralists who are distributed across a wide north-south swath of east Africa, from the Sudan to the Cape, such as the Masai, the Nuer, or at one time, the Zulu or Ngoni people, consumed the blood and milk of their animals, and cereal products, but not much meat.

Cereals

What many people think of when they hear 'fermentation' is alcohol. As indicated, the fermentation of grains to produce intoxicating drinks is a very ancient achievement, no doubt independently invented more than once. Though I will not discuss alcoholic beverages, I must talk about what I consider a different use of cereal fermentation that may be of considerable historical significance. To this day, half of the world's population probably has as their principal foods cereal gruels or porridges. Many peoples are accustomed to ferment the cereals, such as Indian *idli,* in order then to eat them as porridge or as pancakes. Cereals are cooked by steaming and then fermented in much of Africa; nutritively, fermenting them can be highly beneficial. By fermenting cereal gruels, for example, their nutritive density can be increased threefold. Fermentation can also reduce, by excluding oxygen, the toxicity of neighboring micro-organisms. The peoples who ferment millet, sorghum, wheat, maize, rice and some non-cereals do so,

22

though, primarily because they enjoy the tastes created by fermentation, even while the nutritional benefits are real.

In much of Africa today, a gruel of this sort literally defines 'food'. We are often told that people can eat all sorts of things during the day, yet complain of hunger, unless and until this familiar and filling food is eaten. Not all such gruels or porridges fermented. People declare that these gruels *must* be eaten with a sauce or relish, which is itself often fermented. Without eating *both* foods together, people claim they'll still feel hungry. Though this is a common situation, I do not believe its frequency has been sufficiently noted.

In most such cases – for example, where rice or maize or wheat is the cereal – people surely recognize the porridge they make as the core or center of the meal. The sharper-tasting sauce or relish is an indispensable accompaniment. I call your attention to this because I suspect that in agrarian Eurasia, Africa and even the Americas, gruel or porridge, thickened to stew or thinned to soup, and often including or accompanied by some fermented material, may once have been the principal daily fare of ordinary people.

Vegetables

Curiously, perhaps, vegetables are the category of fermented foods probably best known to us moderns, because many of us grew up in families that canned and pickled. The term 'pickle,' enlarged in popular discourse to cover any fermentable or fermented vegetable, includes carrots, beets, green tomatoes, okra, string beans and much else beyond the cucumber.

In the West, surely first place must go to the lowly cabbage, transformed by fermentation into a handsome accompaniment to meat, and equally more famed in Eastern Europe as the main ingredient of soups. Sauerkraut is its most famous form. The great, nearly unknown pioneer of food history, the Swiss/Polish scholar, Adam Maurizio,[11] fully documented the role of fermented soups in Europe. His work, though, is oddly unrecognized there.

Fermented vegetables have, of course, very considerable meaning for the history of nutrition. The 27-month record of scurvy-free travel by Capt. James Cook's crews, whom he forced to eat sauerkraut all the time they were at sea, carried a precious message for all navies. What began among technically limited peoples as a means to keep vegetables edible during long months of drought or food scarcity, eventually turned out to be an important health measure for the whole world, as well.

I cannot turn away from vegetables without at least mentioning Korean *kimchi*. It is difficult to think of another vegetable, fermented or not, that plays so singular a role in the life of an entire people. Until quite recently, *kimchi* was a family-produced and consumed food across the nation. Cwiertka and Moriya (2008) suggest that changes in South Korean society in the last half century have transformed the food system,[12] so that while *kimchi* is still a centerpiece, it is now less and less home-produced. But the main obstacle to mass-production persists, writes Dr Cherl-Ho Lee (2001), an eminent scholar of fermented foods:[13] *kimchi*'s apparent loss of its unique taste, once it is packaged.

Legumes

My first paper on fermentation dealt with legumes.[14] Legumes may have become the best source of protein for the poor, once humans successfully mastered agriculture, and the transition to stable agrarian communities was realized. It was above all agriculture that underlay the rise of stratified societies. And once societies with states did take shape, there is good reason to suppose that the best sorts of animal protein would mostly become the fare of the wealthy and powerful. Accordingly, legumes often were stabilized as a crucial source of protein for the laboring poor. This appears to have been true both in the East and in the West. Legumes, especially beans and peas, have been key staples of both Eastern and Western cuisine for millennia.

Yet in the lengthy history of the West, *no legume has ever been fermented*. Asian and Western worlds differ sharply in this regard. The West has been slow to learn about fermented legumes as well as to try them. In contrast, *tempeh*, a fermented soybean product, is at least as important to Indonesian cuisine today as *kimchi* is to Korean. One is a vegetable and the other a legume, but both are fermented products, and both are central to the cuisines of their respective countries. *Miso* and *natto*, two very different fermented legume products in Japan (together with unfermented tofu) play nearly as central roles in Japanese cuisine. Yet the West remains only barely aware of these foods. The only fermented legume product widely known in the West is soy sauce.

Meat

And finally, meat. We are all familiar with salami, corned beef, pickled herring, smoked oysters, sausages and other fermented animal protein. In the West, there is a long tradition of fermenting ground meat, as in sausages, using micro-organisms. In world outside the West, though, the fermented meats are humbler. The Sudanese, for instance, ferment muscle, offal, bones, fat, gall bladder, hooves, hides and skins, and the period of fermentation is brief.

The desire for meat and for meaty tastes is very great among many agriculturists. Indeed, in some places people will eat meat on occasions that outsiders describe as putrid or rotten. Indeed in some cultures, people express a specific desire for what we might call a putrid smell or taste (Dirar 1993). I will return presently to this matter of 'the taste of rotten'.

Fermentation cases

Most of what I have said so far, because it does not deal concretely with how an indigenous people actually ferments its food, cannot give us any real 'feel' for the practice. But as you can imagine, when people in the Sudan, for example, ferment cow urine, mere words fail to describe the on-the-ground process adequately. The same for, say, south-east Asia, when people in Myanmar, The Philippines, or Java process a large quantity of shrimp for fermentation under a strong sun. I turn to two cases in conclusion.

Sudan

My first case comes from one of the best monographs I have read on fermented foods, *The Indigenous Fermented Foods of the Sudan* by Hamid A. Dirar. Dirar's monograph, dedicated to the women of Africa, has been out for nearly twenty years, though it remains little known among students of food. Professor Dirar gives us a welcome peek at his own professional career, before describing in careful detail the more than *eighty* fermented foods prepared and eaten by the Sudanese people. He mentions that part of his preparation for writing the monograph was having been raised in the countryside by a mother who made all of the fermented foods herself.

Dirar enables us to see something of the conditions under which such foods are produced, and the rationales for their production. This work gives us an overview – narrow to be sure, but powerful, of the food system of an entire nation – as we know now, one on its way to becoming two nations. Dirar provides a pretty close look at those 80 fermented foods. But his book also matters because of what that it tells us, about the Sudanese people and their environment, and the specific role of fermented foods in that society and culture. It shows us why we need to see where fermented foods *fit* within a total food system.

Dirar's work leaves me thoroughly convinced that techniques of preservation must be studied not only in relation to local environmental features, but also in relation to the availability of other non-fermented food during the yearly round, in order to be more fully understood. We need to know in each case if the preserved food is what people may eat alone, or what they eat other food with; at what times or seasons the preserved food is available; its nutritional and aesthetic contribution to total food intake; and so on. Peoples whose life-conditions may leave them hungry or even starving at any time are often obliged to count heavily on their ability to preserve and to store other foods. Extreme climatic conditions, or a scarcity of plant and animal life, sudden or chronic, or plain poverty, can make preserved foods the difference between life and death.

Dirar points out that some 60 of the 80 Sudanese fermented foods either are sorghum (*feterita*), the nutritive underpinning of the Sudanese nation; or they are the relishes, sauces or condiments that turn the traditional boiled sorghum porridge into a more appetizing food, thereby enabling people to eat *even larger* quantities of it. To say it more clearly, the Sudanese poor survive primarily on a diet based on a complex carbohydrate core, made more appetizing by the addition of mostly fermented sauces. The sauces are made out of animal protein, when it is available. But when it is not, they are made from plants, including legumes, that can impart a meaty taste to the sauce.

Dirar's description shares something with that provided long ago by Audrey Richards, the great British anthropologist whose monograph *Land, Labour and Diet in Northern*

25

Rhodesia,[15] discusses food and society among the Bemba people. It was Richards' work on the Bemba that first gave me the idea of comparing the diets of horticultural peoples by using three elements, which I called the core, fringe and legume, and which I saw as a pattern potentially useful for cross-cultural comparison. 'Core' means the basic complex carbohydrate, invariably a cereal or tuber, eaten daily by nearly everyone, and the major source of calories. 'Fringe' means the culturally-specific elements that are added to the complex carbohydrate core to flavor it. They can be salt, alliums, dried or otherwise preserved greens, fungi, insects, and so on; raw, cooked, smoked, fermented, dried, or fresh. Back then I wasn't focused on fermented sauces. Now I plan to take a fresh look at the sauces of the Bemba – Richards calls them 'relishes' – to see whether any are fermented or preserved.

It is common among agrarian peoples to find legumes playing a basic role in such diets. Legumes are often prized for the tastes they add to the meal, but nutritionally, they usually make up for a scarcity of animal protein. One need only think about red and black beans (*frijoles*) in Mexico and the Caribbean, chickpeas in the Middle East, and bean curd in China, Korea, Japan and Indonesia to see what I am driving at. Among the very poor, the legume may supply the fringe of flavor.

One fermented legume in the Sudan that can serve this purpose is *Cassia obtusifolia*, the sicklepod. Only its leaves are fermented, then dried into a hardened mass called *kawal*. It is the liquid expressed from *kawal* that is used to make a sauce for cooked millet porridge. *Kawal* imparts a meaty taste, which the Sudanese adore. It exemplifies three characteristics of indigenous fermented foods that have attracted the interest of food technologists in recent years; such sauces may count heavily in the world's food future, particularly in some of the poorest regions. First, fermentation greatly enriches the nutritional value of the substance used, an advantage that needs no further explanation. Second, this product is made from only the protein-rich *leaves* of a wild plant, an important but hardly-noticed additional food source. Finally, this is solid-substrate fermentation, one which requires no water, an ever-scarcer resource. The sicklepod leaves, which are high in protein and other nutrients, like the leaves in many plants, become the dried product that can then be expressed to yield the liquid used in food. These features matter especially, if one inclines to think that meat in the future is likely to become ever rarer and more costly.

Most of the people Dirar is looking at in his monograph are the rural poor of Darfur. Given their poverty and lack of formal education, their knowledge of fermentation and its crucial place in Sudanese cuisine is easy to understand.

Inuit and Chukchi

My last case is from a remote part of the earth, as challenging environmentally as the Sudan. The peoples of the circumpolar north, from Greenland to Alaska and across Bering Straits to the Chukchi and Yupik people of Russian Siberia, have made remarkable adaptations to their locales. What may be their main fermentation product is even more remarkable. Renee Wissink, who traveled with the Polar Eskimo, writes this way about it:

> … we found the brilliant orange north face of Foulke Fiord almost startling. The orange was lichen, heavily fertilized by millions of dovekies, birds that return each spring to nest along the coast. The dovekies were the key to the Polar Eskimos' survival in the face of all their losses. Using rock blinds and long-handled nets, the Greenlanders caught – and still catch – thousands of the plump little birds. They can be eaten raw or cooked, and for a delicacy, they can be packed a hundred at a time in a sealskin and left to ripen for several months. The result, a fermented combination resembling a mixture of vinegar and the strongest imaginable blue cheese, is called *kiviaq*.[16]
>
> (*Equinox* 5 (4) Sept 2003 [1987]).

Hundreds of miles east in Chukotka, the Chukchi and Yupik of Siberia, about whom Yamin-Pasternak writes,[17] use a related process:

> A lasting supply of meat is prepared by allowing it to age inside a tightly filled and sealed bag made of walrus or bearded seal. Most commonly this recipe… is prepared with walrus meat. While some animal parts – flippers, intestines, brains, whiskers – are consumed shortly following the harvest, wide slabs of flesh are folded into rolls, stuffed inside the skin bags, and stored in subterranean pits over the course of several months. During the winter, the roulettes are consumed with locally gathered sweet roots and fermented greens, providing a complex nutritional blend of protein, vitamins, and carbohydrates. Collectively, this category of food is called "the tastily rotten." When talking about food in Russian, which for the overwhelming majority is now the first language, the enthusiasts of "the tastily rotten" emphasize that these foods are prepared *by being purposefully set to rot into their desirable state*. Contrary to the frequent misunderstanding by outsiders, the former is a salient edible category, very unlike the one referring to foods that are actually considered spoiled and inappropriate for human consumption.

These extreme cases bring us closer to the lives of two of the world's poorer peoples. We surely ought not to be surprised that they have canons of taste, just as do societies with much more. The careful reader may notice that Yamin-Pasternak points to that same delicate culture-specific line, referred to earlier, which separates 'inedible' from 'delicious.' What both Yamin-Pasternak and Dirar underline is the indigenous liking for the *taste* of rottenness. These cases make explicit what was perhaps known before, but not examined ethnographically. I think it necessary finally to point out that in recent years, at least in the case of the fermentation of bird-stuffed sealskins, there have

27

occurred some toxic substitutions, due to ignorance or arrogance, that resulted in serious medical problems. By switching to plastic containers instead of using animal skins and by making other egregious errors, some would-be modernizers have managed to make Alaska the national leader in cases of botulism; a few cases having ended in death.

Conclusions

My aim in the original version of this paper was to comment in a general way upon food preservation. I took the liberty of settling primarily on one form of preservation which, on examination, is revealed as ancient, vital and complex. Microbiologists are fond of telling us that if the human species were to vanish from the earth, the micro-organisms would not be in the slightest disturbed. Yet, they add with some satisfaction, if micro-organisms were to vanish, we humans would miss them terribly, if we survived at all. That we have been able to make those yeasts, molds and bacteria work for us is a tribute to human powers of observation and ingenuity.

In a world in which the powerless must struggle to survive, such humble tools can become hugely valuable. World population, now about 6.5 billions, grows by about 250,000 persons each day, and promises to become a far larger total in the next half century. The implications of this growth are stunning, especially in terms of food security. Like all other forms of preservation, fermentation can soften the handicaps of calendar, season and locale. Unlike some other types of preservation, it adds its ability to widen the range of taste. Most importantly, it can dramatically improve the nutritional value of the product, at the same time increasing its reliability as human food. It can also make possible other economies, such as in time and fuel.

I do not mean here to exaggerate the potential benefits of one preservation technique. But if our global future is of a falling centricity of animal protein in global diet, and increased reliance upon vegetables and legumes, then fermentation can play an augmented role in keeping our species well fed.

I've tried here to suggest by example the remarkable ubiquity, great diversity and rich promise of fermentation for the future. I hope my remarks may inspire in us a greater respect for human imaginativeness.

Notes

1. The author wishes to thank Dr H.T. Huang for his valuable criticism, and Prof. Sveta Yamin-Pasternak, Helen Saberi and Jacqueline Mintz for their help.
2. Fabre, Jean Henri. *The Hunting Wasps*. New York: Dodd Mead & Co., 1915.
3. Mintz, Sidney, 'The anthropology of food: core and fringe in diet', *India International Centre Quarterly 12* (2). 1985, 193–204; 'Die Zusammensetzung der Speise in Frühen Agrargesellschaften: Versuch einer Konzeptualisierung', in Schaffner, M., ed., *Brot Brei und was Dazugehört*. Zürich: Chronos Verlag, 1992, 13–28; 'Food patterns in agrarian societies: the core-fringe-legume hypothesis' (with Daniela Schlettwein-Gsell), *Gastronomica I* (3), 2001, 41–52.
4. Miller, Naomi, & Wilma Wetterstrom. 'The beginnings of agriculture: the ancient Near East and Africa', *The Cambridge World History of Food 2*, 2000, 1123–39.
5. McGovern, Patrick. *Uncorking the Past*. Berkeley: University of California Press, 2009; McGovern, Patrick et al. 'Fermented beverages of pre- and proto-historic China', *Proceedings of the National Academy of Sciences*. USA 101 (51), 2004, 17593–98; Michel, R.H., McGovern, P.E., & V.R. Badler. 'Chemical evidence for ancient beer', *Nature 360*: 1992, 24.
6. Huang, H.T. *Biology and Biological Technology*, part 5, *Fermentations and Food Science*, vol. 6 of J. Needham, *Science and Civilisation in China*. Cambridge: Cambridge University Press, 2000.
7. McGovern, Patrick. *Uncorking the Past*. Berkeley: University of California Press, 2009.
8. Steinkraus, Keith. 'Classification of fermented foods: worldwide review of household fermentation techniques', *Food Control 8* (5/6), 1997, 311–17.
9. Dirar, Hamid. A. *The Indigenous Fermented Foods of The Sudan*. Wallingford: CAB International, 1993.
10. Cronk, T.C, Steinkraus, K.H., Hackler, L.R. and L.R. Mattick. 'Indonesian *tape ketan* fermentation', *Applied Environmental Microbiology* 33, 1977, 1067–73.
11. Maurizio, Adam. *Histoire de l'Alimentation Végétale*. Paris: Payot, 1932. See also Sidney Mintz. 'Heroes sung and unsung: toward a history of the anthropology of food', *CNA Newsletter 25* (2), 2002, 3–8.
12. Cwiertka, Katarzyna, and Moriya, Akiko. 'Fermented soyfoods in South Korea', in Du Bois, Christine, Tan, Chee-Beng, and Sidney W. Mintz, eds., *The World of Soy*. Urbana: University of Illinois Press, 2008, pp.161–81.
13. Lee, Cherl-Ho. *Fermentation Technology in Korea*. Seoul: Korea University Press, 2001.
14. Mintz, Sidney. 'Fermented beans and Western taste', in Du Bois, Christine, Chee Beng Tan, and Sidney Mintz, *The World of Soy*. Urbana: University of Illinois Press, 2008, pp. 56–73.
15. Richards, Audrey. *Land, Labour and Diet in Northern Rhodesia* [1939]. London: Oxford University Press, 1951.
16. Wissink, Renée. 'The Qitdlarssuaq Chronicles, Part 4', *Equinox 5* (4) 1987.
17. Yamin-Pasternak, Sveta. 'The Rotten Renaissance: Aged Foods and the Importance of Their (Re) Acquired Taste in post-Soviet Chukotka'. Unpublished manuscript, 2010.

Bacterial Fermentation and the Missing *Terroir* Factor in Historic Cookery

Ken Albala

Although much credit has been given lately in gastronomic writing to the role of *terroir*, the power of food products to express unique traits reflecting geological, environmental and human factors of production, recognition of bacteria in these processes has been less apparent. Bacteria in the modern consciousness are pathogenic germs to be eradicated from kitchen surfaces, equipment and hands. With the triumph of modern scientific production methods, fermented products such as cheese, cured meats, pickles, bread and wine, have suffered from association with potentially harmful bacteria. In the name of food safety, predictability and product consistency these foods are routinely sterilized and are then inoculated with laboratory-tested, carefully controlled strains of micro-organisms. The unique properties of local bacterial populations are thus obliterated through such seemingly benign processes as pasteurization, or crowded out with super quick-acting starter cultures. The result is bland homogenous food catering to the lowest common gastronomic denominator. Flavorless, characterless, sterile products no longer reflect place but the demands of the industrial marketplace which require long distance shipping, stable shelf-life and, most importantly, uniformity and consistency.

This paper records the practical results of producing fermented products without modern methods or equipment in an effort to reconstruct the historical profile of local bacteria during the course of one year, from fall, 2008 to fall, 2009 at 38 degrees North latitude and 121 degrees West longitude, at Stockton California, located in the Central Valley, a flat arid plain with a Mediterranean climate. Without the use of modern equipment, commercial bacterial strains or the advice of modern do-it-yourself guides, this paper recounts the results of crafting three traditionally hand-made products: sourdough bread, aged cheese and dry salami.

The thesis of this project is simple. When we speak of local flavors and the immense variety of traditionally made fermented products from place to place, we are largely speaking of local bacteria: lactobacilli, streptococci, leuconostoc and dozens of other micro-organisms, molds and fungi that create an entire biological complex that is directly responsible for shaping the flavor-profile of traditional fermented products. The names of these organisms are less important than the crucial role they play through history in giving specific places unique flavors and also in explaining why certain products can only be produced with specific environmental conditions with the right microbiota. This project is intended to suggest modes of research which will initiate a new phase in historical food research. The aim is to reconstruct not only recipes as described in old cookbooks, but the unrecorded methods handed down orally or discovered through trial and error which give us an approximation of the flavors our forebears enjoyed in both the distant and recent past.

Predictably, historic methods developed in Europe, or anywhere on earth for that matter, should not be possible to replicate elsewhere since the local flora differ greatly. But it is precisely in this difference that I intend to support my general thesis. Even given comparable climate, soil, and production methods and all other factors that are believed to constitute '*terroir*', it is the bacteria which are the crucial factor in determining taste. Industrial products can be replicated anywhere, but given the vagaries of bacteria residing on human hands, in the air and on equipment, it will be argued that this is the missing factor in that determines the taste of place.

Let me assert from the outset that the approach here is decidedly unscientific. There was no attempt to isolate and identify specific bacterial strains, no systematic testing of the different microbes in isolation to judge what role they may have played in creating flavor, texture, consistency, etc. I leave this to laboratory science. Rather the intent was to replicate traditional uncontrolled food techniques to show how place does make a difference and how it is precisely the interaction of dozens of microbes in tandem, forming an ecosystem unique to every place and every individual set of hands that ultimately shapes what we think of as *terroir*.

Bread

I will begin with one of the most basic of natural ferments: bread. Contrary to all dictated wisdom in modern baking guides, creation of natural leavening is spontaneous and requires little human intervention. Thrice daily feedings of the starter, temperature and humidity controls, all the factors that commercial bakers, even the best, monitor for consistency would not have been possible in the past. Thus I began with a simple combination of flour and water. Bacteria were present on the flour to start with, on the bowl, in the air, on my hands. Simply feeding a moist slurry of flour and water daily allowed these to thrive and after two weeks it was strong enough to raise bread dough. Unlike baking with commercial yeast, which produces a great deal of lift, but relatively little flavor or texture, especially in the crust, natural leavening makes an entirely different kind of loaf. Denser, darker and with a pronounced sour flavor. This is due to the combination of natural airborne yeast (not exactly wild since they have certainly evolved with human interaction) plus lactobacilli which lower the pH of the starter and kill off certain molds, fungus and other dangerous bacteria, something which no one in the past understood scientifically, but learned merely from trial and error. A dough made with natural leaven may take four or five hours to rise rather than one or two, but it is in this time that the crucial flavor and complexity develops. Baking with this sourdough starter began 4 October 2008 (named Durga for the Hindu Goddess, the unfathomable female principle of unforgiving rage and enduring endless love, whose festival occurs on this day).

This experiment also featured a predictable variable. My co-author (Rosanna Nafziger, *The Lost Art of Real Cooking: Rediscovering the Pleasures of Traditional Food One Recipe at a Time*) who lives 90 miles due west in San Francisco, replicated the procedure using the same feeding schedule for the starter, the same brand of flour (organic King Arthur Bread Flour) and equipment (a peel, baking stone, oven at 550°F, water tossed in the oven before baking to create steam.) The breads were even formed and slashed in the same way. But as everyone knows, San Francisco is home to a unique strain of yeast that thrives in the cold, foggy climate and is said to produce a sourness unlike any other in the world and, according to legend, maintained carefully from the days of the gold rush-era '49ers who were said to have carried their starters into the mountains (where the starter should actually have changed dramatically – a factor left out of the story). In any case, as predicted, the San Francisco- and Stockton-produced breads were absolutely nothing alike. Mine baked to a golden brown, my partner's had a distinct white exterior. Mine was dense with large open holes, hers lighter in color and with smaller holes. And predictably, hers was reported to be decidedly sour, whereas mine had a mere hint of tanginess. Clearly the yeast and, I would suggest, also the bacteria, the climate and the microbes on our hands were all together the crucial factor in explaining the difference between these two breads.

Cheese

For the next experiment I decided to cling closer to the historical sources for the methodology, to produce a traditional aged cow's milk cheese. Cheese is among those natural products that pretty much makes itself – or rather bacteria make it. This seems surprising to modern sensibilities, as we know very well that milk goes bad after a week. Actually, that is only when milk is pasteurized, when it has been heated to kill all the bacteria, good and bad, along with most of the flavor. Pasteurized milk does indeed rot if kept too long, even with refrigeration. But raw milk turns sour and tangy when invaded by lactobacilli. Certain strains cause the milk to solidify into yoghurt, some produce other cultured products like *kefir*, quark, etc. Thus this experiment would only be possible using raw milk, which fortunately is legal in California, though not in most of the US.

To stick as close to historic methods as possible I decided to use only liquid rennet, but no commercial starters, cultures or other additives. After all, I wanted to see what the bacteria would do on their own to milk, and see how people in the past would have made cheese. I decided to make something like a traditional bandaged wrapped white cheddar, rubbed with lard as I know it is successfully done a few miles from my house at an award-winning artisanal dairy – Fiscalini. I saw the procedure there with a class, but was nonetheless intent on taking my cues from historical sources.

I started with classical sources like Columella, found a handful of really useful Renaissance sources like Pantaleone da Confienza in the fifteenth century and Vincenzo Tanara in the seventeenth century, but none of these were even vaguely as detailed as the eighteenth-century English author Josiah Twamley who, in *Dairying Exemplified* of 1784, describes every detail of cheese-making before industrialization. This is a précis of the directions I was able to glean from him and the earlier sources. It is scaled down for home production.

Start by warming two gallons of raw milk over a gentle flame: 90°F is about right. Be careful not to overheat it or you will kill all the good bacteria you want alive. Maintain constant temperature carefully for the whole process. If the milk is too hot, Twamley says you will have 'Sweet, or Funkey Cheese.' The milk is kept an hour at this temperature to allow bacteria to multiply. Next, mix 20 drops of liquid rennet into about a cup of cool water. Then pour into the milk and stir. Let this sit for about 45 minutes. Be sure not to disturb this in any way, or you may prevent coagulation. After 45 minutes, you will see that the curds have set, and it looks solid, perfectly coagulated. Not curdled – as you would see in milk gone bad – but a solid jiggling mass.

Then with a long, serrated bread knife, cut the curds, still in the pot, very gently into long, thin slices, and then cut across again. Don't break up the curds too much, essentially what you have now are long, vertical sticks. Let them sit for 20 minutes. Next, raise the heat to 98°F. Hold it at this temperature for about 30 minutes. You will see the curds gradually sink to the bottom and stick together a bit. It will be ready when the whey is no longer white but 'you will always find the whey quite green', says Twamley. In fall, the whey may take on a bluish hue.

Carefully lift the curds with your hands out of the pot into a fine-meshed colander or sieve – a Chinois shape works nicely. Try not to break up the curds violently or you will cause the fat to drain away too; all you want is the greenish, watery whey to drip out. Let drain about 15 minutes or until the whey stops dripping. Keep the whey for ricotta.

Return the curds, which will now look like cottage cheese, back to your pot. Add two tablespoons of salt and stir to distribute evenly. Leave to rest for another hour. You'll see more whey exude. Pour the curds into your cheesecloth-lined mold, and wrap up like a little wheel or cylinder shape, depending on your mold. Let the remaining whey drip down into the pot. Put a top on the cheese – I cut a circle of rigid plastic but a small plate will work too and weigh it down. Start with a little weight on top and gradually increase until there's a lot of weight pressing down on the cheese. Leave this to drain over night.

Take the cheese out of the press and unwrap. Put it on a reed or bamboo mat, anything that allows the air to circulate underneath, in your cellar or cool storage area (I use the wine fridge) at about 50–55°F and turn a few times a day for two days.

Lastly, you can either rub with oil or wrap the firm and dry cheese in leaves or several layers of clean cheesecloth or thin muslin and then melt about a cup of lard and brush it all around the cheese, saturating the cloth. You can also brush the cheese with melted paraffin wax. Put it back in your cellar, wait 12 months. Then eat.

33

In the course of a year and a half I made six cheeses (two are still aging) and altered certain variables. For example, using pasteurized milk created a cheese which molded and rotted. The right bacteria to cure the cheese wasn't present in the milk and apparently wasn't transferred by my hands or equipment. Bandaged cheeses dried out a little too much but also formed a nice crystalline texture similar to Parmesan. Waxed ones stayed softer and were a little milder. Slight variations in procedure made significant differences in texture and consistency. But the color and flavor of the cheese in every experiment that used raw milk was similar to the Fiscalini cheese made a few miles away. In some side-by-side taste tests, they were indistinguishable. Climate, soil, fodder certainly played a role, but I would contend that most important was the local bacteria in the milk. There is not another industrial cheese (among many) produced in the area that tastes anything like these. And the very fact that an amateur could produce a cheddar comparable to the professionals suggests that bacteria above all was the crucial factor in the expression of *terroir*.

Salami

The last experiment involves hard Italian fermented and aged salami. Reconstructing historical procedures was much more difficult than cheese, mostly because very little has been recorded, and hardly anything in food literature. Cookbooks, for example often tell you how to serve cured meats, and very often give directions for various cooked sausages, but the actual curing was always either done by professionals in cities whose trade secrets were not shared or on a small scale on farms where the pigs were slaughtered. Salumi was simply not something chefs or stewards regularly made. But there are glimpses here and there.

If the origins of salami manufacture are obscure, they are nonetheless just as natural as the discovery of cheese or wine, so let me turn to just a little basic chemistry to explain what's involved. I think it will also help to explain why there are real differences in flavor from place to place, because you are really depending on whatever bacteria and molds happen to thrive in a particular spot. Nowadays, and for the last 50 years or so, as with cheese, manufacturers use standardized commercial starters to get a consistent product and to prevent spoilage. They also tend to speed up the whole process to save money. The result is, to my taste, a really unpleasantly sour one-note salami without much character. The sourness happens because they are looking to lower the pH rapidly to prevent pathogenic bacteria. All these procedures of course ruin the natural and historically rooted flavors. You really need to depend on whatever nature gives you to get complexity and expression of local *terroir*.

Salami is simply chopped or ground meat in a casing of intestine that is aged by salting and drying and bacterial fermentation. In many instances that is all you need – the bacteria in the animal's gut and on the human's hands (lactobacilli, pediococcus, leuconostoc, etc.), combined with the right temperature and humidity, will work perfectly, especially in anaerobic conditions. It needs to be cool, hence slaughter in autumn, usually after St Martin's Mass (11 November). The weather should not be too dry either or the exterior of the salame dries out too fast and the interior spoils, nor too cold. Italy happens to have an ideal climate, the further north you go in Europe the more difficult it can be without the right bacteria and too much humidity – which is why cured meats are more typically smoked in the Alps and northward.

The meat, in this case pork shoulder, is chopped or ground, or even pounded in a mortar and then salted. Historically, it would have been mined salt which has natural minerals, some of which aid in preservation, but if you are thinking of bright red classic salami, then saltpeter (or the modern equivalent sodium nitrite) is also necessary. Mined salt sometimes contains a high amount of nitrates, especially taken from caves where there are bats, but typically saltpeter has to be manufactured. Potassium nitrate is KNO_3 which historically was either mined directly from rock, hence the name *sal petrae*. Or it is made by taking a pile of manure, mixing with it wood ash and other decomposing vegetable matter – especially hay, covering it, and letting it basically compost. It's turned over, and kept moist with urine: a completely natural, if slightly unsavory process. Then, after a year, it is soaked with water, the water drained off, and left to dry into crystals. The principal use for saltpeter is of course not food processing but, when mixed with sulfur and charcoal, gunpowder.

Apart from its anti-pathogenic properties, the nitrite reacts with the myoglobin, which prevents oxidation which turns meat brown. This is not nitrate, but nitrite which is converted into nitrate by microbial action. Which is also why sugar is necessary in curing, not only to offset the flavor of salt, but to feed the micro-organisms that convert the nitrates. Of course how nitrates work in curing meat was not understood until modern times, and even though saltpeter was known to chemists from the late Middle Ages, it is very difficult to say when exactly it began to be used to cure meat. But it is from this time that we begin to find recipes.

Traditionally made salami is relatively unknown in the US since it is illegal to import into the US any raw meat cured less than 400 days – so prosciutto can be imported, salami can't. One hundred days is about when salami turns to rock. But we have domestically produced salami, an excellent example of which comes from the Bay Area – made by Paul Bertolli. I interviewed Paul in Berkeley at the Fra Mani factory in October 2009. Paul came to fame as a chef at Chez Panisse with Alice Waters, and then opened his own restaurant called Olivetto in Oakland. Apparently having become so enthralled by curing meat, he left to work full-time at his own salami factory – and wrote a great cookbook called *Cooking by Hand*.

He has been striving to recapture old salumi-making traditions by rejecting mass manufacture, and quick industrial procedures. Obviously to produce on any scale and follow USDA regulations he has to adopt certain food safety standards and has to have a government inspector on hand all the time. One outbreak of listeria could put him out of business, so the machines have to be scrupulously clean. I wasn't even allowed in the processing part of the facility. But I got a very good idea of how salami is made there, and how different it actually is from traditional salami-making (which incidentally is practically extinct in Italy, as it is in the US).

Paul is part of the more recent wave of producers who are looking for small-scale, artisanal and traditionally manufactured specialities. Well, what does that actually mean? First, Paul told me that the most important factor is the quality of life for the pigs, which directly affects the quality of meat. His are sourced from family farms in the Midwest through Niman Heritage (no longer connected to Bill Niman, incidentally). (Most of the older producers like Molinari just buy wherever the pork is cheapest – usually Denmark.) The Niman pigs are allowed to roam outside on open pasture but have little portable hoop barns that they can go into for giving birth, they are not given antibiotics (necessary when pigs live very close together indoors) nor growth hormones. A sow usually gives birth to about ten to fourteen piglets per litter. They are weaned at six weeks and after about six to seven months are big enough to go to market. That's about 300 lb on the hoof or about 200 lb dressed. Fra Mani processes about 100 pigs per week, and the time from slaughter to production is about a week. The meat never arrives frozen, but is always fresh. The rearing practice and speed from slaughter to processing helps avoid PSE (pale soft exudative) meat, which happens when the pH lowers and the muscle proteins denature resulting in mushy meat. The scale here is also very small. Only twenty people work at this factory – and that apparently helps maintain the quality of the meat

The important part is cutting it into primal sections, avoiding the sinews that would make salami unpleasant to chew. It is then ground with various successively sized blades, because you want some chunks large, others more finely cut to give texture to the finished product. And you want clearly visible knobs of fat, not smeared sections. The final product has about 18–22 per cent fat. Then fermentation cultures are added: staphylococcus, pediococcus, lactobacillus. What these do is bring down the pH so the good bacteria that cure can thrive and the bad bacteria perish. But note, these are commercial starters. They add flavor, texture, color – and consistency. As does, of course, the salt. The pH needs to be an acidic 5.3 to kill salmonella and the like.

The ground meat is then mixed with a paddle, which helps it adhere, then goes into a stuffer, goes in literally by hand into a natural casing only made of pork (not beef middles which can carry e-coli). The section of intestine determines the width of the final salami, ranging from small to sow-bungs which are 120 caliber. All are hand-tied with linen or hemp. The reason for this is that they're all naturally irregular in size and shape and a machine really could not do it well.

Then they are hung to ferment in special chambers that control temperature (about 70–75°F) and humidity for a week, before penicillin mold is introduced to the exterior, similar to blue cheeses. This is essential for flavor as well as for regulating the flow of moisture through the skin. The mold is sort of gatekeeper. The real trick is to dry at a regular pace. If the exterior dries too quickly it prevents the interior moisture from migrating to the surface. If done properly, the salami will lose 40 per cent of its water, becoming harder and shrivelled.

The answer Paul gave me to one particular question was really surprising. He said that these salami are 'uncured', which was baffling. I asked whether he used nitrates to keep deep red myoglobin. He said, 'No, we use celery juice.'

So I am wondering, 'You mean, if I squeeze the water from celery it will prevent botulism?'

'No it's actually concentrated celery juice. But legally there are no 'nitrates' (normally synthetically manufactured) as defined by US law, so it can be labelled as uncured and thus sold in Whole Foods. Only this way can it be labelled organic. But the celery juice is in fact an abundant source of nitrates.'

The stuffed salami is next aged for at least 32 days, or as long as 65 for the *salami gentile*, which is cured in a rather thick casing. Nostrano is aged for 70 days, Toscano for 90–100 days, the typically harder *sopressata* about the same. They are never wrapped in plastic or shrink wrap, because like cheese it needs to breathe. They are sometimes refrigerated at markets, but this is unnecessary.

Despite the small size of the Fra Mani factory, it is still salami made on an industrial scale, and they still have to follow USDA regulations. If the slightest trace of listeria, for example is found, they have to shut down production and do an IVT, intensive verification testing. And every 45 days every piece of machinery and surface is thoroughly inspected and sterilized. And naturally as a business, if anything goes wrong, and a customer gets sick, they are in serious trouble. Nonetheless, I have to admit, and you will see, he does achieve some funky intense flavors.

At home you can be looser with regulations. Listeria is just as likely to show up on your cutting board as in home-made salami, and the same is true of salmonella, and trichinosis is really not a concern any more unless you're using wild boar. So I thought I'd share the much simpler procedure, which is not only less complex, but depends on whatever bacteria you happen to have in your kitchen and of course truly replicates historic methods. It is salami made the old-fashioned way. And I should say here that if you scrupulously use antibacterial soap it will be much harder to ferment anything, because you've killed all the good and bad bacteria.

I have made salami literally by hand with no machinery about ten times in the past year and a half, including with a class of twenty at Boston University and about 30 lb of meat. Start with either beef middles which give you a nice fat salami, or with pork casings. It has to be natural – again we want bacteria. Soak these about half an hour to remove the odor. Then take 5 lb of pork shoulder – you can either buy a whole roasting joint which is a little tricky to cut up and remove all the sinews from; or you can use what are called country ribs, which come from the shoulder or loin; or even pork steaks which are also shoulder cut flat. In either case, I cut the meat into smaller fist-sized hunks and put it in the freezer to keep firm – replicating the winter-time slaughter outside. There should be enough fat on this, which should be about 20–25 per cent. If you need more fat, just add a little fatback, with the rind removed. There are two ways to do this. One is with a meat grinding machine, which is quite tricky because the fat can smear and the meat can be over-worked. I once owned a hand-cranked meat grinder but I tossed it in the trash about a year ago, in a fit of rage. You really want a mix of larger and smaller bits, but absolutely distinct little nubbins of meat and fat. The best method is to get out a good, heavy, very sharp knife and cut it all by hand.

Take a few hunks of meat at a time and put the rest back in the freezer while you work, because if it gets to room temperature it gets slippery and much harder to cut cleanly. Cut the whole thing, fat too, into neat little nubbins about the size of a pencil eraser top or smaller. Here the proportions of cure are very important. Add 3 ½ tablespoons of sea salt, 4 tablespoons of sugar, not to make it sweet, but necessary for the fermentation and 1 teaspoon of pink curing salt, Insta Cure™ #2, sometimes called Prague powder II. The flavorings are up to you: I usually use oregano, pepper and either fennel or a touch of a spice mixture I keep around made of cinnamon, cloves, nutmeg, cardamom and ginger, similar to the French *quatre épices*. Just a pinch of mace would be fine too. Garlic would be classic. Then add a quarter-cup of red wine and mix it all well with your hands. Doing the whole thing by hand is what really introduces the bacteria here. It probably helps that I've got sourdough bread starter on the countertop – and pickles fermenting in the cupboard.

If you really want to learn the meaning of the word hand-made, get a wide-mouthed funnel and push the opening of your casings onto the end, wetting them well first so they slide on. But you don't even need a funnel, it can be done with your hands. Push on about two feet-worth. Tie the end of the casing off in a knot once it is on your funnel. With funnel in one hand, stuff your mixture into the opening and it will gradually fill the whole casing. Remove your sausage and tie off the other end. Twist it in the middle and tie with a string and you will have two foot-long salamis. The 5 lb of pork should make about twelve feet. You can also tie string around the knots which keeps them from untying and you can hang the salamis from the string.

Then hang these in a cool place, at around 55°F with a moderate humidity – also necessary so they don't dry out too quickly on the outside, preventing the inside from drying evenly. A wine fridge works well for this. In about four weeks they should be ready. They will lose about 35–40 per cent of their moisture, so you will have rather small *salametti* at the end. An even longer aging is fine if you want them to be harder. If you see flecks of white mold that's perfectly fine. In fact, you can encourage it by buying a commercial dry salami with mold on it and putting it in with yours. The mold adds to the flavor and helps preservation. It is the gate-keeper, so to speak, regulating the exit of moisture and development of flavor.

If you find the casing a little too chewy, feel free to peel it off. The fat inside the salami will be soft and yielding and balances beautifully with the firm deep red flesh. These will keep several months, becoming even drier and more complex in flavor. They can be stored at room temperature too. I have some that have been hanging in the kitchen since the spring, rock hard but really very tasty if sliced razor thin.

The salami experiment above all other proves that place and local bacteria are a key if not the essential factor in what we call *terroir*. This salami tastes absolutely nothing like any I have tasted in the US or in Italy. It is very slightly sour, quite hard and chewy, with an aroma that I can imagine is the result of whatever this distinct bacterial ecosystem has done to the meat. But it tastes nothing like mass-produced salami or the artisanal USDA-regulated salami now so popular in the US. I wish there were a way to compare it to others made with the same process, but that's a subject for further investigation.

Sources used in reconstruction of techniques

d. 149 BC Cato the Elder, *De re agricultura*.
d. AD 70 Columella, *De re rustica*.
d. AD 102 Martial, *Epigrammata*.
d. AD 217 Galen of Pergamum, *Alimentorum facultatibus*.
4th century AD Apicius, *De re coquinaria*.
d. AD 815 Geber (Jabir ibn Hayyan).
1242 Roger Bacon.
1270 Hasan al-Rammah.
c. 1460 Martino of Como.
1470 Platina (Bartolomeo Sacchi), *De honesta voluptate*.
1477 Pantaleone da Confienza, *Summa lacticiniorum*.
1491 Antonius Gazius, *Corona florida medicinae*.
1535 Agnolo Firenzuola, *In lode dells salsiccia* .
1542 Giulio Landi, *Formaggata di Sere Stentato*.
1549 Cristoforo di Messisbugo, *Banchetti*.
1556 Jodoco Willich (Conrad Gesner), *Ars magirica* and Jabob Bifrons's letter.
1564 Agostino Gallo, *Le vinti giornata di agricultura*.
1569 Hortensio Lando, *Commentario della più notabili e mostruose cose d'Italia*.
1570 Bartolomeo Scappi, *Opera*.
1581 Alessandro Petronio, *De victu Romanorum*.
1584 Giovanni Battista Rossetti, *Dello scalco*.
1586 Baldassare Pisanelli, *Trattato della Natura de Cibi e del Bere*.
1653 Vincenzo Tanara, *L'economia del cittadino in ville*.
1784 Josiah Twamley, *Dairying Exemplified*.

39

Fundolus or Botulus: Sausages in the Classical World

Joan P. Alcock

In the classical world sausages were not recognized as a status food as they were often a way of using offal and other parts of animals, especially pigs, which might otherwise have been discarded. They provided the poor, however, with a cheap source of nourishment, varied their food, and could be a significant part of their diet.

The disdain in which sausages were held can be noted in the standing of the sausage-seller. In Aristophanes' play *Knights*, written in 425 BC, a sausage-seller takes centre stage in a political satire against Cleon and other Greek politicians who had succeeded Pericles in 429 BC. Aristophanes believed such men were unworthy of their position and that they had authorized reckless military adventures by which they hoped to enrich themselves. He dramatized this as a folktale. The house and wealth (Athens) of Mr Demos had been taken over by a slave, Paphlagon (Cleon), who had seduced Mr Demos by flattery, lies and gifts, and alienated his household (political competitors). Two slaves predicted that Paphlagon would be overthrown by someone of a status worse than a tanner, a person despised because hides were soaked in urine and excrement before processing and thus having a smell lingering on the body. A sausage-seller duly appeared, described as loudmouthed and down-market. He admitted cheerfully that his family was low class and that he had made his way by his sharp wits, haggling in the market place and crying his wares in a loud penetrating voice (*Knights* 180). He just wants to soak his tripe and sell his sausages.

His pitch was at the city gates, the haunt of those on the fringes of society. At the end of the play, when Paphlagon is defeated, this lowly status will be his lot. The reference is to the Dipylon gate, which was near the extra-mural cemetery where men traded insults with prostitutes, and sold salt fish, a trade equally despised, and hashed dog and ass meat. (*Knights* 1396) The reference to dog meat was an equally contemptuous and satirical remark because although the Greeks do not seem to have eaten dog meat (Garnsey 1999, 83–85; Roy 2007) it was uncertain whether it was included in sausage meat.

Sausage-selling, although providing a cheap snack, was also regarded as a low-class trade in Rome. Seneca, who had lodgings over a bathhouse, was infuriated by the cries of street traders (*Epistulae ad familiares* 56.2) including those of sausage-sellers whose cries had their own distinctive intonation. Martial (*Epigrams* 1 41 9–10) confirmed this noise, commenting on the 'pie man who bawls as he carries round his warm pans of smoking sausages.' The contempt felt for these men was mainly because they seem to have obtained much of their meat from sacrifices, especially the intestines, offal and other less desirable parts. These parts were appreciated, however, because of their strong flavour. Sacrifices also ensured that large quantities of blood were available for blood puddings.

Sausage-sellers got their meat in other ways. Theophrastus (*Characters* 9.4), in an essay on 'Sponging', remarked that a man got his meat by joking with a butcher and, when his attention was distracted, grabbed some tripe and went away laughing. Aristophanes (*Knights* 424) mentioned that his sausage-seller was not averse to hiding stolen meat in his buttocks. Edward Gibbon, in his eighteenth-century epic *The History of the Decline and Fall of the Roman Empire* (chapter 41, note 101), speaking of the siege of Rome in AD 537, said that the Romans made sausages of mules' flesh, unwholesome though it might be, especially if the animals had died of plague. He also added, rather contemptuously, that Bologna sausages were said to have been made of asses' flesh. As a profession, therefore, sausage-making (entailing dealing with intestines and the interior parts of animals) could be a bloody and messy trade. 'Holy Poseidon,' remarked one of the slaves in *Knights* (146), 'what a trade.'

The most acceptable meat in sausages was pork, which was also regarded as the produce of the most economical animals, probably because pigs can produce a litter of up to twelve piglets a year or even, with a young pig, twice a year. Pliny (*Natural History* 8 77 205) said a sow could produce a litter of twenty piglets although she might not be able to rear them. He remarked of pigs (*Natural History* 8 77 209), 'there is no animal that provides more materials to the eating house; its meat provides nearly fifty flavours while other animals only one.' Varro asked (*De Re Rustica* 2 4 3), 'who cultivates a farm without swine?' and added (*De Lingua Latina* 5. 110) that the pig was the first domestic animal that its owners began to slaughter and salt to keep the meat unspoiled. Ovid (*Fasti* 6 169) said that pork was the only meat consumed at the beginning of history and that it was perhaps reasonable to think that pigs were the first animals to have been domesticated. Pork seems to have provided most of the fresh and preserved meat for the classical world. Pigs needed very little supervision, could eat almost anything and, as has been said, every part of the animal could be used except the squeal.

Pork could not be preserved easily in hot weather and therefore some form of preservation was necessary. Superstition entered into this process: it was best to kill and salt a pig in midwinter before the moon was waning and possibly before the fifteenth of the month. The fifteenth was the Ides sacred to Jupiter and hence a propitious day. Columella (*De Re Rustica* 12 55 1–4) gave instructions for salting pork. A pig must be prevented from drinking for twenty-four hours before being killed so that its flesh would be drier. All bones had to be removed to make the flesh less oily. Hot, coarse salt was rubbed all over the divided pieces of flesh before they were put on a board and pressed with weights to get rid of any blood and water. After three days the weights were removed and more crushed salt was rubbed in, for at least nine days in warm and dry weather, twelve in wet weather. After this the salt should be shaken off and the meat washed (in a pond was suggested) until all the salt had been removed. The pieces must be hung up and smoked to dry out the moisture.

He also gave a simpler method. This was to remove the dead pig's hair either by covering the pig in boiling water or by singeing the body with a flame. The flesh would be cut up and the layers of pork and salt put in a barrel ending with a huge amount of salt on the top. A heavy weight was put on at the top to press out the moisture. Columella said that this meat would always keep for long periods as it remained in its own brine. In a modern experiment (McCormack 2002, 26) emphasized that a great deal of salt was needed for the process in twentieth-century Irish home-curing: 18 kg of salt for wet-curing 100 kg of pig carcass and 25 kg for the same amount for dry-curing. With this amount of salt the meat would keep for a long time but the salt must be removed to make the meat edible.

Cato (*De Agri Cultura* 162 1–3) recommended another method, again placing pork and salt in layers in a barrel so that meat did not touch meat. After five days all the meat should be taken out and reversed so that the top layer was at the bottom. After a further twelve days the barrel should be emptied, the salt brushed off and the meat pieces hung for two days on a *carnarium* (rack). Three days later the salt should be washed out and oil rubbed into the flesh. The pieces needed to be smoked for a further two days before being rubbed with a mixture of oil and vinegar. After this process, Cato assured, 'no moths or worms will touch the meat.' Apicius (1 7 2) said that a mixture of prepared mustard, vinegar (presumably lees of wine), salt and honey (a noted preservative) would help the process; honey also added a touch of sweetness to the meat. 'You will be surprised', he added, presumably at how long the meat would last. Apicius (1 7 1) also gave what might be considered a fast-food method of preservation in winter by merely covering the meat with honey and then hanging it. However meat preserved in this way would keep only a few days during a hot summer.

Classical writers did not know why meat should be preserved in this way, but it was a method that was normal practice. Davidson (1999, 688) provides the explanation, observing that during the salting process, a moderate amount of salt 'allows lactic acid-producing bacteria to grow. This inhibits other bacteria, which cause decay. In turn, this lactic acid produced by "good bacteria" will prevent the growth of "bad bacteria". Eventually the acid becomes so concentrated even the "good" bacteria are inhibited: fermentation stops and the food keeps.' The meat cannot be used for consumption in this condition, as the salt must be removed. Apicius recommended (1 8) cooking the meat twice, first in milk and then in water.

An inn at the corner of the Via di Mercurio in Pompeii has a painting showing men dining at a table. Above them is a *carnarium* from which hang strings of onions, cheeses and a long sausage (Mauri 1960, 134–137; Mau 1899, 395). The sausage is obviously being dried. Drying (Davidson 1999, 256) reduces the water-content of a food to 'a level so low that the micro-organisms and enzymes which cause spoilage cannot function.' This is particularly necessary in order to preserve sausages. Sausages cured in this way have a very long shelf-life as the drying concentrates the salt and lactic acid thereby getting rid of bacteria and rendering them safe to eat without heating.

Smoking was also useful in drying sausages as it deposited a layer on the surface that prevented oxygen making the meat-content rancid. If sausages were hung in smoky kitchens this would be no problem. Ovid (*Metamorphoses* 8 647–648) gave such a description in the story of Baucis and Philemon who unwittingly entertained the gods Jupiter and Mercury in their house where smoked hams hung from a *carnarium* covered with soot from a smoky fire. The middle of a sausage mixture would dry more slowly than the outside and ferment slightly. This was part of the curing process giving most sausages a tangy flavour. Sausages today often use saltpeter (potassium nitrate) as a preservative but this was not used, as far as is known, in the ancient world. Reliance was on salting and drying for preservation.

Smoking could be done lightly or heavily imparting a flavour according to the type of wood used. The Romans preferred beech and oak; the Gauls preferred juniper wood. Sidonius Apollinaris (*Letters* 8 133 41–45), a notable Roman poet who was also Bishop of Augustonemetum (Clermont-Ferrand) in the fifth century AD, mentioned sausages he had encountered in an inn, flavoured with juniper berries. To have this treat Sidonius had to eat them with eyes watering from the steam from the cooking-pans and the haze from the frying-pans in which the sausages were spitting happily.

It is not clear whether Aristophanes' sausage-seller made his own sausages. Probably he did, as he was also a purveyor of blood puddings of which the Greeks and Romans were inordinately fond. When Odysseus returned to his homeland (Homer *Odyssey* 18 44–45) Antinous created goats' paunches for Penelope's suitors filled with fat and blood that he then set before Odysseus. Later (*Odyssey* 20 24–27) Odysseus, unable to sleep, pondering how to kill the shameless wooers of his wife, tossed and turned, 'as when a man before a great blazing fire turns a paunch full of fat and blood swiftly, from side to side, eager to have it toasted quickly.'

There was always plenty of blood available in Rome from the huge number of sacrifices offered at the many temples and shrines or from animals killed in the arena. One advantage of keeping pigs was that their killing produced a huge amount of blood that could be used in blood puddings. An arrangement for slaughtering animals and catching the blood has been reconstructed from remains found during excavations at the site of Augusta Raurica (Switzerland). The animal was seemingly slaughtered on a base from which grooves led to a bowl where the blood was collected. Another groove allowed the blood to be channelled to a waiting recipient (Lachiche and Deschler-Erb 2008, 133, fig 3).

Apicius (2 3 2) had a recipe for a blood pudding consisting of a mixture of six hard-boiled egg yolks, chopped pine kernels, onions and leeks, seasoned with pepper. This mixture was stuffed into an intestine skin and cooked in a mixture of *liquamen* and wine. Today black or blood puddings in Britain (though the British would never refer to blood puddings) include cereal, often oats, to absorb the blood; the French *boudin noir* relies on chopped onion to absorb the blood, as did Apicius' pudding. The Christian writer Tertullian indicated in *Apologeticus* (9 13), written about AD 197, that this way of utilizing blood could be a problem for Christians, for 'we do not include even animals' blood in our natural diet.' This was in accordance with the instructions in the Bible

(*Acts* 15 20 and 29) that Christians should abstain from eating meats offered to idols and 'from things strangled and from blood'. To test if persons were Christian, the Roman authorities offered them sausages full of blood to see if they would be accepted and, as Tertullian said, 'They were well aware that amongst them it is forbidden; but you want to make them transgress.' The phallic shape of sausages also disgusted Christians.

Sausage meat was stuffed into the lining or the intestines of a sheep or a pig's stomach. The small intestine of a calf could also be used or its caul, the thin sheet of fatty tissue from around the intestine. These casings might allow the sausage to expand without bursting when being cooked. This was a danger noted in Aristophanes' *Clouds* (409–411) when Socrates said that clouds might be dispersed by winds blowing them up like a bladder until they burst. Strepsiades commented that this happened to him when he was cooking a sausage and forgot to make a slit. It blew up, then suddenly burst, spattering blood into his eyes and burning his face. If the mixture were merely wrapped in caul this would be like the British faggot, which is made from highly seasoned offal and other meat and sold cooked, ready for frying or poaching.

Sausages would be hand-made using a funnel of some kind, probably made of cloth. The sausage casing would be pulled over the funnel filled with the meat mixture, secured with another strip of cloth and gradually the mixture would be forced into the casing, packed in a tightly as possible. Modern experiments indicate that wetting the inside of a skin would achieve swift results. Casings could be of different lengths but the Romans referred to two main types of sausages, a long one – *botulus* – and a fat bag-like one – *fundolus*. Each sausage was made separately. Varro said (*De Lingua Latina* 5 111) that *fundolus* was derived from *fundus* meaning bottom because this sausage was open only at one end. Aulus Gellius (*Attic Nights* 16 7 11) commented that Laberius in a farce called *Saturnalia* called a long sausage a *botulus*. According to André (1981, 148) a *botulus* is mentioned on an inscription from Pompeii as part of food for slaves. The *botulus* is seemingly like the French *boudin noir* which is poached ready for further cooking. The first mention of a string of sausages occurs, according to Dalby (2003 (b), 70), in the *Life of St Simeon Salos* (8, 52) by Leontius of Naples. Leontius comments on the saint having a string of sausages round his neck and dipping each one into mustard held in his left hand before eating them.

Although the main meat used in sausages may have been from pork products, other meat would also have been used, especially if it came from the animals killed in the arenas. Pork and beef sausages were the only ones mentioned in Diocletian's Price Edict of AD 301 (4 13–16; Frank 1940, 325). The difference in quality is obvious. Pork sausages are priced at 2 denarii for one ounce; beef sausages at 10 denarii for 1 Roman pound. Smoked Lucanian pork sausages were 16 denarii for 1 Roman pound and smoked beef sausages 10 denarii for 1 Roman pound.

The Lucanian sausage was deemed the most acceptable of all sausages. This was a long, spicy, smoked sausage encountered by Roman troops who served in southern Italy in the third century BC and who brought the recipe back with them to Rome.

Cicero in a letter to his friend Papirius Paetus, a wealthy resident of Naples, written in July 46 BC (*Epistulae ad Familiares* 9 16 8), jested that he used to half-ruin his appetite with his friend's treats of Lucanian sausages and olives. Martial (*Epigrams* 13 35) extolled this sausage when eaten surrounded with a white pottage. This pottage may have been made from pulverized beans or, as Giacosa suggests (1992, 13), a kind of polenta made from spelt. Martial satirized (*Epigrams* 4 46) Sabellus at Saturnalia being ecstatic because he has been given some spelt, crushed beans, frankincense and pepper, and Lucanian sausages, together with a Faliscan paunch (? a blood pudding) and other poor gifts – a small box with a few olives and some cups made at Sagundum by a potter's clumsy wheel.

Apicius provided a recipe (2 4) for Lucanian sausage. Pound together pepper, cumin, savory, rue, parsley, mixed herbs, laurel berries (bay berries), and *liquamen*. The berries needed to be roasted and ground to release more flavour. These spices were next pounded into well-beaten meat. Then *liquamen*, peppercorns, plenty of fat and pine kernels were added. The mixture was inserted into a sausage skin, drawn out very thinly and hung in the smoke to dry. This sausage is seemingly the ancestor of the numerous Italian northern sausages, the *luganische* or *lucaniche*, the best being made in Milan and Lombardy, not smoked, however, and being freshly eaten, either grilled or fried (Riley 2007, 302). These are sold in coils by length rather than weight and Anna del Conte (1989) believes that their origins lie in the recipes of Apicius, although the flavourings are not the same. *Salsicca* (Riley 2007, 477), made either commercially or in the home, a partly cured or fresh sausage, can be added to sauces and stews, as was the case in ancient Rome. Some, such as the *salsicca gialla* of Modena, include a huge variety of spices and those of the Val Comino are made from the offal of pigs fed on acorns, a favourite Roman method which added flavour to the pork. The Spanish *chorizo* and the Portuguese *longaniza* use pimentos which give the red colour, while the Spanish *salchichon* is more akin to the Roman version. Dalby (2003, 295) says that a version of the Lucanian sausage is eaten 'from end to end of the Mediterranean and even beyond'.

45

Apicius also used the Lucanian sausage in other recipes. One (5 4 6) was for a stuffing based on a mixture of the sausage, peas and brains. Pepper, lovage, oregano and ginger moistened with *liquamen*, *passum* (a sweetish wine) and wine was pounded together and boiled, and a little of this added to the stuffing mixture, which was then used to stuff a boned chicken. The bird was wrapped in a sausage skin – the calf's caul would be the biggest and most useful – and cooked gently in the oven. Another recipe (5 4 2) put soaked dried peas, sliced Lucanian sausage, tiny pork meatballs, and other meats including pork shoulder into an earthenware pot. To this was added a pounded mixture of pepper, lovage, oregano, dill, coriander and diced onion mixed with *liquamen* and wine. Oil was added, the meats pricked all over to absorb the oil and the mixture was cooked over a low fire. Giacosa suggests (1992 70) that if cabbage is substituted for peas this would be similar to a Milanese dish called *cassoeula* or *bottaggio*.

An Apician recipe (4 2 13), under the title *patina*, meaning that ingredients had to be cooked in a flat, straight-sided dish, was a rather luxurious recipe, which would have delighted the Romans. Lucanian sausages were placed with vegetables, pieces of chicken, boiled brains, halves of hard-boiled eggs, chicken livers, fried fillets of hake, jellyfish, oysters, fresh cheese and pork sausages stuffed with a Terentian sauce (detailed in 8 1 10) made of pepper, laurel berries, rue, asafoetida, oil and *liquamen*, in layers in a dish. To this were added pine kernels and peppercorns and a sauce made of pepper, lovage, celery-seed and asafoetida. A mixture of beaten eggs and milk was poured onto the mixture. The heat might make the mixture set as custard or it could have been heated gently to make it set. To complete the dish, sea urchins were placed as a garnish.

Apicius (2 1 4) created sausages from pounded pig liver, pepper, rue and *liquamen*. These were wrapped in bay leaves, and could be hung in smoke, probably from a *carnarium*, for as long as the cook thought fit, then grilled before being eaten. Other sorts (2 5 1–4) include a variety of ingredients such as brains, various vegetables, spices and herbs. One sausage was filled with a forcemeat, formed into a ring, smoked until it was red, then sprinkled with cumin and *oenogarum* (a sauce made of wine, *liquamen* and spices). Elsewhere (7 3 1) he gave a recipe for livers of pigs fed on figs. Pliny (*Natural History* 8 77 209) said that pigs, according to a method discovered by Marcus Apicius, were forced to eat dried figs. When they were full, they were given a drink of *mulsum* (sweetish wine) and then swiftly killed. Fass (2003, 259) said that this type of sausage resembles tiny smoked Corsican liver sausages called *figatelli*, flavoured with bay leaves, pork fat and garlic, eaten either hot or cold.

Several other varieties of sausages were mentioned in Roman texts. Martial (*Epigrams* 4 46) spoke of Faliscan, and Varro (*De Lingua Latina* 5 111) said that soldiers found this type of sausage in Falerii. He said that there was also a long one (*longavo*) and an *apexabo*, so called because it had a projection at one end like an apex (a pointed cap). Martial (*Epigrams* 1 41 9–10) called the hot sausages sold in the streets *tomacla*, a similar name to those served by Trimalchio. A *hila* seems to have been a long thin sausage perhaps somewhat like *salami de Strasbourg*.

Another sausage was the *tuccetum*, which André (1981, 143) suggested originated in Cisalpine Gaul. Perseus (*Satires* 2 42) asked for strength for his muscular body in old age but lavish dishes and slices of thick *tucceta* 'will get in Jove's way'. Apuleius (*Metamorphoses* 2 7) recounted that when Lucian found Milo's maid Photis cutting up pork innards for stuffing and slicing other meats, he smelt an utterly delicious *tuccetum*. Later (9–22), Lucian recounted the story of a wife who prepared a feast for her lover with expensive wine and seasoned fresh meat with sausage (*tuccetum*) while her husband was dining at the fuller's house next door.

Nutritional value would vary according to the type of sausage and to the different or varying proportion of ingredients included in them. Some would have a high fat-content; some modern sausages have a fat-content of 25 per cent. Beef sausages might have less fat-content than pork sausages, but pig and ox liver would provide stronger flavour. Other sausages were made of very dubious meats but both cured and fresh sausages would have had some nutritional value and a certain amount of protein. If the sausages contained pork and beef liver this would provide both vitamins and minerals (Frost 2001, 242). Liver contains nicotinic acid, folic acid, vitamins B12 and D and some iron. Some sausages were very tough, as sometimes modern salami can be, and salami may contain as much as 45 per cent fat.

Minced meat, *insicia* (Varro, *De Lingua Latina* 5 110) or *insicium* (Macrobius, *Saturnalia* 7 8 1), indicated that some meat was ground before being made into sausages. Even then there might be problems. Macrobius recorded a discussion between Furius Albinus and Disarius. Furius asked why it was difficult to digest minced meat (*insicium*) even though this type of meat made digestion easier by removing all that was heavy and thereby aiding the digestive process. Disarius said that this meat was still hard to digest because mincing lightened it and so it floated as a liquefied food in the stomach instead of adhering to the stomach walls that provided the heat to promote digestion. Also mincing of the meat incorporated air, which had to be disposed of in the stomach before the meat was finally digested. This might have been as good a reason as any to explain why sausages made of dubious meats did not suit every person. Bad teeth in the ancient world also meant that many people avoided eating tough meat or preferred a much softer diet. Soft blood puddings were welcomed as they could be eaten with a spoon, as would rissoles. Apicius provided several recipes for rissoles – peacock, pheasant chicken and sucking pig. Pliny (*Natural History* 28 58 209) prescribed kid's blood included in a pudding (*sanguiculus*) for a coeliac disorder.

47

Sausages were served in a variety of ways. Aristophanes (*Knights* 315) talked of cutting them slantwise and Athenaeus (*Deipnosophistai* 94f, 95c) said Cratinus, Alexis and Antiphanes referred to slices of sausages in plays. He added that a comedy by Cratinus (138e) mentioned sliced sausages hanging from pegs in public buildings for old men to bite off. Martial (*Epigrams* 5 78) suggested sausages were good served with a white pease pudding with pale beans and red bacon. Trimalchio (Petronius, *Satyricon* 49, 66), as was only to be expected, preferred a dramatic setting, ordering his chef to slit open a pig's belly to let sausages and blood puddings pour out. A dramatic relief on the Porte de Mars at Reims showing a pig lying on its back having its stomach slit open indicates what was intended. Trimalchio served them as hors d'oeuvre on a silver gridiron with damsons and pomegranate seeds underneath. These would give the impression of a fire beneath a griddle. Juvenal (*Satires* 10 356) advised that consecrated sausages made from a white pig should be offered at every shrine for a sound body and a valiant heart, which ensured longevity.

Sausages need not be just a humble dish. Athenaeus (*Deipnosophistai* 131 d) mentioned *phuskai*, a sausage made either of wheat flour and meat or barley flour, fat and meat served during a symposium that was part of a wedding feast for Iphicrates, an Athenian general about 370 BC. Elsewhere (269 f) he commented on a play where the river Crathis, flowing near to Sybaris, a town famous for its luxurious living, has its banks lined with food including sausages and hash. He also (268 f) mentioned that Pherecrates (an Athenian comic poet *c.* 440 BC) depicted a fantastic world in his play *The Miners*. Rivers flow with porridge and black broth and good food lined their banks including steaming hot sausage slices sizzling like oyster shells. But to partake of this abundance one would have to enter the underworld, the realm of the dead.

Bibliography

André, J. *L'Alimentation et la Cuisine a Rome*. 2nd edn. Paris: Librairie C. Klincksieck, 1981.

Apicius. *The Roman Cookery Book*. Translated by Flower, B. and Rosenbaum, E. London: Harrop, 1957.

Dalby, A. *Food in the Ancient World from A to Z*. London and New York: Routledge, 2003(a).

_____. *Flavours of Byzantium*. Totnes: Prospect Books, 2003(b).

Davidson, A. *The Oxford Companion to Food*. Oxford: Oxford University Press, 1999.

Del Conte, A. *Secrets of the Italian Kitchen*. London: Bantam Press, 1989.

Fass, P. *Around the Table of the Romans*. London: Macmillan, 2003.

Frank, T. *An Economic Survey of Ancient Rome. Vol. 5 Rome and Italy of the Empire*. Baltimore: Johns Hopkins University Press, 1940.

Frost, F. 'Sausages and Meat Preservation in Antiquity' in *Greek, Roman and Byzantine Studies*, 40, 241–252. 1999.

Garnsey, P. *Food and Society in Classical Antiquity*. Cambridge: Cambridge University Press, 1999.

Giacosa, I. G. *A Taste of Ancient Rome*. Chicago: University of Chicago Press, 1992.

Lachiche, S. and Deschler-Erb, G. 'De la Viande pour les Hommes et pour les Dieux – sa gestion dans deux villes de la Suisse romaine', in *Food and History*, vol. 5, no. 1, 2007, Institute Européen d'Histoire et des Cultures de l'Alimentation: Turnhaut, Belgium: Brepols, 2008, 107–131.

Mau, A. *Pompeii: its Life and Art*. London: Macmillan, 1899.

Mauri, A. *Pompei*. Rome: Navara, 1960.

McCormack, F. 'Distribution of Meat in an Hierarchical Society: the Irish Evidence' in Miracle, P. and Milner N. (eds.), *Consuming Passions and Patterns of Consumption*. Cambridge: MacDonald Institute Monographs for Archaeological Research, 2002, 25–32.

Riley, G. *The Oxford Companion to Italian Food*. Oxford: Oxford University Press, 2007.

Roy, J. 'The Consumption of Dog–Meat in Classical Greece', in Mee, C. and Renard, J. (eds.) *Cooking and the Past. Food and Culinary Practices in the Neolithic and Bronze Age Aegean*. Oxford: Oxbow Books, 2007, 342–353.

Writers mentioned in the text

Aristophanes (*c.* 445–*c.* 385 BC), Greek playwright, comic poet and author.

Athenaeus (active *c.* AD 200), Egyptian Greek author of an imaginary tale of men dining together and discussing topics including food and medicine.

Aulus Gellius (*c.* AD 130–?180), Roman author.

Apuleius (active *c.* AD 155), Roman author of a novel where the hero is accidentally turned into an ass and undergoes a series of adventures.

Cato (234–149 BC), Roman statesman and moralist who wrote on agricultural matters.

Cicero (106–43 BC), Roman statesman and orator.

Columella (active AD 60–65), Roman author who composed a treatise on farming.

Homer (?eighth century BC), Greek epic poet.

Juvenal (active second century AD), Roman poet, mainly of satires.

Macrobius (active around AD 400), Roman writer and philosopher.

Martial (*c.* AD 40–103), Roman satirical writer.

Ovid (43 BC–AD 14), Roman poet.

Persius (AD 34–62), Roman poet.

Petronius (died *c.* AD 69), Roman satirical writer.

Pliny the Elder (AD 23–79), a prolific Roman writer on natural history.

Seneca the Younger (*c.* 4 BC–AD 65), Roman politician, philosopher and dramatist.

Sidonius Apollinaris (*c.* AD 430–*c.* 480), Gallo–Roman poet.

Tertullian (*c.* AD 160–220), Latin Christian writer.

Theophrastus (*c.* 370–*c.* 287 BC), Greek writer of entertaining monologues.

Varro (116–27 BC), prolific Roman writer on agriculture.

Transylvanian Charcoal-Coated Bread:
From Village Staple to Local Hero

Rosemary Barron

To travel on the night train from Budapest into Transylvania is to open a history book. Leaving a city of streets lined with ornate, elegant buildings and waking up the next morning to the sight of compact, carved wooden houses surrounded by exquisitely shaped haystacks, fruit trees and neat vegetable gardens, and horses plodding along the rough roads pulling their flat-bottomed carts, it's easier to imagine how the sophisticated Habsburgs viewed this arcane land on their eastern borders.

I had been invited to Transylvania by an NGO that was familiar with my work and experiences on Crete, thirty years earlier. My task was to identify the area's special foods and artisan food products that contributed to its true 'food story' and help establish ways that these foods and food products could be part of a modern entrepreneurial community; one that would be able to benefit from others' interest in their foods, yet not allow this to destroy their way of life. Which is why, one beautiful, warm May morning, I found myself in a summer-house in the village of Mesendorf, in southern Transylvania, whacking a large charcoal-covered loaf of bread with a heavy stick.

Transylvania or, 'across the woods' (Latin), was regarded by the early medieval Hungarians as a source of mystery and riches, and a formidable natural barrier to enemies approaching from the east. For over one thousand years, until the beginning of the twentieth century, the 'land beyond the forest' – the forest-covered, horse-shoe-shaped Carpathian mountains – was the jewel in the crown of the Hungarian empire. Yet, for Romanians, Transylvania has always been their country's ancestral heartland. Although first settled by the Dacians, a branch of the Thracians, in the second millennium BC, it was the Roman occupation from AD 101 to AD 271 that brought today's language, national identity and culture to Romania. When Rome withdrew its legions, many Romans stayed in Dacia (Transylvania) where, for the following centuries, Romano-Dacians frequently found themselves in the path of migrating Eurasian peoples on their way to the northern and western parts of Europe. In the ninth century, the Magyars, or Hungarians, occupied Transylvania and, over the next ten centuries, the region's history was inseparable from that of its powerful neighbour.

The Saxons (Germans, from the Moselle region) are thought to have first come to southern Transylvania as immigrants in the twelfth century, invited there by King Geza II of Hungary when his empire was under threat from the east by the Cumans, a Turkic people from the northern Caucasus. He gave them land, tax concessions and some autonomy – a bold offer, and a very attractive deal for people in those days. The Saxons brought with them the innovations of an early medieval agricultural revolution that had already taken place in north-western Europe – better farm tools, well-constructed barns, a knowledge of crop rotation, and the skills of the artisan and merchant. They and their Romanian, Jewish, Hungarian and Roma neighbours suffered frequent invasions by the Ottoman Turks, Wallachians and numerous others. Unlike their neighbours, though, self-protection was fundamental to the way the Saxons lived their lives.

They built large churches in their villages that, in times of need, served as fortresses that could withstand attack and siege. High stone walls surround each church citadel, and an inner wall with a strong wooden roof provided storage space for hay and shelter for their animals. When danger approached, the huge bell tolled, warning the shepherds to bring the animals down from the high meadow or the villagers to bring them from the houses to the church. Within each church's fortified walls were a well, vegetable beds and, sometimes, a few fruit trees. The belfry served as a pantry as well as a lookout, a place where villagers could hang their hams and even smoke them when necessary.

To a casual visitor, the architecture of the village houses, running in colourful rows along the orderly streets, is simple, charming and attractive. But it doesn't take long to realize that the houses have no front doors on the street, nor is it possible to surreptitiously peek into windows, for they are above shoulder height. Instead, each house has a massive wooden gate, as high as the house walls, leading into a courtyard and to the front door of the house. Along the sides of the long courtyard are a neat vegetable garden, little wooden houses for the chickens, ducks and geese, and storage areas for wood and animal fodder; towards the end is a pigsty and, behind that, a large barn leading into an orchard. Beneath each house is a large stone cellar lined with wooden shelves to hold the pickles and jams made each summer and autumn, and where the cabbages, onions, potatoes and wine are stored. At the back of the house, and opening on to the courtyard, is a summer-house with a brick or stone oven, where the bread is made and meals are prepared during the warm months. A raised wooden terrace alongside the house provides the family with a place to enjoy a cool breeze in the hot summers and some protection from the cold on spring and autumn evenings.

These practical living arrangements, designed to keep themselves and their communities secure, ensured that these industrious people prospered. However, the tottering Habsburg Empire finally ended with the First World War and a Saxon emigration to Germany began. By the time Ceaucescu's power ended, only a small percentage of the Saxons of the Siebenburgen, or 'seven citadels' (named for the original seven Transylvanian Saxon cities of Bistrita, Cluj, Medias, Sighisoara, Sibiu, Sebes and Brasov) remained.

For the last one hundred years, Transylvania has been largely ignored by its neighbours. Its physical and political isolation from the twentieth-century industrial, and far more prosperous, Western Europe, has meant that centuries-old ways of culinary and cultural survival are still practised. Until only a few years ago, to visit the villages and cities of Transylvania was to travel back in time.

Preserved foods – cured, fermented, smoked, salted, stored in fat – are at the heart of all the cuisines of Transylvania. They make good kitchen sense in an area with an enormous food surplus in its short, hot summers, and little access to the land during its long, and often harsh, winters. The likelihood of several months of sub-zero winter temperatures has also created a local habit of being very careful with fuel. One particular food that has evolved out of this communal need and climatic necessity is a bread that has a longer 'shelf-life' than most other wheat-flour breads. Made from a well-fermented, moist dough and baked at length at high temperature, the loaves quickly develop a protective charcoal coating. Inedible until the baker has whacked the last speck of charcoal from its golden crust, this lovely bread is a feast for the eye as well as for the stomach.

Mrs Bardas only started making bread when, in 1992, she came back to Mesendorf, the village where she was born. Like other young women of that time in similar circumstances, she had left home at fourteen to go on a training course, then returned to work in a textile factory in nearby Sighisoara. The village she returned to had changed for, in the intervening years, both Ceaucescu's regime and the Berlin Wall had fallen. Only a few, mostly elderly, Saxons remained and their age made it very difficult for them to do the work required to maintain their traditional way of life. When she was a child, every family had had a bread oven in their summer-kitchen and Mrs Bardas had loved watching her grandmother and mother making bread. Sometimes, families used to share the work – one week, one family would make bread for several others; the following week it would be the turn of another family. For this reason, Mesendorf, like most Saxon villages, had no commercial bakery. So Mrs Bardas, having discovered on her return how much she loved making bread for her family, now began to make it for her friends, too.

Her first problem was to find a good source for the flour. In the years before Ceaucescu's grandiose experiment with co-operative farms, village bakers would have used a flour from a locally-grown wheat varietal, one that had evolved over the centuries to withstand Transylvania's particular growing conditions. In Sibiu, a young Saxon baker, whose family has returned after forty years in Germany, has instigated the re-planting of this varietal and it will be interesting to taste her breads in the future. Meanwhile, fortunately for Mrs Bardas and her friends who love her bread, there is still a bakery in the nearby village of Bunesti (Bodendorf), where she can buy a quality flour from southern Romania – a region the Romans regarded as their 'bread basket' – at a good price.

Mrs Bardas is able to bake six three-kilogram loaves at one time in her oven; she likes to use it to capacity each time as a great deal of work is needed to heat it to the required temperature. To make the bread, she needs 18 kg white flour, 10 g fresh yeast, a fistful of salt, water, and 500 g *maia*, a piece of dough put aside the last time she made bread, and stored since in a covered jar in a cool place. The water is from the communal well, the only source of water in the village. Bread-making starts the day prior to baking when Mrs Bardas mixes the dough by hand in a huge, shallow bowl, then transfers it to a *troaca* (trough) and thoroughly kneads it. She lightly covers the *troaca* with a clean cloth and leaves the dough overnight, to rise; in the summer-kitchen, night-time temperatures are ideal for this process, but more care is needed in the winter.

Mrs Bardas' summer bread-baking day starts around 5 a.m., her winter one a little later, when she sweeps out the oven with a *maturatorul*, or broom, made from a few branches of an elder tree (commonly found locally), and puts the wood ash to one side. Once she starts the fire inside the oven, it takes about 1½ hours for the oven to reach the right temperature in the summer months, a little longer in the winter. When does Mrs Bardas know the moment is right to start baking? When the inner walls of the oven are glowing just the right colour, she explains. Meanwhile, she checks to see if the dough is to her satisfaction. If it is, she forms it into six round loaves, ready for baking.

When the oven is ready, Mrs Bardas rakes out the fire with a *darc,* or rake, and uses a *lopata,* or baker's peel – a long, flat shovel – to insert, and carefully position, the loaves in the oven. She tightly closes the oven door, to seal in the heat, and spends the next 2½ hours preparing other foods for baking once she has removed the loaves from the oven – perhaps a meat dish, or *cozonac* (a traditional cake made from a sweet dough and walnut or poppy seed paste), or *lichiu* (the remnants of the bread dough, flattened and covered in a sweet egg and milk batter).

Mrs Bardas doesn't touch, or move, the loaves during baking until fifteen minutes before she removes them from the oven. At this point, she opens the oven door for the first time, to check that everything is as it should be. Sometimes there are problems – perhaps the oven wasn't quite hot enough, or was too hot, or maybe the flour hadn't been of sufficient quality, or the viscosity of the dough not quite right. When Mrs Bardas opened the oven door in front of me, all I could see were six charcoal-covered mounds! As I could not see the bread, I had no idea whether the loaves were looking good or not, but she assured me that all was going well.

Using the *lopata*, Mrs Bardas transfers the blackened loaves one at a time to a bench and covers them with a blanket – an essential process, she assures me. I suspect that this creates a layer of steam between the crust and charcoal, loosening it, and thus allowing it to be completely removed. This is one of the processes I plan to pay careful attention to when I make the bread myself. Once a loaf has cooled (but before it's cold), Mrs Bardas needs to remove the covering layer of charcoal. To do this, she beats the bread with a *batator*, or heavy bat. This is not only hard work, but also requires a great deal of patience and skill. Although the loaf isn't delicate, it can, nevertheless, easily lose its magnificent appearance if beaten too enthusiastically, and its flavour, if any trace of charcoal remains. Nothing is wasted – the ash from the fire becomes fertilizer for the family's extensive vegetable garden and flower beds, and the charcoal is mixed with animal feed, much to the delight of the chickens in particular. For the War generation, the charcoal was a substitute for coffee.

These handsome loaves, with their deep golden crusts, will keep for at least a week in a cool place even though, unlike commercial bread, they contain no additives or preservatives. The dough's long, slow rise and fermented character gives the bread a depth of flavour that makes it very satisfying to eat, especially when partnered with *slanina* – pork fat – and slices of onion, the favourite snack of Mrs Bardas' husband.

Our lunch that day was one of those exquisite moments in life when foods and kitchen skills come together at the table, a moment that's the exact opposite of a commercialized 'food experience'. Mrs Bardas arranged platters of home-smoked meats, pickled and fresh vegetables, a few village cheeses and a large tureen of soup along the centre of a splendid wooden table set up in her courtyard. Pride of place was of course given to the magnificent loaves. Our wine was the product of the previous year's grape harvest from the vine shading the terrace, and we dined to the sound of some very happy noises from the summer-house, where the chickens and geese had found the remnants of the charcoal.

Now Romania is part of the European Union, sliced white bread has made its way to the tables of the Transylvanian villages. Yet in the last five years, a growing number of people have become interested in the bread made by Mrs Bardas. For her, making bread is a joy – she gains enormous satisfaction from doing a job well, and happiness from seeing her loved ones eat with such appetite and gusto. Her visitors – foreign and, increasingly, Romanian – particularly please her as she loves their curiosity about her way of life.

Her loaves are now part of a growing regional, community-based food tourism programme that is developing in this fascinating part of Europe. It includes visits with artisans producing buffalo- and sheep-milk cheeses, honeys, wild- and garden-fruit jams, herb teas, fermented pickled vegetables, smoked and cured meats and fats and other pure foods of the village and high meadows, and visitors experience a genuine, heartfelt hospitality while they explore the rather forbidding citadels, beautiful mountain meadows and eerie forests. Attracted by the villagers' self sufficiency, history and food culture, visitors want Mrs Bardas' bread with their local taste-treats, not a commercial sliced-white loaf that they can find anywhere. Her bread is a unique product that's perfectly suited to its environment and making it for family and friends transforms and enriches her life. She is proving that foods with a place in a community's history can not only help us understand that history, they can also play a central role in its future.

Kitchen Notes

I was able to bring to the Symposium two of Mrs Bardas' loaves – one with its charcoal coating removed, one with it still intact.

Using a baseball bat, we tried hard to remove the charcoal covering the second loaf, but it proved impossible, proving Mrs Bardas' point that the loaves had to be loosely covered immediately they were taken out of the oven, and the charcoal removed as soon as the loaf had cooled.

I have made two attempts so far to make the bread here, in England, but have been unsuccessful. This has been due, I suspect, to not heating the oven to the required temperature, for I found it very hard to judge that 'right' moment. To me, on both occasions, it was just a very, very hot oven!

However, the Symposium is a rich source of both knowledge and generosity, and two symposiasts, both keen bread-makers, have offered to join me in my next attempt at making this bread. I plan to find a special thermometer that can measure a greater heat than normal, for I'm very curious to discover exactly what the 'right' temperature is that's needed to create that incredible charcoal coating.

Cultures and Cultures: Fermented Foods as Culinary 'Shibboleths'

Jonathan Brumberg-Kraus and Betsey Dexter Dyer

Fermented foods and drinks, especially if assertively aromatic and prepared in the deep tradition of a particular culture, are what we call 'shibboleths' after the Hebrew word in the Biblical book of Judges used to distinguish one ethnic group from another. That is, fermented dishes quickly and emphatically separate those who belong to the village from those who are visiting (or planning to attack it!). For *our* group, a traditional fermented item like *kimchi*, cheese, beer, or wine can represent the most comforting of comfort food or the most joyful of celebratory food. But for our *guests*, no matter how intrepidly cosmopolitan and open to experiences, that same dish may never become their treasured comfort or joy food. The polite guest may even need to leave the table for a moment to recover enough composure to try another small carefully selected bite under the watchful eye of the gracious and hopeful host. At the very worst the impolite guest will avoid the table altogether, the complete nature of the shibboleth having been revealed.

From our unique paired and integrated point-of-view as a working team of a Professor of Religion (and Rabbi) and a Professor of Biology (and atheist), we explore in our paper the biological origins of cultural preferences for particular fermented foods and drinks with an emphasis on the shibboleths: that is, those fermented cuisines that have been among the most defining and unifying components of human cultures while emphatically excluding other cultures. Using examples especially from Jewish tradition, we will complement the biological analysis with a cultural-linguistic analysis of explanations and justifications that humans have used for their unique preferences. Indeed we find the two aspects (the biological and the cultural) to be inseparably intertwined. The compelling importance of our contribution will be to set a firm and comprehensive foundation for fermented cuisines in general as biologically inevitable shapers (i.e. includers and excluders) of cultural traditions.

Traditionally fermented foods are always transformed by the activities of local microbes, and are always many steps away from 'fresh.' The transformations may be profound: new, unfresh colors, textures (often leaning toward the viscous), flavors entirely devoid of clues as to the original identity of the food and even peculiar sounds since many traditionally fermented foods spend much or all of their life-spans fizzing effervescently. However the odors of fermented foods are typically their most defining properties. Olfaction, a peculiar and primal sense, seems to shoot information directly into the most primitive parts of the brain, bypassing rational contemplation and decision-making and certainly bypassing certain aspects of normal guest-like behavior.

Fermented foods work well as shibboleths for at least three biological reasons:

1. The original fermenting communities of microbes were (and many still are) no more than the indigenous microbes of a particular region and of its human population. Microbes from local soils and waters confer a characteristic '*terroir*' by tumbling into open buckets of milk and vats of grape juice. The indigenous microbiota dwelling in and on humans produce not only familiar body odors and flavors but also those same nuances in fermented cuisines. It is no coincidence that a well-ripened, surfaced-washed cheese can reek of foot odor. The same bacteria cause both.

2. Our senses of taste, smell, touch, sight, and hearing vary according the genes that code for the functions. The normal, ancestral situation was for a continuous lineage of humans to dwell in a small, inbred settlement with a limited travel radius. Such conditions are ideal for concentrating genetic traits including perceptions of food that might lead to strong preferences and aversions. Small, related communities are also ideal for the transmission of cultural information concerning culinary preferences. However, when these groups become less socially and geographically isolated from one another, 'culture' enables them to adapt their genetically inherited preferences in order to negotiate their new experiences of familiarity with the Other as friend or foe. To this end,

3. Humans seem to be genetically predisposed to find causalities and explanations. No matter how serendipitously a particular regional fermented cuisine might have evolved through chance encounters of microbes and food, humans characteristically would be ready with a full explanation: 'This is our cuisine, as our ancestors always made it, and part of our culture', or 'it's OK to eat this but not that from our neighbors, because…' This is the gist of even the most scholarly of commentaries on foods, no matter how elaborate the rhetoric and justification. Jewish commentary is a rich source of such explanations.

The word 'culture' has several definitions, with which their etymologies are intertwined here. The *Oxford English Dictionary* entry indicates an origin for 'culture' concerned with the cultivating of plants and animals (essentially farming) but then the word began to take on connotations of the various parameters of societies such as customs, language, art and religion. And the word 'cult' is a sort of extreme and specific form pertaining mostly to religion and is connected etymologically to culture from the deepest Latin roots. Meanwhile, late-nineteenth-century microbiologists developing techniques for keeping various microbes alive in the lab., decided 'culture' was the right word (both as a noun and verb) for that activity. We have come to understand a certain profound, unexpected and even counterintuitive relationship between *cultures of humans* and *cultures of microbes*, especially fermenting microbes that enhance flavors, aromas, colors and textures of some of the most defining foods and drinks of human cultures.

Cultures of fermentative microbes associate with their own particular cultures of humans. Likewise, cultures of humans have their special microbial cultures. How these relationships were initiated and are maintained are more in the hands (or in the fimbriae) of the microbes than of the humans. That is the counterintuitive part. Humans (being almost unavoidably human-centered) might think that their various fermented foods and drinks are concoctions of their own invention. (Indeed typical recipes for fermented items read like elaborate protocols.) *However it is the other way around.* The relentless (microbe-centered) activities of microbial fermenters make it impossible for fermented cuisines not to have occurred. It was inevitable many times over in human cultures everywhere.

Microbiology students mindful of their experiments are sometimes surprised to discover that the bacteria by which cheese-making is demonstrated on one day in the lab. are virtually the same bacteria that may be isolated from their own skin on another day in the lab.[1] However, many microbiology lab. manuals, which come from a tradition of controlling microbes, do not make this connection. Modern milk processing is all about control and even legislation. However it was not too many centuries ago (and even currently in some indigenous human cultures) when fermentations of all sorts *just happened* to pretty much anything that was not either eaten on the spot or completely desiccated (by long roasting, salt, or exposure to dry air). Which micro-organisms did the fermentations? Whatever bacteria and fungi were available tumbled into milk pails, grain bins, and vats of fruit. Those available were two categories of mostly 'Gram positive' bacteria. One set came from the bodies of humans, the same bacteria that produce odors ranging from pleasantly familiar to repelling. Another set of Gram positives were from the soil, easily brought into the kitchen on hands and feet and on wooden milk pails. In addition to bacteria were indigenous fungi, mostly yeast. The many wild yeasts (now tamed and domesticated for industrial fermenting operations) were just those that can easily be found on decaying plants, in rich humus soils and on normal human skin.

What about the pathogens? Despite garnering most of the publicity about the microbial world, pathogens are rare. Of the estimated millions of bacterial species, only about 50 are human pathogens and these tend to be out-competed by our normal body bacteria and in normal soil communities. Therefore by extension, the rare pathogens are out-competed in any decomposing food such as a bucket of fermenting milk. Indeed most fermented food and drink are preserved and protected against further invasions by less desirable microbes.

A special, related side topic is food poisoning, which we consider to be a summary (often violent) encounter between one's own indigenous bacteria and those of a particular regional, foreign cuisine (i.e., other peoples' bacteria), whether the microbes are characteristic of a particular fermented food or merely local contaminants. Living in an area over a period of time may allow an acclimation and truce between the adversarial microbes and thus a gradual acceptance of the offending regional item. However, humans learn quickly and viscerally (albeit often irrationally) from such encounters and can develop life-long, strong aversions often centered on an acutely recalled odor or flavor. Thus a memory of food poisoning can be a contributor to some of the strongest shibboleth qualities of fermented cuisines.[2]

Although you might be convinced now that body and soil bacteria and yeasts are tumbling by the billions out of the air into pails of milk and vats of fruit at all times, you might nonetheless cling to the idea that somehow fermented cuisines are inventions of our various human ancestors who were cleverly taking advantage of the situation. The other way around, is our conclusion! The first major contribution of our human ancestors was being desperately hungry and willing to eat highly transformed (indeed putrefying) food, frothing with a miasma of microbes. Then, subsequent contributions of humans to the development of regional fermented cuisines centered around the remarkable (probably species-specific) ability of humans to justify elaborately pretty much anything that they are doing, including finding causalities (false or otherwise.) It was inevitable that elaborate customs and traditions (i.e. justifications) would evolve around special fermented foods. Furthermore the shibboleth quality probably did not go unnoticed by our various insular, not well travelled, and somewhat xenophobic ancestors. That aspect would only serve to enhance the culture-building aspects of fermented cuisines: noticing one's very own language, religion, customs, (delicious) fermented foods versus some stranger's very different language, religion, customs, (repugnant) fermented foods. *59* Cultural justifications for these distinctions came about especially when geographic proximity brought groups together regularly, so as to negotiate whether these 'Others' were friends or foes. This is exemplified in our consideration of two traditional Jewish culinary shibboleths: *hametz* and Gentile wine

In Biblical and later Jewish cultural traditions, two food categories, *hametz* (leavened bread) and Gentile wine, exemplify taboos on fermented foods explicitly intended to keep groups separate from one another, i.e. Jews from Gentiles. *Hametz* is prohibited during the seven days of Passover and in the Biblical grain-offering sacrifice (*minhah*): 'It shall be eaten as unleavened cake...it shall not be baked with leaven' (Lev. 6:17–18). Maimonides says that this is because idolaters (that is, non-Israelites) typically used leavened-bread offerings in their sacrifices. The Bible's prohibition against leavened food during Passover makes very clear its purpose of distinguishing God's chosen people from everyone else: 'For seven days no leaven shall be found in *your* houses; for whoever eats what is leavened *shall be cut off from the congregation of Israel*, whether an alien or native of the land. *You* shall eat nothing leavened, in all *your* settlements you shall eat unleavened bread' (Ex. 12:19–20). This implies that unfermented food is *ours* and perfect, while fermented food is *yours*, and less than perfect. Of course, the ancient Israelites ate leavened bread as part of their ordinary daily diet, just like their neighbors, even as Jews did and continue to do today.[3] Therefore we should emphasize that these seasonal and situational prohibitions of *hametz* had more of a didactic, rhetorical function than a practical legal one. They cultivated an *awareness* of difference from neighboring groups, without absolutely restricting contact and significant interaction with them. For the ordinary Israelite in the Biblical period,

> Eating practices were about what Israel could and, particularly, could not eat – not about what they actually did or did not eat. They were…most often about negation – negation of certain evil qualities and, by extension, negation of nations who displayed those qualities…[and sometimes] the nation whose qualities should be avoided could even be Israel herself.[4]

Similarly, post-Biblical references to the *hametz* prohibitions typically apply them metaphorically to personal qualities to be avoided, though perhaps always lurking in the background is the unstated rationale, 'because that's how the Gentiles behave.'

The prohibition of Gentile wine, a sub-category of prohibited Gentile foods, is a post-Biblical Jewish innovation, and an explicit, direct attempt to limit intimate (versus commercial) contact with Gentiles. Under the foreign rule of the Roman Empire, the rabbis especially felt Jewish identity was particularly vulnerable, and thus intensified social boundaries between Jews and Gentiles. The rationales given for prohibiting Gentile wine were that it was *yayin nesekh* ('libation wine') assumed to have been produced for Gentile worship, *avodah zarah* (literally, *foreign* worship); or even if it weren't, drinking *setam yeinam* ('just *their* wine') with Gentiles will lead to intermarriage. The Talmud (b. Avodah Zarah 36b) rationalizes prohibitions against Gentile foods and wine as protection against a slippery slope to intermarriage and idolatry: 'Their bread and oil were forbidden on account of their wine, their wine on account of their daughters, and their daughters on account of "another thing,"' i.e., idolatrous worship.[5] Indeed, some authorities even prohibited Gentile beer, not because it was used for 'foreign worship,' but because it likewise promoted excessive familiarity between Jews and Gentiles. Thus, the prohibition of *fermented* drinks was intended to separate Jews from Gentiles, though by the medieval era, many restrictions on intoxicating drinks other than wine, e.g. on beer, 'boiled wine,' or wine mixed with significant amounts of honey and pepper (*yaynomalin* or *konditon*), were relaxed,[6] both in the Muslim lands and in Christian Europe. Wine *per se* however remained problematic, because of its association with 'foreign worship' or the foreigners who made it, even after some Jewish legal authorities decided that Muslim and Christian worship was not idolatrous.

While both *hametz* and wine function as 'shibboleths' in Jewish tradition to divide Jews from non-Jews, do the peculiar features of biological fermentation *per se* play a role in this cultural-linguistic construction of boundaries? Yes! *Hametz* is the same root as the Hebrew adjective for 'sour' – *hamutz* – the taste of many fermented foods. Rabbinic law extended the prohibition against Gentile wine to cheese (m. A.Z. 2:4–5), pickled fish, and other products preserved in vinegar, ostensibly because the preservative vinegars may come from Gentile libation wine (m. A.Z. 2:6, cf. 2:2), or because they may have been made from non-kosher fish or other animal ingredients. However, these foods also would taste and smell sour or acidic, or in the case of cheese, pungent. But here is where it gets complicated, for the same could be said for the spicy relishes, pickled fish, and other foods made by Gentiles that the rabbis permitted. Still, it is possible that physiological and ecological factors could easily affect or reinforce cultural preferences so that Jews would experience sour or pungent flavors as '*good* sour' or '*bad* pungent.' Though the earlier rabbinic texts we've mentioned don't stress the off-putting smells or tastes of Gentile foods, early modern German sources complained that Jews smell bad like garlic, and in the modern period, 'sours' such as *borsht*, sauerkraut, and *schav* were a notable component of Lithuanian, Polish, and Russian Jewish diets.[7] However, since Eastern European Jews shared this taste for sours and onions with their non-Jewish neighbors, it functioned more as an intra-Jewish culinary shibboleth between Western and Eastern European Jews.[8]

Fermentation also takes time, a point alluded to not only in the reason given for eating unleavened bread on Passover (the Israelites didn't have enough time to let their bread rise when they escaped Egypt), but also in its metaphorical extension to the moral realm. As a verb, *hametz* also connotes 'delay,' as in the saying: '*ke-derekh she-ayn me-hamitzim et ha-matzah, ayn mahmitzin et ha-mitzvah*', which the *Alcalay Hebrew-English Dictionary* translates 'As you must not allow the *matzah* to become sour, so you must not allow the *mitzvah* to become sour by postponement.' Post-Biblical interpretations set up a rich set of symbolic associations between *hametz* and morality. *Hametz* is associated in midrash and kabbalah with the *yetzer ha-ra*, 'the evil inclination.' There's an echo of this in the New Testament's 'beware of the leaven of the Pharisees' (Mk 8:15, cf. I Cor. 5:6–7). In other words, *matzah* symbolizes a good deed, but food allowed to leaven is a deed 'gone bad' – evoking viscerally all the side-effects food gone bad has; it stinks, is slimy, is puffed up, etc.

While the characteristic odors, taste, and appearance of fermentation may be associated with wine and wine-like drinks, Jewish tradition tends to stress the less visible or palpable, more spiritual or essential aspects of wine and its producers. Indeed, acid or piquant flavors or a frothy appearance are important criteria for determining that wine-like liquids are no longer wine, and hence *permissible*, while conversely, wine contaminated by Gentiles must still taste as wine should for it to be prohibited.[9] Certainly the intoxicating effect of fermented wine made or touched by Gentiles plays a role in its prohibition, since drinking with them blurs and breaches the social boundaries between Jew and Gentile. But more important is the assumption behind it: wine and those who produce it somehow share something basic in their essence. While we doubt the classical Jewish sources knew that fermenters and their fermented products shared the same local bacteria, their language 'contamination', and equation of food producers with their products (even though the connections are invisible) prompt the same response: 'quarantining' the Other's 'poison'. This poison is particularly insidious, since one can hardly smell or taste the difference between Jewish and Gentile wine. What makes Gentile wine bad is that Gentiles themselves make it, and consequently, if a Gentile touches Jewish wine, or if Gentile wine gets mixed with Jewish wine, it becomes 'contaminated' and unfit to drink. It is as if Gentiles and their wine share some sort of fundamental essence that is somehow 'bad,' in contrast to Jews and their wine. The Zohar in the thirteenth century explains a mystical, fundamental difference between Jews and their wine, and Gentiles and their wine, and the dangerous consequences of mixing the two, as follows:

> Hence Israel drinks the wine of Israel ...He who drinks is strengthened and whosoever recites a blessing over such wine is exalted in holiness. They do not imbibe *wine made in impurity by the impure for the spirit of impurity rests upon it.* Whosoever drinks such wine thereby pollutes his spirit and makes himself impure. He is not of the side of Israel and he is disqualified from existence in the World to Come ...the realm of 'the treasured wine.' (*Zohar: Shemini* 40a).

For Jews, drinking such wine turns them to 'the other side.' The famous Maharal of Prague in the sixteenth century quotes this passage at length in his polemical sermon against Jews drinking Gentile wine, directing it especially against the Jewish legal authorities who encouraged it by their lenient determination that Christians and Muslims were not idolaters, hence their wine no longer *yayin nesekh.* The Maharal's argument against drinking Gentile wine is basically 'you are what you eat,' but there is a special connection between a people and its wine:

> Wine is not like other drinks that are for the body alone, but rather, wine enlightens the mind. And indeed its aroma is known to have this effect, as our rabbis *z"l* said, 'Let the whole soul praise the Lord,' what thing does the soul enjoy but the body does not? I say aroma. Accordingly Scripture said [wine] is what 'gladdens God and people'[10] for it should be said that wine gladdens God when one makes libations of it on the altar, and people when it enlightens their mind.[11]

He goes on to say that as Jacob 'the good child' and Esau 'the bad child' while still in their mother's womb (according to the midrash) respectively kicked when she passed by a synagogue and bet midrash, or by a Gentile temple, so

> a kind finds its own kind and is aroused by it. For it is attracted by its nature by itself to the thing to which it is attached, without any intention, awareness, or choice, only of its own accord, because anything on its own part is aroused by the thing to which it is attracted.[12]

It is as if the Gentile wine has a mind of its own, or better, of its Gentile maker, and can't help being attracted to idolatry. However, superficially, Gentiles, Jews, and their wines basically look, smell, and taste like they're from the same species. That they are not is a mystical secret, and so have something in common with the process of fermenting wine, according to the Maharal.

Wine is something secret hidden in the grape, which the process of wine-making brings forth, revealing the invisible and making it visible. Hence the Maharal says,

> you will understand the prohibition of *yayin nesekh*, and will not say that the matter of wine is of little consequence, for Scripture has said about it that it 'gladdens God and people' and by saying it 'gladdens God,' it teaches that wine suits someone who separates themselves from what is physical, and all this is because wine comes out of the innermost part of the grape, and what is hidden suits what is divine, which is why *YaYi"N* (wine) is numerically equivalent to *SO"D* (secret).[13]

Wine-liness, as it were, is next to Godliness. The metaphorical fermentation of wine, its makers, and consumers is dualistic; their differences remain secret and invisible until the process reaches the point when variant effects are revealed in the physical demeanors of those who drink the different wines. Indeed, there are even two different kinds of revelations – *giluyim*. The good revelation from the good wine is the disclosure of the mystical secrets of God, occasioned by *our* wine's power to 'enlighten the mind' – in us, the good people. The bad revelation is the *gilui arayot*, literally, 'the revealing of nakedness,' improper sexual relations, the effects of *the Others'* 'fermentation' that has gone too far.[14] 'Foreign worshippers', Gentiles, or Jews 'poisoned' by drinking their wine, are what they drink. Interestingly, while such blurring of boundaries resulting from intoxication is normally discouraged, there is a notable exception in Jewish tradition. On Purim, drinking *Jewish* wine to blur boundaries is encouraged, indeed required. As the Talmud says '*hayav inesh li-besumeh be-Purya ad de-lo yada bein arur Haman le-Baruch Mordechai.*' (A person must get so drunk on Purim that they don't know the difference between 'Cursed be Haman' and 'Blessed be Mordechai', b. Megillah 7b). In other words, there is both 'good' and 'bad' intoxication, just as there is good and bad fermentation. Jewish wine strengthens Jews, but Gentile wine and other kinds of 'bad fermentation' makes them 'go bad.'

As we were writing and discussing this paper together we realized that there was a particular irony in our contention that strong-smelling fermented foods are shibboleths. Brumberg-Kraus noticed that while his Jewish examples indeed used *fermented* foods and drinks to differentiate themselves socially from Gentiles, they said little about them being odoriferous. Dyer suggested two explanations. The first is that one can be remarkably anosmic (the olfactory equivalent of blind) to fermentative odors of one's own cuisine. Therefore there may be no comment at all in cases where it might appear to an outsider that odor should be mentioned. The second is that humans have a rather poor sense of smell and this may go along with an exceptionally impoverished vocabulary for describing odors. The reactions tend to be more visceral than verbal.

The phenomenon of failing to recognize one's own cultural fermented foods as having any particular odor surprised us at first. Although on retrospect, this may be a shibboleth quality. Some of Dyer's students of English descent have informed her that English food must be an exception since nothing in that cuisine is odoriferously fermented! Meanwhile some of Dyer's Asian students could scarcely bring themselves near the table at which the class was having a cheese-tasting of Cheddars and Stiltons. Similarly, Rabbi Brumberg-Kraus at first despaired that he could think of no stinky fermented Jewish foods, at least not in the classical Jewish sources, to support our hypothesis! His Gentile colleague Professor Dyer easily corrected him, reminding him that pickled herring and gefilte fish left at room temperature for any significantly lengthy period of time would cause odors throughout the house. Indeed the advent of large modern refrigerators may sustain the illusion that one's own (and even others') cuisine have no remarkable odors. Chilling dulls odors and therefore may have a dulling effect on perceptions of unique odors. Visits to open markets of developing countries, especially to the fish and meat sections, may be necessary for reacquainting scholars with the truly shibboleth nature of (for example) fish being transformed in the warm sun into a cultural delicacy by microbial fermentations.

Humans, compared to nearly all terrestrial mammals, are exceptionally deficient in genetic ability to detect odors. Typical mammals have at least 1000 genes for olfactory reception and typically all are functional. In humans, about two-thirds of those thousand olfactory genes are mutated beyond use. We manage to get weak whiffs of microbial fermentations with just a few hundred receptors. Apparently this deficit began to evolve when humans became more upright and visually oriented. Most interesting smells are heavier than air and are best detected with a keen nose (dog-like) to the ground. Indeed dogs are good guides to the mostly uninterpretable (to us) olfactory world. While we detect 'notes', dogs (with 1000 functional receptors) revel in symphonies of olfactory input. Luca Turin in *Secret of Scent*, imagines the olfactory world to be enveloping, like a hologram.[15] Human vocabularies for describing olfactory experience are considered to be as impoverished as our olfactory receptors. Nonetheless, there exist systematic attempts such as the 'Wine Aroma Wheel' of A.C. Noble to collect and arrange all useable adjectives.[16] Many are essentially descriptions of microbial decompositions including moldy, earthy, sulfur, lactic, sweaty and wet wool. Even the adjectives evocative of flowers and fruits such as citrus, berry, and floral are microbial by-products that we happen to interpret as fresh scents. Perhaps, as Rachel Herz suggests, this is because we don't use odors to construct abstract schemas of our world. Animals, like rodents, who rely primarily on their sense of smell to negotiate the world, likely do think in smell, and certainly some of our primate ancestors did as well. But for modern humans, vision and hearing–language are the sensory information sources we use to construct abstract representations to make sense and survive in the world. Because we don't rely on odor images in this way, this ability has not been specially selected for and hence has become weak.[17]

What we humans have left of olfaction is so basic that it seems directly connected to the reflexes of the brain. Thus richly transformed microbial products (our delicious fermented food or your disgusting, decomposing food) defy normal vocabulary but rather require immediate, thoughtless reactions (good! bad!) – as true shibboleths. Perhaps this is why (as our learned commentators have shown) fermented foods (if they are not simply eliciting an exclamation) require elaborate, invented vocabularies and convoluted justifications for their inevitable, defining presence in all human cultures.

It's through our cultural-linguistic rationalizations that we construct our 'abstract schemas,' our 'maps' of the world, while our tastes and smells add value to the places on the map through the strong emotional charge our memories of them evoke. These complex maps, such as the Jewish cultural justifications we discussed, compensate for our olfactory deficiencies. We can't always immediately see, taste, or smell what (or who) might kill or love us, but our cultural taboos protect us, when our physiological capacities alone just aren't enough!

Notes

1. The discussion of bacteria that follows comes from Betsey Dexter Dyer, *A Field Guide to Bacteria*. Ithaca, NY: Cornell U. Press, 2003
2. Dangerous strains of microbes that are developed through careless human practices with stockyard animals and with mass-produced vegetables, especially involving cavalier use of antibiotics, have caused some of the most deadly cases of food poisoning on record. These may include invasion well past the intestines into the body and antibiotic resistance. Such stockyard microbes (carelessly encouraged by irresponsible human practices) are *not* part of any culture's normal fermented cuisines and are *not* considered relevant in this paper.
3. John Cooper, *Eat and Be Satisfied: A Social History of Jewish Food*. Northvale, N.J: Jason Aronson, 1993, 4–9, 37–42, 148–151.
4. David Kraemer, *Jewish Eating and Identity Through the Ages*. London: Routledge, 2009, 22.
5. David Kraemer, 68.
6. Solomon ben Abraham Adret, *Torat ha-bayit ha-arokh veha-katsar*, ed. Mosheh ben Yitzhak Me'ir Baron. Jerusalem: Mossad Harav Kook, 1995, v. 2: 512–3 (Spain, thirteenth century).
7. Maria Diemling, '"As the Jews Like to Eat Garlic": Garlic in Christian-Jewish Polemical Discourse in Early Modern Germany', in *Food and Judaism*, ed. Leonard J Greenspoon, et al. Omaha, NE: Creighton University Press, 2005, 215–234; John Cooper, 155–7.
8. Diemling, 228, quoting the complaint of a German Jewish rabbi about the stench of his Polish Jewish cook's gefilte fish.
9. Solomon ben Abraham Adret, 499–503.
10. Judges 9:13, cited in a discussion about the preeminence of wine over other fruits in b. Berakhot 35a.
11. Judah Loew ben Bezalel, 'Drush al ha-Mitzvot', in *Derashot Maharal Mi-Prag*, ed. Moshe Shlomo Kasher (Jerusalem: Makhon Torah Shlema, 1958), 82–3.
12. Ibid., 83.
13. Ibid., 89.
14. Ibid.
15. Luca Turin, *The Secret of Scent: Adventures in Perfume and the Science of Smell*. New York: Ecco, 2006, 9.
16. Ann C. Noble, *Wine I.Q. Learning and Reference Guide*, 1996.
17. Rachel Herz, *The Scent of Desire: Discovering Our Enigmatic Sense of Smell*, 1st ed. New York: William Morrow, 2007, 88.

Continuity in Culinary Aesthetics in the Western Mediterranean: Roman *Garum* and *Liquamen* in the Light of the Local Survival of Fermented Fish Seasonings in Japan and the Western Mediterranean

Anthony F. Buccini

In considering the relationship between the cuisine of Italy in ancient Roman times and that of modern Italy, it is commonplace to note a certain degree of continuity, particularly with regard to the 'classical triad' of the Mediterranean kitchen – bread, wine and oil – for these staple items have remained throughout history central elements in the diets of the region's population.[1] But otherwise there exists a general sense, shared by many food writers, that the cuisine of classical Rome was in an essential way very different from that of modern Italy.

One striking difference is the absence in ancient Roman cookery of a number of foods that feature prominently in modern Italian cookery, including most famously the tomato, as well as other imports to the Mediterranean from the New World in the early modern period, such as beans, zucchini, peppers, etc., or introduced to Italy from the east in the Middle Ages by the Arabs, such as eggplants and spinach, to name but two. Pasta, the single most emblematic element of modern Italian cuisine, was, at least according to most food historians, also unknown in Italy in classical times, having allegedly been developed elsewhere and introduced at some later date.

No less striking than the absence of specific foods is the seemingly very different aesthetic of modern Italian cookery from that in the collection traditionally attributed to Apicius, the most extensive source we have on ancient Roman cookery. Whereas the primary culinary aesthetic of modern Italy can most reasonably be characterized as one of simplicity, with most dishes exhibiting straightforward treatments of one or a few featured ingredients, and with the use of spices and herbs generally highly restrained, the cuisine reflected in the Apicius collection exults in complexity, with many of the recipes including combinations of numerous main ingredients and almost all being finished with complex seasoning combinations or sauces, using multiple spices and herbs and additional liquid flavouring-agents. Of the last mentioned, several are to this day staple ingredients in the cookery of Italy, namely, olive oil, wine and vinegar, but a further one, which along with olive oil is the most frequently used in Apicius, is the famous fermented fish sauce known variously as *liquamen* or *garum*, an ingredient which is virtually unknown in modern Italian cuisine.

The parallel has often been drawn between this use of fermented fish sauces and pastes in the ancient Mediterranean world and the use of unquestionably similar sauces and pastes in modern times throughout south-east Asia. Far less known is the fact that, while widespread use of fermented fish products (FFPs) in Europe diminished greatly in the early Middle Ages, they have continued to be produced and consumed to limited degrees in localities around the western Mediterranean down to the present time. Also little known is the fact that the use of fermented fish sauces and pastes has undergone significant reduction over time in parts of east Asia, including Japan, where FFPs have been largely supplanted as seasoning agents by fermented soybean and wheat products. Yet, in some regions in Japan, as locally in the western Mediterranean, fish-based seasonings have managed to survive.

Regarding culinary continuity across the past two millennia in Italy, the history of the use of FFPs in Asia offers us a possible typological parallel which may shed light on the historical development of the cuisines of the Mediterranean and in particular on the apparent central aesthetic change that the almost complete disappearance of *liquamen/garum* might represent. From this perspective, I consider an important question in the history of the cuisines of the Mediterranean: why did such a fundamental part of ancient Mediterranean cuisines come to be eliminated so thoroughly from the culinary culture of all but a few localities?

I contend that the collapse of large-scale industrial production and distribution of fish sauces in the late stages of the Roman Empire was, in fact, not associated with any significant change in the typology of the cuisine in much of the western Mediterranean region. Specifically, while extensive use of liquid fermented fish seasonings was vastly reduced, other similar glutamate-based – that is, umami – seasonings came to be used more extensively in the popular cuisines of the region, in a very direct sense fulfilling the exact same functional rôle of less-widely available *liquamen,* etc. Put another way, while there was change in the surface realization of the culinary grammar, the deep-structure remained the same across the historians' divide of classical antiquity from the medieval period.

Indeed, *pace* those who claim there is little similarity between the cooking of classical antiquity and that of modern Italy, it is this writer's contention that at the level of the deep-structure of the cuisine, traditional popular cookery in places such as central and southern Italy, Liguria and Provence (France) changed very little over two thousand years and more.

Historical perspectives on fermented fish products

FFPs in Asia
A typological analysis of the wide variety of Asian FFPs has been offered by Ishige (1993, 14ff.). There is a first, basic distinction to be made between those fermented products in which the fish is fermented together with some non-fish element, typically boiled

67

or steamed rice; for such products in general, Ishige uses the Japanese term *narezushi*. The opposing family of products made with only seafood and salt as major constituents he divides again into two categories, namely, those used in liquid form, i.e. fish sauces, and those used in non-liquid form; this last group he further divides between *shiokara*, solid FFPs, and *shiokara* pastes, produced by various means from solid *shiokara*. But in a very real sense, the term *shiokara* is the basic fermented fish product, yielding fermented solid food products and also secondarily pastes; liquids drawn off from the fermented solids yield fish sauces (Ruddle & Ishige 2005, 1ff.).

To the north and east of the core area in south-east Asia, the range of FFPs in use today is limited. According to Ishige 1993 and Ruddle & Ishige 2005, the Koreans and Japanese produce and consume *shiokara* and *narezushi*, while in parts of eastern China, forms of *shiokara* are also known. Of paste products, these authors indicate only the use of shrimp paste in Korea and along the Chinese coast. With regard to fish sauce, outside of a large contiguous area in and around Indochina – southern Myanmar, Thailand, Laos, Cambodia, Vietnam and southern coastal China (to Fujian province) – there appear on the map offered by Ruddle & Ishige (2005, 3) only outlying isolated areas: part of Java in Indonesia, a small area in western Borneo, Luzon in the Philippines, the Shandong Peninsula in China, and central Japan. In this last case, the extent of the Japanese enclave on the map is misleading in that in recent times Japanese production and use of fish sauces has been quite local and limited. To my knowledge, there are only three areas of small-scale production in Japan: on the Noto peninsula in Ishikawa prefecture, where *ishiri* is produced, in Akita prefecture, where *shottsuru* is produced, and in Kagawa prefecture, whence comes *ikanago-shoyu*.

From a nutritional and dietary standpoint, the value of FFPs is substantial. First and foremost, the process of fermentation allows for long-term preservation of otherwise very perishable foods. Nutritionally, FFPs eaten in substantial amounts can represent a major element of a people's diet but even when eaten in more limited quantities, as a relish or as flavouring agents, they are sources of various proteins and vitamins that contribute to consumers' health (Ruddle & Ishige 2005, 10).

From a culinary standpoint, one sees two basic rôles for FFPs: in the case of the *shiokara* products, they can be consumed as snacks, alongside drinks, or as side-dishes within the context of more or less complex meals. The fermented fish pastes and sauces have their main uses as key ingredients in cooked dishes, in compound sauces or simply as condiments to be added facultatively at table to served dishes. In short, fish sauces, added to a bowl of rice or noodles, make for a simple but nutritious, delicious and inexpensive meal: FFPs enhance bland foods with their inherently strong salty and umami flavours.

FFPs in the West

Space does not permit a detailed review here of FFPs in classical antiquity; see Curtis (1991) for discussion. However, judging from the attested recipes for *garum* and related products from classical (and post-classical) sources, it is clear that the basic process for at least certain products was essentially identical to what is carried out in modern times in Asia, with regard to factors such as general ratios of fish to salt, kinds of containers used, method of layering fish and salt, preferred temperatures, use of sunlight and separation of liquids for sauces from residual solids for paste.[2] There can be no doubt that the FFPs of the ancient Mediterranean and those of modern Asia were in essence the same bearers of salty and umami flavours.

As noted, in the recipes of Apicius, fish sauce – there referred to generally as '*liquamen*' – is included with remarkable frequency, so much so that its use there resembles the use of salt in modern European cookbooks. A question then arises: to what degree do the recipes attributed to Apicius reflect popular or ordinary cookery of ancient Rome? Though it is true that some Apician recipes do not involve expensive ingredients and that they were likely consumed more or less broadly, it is also true that many of them call for the use of imported spices and include food items that, even when not *per se* exotic, were clearly relatively expensive, such as fresh meat and fish, and therefore not available to much of the Roman population. A plausible characterization of the social status of the Apician collection is that of Grocock & Grainger (2006, 23), who regard the text as one compiled over a considerable span of time: while many recipes surely reflect the high-status cuisine of the élite, others may well have been more widely enjoyed and perhaps reflect 'urban and cosmopolitan' culinary habits.

Archaeological evidence from Pompeii and Herculaneum confirms the basic truth of the logical conclusion to be drawn from Apicius, namely that the use of fish sauce in Roman cuisine was widespread and frequent, as noted by Curtis (1991, 174). Indeed, in order to satisfy the large demand for salt fish and fish sauce in the Roman world an impressive large-scale industry arose in those areas of the Mediterranean and nearby Atlantic coasts where there were good sources of salt and easy access to migrating schools of appropriate fish, most notably along the coasts of north Africa and Iberia to the west and east of the Straits of Gibraltar.[3] As was the case with olive oil, fish sauces and salt fish were among the commodities that the Romans brought with them to their colonial outposts, however far they lay from the Mediterranean.[4] The large-scale production of southern Iberia and north-western Africa was matched with equally impressive distribution networks, the operation of which can be traced through the archaeological record of the amphorae in which FFPs (and olive oil) were transported throughout the Roman Empire.

During the later imperial period in the West, archaeological evidence indicates a decline in the manufacture of FFPs after a period of peak activity spanning the first and second centuries AD (Curtis 1991, 178). The parallel can be drawn to what happened with olive oil during these centuries: with disruption of trade routes and loss of some markets, production contracted and the use of the Mediterranean products became increasingly limited to core areas near the points of production, where those products had a traditionally firm position in local life since long before the development of industrial production methods and long-distance export. While this decline of large-scale production traceable in the archaeological record is significant, the possibility exists that small-scale domestic production of FFPs and especially products made from small fish, e.g. anchovies, may have continued as before or even expanded, to fill the gap left by cheap industrial products.[5]

Historical trends in production and use of FFPs

From the early Middle Ages on, mention of fish sauce in the west of Europe becomes rare and when the first recipe collections finally appear in the course of the thirteenth or fourteenth centuries, it is conspicuously absent as an ingredient. How could such a prominent feature of the cuisine of a large part of western Europe so thoroughly disappear? It is in this regard that the parallel between Mediterranean and Asian uses of FFPs may be most useful.

In ancient China, fermented meat and fish products were common flavouring agents; the invention of fermented soybean products more than 3000 years ago, including both pastes and liquid sauces (soy sauce), initiated a gradual process by which the fermented meat and fish products were partially replaced by the vegetable-based products (Ruddle & Ishige 2005, 6). With the arrival of Buddhism and its preference for a strictly vegetarian diet, this process of replacement was likely accelerated and, when Buddhism spread to Japan *c.* AD 500, the preference of soy sauce to fish sauce perhaps arose there as well (Steinkraus 1996, 510; Hesseltine 1965, 175). While religious belief was a factor in spreading this trend, Ruddle and Ishige (2005, 5) point to economic and aesthetic factors as further reasons why soy products and especially soy sauce have expanded at the expense of FFPs.

From our own perspective, applying principles of dialectological analysis to the distributional patterns and established historical facts concerning FFPs across Asia today, it looks very much that a once large and contiguous area, extending from central Japan, Korea and the nearby Chinese coast in the north all the way down to Indochina and parts of Malaysia and Indonesia, has been partly divided through the spread of an innovation across most of the northern half of the zone: while *shiokara* has remained popular to various degrees in this northern area, fish sauce has been almost completely supplanted there by soy sauce. In the southern zone, despite the partial acceptance of soy sauce in local cuisines, fish sauces and pastes have maintained their traditional central rôles as flavouring agents. But where replacement has occurred, there has been only a change in the identity of the element, not in its function: fermented soybean products as condiments are to no less a degree than fermented fish condiments providers of salty and umami flavours, used first and foremost to enhance basic starchy and vegetable dishes. Indeed, Ruddle & Ishige (2005, 10) repeatedly emphasize the 'strong correlation between consumption of fermented aquatic products and rice, with FFPs being added to vegetables eaten with rice.' Fermented soy products have in places merely taken over some functions of the aquatic analogues.

70

The essential continuities of cuisine from ancient to modern Italy

With the Asian situation in mind, the apparent elimination of FFPs in the West demands explanation. It is our belief that the virtual disappearance of fish sauce in western Europe has been essentially misunderstood, with the item being confused with its function. In other words, we believe fish sauce and the essential flavours of FFPs were not eliminated from the cuisines of the western Mediterranean but, to a far more significant degree than generally thought, they have been maintained, in part directly through continued use of salted, fermented fish products and in part through increased use of other products which, like soy sauce in Asia, have replaced fish sauce as appropriate providers of salty and umami flavours, used first and foremost – like their Asian counterparts – to enhance basic starchy and vegetable dishes.

Post-classical FFPs in the western Mediterranean

Fish sauce and fish pastes are produced in a few areas around the European shores of the western Mediterranean to this day, albeit in small quantities on an artisanal and/or domestic scale. The most notable production of genuine fish sauce is in and around the town of Cetara in Campania, Italy, where several artisanal producers make fermented fish sauce from anchovies called *colatura di alici*, available now throughout the world as a gourmet item marketed as '*garum*'. Small-scale production of this kind of sauce, along with the residual paste, is known elsewhere in Campania, most notably in the Cilento peninsula. A better known fermented fish paste is the *pissalat* of the Provençal coast around Nice, also made from anchovies with additional flavourings. In neighbouring Liguria, a similar traditional product, *machetto*, is made from anchovies or sardines, though its production, like that of *pissalat*, has dropped off significantly in recent decades.

There are good reasons to assume that current small-scale production of fish sauce and pastes in Italy and southern France are relicts of once more widespread artisanal and domestic practices in the past; clearly, within the past century or so, these products have been in decline but how widespread they were in preceding centuries is a question deserving investigation.

While fish sauce and fish paste are nowadays more local curiosities than broadly popular kitchen staples, there is a fermented fish product that is very much a staple of kitchens throughout the western Mediterranean region, namely, salt-cured 'Mediterranean-style anchovies': 'Cured fillets or whole dressed fish are often packed or canned in oil... The curing process, which involves both salting and fermentation, takes at least six months...' (Gall et al. 2000, 410). These fermented anchovies are produced on an industrial scale in countries around the Mediterranean and elsewhere but also in a smaller-scale, traditional manner in Spain, Italy and France. Perhaps best known is the product of Collioure in the Roussillon region of France, famed for the quality of the fish which are fermented for three months in barrels before packing (Dominé 2008, 359). Though the product itself is '*shiokara*' and neither a paste nor a sauce, these anchovies are used with great regularity as flavouring agents, being reduced to a paste through pounding or, in cooked preparations, heated and dissolved in olive oil in the base (*soffritto*) of innumerable sauces, stews and soups in the cuisines of the region.

The culinary staples of central and southern Italy through time

Even in the prosperous times of the early twenty-first century, the diet of central and southern Italy is far less oriented toward the consumption of meat and dairy products than the diets of northern Europe and North America; cereals, especially in the forms of pasta and bread, provide a relatively larger part of the nutritional needs and legumes, vegetables and fruits are more important than in the Teutonic and Anglo-Saxon worlds. If one goes back just a short way in time, the rôle of meat and dairy products and also of fresh fish was considerably less in Italy than today, particularly among the lower economic strata of society. Boiled cereal products and whole and mixed grain breads, along with those same legumes and vegetables, all augmented by small amounts of fats and animal proteins, constituted the bulk of the Italian population's sustenance, while fresh meats and fish were consumed in significant quantities only among more affluent groups.[6]

It is striking that the dietary landscape of Italy in the early twentieth century corresponds closely to what the dietary landscape of the country most likely was in the first century. That is, one observes that at those two points in history, alongside a diet of the better-off sectors of society, as represented in the cookery of Apicius, in which there was an obvious appreciation of all kinds of fresh meats and a great love of fresh seafood as well, there was, judging from the evidence we have, a diet of the broader masses which was in essence vegetarian, with essentially the same cereal preparations, legumes and other vegetables, augmented by small amounts of fats and animal proteins.[7] A contrast between diets of more and less well-off groups reflected in relatively greater and lesser amounts of fresh meats and fish consumed is surely, in and of itself, hardly surprising, but what is striking is the lack of recognition by many historians and food scholars of the tremendous degree of continuity that we see in the culinary tradition of the less well-off strata in Italy from classical times to recent modern times.

The widely perceived discontinuity of cuisine of Rome and Italy between classical antiquity and later periods, is the result of the confluence of several errant lines of thought. First, the nature of cuisine in classical Rome and Italy has been misconceived by many who overvalue the literary evidence and view it without proper appreciation of the social context whence it sprang. Even if we accept that the cuisine represented in Apicius was not enjoyed exclusively by the very richest Romans, it also is clearly not representative of how the broader population ate. In parallel fashion, the degree to which the various recipe collections of the Middle Ages and Renaissance from Italy reflect in any meaningful way the eating habits of the broader population has also been badly exaggerated – though the Arabizing use of spices, colourings and sweeteners surely was taken up to a significant degree among those who could afford the requisite ingredients and used on special occasions by the less well-off, there is no compelling reason to think these texts were anything but compilations of recipes for the conspicuous consumers of their times. It is therefore logical to assume that there has been essential continuity of the broader population's diet from classical times to modern times, based in part on the traditional exploitation of local resources of staple food items, secondary foods and relatively inexpensive flavouring agents.

The centrality of umami in central and southern Italy

Cuisine, at least for the non-affluent, is to a considerable degree based on what is most affordable and historically that in turn naturally reflects especially locally available products. But there is more involved than just the practical; there are also aesthetic choices that cultures make regarding which flavours and flavour combinations are most pleasing. As environmental factors persist over time, a given cuisine's choice of ingredients will tend to remain the same, but new crops and animals might be introduced from afar which thrive in that cuisine's natural environment and, insofar as they become popular, they change the cuisine. But the most important question is how are new foods used in the recipient culture? To what degree does their use reflect the culinary practices of a foreign culture and to what degree are they adapted and fit into culinary rôles already present in the recipient culture?

As we have seen in the case of the spread of soy sauce in Asia, for various reasons it has replaced fish sauce in many places and this is a noteworthy change in, for example, the cuisine of Japan; it is, however, a relatively superficial change, for the manner of use and the basic flavour contribution it provides matches closely that of the now largely neglected fish sauce.

In the western Mediterranean generally and in central and southern Italy specifically, the decline of the fish sauce industry of imperial Roman times did not lead to any fundamental change in the cuisines of the region. Instead, alongside some continued local use of fish sauce, there was increased reliance on alternative means to fulfil the rôle formerly played by fish sauce. As noted above, salted, fermented anchovy was and is a product that, as used in western Mediterranean kitchens, closely resembles in function and flavour the old fish sauces, providing salty and umami flavours to vegetable and cereal preparations, especially as a dissolved element of the *soffritto*. Umami flavour, borne by glutamate, is found in especially high concentrations in fermented fish and soy products but it is also present in a number of other foods and, of particular relevance here, in foods which have a long history of use in the cuisines of the western Mediterranean (Kurihara 2009). These foods, like fish sauces and fermented anchovies, are broadly used in Italy as ingredients in various cooked dishes, as *companatici* (things eaten with bread) and as flavourings for boiled cereal dishes, including pasta. One important group is that of salt-cured (and in some cases fermented) pork products, such as *pancetta*, *prosciutto*, *lardo* and various local sausages. Another group is comprised of the aged hard cheeses that are an integral part of the flavouring of Italian cuisine; Parmesan cheese is one of the foods richest in glutamate but many other similarly used Italian hard cheeses, including ewes' milk cheeses (*pecorino*), are also strong bearers of umami flavour, as well as having a significant salty flavour element (Di Cagno et al. 2003). Mushrooms and walnuts, two other flavouring agents that have long been popular among all levels of Italian society, deserve mention here too as strong bearers of umami flavour which fill the same rôle as the just-mentioned foods do in many dishes.

While all of the aforementioned umami-bearing 'substitutes' for fish sauce have been used in Italy for a very long time and were surely in use in much the way they are used today in classical times, there is one more recent import to the western Mediterranean and Italy that must be mentioned here. The tomato, introduced to Spain and thence quickly to Spanish-dominated southern Italy in the sixteenth century, is among vegetables one of the highest bearers of glutamate and thus of umami flavour. The concentrated umami element of the tomato in cooked sauces is further enhanced through the frequent addition of one or more of the other umami-bearing agents just mentioned. The remarkable profusion of uses of the tomato in the cookery of Italy and other Mediterranean countries, which began far earlier among the lower strata of society than food historians generally believe, makes perfect sense from the perspective of our argument (Buccini 2006, 134–7). As was the case with other American imports – maize, beans, peppers, zucchini, potatoes – the tomato was adapted to a well-established culinary rôle in the local cuisines, and while these products enriched tremendously those cuisines, they did not change them at the basic level of the culinary 'grammar'.

74

Conclusion

In certain important respects, the traditional diets of Japan and central and southern Italy are strikingly similar: in both, the preponderance of nourishment has come from cereals, supplemented by considerable amounts of vegetables and small amounts of fats and proteins. In order to improve the aesthetic qualities of this simple diet, both cuisines have traditionally relied on the addition of small amounts of strongly flavoured substances bearing salty and umami flavours. A further parallel is that both cuisines formerly relied greatly on FFPs and especially fish sauces as habitual flavouring agents but, albeit for different reasons, now maintain the use of fish sauces only in a few relict areas. In both cuisines, the reduction in importance of fish sauce has not produced any culinary revolution but rather only an essentially superficial change of flavouring agents, a substitution of soy sauce for fish sauce in Japan and in Italy an increased reliance on other native foods – such as anchovies, pork products, cheese – and the more recently acquired tomato, all strong bearers of umami. From this perspective, we can see at the level of the culinary life of the non-élite strata of Italian society a remarkable degree of aesthetic continuity from classical times down to the present.

Notes

1. Many thanks to: Amy Dahlstrom, Ernest Buccini, Erik Hill, and Ichiro Yuhara.
2. See the appended recipes in Curtis 1991, 191ff., also pp. 14–5.
3. E.g., the studies by Ponsich & Tarradell 1965, Ponsich 1988. Note that FFPs were also produced in the eastern Mediterranean and Black Sea but we restrict ourselves here to the western Mediterranean.
4. But, whereas olive oil could only be produced where a Mediterranean climate prevailed, FFPs could be produced in northern Europe and the Romans established salting facilities there (e.g. north-western Gaul). For discussions of fish sauce and olive oil in Roman Britain, see Cool 2006, 58ff.
5. While there is ample textual evidence for production of FFPs in the eastern Mediterranean throughout ancient times, corresponding archaeological evidence is minimal, as in the central Mediterranean. Some production methods and environments are more propitious for leaving an archaeological record. Small-scale production, using small fish, baskets, wooden containers, would leave few archaeological traces.
6. See the chapters by Betri, Taddei, Ciampi and Teti in Capatti et al. 1998.
7. On social stratification of diet in classical Italy, see Garnsey 1999, 113ff., Grant 1999, 16ff.

References

Buccini, Anthony F. 'Western Mediterranean Vegetable Stews and the Integration of Culinary Exotica,' in Hosking, Richard (ed.), *Authenticity in the Kitchen. Proceedings of the Oxford Symposium on Food and Cookery, 2005.* Totnes: Prospect Books, 2006, 132–45.

Capatti, Alberto, Alberto De Bernardi & Angelo Varni (eds.). *Storia d'Italia, Annali 13, L'alimentazione.* Torino: Einaudi, 1998.

Cool, H.E.M. *Eating and Drinking in Roman Britain.* Cambridge: Cambridge University Press, 2006:

Curtis, Robert. *Garum and Salsamenta. Production and Commerce in Materia Medica.* Leiden: Brill, 1991.

Di Cagno, Raffaella, Jean Banks, Liz Sheehan, Patrick F. Fox, E.Y. Brechany, Aldo Corsetti & Marco Gobbetti. 'Comparison of the microbiological, biochemical. volatile profile and sensory characteristics of three Italian PDO ewes' milk cheeses', *International Dairy Journal* 13. 2003, 961–72.

Dominé, André (ed.). *Culinaria France.* H.F. Ullmann, 2008.

Gall, Ken, Kolli Reddy & Joe Regenstein. 'Specialty Seafood Products', in Martin, Roy E., Emily Paine Carter, George Flick, Jr., & Lynn Davis (eds.), *Marine & Freshwater Products Handbook.* Lancaster: Technomic, 2000, 403–16.

Garnsey, Peter. *Food and Society in Classical Antiquity.* Cambridge: Cambridge University Press, 1999.

Grant, Mark. *Roman Cookery. Ancient Recipes for Modern Kitchens.* London: Serif, 1999.

Grocock, Christopher & Sally Grainger. *Apicius. A Critical Edition with an Introduction and an English Translation of the Latin Recipe Text 'Apicius'.* Totnes: Prospect Books, 2006.

Hesseltine, Clifford. 'A Millennium of Fungi, Food, and Fermentation', *Mycologia* 57, 1965, 149–97.

Ishige, Naomichi. 'Cultural Aspects of Fermented Fish Products in Asia,' in Lee, Cherl-Ho, Keith Steinkraus, P.J. Alan Reilly (eds.). *Fish Fermentation Technology.* Tokyo: United Nations University Press, 1993, 13–32.

Kurihara, Kenzo. 'Glutamate: from discovery as a food flavor to role as a basic taste (umami)', *The American Journal of Clinical Nutrition* 90, 2009, 19S–722S.

Ponsich, Michel. *Aceite de oliva y salazones de pescado. Factores geo-economicos de Betica y Tingitania.* Madrid: Editorial Universidad Complutense, 1988.

——, & Miguel Tarradell. *Garum et industries antiques de salaison dans la Méditerranée occidentale.* Paris: Presses Universitaires de France, 1965.

Ruddle, Kenneth, & Naomichi Ishige. *Fermented Fish Products in East Asia.* Hong Kong: International Resources Management Institute, 2005.

Steinkraus, Keith (ed.). *Handbook of Indigenous Fermented Foods.* New York: Marcel Dekker, 1996.

75

Kimchi: Ferment at the Heart of Korean Cuisine, from Local Identity to Global Consumption

June di Schino

This paper offers an overview of *kimchi,* underlining the central role it has played in Korean everyday life.

Kimchi is a unique fermented food which originated from the natural environmental conditions and traditional cooking skills of Korea. Although a wide variety of wild and cultivated vegetables have always been abundant here during the warm seasons, the sub-arctic climate with long, severe winters created the need to invent a way of preserving this important source of food. *Kimchi* is considered to be a prehistoric food and evidence can be traced to simple leafy greens pickled in brine and matured underground in clay vessels dating back to 2030 BC.

At this time cultured green vegetables became widespread, indicating how fermentation was an early transformative and preserving procedure in cookery. Archaeological, archaeo-botanical evidence, as well as wall-paintings dating back to the first century AD, indicate the use of large jars for fermenting foods.

Excavations at the Mirùska temple (Iksan) founded around AD 600 have revealed a collection of large jars (some over a metre tall) buried in the ground, which have been identified as receptacles used for fermentation. Prior to this, a stone casket, still visible today at the Pòpjusa Temple (AD 553) is considered to be one of the first artefacts testifying the origin of *kimjang* (*kimchi*-curing and storage for the winter season).

The first documentary records of fermented foods appear in the *Koguryójòn* section of *Sanguo zhi Weizdonyizhuan,* a Chinese historical treatise written in the third century which describes Korean customs and foods: 'the *Koguryó* people are very good at making fermented foods such as wine, soybean paste, salted and fermented fish', confirming the belief that fermented foods were widely enjoyed at that time. Similar evidence can be found in a fifty-volume work entitled *Samguk sagi,* completed in AD 1145, which recounts that King Shinmun gave gifts including soybean paste and fermented fish to his bride's parents.

The origin of the word *kimchi* is thought to derive from the Chinese '*chimchae*', meaning soaked vegetables, and similarly the word *kimjang* from '*chimjang*' as Chinese ideograms were used in Korea until the development of Han-geul script by scholars under King Sejong (1418–1450) who promoted the arts, science and technology.

In early *kimchi* production, pickling methods were used for turnip, gourd, leek, royal fern, bamboo shoots and *tódók* (*Codonopsis lanceolata*). During the early Koryò dynasty (918–1392) Buddhists suppressed meat in favour of vegetables and *kimchi* became diversified into three kinds: plain, juicy and garnished, utilizing many other varieties of plant such as white radish, cucumber, green onion, watercress and hollyhock. Subsequently, the Chosòn dynasty, which began in 1392, saw a renaissance of culture and agriculture, bringing newer and more widespread methods of cultivating and curing vegetables. Meat taboos ended with the introduction of an innovative delicacy: the pheasant-meat *kimchi*. During this period we still find simple salt-pickled *jangajji*, alongside newer forms like desalinated *singònji*, juicy radish *nabakchi,* which could be eaten almost instantly, and savoury *tongchimi* which required long-term fermentation.

Flavour began to evolve with the introduction of different seasonings like ginger, mustard leaf and garlic, while in order to improve colour, scarlet cockscomb and safflower were added. After 1500 many spices like chilli pepper were introduced into Korea, bringing about a radical change in *kimchi* processing which developed from simple salting to more sophisticated techniques which included salted fermented fish (sometimes blended into a paste) known as *chotkàl* or *jotkàl.*

Geographic and climatic differences influenced the taste and the consistency of *kimchi.* Korean cabbage, large white radish (about the size of a pineapple) and red chilli pepper with its distinctive pungent taste became highly popular ingredients and, when mixed together with *chotkàl,* completely transformed the taste and texture of *kimchi.* An invaluable historical document entitled *Jùngbosallimkyòngje* (1761) illustrates the diverse and imaginative use of vegetables and, for the very first time, lists about 41 different kinds of *kimchi* among which figure: *sungikimchi* (whole cabbage, still very popular today known as *baechu, paechu or paechutongkimchi*), *sobaegi* (stuffed cucumber *kimchi*), *sòkbakji* (radish *kimchi*), and even *suk kkakdùgi* (see below), made especially to meet the requirements of the elderly.

Kimjang is an important socio-cultural event which takes place in late autumn, during which large amounts of *kimchi* are prepared for the long cold winter. High value is attributed to all aspects of togetherness, especially the sharing of food and the convivial context. From a sociological viewpoint Koreans recognize the extreme importance of the family as a unit, especially in its extended form, and the country itself is considered in these terms. Hence families and villages, boroughs and clans all unite to re-enact this centuries-old ritual. No one would think of preparing *kimchi* alone. Generally women of all ages participate, even young girls, as this tradition is carried out by experienced female hands. In this essentially communal context the cabbage is selected, cut, then soaked in sea-salt brine while the seasoning is prepared for the second stage. The ability to prepare *kimchi* is an essential aspect of a young woman's education and will become a primary credential for marriage. It is interesting to note that *Umshikdimibang,* one of the first cookbooks of detailed recipes including *kimchi,* was written by a noblewoman around 1671.

'No kimchi, no party' might seem a facile expression, but in reality no *kimchi* in Korea often dramatically means no food. Rice (*bap*) and *kimchi* make up the staple diet of the Korean population. To show the profound sense of social solidarity present in

Korea even today, on 9 November, 2009 in Seoul, about 2,500 housewives got together to make 50,000 packets of *kimchi* which were donated to the poor as the basis for their winter food supply.

Fermentation and storage have always been vital to Korean foodways and the beautiful ceramic jar, which is a fascinating subject on its own, played a significant role. As the country's climate varies from one extreme to another the need to stabilize fermentation and to preserve *kimchi* for long periods is essential. *Kimchi* jars could be left in a stream to cool, preventing the contents from becoming putrefied, or buried in the earth to utilize natural geophysical warmth. There is an enormous differentiation in these receptacles which are chosen according to a vast range of shapes and sizes: large pots are called '*tok*', smaller ones '*tanji*'. When selecting the appropriate jar, even the season, the date and place of production would be taken into account and the women of each region consider *their* particular jar to be *the one*. There is a theory that the more elaborate the container, the finer the *kimchi* will be.

Korean ceramic culture and *kimchi* are interlinked. The interesting connection is that Korea is renowned for its wonderful dark-glazed ceramics and these earthenware receptacles with the right requisites have played an integral role in food culture since the Three Kingdoms period (57 BC–AD 668). As the pots are not airtight but slightly permeable, they provide the perfect container for facilitating fermentation and storing *kimchi* and other foods. Prior to this usage, and in those regions like the mounainous Kangwan-do where the earth is unsuitable for ceramics, preserving was (and still is) carried out in lightweight wooden jars made of hollowed-out non-toxic willow logs lined with special oiled paper to render the receptacles waterproof.

Kimchi pots do not stand alone. The social context of preservation can even be recognized in the grouping together of *kimchi* pots in a communal area: sometimes several households unite, sometimes a small community creates a site. To protect this 'family of pots' from snow and rain, a tent-like shelter made of rice straw is erected, and is closely guarded. Sometimes cockscomb is planted around the area to ward off the evil spirits which might interfere with the alchemical process of fermentaion.

This study focuses on the development of *kimchi* from a primitive fermented food into a sophisticated selection of delicacies cutting across social, geographic and ethnic barriers. *Kimchi* is consumed daily by every single Korean, not just at lunch and dinner but at breakfast too and children are introduced to this food at an early age.

Kimchi represents the true spirit of Korea. This is well reflected in the unique religious tradition for remembering the dead. This memorial service known as *jesa,* during which ancestral blessings are invoked, is celebrated with special foods, and written records such as *Oneguginsòljo of Koryòso* and *Koryòjo of Sejongshillok* show the significant role of *kimchi*. This specific connection between past, present and future emphasize how *kimchi* has become a *transcendental medium*. Only fresh, crisp *kimchi* (which tend to be less juicy owing to the lack of fermentation) are used in this religious ritual. *Nabak kimchi* made of small white radish is prepared and, in the case of *baechu kimchi,* only the hearts of the cabbage are used. These varieties are arranged 'standing up' in bowls, which is a sign of courtesy in Korean food language.

Buddhism has influenced every aspect of Korean culture including food, which explains the vegetarian tradition of utilizing every root, herb and leaf to make *kimchi.* The foods of the temples reflect these religious principles, hence *chotkal* (fermented salted fish) and *oschincae,* the five 'hot' vegetables: garlic, green onion, rocambole (red *chesnok* garlic), wild leek and *honggyu,* are prohibited for ascetic reasons. *Kimchi* made by monks in the temples is generally lighter and more varied in consistency owing to the addition of steamed barley gruel, potato starch water, pine nuts and sesame seeds. Many temples are renowned for their own particular *kimchi* made with all kinds of wild herbs found in the vicinity, which characterize the taste. The Kúmansa, Songnamsa and Pongùnsa Temples are famous for their *kimchi* and the Yuyòmsa Temple in Kumgang, the Pohyónsa Temple in Myohyangsan and the Taehúngsa Temple in Haenam are also well known for their own specialities.

Korea is also known as *Tongbangyeùijuguk* (the country of courteous people). Not only are gods and ancestors revered but the elderly are honoured too. *Kimchi* is generally appreciated for its crunchiness, but as old people often suffer from dental and digestive problems, special *kimchi* like *suk kkhakdugi* and *suk nabadji* are carefully prepared for them. Vegetables such as radishes are first boiled to soften, then seasoned with fermented young shrimps and mild, ground chilli pepper. This respect for the aged is fundamental in Korean culture and in the past women would even sleep embracing a *kimchi* jar to create a more gentle fermentation. During the long winters a traditional gift is always given to the aged: it is a special white porcelain jar of *kamdongjòtmu kimchi* respectfully offered with home-made rice wine, as a sign of filial piety.

Childbearing is considered the happiest family event and pregnant women follow the most virtuous ways during this time, as behaviour is believed to have a direct effect on the foetus. Mothers-to-be only eat special *kimchi* called *jong kkakdugi,* carefully made of only the very best ingredients. Each vegetable is cut into perfect cubes or slices to ensure the sound body and mind of the child.

In Korea, tradition and courtesy are reflected in all codes of behaviour, including table etiquette which envisages the correct position for each bowl, plate, receptacle and chopsticks on the table, with hot foods served on the left and cold on the right. Koreans have a different table-setting for each season showing recognition and respect for nature. There should always be at least two or three kinds of *kimchi* for each meal; four or five would be better.

Kimchi can be classified by methods, main ingredients, seasons and regions. It is found both in Arctic and tropical zones where history and geography have intertwined with natural conditions (as in Italy) to give birth to the many distinctive regional cuisines of Korea. *Kimchi* is an essentially regional food. The central Kyònggi-do region (Seoul) is influenced by the royal culinary tradition and food tends to be rather aristocratic, with much attention paid to precision cutting. Here we have wrapped *kimchi,* pheasant *kimchi, tongchimi* and ginseng *susam nabaki*. In the south-western Chòlla-do region, where high-quality fruit and fine seafoods abound, we find persimmon as well as green laver and wild lettuce *kimchi*. The predominant flavour tends to be intense and savoury owing to the high quantities of *chotkal* and chilli pepper seasoning. The coldest and most remote region is Hamgyòng-do where kimchi is very mild and juicy. Indigenous fish are widely used to prepare flatfish *kimchi* made with rice gruel, codfish, radish and bean sprouts *kimchi* which are recognized typical foods.

For convenience, *kimchi* could be divided roughly into usual and unusual varieties and four of each will be listed.

- The most common is spicy *baechu kimchi* made of whole, halved, quartered or shredded Chinese cabbage (so-called Korean) with red pepper paste and threads, watercress (nothing like the English kind), green onions and fermented shrimps.
- *Khakdugi* is made of large white radish cut into cubes and seasoned similarly to the above.
- *Oi sobaegi* is stuffed cucumber *kimchi* with green onions, wild leek, salted fermented small shrimp, chilli pepper powder, garlic and ginger.
- *Ssam* is a complex wrapped *kimchi* of chestnuts, abalone, oysters, Indian mustard leaves, pine nuts, *pyogo* mushrooms, manna lichen (rare rock mushrooms) seasoned with chilli pepper and salted fermented croaker fish wrapped up in large cabbage leaves.

Among the unusual types are:

- *Susam nabakji* made of ginseng root (4–5 years old). This simple white-coloured *kimchi* is very juicy and is made with white radish, cucumber and Korean pear. No spices.
- *Yuja Tongchimi* is a juicy citron and radish *kimchi* made with pear and thickened with glue plant. It is flavoured only with Indian mustard leaves, ginger and whole hot green peppers
- *Kamkimchi* is a fruit *kimchi* made mainly of Korean persimmons and green thread onions flavoured with chilli pepper powder.
- *Sòngnyukimchi* is known as 'pomegranate *kimchi*' although it contains none. The name comes from the shape of the thick slices of white radish cut crisscross at regular intervals which is half-enclosed in a cabbage leaf. Pear, chestnuts, watercress, garlic, manna lichen (rare rock mushrooms) and ginger are cut into julienne strips with green onion threads and stuffed into the slits.

The basic categories of *kimchi* ingredients are:

- Raw vegetables: Chinese cabbage (*Brassica pekinesis*), radish, wild lettuce, leek, cucumber, soy beans and sprouts, mustard leaf (which produces a beautiful purple colour).

- Fresh fruits and nuts: apple, pears, persimmons, peanuts, pine nuts, sesame seeds.
- Cereals and starch gruel: barley, wheat, glutinous rice gruel and glue plant (*Gloiopletis tenax,* a type of seaweed) or potato starch water.

Ingredients can be virtually innumerable but *seasoning* is the first priority in *kimchi*-making, as it not only enhances the taste and flavour, it is vital to the storage-life. It is interesting to note that *Yangnyeom,* the word for seasoning which comes from the Chinese, means 'keep in mind it is medicine'. To prepare *kimchi* and marinate fish, coarse bay salt known as *horyeom* as well as *t'aech,* a boiled salt concentrate, is employed. Ground chilli pepper is classified as coarse, medium and fine and as mild, medium and very spicy. Generally the coarse variety is used but all three strengths go to season *kimchi.* The amount of time vegetables are left to salt is extremely important as well as the length of time and speed of fermentation which evidently influence the characteristics of the finished product. A bright red paste made of ground chillies with glutinous rice, dried barley sprouts, *maeju* (made from cooked and crushed soybeans which are left to ferment for up to a year) and salt water is commonly used. Dried chilli pepper cut extremely finely into threads is often added to provide a colourful tone and tang to *kimchi* soups and stews.

At an upmarket department store in Seoul, I was astounded at the sight (and smell) of endless counters displaying giant vats of an extraordinary variety of fermented fish of bright shades of scarlet from which a *very* distinctive aroma emanated. As Korea is surrounded by sea on three sides, the presence of fish (fresh and preserved) is universal: mackerel, sea bream and yellow corvina as well as abalone, squid, oysters, clams, shrimp and mussels abound. *Chotkal,* made of fermented fish and shellfish, is a significant ingredient. In southern regions it is made of anchovies, abalone and octopus, while in northern regions yellow croaker, oysters and shrimp are more popular. The climatic differences of these two regions also play a part in affecting the taste of *kimchi*: the hotter the weather, the hotter the *kimchi* will be as chilli is used in abundance in the hotter climates to prevent the *kimchi* from becoming rancid.

Kimchi differs radically from all other fermented foods in the world and is the only fermented food which represents the core of a nation's cuisine. Like rice or pasta, *kimchi* is a foundation-food that incorporates many other foods, flavours and consistencies. It is said that *kimchi* satisfies every palate as it incorporates the five tastes, sweet, sour, salty, bitter and piquant. Five is a number of symbolic significance in Korean philosophy, and correct *kimchi* should also incorporate five colours.

Kimchi is also the essential ingredient of several dishes such as *kimchi-jjigae* (stew), *kimchi-guk* (soup) or *kimchi-jun* (Korean potato pancake) and fried rice. Today, with fusion cuisine so fashionable, *kimchi* is turning up unexpectedly in hamburgers, pizza and hotdogs. Sushi leaves the Koreans cold: they prepare their own rice rolled in green seaweed laver with *kimchi*, of course. *Kimchi* is also supposed to be an excellent antidote for drunkenness and an ice-cold beverage made from the *tongchimi* variety is supposed to be good for headaches. *Kimchi* always brings cheerfulness, I am told, and instead of saying 'cheese' for a snapshot in Korea, guess what they say? Glamorous girls are also known as '*kimchi* girls'.

It has been said that Korean women can make *kimchi* out of anything edible; a concept which extends towards infinite possibilities as there is the 'right *kimchi* for the right food'. The Kimchi Foundation has classified over a hundred different versions showing a wide range of gastronomic experiences, varying from the light refreshing tang of *Mul kimchi* with almost no seasoning or spices, found especially in the north, to the several explosive varieties of the south.

In 2001 *kimchi* standards were officially defined by the *Codex Alimentarius*. Styles, ingredients, colour and texture are listed in a three-page document in order to protect this food from being taken over by the Japanese who developed a copy of *kimchi* which costs less and exports extremely well. As the Koreans were more than worried, they appealed to the WHO and FAO. This is an international trade issue which began with the dispute in 1996 when '*kimuchi*' was proposed by the Japanese to be the official food of the Olympics at Atlanta. This attempt at gastronomic imperialism is a sore point for the Koreans who are still sensitive about the Japanese occupation of 1910–1945.

As everywhere in the world, advancing technology and the reduced time factor have brought radical changes in food traditions. *Kimchi* jars are fast disappearing from back yards in the cities. In Korea today, ordinary fridges are equipped with a *kimchi* compartment and recently, refrigeration techniques have developed to meet modern needs. The new special *kimchi* fridge rates high as the most desirable appliance for the family. This is strictly an urban phenomenon, as the country towns and villages still preserve in the traditional jar. Although industry mass-produces several varieties of *kimchi* and supermarkets sell enormous amounts, hand-made *kimchi* is still *gimjang*, a family-group tradition transmitted through the generations.

Kimchi differs radically from other fermented foods like sauerkraut, as it has biochemical, nutritional, and organoleptic properties as well as health-related functions. The biochemical nature of this particular fermentation is initiated by various micro-organisms originally present in the raw materials, but is gradually dominated by lactic acid bacteria. Numerous physio-chemical and biological factors influence the fermentation, growth, and sequential appearance of the principal micro-organisms involved in the process. The complex biochemical changes depend on environmental conditions before, during, and after fermentation, producing specific nutritional qualities. I would like to emphasize that Korean *kimchi* is a highly varied, versatile, inexpensive, low-calorie and low-cholesterol food. Moreover it is considered to be one of the healthiest foods, containing high amounts of vitamin C, calcium, lactic bacteria and natural antibiotic substances. An impressive range of *kimchi* has grown increasingly popular in the Americas, Asia and the Middle East, Europe and even Australia, making *kimchi* an internationally renowned food.

Kimchi reflects the global spread of Korean culture, and illustrates the distances within the Koreas. In fact, a 'World Kimchi Fair' is being planned which envisages co-operation between the North and South Korean Ministries of Culture. Throughout the country, cities, towns and villages hold traditional harvest-time events such as *kimchi* festivals, fairs and *kimchi*-making contests. *Kimchi* should be considered as the foundation of Korean cuisine, a culinary substrate rather than a single food and its central importance is reflected in dedicated institutions such as the *Kimchi* Foundation, a *Kimchi* Research Institute, *kimchi* science departments in all colleges as well as two specialized museums. *Kimchi* is so fundamental to the Korean diet that the National Aerospace Research Institute even developed a special space *kimchi* for the first astronaut from Seoul to eat in outer space on the Russian spaceship Soyuz!

Kimchi represents Korean identity. It is much more than a food, it is a philosophy.

Kimchi symbolizes the Korean way of life.

Acknowledgement
I would like to thank Dr Kim Nak Jung, counsellor to the Embassy of the Republic of Korea for his help.

Bibliography

Breidt, F., McFeeters, R.F., Díaz-Muñiz, I. 'Fermented vegetables', in *Food Microbiology: Fundamentals and Frontiers*. Washington, D.C.: ASM Press, 2007, 783–793.
Campbell-Platt, Geoffrey. *Fermented Foods of the World: A Dictionary and Guide*. London: Butterworth, 1987.
Cho, Jinhee, Dongyun Lee, Changnam Yang, Jongin Jeon, Jeongho Kim, and Hongui Han. 'Microbial population dynamics of kimchi, a fermented cabbage product', FEMS *Microbiology Letters* 257, 2006, 262–267.
Chung, Okwha, Judy Monroe, Robert L. Wolfe, and Diane Wolfe. *Cooking the Korean way*. Minneapolis: Lerner Publications, 1988.
Katz, Sandor Ellix. *Wild Fermentation: The Flavor, Nutrition, and Craft of Live-Culture Foods*. Vermont: Chelsea Green Publishing, 2003.
Kent, Rose. *Kimchi and calamari*. New York: HarperCollins, 2007.
Kim, Man-jo, Kyou-Tae Lee, and Ŏ-ryŏng Yi. *The Kimchee cookbook: fiery flavors and cultural history of Korea's national dish*. Periplus, 1999.
Kimchi. Korean heritage series. Seoul: Korean Overseas Information Service, 1995.
Let's go Korea. Seoul, Korean Overseas Information Service, 2008.
Passport to Korean culture. Seoul: Korean Overseas Information Service, 2009.
Lee, Cecilia Hae-Jin. *Eating Korean: From barbecue to kimchi, recipes from my home*. Hoboken: Wiley, 2005.
Lee, Chun Ja, Hye Won Park, and Kwi Young Kim. *The Book of Kimchi*. Seoul: Korean Overseas Culture and Information Service, The Ministry of Culture and Tourism, 1998.
Steinkraus, Keith, ed. *Handbook of Indigenous Fermented Foods*. New York: Marcel Dekker, 1995.
Wood, Brian J. B., ed. *Microbiology of Fermented Foods*. London: Blackie, 1998.

Rotten Vegetable Stalks, Stinking Bean Curd and Other Shaoxing Delicacies

Fuchsia Dunlop

The Chinese city of Shaoxing is best known abroad for its 'yellow wine' (*huang jiu* 黄酒), a mellow brew of glutinous rice that has been made in the region for some 2500 years. Within China, the city, which lies in eastern Zhejiang Province, is also known particularly as the capital of the ancient state of Yue, as the cradle of Zhejiang culture and cuisine, and as the birthplace of the modernist writer Lu Xun, whose stories contain many depictions of Shaoxing life.

In culinary terms, Shaoxing loosely belongs to the regional style known as Huaiyang Cuisine, an umbrella for the diverse cooking traditions of the modern eastern provinces of Jiangsu, Zhejiang and Anhui, as well as Shanghai. More specifically, it is one of the three culinary centres of Zhejiang Province, along with Hangzhou and Ningbo. Each of these cities has its own famous food products, dishes, and culinary predilections.

Shaoxing, like other cities in the Lower Yangzte region, is threaded by canals, and aquatic creatures such as fish, shrimp and eels, as well as water vegetables like lotus and walter caltrop, have been an important part of the local diet since ancient times. Shaoxing wines, as well as the distillers' grains (*jiu zao* 酒糟) that are a by-product of wine-making, give some of the city's most distinctive flavours in dishes such as wine-pickled chicken (*zao ji* 糟鸡) and drunken crabs (*zui xie* 醉蟹). These wine-based dishes, however, are just one aspect of a fascinating and unique culture of fermented edibles, which includes many kinds of preserved and pickled vegetables, dried fish, several bean curd products and fermented vegetables. It is the intense, heady tastes of some of these fermented foods that give Shaoxing cuisine its famous 'stinky' (*chou* 臭) and 'mouldy' or 'rotten' (*mei* 霉) flavours.

Fermentation has been applied in China since at least the Neolithic age. From at least as far back as the third century BC, elements of the technology used in wine-making were applied to soy beans, which, fermented and salted, became *shi* 豉 (now generally known as *dou chi* 豆豉, and still widely used in Chinese cookery). Thick fermented soy sauces, made by adding extra water and wheatflour during the manufacture of *shi*, became known as *jiang* 酱, an ancient term that had originally described fermented relishes made from fish and meat.[1] It was only later, perhaps in the Song Dynasty, that the residual liquid from *jiang* became recognized and appreciated as a condiment in its own right, soy sauce (*jiang you* 酱油).[2] As far back as the earlier Han period (202 BC–AD 9), fermented soybeans seem to have been considered one of the necessities of daily life;[3] centuries later, during the Southern Song, the writer Wu Zimu included *jiang* in his list of seven things people could not do without in their daily lives, alongside firewood, rice, oil, salt, vinegar and tea.[4]

Until recently, the diet of most Chinese people consisted largely of grains, supplemented by legumes and other vegetables. Meat and poultry were generally the preserve of the wealthy, and dairy products (with a few exceptions) not eaten at all. In the absence of such delicious animal foods, strongly-flavoured relishes made from fermented legumes and vegetables were essential for making a mass of bland carbohydrates palatable, or, in Chinese terms, for 'sending the rice down' (*xia fan* 下饭).

Shaoxing has a particularly rich tradition of fermented foods, yet they are much less well-known than its wines. Reference books on Chinese gastronomy that include lists of Zhejiang and Shaoxing specialities tend to mention dishes made with expensive meat, poultry, cured ham or freshwater creatures such as crabs and shrimps rather than everyday specialities such as fermented amaranth stalks and fermented 'thousand layers'. In my research for this paper, I have relied mainly on direct observation and locally-published sources.

I would like to focus on just a few of Shaoxing's fermented foods: *mei gan cai* 霉干菜 (fermented dried vegetable), *mei dou fu* 霉豆腐 (fermented bean curd), *chou dou fu* 臭豆腐(stinking bean curd), *mei qian zhang* 霉千张 (fermented 'thousand layers'), and *mei xian cai gen* 霉苋菜根 (fermented amaranth stalks). They are all cheap and, until recently, ubiquitous foods, made from vegetarian ingredients.

The translations for *mei* 霉 given in dictionaries include 'mould, mildew'[5] and 'damp, mouldy, mildewed',[6] while the menu at the Xianheng restaurant in Shaoxing, where I conducted some of my research for this paper, translates it as 'mildew and rotten'. According to one cookery book, Shaoxing people apply *mei* to any food other than meat or poultry that is soaked or boiled, and then sealed into a vessel and left to ferment naturally.[7]

Mei gan cai 霉干菜 – fermented dried vegetable

Mei gan cai is not a single type but a whole genre of preserved vegetables, made from leaf or stem mustards (*jie cai* 芥菜), potherb mustard (*xue li hong* 雪里蕻), rapes and various kinds of cabbage that are salt-fermented and then sun-dried.

Mei gan cai is widely used in Shaoxing cookery to enhance savoury flavours: one local chef described it to this writer as like a joker in Mah Jong, a tile that can be used in combination with virtually any other ingredient. At its simplest, it can be simmered in water to give a rich, vegetarian broth. Soaked in hot water to soften, it can be used to enliven a potful of bland vegetables like potato, beans or gourds, to which it lends its delicious savoury flavours. It is also used in stir-fries, and as a stuffing for buns and other snacks, and is a vital ingredient in one of Shaoxing's best-known specialities, *gan cai men rou* 干菜焖肉, chunks of slow-cooked belly-pork topped with *mei gan cai* and steamed until their flavours intermingle. *Mei gan cai* is also regarded as something of a panacea in folk medicine, used as a tonic for women who have just given birth, and a cure for

Figure 1 (above). Chou dou fu *(stinking beancurd) on sale in a market.*

Figure 2 (below). Chou dou fu *(stinking beancurd).*

Figure 3 (above). Fermented thousand layers.
Figure 4 (below). steamed pork with fermented thousand layers.

Figure 5 (above). Fermented amaranth stalks.

88   *Figure 6 (below). Fermented amaranth stalks with tender beancurd.*

indigestion, coughs, heatstroke and car-sickness.[8] It is a particularly nutritious form of preserved vegetable, rich in carotene, magnesium and other vitamins and minerals.[9]

During fermentation, the glucosides in the greens break down, releasing a fragrant mustard oil, and their flavours are concentrated as their water evaporates in the sun.[10] The finished product can be kept indefinitely and is often deliberately aged for several years. Younger *mei gan cai* tends to have a yellowish colour and a relatively light, salt-savoury taste. Aged *mei gan cai* can be sleek and almost black, with a strong fermented taste that is a little reminiscent of marmite. One market stall I visited in April 2010 was selling around 40 different types of *mei gan cai*.

Historical sources dating back to the early Qin Dynasty (221–206 BC) make much mention of salt-cured vegetables (腌菜), but no one knows when people started sun-drying these to make *mei gan cai*. According to one of my sources, the earliest reference to it, albeit with a different name, is in a Ming Dynasty text,[11] and a full description, including the name *mei gan cai*, first appeared in 1765 in an account of the making of salted vegetables in winter in the Zhejiang provincial capital, Hangzhou.

For Shaoxing people, *mei gan cai* is a comfort food and a potent symbol of the tastes of home. Although it is cheap and ubiquitous, in imperial times the finest was sent in tribute to the court, and the Qianlong Emperor is said to have longed to taste *mei gan cai* when he visited Shaoxing. Even the immortals, they said, are not immune to its charms: '*wu gan cai* [*mei gan cai*] with plain white rice, when the celestials smell it, they want to descend to earth' (乌干菜，白米饭，神仙闻了要下凡).[12]

89

Mei dou fu 霉豆腐 – fermented bean curd

Fermented bean curd is known in many other parts of China as *dou fu ru* 豆腐乳 or *fu ru* 腐乳 – literally 'bean curd milk'. It has an intense flavour that can seem reminiscent of a very ripe Roquefort cheese – although local observers consider that it is much cleaner, without the 'muttony taste' (*shan wei* 膻味) of cheese, and with a creaminess that disperses cleanly in the mouth without lingering, greasily, as dairy products do.[13] Its texture can be thick and creamy, or slightly curd-like and crumbly.

Mei dou fu is made by leaving cubes of pressed bean curd, often covered with pumpkin leaves or rice-straw to promote mould growth, in a warm, well-ventilated place for a few days until they are covered in hairy white mould. (The moulding can be started by adding a pure culture of Mucor 毛霉 or Rhizopus 根霉 moulds.)[14] The cubes are then laid down in clay jars with salt, a little alcohol and other flavourings, and left for several months to mature.

During their long fermentation, enzymes secreted by the moulds, yeasts and other micro-organisms break the rich proteins in the bean curd down into amino acids, and break some of its starch into simple sugars, which later ferment into alcohol and organic acids. The wine that is added to the jar combines with some of this new alcohol and acid to form fragrant esters, which, along with the residual sugar and alcohol and the amino acids from the protein, give fermented bean curd its distinctive flavour.[15]

Several varieties of fermented bean curd are made and eaten in Shaoxing. The plainest (known in Shaoxing as *bai fang* 白方, 'white squares') is an ivory white colour. 'Red squares' (*hong fang* 紅方, also known as red fermented bean curd or *nan ru* 南乳, 'southern milk') are the most distinctive local variant across the wider southern Yangtze region: here, the moulded cubes of bean curd are mixed with red yeast rice (红曲米), which creates a vibrant crimson sauce that clings to the outer surfaces of the bean curd. 'Red squares' were one of the 'eight great tributes', sent from Shaoxing to the Chinese imperial court, which is why they are sometimes also known as 'tribute squares' (*gong fang* 貢方). In Shaoxing, they also make 'drunken squares' (*zui fang*, 醉方), with added fermented glutinous rice; small 'chess-piece squares' (*qi fang* 棋方); and 'black or green squares' (青方), also known as 'stinking squares', because of their smelly aroma.[16]

Because it is considered to stimulate the appetite and aid digestion, a couple of cubes of *mei dou fu* are often served in a small dish to 'open the stomach' (*kai wei* 开胃) at the start of a meal. *Mei dou fu* is also eaten as a relish to accompany plain steamed rice or noodles, or simply cooked vegetables, meat or seafood. It is also used as an ingredient in sauces and marinades.

Fermented bean curd is documented in Ming and Qing Dynasty texts.[17] According to Shaoxing local legend, however, it was invented 'a few hundred years ago' by the owner of a pickle shop called Qian Tai. This man, a Mr Song, was in the habit of making his own bean curd, and once, having made more than he could eat, he left it sitting around for too long and was dismayed to find it covered in mould. In his annoyance at this discovery, he knocked over and damaged an old wine jar. He ordered one of his workers to chuck the mouldy bean curd into the cracked jar, and the worker, fearing that it would start to stink, threw in a handful of salt too. After a few days a delicious fragrance started emerging from the cracked jar, and fermented bean curd was born.[18]

Chou dou fu 臭豆腐 – stinking bean curd

Stinking bean curd is one of the most notorious of Chinese vegetarian delicacies, as appalling to those unused to it, and as delicious to its fans, as ripe blue cheese. It is enjoyed in a few specific regions of China, including Hunan, Taiwan, and parts of the southern Yangtze region. It is most commonly deep-fried, often at street-stalls which perfume their entire neighbourhoods. Shaoxing street-vendors string cubes of stinking bean curd onto bamboo skewers and deep-fry them until they are crisp and golden. Customers then dip them as they please into chilli paste or sweet fermented sauce. At home or in restaurants, stinking bean curd can also be mashed to a purée, steamed, and served with a little rapeseed oil as a dish to accompany rice.

Chou dou fu is made by soaking pieces of firm, pressed bean curd in a *lu* 卤 – a brine made from decomposing vegetation. The precise constituents of this brine vary according to region: in the Hunanese capital, Changsha, it includes black fermented soybeans, winter bamboo shoots, shiitake mushrooms, salt and wine; in Shanghai, lily flowers, bamboo shoots, wild amaranth stalks and ginger. In Shaoxing, the bean curd is soaked in the liquid left over from making rotten amaranth stalks (see below). The pieces of bean curd decompose slightly in the brine, and their proteins break down into amino acids under the action of bacteria. Hydrogen sulphide produced during the break down of one or more sulphur-containing amino acids is the source of the finished product's disgusting smell. [19]

Despite its plain appearance and off-putting aroma, stinking bean curd inspires incredible passion in its devotees. Mao (2005) recounts the following legend: The Qianlong Emperor, travelling incognito on a secret visit to Shaoxing, was startled by a strange and alluring aroma. He followed his nose and came upon a pedlar doing a brisk trade in deep-fried stinking bean curd. He bought a skewerful, and never forgot its taste. 'He was accustomed to eating exotic delicacies from the mountains and the seas at court, and yet he had never realized that something so utterly delicious could exist, with its stinkiness that assailed the nostrils, and an exotic fragrance that emerged in the mouth.'[20]

Mei qian zhang 霉千张 – fermented 'thousand sheets'

Mouldy 'thousand sheets' is one of Shaoxing's most arresting delicacies. Thin sheets of pressed bean curd, known as 'thousand sheets' in Shaoxing dialect, are blanched in very hot water, rolled up and cut into sections, squeezed dry and then placed on a bamboo mat in a clay vessel, and left to ferment naturally for 3–5 days in a warm, humid place. (Sometimes a layer of rice straw from long-grained, non-glutinous rice is laid onto the bean curd rolls to aid fermentation.)[21] When the fermentation has reached the right point, the bean curd is 'jade-yellow, glossy and bright, with a delicious umami flavour, a tender, yielding texture, and a slightly boozy fragrance'.[22]

The moulded rolls are usually rinsed in hot water, and then steamed with a little Shaoxing wine and salt or soy sauce, and served with a trickle of sesame oil. They have a fierce, dirty smell that reminds this writer of 'Bombay duck', and a thrilling, stingy taste, reminiscent of the rind of an overripe Stilton, with a hint of ammonia, and utterly addictive. They are commonly cooked alone and eaten with plain rice and other dishes, but they may also be steamed with other ingredients, for example on top of a patty made from chopped pork. Like other soy products, *mei qian zhang* is rich in protein and extremely nutritious.

The town of Songsha 松厦, just outside Shaoxing, has been known as the source of the finest *mei qian zhang* for nearly two centuries, since a small producer there attracted the attention of Buddhist monks from the temples of the island of Putuoshan, and of imperial officials. In courtly circles, *mei qian zhang* became known as an 'exotic dish' (*qi cai* 奇菜), but it was also so cheap and so simple to make that it was enjoyed in almost every Shaoxing household.[23]

Mei xian cai gen 霉苋菜根 – fermented amaranth stalks

Young amaranth leaves are widely eaten as a vegetable in China, and in some parts of the country are an essential part of family dinners at *duan wu jie* (the Double-Fifth or Dragon Boat Festival in the fifth lunar month). In Shaoxing and some other areas in Zhejiang, fermentation is used to make a weird and wonderful delicacy from overgrown amaranth stalks, at the end of the growing season.

The stalks are gathered when they are more than a metre tall, and their twigs, leaves and woody bases are discarded, leaving an even, green central section that is then cut into pieces a couple of inches long. After washing, these pieces are soaked for a day or so in cold water, until the water becomes frothy, and then washed again and shaken dry. They are then sealed into a clay jar (known locally as a *beng* 甏) and left in a warm place to ferment. There's an art to timing the fermentation: if it is insufficient, the stalks will be too hard to eat; if it is too advanced, the pulp and skin of the stalks simply dissolves away, leaving nothing but fibrous tubes in a filthy liquid. After a few days (the precise time depending on the ambient temperature), the stalks will have softened and a 'special fragrance' will be detectable at the mouth of the jar. At this point, saltwater is added, and the stalks sealed into their jar for another couple of days, by which time they are ready to eat.[24]

Stalks fermented in the manner described above (known as *dan mei* 淡霉, unsalty or bland fermentation) taste good but don't keep well. Another method, *yan mei* 盐霉 (salt-fermentation), introduces salt at the start of the fermentation. The stalks take longer to mature, but can also be kept for longer.[25] When they are ready, the stalks are typically steamed for about twenty minutes with a little saltwater and some rapeseed oil before eating.[26] Sometimes they are steamed on top of other ingredients, such as tender bean curd or sliced pumpkin.

The *lu*, the liquid produced during the fermentation, smells horrifying, like a drain blocked by rotting vegetation. (The stems themselves, removed from the *lu*, have a more innocuous but still faintly unpleasant smell.) It is, however, a master liquid that can be used to ferment several other kinds of foods, including stinking bean curd (see above), pumpkin, taro and winter melon.

Once steamed, the stalks have an aroma that is oddly disturbing, and a taste that is putrescent and wildly exciting at the same time, especially when served on a bed of innocent milkwhite bean curd.

There seems to be no firm historical evidence about when this delicacy first appeared, but a local legend tells of its origins: During the Spring and Autumn Period (770–476 BC), the Yue state, whose capital was based at the site of today's Shaoxing, was conquered by the state of Wu, and its king, Gou Jian, and his wife were taken to Wu as slaves. In a Yue state left impoverished after the war, people had to grub around for wild vegetables to satisfy their hunger. During this time, an old man gathered a bundle of wild amaranth stalks on Ji Mountain. He ate their tender leaves as a vegetable, but although the stalks were too tough to cook, he couldn't bear to throw them away, so he stashed them in a clay jar. Some days later, he noticed a bewitching aroma coming out of the jar, and he took the stalks and steamed them, and found to his surprise that their flavour far surpassed that of the leaves. Word spread of his discovery, and soon the mountain was shorn of wild amaranth, but people had gathered its seeds and put them into cultivation.[27]

The importance of fermented vegetable foods in Shaoxing

The foods described above are the stars in the firmament of Shaoxing's fermented vegetarian foods, but they are not alone. Soft, yellowish fermented soybeans (*mei mao dou* 霉毛豆) are eaten as a relish before meals; bamboo shoots, wheat gluten and some other vegetables can also be fermented before eating. The Zhejiang climate, with its warmth and humidity, is particularly suited to making such foods. Some of these delicacies are found in other parts of Zhejiang: the people of Hangzhou, for example, sometimes eat moulded thousand layers, and Ningbo is known for its 'three stinks' (*san chou* 三臭: usually stinky bean curd, amaranth stalks and winter melon). It is only in Shaoxing, however, that such foods are seen as central to traditional cooking, and to local culinary identity.

This is perhaps because, although Shaoxing is revered as the cradle of Zhejiang cuisine, Shaoxing cooking is almost always described as having its roots in thrifty, down-to-earth folk cooking. For example, although Mao (2001) makes reference to Shaoxing's refined literary culture in one essay on its cuisine, he notes that the beauty of Shaoxing cooking lies in the 'honest simplicity' (纯朴雅正) of its flavours, its emphasis on the natural and essential tastes of ingredients (自然本味), its roots in rustic folk tradition (乡土民间), and its clever ability to make smelly and rotten things taste fragrant and exotic (臭腐为香奇).[28]

93

One appalling local legend traces the origins of Shaoxing's stinking and fermented foods to when the Yue king Gou Jian, his wife and one of his high officials were enslaved by the neighbouring state of Wu (see above). During the three years of their captivity, the Wu king succumbed to a mysterious illness. Following the advice of his high official, Gou Jian visited the Wu king and made a prediction of his imminent recovery after *tasting* his excrement. The Wu king was so impressed by his diagnosis that he released Gou Jian and his other two slaves, and they were able to return to Yue. 'When news of his shit-eating diagnosis reached Yue,' recounts Mao, 'there was not a subject who did not weep bitter tears. In order to commemorate this shame and humiliation, an official named Wen Zhong suggested that the people of Yue should eat their rice with stinking foods. When Gou Jian arrived back in Yue, and saw for himself the great mass of his subjects eating rotten and stinking foods, he was not only filled with emotion, but vowed himself to "sleep on firewood and eat gall" (卧薪尝胆) for ten years' as a reminder of his nation's bitter travails.[29]

Many of the origin-myths of Shaoxing's fermented delicacies tell tales of extreme poverty, and of the accidental discovery of ways of using fermentation to make spoiled, inedible or overlooked odds and ends of produce taste striking and delicious. One particular story, about the origins of a pickled vegetable, tells of a maid, Peihong, who was in charge of cooking for all the servants in a landlord's household. The landlord was so mean that he only supplied them with spoiled vegetables, which were so disgusting that the staff were barely able to eat. Clever Peihong worked out a way of pickling these vegetables that delighted her colleagues and restored their appetites, but her boss was so dismayed at the amount of food they started to eat that he beat Peihong to death. The Peihong story is a reminder of the importance of tasty fermented relishes in making a mass of bland carbohydrates appetizing, and 'edible'.

Shaoxing's typical flavours are heavier and saltier than those of nearby Hangzhou, presumably because of their origins in a poverty cuisine where the norm was to eat rice with small amounts of intense-tasting but thrifty dishes. In Shaoxing dialect, *cai* (the dishes that accompany rice) are actually known as *xia fan* ('that which sends the rice down'). Fermented soybean foods are not only rich in protein,[30] but particularly rich in the delicious umami tastes that make a vegetarian poverty diet palatable. A small cube of fermented bean curd is enough to lend savour to a whole bowlful of rice: according to Mao, in the past it was the most important relish used to 'send the rice down' in average Shaoxing households.[31] Amaranth is another outstandingly nutritious plant, and fermentation makes its otherwise inedible stalks into a lively and delicious *xia fan* treat. A few fermented amaranth stalks also add umami flavours to bland, nutritious bean curd.

Then and now

Until recently, fermented foods were an essential part of daily diets for Shaoxing people, and by all accounts almost every household made its own *mei qian zhang* and *mei gan cai*. Now, however, the imperative of poverty is fading, and meat and poultry are more widely available. According to Mao Tianyao, spoiled only-children are growing up without learning any of the household skills of their parents and grandparents, and the habit of making these foods is dying out.[32] Tastes are also changing, and although the place of *mei gan cai* in local affections seems secure, foods like fermented 'thousand sheets' and amaranth stalks are falling out of favour with the younger generation, perhaps because they seem old-fashioned, and are associated with the bitter poverty of the past. 'Living standards are rising, and society is developing, so many people don't like these old things anymore,' one middle-aged rickshaw driver told me. Some people I spoke to in Shaoxing thought that *mei* 'thousand sheets' and amaranth stalks were unhealthy, and should not be eaten regularly. Once a critical part of Shaoxing food culture because of their high nutritional value and ability to stimulate appetite and make a humble diet delicious, some of these unusual delicacies may survive only as eccentric treats for gourmets in search of the soul of Shaoxing cooking.

Acknowledgement

This paper could not have been written without the generous support of Mao Tianyao, manager of the Xianheng Tavern in Shaoxing.

Notes

1. Huang (2008, 48–50).
2. Sabban (2000, 1170).
3. Huang (2008, 49).
4. Cited in Freeman (1977, 151).
5. *A Chinese-English Dictionary*, 商务印书馆, Beijing, 1988.
6. *Mathews' Chinese-English Dictionary*, Harvard University Press, Cambridge Massachusetts (1975).
7. Shaoxing Xian Wenlian (1990, 161).
8. Mao (2005, 94).
9. Nie and Zhao (2004, 191).
10. Nie and Zhao (2004, 191).
11. 群芳谱 (A Catalogue of Flowers), cited in Nie and Zhao (2004).
12. Popular Shaoxing saying, quoted by Mao (2005, 94).
13. Personal communications at a comparative tasting of mature cheeses and fermented local products at the Xianheng Tavern in Shaoxing.
14. Nie and Zhao (2004, 177). According to McGee (2004, 496), these moulds are of the genera Actinomucor and Mucor.
15. This account of the fermentation process is from Nie and Zhao (2004).
16. Mao (2005, 86).
17. Nie and Zhao (2004, 178).
18. This account is derived from Mao (2005, 85).
19. Mao (2005, 81).
20. Mao (2005, 81).
21. Mao (2005, 77), Nie and Zhao (2004, 173).
22. Mao (2005, 77). See also Shaoxing Xian Wenlian (1990, 167).
23. Mao (2005, 77).
24. Shaoxing Xian Wenlian (1990, 163); personal account from a professional maker of this speciality.
25. Shaoxing Xian Wenlian (1990, 163).
26. Mao (2005, 87).
27. The story is told in Mao (2005, 87) and Shaoxing Xian Wenlian (1990, 164).
28. Mao (2001, 4).
29. Mao (2005, 79).
30. Soy is the richest vegetarian source of protein, and contains all the essential amino acids required by the human body in the right proportions for absorption and nutrition. See McGee (2004, 485, 496).
31. Mao (2005, 85).
32. Personal communication.

Bibliography

Chang, K.C. 'Ancient China', in K.C. Chang (ed.) *Food in Chinese Culture*. London: Yale University Press, 1977.

Huang, H.T. 'Early uses of soybean in Chinese history', in Christine du Bois, Chee-Beng Tan and Sidney Mintz (eds.) *The World of Soy*. Urbana and Chicago: University of Illinois Press, 2008.

McGee, Harold. *McGee on Food & Cooking*. London: Hodder & Stoughton, 1977.

Freeman, Michael. 'Sung', in K.C. Chang (ed.) *Food in Chinese Culture*, London: Yale University Press, 1977.

Mintz, Sidney W. 'Fermented beans and Western taste', in Christine du Bois, Chee-Beng Tan and Sidney Mintz (eds.) *The World of Soy*. Urbana and Chicago: University of Illinois Press, 2008.

Sabban, Francoise. 'China', in Kenneth F. Kiple and Kriemhild Coneè Ornelas (eds.) *The Cambridge World History of Food*. Cambridge: Cambridge University Press, 2000.

Tan Chee-beng. 'Tofu and related products in Chinese foodways', in Christine du Bois, Chee-Beng Tan and Sidney Mintz (eds.) *The World of Soy*. Urbana and Chicago: University of Illinois Press, 2008.

Jiang Xi 姜习（主任), 1992, 中国烹饪百科全书（北京, 上海, 中国大百科书出版社）.

Jiang Liyang 江礼 yang, 2001, '鲜成糟醉, 田园本味 － 绍兴菜的历史和特色', 茅天尧 (ed.), 绍兴菜（上海, 上海科学技术文献出版社）.

Mao Tianyao 茅天尧, 2005, 品味绍兴 （杭州, 浙江科学技术出版社）.

Nie Fengqiao 聂凤乔 and Zhao Lian 赵廉 (eds.), 2004, 中国中国烹饪大典（下卷）（ 青岛, 青岛出版社）.

Shaoxing Xian Wenlian 绍兴县文联, 1990, 绍兴民间传统菜谱（北京, 中国国际广播出版社）.

Xiao Fan 萧帆(主编), 1992, 中国烹饪辞典（北京, 中国商业出版社）.

Quinces, Oranges, Sugar, and Salt of Human Skull: Marmalade's Dual Role as a Medicine and a Preserve

Elizabeth Field

For the last 1,500 years at least, various forms of marmalade have been enjoyed as a sweetened fruit preserve with long keeping-qualities. The Greeks stored *melimelo* (raw or cooked quinces and honey) in earthenware jars to use during times of scarcity; while for centuries home cooks have boiled together bitter oranges and sugar during the brief mid-winter Seville orange season, to transform into orange marmalade for year-round use.

Just as important, however, is marmalade's age-old use as a remedy. According to the ancient Galenic medical tradition, based on balancing the body's humoral 'complexion' with compensatory foods, quinces, honey, and later sugar, were considered to be 'warming' remedies for stomach complaints, gynaecological problems, dropsy, bladder stones as well as colds and bronchial disorders. Galenic theories prevailed in Greece, the Arab world and southern and northern Europe through the mid-eighteenth century.

Solid, boxed quince and rosewater *marmelada* (similar to today's *membrillo*) was produced in southern Europe (the word 'marmalade' derives from the Portuguese *marmelo* or quince) and imported to England in the late fifteenth century. It was offered in the most élite households as an after-dinner digestive. A medieval northern European honey-sweetened equivalent, chardequince (flesh of quince), spiked with the same 'warming' spices (cinnamon, nutmeg, ginger) as those used in hippocras (a medieval après-feast 'digestive' wine) was similarly extolled as a remedy for various ills.

Solid quince 'digestive' marmalades continued to be recognized as remedies through the early nineteenth century, although they began to be overtaken by orange breakfast preserves in the seventeenth century. It is this period of concentrated overlap of the two marmalade forms, roughly 1600 to 1830, that especially interests me. Here are some examples of how the marmalade transition played out.

First published in 1615, Gervase Markham's *The English House-wife* embraces a number of concurrent social trends, including the strong link between the preparation of preserves and confectionery and the compounding of home medicines among well-born country women in their still-rooms. The ritual of the 'banquetting course', the special final course of a Tudor feast featuring an abundance of sweetmeats, is, to me, a bridge between the two marmalade traditions.

Though the 'banquet,' often served in a separate elegant pavilion, was designed to showcase the beauty of the sweetmeats as well as the host's wealth, the medicinal element was still important. John Partridge, the author of *The Widdowes Treasure* of 1595, wrote:

Virtutis hujus confectionis sequuntur
This decoction is good to eate
alwaies before and after meate.
For it will make digestion good,
and turne your meate to pure blood.
Besides all this it dooth excell,
all windiness to expell.
And all groce humors cold and rawe
that are in belly, stomacke or mawe.[1]

It was the duty of a 'compleat woman' to properly 'order and set forth' the 'banquet.' According to Markham:

> ...you shall observe that March-panes have the first place, the middle place and last place; your preserved fruits shall be disht up first, your pasts [sic] next, your wet suckets [succade] after them, then your dried sucket then your Marmalades, and Cotiniates, then your Comfets of all kinds, Next your Pears, Apples, Wardens, bakt, raw, or rosted, and your Oranges and Lemons sliced; and lastly your Wafer Cakes...[2]

98

Markham provides the requisite recipes: white- and rose-coloured solid quince marmalades that are rolled and twisted into hearts or knots, or flattened and then stamped with flowers or stars; comfit-decorated translucent Genoa paste made from peaches, quinces, apples, pears, plums or 'any fruit you please'; apple tarts; moulded marzipan figures; lemon and orange succades; cookie-like jumbals, wafers and even a transitional form of orange marmalade, in which orange pulp and sugar are boiled till very thick, and, like the old quince marmalades, cooled and poured into wooden boxes.[3]

Of equal prominence are 48 pages of household remedies for afflictions ranging from the plague to baldness. For stinking nostrils: 'Take red nettles and burn them to powder, then adde as much of the powder of Pepper, and mix them very well together and snuff thereof up into the nose; and thus do divers times a day.'[4]

'Banquetting stuffe' also had aphrodisiac connotations. 'Queen Mary Tudor's marmalade' (to help her conceive a son – it didn't work) in *A Closet for Ladies and Gentlewomen* (1608) contains sugar, quinces, candied orange peel, almonds, candied eringo roots, musk, ambergris, rosewater, cinnamon, ginger, cloves and mace.[5] The alleged 'hot, dry' qualities of these spices and aromatics, added to the hot, dry quality of dried fruit and sugar were thought to heat the blood and inflame the libido. According to Roy Porter, female orgasm was widely believed essential for conception.[6]

Two texts from the late seventeenth and early eighteeenth centuries illustrate the divide between authors. Presumably continuing a Galenic tradition (despite a prevailing new medical philosophy espoused by Paracelsus), the English physician

William Salmon's *New London Dispensatory* (1678) includes a Marmelada Cephalica for diseases of the head such as frenzy, madness, apoplexy and migraine. It calls for the salt of a man's skull in addition to quince paste, amber, nutmeg and gold leaf.[7]

Meanwhile, *The Compleat Cook*, compiled from a manuscript by Rebecca Price (1681), offers the thoroughly modern concept of a 'true orange marmalade,' according to C. Anne Wilson, made from sugar and Seville oranges in a 1:1 ratio of fruit to sugar.[8] This is the formula that most marmalade-makers use today to ensure a perfect gel.

The seventeenth century saw La Varenne's introduction of a thinner form of quince marmalade, achieved by reducing its boiling time.[9] This texture has since remained the norm.

In the eighteenth century, Seville orange marmalade became increasingly popular in Scotland, perhaps because Scotland's cool climate precluded the cultivation of quince trees in many areas. Oranges had been arriving in Scottish ports since the late fifteenth century and were regularly purchased by gentry households by the early eighteenth century.[10] The apocryphal story of Janet Keiller, a Dundee grocer's wife who allegedly converted a wrecked ship's cargo of Seville oranges into orange marmalade, and so founded the James Keiller and Son jam and marmalade operation in 1797, attests not only to orange marmalade's growing popularity but to a new consumption pattern of eating marmalade as a breakfast condiment rather than an after-dinner digestive.

A succession of lovely Scottish cookbooks treat orange marmalade increasingly reverently. Mrs McLintock's *Receipts for Cookery and Pastry Work* (1736) includes recipes for a beaten orange and lemon marmalade, in which the citrus peel and pulp are boiled soft and pounded in a mortar, as well as recipes for apple and gooseberry marmalades – but no quince marmalade recipes.[11]

Elizabeth Cleland's *A New and Easy Method of Cookery* (1770) is a bit pernickety:

To make Marmalade of Oranges
Take your oranges, grate them, cut them in Quarters, take the skins off them, and take the Pulp from the Strings and Seeds; put the Skins in a Pan of Spring-water, boil them till they are very tender, then take them out of the Water, and cut them in very thin Slices; beat some in a Marble Mortar, and leave the thin Slices to boil by themselves. To every Pound of Oranges put a Pound of fine Sugar; first wet the Sugar in Water, boil it a good while, then put in Half of the Pulp, keep the other Half for the sliced Oranges; to every Mutchkin of the Pulp you must put in a Pound of Sugar likeways, then put in the grated Rind, boil it till it is very clear, then put it in Gallypots; when cold, paper them. Boil your Chips [shredded orange rind] the same Way, but don't mix the pounded with them.[12]

Susanna Maciver waxes a bit more poetic in *Cookery and Pastry* (1800), where she advises: 'You will know when [the texture] is enough, by its turning heavier in the stirring and of a finer colour: whenever it begins to spark, it is enough...'[13]

99

And John Caird's *Complete Confectioner and Family Cook* (1809) elevates marmalade into an art form: *'The beauty of the marmalade consist in the thinness and transparency of the strips'* [italics his]. His recipe for Cream D'Arcy, a sumptuous ice-cream made from cream, orange marmalade and grated Seville orange and lemon peel, is an elegant representation of Regency desserts.[14]

The evolution of medicinal and culinary marmalades continues unevenly. While *Domestic Economy and Cookery for Rich and Poor,* by a Lady (1827), includes a recipe for 'Carrot Marmalade – Excellent for the Navy,' an anti-scorbutic which calls for boiling carrot zests with sugar and then acidulating it with lemon, vitriol [sulphuric acid], verjuice, tartaric crystal and tamarind,[15] G.A. Jarrin's *The Italian Confectioner* (1820) sticks closely to confectionery. Echoing La Varenne, he declares: 'Marmalade is a half liquid preserve.'[16]

The Victorian era heralded the rise of commercial marmalade. Firms offered many varieties, with the largest concentration in Seville oranges and other citrus fruits. Whatever one believed about the superiority of home-made marmalade – Margaret Dods's *The Cook and Housewife's Manual* (1828) argues for home-made preserves being 'a point of good housewifery,' as well as 'both cheaper and more nicely done' than manufactured marmalades,[17] while Isabella Beeton's *Every-Day Cookery and Housekeeping Book* (1892) counters with: 'The best marmalade is made by Keiller ... it can be bought so cheaply and good it is scarcely worth making it at home'[18] – there was no doubt that orange marmalade was on the British breakfast table for good.

100   Like untold others, the late Oxford Symposium co-founder Alan Davidson had a ritual of making Seville orange marmalade each winter. He simplified his Scottish grandmother's recipe by disregarding its commandments to: 'Warm the Sugar, Warm the Jars, Put the Pips in a Muslin Bag, Skim the Froth, Fiddle with Waxed Discs.' He personalized the recipe to include the addition of one knobbly Kaffir lime to every batch, producing a flavour that 'forty per cent of British people find too sharp.'[19] Result: more marmalade for him, and further testimony that home marmalade-making is every bit as satisfying and therapeutic as imbibing *membrillo* for medicinal use.

Notes

1. Partridge, p. 3.
2. Markham, p. 98.
3. Markham, pp. 88 – 101.
4. Markham, p. 25.
5. *A Closet for Ladies and Gentlewomen*, p. 43.
6. Porter, p. 129.
7. Salmon, p. 617.
8. Wilson, p. 50.
9. La Varenne, p. 479.
10. Plant, p. 93.
11. McLintock, p. 24.
12. Cleland, p. 178.
13. Maciver, p. 151.
14. Caird, p. 54.
15. *Domestic Economy and Cookery for Rich and Poor,* by a Lady, p. 608.
16. Jarrin, p. 53.
17. Dods, p. 422.
18. Beeton, p. 336.
19. Davidson, pp. 75–77.

Bibliography

A Closet for Ladies and Gentlewomen. London: Arthur Johnson, 1608.

Beeton, Isabella. *Beeton's Every-Day Cookery and Housekeeping Book*. London: Ward, Lock, Bowdon and Co., 1892.

Caird, John. *Complete Confectioner and Family Cook*. Edinburgh: John Anderson, 1809.

Cleland, Elizabeth. *A New and Easy Method of Cookery*, 3rd ed. Edinburgh: R. Fleming and W. Gray, 1770.

Davidson, Alan. 'Marmalade: An Unpublished Letter to "The Times"', in *A Kipper With My Tea*. San Francisco: North Point, 1990.

Dods, Margaret. *The Cook and Housewife's Manual*, 3rd ed. Edinburgh: Oliver and Boyd, 1828.

Domestic Economy and Cookery for Rich and Poor, by a Lady. London: 1827.

Jarrin, G.A. *The Italian Confectioner*. London: John Harding, 1820.

La Varenne, François Pierre de. *La Varenne's Cookery: The French Chef; the French Cook; the French Pastry Chef; the French Confectioner*. Trans. Terence Scully. Totnes: Prospect Books, 2006.

Maciver, Susanna. *Cookery and Pastry*. Edinburgh: J. Fairbairn, 1800.

Markham, Gervase. *The English House-wife*. London: George Sawbridge, 1675.

McLintock, Mrs. *Receipts for Cookery and Pastry-Work*, facsimile of 1736 edition. Aberdeen: Aberdeen University Press, 1986.

Partridge, John. *The Widdowes Treasure*. London: 1595.

Plant, Marjorie. *The Domestic Life of Scotland in the Eighteenth Century*. Edinburgh: Edinburgh University Press, 1952.

Porter, Roy. *The Greatest Benefit to Mankind: A Medical History of Humanity*. New York: W.W. Norton, 1997.

Salmon, William. *Pharmacopoeia Londinensis*, or, *The New London Dispensatory*. London: Royal College of Physicians, 1678.

Wilson, C. Anne. *The Book of Marmalade*. Philadelphia: University of Pennsylvania, 1999.

Fermented, Cured and Smoked: The Science and Savour of Dry-Fermented Sausages

Len Fisher

Dry fermented sausages are an integral part of our world-wide gastronomic heritage. Modern examples include Italian *salami, pepperoni*, French *saucisson*, Spanish *salchichón* and Spanish *chorizo*, with a vast number of regional variations. All are produced by fermentation and curing, while some are also smoked. Here I explore how the curing, fermentation and smoking processes contribute to the flavour, texture and shelf-life of the sausage, with a brief reference to a surprising link between fermented sausages and the function of Viagra.

Introduction: the role of water

The earliest records of food preservation by fermentation date back to 6000 BC and the civilizations of the Fertile Crescent in the Middle East.[1] Meat would probably first have been preserved by salt curing, but it just happens that fermentation bacteria such as *Lactobacilli* and *Leuconostocs* can survive and thrive in an appropriately salty environment at the expense of other bacteria.

According to Harold McGee in *On Food and Cooking*,[2] the fermented sausage may have originated with the prehistoric practice of salting and drying meat scraps to preserve them. 'When salted scraps are squeezed together,' says McGee, 'microbe-laden surfaces end up inside the moist mass, and salt-tolerant bacteria that can grow without oxygen thrive there.'

Scientifically, there is a very subtle balance here. Conditions need to be just right for fermentation bacteria to thrive, but not for the growth of dangerous bacteria such as *Clostridium botulinum* or the vegetative cells of other bacteria such as *Staphylococci* that have public health significance.

The dry, salty, well-spiced fermented sausage of the type that this talk is concerned with typically contains 25–35 per cent water,[3] but what really matters for bacterial growth is the *availability* of that water. The salt, sugar and proteins in the sausage can reduce that availability by binding the water to themselves.

Scientists use a quantity called water *activity* (a_w) to measure the effectiveness of the binding. It is really a very simple measure, and comes down to the vapour pressure of the water in the material divided by the vapour pressure of pure water at the same temperature – in other words, the relative humidity in the atmosphere in a closed bottle containing the sausage.

The crucial points are that a_w needs to be less than 0.93 to prevent the growth of *Clostridium botulinum*, and less than 0.85 to comply with food regulations with regard to the growth of other harmful bacteria when acidic foods are stored at room temperature.[4]

The presence of salt helps in this regard. Typical dry-fermented sausages contain more than 4 per cent salt by weight, which is sufficient to reduce a_w to below 0.91.[5] The rest of the job is done mainly by the meat proteins, and here there is an important rule of thumb. The key is the ratio of water to protein by weight.[6] If this ratio is above 3.1, then the water activity is likely to be high enough to support the growth of pathogenic bacteria at room temperature, and refrigeration is not only desirable, but often essential. If the ratio of water to protein is below 3.1, and the salt concentration is sufficiently high, then the sausage can probably be stored safely at room temperature.

Fermentation

Fermentation arises from the presence of *lactic acid-producing bacteria*, which digest sugars and starches and excrete lactic acid and/or alcohol. The lactic acid is primarily responsible for the sharpness in the flavour, and also produces a low pH (between 4.5 and 5) that leads to meat protein coagulation and a firm, cohesive, sliceable product. The flavour is also enhanced by the low fermentation temperatures used for dry-fermented sausages (as low as 38°C), which encourages the growth of bacteria that produce a complex blend of nutty aldehydes and fruity esters to go with the acidity. The final flavour may also be enhanced by a powdery white coating of moulds and yeasts that can grow on the casing during the final drying process.

Curing

The *curing* of meat specifically refers to its treatment with salt and nitrates or nitrites. The salt reduces the availability of water for the growth of pathogenic bacteria, and also provides an environment that is more suited to the growth of lactic acid-producing bacteria and *micrococci*. The latter are needed for the reduction of nitrites or nitrates to produce nitric oxide – a small molecule which has a surprisingly diverse range of natural roles in the human body.[7] It is an important regulator of neurotransmission, and also acts to relax smooth muscle and hence produce vasodilation in blood vessels. This role is a key player in the functioning of Viagra, although the firmness of dry-fermented sausages ultimately arises from quite a different mechanism.

In sausages, nitric oxide reacts with the muscle protein myoglobin to produce the characteristic reddish colours. It also inhibits the growth of *Clostridium botulinum* by reacting with iron-sulfur proteins in the vegetative cells.[8]

Safety concerns have sometimes been raised about the addition of nitrates (Europe) or nitrites (U.S.) to act as 'food' for the *micrococci* to produce nitric oxide. These concerns mostly arise because nitric oxide can react with amines that are natural breakdown products of proteins to produce nitrosamines, many of which are known to be carcinogenic. According to a 1992 study by scientists from the University of Minnesota 'based on available evidence to date, nitrite as used in meat and meat products is considered safe because known benefits outweigh potential risks.'[9] That conclusion appears to remain valid today.[10]

Until the 1950s, each bacterial culture used for fermentation would have been different (as is still the case for many small artisanal manufacturers today – a point that will be explored in relation to food safety and to the different flavours produced). At this stage, the use of pure bacterial cultures in meat products was launched,[11] producing more uniformity. It has also supposedly produced greater safety, although an analysis[12] of the bacterial flora from over 300 southern and eastern European small-scale processing units did not show up many substantial safety concerns among these artisanal manufacturers – begging the question of whether we have sacrificed too much variety in the cause of uniformity and safety.

Smoking

Finally, smoking reduces the water-content through the heat applied, but otherwise only affects the surface of the sausage, where it contributes to colour, flavour and bactericidal properties. *Liquid smoke* can help to mask flavours such as boar taints in pork sausages made from uncastrated male pigs,[13] but traditional smoking generally produces better flavours.

In summary, the preservation and shelf-life of dry-fermented sausages depend on a few relatively simple scientific principles, mostly concerned with providing conditions for the growth of desirable bacteria while inhibiting the growth of those that are less desirable or even positively dangerous. It is only to be hoped that an over-enthusiastic application of those simple principles in the future does not lead to a corresponding simplification in the flavours.

Notes

1. Fox, P.F. 'Cheese: An overview', in Fox, P.F. (ed.), *Cheese: Chemistry, Physics and Microbiology* (Vol. 1), 2nd edn. London: Chapman & Hall, 1993, 1–36.
2. McGee, Harold, *On Food and Cooking*, 2nd edn. New York: Scribner, 2004, 176.
3. McGee, op. cit.
4. U.S. Food and Drug Administration 'Water Activity *aw* in Foods' http://www.fda.gov/ICECI/Inspections/InspectionGuides/InspectionTechnicalGuides/ucm072916.htm
5. Mohamed El Guendouzi, Abderrahim Dinane & Abdelfetah Mounir 'Water activities, osmotic and activity coefficients in aqueous chloride solutions at T = 298.15K by the hygrometric method', *Journal of Chemical Thermodynamics* 33, 2001, 1059–1072.
6. Sebranak, Joseph G., 'Semidry Fermented Sausages', in Yiu H. Hui, Lisbeth Meunier-Goddik, Ase Slovejg Hansen, and Jytte Josephsen, *Handbook of Food and Beverage Fermentation Technology*. New York: CRC Press, 2004, 385–396.
7. A good, scientifically accurate summary may be found in the Wikipedia article 'Biological functions of nitric oxide' (http://en.wikipedia.org/wiki/Biological_functions_of_nitric_oxide).
8. Reddy, D., Lancaster, J.R., Jr., & Cornforth, D.P., 'Nitrite inhibition of *Clostridium botulinum*: electron spin resonance detection of iron-nitric oxide complexes', *Science* 221, 1983, 769–770.
9. Epley, R.J., Addis, P.B. & Warthesen, J.J., 'Nitrite in Meat', *Minnesota Extension Service Report AG-FS-0974-A*, 1992.
10. Sofos, J.N., 'Challenges to meat safety in the 21st century', in *Symposium on meat safety: from abattoir to consumer* (Valencia, Spain) 78, 2008, 3–13.
11. Incze, K., 'Dry fermented sausages', *Meat Science* 49, 1998, S169–S177.
12. Talon, R. et al., 'Traditional dry fermented sausages produced in small-scale processing units and Slovakia. 1: Microbial ecosystems of processing environments', *Meat Science* 77, 2007, 570–579.
13. Stolzenbach, S. et al., 'Perceptual masking of boar taint in Swedish fermented sausages', *Meat Science* 81, 2009, 580–588.

105

The Enigma of Enset Starch Fermentation in Ethiopia: An Anthropological Study

Takeshi Fujimoto

Enset is a prominent food crop in the south-western region of Ethiopia. It is cooked in two different ways. One is to steam-boil the corms and the other is baking (or steaming, etc.) fermented starchy paste elaborately processed from the corms and leaf-sheath pulp. It seems strange that enset is processed for fermentation with a great deal of labour and time although the corms are eaten simply cooked and the crop is harvested throughout the year. This paper, by discussing a case study of enset-related culture in an ethnic group, considers the question. In fact, enset-growing groups vary as to which method of enset cooking is more common. It is suggested that social (population size and density) and ecological (highland/lowland) factors matter.

What is enset?

Owing to its apparent resemblance to the banana, enset [*Ensete ventricosum* (Welw.) Cheesman] is often referred to as 'false banana'. Indeed, both enset and bananas are tree-like, giant but herbaceous plants belonging to the same botanical family (Musaceae). However, enset grows at higher altitudes, mostly over 2,000 metres and sometimes over 3,000 metres above sea level, flowers only once during its final stage at around the age of ten years and does not bear edible fruits.

Whereas wild enset is native to tropical highland Africa, cultivated enset is grown as a crop only by farmers in Ethiopia. It is a minor, non-food crop consisting of a few plants in gardens in north-western Ethiopia, where its leaves are used to wrap cereal breads baked over a griddle. On the other hand, it is a prominent food crop in the south-west, where its underground giant corms, weighing more or less 20–30 kg, constitute the most important local dietary source (fig. 1). The crop is monocropped or intermixed with other crops in gardens of fertile soils surrounding the homes. Enset plays a key role in food security because it is highly drought-resistant and can be harvested throughout the year. Considering the enset-related cultural characteristics as well as the ecological attributes, Shack (1966) referred to a large part of the south-western region an 'enset(e) culture complex area'. The population density of the enset-growing area is more than six times as high as that of the country as a whole (Gascon 1994). Today more than 15 million people, 20 per cent of the total population of the country, rely on this crop (Dohrmann & Metz 2005).

Figure 1. Major Enset Growing Area in Ethiopia.

Kocho (*qoch'o*) is the best-known food made from enset. It is a fermented starchy mixture of pulverized corm and squeezed leaf-sheath pulp that is most commonly baked as unleavened bread. A bacteriological study (Gashe 1987) has revealed that *kocho* fermentation is a type of lactic acid fermentation.[1]

Why is enset starch fermented?

Then a question may be posed: why is enset starch fermented? If a crop is harvested seasonally, it is natural to assume that fermentation is chiefly for storage. But how about enset which is harvested throughout the year once the plant reaches the age of 2–3 years? Or is it for detoxification? Apparently no data are available which suggest that the corm or leaf-sheath pulp contains toxins to remove. Indeed, the corm is eaten after it is just cooked (steam-boiled, etc.). Furthermore, the processes for fermentation are highly labour-intensive and time-consuming. Then why is enset starch fermented although the processes require a great deal of labour and time and the corm can be eaten simply cooked? A taste preference for the acidic flavour of fermented substances can be a contributing factor, which was argued for breadfruit fermentation in Oceania (Pollock 1984, 1992), but is it enough?

In fact, enset-related cultures vary between the ethnic groups in the area. Westphal (1975) classified the 'ensat (enset)-planting complex' into the following four categories, in terms of the importance of the crop: (1) 'enset as a staple food', (2) 'enset as a co-staple, with cereals and tuber crops', (3) 'enset not as a co-staple, with tuber crops dominant and cereals of secondary importance', and (4) 'enset not as a co-staple, with

107

cereals dominant and tuber crops of secondary importance'. The first category covers the eastern side of the enset-growing area. The second occupies the central and largest part of the area. The third and the fourth are found in the south-western and in the north-western corners of the area respectively.[2] Hildebrand (2007) discussed enset cultivation in terms of intensity and identified two levels of intensity, high and low. High-intensity cultivation focuses on enset as a staple crop and involves more than 100 plants that are monocropped and treated with frequent manuring and transplantation. By contrast, in low-intensity cultivation, the crop is grown as a non-staple with about 30 plants interspersed with other crops. And she noted that harvested corm and leaf-sheath pulp are normally fermented and stored for months or years in high-intensity cultivation whereas the crop is cooked in diverse ways (steaming or pit-baking the corm and baking bread from the fermented starch, etc.) and is usually consumed within a week in the low-intensity cultivation. Why should these differences come about?

To consider these matters, I will present a case study of enset-related cultures among the Malo, who live in the middle of the enset-growing area, and among whom I have conducted anthropological fieldwork since 1993.

Enset cultivation among the Malo

The Malo are predominantly subsistence farmers who number approximately 30,000–40,000. They live in a steep mountainous area ranging in elevation from *c.* 600 metres to over 3,400 metres above sea level. The Malo people classify their land into three zones: the 'highland' (*gezze*; above 2,200–2,300m), the 'midland' (*dollo*; between 2,200–2,300m and 1,500–1,600m), and the 'lowland' (*gad'a*; below 1,500–1,600m).[3] Although temperate cereals such as barley and wheat are sown in the highlands, maize and sorghum are dominant in the midlands, and locally domesticated teff millet (*Eragrostis tef*) is sown most extensively in the lowlands. Most of these cereals are consumed locally, and the most common recipe for them is unleavened bread (*boora*) baked on an earthenware griddle. Enset is, however, the most important food crop among over 100 crop species grown by the people. This crop has several distinct traits.

Enset is planted at widely varying elevations, ranging from over 3,000 metres to approximately 1,000 metres, in all three zones. In the highlands, especially in the area approaching the uppermost limit, the crop is cultivated in large numbers, normally in hundreds, and serves as the most prominent staple food. In the midlands, where about 100 plants are grown in one plot, enset remains the most important cultivated crop, but taro, yams and other root crops also play key roles as co-staple food crops. In the lowlands, however, where it is the hottest and driest in the area, it is planted in much smaller numbers (often less than 10) and is just one of the staple food crops, which also include cassava, sweet potato, and so on. Thus, the importance of the crop differs between the elevational zones. Whereas it is cultivated in high intensity in the highlands, it is in low intensity in the lowlands.

Figure 2 (left). Enset plants.
Figure 3 (below). A giant enset corm.

109

Figure 4 (above). Pulverizing an enset corm.
Figure 5 (below). Squeezing enset leaf-sheath pulp.

Like the banana, enset is a perennial. However, in sharp contrast to the banana, enset is harvested for use as food only once, after a long period of cultivation lasting three to six years. Enset cultivation is, therefore, considered to represent an extremely 'delayed return' system, in that most other perennial and all annual crops provide annual harvests.[4] Nonetheless, in return, enset yields an exceptionally large harvest (e.g. Tsegaye et al. 2001). Two remarkable features of the elaborate management of this crop are the regular manuring and repeated transplantation involved in its cultivation.

This crop is planted permanently in small gardens surrounding homes. Although cereals and some pulses are monocropped in large outlying fields with short or long fallow periods and, traditionally, without any manure, many other crops including root and tuber crops, vegetables, spices, coffee and other tree crops, are all planted side-by-side in gardens. Enset is the garden crop that is planted the closest to their round houses. Because virtually all the houses are built on a slope with a flattened base, gardens are divided into upper and lower sections (*kara afna* and *kara omo*) according to their location in relation to the house. Although enset is planted in the upper section of the garden, it is usually grown in the lower section because the soil in the lower garden is more fertile as a result of its constant fertilization by cow dung and urine flowing out of the house through a small channel. Women also use dung from cows and other animals (sheep, goats) housed inside to manure upper and remote garden sections on a regular basis, usually every few months. The bulk of the dung is used to grow enset and coffee, which are often planted in mixed groves around the house.

In addition, enset crops are uniquely propagated and repeatedly transplanted by men. Apart from its use for food, enset corm is also harvested for propagation. Immature plants of about three years of age are used for this purpose. The harvested corm is cut vertically into halves, and then shallowly buried around the edges of the garden, where the soil is rarely manured and is the least fertile. In a few months, adventitious buds (generally mentioned as suckers and locally known as *ooshe*), often numbering in the hundreds, emerge from the halved corms. After about a year, the large shoots are chosen to be transplanted as individual plants, known as *mach'e*, in a more fertile corner of the garden. After one or more years, the plants are again and again transplanted to different locations in more fertile garden plots. Finally, the plants, now referred to as *alo*, may be replanted in empty spots that had previously contained plants that have recently been harvested. Due to this elaborate transplanting and soil fertility management system, enset (and coffee) are maintained as permanent thick groves around the house.

Almost all parts of enset are used for multiple purposes. For example, the leaf can serve as a sheet on which to serve a meal, as a cover for a dish or drink, as wrapping material for freshly baked bread, as a lid for steam-boiling pots, as a mat on which to sit and sleep, and as fodder for cattle (Fujimoto 2005).

Different varieties of this crop have different local names. Thus far, 66 varieties of enset, far more than the 36 varieties of taro (Fujimoto 2009), its closest competitor in this regard, have been identified, making it the crop with the greatest number of local varieties in the land. Interestingly, enset varieties are categorized by gender as either 'male' (*d'iratts*) or 'female' (*maach*). The vast majority (56) of these varieties are regarded as female and only nine male (one variety is unidentified). However, male/female ratios in plant numbers vary according to elevation. Whereas male varieties are more common than female varieties in the highlands and male and female varieties are almost equally common in the midlands, female varieties are dominant in the lowlands. Female varieties tend to be planted in the less fertile upper section of the garden, whereas male varieties dominate in the most fertile lower section of the garden (Fujimoto 1997).

This may beg questions about the criteria used to distinguish between male and female varieties. Whereas female varieties are thin and grow fast until they are harvested (3–4 years), male varieties are fat but require more time (5–6 years), which suggests the latter's higher yield. Malo farmers commonly explain that the most important distinction between male and female varieties is their palatability and they claim that female varieties are more palatable than male ones. Related to this distinction, male and female varieties tend to be cooked in different ways.

Enset processing and cooking among the Malo

As a food, enset is cooked in two ways. One method involves steam-boiling. Enset is harvested by removing the soil around the corm, cutting off the roots extending from the corm, pushing down the whole plant, removing the corm from the plant, and shaving the surface of the corm. Next, the scraped corm is cut into approximately 5 cm cubes until it fills most of a pot. Green vegetables, spices and a little water, are added to the pot, which is then sealed with enset leaves, and placed on a fire over a high flame for about an hour. This method has the advantage of enabling the preparation of a large volume of food in a short time, although it must occur immediately after the plant is harvested because a harvested enset corm rots quickly. Additionally, the dish rapidly loses its culinary appeal when it cools and it easily spoils within a few days. Thus, this meal is often served to participants in co-operative labour parties and at ceremonial occasions such as funerals. Female varieties of enset are usually cooked in this way, whereas male varieties rarely receive this treatment because of their inferior palatability. Malo people prefer steamed-boiled dishes made from some of the female varieties; these are rarely offered to communal gatherings and are usually consumed as part of family dinners. This steam-boiling method is in itself not unique to enset but is commonly used for all root and tuber crops, i.e., taro, yams, cassava, sweet potatoes, Irish potatoes, Oromo potatoes (*Coleus edulis*) as well as for pumpkin.[5] It is the most common and almost the only cooking method for all the local root and tuber crops, except enset. Indeed, the local term for a steam-boiled dish (*kattsa*) also refers to cooked food in general, suggesting that the steam-boiling has long been the most common method of cooking in this area. For cooking enset, steam-boiling is still the most common method in the lowlands, although this is no longer the case in the highlands.

Figure 6 (above). Mixing fermented enset.
Figure 7 (below). Grating fermented enset.

Figure 8 (above). Fermented enset porridge.
Figure 9 (below). A steamed and boiled enset dish.

The second type of enset preparation involves a more complex and labour-intensive pre-cooking treatment that produces lactic acid fermentation using both the underground corm and leaf-sheath pulp. Once fermented, however, the product remains edible for a longer period (over a few months) and provides the basis for a wide variety of dishes.

Like steam-boiling, the harvesting of enset plants is performed by women. However, husbands often help in uprooting the plant because plants used for this use are frequently quite large. With the exception of this operation, however, women perform all the procedures described. First, a work area of about 1 m by 2 m is prepared near the harvested spot in the enset grove by lining with several layers of enset leaves. Second, the shaved corm is placed on this work area and totally pulverized with a 50–60 cm long bamboo scraper (*garme*) used exclusively for this purpose. The pulverized substance is collected in a corner of the work area. This most laborious enset-related process usually takes a woman two to five hours depending on the size of the corm. Then, the outer pseudostem is ripped off and the inner whitish pseudostem is dismantled into 10–20 leaf sheaths. The leaf sheath is decorticated and tied to a slanted plank (*otetts*) on a nearby enset plant and the pulp is squeezed from the leaf sheath using a 30–40 cm long bamboo scraper (*maylishe*). This procedure is performed at the work area or at another location and normally requires two to three hours. During this squeezing process, the enset fiber (*gola*) is also collected for later use in strings, hats, and so on. Next, the pulverized corm and squeezed leaf-sheath pulp are mixed and then wrapped with several layers of enset leaves. These pre-fermentation procedures, which must be completed in one day, normally require an entire day, from about 10 a.m. to around 4 p.m., for a woman to complete. If the harvested plant is large, this work is performed with the aid of a neighbour. In the highlands, where fermented enset is the most important food source, these procedures normally occur in a household once per week or every ten days, whereas they occur only once per month or less frequently in the lowlands.

The resulting substance (*mala*) is left in the enset grove for about two weeks to ferment, a period interrupted only by one mixing at the midpoint.[6] When the material is considered properly fermented, small portions are extracted, wrapped separately, and weighted with heavy stones to be dehydrated in the backyard for a few days.[7] Subsequently, fibres and other small scraps left inside are carefully removed by repeated kneading and chopping with a knife. The pasty material is then elaborately grated with a stone mortar. These post-fermentation tasks, which normally take one to two hours during the afternoon of the day that the material is to be cooked, are again labour-intensive but essential because they greatly affect the taste of the final dishes.

At this point, the prepared fermented paste is ready for cooking as follows:

(a) Unleavened baked bread (*boora*): The prepared material, wrapped in enset leaves, rotates on an earthenware griddle placed over a medium fire for less than one hour (normally 30–40 minutes) to create unleavened disc-shaped bread with a diameter of 40–50 cm and a thickness of 2–3 cm. The bread is then cut into 7–10 cm square-shaped pieces and served with hot spicy vegetable relishes. Three to five pieces constitute a quite substantial meal for one person. In the highlands, this is the most common method of preparing enset. The bread does not spoil quickly and remains fresh for over a week. Students living in school dormitories often visit home during weekends and return to school with several loaves of this bread, usually containing spices. Wheat, sorghum, or other cereal flour may be added to the dough. In such cases, the bread is called *gindittsa*.

(b) Steamed dumpling bread (*d'ufe*): The prepared material can also be steamed as cylindrical dumpling bread with a diameter of *c.* 2 cm and a length of 10–15 cm. Wrapped in enset leaves, it is steamed in a pot often together with ingredients such as enset corms, yam tubers, and pumpkins. Older people remember that this method of cooking was as common in the past as the method of baking unleavened bread is in the present. The decreased importance of this method of cooking is probably related to the decrease in the steam-boiling of root and tuber crops more generally. This dish can also contain wheat, sorghum or other cereal flour.

(c) Roasted grain (*koose*): The prepared material is torn into small shreds or grains using one's fingers. These shreds or grains are then roasted over a griddle while being stirred occasionally. Green vegetables are usually mixed with this dish. Teff flour can be cooked into this dish.

(d) Steamed grain (*aybiza*): Small grains are formed using the process for making roasted grain (*koose*). These are then steamed in a pot using the similar process for making steamed dumpling bread (*d'ufe*).

(e) Porridge (*shendera*) and gruel (*ware*): Finely prepared material can be made into porridge or gruel. Milk and butter can be added to the former, which serves as a special kind of food.

Although root and tuber crops are largely steam-boiled in a pot or baked in the hearth, fermented enset starch tends to be cooked by different methods. It should be noted that most of these dishes (unleavened baked bread, steamed dumpling bread, roasted grain, porridge and gruel) can be made from cereal flours as well. Thus, these methods of cooking may have been originally designed for cereals rather than developed for root and tuber crops, indicating that enset starch becomes like cereal flour through fermentation and the elaborate pre- and post-fermentation treatments. Cooking these dishes does not require as much time or as strong a fire as does steam-boiling root and tuber crops.

It should also be noted that in the lowlands, a region with a lower population density (~130 people per km^2) in which the crop is of minor importance, enset is rarely processed for fermentation and is usually consumed as a steam-boiled dish. However, fermentation and simple steam-boiling methods are employed on more or less equal terms in the midlands. And in the highlands, where enset is the prominent food source in the local diet and the population density is higher (~250 people per km^2), the

Figure 10. Baked unleavened enset bread.

fermentation of enset starch is a more important cooking method than steam-boiling the corm. In other words, starch-fermented dishes are more prominent in areas with abundant enset plantations and a higher population density. A similar tendency, but on a larger scale, has been observed with respect to the whole enset-growing area in south-west Ethiopia.

Conclusion: enset starch fermentation as a process of intensification

Westphal's classification (1975) of the enset-growing area according to the importance of the crop, and Hildebrand's distinction (2007) of high-intensity and low-intensity cultivation of enset were introduced at the start of this essay. It may be further added that high-intensity cultivation of enset tends to be practised in most densely populated areas by large ethnic groups while low-intensity cultivation is practised in rather sparsely populated areas by smaller ethnic groups. For example, the Gurage and the Sidama who practice high-intensity cultivation of enset number over 1,800,000 and nearly 3,000,000 respectively, and their respective population densities are estimated at about 280 and 430 people per km². On the other hand, the Sheko and the Dizi who practice low-intensity cultivation number about 35,000 and 36,000 respectively, and their respective population densities are estimated at 8.1 and 5.8 people per km² (Central Statistics Authority 2005). The importance as a staple and the cultivation intensity of the crop are clearly associated with the population size and density of enset-growing societies, which will be examined in detail. Anyway, social dimensions need to be considered in future discussions.

In addition, large ethnic groups who practice high-intensity cultivation generally live in the highlands, whereas small groups who practice low-intensity cultivation inhabit the lowlands. Even within the same ethnic group, the importance as a staple and the cultivation intensity of the crop as well as the population density vary between the highlands and the lowlands. This ecological factor cannot be overlooked.

Importantly, highlanders living in more densely populated zones who rely on the crop as a main staple mostly employ the starch fermentation method. Although it is not obvious how and to what extent the consumption of fermented enset starch contributes to their population size and density, it is obvious that the fermentation of enset starch is more of a delayed-return system than is the steam-boiling of corms which lowlanders living in more sparsely populated zones mostly employ. As discussed, enset plants used for fermentation, largely the male varieties in Malo society, are cultivated for longer periods (c. 4–6 years) than are the largely female varieties used for steam-boiling the corms (c. 2–3 years). This delayed-return aspect of fermenting enset starch holds not only for cultivation but also for processing. Although the corms are steam-boiled on the day of the harvest, fermenting enset starch requires at least a few weeks before cooking.

Nonetheless, why do large groups living in densely populated areas depend primarily on the method that involves fermenting enset starch? Why do they not steam-boil the corms? These groups have a cultural tendency to regard steam-boiling as a low-grade practice, although this sentiment is not shared by other enset-growing groups. Is the practice of fermenting enset starch merely a matter of cultural preference? I am certain this is not the case.

Steam-boiling (steaming, boiling, pit-baking, etc.) is a simple cooking method commonly used for root and tuber crops. As discussed, this method requires less labour but more wood for fuel (longer cooking time over a high flame). If the population density is low and wood for fuel is abundant, this method is likely to be optimal and favoured. On the other hand, processing corm and leaf-sheath pulp for starch fermentation requires a great deal of labour but, once fermented, the material can be stored for a longer period of time and cooked with less fuel. Fermenting enset starch, which involves lower environmental costs and more human labour, will be appropriate for land that is densely populated and intensively farmed, suggesting that the use of both agricultural land and human labour may intensify as the population of an area increases. In this context, human labour is involved not only in cultivating crops but also in processing them (e.g. for fermentation), although this point has been largely overlooked in the discussion about agricultural intensification.

Hildebrand (2007, 286) also noted that: 'High-intensity cultivation of enset resembles systems of seed-crop production in two primary ways: soil requires the addition of fertilizer and plots are low in diversity.' The study of the Malo suggests that the method of cooking may be added to this. Fermented enset starch, dominant in high-intensity cultivation areas, is cooked like cereal crops rather than like root and tuber crops, and is often mixed with cereal flours. Fermentation of enset starch is therefore not only a matter of micro-organisms or cultural preferences but also of agricultural intensification. This practice carries wider social and ecological implications that need to be examined further.

Notes

1. Using an experimental method, Gashe (1987) identified the major micro-organisms involved in enset fermentation; these are identical to those involved in the lactic acid fermentation of other vegetables, that is, the two groups of lactic acid bacteria: *Leuconostoc* spp. and *Lactobacillus* spp. While the former, *L. mesenteroides*, initiates the fermentation, the latter, including *Lact. coryneformis* subsp. *coryneformis* and *Lact. plantarum*, are prominent following day 15 until the end of fermentation.
2. The first category includes the Gurage, the Hadiyya, the Kambatta, the Tambaro, the Sidama and the Darassa. The second includes the Wolayta (Welamo), the Koyra (Amarro), the Gamo, the Yem (Janjero), the Kafa, the Ari, the Basketto, and the Dime. The third includes the Sheko (Chako) and the Maji. The fourth includes some portions of the Oromo who recently started cultivating enset (Westphal 1975).
3. In the highlands, the average maximum and minimum temperatures are around 20°C and 13°C, respectively, whereas they are around 29°C and 17°C, respectively, in the lowlands. The annual rainfall in the highlands is about 1,700 mm; the figure in the lowlands is about 1,400 mm.
4. The 'delayed-return' system is a term coined by Woodburn (1982) to discuss egalitarian societies comprised of hunter-gatherers. He separated hunter-gatherer economies into 'immediate-return' and 'delayed-return' systems. Food is casually consumed without being elaborately processed or stored in the former system; in the latter system, however, it is normally processed, stored in fixed dwellings and treated as a valued asset which people have rights over. In this paper, these categories are applied to farmer economies, as suggested by Pankurst (1996).
5. Although it is a minor crop, and becoming extinct, the Oromo potato (*Coleus edulis*) is another root crop that has been domesticated and cultivated in Ethiopia.
6. It may be notable that the lactobacilli succeed the *Leuconostoc* spp. as the most abundant micro-organisms in enset fermentation after about two weeks (Gashe 1987).
7. In this way, the fermented substance from one plant is consumed over a few months. In this area, the use of an underground pit for longer storage is not common.

Bibliography

Brandt, S.A., A. Spring, C. Hiebsch, J.T. McCabe, E. Tabogie, M. Diro, G. Wolde-Michael, G. Yntiso, M. Shigeta, and S. Tesfaye. *The 'Tree Against Hunger': Enset-Based Agricultural Systems in Ethiopia*. Washington, DC: American Association for the Advancement of Science, 1997.

Central Statistics Authority (CSA) *National Statistics*. Addis Ababa, Ethiopia, 2005. http://www.csa.gov.et/text_files/2005_national_statistics.htm

Dohrmann, A. and M. Metz. 'Ensät', in Uhlig, S. (ed.), *Encyclopaedia Aethiopica, Vol. 2*. Wiesbaden: Harrassowitz Verlag, 2005, 316–318.

Fujimoto, T. 'Enset and its varieties among the Malo, southwestern Ethiopia', in Fukui, K., E. Kurimoto and M. Shigeta (eds.), *Ethiopia in Broader Perspective*. Kyoto: Shokado Booksellers, 1997, 867–882.

_____ 'Malo ethnography' in Uhlig, S. (ed.), *Encyclopaedia Aethiopica, Vol. 3*. Wiesbaden: Harrassowitz Verlag, 2007, 711–713.

_____ 'Taro [*Colocasia esculenta* (L.) Schott] cultivation in vertical wet–dry environments: diversity maintained by mountain farmers' techniques in southwestern Ethiopia', *Economic Botany* 63(2), 2009, 152–166.

Gascon, A. 'Le miracle de l'ensät: géographie d'une plante peuplante', in Zewde, B., R. Pankhurst and T. Beyene (eds.) *Proceedings of the XIth International Conference of Ethiopian Studies, Vol. 2*. Addis Ababa: Institute of Ethiopian Studies, 1994, 85–98.

Gashe, B.A. 'Kocho fermentation', *Journal of Applied Bacteriology* 62, 1987, 473–477.

Hildebrand, E.A. 'A tale of two tuber crops: how attributes of enset and yams may have shaped prehistoric human-plant interactions in south-west Ethiopia', in Denham, T.P., J. Iriarte, and L. Vrydaghs (eds.), *Rethinking Agriculture: Archaeological and Ethnoarchaeological Perspectives.* Walnut Creek, CA: Left Coast Press, 2007, 273–298.

Pankhurst, A. 'Social consequences of enset production', in Abate, T., C. Hiebsch, S.A. Brandt, and S. Gebremariam (eds.) *Enset-Based Sustainable Agriculture in Ethiopia.* Addis Ababa: Institute of Agricultural Research, 1996, 69–82.

Pijls, L.T.J., A.A.M. Timmer, Z. Wolde-Gebriel and C.E. West. 'Cultivation, preparation and consumption of ensete (*Ensete ventricosum*) in Ethiopia', *Journal of the Science of Food and Agriculture* 67, 1995, 1–11.

Pollock, N.J. 'Breadfruit fermentation practices in Oceania', *Journal de la Société des Océanistes* 40, 1984, 151–164.

_____ *These Roots Remain: Food Habits in Islands of the Central and Eastern Pacific since Western Contact.* Laie, Hawaii: Institute for Polynesian Studies, 1992.

Shack, W.A. *The Gurage: A People of the Ensete Culture.* Oxford: Oxford University Press, 1966.

Tsegaye, A. and P.C. Struik. 'Enset (*Ensete ventricosum* (Welw.) Cheesman) kocho yield under different crop establishment methods as compared to yields of other carbohydrate-rich food crops', *Netherlands Journal of Agricultural Science* 49(1), 2001, 81-94.

Westphal, E. *Agricultural Systems in Ethiopia.* Wageninge:, Centre for Agricultural Publishing and Documentation, 1975.

Woodburn, J. 'Egalitarian societies', *Man* (N.S.) 17(3), 1982, 431–451.

Roman Fish Sauce: an Experiment in Archaeology

Sally Grainger

This paper will report on a recent project undertaken in collaboration with the University of Reading's Departments of Archaeology and Food Biosciences to duplicate, using experimental archaeology, the processes involved in the manufacture of the various kinds of Roman fish sauce, one of the principal types of preserved food in the ancient world. Symposiasts may remember my paper at the 2005 Symposium on Authenticity, in which I described my preliminary experiments in the manufacture of the blood fish sauce known as *garum* and surveyed the current literature. The question that I posed was how authentic was modern fish sauce when attempting to reconstruct ancient recipes. My conclusion was that Roman and modern fish sauces are very similar but different in some crucial ways: (1) the salt levels of ancient sauces are apparently quite low; (2) ancient sauces appear to be ready after just a few weeks rather than the upwards of eighteen months that modern sauces can take; and finally (3) the Romans manufactured fish sauce not only from the ubiquitous small fry *clupeiforms* such as sardine, anchovy, herring and sprat which modern fish sauce is largely made of but from any number of different fish such as mackerel, mullet, tuna, moray eels, oysters and sea urchins.

Roman fish sauce resembles Thai fish sauce in its basic principles: small whole fish and salt are allowed to dissolve and ferment into a liquid sauce through the action of enzymes in the viscera by a process called autolysis. The enzymes present in the viscera convert the solid proteins of the fish meat into water-soluble amino acids and peptides as they dissolve the flesh. As a result the sauce can and should be highly nutritious (Mclver et al. 1982, 1017). The salt levels in modern fish sauce fluctuate between 4/3 fish to 1 salt (33–25 per cent) and even on occasions 1:1, while ancient fish sauce recipes suggest 7:1 fish to salt (15 per cent) (Mclver et al. 1982). Modern fish sauce analysis is now suggesting that the high levels of salt actually inhibit enzyme action resulting in a very slow fermentation process and lower protein levels (Klomklao et al. 2006, 441). The finest south-east Asian fish sauces, *nuoc mam* from Vietnam and *nam pla* from Thailand, continue to use high salt levels which appeal to local tastes but as a result they have to be fermented for up to eighteen months to generate sufficient high-quality sauce to feed the market at home and abroad. Roman fish sauce with its low salt levels and apparently short fermentation process appears able to generate very quickly a nutritious sauce (which would improve the health of the consumer in south-east Asia). Because the safety of the manufacturing process can now be guaranteed, salt levels in south-east Asian fish sauces are beginning to be reduced (Klomklao et al. 2006, 443).

This project, which plans to duplicate Roman fish sauce recipes on a large scale, was also prompted by a need to integrate the vast body of archaeological evidence for fish sauce with the literary and modern evidence so that we can have a comprehensive picture of these sauces in the ancient world.

Evidence for fish sauce in Roman archaeology

Fish bones are often found on Roman sites in amphorae, the two-handled spiked vessels that the ancients used to transport oil, wine and fish products (see figure 1). The bones are common in amphorae from shipwrecks and also in discrete deposits associated with processing sites, retail sites and consumption sites (Desse-Berset and Desse 2000). There has been little agreement among the numerous scholars in archaeology, food history and classics as to the nature of the various products manufactured under the names *garum, liquamen, muria* and *allec* (Curtis 1991, 7; 2009, 713; Corcoran 1963, 206; Studor 1994, 195). However, an understanding of the meaning of these terms is essential if the fish bones associated with these sites are to be attributed to certain products. My research into fish sauce through the literary evidence has led to a definition of the terms which are as follows:

Garum: in Latin, a blood and viscera sauce made from mackerel and other kinds of fish. It is a black and bloody sauce used largely as a table condiment. When of superior quality, it is mentioned by élite writers such as Horace (*Sat* 2.8), Martial (13.103) and Pliny (*HN* 13.93).

Liquamen: in Latin (*garon*: in Greek), a sauce made from whole fish of various sizes, mackerel (when high status) and generally various *clupeiforms* (sardine, anchovy). This sauce sometimes has extra viscera added to aid the liquefaction process. It can be yellow through to dark brown in colour and is largely used as a cooking ingredient in the kitchen and is therefore often unrecognized by the élite in their literature. It is the standard term for fish sauce in the Roman recipe text *Apicius* (Grocock and Grainger 2006, 373ff.).

Allec: a fish paste derived from the manufacture of *liquamen/garon*; bone free.

Muria: a brine derived from salted fish, the poor man's fish seasoning.

The categories I use are somewhat different from other interpretations as the traditional approach is to take the definitions of Curtis as the standard and see *garum* as the generic term in the early period and *liquamen* in the later Empire (Curtis 2009, 713; Étienne 2002, 6). Contrary to this, and as I have argued elsewhere (see Grainger 2007, 93; Grocock and Grainger 2006, 383), I believe that there was a distinct difference between the two terms and that the Greek and Latin terminology referred to different types of sauce.

The fish bones from shipwrecks are often exceptionally well preserved and sometimes even retain organic matter clinging to them. Fish bone experts have had particular difficulty in identifying the differences between a salted fish product and a fish sauce in amphorae from shipwrecks (Desse-Berset and Desse 2000, 92). The natural assumption is that a fish sauce would be a relatively clear liquid and bone-free and so archaeologically invisible (Van Neer and Ervynck 200, 208). In this scenario, the bones are left at the processing sites, such as those found in southern Spain. A leading fish bone expert has determined that salted fish products can be recognized widely in the record through a group of particular criteria, i.e. good preservation of large and whole examples of species such as mackerel and smaller species such as sardine and anchovy (Desse-Berset and Desse 2000, 92). There is also considerable fish bone evidence from wrecks and land sites that have been identified as *allec*, the fish paste residue associated with fish sauce production. This identification has been made either because the bones are from fish too small to be salted whole or when they are badly damaged, which is believed to be caused by the fermentation process (Van Neer and Ervynck 2000, 208; Cotton and Lernau 1996, 231). *Allec* is considered both a residue from the production of a fish sauce as well as a separate marketable fish paste which may or may not contain bone depending on the size of fish and the quality of the product: *allec* was also made from bone-free products such as oysters or sea urchins (Pliny *HN.* 31.95). The association of wreck evidence with *allec* has been noted to be economically illogical as a bony fish paste generally from small *clupeiforms* does not appear to be a product worth shipping across the Mediterranean in bulk, particularly as it is considered a slave ration and low status (Van Neer and Ervynck 2002, 208). Large deposits of discarded and damaged small *clupeiform* bones are regularly found associated with broken amphorae at processing and port sites. This is also considered as the fish paste *allec* though the question as to why the product was discarded is rarely considered. If the bone were integral to the *allec* when purchased and someone had to remove the bones to consume the product then the bones themselves would be discarded in an *ad hoc* fashion at various places of consumption rather than in discrete assemblages as we find them (Bruschi and Wilkins 1996, 167; Dellusi and Wilkins 2000, 56).

It is hoped that many related questions can be answered in the course of the long-term project to manufacture fish sauce. This article will discuss some of the initial experiments. It will pursue two key questions and report on the preliminary findings. The questions are:

1. What are the potential protein levels and, therefore, nutritional value of traditional Roman fish sauces when fermented for 1–2 months compared to modern varieties?

2. What is the nature of the *allec* residue in production and how does the bone evidence from that process compare with some key sites where fish bones have been found?

I will discuss three key sites, two wrecks and one land site (all from the Mediterranean), which contain amphorae holding a processed fish product that may be fish sauce or salted fish. I will then review the experiment and the results of the observational study and laboratory analysis followed by some tentative conclusions.

Grado: second century AD; northern Adriatic coast (Delussi and Wilkins 2000, 60; Auriemma 2000, 10).

The ship held 23–25 tons of cargo which included 600 amphorae. It is not necessary to know the details of the types (see figure 1) beyond the fact that the large capacity amphorae were half-full of bones from whole sardines in exceptional preservation. Other amphorae held whole mackerel of various sizes up to 30 cm and it was noted that there was some intermingling of the species between the vessels. These vessels had thin narrow necks which would mean that not only was it difficult to fit whole fish in but that it would also have been impossible to take them out again without breaking the vessel. The exception was the Dressel 19/6b amphora which had a short stumpy base, round body and narrow neck but small capacity. These smaller vessels were empty but did have an inscription identifying the product as '*Liq(uamen) flos*'. The product inside was therefore a quality fish sauce of some sort. The current interpretation is that the vessels with fish bones represent a salted fish product, whether it was sardine or mackerel, while the empty vessels clearly held a sauce (Delussi and Wilkins 2000, 60). However, one recent commentator made the suggestion that while the fish bones are probably salted fish they may actually represent a semi-processed fish product which may have been made into a sauce later (Auriemma 2000, 43).

124

Cap Bear III (Port Vendres): first century AD; north Mediterranean coast near the Spanish/French border (Desse-Berset and Desse 2000).

This wreck held three types of amphora, mainly for wine. A small collection of sixteen Dressel type 12 amphorae contained whole Spanish mackerel bones in good preservation. The fish were approximately 28–30 cm in size and the product has been identified as salted fish (Desse-Berset and Desse 2000, 80). The Dressel 12 amphora has a particularly interesting shape: the neck is long and thin with an hourglass shape that swells slightly at the rim. The body is also long, relatively narrow, with a stumpy base. It is very hard to imagine this amphora actually being designed to hold a solid salted fish product. Its shape is clearly designed for liquids and unlike the Grado evidence (above), which makes use of a disparate collection of available amphorae, there is a uniform use of 16 vessels suggesting that they were selected or made to order to hold this product.

Cerro del Mar, Malaga, Spain: first century AD (Von den Driesch 1980, 151–54).

At Cerro del Mar in Spain, an early-first-century trench associated with a fish processing factory contained numerous broken *sigillata* amphorae (red-glazed) beneath which was a 10 cm layer of multiple species of fish bone sediment associated with the amphorae. Assigning fish to particular amphorae, however, was impossible. A large quantity of

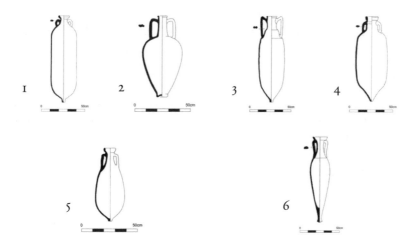

Figure 1. Types of amphora: (1) African 1; (2) Forlimpopoli A; (3) Knossos a/53; (4) Tripolitana 1; (5) Dressel type 19; (6) Dressel type 12.

bones from small *clupeiforms* of 10–20 cm length were badly damaged and broken up. They may represent a fish sauce residue. There were also small mackerel. The fish bone experts disagree as to the interpretation of this material. Cotton and Lernau (1996, 232) and Lepiksaar (1986, n.23) both consider the bones remains of an *allec* fish paste, while Von den Driesch makes the far more likely claim that it is simply the discarded residue of fish sauce production (Von den Driesch 1980, 151–54). In this interpretation Von den Driesch has acknowledged that it may be possible for a liquid fish sauce to be transported with its bones and residue and this could be discarded at the place of sale or consumption rather than at the place of production.

Modern and ancient processing sites

There are the remains of hundreds of fish processing sites in southern Spain around the Straits of Cadiz, and also in north Africa. The sites are uniform in structure and suggest that these factories were active in making a bulk fish sauce in the first and second centuries AD (Ponsich and Tarradel 1965). Large cement-lined tanks of various sizes are arranged around a central area. The remains of pillars suggest that, though open to the air, the tanks were covered with a roof. Most of the factories also have a room that has a furnace facility to heat a hypocaust beneath the floor. It is believed that fish sauce underwent some sort of heating process, though it is clear from the recipes that a cooked sauce was a separate domestic process (Ponsich and Tarradel 1965, 99). The tanks are sealed and have curved edges and corners which we might suspect was to prevent the fish from getting lodged in the corners as well as to facilitate cleaning.

The method of production that the majority of the structures imply is that the fish and salt are placed together in the tank and the resulting sauce, when it has formed, must be removed from above. One imagines the bones and residue remain in the tank. The small-scale method advocated in the *Geoponica* suggests that after 2–3 months a sauce could be taken, while a different source suggests an indeterminate number of days beyond seven. In both these written sources, a close-woven basket is placed over the vessel and the sauce flows into it. How this method is duplicated on a large scale and with what kind of structure is hard to discern.

Modern fish sauce factories

Methods (in present-day south-east Asia) have become very industrialized in recent years, but the traditional factory sites were very similar to the ones we find in Roman Spain. Cement tanks that did not drain from beneath were quite common, but the norm was to have a raised tank with a filtering drain. The fish and salt were placed together and two basic types of production were employed: either the mixture is regularly stirred while being held underneath the brine, or it is compressed with weights (Hung 2007, 1.3). Modern analysis shows that stirring increases the protein yield while the compressing method is particularly efficient and clean as the fermenting fish, which is greasy and somewhat unpleasant, is hidden away. The fish was held down with removable wicker covers which may also have facilitated the removal of the residue. In the compressing method the clear sauce that forms is taken from beneath and poured back into the tank above until it develops the required protein levels. At this point, it is removed and finely filtered. More brine is then added and the semi-dissolved fish residue and bone is stirred and compressed again. In some circumstances it is filtered up to five or six times before the residue is heated to extract the last possible fish flavour and nutrients (Hung 2007, 1.3.1; Curtis 2009, 713). The ancient factories cannot have manufactured a sauce under compression because most tanks were incapable of being drained from below. It must, therefore, have been necessary not only to stir regularly, but also to access the sauce from above.

The experiments

The recipes in the experimental fish sauce production for this project derive from Greek agricultural manuals and the details of the procedure involved will be only briefly referred to (Dalby 2011). The sauces were started in fish tanks in a greenhouse in order to duplicate the temperatures found in southern Spain where the majority of these bulk sauces were made. Daily observation allowed the sauce to be described at each stage of liquefaction and the resulting liquids and residues have now been bottled and the bones dried.

It was proposed that six basic experiments should be conducted, in order to understand what happens to fish under many different conditions, including salted

126

mackerel, sardine without extra viscera, sardine with extra viscera and mackerel cut open to expose the viscera. The precise consequences of the addition of extra viscera to the production of a whole fish sauce of the *liquamen* type has been explored (the viscera sauce (*garum*) was not part of these current experiments), however it will not be possible to discuss all the experiments here.

Fresh whole sardine (*Sardina pilchardus*), 5–20 cm in size, and sprat (*Sprattus sprattus*), 5–8 cm in size, were individually salted at 15 per cent in 10 kg batches and left in the heat of the greenhouse with a loose cardboard cover. A sauce was also made with sardine and extra viscera to observe the differences is speed and efficiency of liquefaction. The observational study resulted in the following conclusions concerning the liquefaction process:

The whole fish shrink and generate a brine which allows the salt to dissolve. The fish never produce enough brine to allow all the fish to be submerged beneath it unless heavily weighted.

Within the space of a week a small number of the sardine had exposed vertebrae and a few had shed all their flesh while the sprat had dissolved into paste within four days.

As the fish dissolved through enzyme action a thick emulsion formed which comprises the fish flesh in suspension.

Evaporation was also a major factor and extra liquid was needed throughout the experiments. The quantity and nature of this extra liquid is crucial to the final quality of the sauce: it could be brine or, as noted in the *Geoponica,* wine.

With the sauce made without extra viscera and with sardine, it was clear that at four weeks, even after the addition of extra liquid, the brine had become saturated with the emulsion of fine particles of flesh and the dissolving process had stopped.

A clear yellowish brown liquid formed in layers throughout the emulsion and also initially on the surface. Over time the paste and bone sank to the bottom.

When this emulsion was finally taken after two months at least two-thirds of the whole fish were still intact though the cavity had burst and a good deal of the flesh had already gone.

This experiment was duplicated with extra viscera but with no extra fluid and while the fish dissolved rapidly, the emulsion also rapidly became saturated with particles of flesh and stopped before all the fish flesh had been shed from the bones. When additional liquid was included, rapid and effective liquefaction took place which left all the bones fully cleaned of muscle tissue within two weeks.

The thick saturated emulsion, without sufficient liquid, initially separated out, with the residue (*allec*) at the bottom and the fine clear liquid at the top. With time this situation reversed and the clear liquid settled at the bottom. This may be because there is an increase in density due to more of the protein from the particles of muscle flesh dissolving into the liquid sauce.

When efficient liquefaction occurs (through sufficient viscera and liquid) the emulsion separates out with some of the residue on the surface and some at the bottom. This means that when the sauce is taken it must be removed as a part-emulsion. This sauce made up of a residue or *allec*, which we may define as a fish paste of particles of muscle tissue, and the clear liquid are therefore likely to be transported together in the amphorae.

It was apparent that extra liquid and extra viscera (when the fish are larger than 12 cm) are crucial to efficient liquefaction. The recipes recorded in the *Geoponica* and *Gargilius Martialis* differ as to the addition of both viscera and liquid. They also differ as to whether a cover and consequently a reduction in evaporation was employed. Of the two recipes in the *Geoponica*, one has extra viscera, is uncovered and has no extra liquid which means that, though liquefaction is improved the reduction in liquid through evaporation results in rapid saturation of the remaining liquid and a very low yield of the first sauce. Which in turn allows for many *in situ* additions of brine to the semi-dissolved residues to make many grades of sauce, in keeping with traditional methods in Thailand. The *Gargilius Martialis* recipe uses larger fish in pieces, no extra viscera (which is unnecessary as the fish are cut open to expose the viscera), no extra liquid and is covered and sealed which would also generate limited volume of initial sauce. The second recipe in the *Geoponica* uses larger fish, has no extra viscera, is covered and adds 2:1 extra liquid which suggest that all the fish will dissolve efficiently in this extra liquid and it will be possible to take substantially more sauce from the bones. This method results in a quantity of *allec* within the layer of bone at the bottom of the tank, once the rest of the sauce has been removed. The sardine bones within this layer (extra viscera experiment) were very well preserved during the process. No obvious damage to their structure was detected though the rapid liquefaction resulted in complete disarticulation. It appears that the *allec* residue at the bottom of the tank was also rich enough to be able to generate a second-quality sauce if diluted. The salting tanks associated with the fish processing factories in Roman Spain and north Africa are on a much greater scale than these domestic vessels and consequently the volume and potential value of this remaining residue is that much greater. It is more than likely, given the fish bone evidence, that the process of generating this second-quality sauce took place away from the factory and in fact in the amphora. This scenario provides a logical reason for the presence of large quantities of what appears to be traded fish sauce residue (*allec*) in the archaeological record at sea. The Grado wreck, containing numerous amphorae full of sardine bones, can be seen as transporting the second-quality sauce being generated in transit, while the small Dressel 19/6b vessels identified as holding a *liquamen flos* could well be transporting the first-quality sauce from those self-same bones. The land-based sites such as Cerro del Mar could therefore represent the debris from the harvesting of that second-quality sauce at a single place of sale or consumption. The damage to the bone associated with these sites is likely to be caused by the process of extracting all the potential sauce either using direct heat or hot brine as is commonly practised in south-east Asia.

It has not been possible to fully access the remaining site at Cap Bear III (Port Vendres) which contained larger mackerel bones of exceptional preservation. However it is clear that the main criteria by which Desse-Berset and Desse identify salted fish is through good preservation. The Grado fish bone evidence is well preserved yet it has been strongly indicated that this ship was carrying fish sauce products, not salted fish. It is also clear from the literary evidence that a high-quality fish sauce was made from whole mackerel and also that this was the most desirable according to Pliny (31.93). There are a few incidences of *liquamen* and *allec* from mackerel on amphora labels but this is in contrast to the vast numbers which record an undesignated fish sauce type and it is also clear from the recipes that *liquamen* was made from a mixed variety of fish. The mackerel bones generated in this project display evidence of changes that may indicate enzyme digestion. These will be compared to those bones from Port Vendres and other wreck sites to ascertain categorically which bones have been subject to enzyme digestion and therefore have been used to make fish sauce.

The laboratory results

Sample	Definition	Protein mg/ml
A1	sardine 1st	22.001
A2	sardine 2nd	16.297
B1	sprat 1st	24.797
B2	sprat 2nd	18.753
A1ℓ	sardine allec 1st	144.648
A2ℓ	sardine allec 2nd	82.500
B1ℓ	sprat allec 1st	113.786
B2ℓ	sprat allec 2nd	73.412
L	squid fish sauce	50.41
A1ℓ+	sardine allec + brine	43.40

The laboratory results reveal substantial differences between the different types of sauce. It is apparent from modern fish sauce studies that colour and taste are governed by protein levels (Mciver 1982, 1019). The sardine variety (A1) was separated from its *allec* within a month of its removal from the bone and is relatively weak in protein compared with a sample of modern fish sauce (L). The sprat sauce was treated the same way and is only marginally better. The *allec* on the other hand is exceptionally high in protein as it is largely made up of particles of muscle tissue which in theory could shed all its protein into any liquid it is suspended in. In order to test the quality of a sauce made from re-diluted *allec*, a small amount of A1ℓ = first quality sardine *allec* is blended with a new 15 per cent brine and left for two months. The resulting protein levels are far higher than the original sauce from which the *allec* was derived and suggest that a sauce stored as an emulsion for the duration of its journey to market is going to improve its quality the longer it is left. It is apparent that the local and small-scale fish sauce manufacturing process in which numerous clear sauces are harvested from the surface of a batch of dissolving fish, leaving the residues behind, will produce relatively weak and inferior sauces.

Conclusion

These fish sauce experiments have provided vital empirical evidence for the possible ways in which a bulk fish sauce could be made in the ancient world. It has been possible to re-evaluate the fish bone evidence from a number of shipwreck sites and suggest that fish sauce may have been transported with its bone which may well explain the trade in so much low-value fish sauce residue. The question posed at the beginning of this paper was to consider how nutritious ancient fish sauces were in comparison to modern fish sauce. The bulk process as reflected in the ancient fish sauce factories of Roman Spain and north Africa does appear to have been superior in quality when harvested as an emulsion and potentially equal to modern protein levels. Spanish fish sauce was considered particularly valuable, according to Pliny (*HN* 31.93). However the local and small-scale process may have produced an inferior product which was far less nutritious. Both varieties of fish sauce played a vital role in the diet of the Romans, though the local and small-scale variety may have been the only fish sauce that lower status consumers could purchase and the health benefits of fish sauce consumption reduced accordingly.

130

Bibliography

Auriemma, R. 'Le anfore del relitto di Grado e il loro contento', *Mélanges de l'École Française de Rome. Antiquité.* 2000, 112: 27–51.

Corcoran, T.H. 'Roman fish sauces', *Classical Journal,* 1963, 58: 204–210.

Cotton, H., O. Lernau, Y. Goren. 'Fish sauce from Herodian Masada', *Journal of Roman Archaeology,* 1996, 9: 223–238.

Curtis, R. *Garum and Salsamenta. Production and Commerce in Materia Medica.* Leiden: Brill, 1991.

_____. 'Umami and the foods of classical antiquity', *American Journal of Clinical Nutrition,* 90 (suppl.), American Society for Nutrition, 2009, 712–18.

Dalby, A. *Geoponika.* Totnes: Prospect Books, 2011.

Delussi, F. & B. Wilkins. 'La conserve di pesce. Alcuni dati da contesti Italiani', *Mélanges de l'École Française de Rome. Antiquité.* 2000, 112: 53–65.

Desse-Berset, N. & J. Desse. 'Salsamenta, garum, et autres préparations de poisson. Ce qu'en disent les os', *Mélanges de l'École Française de Rome. Antiquité.* 2000, 112: 73–97.

Étienne R., Mayet F. *Salaisons et Sauces de Poisson Hispaniques* [Spanish processed fish and fish sauces]. Paris, France: E. de Boccard, 2002.

Grocock, C. & S. Grainger. *Apicius: a Critical Edition with Introduction and English Translation.* Totnes: Prospect Books, 2006.

Grainger, S. 'A New Approach to Roman Fish Sauce', *Petits Propos Culinaires* 83. Totnes, Prospect Books, 2007, 92–111.

Green, K. *The Archaeology of the Ancient Economy.* London: Batsford, 1986.

Hung, Tran Viet. *Decision on the registration of appellation of origin for phan thiet fish sauce,* Ministry of Science and Technology National Office of Intellectual Property, Socialist Republic of Vietnam Hanoi, 30 May 2007 (Translation provided by the EC-ASEAN Intellectual Property Rights Co-operation Programme ECAP II), 2007.

Klomklao Sappasith, Soottawat Benjakul, Wonnop Visessanguan, Hideki Kishimura & Benjamin K. Simpson. 'Effects of the addition of spleen of skipjack tuna (*Katsuwonus pelamis*) on the liquefaction and characteristics of fish sauce made from sardine (*Sardinella gibbosa*)', *Food Chemistry* 98: 2006, 440–452.

Lepsikaar, J. 'Tierreste in einer Römischen amphora aus Salzburg (Mozartsplatz 4)', *Bayerische Vorgeschichtsblatter* 51. 1986, 163–85.

McIver, R., R. I. Brooks & G. A, Reineccius. 'The flavours of fermented fish sauce', *Journal of Agriculture and food chemistry,* 30, 1982, 1017–1020.

Ponsich, M. & M. Tarradel. *Garum et industries antiques de salaison dans la Mediterranée Occidentale.* Paris: Bibliothèque de l'École des Hautes Études Hispaniques 36, 1965.

Studer, J. S. 'Roman fish sauce in Petra, Jordan' in *Fish exploitation in the past,* in W. Van Neer (ed.), *Proceedings of the 7th meeting of the ICAZ Fish Remains Working Group. Annales du musée Royal de l'Afrique Centrale, Sciences Zoologiques* 274. Tervuren, 1994.

Van Neer, W. & A. Ervynck. 'Remains of traded fish in archaeological sites: indicators of status or bulk food?' in Sharyn Jones O'Day et al. (eds.), *Behaviour behind bones:* 203–14. Proceedings of the 9th ICAZ conference, Durham, 2002.

Von den Driesch, A. 'Osteoarchäologische Auswertung von Garum-Resten des Cerro del Mar', *Madrider Mitteilungen.* 21. 1980, 151–4.

A Pickletime Memoir: Salt and Vinegar from the Jews of Eastern Europe to the Prairies of Canada, or Bringing Back the Pickled Lettuce

Alexandra Grigorieva and Gail Singer

Part one

Pickles have a curious reputation. First their shape. They could be a small penis, so eating a pickle makes for slightly audacious optics. I was teased unmercifully as a pickle-eating girl by my naughty older brother and his friends. Further, the strong flavour of pickles has a rather unseemly sexual connotation, especially where garlic and dill are involved. Somehow gherkins, on the other hand, have retained a certain dignity, perhaps because they tend to be small, almost infantile, and thereby elude the more coarse connotations of larger pickled cucumbers. In the twentieth century, while the gherkin was a French and English favourite, the highly aromatic dill-pickled cucumber of Eastern Europeans became the standard-bearer in North America, where outdoor barrels of the fermenting *Cucumis sativus* perfumed the market streets of New York, Chicago and Winnipeg with their powerful aromas.

When I was searching for references to cucumbers and pickles of the past, I was delighted to find serious scholarly work by Corinne Mandel investigating the rôle of the cucumber in European artwork and, consistent with my shallow hypothesis that eating a pickle had some sexual connotation, she demonstrates that the cucumber itself was an erotic device in the works of the Venetian Carlo Crivelli, and the frescoes to be found on the vault of the Chapel of Eleanor of Toledo by Bronzino, amongst other places. Once it's brought to your attention, it's unequivocal.

My own memories of pickles, pickle juice, and pickle-making go back to Winnipeg, Canada, some fifty years ago, when as a child I would sit in the kitchen with my father, Canadian-born of Romanian parents. We would have spent the day at the Farmers' Market on Main Street, where huge baskets of cukes, as they were named, corn on the cob, lettuce, tomatoes, green and red, cabbages and potatoes scented the air with an earthy pungency: the rich, naturally processed dung of free-roaming cattle from the wide, sunny, fertile mid-Canada prairie. The selection of which bushel basket might be ours would be made by tenderly squeezing the dark green, slightly pimpled oblongs: they had to be hard and cool, so that when challenged to retain crispness in the jar, in the brine, nature was on their side. (My father, a reasonably well-educated man, knew nothing of the science of fermentation: micro-organisms on the surface of the cucumbers, coupled with those on the crowns of dill, bathed in salt and vinegar would alter their nature just as they had in his parents' home, and their parents' before them. In spite of his ignorance, he knew exactly what to do.)

There would be a particular verbal exchange between my father and the farmer he might be speaking to: it would be different from the way my father spoke with me or my brother, or mother or Uncle Jack, or Uncle Harry. The farmer was almost invariably Ukrainian. Deep in my father's head was the Ukrainian as enemy: the annihilation of the Jews of the Ukraine was not spoken about, but sat at the back of the minds of the Jews, who were determined, as were the Ukrainians, to make a civilized life in this Canadian prairie city where all sorts of former enemies found themselves eye to eye with question-mark pasts.

Perhaps for those very reasons I don't remember my father ever choosing, or rather being offered, a bad basket of cucumbers. The Jews and the Ukrainians had to re-establish trust.

The bushel baskets of cucumbers, bouquets of dill and heads of garlic came home with us in our 1950 blue Plymouth Deluxe, our first family car. The cucumbers went into the sink where my father patiently scrubbed off the surface dirt. This was one of the tasks I assisted with. Later, if a jar went bad, that is, the pickles were soft or off taste, I would wonder if I had inadequately scrubbed the pickles that went into that jar. The jars and lids were boiled in a large dark-blue speckled canner on the stovetop. It was the largest pot in our house and only emerged from the depths of the basement at canning time. A batch of fresh sealer rings had to be fitted onto the glass lids. They exuded a distinct rubbery odour. My father, with his steady hand, half filled the jars with a broth composed of water, vinegar, salt. I managed to place a generous bouquet of pungent fresh dill crowns in the jar, followed by several cloves of garlic. My father packed the pickles with the finesse of a Japanese gift-wrapper. He could get exactly the right number of pickles in each jar so that they were snug, with only enough room left for a couple of small dry, hot red peppers, and a last sprig of dill. At last the jars were sealed, and transported to the dark, cool basement, to which I would venture on day two, three, four, fascinated by the busy bubbling life within the jars, where fermentation was magically transforming the cucumbers into pickles. (In university I took up the study of chemistry for a brief time, I think inspired by my fascination with that very process.)

But my father was no fool. He knew none of us could wait out the longer metamorphosis. At the end of the night of pickles, two or three more things would happen. Some pickles were placed in jars with water, salt, garlic and dill only: no vinegar. These jars were placed on the back steps with a warning: 'You have to wait until the sun has done its work. No peeking.' Since my older brother never listened to this admonition, neither did I. Sometimes, after only one sunny day, it was August after all, the pickles had begun to turn. They were the elusive 'half-dones' flavoured with the dill and garlic and pepper, as crisp as a fresh McIntosh apple in September, and all the better for consuming them against the explicit instructions of father. He might as well have been telling a cocaine addict not to consume a line of coke left on a coffee-table with a rolled-up dollar bill. My friends would come home with me after school and we would stand around the back door, all eating these homespun delicacies (what in the world did the nice Anglo-Saxon girls tell their mothers?!), saliva dripping from our mouths, as we crunched our way through the pickles. There were never any repercussions for this sin of theft, as long as we didn't consume the whole jar. I assume my father took it as a compliment.

Another thing that happened at the end of the pickling night was several jars got all the same ingredients as the cucumbers, but the cucumbers themselves were replaced by carrots. These would take longer to 'cure' and it was sometimes not until December that the carrots were opened and demolished.

But it is my father's almost instantaneously 'cured' pickled lettuce that I would most like to explore. In those days, the 1950s and '60s, a green salad usually consisted of iceberg lettuce and Kraft Dressing, the latter an improbable hue of neon orange – no wonder the lack of enthusiasm for ordinary salad. No wonder, too, my father remembered the taste of the pickled lettuce of his childhood (just as I remember it from mine!) and determined the perfect balance of sweet and sour – simply vinegar, sugar, salt and water (with a hint of garlic) – and forever after provided us with Mason jar after Mason jar of pickled lettuce throughout the late summer, early fall and even winter. Little did he know that he was amongst the few who carried on this tradition. (Little did he further know that he was enjoying perhaps a distant variation on a brine-and-vinegar recipe proposed for pickled lettuce by the Roman writer Columella[1] in the first century AD – albeit for a rather different lettuce.)

And it is this pickled lettuce of our mid-prairie city in mid-Canada that has become the culinary memory challenge. I asked dozens of fellow former Winnipeggers if they remembered pickled lettuce, and it was as if I were asking them if they remembered their first taste of milk. Long minutes into the conversation, they might blurt out 'Salata' (that was the name my father used for it) or 'Mmmmmm, very soft and yielding to bite into ... no! I don't remember.' Or even '... perfect balance of sweet and sour ... no, I don't know anything about pickled lettuce.' Had they been brainwashed? Nothing appears in the dozens and dozens of Jewish cookbooks I've looked through either. One vague possibility I entertained is that the soporific effects of the lettuce as noted by physicians of classical antiquity had been unleashed. (I jest. Those soporific effects were long gone from the modern iceberg lettuce, which, by the way, I used to think was named for our very long, indeed icy, winter.)

I began to take this quest of finding another authentic recipe very seriously. I contacted an old friend, Dolly Reisman, whose late father, I recalled, had been a superb pickle-maker. She remembered that he had made pickled lettuce a very long time ago. She would ask other members of the family if they recalled when, and why, he stopped. In the meantime, I ran into some old friends from Winnipeg. Did they remember pickled lettuce? 'Sure,' they pronounced, they remembered that Dave and

Dorothy Kaplan made pickled lettuce. I got in touch with them. Dave remembered that the recipe which his wife kindly made for him, was originally from his father. 'Who was from where?' I asked. Dave had to look this up. He couldn't remember the name of the small town. He remembered that the government of Canada had told him the town no longer existed, but they could find the original name. He called me back and so did Dolly. The two grandfathers who brought the pickled recipe to Canada, one to Toronto, the other to Winnipeg, over a thousand miles apart, were from the same town: Małe Siedliszcze (south-east of Kostopol, Rivne province, now in the Ukraine, but part of Poland before World War II). How did my own father come by this recipe? In my grandparents' day in their unstable border homeland I do not know what particular duress they endured: it was never spoken about. They were not privileged people, but I would assume that they had lettuce in some subsistent patch of garden. Pickling lettuce was a wonderful way to keep something green on hand, something cheap, something that required little effort to compose. Eastern European Jews didn't like dogs, but they did keep geese to guard their homes and eventually supply food. Geese loved lettuce, so it behoved the geese-keepers to grow the most succulent lettuce.

Though the texture of lettuce is soft, the memory of the perfect balance of sweet, sour and salty recalls the pleasures of the eating of the slightly soggy but very tasty alternative to the crisp, tasteless lettuce with which we began, and which we can easily forget. I have wondered if it was the ease of transforming the lettuce into its tasty state that has led to lettuce amnesia. Or perhaps only a few of us had a parent like mine whose memory was preoccupied with the tastes of childhood, despite the absence of those tastes from the conventional current cuisine. Maybe coleslaw or pickled cabbage sufficed for most people. I asked the mother of a childhood friend. She said, 'Yes, I remember pickled lettuce, *salata*. Yes, I imagine your father would have made it. We never made it, but I do remember it. Perhaps it's a class thing.' I am certain she is right. It's so tangy, and easy. Beneath some people's culinary radar.

Now here we are a century later reviving that lost art. Pickled lettuce is the perfect modern food. It is universally accessible, requires no additives, takes 24 hours to cure, needs only slight cooling. Its juice is healthy. My medical sources recognize our attraction to pickle juice, be it from lettuce or dill cucumbers. They spoke to me of the need historically, perhaps by the workers in the fields of the steppes, for such a drink in the heat of summer with little respite from the relentless sun. One medical scholar, Dr Arnold Naimark, former Dean of Medicine at the University of Manitoba, former President of the University of Manitoba, and Member of the Willcocks Institute of Science, called it natural Gatorade – a drink that athletes and long-distance runners use to replenish electrolytes. Current clinical practitioner in the field of metabolism and diabetes, Dr Aubie Angel added that the bonus in dill pickle juice is the potassium that has leached out of the cucumbers, enriching the tasty ocean which the pickles inhabit. At Brigham Young University, extensive experiments have been undertaken to try to explain why pickle juice seems to be so effective in combating cramp in runners.

135

According to Dr Kevin C. Miller, PhD, ATC, the lead author, something in the acidic juice, perhaps even a specific molecule of some kind, may be lighting up specialized nervous-system receptors in the throat or stomach, he says, which, in turn, send out nerve signals that somehow disrupt the reflex mêlée in the muscles. I thought to myself, 'How could anything that tastes so good, also be good for you?' Of course we now think of the high quantity of salt in the pickle juice as a challenge to our blood pressure. But that doesn't mean the pickle juice doesn't still have a heavenly flavour. In fact I daresay it is the salt brine that bathes the cucumber that latches into our memory and brings back both the events of the past (the youthful time of eating pickles with abandon), and the very – incomparable – sensation of biting into the crisp fresh, gently altered cucumber, which has just barely absorbed its salty, dilly, garlicky bath. The cucumber hasn't been overwhelmed by its 'soup', rather the ingredients have melded with the texture and potential of the ancient, stalwart little tempter.

Recently, I discovered a way to consume the pickle juice that might be less unhealthy, in that the quantity of salt is reduced because the quantity of juice itself is reduced, in order to marry it to another liquid. I mixed the pickle juice from my home-made half sours which I make in the fall and immediately refrigerate in order to keep the level of (fermentation) sourness low, with vodka, to produce a pickletini. It is nice with a slice of cucumber floating on top, and not so different in spirit from a 'dirty martini' made from olive juice and vodka, or gin for those who prefer gin. It has more recently come to my attention that in certain bars in NYC, the 'hot' bars, pickle juice has become the latest fad, mixed with whiskey, gin, tequila and other alcoholic beverages. One of the largest global distributors of alcoholic beverages in the world is about to launch a campaign to promote this 'new' idea. I'd like to rush my near-perfect pickle juice to the biggest grocery chains: I might make millions of dollars. That brings me to the end of my recollections as I become overwhelmed by the craving for a pickletini.

Gail Singer

Part two

When I discovered that people in online Russian cooking communities were looking for a pickled lettuce recipe to revive fabulous lettuce memories of their childhoods I first assumed that it must have been a forgotten Russian recipe. It turned out to be a very homey dish. Lettuce was briefly fermented at room temperature in plenty of water with salt, sugar, dill and garlic. A piece of dark rye bread wrapped in a bit of cheesecloth was often added to facilitate the fermentation. The result was a slightly greenish refreshing lettuce drink that definitely belongs to the varied east European *kvas* family of fermented drinks, such as Russian malted rye *kvas*, apple *kvas*, pear *kvas*, mint *kvas* and so on, Polish and Ukrainian beetroot *kvas*, Romanian and Moldovan bran *kvas*. This drink was sometimes called '*salat*' – the Russian word for lettuce. It was enjoyed during hot summer days, with or without limp fermented lettuce leaves. Sometimes such fermented lettuce was also made with a bit of vinegar which made the resulting drink taste more like proper pickle juice.

Both fermented drinks and pickle juice have many uses in traditional Russian cuisine: be it enjoyed on their own or made part of other dishes. Very salty but no-vinegar pickle juice from sour cucumbers (dill-pickles) was often used for hot soups. Low-salt and no-vinegar pickle juice from pickled fruit (*mochenya*) such as cowberries, cloudberries, apples, pears, plums and so on was mostly drunk plain. Numerous *kvas* varieties were traditional Russian soft drinks to be had in all seasons, but some of these were also used as a base for cold soups. However, when I consulted Maksim Syrnikov, the best traditional Russian cuisine expert and researcher there currently is, he assured me that he never encountered anything lettuce-related in his expeditions for regional Russian recipes, nor did he ever see anything like a pickled lettuce recipe in his extensive collection of Russian cookbooks.

So I was very excited when I found out that 'salata' (pickled lettuce) was a prominent feature of my friend Gail Singer's Jewish-Canadian childhood. And after I started asking around people that participated in fermented lettuce online discussions in Russian it turned out that the only persons who are aware of this dish hail from Jewish families mostly from just a few regions of Ukraine within the Pale of Settlement (although there are a couple of reports of this tradition existing among Moldovan Jews too). Non-Jewish people from Ukraine and Moldova whom I asked didn't know a thing about it (and actually never remembered much lettuce usage in their respective cuisines at all). Ukrainian, Moldovan and Romanian cookbooks were also silent on the subject of pickled lettuce or fermented lettuce drinks, as were books on Jewish cuisine both in Russian and English, Old World and New World. Even Claudia Roden's comprehensive work had no lettuce references. The only printed pickled lettuce appearance that has surfaced so far is from a 1972 Soviet fruit and vegetable cookbook *Dary Leta* published in the Ukraine,[2] but the recipe there is a bit bizarre as if its authors, Mitasova and Rozentsvaig (again, at least one of them is Jewish, judging by the surname) have heard of the tradition but never experienced it first-hand: lettuce is fermented with salt, garlic and dill in ready-made brown rye *kvas,* which is never the case in other sources – lettuce *kvas* was usually the result of lettuce fermenting in water.

We have by now collected 40 lettuce reports and it can be safely assumed that both *salata* (pickled lettuce) and *salat* (fermented lettuce drink) are variations on the same theme and that this almost-forgotten dish essentially belongs to the east European Jewish tradition. There are 19 vinegar-based variations and 21 fermented variations. Vinegar-pickled and rye bread-fermented lettuce recipes criss-cross and merge: of nineteen vinegar-based variations three refer to the lettuce drink rather than sweet and sour leaves and the same is true in reverse for fermented variations, five out of twenty-one are not about lettuce drink at all, the desired result is just pickled lettuce leaves. I have arranged all the information in two tables at the end of the article (table 1 for vinegar-based lettuce variations, table 2 for fermented ones), unfortunately data are often incomplete as many of my informants do not know the exact recipe, having only memories of their respective childhoods to rely upon. Still, I've tried not only to list all the ingredients they remember, but also to specify the particular name (if any) for pickled lettuce, serving traditions linked with this dish, and geographical origins of my informants' families, whenever possible. Here's a map of eastern Europe marked with the numbers of reports per region. Reports from unspecified Ukraine regions (4), and from unspecified ex-USSR Jewish families (3) are marked separately.

Now we come to an interesting question. Why bother pickling lettuce at all? Most of the pickling traditions we know of exist for preserving foods. But pickled or fermented lettuce is a very short-lived thing as preserves go, it is ready in a day or two and it tastes good for several days only. Its wilted texture is also contrary to the classic European fashion of fresh, crisp, green (often lettuce-based) salads dressed just before serving that has existed at least since the seventeenth century. Another thing is that there is almost no evidence of lettuce in any form being part of traditional Ukrainian, Moldovan or Romanian cuisine. So how did lettuce appear in the Jewish culinary tradition of this geographic area?

To make a long story short we'll have to go back to the times of the Roman Empire. Lettuce, like chicory, belongs to the Compositae botanical family and in those days they were probably almost equally bitter. (It was only in the seventeenth century that

this bitterness was significantly reduced by selection,[3] which probably partly accounts
for the rising popularity of green salads.) But the Romans had a liking for bitter tastes,
or at least considered it to be beneficial for one's health. So both lettuce and chicory are
often mentioned together in Latin sources, be it the recipes of Apicius or of Columella.
Apician recipes mitigate the bitterness of lettuce with vinegar and honey sauces.[4] As
for Columella, he actually pickles lettuce: either dry-curing it in salt or in a brine-
and-vinegar mixture. Another interesting thing found in Columella is the importance
of growing lettuce as a feed for young geese or goslings before they can start grazing
properly.[5]

In its heyday, the Roman Empire included the territory of modern western
Hungary, the part of the country that is now called Transdanubia which is especially
famous for its geese for foie gras and its vines,[6] both presumably hailing back to
Roman times. Incidentally, one of my Moldovan sources revealed that although lettuce
was readily available everywhere, his grandmother used to plant lettuce between her
vines (Moldova is also a country of viticulture) to feed the poultry with. The family
used some of it in vegetable salads if there was plenty. Apparently, use of lettuce in
modern poultry-rearing is quite widespread and must have been even more so in the
time when no commercial poultry feed was available.

If traditions of geese-raising in Transdanubia were started by the Romans they
could well have included planting lettuce for goslings, maybe even between the
vines as it is still sometimes done in present-day Moldova. It also may be that the
population consumed extra lettuce the old Roman way – with vinegar and honey to   *139*
mitigate its bitter flavour. That might even be the distant origin of traditional and
ubiquitious Hungarian *ecetes saláta*: lettuce leaves pre-soaked in a special dressing made
with vinegar, water, sugar, salt, pepper and bit of minced onion before being served
sprinkled with a little oil.[7] George Lang even adds a note to this recipe:

> This salad is different from the Western ideal; crispness is replaced with a texture
> like that of a cooked vegetable that has been marinated. The leaves are supposed
> to be limp...[8]

Now this actually reminds us strongly of the sweet and sour Jewish pickled lettuce we
have been talking about before, where vinegar is also sometimes cut with water (one
source from a Jewish settlement in Moldova also specified a bit of oil and pepper).
It's just that the minced onion is replaced with garlic and lettuce leaves are usually
roughly torn (so in some Jewish families this dish was lovingly called in Yiddish
shmates – 'rags') and allowed to sit in their dressing for about a day. The reason for
this pre-soaking or light pickling was that it also (together with the sweet and sour
flavouring) tended to considerably reduce the bitterness of old lettuce varieties (some
of my Jewish-Ukrainian sources specifically remember that in Soviet times lettuce
that was used for this dish was also always bitter and almost inedible on its own). It is
no longer necessary to do it because modern lettuce varieties are usually quite bland

but the acquired taste for sweet and sour limp, soggy lettuce is still a fixture both in Hungary and in a few Jewish families of eastern European origin where this tradition is remembered.

Jews have been attested in Hungary at least since medieval times. And even now in anti-semitic Hungarian circles they still have the nickname goose-eaters (*libások*).[9] Hungarian cuisine currently includes some unmistakably Jewish dishes like goose *cholent*, and it is quite possible that Jewish cuisine has absorbed quite a few Hungarian dishes along the way, including sweet and sour lettuce and stuffed goose neck (a dish popular in many geese-raising areas, such as the French Dordogne). But the life of Jews in Hungary, as in other countries, was often fraught with difficulty and danger, there were many persecutions and expulsions. As far back as the fourteenth century, Hungarian Jews were constrained to leave the country and move east to the territories that now belong to Romania, Moldova and Ukraine. And so it went on in waves — re-admittance to Hungary in milder times and then new persecutions and new expulsions.

The further east Jews went, the poorer they became. Geese became an unaffordable luxury but many families had to raise chickens to survive in the small towns – *shtetls* – where they settled. And presumably that's how lettuce travelled east too – as vital chicken-feed, that could be used as a supplement for human diet. In the non-viticultural areas of Ukraine, around Kiev, wine vinegar for pickling lettuce must have been gradually replaced by the aromatic light brine and rye bread fermentation familiar from neighbouring Slavic *kvas*-making traditions. Indeed other kinds of *kvas* were often

140 made in those Jewish settlements. Sholem Aleichem mentions a Jewish lady in his *shtetl* who was famous for the excellence of her apple *kvas* in the nineteenth century and one of my sources, an old lady, remembers her mother that was born in another tiny *shtetl* nearby making beetroot *kvas* for a special Jewish holiday in summer in Soviet times. Just before the Second World War, judging by an eye-witness account,[10] *shtetls* in the USSR were much the same as they were in the stories of Sholem Aleichem, somnolent, with chickens roaming the dusty streets and people looking after little patches of kitchen gardens in their yards (although both men and women now went to work, of course). So this Jewish *salat* lettuce *kvas*, very cheap and easy to make, must have been vastly popular there too.

The fact that there is almost no trace of lettuce *kvas* and pickled lettuce left in public memory is largely due to the ravages of the Second World War. Thus, according to the website of Yad Vashem, The Martyrs' and Heroes' Remembrance Authority,[11] whereas there were 1.5 million Jews living in the Soviet Ukraine alone before the war, only 100,000–120,000 Jews were left in the whole of the USSR afterwards and, 'alongside the immense number of deaths, the Holocaust in the Soviet Union also resulted in the elimination of the *shtetl* – that for centuries had embodied the Jews' unique way of life in Eastern Europe.' The *shtetl* cuture was irrevocably lost and most of its traditions with it. No wonder we have so few memories of what must have been once a summer staple either in pickled or in *kvas* form in many eastern European Jewish families. As for the eastern European Jewish families that made it to the New World before the war, for most of them pickled lettuce was probably too humble a dish, a not-so-pleasant reminder of Old World poverty and hardships.

Alexandra Grigorieva

To conclude
Lettuce (even bolted) is mostly no longer bitter. Jewish vinegar-pickled lettuce or lightly salty fermented lettuce drink is mostly no longer made in Ukraine, Moldova, Romania or Hungary. The few people that still persevere with these culinary traditions live well away from the original *shtetl*-land of their forefathers in Israel, Canada, US, Russia, and even Germany. Still, it is good to know that we've managed to share these memories with you and that the pickle juice with pickled lettuce floating in it (or lettuce *kvas* with leaves) that used to accompany the meat dish in the lost world of *shtetl* is snatched from oblivion by our research efforts and will perhaps be remembered as an integral part of the east European Jewish Heritage. Cheers!

Notes

1. *De re rustica* (On Agriculture), 12.9 *Lactucae conditura* (second recipe, two parts vinegar to one part brine).
2. My thanks to Jake Bukhanov for passing on this information.
3. See article on lettuce in *The Oxford Companion to Food*.
4. Apicius 3.18.1–3.18.3.
5. Columella 8.14.
6. See George Lang's *Cuisine of Hungary*.
7. Compare to this Hungarian Jewish lettuce recipe http://kosherfood.about.com/od/koshersaladrecipes/r/lettuce_saba.htm, the essentials are the same.
8. Op. cit., p. 331.
9. http://en.wikipedia.org/wiki/Hungarian_Jews
10. See the memoir of a Jewish refugee from Poland, Toby Kladowski-Flam.
11. http://www1.yadvashem.org

Select Bibliography

Apicius. A Critical edition with an Introduction and an English Translation of the Latin Recipe Text Apicius (ed. by Christopher Grocock and Sally Grainger). Totnes, Devon: Prospect Books, 2006.

Barer-Stein, Thelma. *You Eat What You Are: A Study of Ethnic Food Traditions*. Toronto: M&S, 1979.

Columella, Lucius Iunius Moderatus. *De Re Rustica* (On Agriculture, in 3 volumes). Harvard: Harvard University Press, Loeb Classical Library, 1941, 1954-1955.

Dalby, Andrew. *Food in the Ancient World from A to Z*. London and New York: Routledge, 2003.

Davidson, Alan. *The Oxford Companion to Food* (2nd edn, ed. Tom Jaine). Oxford: Oxford University Press, 2006.

Food Culture: Tasting Identities and Geographies in Art (ed. Barbara Fischer). Toronto: YYZ Books, 2004.

In Memory's Kitchen: A Legacy from the Women of Terezin (ed. Cara De Silva). New York: Jason Aronson, 1997.

Kladowski-Flam, Toby. *Toby: Her Journey from Lodz to Samarkand (and beyond).* Toronto: Childe Thursday, 1988.

Lang, George. *George Lang's Cuisine of Hungary* (2nd edn). New York: Wings, 1994.

Malaguzzi, Silvia. *Food and Feasting in Art.* Los Angeles: The J. Paul Getty Museum, 2008.

Mandel, Corinne. 'Food for Thought: on Cucumbers and their Kind in European Art', in *Food Culture* (ed. Barbara Fischer). Toronto, 1999, p. 53.

Melnik, V. *Moldavskaya Kukhnya* (Moldavan Cuisine, in Russian). Kishinev: Kartia Moldovenyaske, 1961.

Mitasova, N. T. and Rozentsvaig, M. L. *Dary Leta: Fruktovo-Ovoschnoy Stol* (The Gifts of Summer: Fruit and Vegetable Bonanza, in Russian). Kharkov: Prapor, 1972.

Naomi Cook Book (4 editions). Toronto: 1928, 1932, 1948, 1960.

Roden, Claudia. *The Book of Jewish Food: An Odyssey from Samarkand to New York.* New York: Knopf, 1997.

Roman, Radu Anton. *Savoureuse Roumanie.* Suisse: Noir sur Blanc, 2004.

Schwartz, Oded. *In Search of Plenty: A History of Jewish Food.* London: Kyle Cathie Ltd, 1992.

Sholem Aleichem. *S Yarmarki* (From the Fair, in Russian). Moscow: GIKhL, 1960.

Syrnikov, Maksim. *Russkaya Domashnyaya Kukhnya* (Russian Home Cooking, in Russian). Moscow: EKSMO, Kniga Gastronoma, 2009.

——. *Nastoyaschaya Russkaya Yeda* (Real Russian Food, in Russian). Moscow: EKSMO, 2010.

Winnipeg Hadassah Shoppers' Guide and Cook Book (3 editions). Winnipeg: 1956, 1957 and 1961.

Selective Online Sources

http://www1.yadvashem.org
http://community.livejournal.com/easycooks/1273208.html
http://community.livejournal.com/oede/332869.html
http://community.livejournal.com/kitchen_nax/2739094.html
http://community.livejournal.com/md_kitchen/29664.html
http://community.livejournal.com/gurman_il/423971.html
http://community.livejournal.com/ladies_il/2350759.html
http://kosherfood.about.com/od/koshersaladrecipes/r/lettuce_saba.htm
http://www.grouprecipes.com/38937/pickled-lettuce-side-dish.html

Table 1. Jewish pickled lettuce: vinegar-based variations

	Geographical origin	Name and serving tradition	Pickling agent	Water	Salt	Sugar	Garlic	Dill	Other
1	Hungary unspecified*	Sweet and Sour Lettuce Salad, dresses up meat sandwiches or makes a flavorful side dish	vinegar	+	+	+			
2	Romania unspecified**	'salata' (lettuce), lettuce leaves	vinegar	+	+	+	+		
3	Romania, later Soviet Moldova	lettuce leaves	vinegar		+	+			
4	Moldova unspecified	lettuce leaves	vinegar		+				pepper, sunflower oil
5	Ukraine unspecified***	Pickled Lettuce Side Dish, with steak or fish	boiling vinegar marinade	+	+	+	+	+	red & black pepper, sunflower or oil
6	Tulchyn, Vinnytsya province, Ukraine (not far from Moldova)	'shmates' (rags), lettuce leaves as a side-dish for meat course, pickle juice thrown away	boiling vinegar marinade	+	+	+	+	+	
7	Ananiv, Odessa province, Ukraine (Moldovan Autonomous Rep. 1924–1940)	leaves eaten with sweet and sour pickle juice	vinegar			+	+		
8	Uman, Cherkasy province, Ukraine	'shalote', probably corrupted 'salat' (lettuce) lettuce leaves	no vinegar, but citric acid and boiling water marinade	+	+	+	+	+	celery stalks and leaves
9	Donetsk province, Ukraine	leaves eaten with meat course or *kielbasa* sausage sandwiches	vinegar	+	+	+			

* http://kosherfood.about.com/od/koshersaladrecipes/r/lettuce_saba.htm
** Gail Singer's father's recipe from her Jewish Canadian childhood in Winnipeg.
*** http://www.grouprecipes.com/38937/pickled-lettuce-side-dish.html: the only recipe without underlined Jewish connection, but still it is quite probable since its author is from Ukraine.

	Geographical origin	Name and serving tradition	Pickling agent	Water	Salt	Sugar	Garlic	Dill	Other
10	Pavlohrad, Dnipropetrovsk province, Ukraine	leaves eaten with meat course or *kielbasa* sausage sandwiches	vinegar	+	+	+			
11	Małe Siedliszcze shtetl, Rivne province (south-east of Kostopol), Ukraine	lettuce leaves	vinegar						
12	Małe Siedliszcze shtetl, Rivne province (south-east of Kostopol), Ukraine	lettuce leaves	vinegar						
13	Radomyshl, Zhytomyr province, Ukraine	lettuce leaves	vinegar with hot water	+	+	+	+	+	
14	Kamenka, Kiev province, Ukraine	lettuce leaves sometimes mixed with macaroni	vinegar	+	+		+	+	
15	probably Kharkiv province, Ukraine	lettuce leaves	lemon juice with warm water	+	+	+	+	+	
16	ex-USSR unspecified	lettuce leaves	vinegar	+	+	+	+	+	
17	probably Dnipropetrovsk province, Ukraine	refreshing drink served with lettuce leaves floating in it at dinner	vinegar	+	+		+		
18	ex-USSR unspecified	refreshing drink	vinegar	+	+	+	+	+	
19	Yablonets, Zhytomyr province (between Novohrad-Volynskyi and Korosten), Ukraine	refreshing drink	vinegar diluted with tepid water NB lettuce first presoaked in salted water	+	+	optional	young greens shoots too	+	green onions

Table 2. Jewish pickled lettuce: fermented variations

	Geographical origin	Name and serving tradition	Fermenting agent	Water	Salt	Sugar	Garlic	Dill	Other
1	Kiev and Vinnytsya province, Ukraine	*'shmates'* (rags), refreshing drink with a meat course	no	+	+	+	young greens shoots too	+	
2	Kiev, Ukraine	refreshing drink		+	+	+	+	+	
3	Kiev, Ukraine	refreshing drink	rye bread	+	+	+	+	+	
4	Kiev, Ukraine	refreshing drink	rye bread	+			+	+	
5	Kiev and Zhytomyr province (Novohrad-Volynskyi and Ovruch), Ukraine	*'salat'* (lettuce), refreshing drink	rye bread	+	+		+	+	
6	Kiev, Ukraine	*'salat'* (lettuce), refreshing drink	previously made lettuce *kvas*	+			+	+	green onions
7	Korets, Rivne province, Ukraine	*'salat'* (lettuce), refreshing drink	previously made lettuce *kvas*	+			+	+	green onions
8	Shpola, Cherkasy province, Ukraine	refreshing drink		+			+	+	
9	Frampol shtetl (near Kamianets-Podilskyi) Khmelnytskyi province, Ukraine (near Moldova)	refreshing drink	hot water and rye bread	+			+	+	
10	Polonnoe shtetl, Zhytomyr province, Ukraine	refreshing drink to accompany main course	warm water and rye bread	+	+		+	+	
11	Cherniakhiv, Zhytomyr province, Ukraine	refreshing drink	yeast and maybe rye bread	+		+			
12	Ukraine unspecified	refreshing drink	rye bread	+	+		+	+	
13	ex-USSR unspecified	refreshing drink		+	+		+	+	

	Geographical origin	Name and serving tradition	Fermenting agent	Water	Salt	Sugar	Garlic	Dill	Other
14	Ukraine unspecified	served with meat course	rye bread	+	+				
15	Slavuta, Khmelnytskyi province, Ukraine	refreshing drink to be enjoyed with lettuce leaves	rye bread	+	+		+	+	sour cherry or black currant leaf, maybe horseradish root
16	Zhytomyr, Ukraine	refreshing drink to be enjoyed with lettuce leaves or without usually with meat course	rye bread	+	+		+	+	
17	Kiev, Ukraine	lettuce leaves	rye bread	+	+		+	+	
18	Kiev, Ukraine	lettuce leaves usually with meat course or on their own as a green salad		+	+				
19	Lviv, Ukraine	lettuce leaves usually with meat course or on their own as a green salad		+	+				
20	Kharkiv*, Ukraine	lettuce leaves	rye bread *kvas*		+		+	+	
21	Ukraine unspecified	lettuce leaves pickled with cucumbers ('half-dones')		+	+		+	+	cucumbers and horseradish

*From a cookbook printed in Kharkov in 1972.

146

Sausage in Oil: Preserving Italian Culture in Utica, NY

Naomi Guttman and Max Wall

With plenty of means to extend the shelf-life of food, preservation techniques like making sausage are no longer an existential necessity in the home. Yet in Utica, New York, which has a strong Italian-American identity, families continue a tradition of dry-cured sausage-making brought over from southern Italy by their grand- and great-grandparents at the beginning of the twentieth century. Early in the year, when winter conditions are right, these families get together to make fifty to a hundred pounds of sausage which they hang in their attics to dry and then preserve in oil. In interviews with several Utica families, our paper explores the recipes, techniques, and cultural significance of traditional dry-cured sausage-making in this community, how it has changed and developed over the decades, and what keeps it alive today.

Dry-curing these spiced pork sausages is, in effect, a fermentation process. Uticans keep to tradition, combining selected spices with salt which acts to release water and create an environment that promotes the growth of lactic acid-producing bacteria. An optimal substrate for the growth of bacteria, meat is highly susceptible to microbial spoilage. Thus, storing this perishable food requires specific techniques to reduce or eliminate microbial growth. Traditional techniques such as curing, fermenting and drying are ancient and effective methods for preserving both nutritional function and organoleptic quality. In times when meat was rare, these techniques were once practised out of necessity. In the current food environment, traditional techniques take on a new meaning so that their original function of nutritional preservation is being replaced by that of cultural preservation.

The Giruzzis

Frank and Rocco Giruzzi are cousins, born in the 1930s, who grew up in East Utica – the old Italian neighborhood. Frank's grandparents came from the Basilicata region and the origin of sausage-making is, as Frank puts it, 'making it through the winter': 'These people were from the poorest area of Italy. They butchered the pig in the winter and used everything.' Sausage was 'the winter supply of food,' says Frank, and the continued practice of sausage-making is 'a direct line to where these people came from. It's not a lost art. … It's a communal activity – now it's the fourth generation. My son got it from my father. He's the one that makes the sausage.'

The process really begins with the peppers – a key ingredient in almost all the local family recipes. Rocco grows his own hot peppers, dries them and grinds them. 'Some people buy sweet red peppers (bell peppers) and dry those. It depends what you want.'

One cousin uses black pepper and even puts cheese in his sausage, 'but that's a Sicilian thing,' says Frank. In addition to salt and different varieties of pepper, the recipe usually includes fennel seed – also sometimes home-grown – and red wine. Rocco trims his pork butt of all the fat he can, making a very lean sausage. One-hundred pounds of pork butt makes about 38 lb of sausage once all the fat and water have been extracted in the process. Once the sausage is seasoned, they fill the casings (hog intestine), and tie them off in links. Rocco pricks the casings, then leaves the sausages in a tray in the attic overnight before hanging them from the rafters in loops the following day. This gets rid of a good quantity of water. 'The conditions for drying are coolness, air movement, some humidity, but not a lot,' says Frank. 'In the old days, every other house in Utica had an attic suitable for drying. With the advent of insulation, this is no longer the case. You need some heat coming up to dry it, but you also need cool humid air circulating to keep it fresh. They used to be hung in caves in Italy,' says Frank. Some people now hang the sausage in their refrigerators, 'but this is a real pain,' says Frank, and it changes the taste. Once the sausage is cut down – after two to three weeks of drying – it is preserved in vegetable oil. 'Olive oil is no good,' Frank tells me. 'It gets cloudy.'

In Utica, each sausage-maker has a slightly different recipe of which he is proud, and each family secretly cherishes its own variation. It is customary to share sausage with other families, tasting and, secretly, comparing. Bringing home-made sausage to Super-Bowl parties and Easter celebrations is the norm; but when a friend suggested a sausage 'competition,' Frank Giruzzi thought it was a bad idea. 'You could have a sausage 'exposition,' he says, 'but you can't say any one sausage is "the best". It's a loving process. Each link gets handled, fondled. When it's bad, you know it and you have to throw it away and start over.' Both cousins agree that sausage-in-oil should not be sold. This sentiment underlies a practice of exchange known as the 'economy of the gift,' parallel to the commercial economy, which privileges a system of non-monetary exchange between families and focuses on passing the ritual to the next generation. You don't sell sausage to your friends, but give it in a spirit of generosity and love.

The Wereszynskis

Down on Lansing Street, Gary and Jennifer Wereszynski still hang their yearly batch of sausage in the un-insulated attic. The ceiling in the attic is lined with crossbeams, out of which rows of nails poke out at two-inch intervals. More boards are strung across the roof-beams and these are dotted with nails as well, the only evidence of the hundreds of pounds of sausage which have hung here over the years. This year's batch was only about 20 lb, a small batch in comparison with previous years which have sometimes been as large as 240 lb. Avid sausage-makers, Gary and Jennifer had even hoped to sell their sausage commercially – but, as Gary lamented, 'There were too many regulations. We couldn't hang them in the attic, and that's where the flavor comes from!'

Sausage-making has been passed down through Gary's family on his mother's side. His great-grandfather came to America in 1892 from the town of Palermo on the northern coast of Sicily. He brought the tradition of Sicilian sausage-making with him, starting a meat market with his sons that eventually went out of business because, as Gary admits, 'They were better sausage-makers than business men.'

Though the tradition comes from his mother's side, when Gary was growing up it was his father who became the family's most enthusiastic sausage-maker. Gary's father worked his way through college as a butcher and even now, as Gary and Jennifer attest, shaking their heads in awed disbelief, 'he could bone a pork butt in two minutes flat.' Gary remembers when he was a kid the whole family would gather at his uncle's house on Lansing Street once a year for two full days of sausage-making. On day one they boned the pork, trimmed the fat, ground the meat, and mixed in the spices. On day two they stuffed and hung the sausages in the attic. Gary now owns that house on Lansing Street, and still hangs the sausage in the attic. Though much is the same, there have been a few changes over the years.

These days everything, from the grinding to the stuffing, is done in one day, using an automatic grinder which puts the meat directly in the casing. This machine weighs 400 lb, and needs two people to operate it, one to stand above and feed the meat into the grinder and other to make sure that the casing is filling just right. Jennifer mentions that the grinder processes the meat quickly and that communication is essential between the person on the casing end and the person above, pushing the meat in. When asked whether it's a steep learning curve they both laugh, recalling mishaps of exploding casings. Gary demonstrates how you have to hold the end of the casing just so and massage the incoming sausage to make sure that it fills out the space, but doesn't overfill – an art that takes experience to master. Jennifer notes that an important step is to have a glass of wine while you work and Gary nods in agreement, adding 'well, maybe more like two or three.'

This year's event was hosted by Gary's parents: Nancy Wereszynski and Gary Sr. who once lived in Utica, but now live nearby in the town of Westmoreland. As everyone arrives, the family convenes in the kitchen, gathered round a tomato pie, another signature dish of Utica, and the newest batch of stuffed peppers in oil – a family recipe. Jim and Sam arrive (Jim is Gary's godfather, though he calls him an uncle). Jim's grandmother, Carmela Dellitto, was from Basilicata and he recalls that she kept up other traditional Italian practices such as making wine and baking Easter bread.

When asked why his family still makes sausage, Gary Wereszynski responds: 'It's a great excuse to get together with the family and partake in a little bit of old world history and culture that helped form our identity. In this fast-paced world that we live in, it's nice to take a step back in time and experience the true essence of life: family, friends, culture, tradition and great, slowly prepared food.' Even Gary's brother, who now lives in Washington DC, braved the biggest snowstorm in years to be home for the day of sausage-making.

After the knives have been sharpened, the party moves downstairs to the basement. On the table are five vacuum-sealed pork butts, which, after boning, comes to around

40 lb. Out of the initial weight of the pork butt about half goes into the casing (fat and bone gone) and then half of that is left after drying. These days they throw away all of the fat they cut from the butt. In the old days, Jim says, they used to render the lard, and then use it to start tomato sauces, or to fry rolled pig skin into fritters which would be served on pizzas.

While the men in the Wereszynski family bone the pork, Jennifer measures out the seasoning. First, the fennel must be soaked red wine. Then the salt is added, and the two kinds of pepper (equal parts Utica grind, red and black), and finally the sugar. After the first grinding, Jim hand-mixes the seasoning into the meat. This is a difficult process because everything needs to be well mixed, but the meat is still near freezing, so it's hard on the hands. When all of the meat is mixed the family cooks a little bit just to make sure everything tastes right. If all goes well, the sausage should taste a little too salty before drying.

Once everyone has approved the taste, the ground meat must be stuffed into the casing. While Gary Jr. pushes the meat into the stuffer, Jim squeezes the casing to make sure that just enough meat is filling in at one time. Finally, the sausage is tied off into links. This is usually the grunt work where hands are chaffed and patience is tried. All in all, though, things go smoothly.

By four in the afternoon Gary and Jennifer go down to Lansing Street to hang the sausages in the attic. When Gary and Jennifer hung the sausage in their own house, Gary would check on them daily. Jennifer recalls that he would go up every evening with his paper and check for broken links, squeezing each length to feel how it was progressing. Gary adds, 'It's like I talk to them.' He explains that you can tell when a sausage is done when it is hard to the touch, this is usually after about thirty days or so of drying. However, on this day the temperature in the attic is 55°F. A hundred years ago, this unseasonable weather would have spoiled the entire batch, a devastating blow for a family trying to get through the winter. By contrast, Gary and Jennifer put the sausage in the fridge and come back to hang them in the attic a day later, declaring the day a success. This is perhaps the clearest indication that the purpose of sausage-making is no longer nutritional but cultural preservation. What is important these days for a successful day of sausage-making is not the conservation of edible calories, but rather the ritual that binds family and friends together.

The Noles

Dean Nole's family came to Utica from the town of Laurenzana in Basilicata. Like the Giruzzis, Nole points out that sausage-making doesn't begin with the slaughter of hogs, but with the drying of peppers in September. In his family they use sweet red peppers which they grind to a paste and mix with fennel seeds from Italy. In the old days, his grandparents would boil down the fat from the pork butts and use it to preserve the sausages in jars. 'They would also put a little ground red pepper into the fat, so it would come out pink and would give the sausage more flavor when it was rendered.'

A local pastry chef and restaurateur, Dean has spent a lot of time in Italy and though he appreciates the allegiance to the old ways, he now dries the sausage in the cooler instead of in the attic and Cryovacs instead of preserving in oil. 'It comes out perfect,' he says. Though the drying takes longer, it tastes the same as when it first comes down from the attic and you don't have to worry about anything rotting. 'The old-timers would not have liked it because it changes the flavor,' but to dry it in the attic is risky: 'If you get holes, it will rot; if the weather warms up, you have to put in fans; if it gets too cold, you have to hang up sheets to keep the sausage from freezing. … People can get sick,' he says.

Though Dean plans to pass this tradition on to his children, he worries that in the current food environment, it will be a struggle to maintain this sausage-making culture. 'I see the young people at the grocery store. They don't even know what they're buying.' Whereas with commercially made sausage the process is a mystery, family sausage-making brings one into a hands-on relationship with the ingredients, beginning with boning the pork butt, removing the gland, and grinding the meat. Salt and spices are measured, wine and sugar go in, and everything is mixed manually. In other words, making sausage means engaging in an intimate process, something that has become completely foreign to young consumers who routinely buy pre-packaged prepared meals. Despite these worries, we came across one family in Utica that has recently rediscovered the tradition of sausage-making and is beginning to embrace this process once again.

The Fiorentinos

Tom Fiorentino lives with his wife Lori and three of their five children in a renovated farmhouse. In the kitchen, Tom stuffs the sausage casings with the help of his friend Mike Shue who has never before had the honor of participating because there are usually more family members around. Tom is partly pleased: it's less crazy. The stuffer is an old hand-cranked cast iron machine that belonged to Tom's great-grandmother and is bolted to a block of wood which is itself held onto the granite kitchen counter with a vise. Tom's daughter is visiting home from college – she would never miss the sausage-making. Also present are his mother, Nicki Fiorentino and his three sisters, Mary Beth, Carol and Anne. His sister-in-law, Ellen Fiorentino is also there, as are Tom's cousin Larry, and his aunt Nina. Tom is one of six children; missing are his brother, Matt, who is attending a basketball championship, and his brother, Gene, who passed away in 2003. In fact, when I query Tom about the roots of this tradition, he says that he took it over from his uncle Francis when his brother Gene died because he had vowed to Gene 'to keep the family together.' 'Once people start to go,' he said, 'it's important.' In addition to this yearly sausage ritual in the winter, Tom organizes a midsummer barbeque, using his three barns as shelters for the party-goers. About the sausage-making, he says that it's gratifying that the kids remember it and like it, that his daughter says she wouldn't miss it. When I ask whether she'll be keeping this tradition up herself when she has a family she says yes, 'with my brothers.'

Tom's family is originally from the town of Amato in Italy's Calabria region but the family sausage-making wasn't part of his life as a child. His mother Nicki says that in her home (her father is from Naples and her mother from Sicily), they didn't make sausage-in-oil: 'Maybe a cousin did it, but it wasn't a big family thing,' and that she only started making fresh sausage on her own with her father-in-law's grinder when her kids were small, but she never dried it. It was her brother-in-law Francis (or Frannie) who started making sausage, but only as an adult.

The family gathers around the island to curl the sausage around in a coil and once it is done, they take turns tying up the links which will be taken upstairs to the attic. I ask Tom if he spreads newspaper under them and he smiles slyly and says, 'I say I do'; I ask him whether he pricks the sausage or goes up to check on it while it cures, and he shakes his head – 'No – I just leave it alone.' The recipe he uses is from his uncle Francis: he used only red pepper paste he made himself from dried sweet peppers, and salt. Tom says that this is a Calabrian-style sausage. He also makes another type with cracked black pepper and fennel, and then vacuum-seals it instead of preserving it in oil.

On this sausage-making day in late February, the table is a groaning board of Italian specialties, including Nicki's home-made bread, *caponata*, olive salad, salami and *capicola*, fried peppers, eggplant parmesan, and shrimp with lemon and wine. More dishes arrive as the afternoon progresses. Tom's ten-year-old daughter is saving her appetite for cheese cake. Cousin Larry brings 'Fiorentino Brothers Wine' made two years ago from fresh grapes.

Frannie's window, Nina, prefers her Côtes du Rhône. Nina is the daughter of Russian immigrants and says she never knew what food was until she married into the Fiorentino family. 'Frannie was a superb cook and a perfectionist; if it didn't come out right he threw it away and started over. In our house we never ate anything processed.' And their house was always full of company. Tom reminisces about sitting on Uncle Fran's porch on beautiful summer or fall evenings, talking, eating, laughing and smoking cigars.

Frannie was inspired to make sausage-in-oil after visiting relatives in Montreal. Italian immigrants, cousins Joe and Felicia Caliguire from Amato, taught Frannie how to make sausage-in-oil and *capicola*. 'Frannie's parents made liqueurs and pickled green tomatoes, but not the sausage.' Now Nina's son, Phillip, joined her nephews Tom and Larry for sausage-making: they grind and stuff together, but each brings his own spice mix. When her nephew Gene, Tom's brother, got sick, he asked the family to keep getting together and this winter sausage-making ritual became the glue.

There are places in Utica that sell sausage-in-oil, and also places where you can buy all the ingredients premixed and ready-to-hang, but it seems that people prefer to do it themselves. 'Why bother?' Nina says, 'It's like quilting: do it by hand all the way or don't do it at all.'

Ultimately, however, for Tom Fiorentino it's not about the sausage or passing on a culinary tradition so much as it is maintaining family ties: 'at the end of the day, and perhaps ironically given the topic of your paper,' he writes in an email, 'it is less about making sausage and more about family staying together. It gets harder and harder every year with all of the distractions ... but we keep at it.' Tom is gratified that the two children who are away from home call to ask about when the family will be getting together, and he is convinced that this new tradition will prepare them for the job of preserving family ties once he and his wife are gone.

Conclusion

While the continued practice of making sausage-in-oil connects members of the Italian community to their ancestral home and to memories of times when sausage was an important dietary staple, its main function today is to bind families and stabilize community. Whether passed down from generation to generation, or recently rediscovered, the sausage-making ritual is constantly renovated according to need and circumstance. More than a means to an end, sausage-making allows practitioners to engage in competition, celebration, and a gift economy, transforming a strategy of survival into a form of family and community preservation.

Boza, Innocuous and Less So

Priscilla Mary Işın

Boza is an ancient type of beer, often of thick consistency, made by fermenting millet, wheat, rice or other cereals. It contains no hops and usually the cereal is not malted. The alcohol-content varies according to the length of the fermentation period. It can be traced back to the Sumerians, Egyptians and Hittites, and has changed little over the intervening millennia. It is still a traditional beverage in many parts of Asia, Africa and eastern Europe, ranging from Serbia to China and the Crimea to central Africa. The Turkish term boza has become the generic name for these beers. The geographical dissemination of the word boza includes western and central Asia, Russia, and central Africa, as well as the lands that were once part of the Ottoman Empire.

Boza made in Turkey today is the type known in the past as *tatlı* boza (sweet boza); a tangy-sweet beverage with the consistency of thick soup and a negligible alcohol-content. It is drunk chilled, sprinkled with cinnamon or ginger, and often accompanied by roasted chickpeas. It is only sold during the winter months, traditionally by street-sellers in the evenings. One particularly famous brand, Vefa, which dates back to the nineteenth century, is now sold in plastic bottles in supermarkets. Commercial boza is always made from millet, while at home it is made from *bulgur* (boiled and dried cracked wheat). A considerable quantity of sugar is added, equivalent to between a third to half the quantity of cereal by weight.

In the past boza was frequently made with barley (Thevenot 1687, 33), and the two earliest Turkish recipes for boza, recorded by the Ottoman physician Şirvânî in the first half of the fifteenth century, are for boza made with rice and barley respectively (Şirvânî 2005, 248–249). In its many adoptive homelands boza has been made from whichever grain was available: oats, wheat, buckwheat, maize, millet or even pea-flour, the latter recorded for Albania and Georgia (Morewood 1838, 505). In the past honey or *pekmez* (grape molasses) were more commonly used than sugar (Şirvânî 2005, 248–249; Abdülaziz Bey 1995, 152; Musahipzade Celâl 1946: 90). Boza with a high alcohol-content called *mırmırık* boza was sold in dedicated taverns called *bozahane*.

The word boza first appears simultaneously in three early fourteenth-century written texts in Chinese, Arabic and Turkish, although boza itself is far older and is recorded in central Asia in the eleventh century under the Turkic name *buxsum* (Mahmud al-Kashgari 1984, III 82).

A Chinese dietary manual with a strongly Turkic influence presented to a descendant of Qubilay Qan by his physician in 1330 describes boza as 'slightly sweet and piquant in flavor', which sounds precisely like the sweet boza made in Turkey today (Buell 2000, 529):

Sürma Liquor: It is also called Boza. It is slightly sweet and piquant in flavor. It is good for augmenting the ch'i and controlling thirst. If too much is drunk it makes a person fat and produces phlegm.

In 1333 the Moroccan traveller Ibn Battuta was served boza made of millet in the Crimea, when the region was under Ilkhanid rule. After one taste he refused to drink any more for religious reasons (Ibn Battuta 1953, 474–5):

These Turks ... have also a fermented drink which they make from the grain of the *dugi* (hulled millet) ... I tasted it and finding a bitter taste in it left it alone. These people are Hanafis and *nabidh* (fermented liquor) is permissible according to their doctrine. They call this *nabidh* which is made from *dugi* by the name of *buza*.

The third reference to boza at this period is a Turkish text on the healthy properties of foods written in the 1330s or 1340s (Ertaylan 1960, 20).

The word boza has found its way into more than twenty languages in central Asia, eastern Europe and north Africa. As well as Turkic languages like Chagatay, Uzbek and Kirgiz, and numerous Finno-Ugric languages, boza is recorded in Mongolian, Tajik, Arabic, Afghan, Persian, Urdu, Russian, Ukrainian, Georgian, Hungarian, Rumanian, Bulgarian, Serbocroat, Macedonian, Polish, Czech, modern Greek and Albanian (Doerfer 1963, 337–341; Laufer 1929, 57). It is also recorded in western European languages – French, Spanish, Portuguese, French, English and German – usually defined as a kind of Turkish beer made with millet (Laufer 1929, 57).

The possibility that the word 'booze' derives from boza was discussed by the linguist Berthold Laufer in his 'Brief Notes on the Possible Oriental Origin of Our Word Booze', and while not finding the evidence conclusive he nevertheless comments that 'the coincidence itself is suggestive' (Laufer 1929).

The antiquity of boza in Asia is suggested by its use in harvest rituals in the Caucasus region. Among the Turkic Kumuk people of Daghestan and the Circassians, boza was ritually drunk at the harvest feast held before the fields were mowed (Tavernier 1684, II 128–9):

The Drink of the Sherkes (Çerkes) is Water and Bosa. Bosa is a Drink made of Millet as intoxicating as Wine, which they want in the Country ... The Principal of all the Feasts which the Comouchs and Sherkes or Cirkassians make, is that which they make at the end of Autumn, after this manner. Three of the ancientest of the Village are appointed to manage it, and ... the three old men stand upright before a Table, and all the People, Men, Women and Children behind them. When the Table upon which the Meat stands, is brought in, two of the three old men cut off the Legs and the roasted Gathers, and hold them up above their

155

heads, and the third holds up a great Cup of Bosa in the same manner, to the end to that people behind may see them. When the people see the Meat and Bosa so lifted up, they prostrate themselves upon the ground

In Circassia boza replaced wine in the Eucharist for Circassian Christians at Pshat, as described by James Stanislaus Bell in the early nineteenth century (Bell 1840, I 85):

> The congregation placed themselves on their knees at some little distance in front of the cross, and say their prayers, after which two old men advance to the cross with bread or pasta, and a fermented liquor called shuat or bosé, in their hands. They pray for a blessing upon these, and then distribute them among the people.

Further evidence that boza was regarded as sacred by peoples in this region is that an order of dervishes in the Crimea shaved their moustaches so that the boza would not be be defiled by contact with body hair (Evliya Çelebi 1996–2007, VII 243).

According to a sixteenth-century Turkish source, the Tatars attributed boza's invention to Hızır (Al-Khidr), a spiritual guide in Islamic tradition who is identified by some scholars with the Green Man (Âli 1978, 149; Wikipedia 'Khidr'). Other invention myths attribute boza to Yazid bin Mu'awiyah, founder of the Umayyad dynasty, Tatar Salsal, and a thirteenth-century Turkish hero called Sarı Saltuk (Evliya Çelebi 1996–2007, I 312, IV 274, VIII 301).

In Thomas Blount's *Glossographia* (1656) boza is defined as 'Boza, a drink in Turky made of seed, much like new mustard, and is very heady.' That millet was unfamiliar in seventeenth-century Britain is confirmed by the British diplomat Sir Paul Ricaut, who merely describes it as 'a certain seed' (Ricaut 1686, 110):

> the riotous and dissolute (among the Tartars) are addicted to strong Waters, and a drink called Boza made of a certain seed (which drank in a great quantity doth intoxicate, and is now much in use amongst the Turks.

Hans Dernschwam, a German who travelled to Turkey in the mid-sixteenth century, recognized both millet and boza, which he had come across in Hungary and Zekelland, a region of Transylvania inhabited by the Turkic Szekler people, but held it in low esteem (Dernschwam 1923, 104):

> They also make boza like in many different places in Hungary and Zekelland. It is made of millet, a miserable drink.

Like Dernschwam, Charles Thompson, who visited Istanbul in 1733, was not impressed by boza, which he described as 'thick and disagreeable' (Thompson 1744, II 147).

Sweet boza

Sweet boza was 'as pleasant to swallow as a bowl of rosewater', as white as milk and so smooth and thick that not a drop would seep through a napkin. The smooth texture was achieved by sieving, hence the terms *süzme boza* (strained boza) to describe good quality boza. Since it was kept in great wooden boxes, each large enough to hold a man, it was also known as *kutu bozası* (box boza). Customers brought their own copper or earthenware pots to be filled, and drank the sweet boza sprinkled with cinnamon, cloves, ginger or nutmeg (Evliya Çelebi 1996–2007, I 313, II 108, VII 234).

The tradition of drinking sweet boza in winter is probably due to the fact that it would quickly over-ferment in warm weather. Today boza is always refrigerated before drinking and in the past it was chilled with snow (C.SM 160/8031). The twentieth-century Turkish writer Burhan Felek said he could never understand why boza was drunk in winter, but recorded a popular maxim to the effect that 'pickled cabbage and boza spoil once March is over' (Felek 1985, 102).

Boza was made for Sultan Mehmet II (1451–1481) from either millet or rice, and sweetened with honey or rock sugar. A kind of helva was made with boza for the same sultan, although nothing else is known about this surprising pudding (Barkan 1979, 224). Apparently unaware of this precedent, an Istanbul cook has invented a twenty-first century equivalent of this pudding, consisting of whipped cream and boza served with raspberry or chocolate sauce (Başaran 2010). In the seventeenth century the quantities of boza being made at the palace were huge, kitchen registers recording purchases of 6.7 tons of rice for making boza in 1626, for example (Bilgin 2002, 68).   *157*

In Istanbul boza was commonly drunk on winter evenings at gatherings of family, friends and neighbours (Öztekin 2006, 200–201; Abdülaziz Bey 1995, 161, 214–5). The boza was served with roasted chickpeas, and elderly people with insufficient teeth to crunch chickpeas sprinkled roasted chickpea flour on top instead (Abdülaziz Bey 1995, 152; *Tarih Hazinesi* 1950, 2: 88).

Boza was also widely made in provincial Ottoman towns and cities, mostly by small tradesmen but also on a larger scale. Boza was a good investment and a state-owned boza manufactory in Edirne generated revenues of 200,000 akçe for the Treasury in 1477. Other state-owned boza manufactories are recorded in Bursa in 1454, Kızanlık (Bulgaria) in 1515, and no less than 23 in Edirne in 1519 (Oğuz 1976, 733–734).

Intoxicating boza

The alcoholic type of boza, known as *ekşi boza* (sour boza) or 'Tatar boza', was stronger than wine according to some observers (Withers 1737, 762). Jean Thevenot (1633–1667), who travelled widely in the Levant in 1655 and 1656, remarked:

> In the Countrey, about Constantinople, and all over the Archipelago, they have plenty of good Wine. They have besides another Liquor, which they call Boza, made of Barley or Millet, and Tasts somewhat like our Beer, but not so pleasantly;

I tasted of it once, but found it to be very bad; and none but the meaner sort of people drink it, because it is very cheap. This Drink makes them drunk.

(Thevenot 1687, 33)

The intoxicating effects of boza are confirmed by a case history related by the fifteenth-century physician Şerefeddin Sabuncuoğlu of Amasya. He treated an artist who had fallen into such a heavy stupor after drinking boza that he awoke with his hand paralysed from sleeping on his right arm (Serefeddin Sabuncuoğlu 1999, 29).

Analyses of 16 samples of boza collected from around Cairo in the 1920s were found to have an average alcohol-content of 7.1 per cent (Hornsey 2003, 46).

Dr Leonhart Rauwolff, who travelled in Turkey and the Middle East in 1573, said that the beer made of barley or wheat 'make the Turks so merry and elevated, that as our clowns do when they drink beer, they sing and play on their hautboys, cornets and kettle drums' (Rauwolff 1693, 95).

Inspiring the drinker to sing was one of the most marked features of boza intoxication. Tatar boza made in the Crimea was so strong that a single mugful caused a man to burst into song (Evliya Çelebi 1996–2007, VII 197), and one of the names used for boza in Nubia was *om belbel*, meaning 'mother of nightingales' in Arabic (Burckhardt 1819, 218).

Bozahane (boza houses) were establishments much like taverns, frequented by sailors, muleteers, porters and other working-class people. They were not places where gentlemen liked to be seen, and Evliya Çelebi was 'prostrate with shame' when he inadvertently entered a boza house in Ankara in the mid-seventeenth century (Evliya Çelebi 1996–2007, II 227). However, in the sixteenth century Âli reports that well-bred people might drop by a boza house on winter days to eat a kebab and drink a cup of boza flavoured with nutmeg, but would certainly not stay to enjoy the company (Âli 1978, 184). Only in Bursa were *bozahane* respectable, boasting elegant establishments with patterned tiles covering the walls, decorated ceilings, divans and singers and musicians to entertain the clientele (Evliya Çelebi 1996–2007, II 18–19).

Tatar boza was banned time and time again over the centuries, to little effect. On 16 September 1567 an order was issued prohibiting this type of boza – along with wine, whores, musical entertainments, backgammon and chess – in the holy district of Eyüp on the Golden Horn (Oğuz 1976, 734; Sertoğlu 1992, 85). The same year another edict was passed banning Tatar boza throughout Istanbul (Ahmed Refik 1988a, 141). After a ban on wine shops in Ankara in 1584 the boza shops stepped in to fill the gap, as a contemporary court record shows (Oğuz 1976, 735; Ongan 1958, 6):

When the boza-seller Haydar bin Abdullah was brought before the judge and was accused of drunkenness, he declared that he had drunk no wine but only boza. Witnesses, including Hacı Sinan bin Taşçı and Ali Dede Ibn Mehmed, informed the court that the boza made by the accused was more intoxicating than wine. Assistant judge Dede Halife was sent to inspect the boza shop, and reported that it was no different from a tavern with music playing and drinkers shouting. Incidents like this led to a ban on boza houses in Ankara, and jars and bowls belonging to one boza house were smashed when it was closed down in 1588.

(Ongan 1974, 894)

In 1594 the authorities were notified that some houses in Koca Nişancı in Istanbul had been turned into *bozahane*, where planks ripped off the walls of local houses were being used as fuel to cook boza and kebabs. The court ruled that the delinquents should be imprisoned and sentenced to the galleys (Ahmed Refik 1988b, 18). Sultan Murad IV went to the extreme of introducing capital punishment for those caught drinking boza, coffee or wine, but even this draconian measure failed to stamp out boza drinking (Evliya Çelebi 1996–2007, I 92–3)

Food provided at *bozahane* included kebabs (Âli 1978, 149; Ahmed Refik 1988b, 18), flat and loaf bread, *hoşaf* (fruit compote), and offal including *çevren* (minced liver wrapped in caul fat), *şirden* (stuffed abomasum, the fourth chamber of the stomach in cattle), minced liver balls, and grilled or roasted spleen, kidney, heart and intestine (Evliya Çelebi 1996–2007, I 54, 190, 247).

The amount of boza that aficionados, particularly Tatars, were able to consume was a source of amazement. Evliya Çelebi saw a barrel and a ladle hung over the gate of a *han* (khan or caravanserai) in Bursa with a sheet of paper explaining: 'He who drinks boza by the barrel is an ox. He who drinks by the ladle is a man.' These were mementos of a customer who had drunk an entire barrel of boza for a wager. In the Crimea, Tatars regularly swigged 20 litres of boza, and for a wager had been known to drink 120 litres and eat an entire roast sheep. Despite their huge consumption of boza, the Crimean Tatars did not approve of drunkenness, and misbehaving boza louts were strictly dealt with. Each *bozahane* appointed a respected elderly customer as referee, and anyone involved in a drunken brawl was thrown out and never admitted again (Evliya Çelebi 1996–2007, II 15, VII 215, 235, 341).

Istanbul's porters, legendary even today for the extraordinary loads they can carry on their backs, were also renowned in the past for the quantities of boza they consumed. After eating an entire roast lamb and drinking 40 pots of boza they were able to carry loads weighing over a thousand kilos. A *bozahane* in the dock area of Unkapanı had a barrel large enough to accommodate three men hanging by a chain over the door as a souvenir of a Turkish porter from the Black Sea town of Bartın, who for a bet had drunk an entire barrel of boza in one day (Evliya Çelebi 1996–2007, I 255, 313).

The fifteenth-century poet Melîhî gave up wine at the command of Sultan Mehmet II, and turned to boza and marijuana instead. But these proved disappointing substitutes (Onay 2000, 126–7):

A curse on boza and marijuana
Hurrah for the rose-red wine

Boza from bread

Although today Turkish boza is made by boiling coarsely ground millet or *bulgur*, boza made from bread (*ekmek bozası*) was a popular variety mentioned by the poet Tirsî (*d.* 1727). A dictionary dated 1901 defines boza as being made from fermented millet dough (Şemseddin Sâmî 1901, 313), and a gourmet version was made from *francala* (French loaves) and sweetened with sugar instead of *pekmez* (Abdülaziz Bey 1995, 152–4).

Egyptian *ekmek bozası* was made from loaves of lightly cooked barley, wheat or sorghum bread (Lane 1927, 1010 n. 51). Burckhardt, who travelled widely in Egypt and the Middle East between 1809 and 1815, described the method for making boza from bread as follows:

> The intoxicating liquor which they drink is called Bouza (بوزة). Strongly leavened bread made from Dhourra is broken into crumbs, and mixed with water, and the mixture is kept for several hours over a slow fire. Being then removed, water is poured over it, and it is left for two nights to ferment. This liquor, according to its greater or smaller degree of fermentation, takes the name of Merin, Bouza, or Om Belbel (أمبلبل), the mother of nightingales, so called because it makes the drunkard sing. Unlike the other two, which being fermented together with the crumbs of bread, are never free from them, the Om Belbel is drained through a cloth, and is consequently pure and liquid. I have tasted of all three. The Om Belbel has a pleasant prickly taste, something like Champagne turned sour.
>
> (Burckhardt 1819, 218, 236)

Ekmek bozası may be the most ancient variety of boza, since the Sumerian word for brewer is LU.KAS + NINDA, which literally means 'man of the beer loaf' (Hornsey 2003, 81).

Boza for fighting men

Soldiers belonging to the Janissary Corps, backbone of the Ottoman army, were keen boza drinkers, and when the army was on campaign boza-makers ranked among the most indispensable camp followers, along with saddlers, farriers, cooks and barbers (Evliya Çelebi 1996–2007, I 285, 313). At the long Turkish siege of Candia in Crete (1666–1669), the encampment outside the walls was a town in itself, with grocery shops, olive oil shops, butchers, water-sellers, coffee houses and *bozahane* (Evliya Çelebi 1996–2007, VIII 180, 190).

The connection between soldiers and boza was close, since Sarı Saltuk, an epic hero of the early Ottoman conquests, was regarded as the patron saint of boza-makers. Since boza provided strength and heat to the body and satisfied hunger it was an important source of nutrition for fighting-men. However, boza was not all good news. In the seventeenth century, Abaza Paşa lost Ahıska Castle, 'that last outpost of Islam', to the Persians because it had been impossible to get the janissaries out of the boza houses to put up a defence (Evliya Çelebi 1996–2007, I 95, 312–3).

While the army lost some of its soldiers to the boza houses, the latter were simultaneously losing customers to the navy. Naval recruitment officers would visit boza houses and taverns in search of recruits. When their victims were sufficiently drunk the officer would secretly put a hundred or so piasters into their purses, accuse them of accepting state money and pressgang them as galley oarsmen (Evliya Çelebi 1996–2007, I 223).

Boza-vendors

In Istanbul boza was sold by street-vendors, equipped with mugs, a cinnamon pot, and a small jug of water for washing the mugs kept in a curved box strapped around their waist, a lantern, and carrying a *güğüm* (large lidded jug made of copper) in each hand (Abdülaziz Bey 1995, 152–4). However, an eighteenth-century picture shows a boza-seller carrying a jar of boza on his shoulder. These itinerant boza-sellers were almost invariably Albanians.

As a way of attracting customers, vendors declaimed poetry as they walked the streets at night. The following verses were composed by a nineteenth-century boza-seller named Hacı Zeynel (Abdülaziz Bey 1995, 153):

My boza is yellow
Fermented with millet
Old ladies love it
My boza smooth and thick

My boza is fine as bone marrow
My jar has a leak
Four okkas for two piastres
My boza smooth and thick

My boza gives strength
You'll know if you try it
Grand houses buy my boza
My boza smooth and thick

My boza is white as milk
Boza like this is hard to find
Summer is coming so hurry to buy
My boza smooth and thick

My boza is *mırmırık* [the alcoholic type of boza.]
Take heed and be warned
Don't miss your chance to taste
My boza smooth and thick

My boza contains grape molasses
Nought but truth I speak
Come and taste it, my dear
My boza smooth and thick

I sell what my master makes
I always taste it first
Once it's sold I go to bed
My boza smooth and thick

The famous singer Şamram Hanım of the late Ottoman period was inspired by these poems to sing a music hall song in the *nihâvend* mode about boza (Koçu 1958–73, 3050):

I make boza out of millet
Wandering the streets I sell it

When all is sold and gone
I please myself in my own room

There is boza both sour and sweet
And cinnamon too if you wish

When you drink some boza
It arouses good cheer

Try it for yourself and see
If I am deceiving you

My name is boza-seller Şamram
A maker of boza I am

I am tired of wandering
No energy left for walking

Whoever drinks my boza
Desires to try some more

Now it is time for me to go
My masters are awaiting me

Two recipes

To conclude, here are two recipes for boza. The first is my Aunt Gezgen's recipe for home-made boza:

Put half a kilo of bulgur in a saucepan and water to cover, cook until soft, adding water if necessary. Strain through a wire sieve. Add 1 cup of sugar and 1 cup of old boza, stir and cover. Set aside. If left in a cool place it will take 3 days to ferment, if in a warm place 2 days. Taste once in a while and add a little more sugar if necessary.

The second recipe is that used by Zeynel Güneş, of Macedonian extraction, who owns our local boza shop in the Istanbul suburb of Kozyatağı. He makes boza from millet which has been coarsely ground like semolina (apparently boza made from wheat spoils quickly). The millet is boiled for 10 hours then the boza culture is added and left to ferment for 3 days. To obtain a more fermented variety, which he calls *ekşi* boza (sour boza), it needs to be left for 7 days.

References

Abdülaziz Bey. *Osmanlı Âdet, Merasim ve Tabirleri*. Eds. Kâzım Arısan and Duygu Arısan Günay. 2 vols. Istanbul: Tarih Vakfı, 1995.

Ahmed Refik. *Onuncu Asr-ı Hicrî'de Istanbul Hayatı (1495–1591)*. Istanbul: Enderun Kitabevi, 1988a.

——.*Onbirinci Asr-ı Hicrî'de Istanbul Hayatı (1592–1688)*. Istanbul: Enderun Kitabevi, 1988b.

Âli, Gelibolulu Mustafa. *Ziyafet Sofraları (Mevaidü'n-nefais fî kavâidi'l mecâlis)*. Istanbul: Tercüman 1001 Temel Eser, 1978.

Barkan, Lütfi Ömer. 'Istanbul Saraylarına ait Muhasebe Defterleri', *Belgeler*, IX 13, 1–380. Ankara: Türk Tarih Kurumu, 1979.

Başaran, Vedat. 'Yüzyılların Lezzeti Boza', *Skylife*. Istanbul: THY, January 2010.

Bell, James Stanislaus. *Journal of a Residence in Circassia during the years 1837, 1838 and 1839*, 2 vols. London: Edward Moxon, 1840.

Buell, Paul, Eugene Anderson and Charles Perry *A Soup for the Qan: Chinese Dietary Medicine of the Mongol Era as seen in Hu Szu-Hui's Yin-Shan Cheng-Yao*. London and New York: Kegan Paul, 2000.

Burckhardt, John Lewis. *Travels In Nubia*. London, Association for Promoting the Discovery of the Interior Part of Africa: John Murray, 1819.

C.SM 160/8031 1140 C 15 (Ottoman Archive document dated 29 January 1728).

Dernschwam, Hans. *Tabebuch Einer Reise Nach Konstantinopel und Kleinasien (1553–1555)*, trans. Franz Babinger. Munich and Leipzig: Verlag von Duncker & Humblot, 1923.

Doerfer, Gerhard. *Türkische und Mongolische Elemente im Neupersischen*. Wiesbaden: Franz Steiner Verlag, 1963.

Eren, Hasan. 'Eski Türk İçkileri', *Dördüncü Milletlerarası Yemek Kongresi*. Konya: Konya Kültür ve Turizm Vakfı, 1992.

Ertaylan, İsmail Hikmet. *Tabiatname*. Istanbul: Istanbul Üniversitesi Edebiyat Fakültesi, 1960.

Evliyâ Çelebi. *Evliyâ Çelebi Seyahatnâmesi* eds. Seyit Ali Kahraman, Yücel Dağlı and Robert Dankoff et al., 10 vols. Istanbul: Yapı Kredi Yayınları, 1996–2007.

Felek, Burhan. *Gecmis Zaman Olur ki*. İstanbul: Felek Yayıncılık, 1985.

Hornsey, Ian Spencer. *A History of Beer and Brewing*. Great Britain: Royal Society of Chemistry, 2003.

Ibn Battuta. *The Travels of Ibn Battuta, AD. 1325–1354*. London: Hakluyt Society, 1953.

Koçu, Reşat Ekrem. *Istanbul Ansiklopedisi*. Istanbul: Istanbul Ansiklopedisi ve Neşriyat Kollektif Şirketi, 1958–1973.

Lane, Edward William. *The Arabian Nights Entertainments or The Thousand and One Nights*. New York: Tudor Publishing, 1927.

Laufer, Berthold. 'Brief Notes on the Possible Oriental Origin of Our Word Booze', *Journal of American Oriental Society*, XLIX, 1929, 56–58.

Mahmud, Kaşgarlı. *Divanü Lûgat-it-Türk Tercümesi*, trs. Besim Atalay, 4 vols. Ankara: Türk Dil Kurumu Yayınları, 1986.

Mahmud al-Kashgari. *Compendium of the Turkic Dialects (Diwan Lugat at-Turk)*, ed. and trs. Robert Dankoff in collaboration with James Kelly, 3 vols. Cambridge, Mass.: Sources of Oriental Languages and Literature, Harvard University Press, 1982–1985.

Morewood, Samuel. *A philosophical and statistical history of the inventions and customs of Ancient and Modern Nations in the Manufacture and Use of Inebriating Liquors, with the recent Practice of Distillation in all its varieties: together with an extensive illustration of the consumption and effects of opium, and other stimulants used in the East, as substituttes for wine and spirits*. Dublin, 1838.

Musahipzade Celâl. *Eski Istanbul Yaşayışı*. Istanbul: Türkiye Yayınevi, 1946.

Oğuz, Burhan. *Türkiye Halkının Kültür Kökenleri*. vol. I. Istanbul, 1976.

Onay, Ahmet Talât. *Eski Türk Edebiyatında Mazmunlar ve İzahı*, ed. Cemal Kurnaz. Ankara: Akçağ Yayınları, 2000.

Ongan, Halit. *Ankara'nın I Numaralı Şer'iye Sicili (14 Mayıs 1583–12 Şubat 1584)*. Ankar:, Ankara Üniversitesi Dil ve Tarih-Coğrafya Fak. Yayınları, 1958.

——. *Ankara'nın İki Numaralı Şer'iye Sicili (20 Kasım 1588 – 11 Temmuz 1590)*. Ankara: Türk Tarih Kurumu, 1974.

Öztekin, Özge XVIII. *Yüzyıl Divan Şiirinde Toplumsal Hayatın İzleri: Divanlardan Yansıyan Görüntüler*. Ankar:, Ürün Yayınları, 2006.

Rauwolff, Leonhart. *A Collection of Curious Travels and Voyages in Two Tomes, The First containing Dr. Leonhart Rauwolff's Itinerary into the Eastern Countries, as Syria, Palestine, or the Holy Land, Armenia, Mesopotamia, Assyria, Chaldea Etc.* tr. Nicholas Staphorst, ed. John Ray. London, 1693.

Ricaut, Paul. *The History of the Present State of the Ottoman Empire*. London: printed for R. Clavell, J. Robinson and A. Churchill, in St. Paul's Church-Yard, and Avemary-Lane, 1686.

Sertoğlu, Midhat. *İstanbul Sohbetleri*. Istanbul: Bedir Yayınevi, 1992.

Şemseddin Sâmî. *Kâmûs-ı Türkî*. (facsimile of the 1901 edn) Istanbul: Enderun Kitabevi, 1989.

Şerefeddin Sabuncuoğlu. *Mücerrebname*, ed. İlter Uzel and Kenan Süveren. Ankara: Atatürk Kültür Merkezi, 1999.

Şirvânî, Muhammed bin Mahmud. *15. Yüzyıl Osmanlı Mutfağı*, eds. Mustafa Argunşah and Müjgân Çakır. Istanbul: Gökkubbe Yayınları, 2005.

Tarih Hazinesi 2, ed. İbrahim Hakkı Konyalı. Istanbul, 1950.

Tavernier, Jean Baptiste. *'The Persian Travels', Collections of Travels Through Turkey into Persia and the East Indies and also of the kingdoms that encompass the Euxine and Caspian seas*. 2 vols. London: printed for Moses Pitt at the Angel in St. Pauls Church-yard, 1684.

Thevenot, Jean. *The Travels of Monsieur de Thevenot into the Levant 1655–56*. London: printed by Henry Clark, for John Taylor, at the Ship in St. Paul's Church-Yard, 1687.

Thompson, Charles. *The Travels of the Late Charles Thompson Esq, Containing his Observations on France, Italy, Turkey in Europe, the Holy Land, Arabia, Egypt and many other parts of the World*, vol. 2. London: printed by J. Newbery and C. Micklewright, 1744.

Wikipedia 'Khidr'

Withers, Robert. *A Description of the Grand Seignor's Seraglio or Turkish Emperor's Court*. London, 1737.

www.rachellaudan.com

Fermentation as a Co-evolutionary Force

Sandor Ellix Katz

This paper addresses fermentation as an integral factor in the evolution of human beings and human culture. The fermentation processes used around the world to create distinctive and functionally important foods and beverages have developed not only in diverse culinary traditions, but also in the broader contexts of our biological and cultural evolution. Culinary fermentation practices are the products of human beings' co-evolution with our natural environment, arising within a web of symbiotic relationships with plants, animals, fungi, and bacteria. Successful coexistence with microbes is a biological imperative. The fermentation arts are human cultural manifestations of this essential fact.

Fermentation is the transformation of food by various bacteria and fungi. People harness this transformative power in order to produce alcohol, to preserve food, and to make it more digestible, less toxic, and/or more delicious. Fermentation has played an instrumental role in human cultural evolution, as we shall explore; it is important to recognize, however, that fermentation is a natural phenomenon much broader than human culinary practices. Our own bodily cells are capable of fermentation. Humans did not create fermentation; it would be more accurate to state that fermentation created us.

Biologists use the term fermentation to describe anaerobic metabolism, the production of energy from nutrients without oxygen. Fermenting bacteria are thought to have emerged relatively early from the primordial pre-biotic soup. The work of biologist Lynn Margulis and others has convinced many biologists that symbiotic relationships between fermenting bacteria and other early single-cell life forms became permanently embodied as the first *eukaryotic* cells, of which plants, animals, and fungi are comprised.[1] As Margulis and Dorion Sagan explain in their book *Microcosmos*, the symbiosis may have begun as a predator-prey relationship:

> Eventually some of the prey evolved a tolerance for their aerobic predators, which then remained alive and well in the food-rich interior of the host. Two types of organisms used the products of each other's metabolisms. As they reproduced inside the invaded cells without causing harm, the predators gave up their independent ways and moved in for good.[2]

Evolution derived from such symbiosis is known as *symbiogenesis*.

Bacterial fermentation processes are part of the context for all life; fermentation plays such a broad and vital role in nutrient cycling that all beings co-evolve with it, ourselves included. 'For the past [billion] years, members of the Bacteria superkingdom have functioned as a major selective force shaping eukaryotic evolution,' state molecular biologists Jian Xu and Jeffrey I. Gordon. 'Co-evolved symbiotic relationships between bacteria and multi-cellular organisms are a prominent feature of life on Earth.'[3] The importance of bacteria and our bacterial interactions cannot be overstated.

Like all multi-cellular life forms, the human body is host to an elaborate indigenous biota, without which we could not function or survive. Some geneticists argue we are 'a composite of many species,' with a genetic landscape that encompasses not only the human genome but also those of our bacterial symbionts.[4] Bacteria outnumber the bodily cells containing our unique DNA by more than ten to one.[5] The vast majority of these bacteria – 100 trillion (10^{14}) in number – are found in our intestines.[6] Bacteria break down nutrients we would not be able to digest,[7] and play an important role, just recently recognized, in regulating the balance between energy use and storage.[8] Intestinal bacteria produce necessary nutrients for us, including B and K vitamins.[9] They provide us with vital defense by 'outcompeting invading pathogens for ecological niches and metabolic substrates.'[10] In addition, intestinal bacteria are able to modulate 'expression' of some of our genes, related to 'diverse and fundamental physiological functions,'[11] including immune response. Between intestinal bacteria and the immune cells in the intestine linings, 'evidence of an active dialogue is rapidly unfolding.'[12]

That's just bacteria in our intestines. On our bodies' surfaces and in our orifices, microbial communities exist in a great range of distinct niches. The human vagina secretes glycogen that supports an indigenous population of lactobacilli, which ferment the glycogen into lactic acid, thereby protecting the vagina from pathogenic bacteria. 'The presence of lactobacilli as a part of the normal vaginal flora is an important component of reproductive health.'[13] Even our reproduction requires fermentation! Our indigenous bacteria protect us everywhere, aiding our function in myriad ways that are just beginning to be understood. From an evolutionary perspective, this extensive microbiota 'endows us with functional features that we have not had to evolve ourselves.'[14] This is a miracle of co-evolution.

Bacteria are such effective co-evolutionary partners because they are adaptable and mutable. In contrast to our eukaryotic cells, with fixed genetic material, prokaryotic bacteria have free-floating genes, which they frequently exchange. Some microbiologists consider it inappropriate to view them as distinct species. 'There are no species in prokaryotes,' state Sorin Sonea and Léo G. Mathieu.[15] 'Bacteria are much more of a continuum,' explains Lynn Margulis. 'They just pick up genes, they throw away genes, and they are very flexible about that.'[16] Sonea and Mathieu explain: 'Each bacterium can be compared to a two-way broadcasting station, using genes as information molecules.' Genes 'are carried by a bacterium only when needed…as a human may carry sophisticated tools.'[17] Margulis and Sagan summarize: 'All the world's bacteria essentially have access to a single gene pool and hence to the adaptive mechanisms of the entire bacteria kingdom.'[18]

Humans are not unique in having co-evolved with bacterial symbionts. Plants also co-evolved with and are dependent upon bacterial partners. A symbiotic relationship between photosynthesizing cyanobacteria and other prokaryotes is thought by many to be the origin of the photosynthesizing chloroplasts in plant cells.[19] The soil around plant roots comprises what is known as the *rhizosphere*, where plants find sustenance through elaborate interaction with the multifaceted soil food web. Roots and their surfaces for soil interaction are far more elaborate than meets the eye. A single rye plant, growing but a season, has millions of rootlets, running an estimated 680 miles, and each of the rootlets is covered with still smaller root hairs, numbering in the billions on each plant, altogether running 6,600 miles.[20] All these microscopic root hairs release *exudates* into the soil, highly regulated excretions including sugars, amino acids, enzymes, and many other nutrients and unique chemical compounds, creating a very selective environment in which they 'literally call the proper bacteria to the area where [the plant] is growing,' according to naturalist Stephen Harrod Buhner.

Because we have co-evolved with both plants and animals by eating and thus interacting with them, our histories encompass not only the plants and animals themselves but their microbial associates. It is the ubiquitous presence of these life-forms, present from the very beginning but invisible until the past few centuries, which results in the ferments, nearly all prehistoric, that we love to eat and drink. The ferments, in spontaneously occurring forms, predate our consciousness of how to manipulate conditions so as to guide their development. But our consciousness did develop, and as part of that, so did the fermentation arts. The ferment itself, and our ability to produce it, is as much a product of co-evolution as the person, plant, yeast, or bacteria. Thus co-evolution encompasses even culture.

167

***

What exactly is culture? In contrast to the realm of biological reproduction, where information is coded and copied as genes, in the cultural realm information is encoded as memes. Memes are transmitted through words, concepts, images, processes, abstractions; stories, pictures, books, films, photographs, computer programs, ledgers; secret family recipes; life lessons, like learning to identify edible plants, learning to garden, learning to cook, learning to fish, learning to procure and preserve food resources; fermentation.

It is largely our history of interacting with plants (and associated microbes) that gives rise to what we call 'culture.' After all, the word culture comes from Latin *cultura*, a form of the verb *colere*, to cultivate or till. The first definition of culture in the *Oxford English Dictionary* is simply: 'The cultivation of land, and derived senses.' Through these derived senses, and the many varied manifestations of cultivation, ideas of what could be cultivated grew. People learned to culture milk, pearls, and cells. We practice aquaculture, viticulture, and horticulture, not to mention popular culture. Many people work hard to imbue their children with culture. Sometimes people decry cultural appropriation or defend cultural purity. Culture begins with cultivating the land, planting seeds, bringing intentionality to cycles that we act to perpetuate. Indeed, a more ancient origin of the word culture is the Indo-European root 'kwel,' meaning 'to revolve,' from which cycle, circle, *chakra*, and many other words, from many languages, are derived.[21] Culture is cultivation, but it is not an isolated act; it is, by definition, part of a cyclical ongoing process, passed from generation to generation.

As my exploration of fermentation unfolds, I keep coming back to the profound significance of the fact that we use the same word (culture) to describe the community of bacteria that transform milk into yoghurt, as well as the practice of subsistence itself, language, music, art, literature, science, spiritual practices, belief systems, and all that human beings seek to perpetuate. Successful coexistence with microbes in our midst is a biological imperative. The fermentation arts are cultural manifestations of this essential fact. If we are to enjoy surpluses of food, then we must have strategies for preserving them in the presence of the microbial ecology, such as it is. Clearly, as a group, fermented foods and beverages are more than incidental culinary novelties. They appear to be found in some form in every culinary tradition (I have searched without success for examples of cultures that do not incorporate any form of fermentation), and are central features of many, perhaps even most, cuisines. Immigrants, crossing continents and oceans with only the belongings they could carry, have often brought their sourdoughs and their milk cultures with them. They are embodiments of culture not lightly abandoned.

168

How can we even imagine the cultural realm without alcoholic beverages? 'Their pre-eminence and universal allure – what might be called their biological, social, and religious imperatives – make them significant in understanding the development of our species and its cultures,' states anthropologist Patrick E. McGovern, who has identified alcohol residues in 9,000-year-old pottery shards. 'Our species' intimate relationship with fermented beverages over millions of years has, in large measure, made us what we are today.'[22] Though some religions and nations ban alcohol altogether, thus defining themselves in opposition to it, alcohol is known and used everywhere, and of widespread importance in ritual, ceremony, and celebration. Most people seem to enjoy manipulating our gift and burden of consciousness, and do so by whatever means available. Alcohol has been far and away the most widely available and widely used intoxicant.

We do not know the origins of alcohol. The alcohol that Professor McGovern identified from the Neolithic settlement of Jiahu in China was made from a mixture of rice, honey, and fruit.[23] It would appear that these early human alcohol-makers were combining available carbohydrate and yeast sources, however they might have conceptualized it. Is it possible that, rather than humans 'discovering' alcohol and mastering its production, we evolved always already knowing it? Many animals have been documented consuming alcohol in their natural habitats. One of them, a daily consumer of alcohol in the Malaysian jungle, is the pentailed treeshrew (*Ptilocercus lowii*). Interestingly, this mammal is considered to be 'the morphologically least-derived living descendent of early ancestors of primates,' regarded as a 'living model' for the ancestral lineage from which primates radiated. The alcohol these treeshrews consume occurs, naturally, on the bertam palm (*Eugeissona tristis*), on 'specialized flower buds that harbor a fermenting yeast community.'[24] And the treeshrews are pollinators for the bertam palm. This tree, its pollinating shrews, and the fermenting yeast community all co-evolved this arrangement together. It would be absurd to think of one species as the primary actor.

Our primate and humanoid ancestors in Africa presumably ate lots of fruit, which ferments when ripe, especially quickly in the warm and wet jungle climate. Biologist Robert Dudley theorizes that our precursors were routinely exposed to alcohol in fruit, and that 'this exposure in turn elicited corresponding physiological adaptations and preferences over an evolutionary time scale that are retained in modern humans.'[25]

While alcohol is present in fruits at low concentrations compared to alcoholic beverages, the fleeting availability of seasonal fruits encourages gorging. I know I respond to plentiful ripe berries that way. I am not unique in this regard. Addiction researcher Ronald Siegel describes 'a menagerie of jungle beasts' responding to fallen, split, fermenting durian fruits in Malaysia, and eating it to the point of visible disorientation.[26] Maybe our progenitors partook in similar festivities; if so, then our human lineage, rather than discovering alcohol, knew it all along, evolved with it, and applied our growing conceptual capabilities and tool-making skills to assuring a steady supply. Understanding how to manipulate conditions to make alcohol, and being able to share that information, are huge milestones in our cultural evolution.

169

Even more important, or at least more necessary at a day-to-day level, is the cultural information required to effectively store food. At least a rudimentary knowledge of food storage strategies is required in order to survive without daily hunting and gathering. The only way humans could escape from daily preoccupation with feeding themselves is by acquiring the ability to preserve food for the future.

The very fact of food storage requires huge conceptual leaps: thinking about the future, understanding that an action now can result in a benefit later, and being able to communicate about that process. In emergent human societies, cultural information, transmitted via symbol and language, enhanced ancient co-evolutionary relationships. Genes were supplemented by memes as vectors of co-evolutionary change. Information about cultivation, storage, and processing could be communicated and taught. Major technological advances such as pottery vessels were creative solutions to challenges of fermentation and storage. Food storage capabilities reinforced the logic of generating surplus food. And surpluses drove the need for more effective storage strategies. Specialization and elaboration ensued.

Food storage does not necessarily involve fermentation. In many cases it primarily consists of keeping foods dry but not too dry, cool but not too cold, and dark. But it is not easy, with limited technology, to create ideal conditions for storage. Learning the lessons it takes to dry and store food effectively involves errors and accidents: seeds and grains getting moist, encouraging germination and/or molds; fruits and vegetables fermenting and/or rotting; milk aging in various environments; meats and fish faring quite differently depending upon moisture and salt-content. A necessary aspect of co-evolving with the more limited range of plants and animals that agricultural societies increasingly came to rely on for food was learning to understand the dynamics of how they aged under different storage conditions. Settling into a sedentary life primarily subsisting on agricultural crops and/or milk or meat animals requires such an understanding.

Distinctions between fresh and rotten food – and the creative space between those extremes – are fundamental narrative themes across human cultures.[27] Understanding what is and isn't appropriate to put in our mouths is some of the earliest cultural information we each acquire as babies. The contrast between food that is rotten and food that is fresh is a fundamental life-lesson for survival. In the creative space between those binary opposites is the food that is effectively preserved, the cultured foods, the ferments so deeply embedded in our cultural particulars. Cultural evolution is part of our co-evolutionary tale.

***

To me, what is fascinating about the concept of co-evolution is the recognition that the process of becoming is infinitely interconnected. As a dynamic between two species, co-evolution has been described as 'an evolutionary change in a trait in the individuals of one population in response to a trait of the individuals of a second population, followed by an evolutionary response by the second population to the change in the first.'[28] Life, however, is never so simple as to be limited to just two interrelated species; co-evolution is a complex and multivariable process through which all life is linked.

All the plants our hunter-gatherer ancestors ate, like those our primate ancestors ate, consisted of unique chemical compounds, along with enzymes, bacteria, and other associated microbial forms, to which our ancestors and their microbiota adapted (or not). The plants' co-evolutionary histories do not revolve exclusively around us. For instance, could certain large fruits have evolved to attract the attention and seed-spreading potential of extinct megafauna, to our enduring benefit?[29] Some plants we eventually co-evolved with in ways we came to describe as domesticated. 'We automatically think of domestication as something we do to other species,' writes Michael Pollan in *The Botany of Desire*, 'but it makes just as much sense to think of it as something certain plants and animals have done to us, a clever evolutionary strategy for advancing their own interests. The species that have spent the last ten thousand or so years figuring out how best to feed, heal, clothe, intoxicate, and otherwise delight us have made themselves some of nature's greatest success stories.'[30]

The influence of co-evolution changes all involved. To say that one species is the creation or the master of another is a self-serving oversimplification. What we call 'domestication,' like any co-evolutionary process, has repercussions for all parties.

Co-evolutionary success can lead to very specialized relationships. Treeshrews eating the fermenting nectar while pollinating bertam palms, discussed already, is one vivid example. With the major human food crops, we've become 'obligate agents': 'sufficiently dependent upon certain plants so that [our] survival, at new densities, is dependent on the survival of the plants.'[31]

In that dependence, in all our cultural particulars, we are manifestations of co-evolutionary processes with the plants as much as they are manifestations of co-evolutionary processes with us. Humans are not the only actors in these relationships. Nor are plants the only other life-forms to benefit from their close association with us. How about *Saccharomyces cerevisiae*, the primary yeast used to produce alcoholic beverages and bread? *S. cerevisiae* is rarely, if ever, found in nature outside of human environments.[32] This suggests that some ancestor of our beloved yeast evolved, through its long association with humans and our willingness to grow and process plants to its preferred specifications, in huge quantities, to feed it generously and cultivate it continuously over the course of millennia, into the co-evolutionary partner we now know as *S. cerevisiae*.

Fermented foods are not exactly human inventions. They are natural phenomena that people observed, although in different places, very different phenomenon were observed, due to differences in what plants were grown and how they were processed and stored. The distinctness of cultures arises out of the specificity of place. In China, rice and millet were developed, and their complex carbohydrates came to be digested by molds into simple sugars for alcohol fermentation. In the 'Fertile Crescent' of the Middle East, it was barley and wheat that developed, and a very different method, germination (malting), came to be used to digest them into sugars for fermentation. Although in different regions the foods, micro-organisms, and processes vary widely, Hesseltine and Wang of the US Department of Agriculture state: 'Fermented foods are essential parts of diets in all parts of the world.'[33]

***

The biological reality – that bacteria are our ancestors and the context for all life; that they perform many important physiological functions for us; and that they improve, preserve, and protect our food – contrasts sharply with the widespread perception of bacteria as our enemies. Because the earliest triumphs of microbiology involved identifying bacterial pathogens and developing effective weapons against them, our culture has embraced a project that I call the 'War on Bacteria.' Beyond antibiotic drugs that individuals take, sometimes for important reasons (but typically over-prescribed), we routinely feed antibiotics to livestock, chemically sterilize our water, and use antibacterial soaps marketed with the seductive promise of killing 99.9 per cent of bacteria.

The problem with killing 99.9 per cent of bacteria is that most of them protect us from the few that can make us sick. Continuous indiscriminate killing of bacteria in, on, and around our bodies makes us more vulnerable to infection. Because of bacteria's genetic mutability, pathogenic bacteria are rapidly developing resistance to commonly used antibacterial compounds. The constant generalized assault of bacteria, and the ideology that fuels it, is misguided and dangerous.

As a result of the War on Bacteria, our bacterial context is rapidly shifting. One bacterium formerly ubiquitous in humans, *Helicobacter pylori*, which resides in the stomach, is now found in fewer than 10 per cent of American children, and may be headed toward extinction.[34] *H. pylori* has been correlated with various gastrointestinal problems, which have decreased along with the bacteria's incidence in the population. But even though *H. pylori* may contribute to problems for us, it is part of us and we co-evolved dependent upon it for certain regulatory functions. Among the roles this particular bacteria is thought to play (or have played) in our bodies is regulating stomach-acid levels, certain immune responses, and the hormones that control appetite. The disappearance of *H. pylori* may be implicated in increased levels of obesity, asthma, acid reflux, and esophageal cancers.[35] 'The accuracy of classifying commensal bacteria as "detrimental" or "beneficial" remains highly speculative,' cautions epidemiologist Volker Mai.[36] We eradicate our evolutionary partners at great risk.

The practice of fermentation offers opportunities to cultivate not only the specific bacterial and fungal communities necessary for the ferments, but a consciousness of ourselves as co-evolutionary beings, part of a greater web of life. Biologist Edward O. Wilson has dubbed such consciousness *biophilia*.[37] While this word may be new, such a consciousness has been part of humanity since the beginning. Unfortunately, we have become increasing isolated from the natural world, lacking interaction with animals, plants, and bacteria in our midst. Rather than continuing to distance ourselves from the larger web of life, we must reclaim these relationships. Fermentation is a tangible way of cultivating this consciousness and these relationships.

The trend in human culture has been toward ever-increasing specialization, with diminishing numbers of people involved in food production. Often this is cited as evidence of progress, liberating us for higher callings. Agriculture has largely disappeared from our lives, along with fermentation, both relegated to specialists far from mainstream view. We have applied the model of mass production to our food, and it has been a terrible failure. It is destroying the earth, destroying our health, and depriving us of dignity. With respect to food, the vast majority of people have been reduced to consumers, dependent upon an infrastructure of global trade, monocultures, synthetic chemicals, and biotechnology.

Much of the twentieth-century literature of fermentation promoted moving production away from small-scale community-based cottage industry into factories, and replacing traditional starter-cultures passed down from generation to generation with laboratory-bred improved strains, in the name of improved hygiene, safety, and efficiency. My objective is exactly the opposite: I want to encourage a reclaiming of fermentation in our homes and in our communities, as a means of reclaiming food, and with it a broad web of biological connections. Rather than fermenting just grapes, barley, and soybeans, let's ferment acorns, turnips, sorghum, or whatever food surpluses we can access or create. No single household can make all these foods on an ongoing basis. Let's not confuse reclaiming our food with the myth of household self-sufficiency. Reclaiming food means reclaiming community, with specialization and divisions of labor at a human scale, promoting awareness of resources and local exchange. This is not intended as xenophobia or opposition to foreign trade. Exotic foods are thrilling treats; it's just inappropriate and destructive to organize our lives around them. All things, including alcohol and global trade, in moderation.

As evolutionary beings, we must recognize in bacteria not only our cellular origins and mutualistic partners, but our best hope for biological pathways into the future. How else can we adapt to all the toxic compounds we are creating? Bacteria have already been found to decompose many pollutants, including rubber tires,[38] organophosphorus compounds used in pesticides, plasticizers, jet fuel, and chemical warfare,[39] and phthalates used in plastics and cosmetic products.[40] Fungi also offer promising adaptive potential.[41] If our evolutionary imperative is to adapt to shifting conditions, then we must embrace and work with micro-organisms rather than attempting to eradicate them; or imagining that we can engineer them to our will in precise and predictable ways. Co-evolution has repercussions for all involved, far too compounded to be predictable. We cannot control co-evolutionary fate; we can only adapt to shifting conditions as best we can.

There is no generic formula for adapting to change. Yet we must. We can only transform by looking beyond the seductions of cultural innovation – the television, the computer, even the printed page before you – and reclaiming our cultural roots and biological inheritance. We must build community not only with people, but by restoring our broad web of co-evolved relationships. Fermentation gives us the opportunity to get to know and work with a range of micro-organisms with which we have already co-evolved. Into the future they go, with us or without us.

173

Notes

1. E. G. Nisbet & N. H. Sleep, 'The Habitat and Nature of Early Life', *Nature* 409: 1089 (2001).
2. Lynn Margulis and Dorion Sagan. *Microcosmos*. New York: Summit Books, 1986, 131–2.
3. Jian Xu and Jeffrey I. Gordon, 'Honor Thy Symbionts', *Proceedings of the National Academy of Sciences* 100: 10452 (2003).
4. Fredrik Bäckhed, et al., 'Host-Bacterial Mutualism in the Human Intestine', *Science* 307: 1915 (2005).
5. D. C. Savage, 'Microbial Ecology of the Gastrointestinal Tract', Annual Review of *Microbiology* 31: 107 (1977).
6. Ruth E. Ley et al., 'Ecological and Evolutionary Forces Shaping Microbial Diversity in the Human Intestine', *Cell* 124: 837 (2006).
7. Steven R. Gill, et al., 'Metagenomic Analysis of the Human Distal Gut Microbiome', *Science* 312: 1357 (2006).

8. Bäckhed.

9. Hill, M. J., 'Intestinal Flora and Endogenous Vitamin Synthesis', *European Journal of Cancer Prevention* 6 (Suppl. 1): S43 (1997).

10. S. C. Leahy, et al., 'Getting Better with Bifidobacteria', *Journal of Applied Microbiology* 98: 1303 (2005).

11. Lora V. Hooper et al., 'Molecular Analysis of Commensal Host-Microbial Relationships in the Intestine', *Science* 291: 881 (2001).

12. Denise Kelly et al., 'Commensal Gut Bacteria: Mechanisms of Immune Modulation', *Trends in Immunology* 26: 326 (2005).

13. E.R. Boskey, et al., 'Origins of Vaginal Acidity: High D/L Lactate Ratio is Consistent With Bacteria Being the Primary Source', *Human Reproduction* 16(9): 1809 (2001).

14. Bäckhed.

15. Sorin Sonea and Leo G. Mathieu, 'Evolution of the Genomic Systems of Prokaryotes and Its Momentous Consequences', *International Microbiology* 4: 67 (2001).

16. 'Interview with Lynn Margulis', *Astrobiology Magazine*, October 9, 2006.

17. Léo G. Mathieu and Sorin Sonea, 'A Powerful Bacterial World', *Endeavour* 19(3): 112 (1995).

18. Margulis and Sagan, 16.

19. Ibid., 133–6.

20. Stephen Harrod Buhner. *The Lost Language of Plants*. White River Junction, VT: Chelsea Green, 150.

21. *American Heritage Dictionary of the English Language*. Fourth Edition. 2000.

22. Patrick E. McGovern, *Uncorking the Past*. Berkeley, CA: University of California Press, 2009, xi–xii and 281.

23. Patrick E. McGovern, et al., 'Fermented Beverages of Pre- and Proto-historic China', *Proceedings of the National Academy of Sciences* 101: 17593 (2004).

24. Frank Wiens et al., 'Chronic Intake of Fermented Floral Nectar by Wild Treeshrews', *Proceedings of the National Academy of Sciences* 105: 10426 (2008).

25. Robert Dudley, 'Fermenting Fruit and the Historical Ecology of Ethanol Ingestion: Is Alcoholism in Modern Humans an Evolutionary Hangover?' *Addiction* 97: 384.

26. Ronald K. Siegel, *Intoxication*. NY: Pocket Books, 1989, 118.

27. See Claude Lévi-Strauss, *The Raw and the Cooked*. New York: Harper & Row, 1969.

28. D. H. Janzen, 'When is it Coevolution?' *Evolution* 34: 611 (1980).

29. See Connie Barlow. *The Ghosts of Evolution*. New York: Basic Books, 2000.

30. Michael Pollan. *The Botany of Desire*. New York: Random House, 2001, xvi.

31. David Rindos, *The Origins of Agriculture*. Orlando, FL: Academic Press, 1984, 159.

32. Ann Vaughan-Martini and Alessandro Martini, 'Facts, Myths and Legends on the Prime Industrial Micro-organism', *Journal of Industrial Microbiology* 14: 514 (1995).

33. C. W. Hesseltine and Hwa L. Wang, 'The Importance of Traditional Fermented Foods', *BioScience* 30(6): 402 (1980).

34. Martin J. Blaser, 'Who Are We? Indigenous Microbes and the Ecology of Human Diseases', *European Molecular Biology Organization Reports* 7(10): 956 (2006).

35. 'The Twists and Turns of Fate', *The Economist* 388(8594): 68 (2008).

36. Volker Mai, 'Dietary Modification of the Intestinal Microbiota', *Nutrition Reviews* 62(6): 235 (2004).

37. Edward O. Wilson, *Biophilia*. Cambridge: Harvard University Press, 1984.

38. Akio Tsuchii, et al., 'Degradation of the Rubber in Truck Tires by a Strain of Nocardia', *Biodegradation* 7: 405 (1997).

39. Brajesh K. Singh and Allan Walker, 'Microbial Degradation of Organophosphorus Compounds', *FEMS Microbiology Reviews* 30(3): 428 (2006).

40. S. Y. Yuan, et al., 'Occurrence and Microbial Degradation of Phthalate Esters in Taiwan River Sediments', *Chemosphere* 49(10): 1295 (2002).

41. See Paul Stamets, *Mycelium Running*. Berkeley: Ten Speed Press, 2005.

Yeast Are People Too: Sourdough Fermentation from the Microbe's Point of View

Jessica A. Lee

An unbaked loaf of sourdough bread is a garden, home to micro-organisms of diverse species and functions. It is an intimate working relationship between microbes and humans; it is also a potent reminder of the culinary benefits of biodiversity.

Fermentation is primarily the business of yeast and bacteria. We humans aren't actually very good at it; we cultivate microbes to do the biochemical work for us. So while fermentation is often seen as a craft, it may in fact more accurately be described a sort of micro-agriculture.

Michael Pollan wrote *The Botany of Desire: a Plant's Eye View of the World* (2001) with the purpose of bringing attention to the lives and needs of the plants we eat. In his book, Pollan illustrates that agriculture is not simply a practice in which humans manipulate plants to express the traits we find desirable, but one in which plants evolve traits that coerce humans to aid the survival of their species – and also in which the traits of plants help to shape human history. In a similar fashion, humans and our food are changed by the microbes we work with, just as much as those microbes are changed by us.

We have done this bread-making thing, harnessing the microbes we find around us, for as long as history has been recorded. However, it is only in the last few decades that we have developed the techniques to be able to understand in greater chemical and biological detail what exactly happens within bread dough, and to use our new knowledge to improve bread further. Here, I will give an introduction to that knowledge, in hopes of encouraging bakers to think more as microbes might.

Bread-making is the work of micro-organisms

Unlike cookies, cakes, and quickbreads, yeast-leavened bread is a baked good that requires the participation of biology in the kitchen. And sourdough bread is defined by that biology. The word 'sourdough' is sometimes used to refer to any bread leavened with 'wild-caught' yeast rather than the commercially-cultivated *Saccharomyces cerevisiae*; or sometimes to the distinctive profile of flavor, texture, and keeping qualities associated with bread made acidic by any means. However, here we use sourdough to refer specifically to the community of micro-organisms which together leaven and acidify the dough: a diverse consortium of yeasts and lactic acid-producing bacteria.

Before the invention of the term 'sourdough', it was the only method by which bread was made, for most of history, before the advent of commercial baker's yeast production. Bread has always been leavened with yeasts captured from the environment, and bacteria are often captured at the same time. However, sourdough bread is nowadays a novelty rather than the default method of production; the default is now bread made with commercial yeast grown as a monoculture – a single species – and with no significant bacterial activity. The popularity of 'conventional' bread is due partly to the simplicity and regularity of the process, and partly to the wide appeal of the mild flavor and very regular texture achievable without bacterial activity. Sourdough therefore finds itself in the small-scale, artisanal niche, and is appreciated for qualities such as complex flavor, rugged texture, and good shelf-life.

All of those special qualities of sourdough bread may be attributed to the complex communities of yeast and bacteria that build it. And an obvious but often-overlooked fact is that sourdough micro-organisms are interested in nothing more than their own survival and reproduction. It just so happens that many of the processes they carry out for survival contribute to an excellent artisanal product. A baker, therefore, has an interest in understanding those microbial processes, in order to facilitate the success of the micro-organisms that will make the best bread. The creation of a good sourdough is a symbiosis between baker and microbes.

Colonization: what starts a starter?

The assemblage of diverse yeast and bacteria that leavens sourdough bread first begins its relationship with the baker when the organisms colonize the flour-water batter that will become the starter. The baker combines flour and water and allows the mixture to sit for hours or days until microbial activity is observed, in the form of bubble formation, sour or alcoholic smell, and thinner texture (these are all signs of microbial activity, the specifics of which are described below). This formation of a 'spontaneous sourdough' is actually one of ecological succession, as will be described below.

Where did the bacteria and yeast come from to begin with? *Everything is everywhere, and the environment selects.* This is known as the Baas-Becking hypothesis, after the Dutch microbiologist who used the words to describe his observation that all micro-organisms are ubiquitous but that the characteristics of any particular environment determine which ones succeed at being most abundant there. Bacteria and yeast are on particles of dust in the air; on the bowls and spoons used to mix the batter; in the flour itself; in ingredients such as fruit or yoghurt sometimes added to help kick-start the process. Then, of all of the microbes that find their way into the burgeoning starter, only a few kinds are able to survive in the world of the flour-water paste.

The initial several hours after inoculation see rapid changes in the microbial community. But once an active sourdough starter has been established, the community of micro-organisms remains quite stable in abundance and composition (Stolz 2003). It consists primarily of one or a few species of yeast, and up to several species of bacteria, almost exclusively lactic acid bacteria. Table 1 lists common sourdough micro-organisms; no one sourdough contains all of these species, but the many species are found in sourdoughs from around the world. Once the population has reached stability, microbial counts tend to range $10^7 - 10^9$ live active bacterial cells per gram of dough, and $10^2 - 10^7$ yeast cells (Siragusa et al. 2009).

Yeast	Bacteria
Candida boldinii	Enteroccocus mundtii
Candida guilliermondii	Lactobacillus acidophilus
Candida holmii	Lactobacillus amylovorus
Candida kruseil crusei	Lactobacillus brevis
Candida milleri	Lactobacillus buchneri
Candida stellata	Lactobacillus casei
Candida tropicalis	Lactobacillus casei
Hansenula anomala	Lactobacillus confusus
Hansenula subpelliculosa	Lactobacillus crispatus
Hansenula tropicalis	Lactobacillus crustorum
Pichia polymorpha	Lactobacillus curvatus
Pichia saitoi	Lactobacillus delbrueckii
Saccharomyces cerevisae	Lactobacillus farciminis
Saccharomyces dairensis	Lactobacillus fermentum
Saccharomyces ellipsoideus	Lactobacillus fructivorans
Saccharomyces exiguus	Lactobacillus hammesii
Saccharomyces fructuum	Lactobacillus helveticus
Saccharomyces inusitatus	Lactobacillus johnsonii
Torulopsis holmii	Lactobacillus namurensis
Saccharomyces chevalieri	Lactobacillus nantensis
Saccharomyces curvatus	Lactobacillus parabuchneri
Saccharomyces inusitatus	Lactobacillus paracasei
Saccharmoyces panis fermentati	Lactobacillus paralimentarius
Candida norvegensis	Lactobacillus plantarum
	Lactobacillus pontis
	Lactobacillus reuteri
	Lactobacillus rossiae
	Lactobacillus sakei
	Lactobacillus sanfranciscensis
	Lactobacillus spicheri
	Leuconostoc mesenteroides
	Pediococcus acidilactici
	Pediococcus pentosaeceus
	Weissella confusa
	Weissella cibaria

Table 1. Micro-organisms commonly found in sourdough cultures. Data from Scheirlinck et al. (2007); Maloney and Foy (2003); Stolz (2003).

The baker may exert some control over the factors that determine what survives: the kind of food available (that is, variety of flour and/or added sweeteners); the mechanisms of breathing that are possible (how well the batter is aerated); the temperature; how much starvation the organisms must endure (the fermentation time before dough refreshment); and the physical nature of the substrate (the hydration of the dough) (Stolz 2003). In the end, by setting his fermentation parameters and then attracting all the potential participants he can, the baker will automatically end up with the population that is best adapted to survive in his particular dough.

Importantly, the baker's choice of fermentation parameters is not the only force that controls these factors. All the organisms in the starter are simultaneously struggling to survive, and at the same time, they too are shaping their environment in ways that make it either more or less hospitable to other organisms. There is evidence that certain combinations of yeast and bacteria species are more likely to coexist than others; however, results from different studies sometimes disagree about the associations they observe (Scheirlinck et al. 2008).

In opposition to the Baas-Becking hypothesis is the argument that biogeography may play a role – perhaps not everything is everywhere, and location does matter. Certainly, the importance of environmental selection in narrowing down a sourdough's inhabitants is clear: only a handful of genera of yeast and bacteria have ever been found in any sourdoughs anywhere (evident in Table 1). However, within those genera, the role of selection is less clear, and there is growing evidence that in fact what determines whether *L. plantarum* or *L. sanfranciscensis* flourishes in a certain sourdough is simply who got there first: Scheirlinck and colleagues, in their survey of traditional Belgian sourdoughs, found the sourdough microbial community to be more dependent on bakery environment than on dough composition (2007). This indicates that regardless of dough makeup and fermentation conditions, a baker may have even more control over the population of his sourdough by his choice of inoculum.

In any stable sourdough starter, regardless of the species makeup of the microbial community, you will find the same basic processes always being carried out by someone or other. In the sections that follow, we discuss the daily business that goes on in a sourdough community.

A day in the life of a sourdough: how microbes eat

Upon being born in a sourdough, a microbe finds itself in a world of carbohydrates, proteins, fats, and water. The same basic ingredients are present in a liquid starter or in a solid bread dough; figure 1 presents an image of the maze that is the solid dough, a network of proteins with suspended starch grains.

A microbe's first line of business is to eat, in order to generate energy. Like humans, yeast and lactobacilli get their energy from carbohydrates – eating, in fact, a very small portion of the very bread dough they live in, and simultaneously excreting their waste into it, before we consume it. As unappetizing as this sounds, the changes that microbes work on sourdough bread are for the better – they break down molecules to change the texture and digestibility of the bread, and create new molecules to change its taste and storage properties.

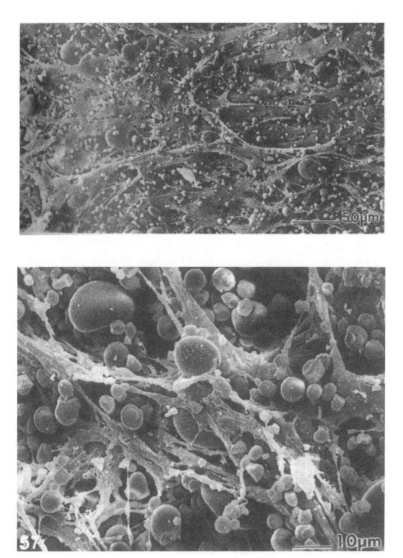

179

Figure 1. (top) Scanning electron microscopy image, optimally kneaded dough. (bottom) Scanning electron microscopy, highly overkneaded dough. From Belitz, Grosch and Schieberle (2009).

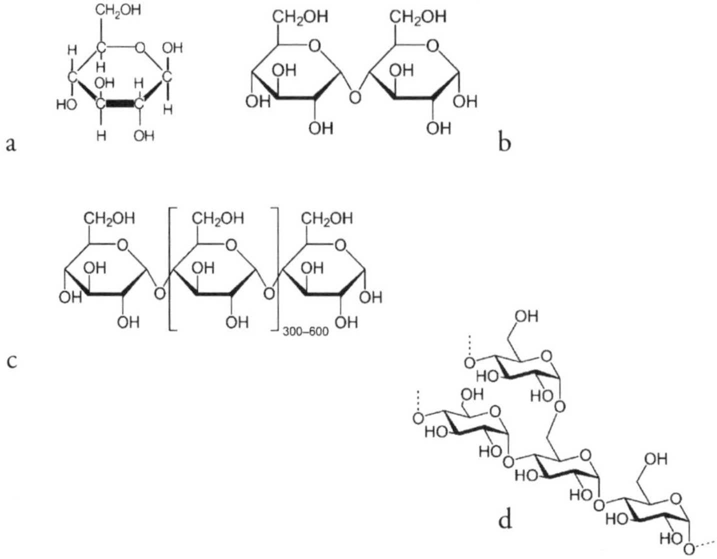

Figure 2. Chemical structures of a) glucose; b) maltose; c) amylose; d) amylopectin.

The main source of carbohydrates in bread dough is starch, which makes up approximately 70 per cent of wheat flour by weight (McGee 2004). Starch is composed of long chains of glucose molecules strung together into molecules called amylose and amylopectin, protected inside starch granules. Upon milling, the granules are damaged and starch becomes more physically accessible, but the long chains remain chemically unusable to yeast and bacteria until they are broken down into smaller fragments. This job is done by the enzymes α- and β-amylase and maltase, which chop the bonds between the monomers to release smaller sugars: primarily the single sugar glucose and its disaccharide counterpart, maltose. (Figure 2)

Elegantly enough, most of the breakdown of starch is done by enzymes furnished by the wheat grain itself. A wheat grain carries amylases and maltases in preparation for the day it will germinate, when it will need to break down the stored starch into glucose to give the growing plant quick energy (Taiz and Zeiger 2002, 484). Of course, a wheat grain that has been milled into flour will never germinate, but the enzymes are still present and active in the bread dough.

The fate of carbohydrates: yeast fermentation

Yeast have two ways of eating. Like animals, they can use oxygen to turn glucose into carbon dioxide gas. This process, called respiration, is the most efficient way of obtaining energy from glucose, so in the presence of oxygen yeast will always respire. For every molecule of glucose, six molecules of oxygen are consumed and six molecules each of carbon dioxide and water are produced:

$C_6H_{12}O_6 + 6\ O_2 \rightarrow 6\ CO_2 + 6\ H_2O$
1 glucose + 6 oxygen → 6 carbon dioxide + 6 water

However, in the absence of oxygen, they can still obtain energy from sugar by a less efficient method: fermentation. Fermentation is a general term for several ways of metabolizing sugar without oxygen. Yeast carry out ethanol fermentation: they turn one molecule of glucose into two molecules of ethanol and two molecules of carbon dioxide:

$C_6H_{12}O_6 \rightarrow 2\ C_2H_5OH + 2\ CO_2$
1 glucose → 2 ethanol + 2 carbon dioxide

Without oxygen, yeast are unable to break apart all of the C atoms, leaving quite a bit of chemical energy in ethanol.

A bread dough is a heterogeneous environment, with both air pockets and regions of dough that oxygen cannot penetrate; therefore, both respiration and fermentation take place in bread.

In a conventional bread dough, at its fastest, a gram of commercial baker's yeast can ferment 0.3–0.7 g carbohydrates per hour. In the entire course of fermentation, the sugar consumed by the yeast is equivalent to about 3 per cent of the total flour weight. That means that in a one-pound loaf, approximately 5 g of carbon dioxide is produced, equivalent to 1500 cm³ (more than half a gallon) of gas at atmospheric pressure. Most of this remains dissolved in the dough or in small bubbles – dependent on the structure of the dough – until baking. An equal amount of sugar is converted to ethanol at the same time (Maloney and Foy 2003).

Sourdough yeast are almost certainly slower at these processes than standard bakery yeast, as they have not been bred for optimum efficiency in conversion of sugar to CO_2 or ethanol. Instead, they compromise efficiency for other fitness advantages, such as acid-tolerance or the ability to consume a diverse range of energy sources.

The fate of carbohydrates: bacterial fermentation

All of the above processes occur in every yeast-raised bread, both conventional and sourdough. However, as mentioned above, the distinguishing characteristic of sourdough is the population of lactic acid bacteria it harbors alongside the yeast. Unlike yeast, lactic acid bacteria cannot use oxygen to break glucose all the way down to carbon dioxide; they make their living only by fermentation. But instead of producing ethanol, they produce, as their name suggests, lactic acid:

$C_6H_{12}O_6 \rightarrow 2\ CH_3CHOHCOOH$
1 glucose → 2 lactic acid

Bacteria that produce only lactic acid are classified as *homofermentative*. *Hetero-fermentative* bacteria produce both lactic acid and either acetic acid or ethanol:

$$C_6H_{12}O_6 \rightarrow CH_3CHOHCOOH + C_2H_5OH + CO_2$$
1 glucose → 1 lactic acid + 1 ethanol + 1 carbon dioxide

or

$$C_6H_{12}O_6 + O_2 \rightarrow CH_3CHOHCOOH + CH_3COOH + CO_2 + H_2O$$
1 glucose + 1 oxygen → 1 lactic acid + 1 acetic acid + 1 carbon dioxide + 1 water

The concentration of oxygen present determines whether more ethanol or more acetic acid is produced (Kandler 1983). Both homo-fermentative and hetero-fermentative bacteria may be found in sourdough bread.

The fact that both yeast and bacteria like to eat glucose would seem to be a perfect set-up for a competitive relationship, rather than the successful coexistence that we observe in sourdough. The answer lies in the fact that, as mentioned before, the glucose in the above equations is actually not very abundant in bread dough, but rather it is the product of substantial work that the microbes must put into breaking down larger molecules and subsequently importing them into the cell interior. Carbohydrate degradation and transport is one of the main differentiating features among microbial species. Each species of micro-organism has the capability to process a different suite of carbohydrates to obtain the glucose it ultimately eats, so different species often do not compete for the same substrate.

Maltose is one of the most common sugars found in bread dough, but it must be broken down into its constituent two molecules of glucose before it can enter the fermentation or respiration pathways. Because consuming pure glucose saves that step, when it does happen to be present many organisms will shut down their ability to use other substrates so that they can concentrate on consuming as much glucose as possible – a behavior known as 'glucose repression' (Maloney and Foy 2003).

Typical San Francisco sourdough provides just one example of the interlocking metabolic relationships in yeast and bacterial consortia. Many yeasts, including the *S. cerevisiae* sold commercially, are able to recognize the disaccharide maltose and transport it into the cell, where it is then broken down into two molecules of glucose and used for energy. However, *S. exiguus*, a species of yeast commonly found in San Francisco sourdough, cannot. At the same time, *L. sanfranciscensis*, one of the lactic acid bacteria most commonly found in sourdough, prefers maltose to glucose. It takes one molecule of maltose into the cell, breaks it down into two molecules of glucose, and then commonly uses one of those glucose molecules and excretes the other. Consequently, glucose-eating yeast nearby, such as *S. exiguus*, thrive (Neubauer et al. 1994). It may well be that *S. exiguus* simply lost the ability to consume maltose because it had no need to, and in fact is better off not competing with the bacteria with whom it coexists. At the same time, the high concentration of glucose in the immediate vicinity triggers glucose repression in most other organisms, so that they lose their ability to consume maltose, leaving *L. sanfranciscensis* (which is not subject to glucose repression) alone to consume maltose without competition (Stolz et al. 1993, Wink 2009).

An acid environment

Every time a sourdough bacterium eats, it produces acid. Although acid appears to be simply a byproduct of the way bacteria obtain energy, it also constitutes one of the most important chemical characteristics of the sourdough environment.

In a sourdough microbial community, acidity acts as a powerful weapon to keep other organisms at bay. The pH in a sourdough starter can fall as low as 4 or lower, and sourdough bacteria are tolerant of acidic environments but many other bacteria are not. Once bacteria start producing acid, they quickly clear the field of competitors so that they can continue to reproduce and to generate yet more acid.

So while the single cell sees acid production as having mainly to do with energy production, from the perspective of the population it also serves the purpose of self-defense, and confers such an evolutionary advantage that it would be unfair to call it just an accidental byproduct of metabolism.

The fate of proteins

Like humans, bacteria and yeast not only need to eat carbohydrates to get energy; they also need to consume proteins in order to build new cells. And as with sugars, microbes generally do not consume proteins whole, but need them broken down into their building blocks (amino acids).

About 10 per cent of wheat flour is composed of the long protein chains glutenins and gliadins. To the wheat grain, they are a way of storing protein for the future baby plant; in the bread dough, they interact to form the elastic gluten matrix that traps gas and enables bread to rise. Lactic acid bacteria possess proteases – enzymes to break down proteins into their constituent amino acids (Gerez et al. 2006). This means that as microbes do their job mining amino acids from the dough they are in fact gradually tearing down the walls around them bit by bit. And their activity is strikingly evident in the changes in the texture (rheological properties) of the dough after fermentation: sourdoughs are measurably softer than doughs fermented only with yeast (Martinez-Anaya 2003). To the baker or bread consumer, these changes can be construed as either positive or negative, depending on the desired texture; to the micro-organism, the main benefit is nutritional.

Studies investigating the role of sourdough in bread dough rheology have revealed that, in fact, bacterial enzymes are not responsible for most of the protein breakdown that occurs during sourdough fermentation (Theile et al. 2004). But sourdough bacteria are still ultimately responsible for protein breakdown in another, indirect way: once again, it is a function of their acid-producing behavior.

183

Just as wheat grains contain enzymes to break down starch and release sugar upon germination, they also contain enzymes to break down gluten and release smaller peptides for the growing baby plant to use (Bottari et al. 1996). Importantly, they are at their most active at low pH (around 4.5) (Belozersky et al. 1989). Though rarely seen in conventional bread dough, this is just the pH that lactic acid bacteria create in sourdough.

So here is yet another way in which bacterially produced acids – ostensibly just a waste product from their method of getting energy – are in fact essential to their survival: without those acids, they would not be nearly so successful at getting the protein they need. And, of course, this particular evolutionary advantage – exceptional protein procurement through acid production – only plays out in the environment of the bread dough. In dairy or meat products, such acid-loving plant proteases are not present, so, unable to manipulate the enzymes of others, bacteria must make their own (Christensen et al. 1999).

As mentioned before, proteolysis in sourdough bread affects dough rheology; but human interest in this proteolysis goes beyond that of bread dough quality, to that of human health. The disease of greatest concern to potential bread-eaters is probably celiac disease, an autoimmune disorder in which the products of the digestion of gluten in the stomach cause an allergic reaction at the stomach lining and unpleasant symptoms, including abdominal discomfort and malabsorption (Sabatino and Corazza 2009). Today, there is still only one effective treatment: lifelong avoidance of all gluten-containing foods. However, interest has arisen in the proteolytic properties of sourdough bread. Preliminary investigations, such as those by Di Cagno and colleagues (2004), have found that some sourdough breads can be tolerated by celiac patients; others have found that culturing wheat flour with a combination of extracted fungal proteases and certain live sourdough bacteria can make the toxic peptides all but disappear, and that both bread and pasta of decent culinary quality can be made from treated flour (Rizzello et al. 2007, De Angelis et al. 2010). Further investigations are necessary, however, to bring the process to commercial viability.

Making flavor

There is no end to the list of important functions that dough acidification plays in sourdough bread. Not the least, of course, is the sour flavor from which sourdough gets its name. This flavor is also dependent on the environment the bacteria live in: for instance, a higher concentration of acetic relative to lactic acid provides a sharper flavor, and, as explained above, bacteria produce more acetic acid when provided with more oxygen.

Stepping away from the acid question temporarily, another remarkable talent of sourdough micro-organisms is the production of many other complex flavor compounds; see table 2 for a brief list of some of the compounds and their associated flavors. Most of these molecules are simply 'secondary metabolites' – byproducts of

	Compound	Flavor	Produced by bacteria or yeast
alcohols	ethanol	alcoholic	either
	n-propranol	fusel-like, burning	either
	n-pentanol (amyl alcohol)	fusel-like, burning	yeast
	n-hexanol	alcoholic	either
carbonyls	acetaldehyde	pungent	yeast
	propionic acid	rancid	either
	n-butyric acid	rancid butter	either
	i-butyric acid	sweaty	either
	n-valeric acid	rancid butter	either
	hexanoic acid	unpleasant, copra-like	yeast
	acetone	aromatic, sweet	either
	methylpropanal	malty	yeast
	2-methyl-1-butanal	malty	yeast
	3-methyl butanal	malty	yeast
	2,3-butanedione (diacetyl)	butter	yeast
	3-hydroxy-2-butanone (acetoin)	butter	only both
	n-hexanal	fruity	either
	trans-2-heptanal	green, fatty	either
	methional	malty	yeast
esters	ethyl acetate	ether, pineapple	either
	2-acetyl-1-pyrroline	roasty	yeast
	i-amyl acetate	fruity	yeast
	phenethyl acetate	fruity	yeast
	2,3-methylbutyl acetate	apple peel, banana	yeast
	n-hexyl acetate	pear, bittersweet	only both
	ethyl *n*-propanoate	rum, pineapple	only both
	ethyl *n*-hexanoate	pineapple, banana	either

185

Table 2. Flavoring compounds detected in sourdoughs. Compounds produced by yeast; either yeast or bacteria; or only in the presence of both. Data from Maloney and Foy (2003).

sundry metabolic activities, especially the processing of amino acids (Maloney and Foy 2003). Many of these flavoring compounds remain in the final bread; in addition, the baking process contributes greater flavor to the crust through Maillard reactions – the heat-induced combinations of sugars and the amino acids released by the bacterially mediated proteolysis described above (McGee 2004).

In general, the greater the microbial diversity in a sourdough, the more different processes that can occur, and therefore the more complex the flavor profile (De Vuyst et al. 2002). As table 2 shows, some flavor compounds are detected only in doughs inhabited by both yeast and bacteria. In addition, longer fermentation times allow for microbes to produce more secondary metabolites. These are both reasons that conventional bread, made with only *S. cerevisae* and short fermentation times, has a simpler flavor profile than traditional sourdough breads.

Fighting spoilage

That sourdough bread spoils more slowly than conventional bread has long been an accepted fact. Of course, there is significant interest in the mechanisms behind sourdough keeping-properties, and in the possibility of harnessing those mechanisms to improve any bread even without the full sourdough process. The main culprits of bread spoilage targeted by scientific study are the *Bacillus* species, several of which are blamed with causing 'ropiness' in baked bread: 'unpleasant fruity odor, followed by enzymatic degradation of the crumb that becomes soft and sticky because of the production of extracellular slimy polysaccharides' (Pepe et al. 2003).

We have already discussed the self-defense strategies of sourdough bacteria that allow them to dominate the living bread dough community; the inhibition of *Bacillus* invasion in baked bread, after the native lactic acid bacteria have been cooked to death, is yet another issue. However, studies indicate that the two main weapons of sourdough bacteria self-defense do live on through the baking process and are likely the cause for the bread's keeping properties. These weapons are acidity and antibiotic compounds. The mechanism of acidity production is the same that has been discussed previously. In addition, many lactic acid bacteria, especially *L. plantarum, L. bavaricus,*and *L. curvatus,* have been found to be capable of inhibiting *Bacillus* growth by the production of antibiotic compounds that they excrete – small, protein-based molecules called bacteriocins. Many of these bacteriocins are heat-resistant and thus probably survive baking (Corsetti et al. 2004, De Vuyst and Leroy 2007, Lavermicocca et al. 2000).

The choice of conventional yeast-bread over sourdough for flavor or ease of production requires a compromise in keeping qualities. Chemical preservatives are one solution; however, growing consumer demand for 'all-natural' foods has prompted greater interest in the use of compounds derived from sourdough bacteria, and the possibility of isolating the compounds for use even in bread fermented without lactic acid bacteria. Although many potential anti-rope bacteriocins have been identified in the laboratory, only a few have been proven to work in bread. Among these is nisin, produced by *Lactococcus lactis* (common in dairy products), which kills other bacteria by poking holes in their cell membranes (Lubelski 2008). The commercial success of nisin raises hopes for future developments with other bacteriocins.

The search for novel biological anti-spoilage agents among sourdough microbes is not unlike the search for biological pesticides among soil-associated bacteria that produced *Bacillus thuringiensis* as an extremely popular insecticide, or even the search among rainforest plants for the next million-dollar pharmaceutical drug. Sourdough microbiota are an equally valuable repository of genetic and biochemical diversity, and the remarkable properties of the bread they produce may be interpreted as a sensual reminder of the value of biodiversity in the food we eat. Sourdough microbes and humans have led a symbiotic existence for millenia, with humans have creating an environment in which the micro-organisms may thrive, and micro-organisms working to transform their living environment into bread rich in flavor, toothsome in texture, free of pathogens, and slow to spoil. It is only natural that interest in traditional sourdough baking is re-emerging in conjunction with interest in traditional forms of sustainable agriculture and the resurrection of heirloom crops and animals; sourdough micro-organisms are equally important teammates in food production.

Bibliography

Belozersky, M. A., Sarbakanova, S.T., and Dunaevsky, Y.A. 'Aspartic proteinase from wheat seeds: isolation, properties and action on gliadin', *Planta* 1989, 177, 321–326.

Bottari, A., Capocchi, A., Fontanini, D., and Galleschi, L. 'Major proteinase hydrolysing gliadin during wheat germination', *Phytochemistry* 43, 1996, 39–44.

Christensen, J. E., Dudley, E.G., Pederson, J.A., and Steele, J.L. 'Peptidases and amino acid catabolism in lactic acid bacteria', *Antonie van Leeuwenhoek* 76, 1999, 217–246.

Corsetti, A., Settanni, L. and Van Sinderen, D. 'Characterization of bacteriocin-like inhibitory substances (BLIS) from sourdough lactic acid bacteria and evaluation of their *in vitro* and i*n situ activity*', *Journal of Applied Microbiology* 96, 2004, 521–534.

De Angelis, M., Cassone, A., Rizzello, C.G., and others. 'Mechanism of Degradation of Immunogenic Gluten Epitopes from Triticum turgidum L. var. durum by Sourdough Lactobacilli and Fungal Proteases', *Applied and Environmental Microbiology* 76, 2010, 508–518.

De Vuyst, L. and Leroy, F. 'Bacteriocins from Lactic Acid Bacteria: Production, Purification, and Food Applications', *Journal of Molecular Microbiology and Biotechnology* 13, 2007, 194–199.

De Vuyst, L., Schrijvers, V., Paramithiotis, S., and others. 'The Biodiversity of Lactic Acid Bacteria in Greek Traditional Wheat Sourdoughs Is Reflected in Both Composition and Metabolite Formation', *Applied and Environmental Microbiology*, 68, 2002, 6059–6069.

Di Cagno, R., De Angelis, M., Auricchio, S., and others. 'Sourdough Bread Made from Wheat and Nontoxic Flours and Started with Selected Lactobacilli Is Tolerated in Celiac Sprue Patients', *Applied and Environmental Microbiology* 70, 2004, 1088–1096.

Di Sabatino, A., and Corazzal, G.R. 'Coeliac disease', *The Lancet* 373, 2009, 1480–1493.

Gerez, C.L., Rollan, G.C., and Valdez, G.F. 'Gluten breakdown by lactobacilli and pediococci strains isolated from sourdough', *Letters in Applied Microbiology* 42, 2006, 459–464.

Kandler, O. 'Carbohydrate metabolism in lactic acid bacteria', *Antonie van Leeuwenhoek* 49, 1983, 209–224.

Lavermicocca, P., Valerio, F., Evidente, A., and others. 'Purification and Characterization of Novel Antifungal Compounds from the Sourdough Lactobacillus plantarum Strain 21B', *Applied Environmental Microbiology*, 66, 2000, 4084–4090.

Lubelski, J., R. Rink, R. Khusainov, and others. 'Biosynthesis, immunity, regulation, mode of action and engineering of the model lantibiotic nisin', *Cellular and Molecular Life Sciences* 65, 2008, 455–476.

Maloney, D. H., and Foy, J.J. 'Yeast Fermentations', in *Handbook of Dough Fermentations*. New York, NY: Marcel Dekker, Inc., 2003, pp. 43–62.

Martinez-Anaya, M. A. 'Associations and interactions of Micro-organisms in Dough Fermentations: Effects on Dough and Bread Characteristics', in *Handbook of Dough Fermentations*. New York, NY: Marcel Dekker, Inc., 2003, pp. 63–95.

McGee, Harold. *On Food and Cooking: the Science and Lore of the Kitchen*. New York, NY: Scribner, 2004.

Neubauer, H., Glaasker, E., Hammes, and others. 'Mechanism of maltose uptake and glucose excretion in Lactobacillus sanfrancisco.', *Journal of Bacteriology* 176, 1994, 3007–3012.

Ng, H. 'Factors Affecting Organic Acid Production by Sourdough (San Francisco) Bacteria', *Applied and Environmental Microbiology* 23, 1972, 1153–1159.

Pepe, O., Blaiotta, G., Moschetti, G., and others. 'Rope-Producing Strains of Bacillus spp. from Wheat Bread and Strategy for Their Control by Lactic Acid Bacteria', *Applied and Environmental Microbiology* 69, 2003, 2321–2329.

Pollan, M. *The Botany of Desire: A Plant's Eye View of the World*. New York, NY: Random House, 2001.

Rizzello, C.G., De Angelis, M., Di Cagno, R., and others. 'Highly Efficient Gluten Degradation by Lactobacilli and Fungal Proteases during Food Processing: New Perspectives for Celiac Disease', *Applied and Environmental Microbiology* 73, 2007, 4499–4507.

Scheirlinck, I., Van der Meulen, R., Van Schoor, A., and others. 'Influence of Geographical Origin and Flour Type on Diversity of Lactic Acid Bacteria in Traditional Belgian Sourdoughs', *Applied and Environmental Microbiology* 73, 2007, 6262–6269.

——. 'Taxonomic Structure and Stability of the Bacterial Community in Belgian Sourdough Ecosystems as Assessed by Culture and Population Fingerprinting', *Applied and Environmental Microbiology* 74, 2008, 2414–2423.

Siragusa, S., Di Cagno, R., Ercolini, D., and others. 'Taxonomic Structure and Monitoring of the Dominant Lactic Acid Bacteria Population during Wheat Flour Sourdough Type I Propagation by using Lactobacillus sanfranciscensis Starters', *Applied and Environmental Microbiology* 75, 2009, 1099–1109.

Stolz, P. 'Biological Fundamentals of Yeast and Lactobacilli Fermentation in Bread Dough', in *Handbook of Dough Fermentations*. New York, NY: Marcel Dekker, Inc., 2003, pp. 23–42.

Stolz, P., Böcker, G., Vogel, R.F., and Hammes, W.P. 'Utilisation of maltose and glucose by lactobacilli isolated from sourdough', *FEMS Microbiology Letters* 109, 2003, 237–242.

Thiele, C., Grassl, S., and Ganzle, M. 'Gluten Hydrolysis and Depolymerization during Sourdough Fermentation', *Journal of Agricultural and Food Chemistry* 52, 2004, 1307–1314.

Taiz, Lincoln, and Eduardo Zeiger. *Plant Physiology*. Sunderland, MA: Sinauer Associates, 2002.

Wink, Debra. 'Lactic Acid Fermentation in Sourdough', *The Fresh Loaf*, 2009, <http://www.thefreshloaf.com/keyword/lactic-acid-fermentation> [accessed May 23, 2010].

Corned Beef: an Enigmatic Irish Dish

Máirtín Mac Con Iomaire and Pádraic Óg Gallagher

'I've been going to America for twenty years now, and I can't believe how many times I've had to emphasize that we don't just live on corned beef, potatoes and cabbage in Ireland'.[1]

Corned beef and cabbage, which is consumed in America in large quantities each Saint Patrick's Day (17 March), is considered by most Americans to be the ultimate Irish dish. However, corned beef and cabbage is seldom eaten in modern-day Ireland. It is widely reported[2] that Irish immigrants replaced their beloved bacon and cabbage with corned beef and cabbage when they arrived in America, drawing on the corned beef supplied by their neighbouring Jewish butchers, but not all commentators believe this simplistic explanation.[3] This paper will trace the origins and history of corned beef in Irish cuisine and chart how this dish came to represent Irish cuisine in America. The name corned beef originates in seventeenth-century England, derived from corns – or small crystals – of salt used to salt or cure the meat. The paper will discuss the anomaly that although corned beef was not widely eaten in Ireland, it was widely exported, becoming one of Ireland's leading food exports, mostly from the city of Cork. Irish corned beef provisioned the British navy for over two centuries and was also shipped to the colonies. There is evidence of a strong trade in Irish corned beef as a staple for African slaves in the French West Indies and in other French colonies. Irish corned beef also became a staple in Pacific islands visited by the British navy, where it is called keg. These Pacific Islanders later corned their own beef, but sailors labelled it 'salt junk.'

Kurlansky (2002, 125) notes that despite giving corned beef its name, the English did more harm to its good name than the Pacific Islanders, by canning it in South America. He notes that the Irish 'continued to make it well, and it has remained a festive dish there with cabbage for Christmas, Easter, and St Patrick's Day, the three leading holidays.' The entry on corned beef in *Larousse Gastronomique* actually states 'cured beef, of American origin, which can be sold in cans.' In more recent times, tinned corned beef, or bully beef, has been imported from former colonies to Ireland, most of which was eaten in sandwiches or salads. Davidson (2006) points out that much of modern canned corned beef came from the river port of Fray Bentos in Uruguay where Justus von Liebig had set up a processing plant in 1866 to produce meat extract that was later known as Oxo. In 1924, the Fray Bentos firm passed into British hands and by the height of World War Two, in 1943, over 16 million cans were exported from this town that called itself 'the kitchen of the world'. Cattle remain important to the economic welfare of Ireland. Over 460,000 tonnes of beef (excluding offal) were exported from Ireland in 2009, more than half of that amount going to the UK market, with France, Italy and the Netherlands as the next largest importers of Irish beef.[4] However, it is the freshly salted joints of Irish beef – principally brisket or tail end (silverside or topside) – that is the main focus of this paper.

Early beginnings

Cattle have been central to the Irish way of life for centuries, and have fed on the rich green grass that grows so abundantly in Ireland's damp, temperate climate. Scientists have radio carbon-dated a cow bone found in an archaeological dig in County Kerry to 4,500 BC. This places the Irish as early adapters to cow's milk consumption, considering that the estimated dates given for humans' first consumption of cow's milk in the Near East is 5,000–7,000 BC, when they developed the enzyme needed to digest it.[5] The Irish obsession with cattle is evident in Irish place-names. *Bó* and *tarbh* are the words in the Irish language for cow and bull respectively. The word *bóthar* is Irish for road and a road was defined in width by the length and breadth of a cow. The word *buachail* which means boy is derived from *bua* (cow) and *chaill* (attendant), literally meaning cowboy or herdsman. Bovine Irish place-names include Ardboe, Drumbo, Lough Bo, Drumshambo, Inishbofin, Clontarf and also the river Boyne (from *Bóinne*, Boann, or Bovinda – the goddess of the white cow). The Irish language name for Westport in County Mayo is *Cathair na Mart* – literally 'the city of the beef'.

190

Cattle were a measure of wealth in Gaelic Ireland. This led to many famous cattle raids in Irish mythology, but also, notes Sexton (1998, 27), militated against the consumption of beef during the early medieval period (AD 500–1200). Cattle raids, according to Mahon (1998, 3) were 'less a method of warfare than a sortie into another tribe's territory in which a young man might test his manhood.' They were also part of the ceremonial inauguration of a prince or chieftain and are mentioned no less than 402 times in the *Annals of Ulster*. The most famous Irish cattle raid is *Táin Bó Cuailnge* (The Cattle Raid of Cooley) where Queen Meadhbh of Connacht attacked the men of Ulster in search of a prized Brown Bull of Cooley, so that her wealth would be more than that of her husband. This legendary epic is a part of *Lebor na hUidre*, the book of the Dun Cow, the oldest extant Irish manuscript, dating from the eleventh century. Legend has it that the vellum in this book came from the hide of St Ciaran of Clonmacnoise's pet cow, hence the name. Cattle were used in payment or in barter and are mentioned as such in the seventh- and eighth-century Brehon Laws, where beef eating is associated mainly with the aristocratic classes.

Kelly (2000, 336, 341) points out that salted beef (*bósall*) is rarely mentioned in ancient texts, which is not surprising since salting an entire bullock would have required a large amount of salt. He also notes that there is no mention of salt mines or salt pans in pre-Norman texts and suggests that salt was produced from 'sea ash', the result of burning seaweed. The ancient text *Críth Gablach* refers to the use of sea ash for salting joints of meat, and the twelfth-century poem *Aislinge Meic Con Glinne* provides evidence that beef was salted as well as bacon (Jackson, 1990):

> Wheatlet, son of Milklet,
> Son of juicy Bacon,
> Is mine own name.
> Honeyed Butter-roll
> Is the man's name
> That bears my bag.
> Haunch of Mutton
> Is my dog's name,
> Of lovely leaps.
> Lard, my wife,
> Sweetly smiles
> Across the kale-top.
> Cheese-curds, my daughter,
> Goes round the spit,
> Fair is her fame.
> Corned Beef, my son,
> Whose mantle shines
> Over a big tail.

Kurlansky (2002,124) discusses the trade in salt between Ireland and France from the Middle Ages, which would explain how the growth of large-scale corned beef and bacon industries became possible.[6] The Gaelic reverence for cattle would explain why so little beef was eaten in the Irish diet, which centred on white meats (milk, butter and dairy produce) which did not require the death of the animal. Fynes Moryson, the English travel writer, for example, writing in the early seventeenth century, states:

> They feede most on Whitemeates, and esteeme for a great daintie sower curds, vulgarly called by them Bonaclabbe. And for this cause they watchfully keepe their Cowes, and fight for them as for religion and life; and when they are almost starved, yet they will not kill a Cow, except it bee old, and yield no Milke.
>
> (Moryson 1908, vol. 4, 200–201)

Lucas (1960) notes that the majority of herds were cows, suggesting that bull calves were killed at birth. Sexton (1998, 28) therefore proposes that there must have been a high consumption of veal throughout the calving season among the Gaelic farmers with substantial herds. Noting evidence from Irish legal texts, she also suggests that some herds of bullocks must have been kept for aristocratic tables. Ireland is a lush country where grass grows nearly all year round and is ideal for cattle production. Andrews (2010) cites a Tipperary farmer who suggested his field of grass was so fertile 'it would fatten a bicycle!' Mahon (1998, 7–8) notes evidence that beef was salted and buried in bog holes, a practice common for the preservation of butter. She also points out that corned beef was a festive dish.

The Cattle Acts and emergence of corned beef industry

In early-modern times, significant numbers of live cattle were exported to England. Between 24 June 1663 and 24 June 1664, some 76,754 oxen were exported from Ireland.[7] There was also a growing provisions trade in salt beef to the West Indies from the late 1650s with the growth of the tropical sugar economies. Intense lobbying by (northern) English cattle breeders led to the enactment by Parliament of the Cattle Acts of 1663 and 1667 prohibiting the export of cattle and cattle products to England. The first Cattle Acts placed a prohibitive duty on cattle exports to England between July and December. The 1667 Act led to an outright exclusion of exporting live animals to England from Ireland, which drastically lowered the price of beef in Ireland available for sale and export as salt or 'corned' beef (Cullen 1972, 13–18). Mandelblatt (2007, 26) notes that this change in prices was of great benefit to the incipient Irish provisions trade. Salt beef was central to this provisions trade, indeed Truxes (1988, 26–7) points out that between 1660 and 1688 Irish salted beef was the most important commodity traded from the British Isles. No other products carried from the English ports or from London matched the export volume of Irish corned beef.

192

Salt obviously played a major role in the production of corned beef and Ireland had a major advantage over both England and France because it enjoyed a much lower rate of salt tax, nearly one-tenth that of England. Ireland only imported the best dry high quality white salt from Portugal, Spain or the south-west of France. Salted provisions dominated Irish transatlantic trade right up to the American Revolution (Cullen 1972, 103; Truxes 1988, 147). Cork city developed a highly skilled and efficient provisions industry utilizing its envied skills in curing, packing and scrutiny of product that ensured consistency and high quality of product when it reached the West Indies. There were salt beef industries based in other port cities such as Dublin, Belfast and to a lesser extent Waterford, but by 1668 Cork's annual shipment of salt beef (16,960 barrels) represented half of Ireland's entire colonial beef exports (Mandelblatt 2007, 27). Cork beef also reached higher prices than that of the other Irish port cities, and remained the leading source of beef entering New York and Philadelphia, despite growing influence of Belfast merchants in trading with mainland America (Truxes 1988, 154).

Truxes (1988, 24) identifies three stages in Ireland's transatlantic trade between 1660 and 1731. The first phase 1660–88 was a time of massive colonial expansion in sugar monoculture in the West Indies. This industry was driven by a huge increase in slave trade from West Africa. Louis XIV's 1685 *Code Noir* mandated the food requirements of slaves working on French colonial sugar plantations. This edict decreed that each slave should be provisioned with 'two pounds of salt meat' (*deux livres de boeuf salé*), but there is debate as to how strictly it was enforced (Mandelblatt 2007, 28). The main consumers of Irish salt beef in the British West Indies were white planters and settlers with the slaves there provisioned on salt fish from Newfoundland. Ships bringing salt beef from Ireland to the Caribbean would then bring rum from the West Indies to Virginia or New York and return to Ireland laden with flax seed for the Irish linen industry.

The second phase identified (1688–1714) was a time of major turmoil in Ireland and of military campaigns in Europe. The struggle between James II and William III caused widespread destruction and confusion in the country. The Anglo-French war of 1689–97 brought about severe restrictions on overseas trade. Special licences were issued for West Indies export but French privateers played havoc with this trade up to the mid-1690s. A major outbreak of distemper in 1688 depleted Irish livestock herds and it took nearly eight years to sufficiently rebuild herds to re-enter the West Indian market. Irish salt beef, however, regained its pre-war level within two years. The final phase, according to Truxes, was from 1714–31. The period after the Treaty of Utrecht saw a surge in transatlantic commerce, but it was short-lived as Ireland fell into its most serious economic depression of the eighteenth century. Nevertheless transatlantic trade increased by more than 40 per cent on average in the four years ending 1731, over the average of the four years ending 1714 (Truxes 1988, 24).

So important was the trade in cheap Irish salt beef that both the English and French Parliaments enacted laws specifically around it. The French wrote a decree into law allowing its ships bound for the colonies to load beef in Irish ports, and also to allow Irish beef be landed, stored and re-shipped from the ports of La Rochelle, Nantes and Bordeaux without incurring taxes. Anglo-Irish landlords saw exports to France, despite the fact that England and France were at war, as a means of profiting from the Cattle Acts (Mandelblatt 2007, 26). English expansion in the colonies also demanded Irish beef and during the 1760s and 1770s, 65–75 per cent of all Irish beef was purchased by the English and French colonies combined (Cullen 1972, 53–55). During the eighteenth century, wars played a significant role in the growth of exports of Irish beef. Irish salted beef was in demand by the Navy for two reasons, firstly its longevity at sea and secondly its competitive price.

Different grades of salt beef and their markets

The slaughter of cattle in August marked the beginning of the salt-beef season which ended generally in October (Mandelblatt 2007, 27). The three basic grades of salt beef were determined by the weight of the animal. 'Small beef' was the lowest grade and came from underweight animals usually slaughtered first. Next came 'cargo beef' or common mess beef and the top grade 'best mess beef' was produced from the heaviest cattle and generally slaughtered towards the end of the season. 'The beef was cut into eight pound pieces, graded, salted and packed into casks, the lower grades receiving more of the unpopular cuts such as necks and shanks. The casks were left stand for four or five days and then sealed by a cooper' (Mandelblatt 2007, 27; Truxes 1988, 151–2). Lord Chief Baron Edward Willes described these grades in one of his letters (*c.* 1757–1762) to the Earl of Warwick,[8]

> I had the curiosity to enquire how they dispose of all parts of the ox slaughtered for exportation, and was informed, they had two methods of doing it. If it was for merchants service, the whole beef, neck as well as other coarse pieces were barrel'd up together, but if it for the English Navy, the necks and coarser pieces were not put into the barrel. They have a third sort which they call French beef, that is old cows and beeves that but half fat, which in time of peace they sell to the French. This sort of beef turns black and flabby, and almost to a jelly (no wonder sailors fed with this meat can't face our honest English Tars, who have so much better and more substantial food in their bellies).

By 1800, England had become the main market for salted beef and pork products. This was in some way due to the provisioning of the Royal Navy but also the West Indian market was, since the 1780s, procuring more of its provisions from north America (Cullen 1972, 103). The decline continued and by 1815 exports of beef were a quarter of their 1770 peak. By the 1840s, pork and beef exports outside the British Isles were less than three per cent of their 1780 levels. From the mid-nineteenth century, one of Ireland's leading exports was its people.

Immigration

The first great wave of Irish immigration to America occurred in the 1600s during the new country's colonization, with the arrival of 100,000 predominantly young Catholic men. Moloney (2002, 6) points out that there was no word in the Irish language for willingly departing the homeland, and that up to the early twentieth century the only term for leaving was *deoraí* – exile. A second wave of immigrants known as the 'Scotch-Irish' settled from Pennsylvania to Georgia between 1710 and the early 1900s. They were descendants of Protestant farmers from England and the lowlands of Scotland who had only been in Ireland for a few generations. The largest wave of immigration to America was in the years of, and shortly after, the Great Famine (1845–1849) when over a million Irish left Ireland for America, tens of thousands of whom died on board the 'coffin ships' that transported them. Moloney (2002, 14) notes that these were the first ethnic immigrant group in the United States 'to carve their future largely from the urban industrial landscape.' These immigrants arrived in America to witness large-scale anti-Irish bigotry, but within a few generations they managed to carve out success at all levels of American politics. Businessmen and fraternal Irish-American organizations such as the Ancient Order of Hibernians helped fledgling politicos rise within the wing of the Democratic Party in places such as Tammany Hall. The first St Patrick's Day Parade in New York City was held by Irish soldiers in the British Army in 1762,[9] but by the mid-nineteenth century it became an event that was celebrated by an even more diverse crowd. Perhaps the proximity to St Patrick's Day influenced President Lincoln's consumption of corned beef, cabbage and parsley potatoes at his inauguration dinner (4 March 1861). Evidence in humorous songs from the early twentieth century links the Irish with other ethnic groups in America. Irish-Jewish connections appear in songs such as the 1910 *It's tough when Izzy Rosenstein Loves Genevieve Malone*, the 1911 *My Yiddish Colleen*, and the 1912 song by Jerome and Schwartz called *If it Wasn't for the Irish and the Jews*:

> Talk about a combination, hear my word and make a note
> On St Patrick's Day, Rosinsky pins a shamrock on his coat
> There's a sympathetic feeling between the Bloom's and MacAdoos,
> Why Tammany would surely fall
> There'd really be no Hall at all
> If it wasn't for the Irish and the Jews.

(Maloney 2002, 37)

Perhaps this inter-ethnic cross-co-operation might explain the Irish purchasing corned beef from Jewish butchers in American cities. The most likely reason for the popularity of corned beef over bacon, however, is the fact that corned beef, a luxury product at home, was available cheaply in America. Andrews (2010) suggests that bacon would have been equally available from German butchers in American cities as corned beef was from Jewish butchers. The traditional festive link between corned beef and St Patrick's Day would also help to embed it as an Irish dish in the American psyche.

Corned beef in modern Ireland

There are a number of terms (salt beef, pickled beef, hung beef, Pocoke beef) used to describe corned beef. There is also a variation of corned beef in which spices are added to the curing process to produce spiced beef, which was and still is particularly popular around the Christmas period. Some evidence is available from manuscripts in the National Library of Ireland. The O'Hara of Annaghmore Papers (MS 36,375/1/2/3), dated 1817, has a reference to Christmas Beef which is probably both salted and spiced. Both corned beef and spiced beef are ideal twin-purpose meats that can be eaten hot with dinner or served cold as an impromptu dish when guests visit during the festive period, or for picnics. In the Headfort Papers (MS 25,370) dated 1953, both salt beef and corned beef are mentioned for a 'picnic lunch going to the Navan Show for 8 ... sandwiches, lamb, corn beef, mustard, cold egg, whole tomato, lettuce, fruit cheese, biscuits, coffee.'[10] There seems to be regional and also socio-economic variations concerning the consumption of corned beef. Daniel Corkery notes in his work *The Hidden Ireland* that it was commonplace in large aristocratic households, during the eighteenth century, to salt their own beef in large stone troughs after slaughter for later consumption.[11] He notes that the Martin family would kill a bullock once a month. Cullen (1981) points out that the bulk of the beef consumed by the population at this time was salted, with fresh beef as a rare and luxurious treat for all classes. Indeed, on 27 December 1829, Amhlaoibh Ó Súilleabháin notes in his diary that he feasted on slices of corned beef with white cabbage, spit-roasted goose with bread stuffing, leg of mutton with turnips, bacon and chickens, and a roast snipe washed down with some hot port and whiskey (de Bhaldraithe 1970, 61). On 19 October, the diarist ate '*mairtfheoil méithe agus caoirfheoil cumhra*' (succulent beef and fragrant mutton) with the parish priest in the house of Michael Hickey. He also noted that on 15 March 1831, he hung five joints of beef, six ox tongues and half a large pig. Was he preparing them for St Patrick's Day?

The butchery of larger animals has historically been more common in cities where there is a large population to consume it. Dave Lang,[12] development officer for the Associated Craft Butchers of Ireland, suggests that some pockets of the country such as Dublin and Cork are stronger for corned beef and that some pockets particularly in the northern counties have little or no knowledge of it. He recalls 40 years ago, as an apprentice butcher in Buckley's in Dublin's Moore Street, they would corn 56 tail ends a week. Meat was cut differently then. The tail end was cut straight across and included the topside and the silverside, which are now seam-butchered. Of all Irish cities, corned beef has had a long and distinctive regional association with Cork. Paul Murphy,[13] a fourth-generation butcher at P. Coughlan Family Butchers in Cork's English Market, sells over 300 lb of boneless corned beef, silverside and topside each week. He also sells corned brisket on and off the bone. He had stopped selling brisket corned beef on the bone with about four inches of fat on it, but started selling it again in recent years, as 'all the old people all ate it.' He remembers his grandfather slicing and eating this fat on bread after a few drinks and notes that he lived till he was 98 years old, 'no talk of cholesterol tablets!' Brisket is a cheaper cut than the tail end and also needs more cooking. Murphy notes that although he sells small amounts of spiced beef weekly, at Christmas he would sell 2000 lb of spiced beef over a ten-day period.

Margaret Byrne who grew up in Dublin in the 1930s and 1940s recalls eating both corned beef and bacon regularly with cabbage and potatoes but suggests that the consumption of corned beef began to decline when people started buying their meat in supermarkets rather than from their local butchers.[14] She noted that it was mostly silverside that was eaten and that she was often disappointed by how much the joint would shrink during the cooking process. Fergal Quinn, who opened the Superquinn chain of supermarkets with a store in Dundalk and in Finglas in 1960, pointed out that corned beef was a big seller when he first opened but lost market-share as the years passed.[15] Tony Byrne, a craft butcher in Rathgar, Dublin, noted that corned beef had been a 'once a week' dinner among many of his customers, but that although he still sold corned beef, bacon is far more popular nowadays. He attributes this to the fact that bacon is cheaper. Liam Mac Con Iomaire who grew up in West Galway in the 1930s and 1940s has no memory of eating corned beef, noting that bacon and either lamb or mutton were the main meats, along with poultry and fish, that they consumed.[16] Their cattle were sold at market rather than slaughtered at home. It was not until he came to Dublin and married that he began to eat corned beef regularly.

Corning the beef

Eliza Acton, in her *The People's Book of Modern Cookery* (34th edition, *c*. 1902) has a number of methods for salting and pickling beef in various ways including 'Hamburgh Pickle, Hung Beef, Collared Beef, and Spiced Beef'. What they all have in common is a combination of salt, saltpetre, sugar and various spices. McGee (1988, 103) notes that salt has been used for thousands of years to inhibit microbial growth, which was especially important in the years before refrigeration. He reiterates the English origin of the term corned beef coming from 'corns' or whole grains of salt and points out that, beginning in the sixteenth and seventeenth centuries, nitrites began to be added to the curing process in the form of a nitrate salt, saltpetre. Paul Murphy, previously mentioned, notes that they stopped using saltpetre in his family's business years ago, but recalls buying it in the chemist shop as a boy for the making of corned beef. He recalls that when two older boys went to buy the saltpetre one day, they were detained by the police on suspicion of making explosives! The saltpetre changed the pigment of the meat, so nowadays Murphy adds some colouring to his brine made from coarse salt because 'psychologically people want to see the bloom on the corned beef.' He advises his customers today that there is no need to soak his corned beef as it is not half as salty as it was in the past, when refrigeration was not as widespread.

197

Summary and conclusions

From ancient times in Ireland, cattle were highly prized as a sign of wealth, which militated against the consumption of beef during the early medieval period (AD 500–1200). Evidence exists in legal and other texts, however, that both fresh beef and salted beef were eaten in Ireland, particularly among the aristocracy and at festive occasions. The Elizabethan period witnessed the end of the traditional Gaelic way of life in most of Ireland and cattle became an economic commodity that was exported to the English markets. The growth of sugar plantations in the West Indies and the introduction of the Cattle Acts (1663, 1667) led to the setting up of commercial corned beef industries in Irish port cities, most significantly in the city of Cork, which prospered for nearly two centuries. Different grades of Irish corned beef provisioned the British Navy for centuries and were also shipped by the French to their colonies. Competition from mainland America in the late eighteenth century was one factor in the demise of the trans-Atlantic trade in Irish salt beef.

Irish salt beef was introduced by the British Navy to the Pacific Islands where it became known as 'keg' and began to be poorly copied and labelled 'salt junk' by the sailors. The setting up of beef processing plants in South America in the late nineteenth century led to the widespread introduction to England of canned 'bully beef'. When sold as corned beef, it damaged the name of the salted joints of beef that Cork and Ireland had been previously known for. This canned corned beef was widely distributed as pack-rations during World War Two, which led to its popularity and widespread assimilation into the food habits of various nations. The entry for corned beef in *Larousse Gastronomique* only mentions the canned American version and has no reference to the earlier Irish salt beef tradition. This paper identifies that corned beef has always been an aristocratic food in Ireland and particularly a festive dish eaten at Christmas, Easter and St Patrick's Day. It suggests that the most probable reason for the popularity of corned beef among the Irish Americans was not the lack of availability of bacon, as sometimes argued, but that corned beef was widely available at a reasonable price. Irish immigrants aspired to better themselves in America and part of this betterment was the consumption of foodstuff they might not have been able to afford at home. This along with the fact that corned beef has long been associated with St Patrick's Day has led to the widespread but erroneous view among many Americans that Irish cuisine consists almost exclusively of corned beef, cabbage and potatoes.

Notes

1. Darina Allen in her introduction to Colman Andrews (2010), *The Country Cooking of Ireland.*
2. Numerous websites and articles provide this simple explanation of why corned beef was so popular among the Irish Americans.
3. See Andrews (2010).
4. Information from Bord Bia (Irish Food Marketing Board).
5. Murphy, K. (2010) 'Land of Milk not Money', *The Irish Times* (13 March) pp. 12–13.
6. Development of the bacon industry in Ireland has been previously discussed in the 2002 Oxford Symposium paper 'The Pig in Irish Cuisine past and present'.
7. Thanks to Tara Kellaghan for this reference from the correspondence of the 1st Duke of Ormonde, MS. Carte 68 from the Bodleian Library, Oxford.
8. Cited in Sexton (1998, 30).
9. www.history.com/topics/st-patricks-day.
10. Many thanks to Dorothy Cashman for this reference.
11. Cited in Cowan and Sexton (1997, 29).
12. Telephone correspondence 27 April 2010.
13. Telephone correspondence 27 April 2010.
14. Personal correspondence 21 April 2010.
15. Personal correspondence with Senator Fergal Quinn 26 April 2010.
16. Personal correspondence 21 April 2010.

Bibliography

Andrews, C. *The Country Cooking of Ireland.* San Francisco: Chronicle Books, 2010.

Cowan, C. and R. Sexton *Ireland's Traditional Foods.* Dublin: Teagasc, 1997.

Cullen, L. M. *An Economic History of Ireland since 1660.* London: Batsford, 1972.

——. *The Emergence of Modern Ireland 1600–1900.* London: Batsford Academic, 1981.

Davidson, A. *The Oxford Companion to Food.* 2nd edn, New York: Oxford University Press, 2006.

De Bhaldraithe, T. *Cín Lae Amhlaoibh.* Baile Átha Cliath: An Clóchomhar, 1970.

Jackson, K. H. (ed.) *Aislinge Meic Con Glinne.* Dublin: Dublin Institute for Advanced Studies, 1990.

Kelly, F. *Early Irish Farming.* Dublin: Dublin Institute for Advanced Studies, 2000.

Kurlansky, M. *Salt: a world history.* London: Jonathan Cape, 2002.

Lucas, A. T. 'Irish food Before the Potato', *Gwerin*, III (2), 1960, pp. 8–43.

Mahon, B. *Land of Milk and Honey.* Cork: Mercier Press, 1998.

Mandelblatt, B. 'A Transatlantic Commodity: Irish Salt Beef in the French Atlantic World', *History Workshop Journal*, 63, 2007, pp. 18–47.

McGee, H. *On Food and Cooking.* London: Unwin Hyman, 1987.

Moloney, M. *Far from the Shamrock Shore.* Cork: The Collins Press, 2002.

Moryson, F. *An Itinerary.* Glasgow: MacLehose, 1908.

Sexton, R. *A Little History of Irish Food.* Dublin: Gill & Macmillan, 1998.

Truxes, T. M. *Irish-American Trade 1660–1783.* Cambridge: Cambridge University Press, 1988.

199

Shad Planking: the Strangely American Story of a Smoked Fish

Mark McWilliams

The biggest event on the Virginia political calendar involves a lot of smoke. Not tobacco smoke, as one might expect from the home of Philip Morris, maker of Marlboros, or even barbecue smoke, although that comes closer to the mark. The event is the annual Shad Planking, and the smoke is cooking hundreds of shad nailed to hardwood planks, to be served alongside fried fish, fried shad roe, coleslaw, corn muffins, sweet pickles, iced tea, and beer. In this paper, I will trace the history of shad planking, consider its importance in early American culture, and briefly discuss the shad's odd role in modern Virginia politics.

The Shad Planking began in the 1930s as a celebration of the shad run, the annual migration of the ocean fish up the freshwater rivers of their birth. The event marked the beginning of the fishing season, but soon came to mark the beginning of the political season as well. Candidates for local and state office turned up to gather support from politically connected attendees and regular voters alike. Long restricted to white men, the gathering changed in 1977 with the attendance of L. Douglass Wilder, who would become the state's first black governor, and Megan Rosenfeld, a female journalist. While attendance has since become far more diverse, the gathering remains overwhelmingly partisan, with diners wearing all manner of campaign regalia and the surrounding countryside covered in political signs. (Indeed, 'shad planking' has become regional slang for blanketing areas with political advertisements.) Though both Republicans and Democrats attend, the event has long been a conservative stronghold.

But the shad planking preserves food customs as well as political ones. Planking goes back to Native American techniques for preserving fish. These Native traditions are perhaps best known in the American north-west, where tribes preserved large catches of the annual salmon runs. But they were arguably as important in the east to preserve the similarly large catches of shad for consumption during the rest of the year. While we should be suspicious of what Anne Mendelson calls 'the myth of exchange,' many sources claim that planking developed from Native techniques for smoking and drying shad and other fish.[1] For example, William Penn, the founder of Pennsylvania, negotiated with the Lenape over the Schuylkill (a major shad fishing ground) in the 1680s, and later noted that shad are 'excellent Pickled or Smoked.'[2] Here Penn refers both to pickling, a European preservation method, and smoking, a Native method.

(There is another story for the origin of planking that removes the Native influence, though it stretches belief in any number of ways. In 1889, the Colony of the Schuylkill, a Pennsylvania fishing club dating to the 1730s, published a club history claiming that planking was created in the 1760s by an apprentice caterer, who nailed a shad to an 'old oaken rudder,' marinated it, and roasted it before a fire.)[3]

Like the salmon, the shad is an ocean-dwelling fish that returns to its native freshwater rivers to spawn. Early reports by Europeans claimed that the spring shad runs filled eastern American rivers 'thick enough to walk across.' At that time, the shad runs 'numbered in the tens of millions, featuring so many fish that the rivers were described as "black" or "boiling."' 'Boiling' seems accurate, given that the 'the fish are propelled,' writes Robert H. Boyle in his natural history *The Hudson River,* by '"ancestral fury."' The shad itself is an impressive fish: the largest herring in the continent, the silver-colored shad can reach almost a meter long and weigh over five kilograms. In early spring, the shad gather off the mouths of their native rivers, waiting for their bodies to adjust until the brackish water reaches the right temperature. Of course, other parts of nature are also waiting for this change: thus fishermen can time the shad run, watching 'the banks for the yellow forsythia and white-budded shadbush that blossom when the water temperature rises a few degrees above [10°C], luring shad from the Atlantic.' In Massachusetts, Henry David Thoreau explains, 'The shad make their appearance early in May, at the same time with the blossoms of the pyrus, one of the most conspicuous early flowers, which is for this reason called the shad-blossom. An insect called the shad-fly also appears at the same time, covering the houses and fences. We are told that "their greatest run is when the apple-trees are in full blossom. The old shad return in August; the young, three or four inches long, in September. These are very fond of flies."'[4]

The fish that come up the rivers are notoriously bony – shad have 769 bones, by one count, 'most of which are small 'Y' shaped bones which are found where most fish fillets would be bone-free.' According to Jim Cummins, these bones were the defining feature of the fish to the Native Americans: '"Tatamaho" was the Algonquin name for the American shad. According to legend, an unhappy porcupine asked the Great Spirit to change it into another form. The Great Spirit's wisdom was to turn the porcupine inside out as a fish (the shad) [....] Tatamaho roughly translates to "inside-out porcupine."'[5]

Despite this boniness, the shad run soon became as important for the English settlers as it had been for the Natives they displaced. Though relatively few know of the shad now, earlier Americans were well aware of their history. Noting that 'Salmon, Shad, and Alewives were formerly abundant here, and taken in weirs by the Indians, who taught this method to the whites,' Thoreau reminds us that shad are mentioned in Edward Johnson's *Wonder-Working Providence,* which covers the 1630s and 1640s. The Concord River, Johnson notes, 'streames with Fish, it being a branch of that large River of Merrimeck. Allwifes and Shad in their season come up to this Towne.'[6]

Thinking of the continent's early settlers, Thoreau finds it pleasant to be 'reminded of these shoals of migratory fishes, of salmon, shad, alewives, marsh-bankers, and

201

others, which penetrate up the innumerable rivers of our coast in the spring, even to the interior lakes, their scales gleaming in the sun; and again, of the fry which in still greater numbers wend their way downward to the sea.' Indeed, the abundance of shad and other fish proved useful in recruiting Englishmen to settle the New World: 'And is it not pretty sport,' wrote Captain John Smith, who was on this coast as early as 1614, 'to pull up twopence, sixpence, and twelvepence, as fast as you can haul and veer a line? [...] And what sport doth yield a more pleasing content, and less hurt or charge, than angling with a hook, and crossing the sweet air from isle to isle, over the silent streams of a calm sea.' The experiences of the early European settlers supported Smith's boast. Fishing in the Potomac in 1612, for example, William Strachey reported catching 'Shad, a great store, of a yard long and for sweetness and fatness a reasonable food fish.'[7]

But the ease of fishing for the abundant shad could count against it as well. Although 'sapidissima, the Latin species name of American shad, means "most delicious,"' shad 'was so plentiful in colonial times that the fish was considered "common" and wasn't eaten in polite circles.' Jim Trager recounts this period in the area around what would become New York City:

> [...] in the Hudson where once the fish was so abundant in early spring that 3000 were taken in a single haul. To the early Dutch of Nieuw Amsterdam, shad was known as elft, the eleven fish, because the first shad on the Hudson was traditionally caught on the 11th of March. Probably for the reason that it was so easy to come by, shad was disdained. It was never served to guests in the 1600s, and while plenty of delicious shad were caught and eaten, few people admitted they ate it, as if eating anything so common were a social gaffe.

Here Trager – and many other sources – seem to get a key fact wrong. The early Dutch settlers did call the shad *elft*, but for quite different reasons: according to tradition, the settlers knew ten types of fish, and thus named the shad 'eleven' when they encountered it, according to Adriaen van der Donck's account, published in 1655. (Similarly, 'striped bass was *twalft* [and] drum was *dertienen*.') Trager's mistake makes sense, however, given the tendency to date things by the shad run. For example, German settlers on the Susquehanna, one of the great shad rivers, referred to *Maifisch* or *Moifish*, or Mayfish. They were unconsciously following Native tradition: the Lenape word for March (which, of course, would not directly match the European calendar) means 'the month of the shad.' Trager is certainly right, however, about the vast numbers of shad. Indeed, shad were so abundant that throughout the 1600s – and to this day in some places – shad were used as fertilizer. Such attitudes are common whenever even a valued commodity is oversupplied, but interestingly this rejection of shad ended long before the supply dwindled.[8]

Indeed, until over-fishing dramatically depleted the annual yields, shad played an important part in the economic and culinary life of the eastern United States, and arguably contributed to American independence. The traditional (if now contested) account of Valley Forge holds that the starving American soldiers were saved by the spring shad run up the Schuylkill River. (Such events lend credence to the claim made by the title of John McPhee's book on the shad: *The Founding Fish*.) Some historians have even argued that George Washington selected the site in part because it was well situated to catch the shad he feared might prove crucial to his force's survival.[9]

Washington, after all, had been a commercial shad fisherman, trading his preserved shad throughout the eastern seaboard and the Caribbean. One of the aspects he most loved about Mount Vernon, as Washington noted in a letter to a friend, was its location 'on one of the finest rivers in the world—a river well stocked with various kinds of fish at all seasons of the year, and in the spring with shad, herring, bass, carp, sturgeon, etc., in great abundance. The borders of the estate are washed by more than ten miles of tide-water; several valuable fisheries appertain to it; the whole shore, in fact, is one entire fishery.' Touring Mount Vernon decades after Washington left the presidency, a visitor marked where 'every year many barrels marked with his brand, and filled with shad or herring, were shipped from this spot for foreign ports.'[10]

Washington's little-known career as a shad fisherman suggests the economic importance of the fish, but it was perhaps even more important to gourmands. In the spring of the new republic, 'congressmen sailed down the Potomac to enjoy great feasts of fresh-caught shad in the spring.' Thomas Jefferson – born in aptly named Shadwell, Virginia – carefully noted the annual shad run in his diary, even during his presidency, and found them 'as good a fish' as any he knew. Sarah Josepha Hale, the renowned cookbook author and editor of *Godey's Lady's Book*, agreed, calling shad 'a delicate and delicious fish.' And Daniel Webster, one of the leading antebellum politicians, was known to brag about his planked shad.[11]

Colonists had adopted the Native method of planking the fish in addition to using their own technique of salting down barrels of shad. While salting allowed the colonists to preserve greater quantities of fish, many expressed a preference for shad planked and smoked, a technique that remained popular throughout the nineteenth century, as this 1894 article from *The New England Kitchen Magazine* explains:

> THERE is still some contention among epicures, says the New York *Tribune*, as to which river produces the best shad, – the Connecticut or the Hudson ; but the consensus of opinion is generally in favor of the large, fine fish that is caught in the stream further down East.
>
> There is also a divided opinion as to which is the best method of cooking this fish. Planked shad has many adherents.
>
> This method is really a kind of broiling. The fish is flattened and kept in place, flesh side outward, on a hardwood plank, by two steel bars. It is sprinkled with a little butter and seasoning, and in this condition is exposed to the fire. The skin side of the fish is cooked by the heating of the plank which is placed

203

upright from the fire, and sometimes becomes even slightly charred, though this is evidence of the heat being too intense.

Exactly the same result may be obtained by placing the shad in a broiler and covering it with a dripping pan while it slowly broils, with the flesh side to the fire, for fifteen minutes.

Before cooking shad in any way it should be thoroughly trimmed, seasoned with a little salt, the merest dash of cayenne, if you wish cayenne at all, and rubbed with sweet oil; it should be left in this marinade for at least ten minutes on the ice. The sooner the fish is broiled after it is caught the better.[12]

Many nineteenth-century American cookbooks include recipes for planked shad, along with preparations for the fish broiled, baked, and fried. Though the shad is notoriously bony, cooks found its flavor worth extra effort. And of course the roe is particularly prized: shad roe's appearance at the local fish-counter remains a sign of spring throughout the mid-Atlantic.

Shad roe is only a fleeting sign of the season, though, perhaps due less to the short duration of the shad run than to declining yields due to damming, over-fishing, and pollution. Even in the mid-1800s, as fishermen still hauled in seemingly as much shad as they could want, some observers were already seeing leading indicators of a human impact on the shad. In 1849, Henry David Thoreau found the shad runs on the

Figure 1. This 1903 Macy's advertisement testifies to the popularity of shad planking, although the plank shown here is better suited to the oven-cooking recommended in some cookbooks. (Newspaper advertisement reproduced in "In and About New York Stores," The House Furnishing Review 23 (January 1903): 343.)

-Concord and Merrimack much diminished; he lamented that 'the canal at Billerica, and the factories at Lowell, put an end to their migrations hitherward; though it is thought that a few more enterprising shad may still occasionally be seen in this part of the river.' Thoreau recorded efforts to open the dams built for the factories during the time of the shad runs, but apparently such efforts failed: 'It is said, to account for the destruction of the fishery, that those who at that time represented the interests of the fishermen and the fishes, remembering between what dates they were accustomed to take the grown shad, stipulated, that the dams should be left open for that season only, and the fry, which go down a month later, were consequently stopped and destroyed by myriads. Others say that the fish-ways were not properly constructed.' Short of vigilantism ('who knows what may avail a crow-bar against that Billerica dam?'), Thoreau held little hope for a human solution ('Perchance, after a few thousands of years, [...] nature will have levelled the Billerica dam, and the Lowell factories, and the Grass-ground River run clear again'), and seemed just as concerned about the impact on local culture as about the fate of the fish themselves:

> One would like to know more of that race, now extinct, whose seines lie rotting in the garrets of their children, who openly professed the trade of fishermen, and even fed their townsmen creditably, not skulking through the meadows to a rainy afternoon sport. Dim visions we still get of miraculous draughts of fishes, and heaps uncountable by the river-side, from the tales of our seniors sent on horseback in their childhood from the neighboring towns, perched on saddle-bags, with instructions to get the one bag filled with shad, the other with alewives.

While damming certainly affected the shad run, the fishermen about whom Thoreau worried caused just as much trouble.[13]

Fishermen hauled in ever greater numbers of fish to meet the growing demand for American shad. Combined with damming, these increased yields radically affected the fishery. McPhee notes, 'Across the years 1825 to 1875, the spring migrations of American shad declined by eighty per cent.' The shad harvested were also decreasing in size, meaning that the fish were being caught at younger and younger ages as the stock of older, fully developed fish disappeared. As a result, a same barrel that 'held forty shad' in 1840, 'held a hundred shad' in 1870. Such significant declines triggered concern. The closing decades of the 1800s saw some efforts at protecting the shad and renewing the fishery through artificial insemination and other tactics. But without meaningful limits on fishing, such efforts were doomed as technology increased yields to unsustainable levels. By the opening decades of the 1900s, McPhee notes, 'Steam winches were hauling in the fish. On railway spurs, freight trains were waiting to carry them to market. Seines were two miles long, three miles long. Charles Hardy calls this "a final cashing in on a once renewable resource."' Yields plummeted up and down the eastern seaboard. On the Delaware River, for example, 1916 was the last year when the yield approach a half million metric tons of shad.[14]

What damming and over-fishing started, pollution threatened to finish. By the late 1960s, the Hudson was so polluted that shad were caught only for roe, with the fish itself sold for cat food. Pollution on the James River, especially from DDT, decimated the fish populations. Similar effects were seen in other rivers crucial to the shad run. In 1970, Jim Trager notes, 'our total shad catch is now a mere one-tenth of the [22,226 metric tons] landed between Maine and Florida in 1897, and the quality of the fish can hardly be compared.' Although the situation improved after the 1970s, when DDT was banned and the Environmental Protection Act passed, yields have again dropped disturbingly. On the James, for example, 'Currently, shad are at a near all-time low with only 6% of the numbers seen just 25 years ago. The cause of the recent decline in the James and other rivers is not yet known.'[15]

This decline, along with the other blows the shad population has suffered, has slowly reduced awareness of the fish. Outside of aficionados, few seem to have even heard of shad. And yet the aficionados remain. The shad may be far less common in contemporary cookbooks than in their nineteenth-century predecessors, but when shad appears, it is celebrated. In his 1961 *The New York Times Cook Book*, for example, Craig Claiborne exclaims, 'Shad and shad roe are among the noblest gifts of spring.' He does bemoan the notorious bones, but recommends professional help, even if it's hard to come by: 'There are only about a dozen professional shad boners in New York, and if the cost of boned shad seems somewhat elevated, it is justified.' Claiborne includes recipes for shad baked in cream, stuffed baked buck shad (stuffed with an onion, celery, breadcrumb mixture), baked shad with spinach stuffing, and two planked shad dishes: one for butterflied shad, basted with butter and cooked in a hot oven on an oiled oak or hickory board, and another stuffed with a shad roe dressing (roe, onion, parsley, and Parmesan). Both planked dishes are to be served with Duchesse Potatoes (mashed with butter, eggs, and nutmeg). And, as might be expected, Claiborne also includes six recipes for shad roe.[16]

Decades later, one of Claiborne's successors at the *Times* food section, Molly O'Neill, again took up the shad's cause. She no longer expresses any hope of finding a professional to bone the fish, but the trouble seems to be worth it: 'The female shad filets are fat, easy to fry, and have a delicate flavor and fine flake. The male filets are smaller, though tasty. The roe is easiest to handle if left to rest in ice water for fifteen minutes, then quickly (and carefully) blanched. Lightly dusted with seasoned flour and fried, it is as pungent as other forms of caviar, though gamier and smaller grained.' Perhaps even more than the flavor, O'Neill celebrates the shad's role in the rituals of spring for communities near shad rivers like the Hudson:

> Generally, by late April and early May, the shad run is steady enough to incite shad fries along the mid-Hudson. In the style of a church supper, fishermen and their wives fire up coals under halved oil drums in parking lots or flat grassy

spots near the river. They fry slabs of bacon and then, after dusting the shad roe in flour, fry it in the grease. In some Hudson River towns, shad fillets are fried, too, but more often the fillets are tacked to a pine plank upwind from a hardwood fire. A planked shad looks like a crucifixion. River men tend to eschew whatever shamanistic properties the nailed, splayed, and smoked filet might have, preferring to eat fried roe on sandwich buns topped with bacon. Everyone else lines up for plates heaped high with planked shad, fried roe, bacon, baked potatoes, and coleslaw. It is the Thanksgiving meal of spring along the Hudson.

Shad plankings like the one O'Neill describes here are a staple of spring festivals along the east coast. Along the Delaware, for example, Lambertville, New Jersey hosts the annual ShadFest to celebrate the area's arts community along with the shad run.[17]

But the nation's most famous shad planking is in southside Virginia. Hosted by the Wakefield Ruritan Club, the event long ago became a Virginia institution, both for the traditional food and for the increasing role the event came to play in state politics. According the club, the annual festival 'traces its origin to the early 1930s when a group of friends gathered together at Wrenn's Mill in Isle Of Wight County during the spring running of the shad in the James River. They planked the shad after the tradition of native Virginia Indians and they talked politics after the tradition of their fathers before them.'[18] The event is relatively small — turnout can be as high as four thousand people in a year with an important election — but the shad planking's impact in state politics is disproportionate. In the pine woods characteristic of the tidewater, candidacies are announced, alliances formed, and funding arranged. The attendees are a strange mix of local folks, political insiders, and the culinarily curious.

My allegiance is to that last group. This April I attended the Shad Planking, arranging (through the kindness of Robert Bains, the event's chairman) to shadow Carl Nyman, the man in charge of the planking itself. Told to show up around 5.30 a.m., I found a sizeable crew already at work. The shad planking team is divided into committees – including the Frying Committee, the Serving Committee, and the catch-all Labor Committee, among others – with each group in charge of a specific aspect of the event. When I arrived, the fire had been lit about half an hour earlier, and was already going strong. Often, as this year, the blaze is so high that a few of the rafters catch fire. Luckily, the local volunteer fire department is on hand to save the building from harm.

Approximately 34 meters long and two wide, the fire is built under a purpose-built pavilion. The main fire burns white oak that has aged a year; green logs of the same wood are added for smoke when the planks are turned toward the fire several hours into the cooking. Within an hour or so of lighting, the fire is so hot that rain immediately steams off the shed's metal roof. Over the course of the day, the fire will consume three to four cords of wood. The planks are made of white oak too, and are cleaned and culled the day before the planking. This year they used about 160 planks. In addition to losses as planks age and split, a few planks disappear each year, presumably taken as souvenirs.

207

The club orders a little over 900 kilograms of shad. This year, that worked out to about 320 fish. Until about ten years ago, the club bought whole fish and scaled them the day before the planking, a monumental – and monumentally messy – process. Since they used whole fish, the roe for the fried-roe stand came from the females. Now, due to concerns of local health inspectors according to club members, they buy dressed fish ready for planking and order roe separately. Whether due to tradition or resistance, the relevant committee is still called the 'Nailing and Scaling Committee.' The new process can lead to mishaps, since the professionals know less about preparing fish for planking than the club members. This year, for example, some fish were butterflied through the back instead of the traditional way through the belly. Far more importantly, the fish arrived without tails, presenting a real challenge to a group whose guiding mantra is 'nail the tail.' This mistake resulted in frantic efforts at the beginning of the nailing, as the nailers worked to figure out the best way to compensate. Traditionally, they put three nails through the tail and one through each wing; this year they found the best system was three nails per side. There's a culinary cost as well, since, as Carl pointed out, 'the tails make good eating. Eat like a potato chip.'

Beginning at 6 a.m., ten to twelve club members remove the dressed fish from ice and nail them to the planks, two fish per plank. The nails have to be driven carefully through the fish but not all the way into the plank since they'll be removed with pliers later in the cooking process. Another five or six members carry the planks to the fire, where they are carefully spaced along the flame by the cooking committee. The fish begin cooking facing away from the fire. Within fifteen minutes, the planks heat up enough to begin cooking the fish. By 7.15 or 7.30 a.m., the fish are stuck to the planks.

After the fish are placed by the fire, the workers sit down to breakfast prepared by the Kitchen Committee. The main room of the clubhouse quickly fills with men sitting down before plates of scrambled eggs, crisply-cooked bacon, hot biscuits, and peppery potatoes. Only when everyone is seated does it become obvious how the planking binds this rural community together. Men too old to help join others that seem too young to work with the volunteer fire company whose shirts they wear; black and white dine side by side, either oblivious to or defiant of the Confederate History Month supporters setting up outside, preparing to distribute craft beer and Confederate battle flags. I sit with two men, a CPA and a retired computer programmer, who grew up around Wakefield but now live in Maryland, and return every year for the planking. Over breakfast the men tell me about the event's history. The planking was private until the mid-1970s. Even the politicians who came appeared by invitation only, until the local delegate to the Virginia General Assembly asked if he could invite all the state representatives. The club took a vote, and the event began to open to the public. Not coincidentally, that change led directly to widening the event beyond its exclusively white male roots. Now the event still binds the local community together – indeed, perhaps more inclusively than before – but there seems to be more of a split between those working the planking and those attending it.

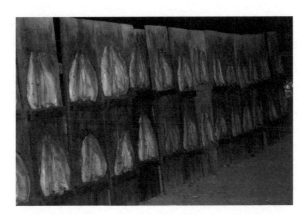

Figure 2. Planked shad facing away from the fire. (Author's photograph.)

Around 10.30 a.m., once the 'oil is running pretty good,' the fish get a heavy coating of table salt; much of the salt will run off during basting. The sauce is an almost black concoction of 'pepper, pepper, and some more pepper along with a little butter and some pepper.' The dark color comes from Worcestershire sauce. Prepared beforehand and cooked down in a barrel heated over a small fire, the sauce is mopped onto the salted fish around 11.30 a.m. and then the shad are turned toward the fire. Though each step is methodically managed, Carl maintains that 'you can't mess it up unless you try to hurry it.'

209

While the fish smoke for another couple of hours, exhibitors arrive to set up. In addition to the Confederate History Month supporters, there are four or five groups devoted to some version of 'Defending Your Right to Defend Yourself.' The Lieutenant Governor and the Governor, both Republicans, have teams working beer trucks; later the Lieutenant Governor will give out hot dogs as well. It's a small crowd this off-election year, and perhaps a more completely hard-right crowd than usual. To get a beer, you have to express your allegiance to the sponsor, and soon people are increasingly covered in political stickers that measure either their devotion or their consumption. Luckily the Jim Beam Bourbon tent requires no political commitments. A band – good old boys playing '80s music – sets up and starts to play, getting the crowd ready for the speeches that will come later.

But I'm here just for the food. There are a few others like me, including one older gentleman from South Carolina who had been eating shad all his life but never had one planked and figured the time had come. The rain that has been threatening all morning starts just as the fried-roe table opens, and soon tents are full of folks dipping the crispy pieces into the same sauce used to baste the fish. Carl had warned me that the roe gets overcooked when deep-fried, and he's right, but it still makes good eating.

And a fine appetizer: soon we move from the tents to the serving line. Each attendee gets a plate piled high with food, planked shad buried under fried fish. The weather has gotten worse as the food has gotten better: this is delicious. The coleslaw, beans, and pickles cut the richness of the fried fish. The shad itself is extraordinary: neither as smoky nor as spicy as I expected from the cooking process. Indeed, under the browned surface the fish was still delicate, almost sweet. And every bit as bony as advertised: tons of bones, several in every bite, making for messy eating. No one seemed to care, though, as the diners were all bowed over their own plates, setting politics aside for a few moments to share a fine and historic meal.

Notes

1. Anne Mendelson, 'The Lenapes: In Search of Pre-European Foodways in the Greater New York Region', in *Gastropolis: Food & New York City*. Ed. Annie Hauck-Lawson and Jonathan Deutsch. New York: Columbia UP, 2009, 28.
2. Qtd. John McPhee, *The Founding Fish*. New York: Farrar, Straus, and Giroux, 2002, 156.
3. McPhee 157.
4. 'A Natural and Cultural History of Shad', Brandywine Conservancy Environmental Management Center, Chadds Ford, PA: http://www.brandywineconservancy.org/shad-history.html; Molly O'Neill. *A Well-Seasoned Appetite: Recipes from an American Kitchen*. New York: Viking, 1996, 53; Henry David Thoreau. 'A Week on the Concord and Merrimack Rivers', in *A Week on the Concord and Merrimack Rivers; Walden, or, Life in the Woods; The Maine Woods; Cape Cod*, ed. Robert F. Sayre. New York: Library of America, 1985, 72.
5. Jim Cummins, 'A Compilation of Historical Perspectives on the Natural History and Abundance of American Shad and Other Herring in the Potomac River', Interstate Commission on the Potomac River Basin, http://www.potomacriver.org/cms/wildlifedocs/PotomacShadHistory032010.pdf: 3 –4.
6. Thoreau 11; Edward Johnson, *Johnson's Wonder-Working Providence 1628–1651*. Ed. J. Franklin Jameson. New York: Charles Scribner's Sons, 1910, 110.
7. Thoreau 72; Thoreau 72–73; qtd. Cummins 5.
8. O'Neill 54; James Trager, *The Foodbook* (New York: Grossman, 1970): 220; Adriaen van der Donck, *A Description of New Netherland*, ed. Charles T. Gehring and William A Starna, trans. Diederik Willem Goedhuys (Lincoln, NE: U Nebraska P, 2008): 58; Betsy McCully, *City at the Water's Edge: A Natural History of New York* (Piscataway, NJ: Rutgers UP, 2007): 80; McPhee 344; McPhee 170.
9. See McPhee 170–182.
10. 'Mount Vernon as It Is', *Harper's New Monthly Magazine* 18: 106, March 1859, 442, 434.
11. Trager 220; McPhee 187–188; Sarah Josepha Buell Hale. *The Good Housekeeper*. Boston: Weeks, Jordan & Co., 1839, 55; Montauk, Reply to 'Webster Chowder', *The Magazine of American History* XI: 6, May 1884, 460.
12. 'Planking Shad', *The New England Kitchen Magazine* I: 2, May 1894, 93.
13. Thoreau 28–29.
14. McPhee 224, 224, 228.
15. Trager n. 5 222; Trager 223; 'Fish and Wildlife', *2009 State of the James Report*, James River Association: http://www.jamesriverassociation.org/the-james-river/state-of-the-james/fish-and-wildlife.
16. Craig Claiborne. *The New York Times Cook Book*. New York: Harper & Row, 1961, 247.
17. O'Neill 53–54.
18. 'Shad Planking', Wakefield Ruritan Club, Wakefield, VA: http://www.shadplanking.com/.

Smoke and Mirrors? Montreal Smoked Meat and the Creation of Tradition

Alan Nash

My interest in the topic of Montreal smoked meat is not a surprising one; indeed, to those who know me, it would seem surprising if I were not interested in it. I live a short block away from Schwartz's – arguably the most famous smoked meat restaurant in Montreal – and at least once a week, upon leaving the house to go to work, I am greeted with the smell of beef brisket being prepared in Schwartz's legendary smoke-house. It is a smell that not only piques my appetite but also my curiosity, because – when I get to work – I am conducting research into the changing world of Montreal's restaurants since the 1950s and I am made all too conscious of the questions that Schwartz's poses for such research.

Simply put, these force us to ask how it is that a product – smoked meat – that was once the preserve of a small minority of the community, the city's Jewish population, has not only become embraced by a much wider cross-section of Montreal's populace, but also how the food of one small segment of that city has come to be propelled to such an 'iconic' status that it has now become seen by almost anyone you care to ask as representative of that entire city to outsiders and tourists alike.

Montreal smoked meat

What exactly is Montreal smoked meat? How exactly is it different from its great rival, New York pastrami? It is helpful to begin an answer to these vexed questions by turning first to Harold McGee's classic *On Food and Cooking*, where he observes that 'the preservation of meat from biological spoilage has been a major challenge throughout history'. The four basic methods of drying, salting, smoking and fermentation have been developed, and, in McGee's words, 'out of these crude methods to starve off spoilage have come some of our most complex and interesting foods' (McGee 2004, 172).

Sadly, smoked meat is not among these foods (he prefers the dry-cured hams and fermented sausages), but it is a nevertheless a product that exemplifies some of the challenges of meat preservation. Indeed, because smoking only affects the surface of the meat, it is a process that has long been used in conjunction with salting and drying – 'a happy conjunction', McGee notes, since salted meats are eventually prone to going rancid (McGee 2004, 175).

In more specific terms, the actual origins of the smoked meat business in Montreal itself appears to owe its origins to Jewish immigrants from Eastern Europe who, in the late nineteenth century, brought with them a familiarity with the meat known variously as *pastrama* in Armenian, *pastirma* in Turkish, *pastram* in Romanian and *pastrami* in Yiddish (Shephard 2000, 74). Referred to as 'smoked meat' in Montreal, it was a product 'which can be differentiated from pastrami or corned beef by its higher ratio of fat and spice, which connoisseurs will attest accounts for its superior taste' (Brownstein 2006, 17). Certainly, today's American pastrami differs from Montreal smoked meat. According to Josephine Bacon, pastrami is made from superior cuts of beef and usually dry-rubbed with a mixture of spices and then refrigerated for up to ten days before smoking (Bacon 2004, 240) – a series of distinct differences when compared with smoked meat preparation, as we shall see.

According to expert opinion, there are two basic ways of making smoked meat. Eiran Harris, perhaps *the* historian of Montreal smoked meat, describes the more traditional process, or 'dry cure', in the following steps. (1) Following kosher practice (in which the only acceptable meat from permitted animals is that untainted by blood), the preferred cuts of meat were taken from the forequarters of the animal, usually a steer. Fattier cuts (known as 'the plate') were used for pastrami; the brisket was used for Montreal-style smoked meat. (2) The briskets were rubbed with salt and spices. (3) The briskets were then put into wooden barrels, where they soaked in their own juices, for between 12 to 20 days. (4) Hung from racks, the briskets were placed in a smoke-house where they were cooked for six to nine hours. According to Harris, 'this form of cooking caused a 25 per cent loss in volume, but resulted in the unique quality and flavour of Montreal-style smoked meat' (Harris 2009).

Evidently, this process was not fast enough for some. 'Eventually the American need for speed was applied to smoked meats' – and the so-called 'wet cure', in which the soaking period was reduced to as little as four days, was developed (Harris 2009).

According to Harris, Montreal-style smoked meat has always been prepared using the older-fashioned 'dry cure', although even its producers could not resist the addition of another American modification, heated smoked meat. This results when the cooked briskets are steamed for three hours before being sliced and served – a step that replaced the 25 per cent of volume that the brisket had lost in cooking, added to the meat's flavour and added to its tenderness.

Schwartz's smoked meat

Any investigation of Montreal smoked meat must also be the story of how the reputation of one small restaurant founded in 1928, Schwartz's Hebrew Delicatessen, has developed to such an extent that this one establishment is now seen as an encapsulation of the entire phenomenon within its rather spartan 61-seater deli. Debates about the best smoked meat in Montreal are hard to settle, but no one doubts that the secret of Schwartz's success must lie in a heady combination of its ability to serve top-quality smoked meat, and the publicity that has come to surround both the food and the place. As one recent authority on marketing has observed on the basis of a case-study of Schwartz's success:

It is highly unlikely that anyone present in the restaurant has just walked in by chance. They have all, in one way or another, been drawn here by Schwartz's continuity between what it promises and what it delivers. ... The reputation survives because one's experience of Schwartz's lives up to the good things people have to say about it.

(Cesvert, 2009, 31–32)

And should anyone wonder what 'good things' people have said, the most famous accolades can be seen not only on the restaurant walls but repeated to such an extent in tourist guides, websites and newspaper columns that, long bereft of their original sources, they have come to have a currency of their own. According to Cesvert (2009, 31–32), the most quotable include: 'A Beef on Rye to Freeze to Death For' (*The Financial Times*); 'The best place in the Milky Way to sample smoked meat sandwiches!' (*Time Magazine*); 'When you're in Montreal, you must go to Schwartz's' (*The New York Times*); and, last but by no means least, 'A Montreal legend for 75 years. So what's the big deal? It's the *viande fumée* that overwhelms two slices of rye' (*The National Geographic*). Small wonder, perhaps, that the restaurant is the focus of a 90-minute documentary video (Elson and Lazar 2007) and the subject of a theatre production to open in Montreal's Centaur Theatre in January 2011 entitled *Schwartz: The Musical*.

If mere words are not enough, those patient enough to endure the weekend line-ups to get inside Schwartz's can be treated to the sight of celebrities such as Harvey Keitel adding mustard to his order of 'a medium and fries', and (to quote the deli's own website) other luminaries such as Angelina Jolie, Celine Dion and most of the Rolling Stones.

As *the* place for *the* food, the epicentre of smoked meat in the city, there is thus no doubt in the minds of many that Schwartz's *is* Montreal. It is an elision of place and food at which geographers who study 'the love of place' and advertising gurus who work up 'place branding' schemes can only marvel.

Smoked meat and place: the theory of 'iconic foods'

An initial perusal of the academic literature suggests that restaurant scholars have not greatly concerned themselves with questions that surround the processes by which one specific group's ethnic cuisine has come to dominate a place. Indeed, scholars who have examined the rise of what have been called 'ethnic restaurants' have had to face the enormous burgeoning of both sheer number and type of ethnic cuisines that have occurred in North American cities in general and in Montreal in particular since the 1950s (Lemasson 2009, 326–332; Nash 2009). In developing theories to account for this, they have leaned instead on explanations of a heightened ethnic diversity in people's eating habits – perhaps because of increasing immigration or the rise of a fashion for eating 'the other' – rather than the apparent *focusing* of such habits upon the cuisine of one group that the rise of institutions such as Schwartz's appears to represent.

213

Ironically perhaps, if we turn to scholars of ethnic cuisines themselves, we see the general tendency for such ethnic foods is to be abandoned by their own ethnic groups – except for festive occasions and religious events – rather than supported in ever greater numbers. Thus, commenting on the experiences of East European Jews once they settled in the United States, Haskia Diner remarks that although they emigrated primarily in response to economic conditions and anti-Jewish violence in Europe, it was 'an act best understood as a search not just for bread, but for meat and fish, noodles and soups and all the sweet stuffs that the less well-off got only at sacred time' (Diner 2001, 176). As Sidney Mintz has remarked in the moving preface to his book *Tasting Food, Tasting Freedom*, 'the rural poor of Eastern Europe were chronically starved for animal protein' (Mintz 1996, xvi). In other words, poor immigrants to North America would have found it bizarre that their heritage cuisines would again be popular even within their own ranks.

Perhaps the best statement of the quandary we face in accounting for the wider popularity of a particular ethnic cuisine comes from Jennifer Berg's 2009 study of the evolution of what she has termed New York City's Jewish 'food icons'. Noting that an icon is a tangible sign of something bigger, Berg argues that 'when consumed or even just imagined, a specific iconic food immediately suggests links to specific places' (Berg 2003, 243–244; 2009, 253).

Applying this concept in the opening pages of her account, Berg remarks that not only is New York represented by a very few 'iconic foods', but that these products themselves have come from only one immigrant group. As she found through a year of asking New Yorkers about the foods they most associated with that city, most reported simple foods such as bagels, deli, cheesecake, knishes, Nathan's hot dogs, egg creams and pizza – all 'simple, inexpensive foods' that 'originated from one immigrant group and became popular during the same era'; 'all foods that today serve as icons and cultural markers for New York' (Berg 2009, 252–3).

To ask why particular foods have become iconic, for whom they are iconic and how iconic food status is achieved are questions that Berg suggests have to be approached historically. Thus, with the exception of pizza, all of the foods that Berg lists as iconic originated as simple, everyday foods in eastern and central Europe, from where they were brought into New York during the period of mass migration between 1880 and 1920. Only once in New York are these foods then taken up and popularized by the city's Jewish immigrants. From the 1920s to the 1950s, New York's Jews sought neither to identify themselves with nor distance themselves from these foods (a period Berg calls one of 'symbolic passive acceptance'). However, between approximately 1950 and 1970, when many Jews were leaving New York for more prosperous accommodations beyond its confines, 'the seemingly benign foods eaten during the tenement days' found themselves rejected as part of the abandonment of that former lifestyle. The final phase of this chronology sees both these trends reverse as large numbers of the Jewish community return to live in the big city and, in a wave of nostalgia, come to embrace the foods of their grandparents.

According to Berg's reading of the story, the fame of New York's iconic foods is somewhat simpler to explain when it comes to the much wider world of the city's non-Jewish community. Thus, 'as the production and consumption of egg creams, bagels, deli, cheesecake, knishes, and hot dogs increased across ethnic groups during the twentieth century they became accepted as non-specific New York fare'. Acculturation and assimilation clearly occurred as minority groups took on the mores of the majority, but there was clearly also a two-way flow between such groups and immigrant foods also, it seems, held their own attractions for that wider group. One of the main appeals was the cheapness of such fare, and Berg argues 'New Yorkers subconsciously adopted simple and inexpensive immigrant foods as their own, transforming them along the way from fast, reasonably priced food to New York City icons' (Berg 2009, 254). Interestingly, the majority of these iconic foods are now associated with restaurants and, in this respect, it is worth noting the comment by a recent historian of the hamburger that 'dishes don't become iconic by being served at the dinner table ... Totems exist in the public place' (Ozersky 2008, 15).

Reflecting upon the wider significance of iconic foods, Berg opines that

> all these foods ... are inextricably linked to New York. They possess iconic status in the twenty-first century in part because they represent New York City's mythical success story. Once scorned food from early-twentieth-century immigrant groups, they now symbolize the city's embracing of immigrants and the social mobility of the underclasses. New Yorkers need not consume these foods regularly to appreciate their value as a symbolic representation of their identity.
>
> (Berg 2009, 254)

As can be seen from quotations such as these, her remarks so clearly resonate with the situation of smoked meat in Montreal that there can be little doubt that our discussion of smoked meat must draw upon both her concept of iconic foods and her approach to its evolution in its particular setting of Montreal.

A history of Montreal smoked meat

The history of smoked meat in Montreal is a tale full of legends and half truths. We are fortunate, however, to have available Lara Rabinovitch's 2009 interview with Eiran Harris, the Archivist Emeritus of the Jewish Public Library in Montreal and a long-time scholar of the subject (Harris 2009).

According to Harris, the most likely pioneer of Jewish-style smoked meat production in the city was neither 'Old Man Kravitz or Old Man Wiseman' as popular opinion believed, but Aaron Sanft, an individual who had emigrated to Montreal and established the city's first kosher butcher's shop in 1884. Sometime over the next decade – when his store placed the earliest-known advertisement in Montreal for the product – Sanft introduced the city to a type of smoked meat prepared in his homeland of Romania.

Interestingly, delicatessen-restaurants serving smoked meat in Montreal do not predate 1908 when Hyman Rees (an immigrant from Lithuania) opened the British-American Delicatessen Store on St Lawrence Boulevard (to give The Main its more formal name). By 1921, there were as many as 19 delicatessens in Montreal, according to statistics Eiran Harris derived from *Lovell's Montreal Directory*, and that number continued to increase to 35 by 1926, before apparently levelling off by 1932 at a figure of 45 – a total that would remain relatively constant, according to Harris, 'for many years' thereafter (Harris 2009). By 1951, according to my own research using the city's classified telephone directories (*The Yellow Pages*), some decline had set in because only a maximum of 21 restaurants can be categorized as Jewish in that year (Nash 2009, 18).

Among those numbers are included several delicatessens that were later to become important Montreal institutions in their own right. One of the most well-known was Bens Delicatessen – traditionally written without an apostrophe – a business that the owner, Benjamin Kravitz, sometimes claimed he had started as early as 1908 (Weintraub 1996, 133; King 2000, 127; Brownstein 2006, 19). However, according to the more sober evidence of the city's street directories, this could not have occurred until at least 1912, at the earliest – the year that Kravitz established his wife, Fanny, in a fruit and candy store at 1208 St Lawrence Boulevard (Harris 2009).

Certainly, whatever the verity of Kravitz' precise recollections, there is no doubt that he had a talent for spotting prime locations, and in many ways his choices can be seen as important reasons for, first, the development of smoked meat's popularity outside of the Jewish community and, second, its subsequent rise to 'iconic food' status. Located in the heart of Montreal's garment district, and immediately adjacent to an eight-storey block of clothing manufacturers, his store was soon able to cater to the workers' demands for something substantial for lunch by producing (at his wife's suggestion) the type of smoked meat he knew from his native Lithuania.

The parallels with the development of iconic foods in New York are telling. As was shown in the previous section, one of the important factors in the early success of such foods was their ability to appeal to wider communities, an appeal made much more attractive by the cheapness of the food product. In this way, to re-word Berg's observation quoted above: Montrealers 'subconsciously adopted simple and inexpensive immigrant foods as their own, transforming them along the way from fast, reasonably priced food to ... icons' (Berg 2009, 254).

By 1929, in an additional step that would propel smoked meat far beyond its original client community, Bens moved again to an address downtown. Despite the Depression, which caused a number of the delicatessens on St Lawrence Boulevard to close, Bens' new location was one that enabled it to prosper by meeting the demands of the city's nearby nightclubs and theatres and the restaurant became the haunt of performers such as Paul Whiteman and Red Skelton when they were in town. Bens was even able to provide free smoked meat sandwiches to the unemployed during this period. In his memoir of life in Montreal in the 1940s and 1950s, William Weintraub notes that Bens was a favourite for late-night dining since it was open for 23 hours a day (the remaining hour was for cleaning) and was 'a pioneer in fast food'. He adds

> Its smoked meat sandwiches were much appreciated by show-business people, after the show, and some of them would even take briskets of Bens smoked meat back to New York, to show pastrami eaters down there what the real thing tasted like.
>
> (Weintraub 1996, 133)

The restaurant expanded several times in the 1950s and, despite Benjamin Kravitz's demise in 1956 and his wife's death in 1968, continued under their three sons' ownership until the business closed in 2006 and the site was redeveloped as a hotel and apartments.

Schwartz's – now the best-known of all Montreal smoked meat restaurants – was a relative latecomer on the scene. Established as the Montreal Hebrew Delicatessen at 3877 St Lawrence Boulevard by Reuben Schwartz on the very last day of 1927, the store was almost immediately a victim of Schwartz's gambling habits and the Depression. However, the combination of a takeover in 1932 (by his friend, the musician Maurice Zbriger) and the reduction of costs (by surrendering the delicatessen's kosher certification, for example) was enough to enable the fledgling business to survive, and Reuben Schwartz continued to run the business as its manager until his death in 1971. It did not hurt that Schwartz, according to Harris, also 'possessed one great asset: the secret recipe for making smoked meats which he brought from Romania'. More recent developments, as we have already reported in a previous section, have seen Schwartz's business succeed to such an extent that, by 2009, according to another recent commentator, it was possible to say 'it is smoked meat that has made Schwartz's arguably the most famous restaurant in all of Canada' (Sax 2009, 196).

217

The rise of smoked meat to the status of an iconic food in Montreal is, as we have seen, a phenomenon of the last fifty years or so. Thus, a tourist arriving in the city in the early years of the twentieth century would not have heard about smoked meat, or – for that matter – any of its delicatessens. My 1922 Baedeker, for example, recommends only a dozen or so restaurants (mostly the grill-rooms of larger hotels, such as the Ritz-Carlton) and apart from observing that the Jewish population forms about six per cent of the city's population of 607,063, makes no mention of St Lawrence Boulevard or its food as a tourist attraction. Apart from a few brawls in one or two delicatessens, neither does resident *bon vivant* Al Palmer, whose recollections of city life in the 1930s and 1940s concentrate on the city's growing reputation for sin and jazz (Palmer 2009). Even as late as 1955, the American Tourist Association's recommended eateries in Montreal ran only to spaghetti and chop houses (Nash 2009).

However, as we have seen, by the 1950s something is stirring and we have noted Ben Kravitz's prescient re-location of his eponymous delicatessen downtown, from where –

on the basis Weintraub's eye-witness account – we know its smoked meat began to reach a much wider audience and was sought after for its cheapness and quality. However, for delicatessens outside the city core, progress was much slower and we can read the testimony of Schwartz's restaurant staff who recall that they were serving far more steaks than smoked meat orders in that establishment as late as the 1950s (Brownstein 2006).

The year of *Expo' 67*, the World's Fair of 1967 in Montreal, is often considered a watershed in the city's restaurant history, the many pavilions from around the world serving to introduce Montrealers to a wider world of cuisines. While I have not been able to detect the 'Expo effect' in the city's growing number of ethnic restaurants during that period, it is significant that Schwartz's staff do point to that event as marking the beginnings of that restaurant's wider fame (Brownstein 2006; Nash 2009).

As for smoked meat itself, by the mid-1980s its place as a food icon is assured: the official tourist guide to Montreal in 1987 remarking, for example, that the visitor should 'try French bread in Montréal or a bagel: both are reputed to be the best on the continent. So is the smoked meat' (Montreal 1987, 69).

Conclusions

> Before the advent of *poutine* [a mixture of french fries, cheese curds and gravy], smoked meat was probably Montreal's best-known food….
>
> (Trillin 2009, 68)

In this paper, we have been able – all too briefly – to sketch out the history of Montreal smoked meat, its growing popularity and the rise of the most famous institutions that serve this product. Drawing a close parallel with Berg's work on New York, this paper suggests that Montreal smoked meat can clearly be identified as an 'iconic food'. As such, of course, it becomes more than simply food – it becomes part of the identity of a place.

As such, of course, Montreal smoked meat has a significance to a population much larger than merely its regular consumers. As Berg observes, one of the qualities of an iconic food is that it no longer needs to be eaten very often for its devotees to maintain their identification with it. Just as with Benedict Anderson's notion of the 'imagined community' that unites people who although they may never have met each other believe they share some common bond, so 'iconic foods' can become part of the matrix of cultural bonds that can construct social identities in place, maintain them amongst the diasporic communities of those who have left, and can serve as highlights caught in the 'tourist gaze' of those visitors who seek a distinctive experience.

However, before concluding, it is useful to make one further addition to the discussion and that concerns the French historian Pierre Nora's notion of *lieux de mémoire* or 'sites of memory'. While few scholars have so far made use of his ideas in the context of food studies (Ory 1997), Nora's views of how the public come to articulate memory around certain agreed-upon narratives has been a powerful one with which to come to understand how 'History' becomes re-interpreted through the popular gaze. Put simply, the importance of an event or a person owes far less to the supposed truth of a professional historian's evaluation of its significance than it does to its perceived value in the popular imagination.

In this sense, it could be argued that it is Montreal's agreed-upon story of a tolerance of difference that has allowed ethnic cuisine – rather than indigenous or North American foods – to represent the city, and that this narrative has subsequently enabled one particular type of immigrant food – smoked meat – to be seen as the 'iconic' food eaten in the city. The fact that the majority of Montrealers do not choose to eat smoked meat is not the point – what is important is that this is how Montrealers have agreed that they would wish visitors to eat, and to remember, their city. Parallels are not hard to find: on St Patrick's Day, it is said that everyone in Montreal is Irish. Certainly, just as invented histories rework the past, there is no reason why types of food or cuisine may not similarly serve as *lieux de mémoire* in the creation of a tradition – a 'culinary tradition' readily utilized by place marketers and tourists alike.

Calvin Trillin's observation that smoked meat is currently losing dominance to *poutine* can itself be seen as the latest extension of these symbolic notions in the political sphere, as *poutine* (arguably, representing the food of a nationalist Francophone population, and one literally invented sometime in the 1950s) seeks to supplant smoked meat as the ambassador of the city. In this respect, it is not perhaps without significance that the underlying theme of 2011's *Schwartz: the Musical* is the English-speaking population's difficulties living amongst a French-speaking majority in Montreal. Political considerations aside, the rise of *poutine* clearly illustrates that the concept of iconic food is certainly not a static one.

219

Bibliography:

Bacon, J. 'Pastrami', in Smith, A.F. (ed.), *The Oxford Encyclopedia of Food and Drink in America*. New York: Oxford University Press, vol. 2, 2004, 240–241.

Berg, J. 'Iconic Foods', in Katz, Solomon H. (ed.), *Encyclopedia of Food and Culture*. New York: Scribner, vol. 2, 2003, 243–244.

_____. 'From the Big Bagel to the Big Roti? The Evolution of New York City's Jewish Food Icons', in Hauck-Lawson, A. and J. Deutsch (eds.), *Gastropolis: Food and New York City*. New York: Columbia Press, 2009, 252–273.

Brownstein, B. *Schwartz's Hebrew Delicatessen: The Story*. Montreal: Véhicule Press, 2006.

Cesvert, B. *Conversational Capital: How to Create Stuff People Love to Talk About*. Upper Saddle River NJ: FT Press, 2009.

Diner, H. R. *Hungering for America: Italian, Irish, & Jewish Foodways in the Age of Migration*. Cambridge: Harvard University Press, 2001.

Elson, R. and B. Lazar (dirs.) *Chez Schwartz*. [A film by Garry Beitel], Montreal: Les Productions du Boulevard Inc., 2007.

Harris, E. 'Montreal-Style Smoked Meat: An interview with Eiran Harris conducted by Lara Rabinovitch, with the co-operation of the Jewish Public Library', *Cuizine: The Journal of Canadian Food Cultures* vol.1 no. 2, no pagination [e-journal article accessed on 2 March and 8 April 2010 at www.erudit.org/revue/cuizine/2009/v1/n2/037859ar.html]

King, J. *From the Ghetto to the Main: The Story of the Jews of Montreal*. Montreal: The Montreal Jewish Publication Society, 2000.

Lemasson, J.-P. 'Montréal: oasis gastronomique ou capitale culinaire?' in Delorme, P. (dir.), *Montréal, aujourd'hui et demain: Politique, urbanisme, tourisme*. Montreal: Liber, 2009, 323–344.

McGee, H. *On Food and Cooking: The Science and Lore of the Kitchen*. New York: Scribner, 2004.

Mintz, S. *Tasting Food, Tasting Freedom: Excursions into Eating, Culture and the Past*. Boston: Beacon Press, 1996.

Montreal Tourist Guide 1987–88. Montreal: Greater Montreal Convention and Tourist Bureau, 1987.

Nash, A. 'From Spaghetti to Sushi: An Investigation of the Growth of Ethnic Restaurants in Montreal, 1951–2001', *Food, Culture and Society* 12 (2), 2009, 5–24.

Ory, P. 'Gastronomy', in Nora, P. (dir.), *Realms of Memory: The Construction of the French Past*. New York: Columbia University Press, 1997, 443–467.

Palmer, A. *Montreal Confidential*. Montreal: Véhicule Press, 2009.

Ozersky, J. *The Hamburger: A History*. New Haven: Yale University Press, 2008.

Sax, D. *Save the Deli: In Search of Perfect Pastrami, Crusty Rye and the Heart of Jewish Delicatessen*. Toronto: McClelland and Stewart, 2009.

Shephard, S. *Pickled, Potted and Canned: How the Art and Science of Food Preserving Changed the World*. New York: Simon and Schuster, 2000.

Trillin, C. 'Canadian Journal: Funny Food', *The New Yorker* (23 November), 2009, 68–69.

Weintraub, W. *City Unique: Montreal Days and Nights in the 1940s and 50s*. Toronto: McClelland and Stewart, 1996.

Tempeh: the Past, Present and Possible Future of a Fermented Soybean

Sri Owen and Roger Owen

Soybeans (*Glycine max*) were probably domesticated in northern and central China at least four and a half millennia ago. Their value as food plants must have been quickly recognized and farmers, who have a claim to be respected as this planet's first scientists, learned to breed varieties which would flourish under contrasting regimes of climate, soil, and day length. Northern soybeans still know, by the number of daylight hours, when to flower and set seed, thus ensuring that they have nothing urgent to do during the cold months. Their cousins that now grow in the tropics have undergone many centuries of selection and cross-breeding. The genealogy of the family is likely to be as complex as that of any nation of *Homo sapiens*: there are dozens of sub-species and varieties, and in parts of Asia one can find ancient races of wild beans growing not far from fields of recently developed cultivars that have been tailored for specific industrial purposes.

Soybeans are now said to be the world's most widely cultivated food plant. Their appeal lies in their high nutritional value, with the bonus that, as legumes, they improve the fertility of the soil they are grown in by absorbing and 'fixing' atmospheric nitrogen. They are viewed with suspicion by some environmentalists because so much tropical forest is being cleared to make space for them. Worse still, the bulk of the harvest is destined to become either biofuel or animal fodder. Worst of all, most soybeans now in cultivation are damned as GM crops, the pawns of multinational corporations.

The authors sympathize with some of the environmentalists' strictures, and are troubled by the problem of how far the small farmer should be free to grow what crops he chooses. But world population is growing fast and must be fed. Many species of legume contribute to our diet, and come to table in one form or another, some recognizable, others processed and transformed even beyond detection. Plain boiled soybeans – in their shells if immature, otherwise shelled and cooked as if they were sweet corn – are palatable and quite nourishing, but their most valuable nutrients pass straight though the human gut and are not available to the body. Soya 'milk' is drunk in south-east Asia, mainly by children, as a kind of substitute for cow's milk, or is made, throughout much of today's world, into tofu (*tahu* in Indonesian): these too are good, but the body still cannot make as much use of them as it should (Shurtleff and Aoyagi 1979).

221

The best way of getting round this problem is to ferment the beans and thus transform the chemistry of their nutrients. People in south-east and east Asia have been doing this in a variety of ways for a long time: soy sauce is a popular example. People in the West do it by feeding soybeans to cattle and then eating the beef, but this method, though tasty, is extravagantly inefficient and may prove to be unsustainable. Several other soybean products, long established in the East, are achieving modest but increasing popularity in the West. One of these is *tempeh*, often described as 'an Indonesian fermented soybean cake'. (In Indonesian, the word is spelled *tempe*; Westerners add the final 'h' to remind everyone that the word has two syllables.)

Most people in the West now seem to have heard of *tempeh*, many know what it is, and a few can even tell you where to buy it. This is especially true in North America, where it is becoming established as a health food and is in medium-scale commercial production. Some of the claims made for it as health-giving, high in nutrients, and 'delicious' are disputed, and on websites (in particular) many misleading statements are to be found. In south-east Asia, *tempeh* is more widely known, and in many areas is practically a staple food, dating back perhaps two millennia – or perhaps only two centuries: no one is quite sure. Different people may have very different reasons for eating it. It can be made from quite a wide range of legumes, but soybeans are the most used. It is usually described as a solid block of beans, held together by the mycelium, or microscopic vegetative threads, of a fungus, *Rhizopus oligosporus* or *R. oryzae*. These threads penetrate not only the husk or hull of each bean but the outer layers of the cotyledon, allowing enzymes to draw nourishment for the fungal spores while also changing the chemistry of the beans in ways that are beneficial to humans. *Tempeh* clearly invites comparison with at least two other Asian fermented soybean foods: Japanese *natto*, and Korean *meju* (see the 'visitkorea' website). *Natto*, fermented with *Bacillus natto*, is softer than *tempeh*, and has a strong smell, whereas *tempeh*, by itself, smells and tastes bland and has a firmer texture, sometimes described as 'sliceable'. *Meju* is closer to *tempeh*, being fermented with *Aspergillus oryzae*, but the process used to make it results in a hard, dry block, traditionally hung from the rafters to ripen and mature.

Our focus in this paper is on *tempeh*'s place in the world, in the traditional food cultures it came from and in today's world at large. We are not going to suggest that soybean *tempeh* is unique among foods, or indispensable to health. We are not biochemists and don't intend to venture into comparative nutritional statistics, except to note that *tempeh*'s particular benefits appear to lie in two areas where research is still ongoing and conclusions disputed.

One of these concerns vitamins, in particular vitamin B_{12}, which we all have to have, in very small quantities, every day throughout life. Plants don't use it, so there is no vegetable source for this: vegetarians and vegans usually take vitamin supplements. Tiny, but adequate, amounts of B_{12} have often been detected in *tempeh*, but the source now seems certain to be harmless bacteria that have jumped ship from the fungus and gone on multiplying in the beans (Shurtleff & Aoyagi 1984; Liem, Steinkraus, and Cronk 1977).

The other area of uncertainty is that of complementary amino acids – that is, building blocks of essential proteins (Univ. of Arizona website). These are vital: if the body is not replenished with them each day, it will eventually start to cannibalize itself, to raid its own tissue (muscle, in particular) in order to rush the proteins to the organs that most require them. A cereal and a legume, however, can together deliver to the body the essential amino acids for this protein synthesis. In particular, rice, even brown unhusked rice, is low in lysine but high in methionine. With soybeans, it's the other way round, so if you eat both, you get, without any further effort on your part and without any biochemical knowledge whatever, a nice balance of these vital components. What is less easy to explain is why fermentation of the beans, into soy sauce or tofu or *tempeh*, greatly increases the good effects of this cereal-legume partnership. Rice and fermented soybean products – *tempeh*, soy sauce (*kecap* in Indonesian, pronounced 'ketjup), *tauco* (pronounced 'tao-tjo: fermented salted soybeans), and others – do this for the human population of most of east and much of south-east Asia. A diet of *tempeh* and rice has proved its value in famines, during wars, and in prison camps: it is by no means a 'complete' diet but it will sustain life for months, or indefinitely if it is eked out with other foods from time to time.

The big picture is one in which, all over the world at roughly the same time, humans switched from wild foods to foods they themselves cultivated – from being hunter-gatherers to being farmers. In different regions, they bred staple cereal crops that suited local conditions. They also developed varieties of legumes that 'complemented' the cereals and resulted in well-fed, healthy human populations. Groups that failed to do this were unlucky and their numbers dwindled. In east Asia, rice and soybeans established themselves as especially valuable partners, and populations that depended on them thrived and continue to do so. It's worth noting also that plain soybeans combine with cereal fodder in the guts of cattle to provide the protein the animals need. This is because cows are ruminants, with several stomachs in which food is fermented; at one point in the digestive process, therefore, the resulting protein becomes available for general use. In the human apparatus, absorption of the amino acids from unfermented beans takes place in the small intestine and is lost by excretion – an example perhaps of how evolution can produce an imperfect solution to a problem, which *Homo sapiens* can then sort out: an interesting speculation for the philosophers.

223

***

Tempeh is easy, if somewhat laborious, to make at home, and even if you cost in your time, labour and fuel, the result will still be cheaper and (with a little practice) better than you can buy from a health-food shop – though factory-made *tempeh* is perfectly acceptable. You can buy the uncooked beans in 2 kg bags at your nearest Asian food shop. The only other thing you need is a reliably pure strain of the 'starter' mould –

usually in the form of microscopic mould spores mixed with rice powder. The common name in Indonesian for any such yeast-like starter is *ragi*. It is possible, as with bread or beer yeast, to use a little of the previous batch of product to start fermentation of the next batch, but this brings the risk of contamination by unhelpful and possibly toxic mould species. *Tempeh* is always cooked before it is eaten, but this does not give complete protection against such toxins. In any case, it must be cooked while fresh unless it can be refrigerated or frozen. If fermentation is allowed to continue, the mould will turn blackish and the *tempeh* will not only look but taste unattractive; toxins will then develop. *Tempe bosok*, 'rotted *tempeh*', can be cooked up into something resembling a delicacy, but it does not appeal to many who are unaccustomed to it.

Essentially, the beans have to be washed, de-hulled, soaked, cooked, cooled, inoculated, packed, and allowed to ferment. Shurtleff and Aoyagi (1979) describe a simple sequence of actions which, within the space of about 48 hours, reliably provides the home *tempeh*-maker with high-quality product. *Tempeh* starter, in powdered form, is obtainable by mail order from at least one firm in the UK and several in the US; the powder is usually rice flour, to which the micro-spores adhere. It is quite expensive (currently £21 for 50 g), but 50 g will inoculate at least six 2 kg bags of soybeans. Each of these makes about 3.6 kg of *tempeh*: the gain in weight comes from water absorbed by the beans in cooking. The process is described in some detail in *The Rice Book* and in *Sri Owen's Indonesian Food* (the latter benefiting from Gus Filgate's helpful colour photographs).

Writers on *tempeh*, even the most sternly academic, often seem to feel an obligation to promote it as a gourmet food. The words 'tasty' and 'delicious' occur again and again, and 'nutty' seems to get copied from paper to paper. A website refers to 'its distinctively nutty taste and nougat-like texture,' an article in a learned journal says it has 'a somewhat nutty flavor and a texture similar to a chewy mushroom' (Dinesh Babu et al., 2009). The enthusiasm is not universal, however; a health-food web page (Wellsphere) says that, 'The secret to *tempeh* is to boil it for about 45 minutes. That softens it and gets the bitter taste out.' These judgments are alike in that they misrepresent *tempeh*. Raw, it does taste rather bitter, and it is somewhat indigestible. Plain boiled *tempeh* is bland, with little taste or flavour, and a rather neutral texture and mouthfeel, pleasant but unexciting. Its claim to gourmet status is its facility in absorbing and giving back flavours of ingredients it is cooked with. The most popular cooked *tempeh* is *tempe goreng* – fried *tempeh*. You slice the *tempeh* thinly into 2 cm squares, and marinate the slices for about 30 minutes in a mixture of hot water and tamarind water with crushed garlic, shallots, chillies, and salt. Then drain, dry them with kitchen paper, and deep-fry a few pieces at a time. Alternatively, the marinated *tempeh* slices can be coated with a simple batter of rice flour and water before deep frying. You can use *tempeh* as a substitute for meat in many dishes; *rendang tempe* is a vegetarian version of beef rendang, just as tasty and very tender. *Tempe bacem* ['ba-tj'm] is the favourite of people in Central and East Java. But we must not get carried away at this point with enthusiasm for *tempeh* recipes. Only remember that *tempeh* must be cooked, and, whatever the enthusiasts say, it needs to be spiced up.

***

The origins of *tempeh*, in time and place, are much discussed (e.g. Shurtleff 1984; Matsuyama 2001). My guess is that somebody, somewhere, boiled up a pan of beans and then forgot about them, returning maybe a couple of mornings later to find they had become – at least to the depth of a centimetre or two – a knobbly, whitish-yellow chunk, with a soft, slightly velvety surface. But that would most likely happen in a warm climate, friendly to airborne mould spores which would settle on the beans as they cooled, then multiply quickly in a favourable ambient temperature. Or the beans can be inoculated by wrapping them in teak leaves whose undersides are hosts to colonies of the spores. Such processes can be discovered by chance many times over in different places, and leave no traces by which future generations could date them. It's hard to imagine how a lump of *tempeh* could be fossilized. Maybe we shall discover the remains of some prehistoric person who ate *tempeh* for his or her last meal.

Was *tempeh* first made in China or in Java? It seems to us unlikely that it appeared by chance in the northern parts of China, surely too cold for accidental fermentation; even the southernmost mainland provinces only just extend into the region of the tropics. A leading authority on *tempeh*, Jonathan Agranoff, informs us that 'there are ancient *prasasti* [inscriptions] in East Java that mention soybeans, which almost certainly came from China,' and adds that he has found *tempeh* still being made today in northern Sulawesi without the use of *ragi* – presumably relying on airborne spores (personal communication). Early Chinese written sources do mention soybeans as an important food crop, but imply that they were not highly rated: like many legumes, they cause flatulence and were regarded as a staple diet for the poor, or perhaps for the better-off in famine years. They appealed to Buddhist monks, who were supposed to avoid meat and fish, and who were very likely among the first to find ways of making the beans both tasty and more digestible – soy milk is good, soy sauce even better, though more complicated to make. Buddhist missionaries are credited with introducing soya to Korea and Japan in the early centuries of the Common Era, and either missionaries or traders (or people who were both) were certainly active in Java and Sumatra from about the sixth century CE or earlier. In tracing the history of Asian foodways, we must never lose sight of the intense economic activity which engaged so many folk at all levels of society from around the fifth century BCE onwards, and in which we recognize the roots of the modern world.

Tempeh, unlike many other fermented soybean products, is perishable, so it can never have been an item of trade over distances much greater than a kilometre. Even on a commercial scale, in its country of origin it has been until recently a cottage industry. But the knowledge of how to make it could travel in any direction at any time. The closest we can come at the moment to *tempeh*'s origin is to say that it was probably accidental, may have happened many times in different places, and is perhaps most likely to have occurred in Java or Sumatra. However, the product may not have been soybean *tempeh*; many other legumes can be fermented in the same way. Shurtleff & Aoyagi (1989) say that the second most-favoured *tempeh* in Java, after soybean, is made from velvet beans (*Mucuna pruriens*). Matsuyama (2001) points out that there is no contemporary written record of soybeans in south-east Asia until the *Herbarium Amboinense* of the celebrated Rumphius (Georg Eberhard Rumpf), compiled in the decades after his arrival in Ambon in 1654 but not published until 1741, nearly 40 years after his death. Rumphius mentions *Zwarte Boontzes*, and Dutch shipping records refer frequently to *swarte boontjes* from the 1640s onwards; small black soybeans still grow wild in parts of Java, and though they are not highly rated today as food they must certainly have been eaten in the past. Matsuyama adds that the word *kědělai*, derived from India, does not occur in any of these Dutch sources, and concludes that the seventeenth century saw the first major migration of Chinese workers and traders to the north coast of Java, where they had to make their favourite fermented soybean products with the inferior local beans. He goes so far as to write, 'In its main characteristics *tempe* is similar to *dan.dou.chi* in China' (a Chinese medicine: black soybeans, steamed, then fermented, but not formed into a solid block). This clearly implies that *tempeh* originated, at least indirectly, in China, which is possible, but in our view is certainly not proven.

Albala (2007) says yellow soybeans were introduced to Indonesia 'about a thousand years ago and temp-eh may be nearly as old, though written references date only to a few centuries ago'. He doesn't say, however, where these references can be found, though one probably occurs in the *Serat Centhini*, a Javanese text dating from the early nineteenth century. At about the same time, Raffles (1817) writes with an empire-builder's enthusiasm about Java's richness and variety of natural produce, but dismisses legumes in one sentence: 'The bean, or *káchang*, of which there are many varieties, is an important article of food.' Several pages later, in a detailed and appreciative description of Javanese food, he says, 'The Chinese prepare from the *gedelé* a species of soy, somewhat inferior to that brought from Japan.' In modern Indonesian, *kacang kědělé* are soybeans. He then names and describes *trasi* (or *balachan*, in various spellings), the fermented fish (or shrimp) paste and its by-products which are still essential today to south-east Asian cooking. But he never mentions *tempeh*, though he must surely have met it, if it existed, and it is difficult to believe that it would not have aroused his curiosity. A century or more after him, Burkill (1935) describes *tempeh* in more detail than one would expect, considering that he was writing about economic products that the British might be able to exploit in Malaya, and makes it clear that *tempeh* 'occupies a very important place in the diets of those who live in central and east Java.' He does not give an opinion about where it originated, and he hardly ever speculates on any product's prospects in the UK market. He names *Aspergillus oryzae* as the agent of fermentation, and describes two ways of making *tempeh*, one quick, the other more painstaking and reliable because the beans are inoculated by spores that have been bred on young teak leaves which are then 'cut fine' and their fragments scattered over the beans. This technique is still widely used.

Tempeh is not only a main-dish ingredient, it is also the basis of many popular snacks, and snacking, always rife in Indonesia, is gaining ground in today's downturning economic climate. Matsuyama quotes, from a Javanese version of the *Ramayana* (of uncertain date), a description of street food outside a temple, with a female vendor selling drinks, and all kinds of snacks, including sticky rice and fermented rice-cake (presumably similar to the modern *tapé*, fermented cooked rice – very mildly alcoholic). There is no suggestion that *tempeh* was also on her tray, but it well may have been.

In recent times, *tempeh* has made some impression in Japan. Dr Kiku Murata, of Osaka City University, did a considerable amount of work on *tempeh* in the 1960s, and her efforts led indirectly to the foundation of the Japan Tempeh Research Society in 1984. By that time, *tempeh* was already going into commercial production in Japan, and a patent is said to have been applied for, though we are not aware that the industry has made very much progress in that country in the quarter-century that has elapsed since. A thorough search of the web has, however, led us to two newspaper reports (*Brunei Times, Jakarta Post*) of a thriving *tempeh*-making business located an hour's drive from Kyoto, established and run by an Indonesian, with his Japanese wife.

***

Can we put some figures on *tempeh* production and consumption, preferably across a span of years which will indicate whether it is gaining or losing ground, or just marking time? There is no doubt that, in the world of the commercial soybean, *tempeh* is a small player. Furthermore, because most production, even today, takes place at cottage-industry level, all statistics must involve an uncertain amount of guesswork. In 1975, *tempeh*-makers were organized into a co-operative known, like most such collectives in Indonesia, by an acronym: KOPTI. Its membership in that year was stated to be 40,000 (Nout and Kiers 2005). In 1986, total *tempeh* production was estimated at 'between' 154,000 and 500,000 tons – a generous margin of error. Two years later, a different authority decided that the average Indonesian consumed about 8.8 kg per year of tempe *and* tofu (International Trade Centre 2006). The country's population in that year was 172,000,000, so the total production of these soybean products must have been a little over 1.5 million tons. Steinkraus (1996), whose big book is highly regarded by all writers on fermented foods, states that in 1988 approximately 764,000 tonnes of *tempeh* was consumed in Indonesia – that is, about 6.45 kg per head, or 17.7 gm per day. But that would require the population to be under 120 million, which must be too low. Today's population, by the way, has passed the 240 million mark, a rate of increase that seems to support claims that *tempeh* is good for you.

KOPTI is almost certainly the ancestor of today's INKOPTI, the Indonesian Federation of Co-operatives of *Tempeh* and Tofu Makers which, in September 1999, announced that it had signed a contract with Cargill to import 200,000 tons of soybeans from the United States for the benefit of its 43,000+ members (endonesia. biz website). It may be worth mentioning here that though Indonesia declared self-sufficiency in rice in 1984, it has never attempted to become self-sufficient in soybeans. It's not easy to find out, from sources available on the Internet, how much *tempeh* was produced in a given year, but not difficult to find how much money was involved: the published figures for 2009 (Biro Rencanaan website) list all 32 Indonesian provinces, showing the net profits made by *tempeh* producers in each of the two previous years in millions of rupiah (one million rupiah is currently worth about £72 in our own battered currency). One can see at a glance where *tempeh* is big business: West Java (more than Rp.988 million, but falling); Greater Jakarta (approaching Rp.331 million, but falling quite sharply); East Java (close to Rp.298 million, and rising fast); and, heavens above, East Kalimantan (Indonesian Borneo; nearly Rp.233 million, and rising – whoever thought of Kalimantan as a top *tempeh* producer?). For the whole country, net profit rose from Rp.3.47 billion to Rp.5.04 billion in a year, say Rp.1.5 billion, a little over 35 per cent – not bad for a cottage industry, though of course some of the 'cottages' are by this time well-funded industrial plants. To emphasize the breadth of the production spectrum, Nout and Kiers (2005) state that the daily output of 'small Indonesian shops' was likely to be anywhere between 10 kg and 2000 kg.

228

We should bear in mind also that population densities vary enormously from region to region, and that in some areas *tempeh* is held in great esteem while in others it is regarded as food for the poor or the famine-struck; west and east Java have always had more regard for it than the centre of the island, just as north and south Sumatra rate it more highly than west Sumatra. *Tempeh*, as a 'convenience' food, is said to be more popular in the cities, but we frankly cannot explain how or why the small 'Special Region' of Yogyakarta (special because it still has its hereditary Sultan) was able to multiply its net profit almost fifty-fold in a year. Another table shows the labour force employed in the co-operatives, classified as managers and operatives: the overall total in 2008 was 357,000, a reduction on 2007 of 14,400, with wide disparities among the regions. Falling employment is as likely to reflect mechanization as it is falling demand, but the report does not attempt to analyse the statistics in any depth.

By 2005, average annual consumption of *tempeh* per head was estimated to have risen to between 7 kg and 12.5 kg, and 860 factories were hard at work making it; there were almost twice as many, however, making tofu (International Trade Centre). In 2008, *tempeh* consumption was reported to be increasing, in Indonesia (Sidharta 2008) as well as in North America and Europe, though dependable production figures are still not easy to pin down.

In this paper, we have focused our attention on Indonesia, but *tempeh* is also made in neighbouring countries, in much more limited quantities and for a much smaller market. We have barely touched on *tempehs* which are made from other legumes, such as *tempe benguk*, made from the seeds of *Mucuna pruriens* (the velvet bean or 'cowitch'), or from the waste products of other processes – *tempe gembus*, for example, is based on the sediment from tofu making, while *oncom* ['on-tjom] is made, usually, from peanut presscake, the solids left over after oil has been pressed from the nuts. These are all nourishing and tasty foods in their way, but it is *tempeh* which, surely, any marketing department would seize on as the food of the future.

Bibliography

Albala, K. *Beans: A History*. Berg, 2007.

American Soybean Association / United Soybean Board: *Southeast Asia Soyfoods Directory, 2003–4.*

Biro Perencanaan [Planning Office], Jakarta: *Statistik Perkoperasian 2009*, www.depkop.go.id

Burkill, I.H. *A Dictionary of Economic Products of the Malay Peninsula*.1935, reprinted 1966 by the Governments of Malaysia and Singapore.

Dinesh Babu, P, R. Bhakyaraj and R. Vidhyalakshmi. 'A Low Cost Nutritious Food '*Tempeh*' – A Review', in *World Journal of Dairy & Food Sciences* 4 (1): IDOSI Publications, 2009, 22–27.

International Trade Centre / UNCTAD / WTO: *Indonesia: Supply and Demand Survey on Food Products*, 2006.

Liem I.T.H., K.H. Steinkraus, and T.C. Cronk. 'Production of Vitamin B–12 in *Tempeh*, a Fermented Soybean Food', *Applied and Environmental Microbiology*, December 1977.

Matsuyama, A. *The Traditional Dietary Culture of Southeast Asia*. Kegan Paul, 2001.

Nout, M.J.R. and J.L. Kiers. 'Tempe fermentation, innovation and functionality: update into the third millennium', *Journal of Applied Microbiology*, Volume 98, Issue 4, 2005, pp. 789–805. (An excellent article – section 2 ('Introduction') contains a great deal of general information about soy-based foods.)

Owen, S. and R. 'Three Staples of Indonesia: Rice, Coconuts, *Tempeh*', in *Staple Foods, Proceedings of the Oxford Symposium on Food History 1989*. Prospect Books, 1990.

Raffles, T.R. *History of Java*. 1817, reprinted by OUP, 1988.

Shurtleff, W. and A. Aoyagi. *The Book of Tempeh* (Professional Edition). Harper & Row, 1979 (freely available on-line).

_____. *History of Tempeh*. The Soyfoods Center, 1984 (available online, with much other material, at: http://www.soyinfocenter.com/)

_____. *History of Miso, Soybean Jiang (China) Jang (Korea) and Tauco / Taotjo (Indonesia) (200 BC – 2009)*. An extensively annotated bibliography and sourcebook, 2009 (available online from the Soyinfo Center at http://www.soyinfocenter.com/bibliographies.php).[NB 6.8 MB on disk; 1348 pages. A huge document, containing much historical information on *tempeh*.]

Sidharta, M. 'Soyfoods in Indonesia', in du Bois, Tan, and Mintz (eds.) *The World of Soy*. University of Illinois Press, 2008.

Sorosiak, T. 'Soybean', in Kiple and Ornelas (eds.) *The Cambridge World History of Food*, vol. 1. CUP, 2000.

Steinkraus K.H. (ed.), *Handbook of Indigenous Fermented Foods*. Marcel Dekker Inc., 1996.

Toussaint-Samat, M, translated by Anthea Bell. *History of Food*. Blackwell, 1994.

Ying-shih Yü, in K.C. Chang (ed.) *Food in Chinese Culture*. Yale, 1977.

Websites

Biro Perencanaan: www.depkop.go.id
Endonesia: http://www.endonesia.biz/mod.php.mod=publisher&op=viewarticle&cid=14&artid=130
(if this URL doesn't work, go to http://www.endonesia.biz/ and type '*tempeh*' in the search box)
Ganie, Suryatini N.: http://www.planetmole.org/indonesian-news/*tempeh*-in-indonesia.html
Soyfoods Association of North America: http://www.soyfoods.org/products/sales-and-trends
Tempeh in Japan, *Brunei Times*: http://www.bt.com.bn/en/life/2009/02/21/tempting_japan_with_*tempehs*_goodness
Jakarta Post: http://www.thejakartapost.com/news/2008/12/01/rustono-king-*tempeh*-kyoto.html
University of Arizona: http://www.biology.arizona.edu/biochemistry/problem_sets/aa/aa.html
Visit Korea: http://www.visitkorea.or.kr/enu/SI/SI_EN_3_6.jsp?gotoPage=1&cid=258790
Wellsphere: http://www.wellsphere.com/heart-health-article/good-*tempeh*-finally/397309

Tempeh starter

In the UK, we have for many years bought from:
Murphy & Son Ltd., Alpine Street, Old Basford, Nottingham NG6 0HQ; http://www.murphyandson.co.uk/

In the USA, Google turns up a few, including:
http://www.gemcultures.com/ (Lakewood, WA)
http://www.healthy-eating.com/gluten_*tempeh*.html (Summertown, TN).

Artisanship and Control:
Farmhouse Cheddar Comes of Age

Bronwen Percival and Randolph Hodgson

Any self-conscious connoisseur will tell you that artisanship is its own reward. In an age of industrialized food stripped of its individuality and made by factories rather than individuals, the very image of the gnarled peasant has fantastic social – and commercial – currency. In this fantasy world, true artisans use innate instinct to produce foods that simply express the goodness of their raw materials. Using technical knowledge is profane, and the need for control suggests that something might not be quite right with those raw materials.

The modern industrial dairy attempts to treat production of cheese as a simple engineering problem, an illusion of control that rests on eliminating the variables one by one until an acceptably consistent product can be made. British and American dairy research and development has accordingly seized as its Holy Grail techniques for the ever more rapid production of inexpensive and consistent cheese.

Resisting pressure to mechanize their production and retaining the methods used by their parents and grandparents has left the few remaining farmhouse Cheddar-makers with a priceless inheritance, and today they make some of the world's best cheeses. Now they – like many other farmhouse cheese-makers – find themselves in an uncomfortable middle ground, carrying forward a set of inherited practices with dogged determination in the face of extraordinary change to the industry at large. Ritual propagation is fine as long as nothing ever changes or goes wrong, and while we might imagine that peasants living outside of time on mountaintops may get by all right, in reality it does not tend to work out nearly so well. The same technical know-how eschewed by those lusting after a vague idea of 'artisanship' is actually the key to making world-class cheese on any scale.

The state of play

Over 99 per cent of the Cheddar currently produced in the UK is made in factories and destined for supermarket sale or further processing. Under these conditions, efficiency and consistency are paramount. Production is centralized in huge factories, the largest of which produce up to 60,000 tonnes per year. Milk is shipped in from around the country, standardized to a precisely-defined fat and protein-content, and pasteurized. Cheese-making is done in closed vats, controlled remotely by an operator in front of a computer. Dried and uniform lactic acid starter cultures are used for the fermentation, often alongside non-acidifying 'adjunct' starters designed to impart a desired flavour profile. The finished blocks of curd are finally sealed in plastic and stored in cold for a several months before being released for sale. By standardizing the raw materials and using an apparatus designed consistently to repeat a defined process, fairly consistent cheeses are turned out. With over £1 billion spent on Cheddar in the UK market in 2009,[1] it comes as no surprise that the dairy research industry is firmly focused on the needs of large industrial cheese-makers, for whom a small increase in yield and consistency may result in a significant increase in profitability.

In contrast, producers of farmhouse Cheddar have self-consciously conserved the techniques taught to them by their parents and grandparents. While they are aware that some of their practices have changed subtly over time to accommodate modest increases in scale of production, the broad strokes have been conserved. In 2003, the three makers of the most traditional form of Somerset Cheddar – the Keens, Jamie Montgomery, and the Calvers of Westcombe Dairy – came together, prompted to define the key points of their recipe as part of an application for a Slow Food Presidium. Despite the close proximity of their farms and their joint membership in industry organizations such as the Specialist Cheesemakers Association it was the first time that they had ever sat down together to discuss the cheese and the key points that make it unique. During the sessions, the three parties came up with the following list of key attributes that defined their Artisan Somerset Cheddar as unique and different from the factory-produced Cheddar that constitutes the norm today:

232

Made in Somerset. Large cheese factories are often forced to draw their milk from a catchment area the size of Great Britain.

Made from the raw milk of their own cows. The sheer scale of the large factories would make this a very difficult – not to mention expensive – proposition.

Acidified using traditional pint starters. A key point of difference between the Artisan Somerset Cheddar-makers and many of the large factories is their use of pint starters: complex, multi-strain distillates of lactic acid bacteria that are responsible for acidity production during cheese-making. A specialist laboratory has been set up by Cheddar-makers A.J. and R.G. Barber Ltd 'dedicated to the preservation of the natural mixed-starter cultures historically used for making cheddar'[2] and these are some of the best and most interesting starters on the market today, although they are both expensive and labour-intensive to use.

Set with animal rennet. Because it is less expensive, most cheeses made for the mass market today are made with vegetarian coagulant, either derived from moulds such as *Mucor miehei* or synthesized in laboratories using recombinant DNA technology. According to Paul Kinstedt, professor of Nutrition and Food Sciences at the University of Vermont, 'Calf rennet is considered by many to be the standard against which all other coagulants are compared and is generally recognized to produce superior aged cheeses.'[3]

Cheddared by hand. 'Cheddaring' is a labour-intensive process involving the repeated stacking of blocks of curd during the second stage of acidification in order to assist drainage and develop the correct structure. It is feasible for small dairies to employ cheese-makers to do this by hand; in large factories the same process is often carried out by a 'Cheddarmaster', a large conveyor belt system with the capacity to cheddar up to 10 tonnes of curd per hour.[4]

Cloth bound. Bound in butter muslin and rubbed with lard to seal them, cloth-bound cheeses have a breathable rind that allows for moisture loss and flavour development during aging. The drawback is that tiny fissures in the rind may allow mould spores to enter the cheese, causing internal blueing that supermarkets will reject. In order to limit moisture loss and eliminate the potential for wastage due to blueing, most factory Cheddar is made in block forms and matured in sealed plastic bags.

Aged at least ten months before sale. A well made farmhouse Cheddar will last up to two years, though many are at their best at around a year to 18 months of age. A correctly made Cheddar that is sold before it is ten months old will not yet have had the chance to break down into a flavourful and expressive cheese. By contrast, 'mild' supermarket Cheddars will spend significantly less time maturing in a cold store before they are sent to market.

With such strict standards and labour-intensive production, it is not difficult to understand why Artisan Somerset Cheddar accounted for only just over 0.1 per cent of the 238,000 tonnes of Cheddar produced in the UK in 2009.[5]

233

It is also no surprise that cheese-makers working with raw milk and manual methods are doubly subject to variations and inconsistencies. Cheese-making is extraordinarily complex, with many interdependent factors at play and raw materials that vary from day to day. As raw materials change, so must the methods correct for the changes and produce a consistent product. In other words, doing the same thing every day to different raw materials will result in quite variable cheeses. While to a certain extent batch variation is one of the things that makes the cheeses unique and special, it is also quite possible to topple over the edge of 'variation' and into the realm of 'problem.' Even a seemingly insignificant change or series of changes in the milk or the method can have mysterious and disastrous results: cheeses can turn out wet and sticky or dry and tasteless, develop a fiery afterburn, or end up prone to extensive blueing and internal bruising. As one might imagine, the production costs of farmhouse cheese are immense compared to factory-produced cheeses, and quality problems cost huge amounts in damage and wastage. They are also time-consuming to sort out – it can be months before the effect of a change in the recipe can be evaluated in a ripe cheese – which can result in further crippling lost sales as customers choose to buy something else that is tasting better in the meantime.

Each of the farmhouse Cheddar-makers draws upon a combination of information from make records and accumulated personal experience when problems arise. There are also technical advisers and graders available to help solve problems, but often their utility is limited by the fact that many of them were trained in large factories rather than in a farmhouse cheese-making environment. At a certain point, deduction from first principles and individual experimentation is an inefficient way for a farmhouse cheese-maker faced with production problems to solve them and get back on track.

For specialist retailers like Neal's Yard Dairy, commercial success hinges upon the consistent availability and quality of its star suppliers' cheeses; it is difficult if not impossible to source anything similar elsewhere, hence the imperative to share information and support cheese-makers as they attempt to solve their production problems.

Looking to France

Frustrated with the lack of technical support for farmhouse cheese-makers in the UK, we looked to France, where cheese-making with raw milk has not suffered the schism from the mainstream scientific and technical community that it has in the UK. Behind a pervasive discourse of tradition and cultural heritage, French farmhouse cheese-makers are hugely sophisticated technicians who take full advantage of a vibrant research scene and technical support network. In cheese-making regions throughout France, producers' groups and schools provide technical support for both small- and large-scale cheese-makers working with raw milk, while dairy scientists examine the behaviour of naturally occurring lactic acid bacteria in milk, the use of continuous whey starter cultures, and the utility of wooden boards for maturing. There is widespread acceptance and understanding among both cheese-makers and scientists that these farmhouse cheese-making techniques are much more complex and sophisticated than industrial cheese-making practices relying on standardized raw materials for consistency.

Assistance appeared in the form of French dairy consultant Ivan Larcher, formerly a cheese-making instructor at the Centre Fromager de Carmejane in south-eastern France. Though he had no previous experience with making classic British cheeses such as Cheddar, Larcher was well-placed to examine their methods from an informed technical perspective, and the cheese-makers were eager to start the dialogue. Through a series of ad-hoc workshops with Cheddar cheese-makers at different farms, including Bwlchwernen Fawr in Wales and Westcombe Dairy in Somerset, they have gone back to examine the tenets of raw milk Cheddar cheese-making and develop a body of knowledge of cause-and-effect to augment the received wisdom on which they were raised.

Looking back

Part of the excitement of looking to France for inspiration is access to its sophisticated network of farmhouse-cheese instructors who occupy the centre of the French cheese industry, and whose technical knowledge can be applied just as successfully to British cheeses. A second route to understanding Cheddar is to look back to texts written to guide cheese-makers in the cheese's heyday.

Early twentieth-century Somerset boasted a community of cheese-making schools and instructors with a technical focus that would be very much at home in France today. It was an exciting time: dairy scientists were beginning to define practical methods to increase consistency of production, and in many cheese-making counties, local authorities had set up a network of dairy schools and colleges, complete with legions of instructors, graders, and consultants, who 'on request ... would visit the farms and make the cheese in their efforts to set things right.'[6] These schools and instructors maintained links with agricultural research institutions and reported these institutions' findings to the cheese-makers with whom they worked so they might be put into practice. In short, farmhouse cheese-making was at the very centre of the dairy industry. Written in 1917, Dora Saker's textbook *Practical Cheddar Cheese-making* was a product of this social milieu.[7] Rediscovered recently in a pile of reference books that had sat gathering dust for many years, it has quickly acquired cult status amongst farmhouse cheese-makers.

Saker's book is fascinating for a number of reasons. Of utmost interest to the cheese-makers themselves are the methods espoused therein. While some are quite familiar, other aspects appear utterly foreign.

For Saker, good cheese is all about cleanliness and control. She focuses heavily on the importance of a clean milk supply, handled carefully so as to avoid taints. Cheese should only be made by a skilled practitioner who observes and understands the variations within the milk, the changing temperature of the dairy, and the variations over the seasons of the year, and who coaxes them into a consistent product by choreographing the delicate interplay between acidity development and moisture loss during the make. It was at around this time that the first tests for acidity were developed. The acidometer, which is still used in most small dairies today, had just arrived on the scene, but Saker also presents alternative tests that gave farmhouse cheese-makers the information required to control their makes without the need for sophisticated and expensive equipment.[8]

For Saker, the best cheeses are made on a farmhouse scale, not because they are 'artisan' but because it is at this level where the factors above are capable of coming together most successfully. It was also around this time that the first cheese factories were beginning to appear, and she had none too high an opinion of them:

> We find the best cheese made in individual farmhouses... the cause of inferior factory cheese is easily seen. The vendors of milk in many cases are thoroughly careless in the production of the same, as they are not troubled with the after results. It goes to many factories unstrained, warm, and in vessels that are not thoroughly cleansed ... this milk on reaching the factory is mixed with pure milk and contaminates the whole. Next at the factory ... the labour in many cases is unskilled. The cheese-maker (often a man who has previously attended to the boiler and just gleaned scraps of information) has no idea of the elementary rules governing the control of milk for cheese-making.[9]

In 1917, the best cheeses were made at the farmhouse level because that was where conditions permitted the closest contact with and most control over variable raw materials. By 2003, the situation had changed: factory cheese had been brought under control by stripping out the variables: milk was pasteurized and standardized, large amounts of uniform starter culture were used, and a great deal of mechanization helped to ensure that the process continued down the same narrow path over and over again.

An interesting exercise is to consider how the tenets of the Artisan Somerset Cheddar Presidium written in 2003 compare to Saker's definition of good Cheddar in 1917:

Made in Somerset. Dora Saker would agree that where the cows live and what they eat have a great impact on the raw milk and cheese – she spends a great deal of space talking about the effect of the soil type on the qualities of the milk and its implications for cheese-making, though she does not suggest that Somerset is better than anywhere else for milk production *per se*. In fact, Saker states that 'Cheddar has been made in Scotland only during the last sixty or seventy years, but such attention has been given to the process that in competition with the Somerset-makers the Scotch often come out victorious.'[10]

Made from the raw milk of the dairy's own cows. This is indeed one of the Somerset Cheddar-makers' most important and unique attributes, and is consistent with what Saker would have counselled cheese-makers to search out for best results in 1917. (Saker talks briefly about pasteurization as a route to complete control over the milk, but points out that it has technical drawbacks such as leading to a soft curd with poor ability to expel moisture, and that the flavour is 'never so strong' as that of unpasteurized cheese.[11])

Made using animal rennet. Calf's rennet remains the gold standard for cheese-making now, just as it was in 1917. Saker briefly touches on alternatives to commercially produced animal rennet, whose only drawback for her is its expense. These include pepsin extracted from pigs' stomachs and a substance called Subrenna, both of which were cheaper than calf's rennet but had technical drawbacks relating to excessive moisture being retained by the curd.

Made using pint starters. Starters were just coming into popular use in 1917, and her description of preparation of starter is strikingly similar to the methods used by the farmhouse Cheddar-makers today, albeit without the aseptic technique.

Cheddared by hand and clothbound. Dora Saker would likely have been perplexed by the inclusion of these points in the Presidium, as no alternatives existed in 1917; for her it would have been akin to saying that the cheese must be made with milk!

Aged at least 10 months. Again, this is consistent with Saker's expectations of the cheese. She says, 'Good cheddar should keep 12 months and should be capable of being sent to any part of the world without damage.'[12]

236

Saker's two overriding principles – cleanliness and correct alignment of acidification with moisture loss – do not appear in the Presidium. The first omission is not difficult to understand as cleanliness would have been taken for granted by the Presidium writers: *of course* the milk was gathered in sanitary conditions, filtered, and not allowed to sit around warm for hours before use! Equipped with HACCP plans and quality management systems, they are testament to the fact that Dora Saker's first gospel had been utterly embraced by the end of the twentieth century, to the point that nobody even thought to mention it.

Saker's other main point, about alignment of acidification with moisture loss, is quite a technical one, but it betrays how farmhouse Cheddar has imperceptibly drifted in the last 90 years. Saker herself was writing during a period of change. During the late nineteenth and early twentieth centuries, the methods for making Cheddar were being formalized, and Saker's and her colleagues' mission as dairy instructors, graders, and technologists was to help the myriad – and often not very conscientious or skilled – cheese-makers of Somerset make better and more consistent cheeses. It was not only in the early factories that quality was patchy, but in the small farmhouse dairies as well:

> It is a lamentable fact that the class of cheese turned out is still anything but uniform, and the dairies where first-class cheese is made are in the minority. The greater part of the cheese produced must be termed second rate.[13]

The original method of making Cheddar was to rely on the naturally-occurring lactic acid bacteria present in the raw milk to promote a slow and steady acidification, and under the best conditions the results of this method were very good, though there were multiple ways in which it could go wrong – the very idea of it would likely send a modern dairy health inspector into shock. Dora Saker and her colleagues recognized that use of starter had the potential to improve the consistency of the cheeses, so that even the worst cheese-makers would be able to make a saleable product. At the same time, she was aware that starters could be used improperly:

> Starters [have been] much abused, many cheese-makers adding a large quantity without judgment, with the consequence that over-acid cheese was produced and starters fell in bad repute ... the quantity required varies usually ¼–1%...the cheese should be ready to vat [mould] 7–8 hours after adding the starter.[14]

These technically specific details have provoked a fair amount of soul-searching on the part of the current generation of farmhouse Cheddar-makers. Simply stipulating 'use of pint starters' denotes something unique and special compared to the direct-vat starters employed by many large factories, but Saker's book provides specific evidence that the amount of starter and the way it is used has changed significantly. It is common for today's Cheddar-makers to use up to eight times as much starter by volume and to

237

complete the acidification several hours more quickly, and while those may sound like small changes, they have pronounced effects on the structure, texture, and flavour of the finished cheeses.

As a result of the groundwork laid by the use of less starter and time taken letting the milk ripen before adding rennet, the later stages of the process unfold in a very different way, producing a curd structure utterly different from that seen in today's Cheddars. Whereas it is common for today's Cheddar curds to be friable and mottled at the end of the cheddaring process, Saker specifies:

> The curd... should be in thin sheets and resemble chamois leather, velvety to the touch, smooth in texture, the joining of the granules of curd hardly discernible.[15]

The experimental workshops held by the Cheddar-makers over the past two years have focused on adjusting the progress of the make relative to the acidification process, with some quite striking and fascinating results.

The road ahead

It is an exciting time for British farmhouse cheese-makers. By drawing upon Continental technical expertise and newly rediscovered historical sources, they are beginning the process of truly understanding and taking control of their recipes. This technical renaissance will be played out in different ways. Some cheese-makers will attend the workshops and read the books, then return to making their cheese as they were before, but with a new appreciation for what makes it what it is. Others are already in the process of using the information now available to take their methods apart, experiment, and rebuild their cheeses one step at a time.

The purpose of these endeavours is not to slavishly recreate a 'more traditional' cheese, or make 'Cheddar how it was in 1917,' as if such a thing could even be conceived. Saker's book is evidence enough that Cheddar was not and never has been a static entity, and a cheese-maker one hundred years her senior would probably barely recognize the cheese she was teaching her students to make. Likewise, read between the lines in her textbook and it is very clear that the average Cheddar at the turn of the twentieth century was not nearly as palatable as the average Cheddar at the turn of the twenty-first. Rather than chase an idealized fantasy of an 'authentic' Cheddar, the goal of the workshops and experiments is to take some already-fantastic cheeses and understand what makes them tick, and then to find ways to help them express themselves more lucidly.

The deeper and more subversive message from Dora Saker is that 'artisanship' itself is a thoroughly modern social construction. Those who trade on the 'artisanal' nature of their goods would do well to remember that it cannot exist in a world without industrialization, as it is simply the 'anti-industrial'. The idea of 'artisanship' as an intrinsic virtue did not exist in Dora Saker's world. Cheeses were good because they were well-made. Farmhouse cheeses were better than factory cheeses because the farmhouse cheese-maker was more likely to have control over her raw materials, expert knowledge and skills, and a vested interest in the excellence of her finished products. And that was it. Dora Saker was in fact quite progressive, as shown by her capacity to spread the gospel about starters so soon after their arrival on the scene and her insistence on consistency. More importantly, she was utterly technical, focused on the process at hand, the skills required, and the integrity and quality that were hallmarks of a well-made cheese.

It is time to abandon false pretences about grizzled artisans and products that make themselves, for artisanship is truly about control. With small scale comes connection with one's own raw materials and sensitivity toward their minute differences from day to day. Good raw materials and received wisdom are a powerful combination, as the Cheddar-makers can attest. But only with knowledge of the inner workings of the process – the ability to read the causes and intuit their effects, and to theorize about how the process *should* be affected if this or that variable were changed in whatever way – can one correct for and control the process to make a consistently brilliant product. Under the tutelage of a French cheese consultant and a Somerset County Council dairy instructor's textbook, those pieces have started to fall into place. It is going to be an exciting ride.

Notes

1. http://www.dairyco.org.uk/datum/consumer/cheese-market/cheese-market.aspx (accessed April 2010).
2. http://www.marylandfarm.co.uk/thecultureofchee.html (accessed April 2010).
3. P. Kinstedt, *American Farmstead Cheese: The Complete Guide to Making and Selling Artisan Cheeses*. Chelsea Green, Vermont, 2005, 82.
4. http://www.spxflowtechnology.com/industries%20served/sanitary/sanitary_systems_cheese.asp (accessed April 2010).
5. http://www.dairyco.net/datum/dairy-processing--trade/dairy-product-production/uk-dairy-product-production.aspx (accessed April 2010).
6. F.W. Foulkes, *Hooked on Cheese*. Shrewsbury: Shropshire Libraries, 1985, 34.
7. D.G. Saker, *Practical Cheddar Cheese-making*. St Albans: The Campfield Press, 1917.
8. These include techniques such as 'the rennet test,' which involves testing the readiness of milk for renneting based upon the time it takes for a piece of straw to stop spinning in a small volume of milk to which a large amount of rennet had been added. 'The hot iron test' uses a piece of hot metal to test the acidity of the curds at a later stage by measuring the length to which their melted threads are capable of stretching. While these procedures may sound rather crude, they represent a level of measurement that is hard to match even with expensive pH meters today.
9. Ibid, p. 39.
10. Ibid, p. 38.
11. Ibid, p. 89.
12. Ibid, p. 82.
13. Ibid, p. 39.
14. Ibid, p. 39.
15. Ibid, p. 50.

Dried, Frozen and Rotted: Food Preservation in Central Asia and Siberia

Charles Perry

Northern Eurasia is generally unsuitable for agriculture. Most of its inhabitants have traditionally lived a wandering life as herdsmen or hunters, outside a few areas where large annual fish spawns made it possible to live in year-round villages. Food preservation has always been a desperate necessity, and a good deal of ingenuity has been invested in preserving the available ingredients. This was not often appreciated by eighteenth- and nineteenth-century visitors, who regularly complained about the leathery texture of dried fish, reported that fishing villages could be smelled several kilometers away and speculated gravely on the reasons for the prevalence of tapeworm in Siberia.

The northern tier of this region, located mostly above the Arctic Circle, is inhabited by, from west to east, the Lapps of northern Scandinavia; the distantly related Komi just west of the northernmost Ural Mountains; the northern Samoyeds (Nenets and Nganasan) of the Yamal and Taimyr Peninsulas; the Yakuts, the most numerous people of Siberia, in the Lena, Yana, Indigirka and Kolyma river basins; and the Chukchi, Koryak and Itelmen of far north-eastern Siberia and the Kamchatka Peninsula. There are also small remnant populations of Yukaghirs and Yupik Eskimos in the far north-east.

The middle tier consists of the Khanty and Mansi (distantly related to the Hungarians) of the Ob River and its tributaries; the Kets, Selkups and Dolgans of the Yenisei and its tributaries; the Tungus (belonging to two groups with the distractingly similar names Evenk and Even) who herd reindeer in a 2.5 million square-kilometer area extending from the Yenisei to the Sea of Okhotsk; and small groups speaking Manchu-Tungus languages in the lower Amur River region (the Manchus, immediately to their south in Manchuria, used to speak a related language). The Nivkh inhabit Sakhalin Island, a northern extension of the Japanese chain offshore of the Amur delta.

In the southern tier live nomadic Turks (Kazakhs, Kyrgyz and Siberian Tatars) and Mongols such as the Khalkha of Mongolia proper and the Buriats of the Lake Baikal region. Between them, in the Altai and Sayan Mountains, are the small Turkish-speaking Altai, Shor, Khakas and Tuva groups, partly pastoral, partly hunting-gathering and (uniquely for this area) partly agricultural.

The Turks and Mongols occupy the vast central Asian grasslands, herding horses and sheep and, to a less important degree, goats and camels. They sometimes fish, but fish is a despised food and the term 'fisherman' (*baliqchi*) is used as an insult. The ease of travel on the steppes has meant that Turkic and Mongolian foods and techniques have spread quite far, reaching even the sedentary Manchus of far north-eastern China.

The Yakuts, an offshoot of the steppe culture, raise cattle and horses (with a fair amount of difficulty) along with reindeer in their far northern territory. The Tungus mostly herd reindeer, though some are horse or sheep herders and some fish. Reindeer are wonderfully adapted to the subarctic forests and tundra, and four groups living at the northern margins of Siberia (the Nganasan, the Tundra Nenets, and sections of the Chukchi and Koryak) live almost entirely off their herds. However, monoculture is rare in this precarious environment. Most reindeer herders also hunt or fish or both.

In far north-eastern Siberia, a few groups live exclusively by hunting. The Yukaghirs are forest hunters, and the coastal Chukchi and Koryak and the Yupik Eskimos hunt marine mammals such as seals, walrus and whales. They rarely if ever eat fish.

Some groups appear to have lived where they are from time immemorial, such as the Lapps, Khanty, Mansi, Itelmen and Nivkh. The herding peoples, by contrast, have been expanding northward for the last 1,500 years or so. The domestication of the reindeer has probably had as great an effect upon Siberia as the introduction of the horse upon the American Great Plains.

In what follows the present tense is used, though many traditional practices have understandably disappeared.

Plant foods

The people of northern Siberia and the Altai Mountains often gather roots, particularly of daylily and adder's tongue, and preserve them by drying or freezing. The Chukchi and Yakuts regularly steal roots from fieldmouse burrows,[1] being careful not to take them all, lest this source of food dry up (or, as the Chukchi believe, lest the mice retaliate by magic).[2]

241

The Nivkh and the Komi preserve mushrooms by salting,[3] and the Komi also dry them without salt: с'öд тшак (s'əd chak), literally 'black mushrooms.'[4] Pine sapwood is consumed in many parts of the far north; it is a source of sucrose and fructose, particularly in autumn and winter. Conveniently, the sugar level is highest near the bark.[5] The forest Lapps scrape sapwood (guolmas) 'so that it looks like fine linen,' then dry it in the sun, bury it in birch bark boxes, cover the pit with sand and build a fire over it for a day. The bark turns red and they eat it 'like candy'.[6]

The Chukchi and Koryaks store great quantities of partially digested moss from reindeer stomachs by boiling and then drying it. They also pound willow leaves with the reindeer moss gruel and ferment it in sacks. This is eaten like salad with dried meat.[7]

Milk

The only groups that do not milk their herds are the Samoyeds, Chukchi and Koryaks. Lactose intolerance might be suspected, but among the last two groups, the reason might easily be that their reindeer are only semi-domesticated and may not stand for milking.

All the Turkic peoples preserve yoghurt by draining the whey from it and then sun-drying into hard balls or lumps called *qurut*. This is generally consumed by grinding it into a powder and adding to soup. In the eastern Altai, the Tuva further preserve *qurut* by smoking.[8] The Turks also make a sort of cheese called *bishlaq* by boiling yoghurt to curdle it and then drying the curds. This will keep but is often consumed fresh.

Both these products have been adopted by the Mongols, and the word хурут or нурууд (*khurut, huruud*) is particularly widespread in the Mongolian languages. It is one of the steppe products to have reached Manchuria, where *kūru* is 'a type of sour cake made from cow's or mare's milk and liquor'.[9]

The Mongols also make some preserved dairy products with names that evidently derive from the Turkish root *aghar-* 'to become white.' One is Khalkha Mongol ааруул (*aaruul*), 'a thick cheese made from boiled curds,' which sounds a lot like *bishlaq*, though the word *byaslag* is also known, explained as 'cheese made of curds which are dried after their whey has been pressed out,' [10] The distinction is also said to be that *byaslag* is made from whole milk, *aaruul* from skim.[11] *Aaruul* is often rolled into worm shapes (хорхой ааруул), Another product is Classical Mongolian *agharcha*, Khalkha аарц (*aarts*), Buriat айрхан (*ayrhan*) 'curd cheese' (*tvorog*),[12] which entered Tungus as аарца (*aartsa*) or аарча (*aarcha*), eventually reaching Manchu as *arcan* 'cream, milk, thickened with wine and sugar'.[13]

One native Mongolian preparation has been borrowed by others, *ejegei* or *eezgei*, 'curds.' The Baraba Tatar ачагай (*achagay*) is 'a thick clabber cooked in the oven and fried brown, then dried in the sun to a thick mass'.[14] The Kazakhs, Khakas and Kyrgyz boil milk with yoghurt or beestings added to curdle it and strain the curds.[15] As another instance of the spread of nomad foods, this word has reached Manchu as *ejihe* ('a food made from dried cream').[16]

The Yakuts allow yoghurt to age and grow stronger through the summer, making a thick substance called *tar*, which they often enrich with other ingredients such as berries, wild sorrel, the bones of horses, cows and fish, and chopped, boiled pine sapwood. Lactic acid softens the bones to the consistency of gristle. In winter, the *tar* is frozen. For use, it is diluted and mixed with powdered sapwood to make a soup called *butugas*. If chopped sapwood is added ('like noodles') instead, the soup is called *yuere*.[17]

Reindeer milk is often preserved by freezing, sometimes (among the Lapps) by drying or making cheese.[18] It is extremely rich, with a butterfat-content of 17 per cent, and the Lapps churn it into butter, which they store in tubs. The Turks and Mongols make butter from sheep and goat milk and preserve it by sewing it in leather sacks. Whichever sort of container the butter is stored in, it eventually oxidizes. Fortunately, the flavor of rancid butter is appreciated in northern Eurasia (as it is also in Morocco, Ethiopia and Tibet).

Another process could be considered a way of preserving milk: fermentation. The only milk suitable for this is mare's milk, which is very low in fat but high enough in sugar to make a sort of milk wine, the kumis (*qïmïz*) of the horse-herding peoples.

Kumis can be distilled to make a product that keeps even better and is even more remote from the idea of food, mare's milk brandy (*araq, arakhi*). The technique of distillation was enthusiastically received in Siberia, where brandy has been made from anything that will ferment.

Blood

Blood is nearly as nutritious as flesh, and nomads never waste it. Mostly they mix it with fat (blood is relatively deficient in calories) and sometimes also milk to make blood sausage, called *qan* in the Turkic languages, шавай *(shavay)* or нярам *(hiaram)* in Mongolian and буюксэ (*buyukse*) among the Tungus. A Khalkha Mongolian expression meaning 'to be well satisfied' is *shavay n' hanah*, 'to bleed blood sausage'.

The Lapps make blood sausage, and they also boil blood to thicken it and store it in firkins or reindeer stomachs – blood has been an article of commerce in Lapland.[19] The Yukaghir and Chukchi store blood in leather containers where it freezes in winter or ferments in summer.[20] The Nenets Samoyeds freeze blood in the open air and cook it as soup or pancakes.

Sausage

The Turks make the familiar sort of sausage of ground meat and fat, called сужук (*suzhuk*) by the Kazakhs, чочых (*chochïkh*) by the Khakas and кыйма (*qïyma*) by the Altai and others; the Buriat Mongols have borrowed this last as хиймε (*khiyme*). The most typical central Asian sausages, however, are the horsemeat sausage карта *(karta)* and казы (*qazi*), made primarily from horse belly fat (which is bland but quite pleasant). The Tungus also make ground-meat sausage, кучи (*kuchi*).

243

Fat

The colder the climate, the greater the need for calories. Reindeer meat is rather low in fat, though a well-pastured reindeer will develop a good layer of subcutaneous fat, and the Lapps and the Nenets store what fat they can accumulate in reindeer stomachs; the Lapps serve melted fat as a sauce for reindeer meat.[21] The Koryaks and Itelmen store whale and seal blubber in pits (which is probably as much a way of preserving it from animals, including their dogs, as from spoilage). The Nivkh store seal blubber in seal stomach, лаӈртʻомсиф (*laŋrt'omsif*).[22] As with butter, none of the blubber preservation methods prevents spoilage, and the resulting sour and rancid flavors are relished.

Jerky

Drying is an uncommon way of preserving meat among the Turkic nations, though the Kazakhs make a salted, smoked horsemeat called сур эт (*sur et*).[23] However, jerky is very characteristic of the Mongols, whose method is to cut the meat in thin strips and hang them on frameworks of sticks to dry in the wind. Their name for this product – Classical Mongol *borcha*, Khalkha борцэ (*bortse*), Buriat борсо (*borso*) – has spread to the lower Amur: Negidal барча (*barcha*), Nanai борци (*bortsi*) and Manchu *borchilaha*. Since jerky is frequently pounded to bits for cooking in soup, the Khanty, Mansi, Khakas and Tungus often keep it in ready-pounded form.

Drying meat is practised throughout northern Asia by everyone from the Lapps to the Eskimos, who dry whale and walrus meat. Where salt is available, it may be salted, and in some places it is optionally smoked. The Nganasan also mix it with fat as a preservative.[24] The Tungus call dried meat хуликта (*khulikta*) or хулта (*khulta*), among other names (the Mongolian term *barcha* is known); хо̄ро̄чо̄ (*khōrōchō*) or хо̄рча̄ (*khōrchā*) more specifically means pounded jerky. The Chukchi know the Mongolian and Tungus practice of cutting meat in thin slices for drying, but they consider it excessively laborious and make jerky only in spring, when the meat will dry successfully in thicker slices.[25]

Frozen meat

One convenience of a frigid climate is that meat may simply be frozen. For eating, slices are shaved off with a knife, hence the usual Russian name for this product, строганина (*stroganina*), from the verb 'to shave.' This is practised by all the reindeer-herding people and the seal- and walrus-hunters of the far north-east. In the Altai, the Khakas freeze assorted horse parts, ысты (*ïstï*), as well as loaves of ground meat, хыйма (*khïyma*). [26]

Fermented (soured) meat

In the far north-east, meat is often preserved (if that is the word to use) by storing it in leather sacks or wrapping it in grass and burying it in pits, where it ferments. The coastal Chukchi[27] and Koryak[28] consider sour seal flippers a delicacy. The Chukchi sew pieces of walrus meat weighing up to 80 kg in walrus skin and store them in pits to make semi-fermented walrus (*k'opalgyn*).[29] The Eskimos also eat fermented whale and walrus meat.

It might be noted that until recently, Russians living in northern Siberia have often buried meat, dumplings and other foods to preserve them (though not with the intent of souring), simply because of the harsh climate. In winter, the soil is as hard as iron, and when it thaws, it heaves and becomes mushy, so digging a cellar was impractical.

Dried fish

All the fishing people preserve their catch by drying. It is such a basic food to the Nivkh that they have an elemental word for it, ма (*ma*). The Russian word for dried fish, юкола (*iukola*), is borrowed from the Mansi ёхӯл (*yokhūl*).

In many places, fish is purely wind-dried in the Mongol manner, salt being unavailable.[30] Salting is traditional among the Lapps, Khanty, Mansi and Nivkh; the last distinguish salted fish тафтьси ч'о (*taft'si ch'o*) from ма. Often dried fish is lightly smoked. Since smoke repels the insects that plague the tundra during the fishing season,[31] this practice may have originated as a way of preserving the fish from them, rather than from microbial spoilage.

Dried fish is often powdered for convenience in cooking, particularly by the Tungus, the Kets and the Selkups.[32] The Khanty and Mansi also dry fish heads and pound them. 'Ostyak bread' (Ostyak being an older name of the Khanty) is made from a mixture of flour and ground fish heads.[33]

The Russian name for powdered dried fish, порса (*porsa*), looks as if it derives from the Mongolian word for jerky, but the picture is clouded. It may come from a word current in some Turkish languages, such as the Yakut барча (*barcha*) or Khakas порча (*porcha*),[34] which might ultimately derive from the Persian word *parcheh* 'piece'; cf. the Yakut verb барчаты-, 'to smash into small pieces'.

Dried roe

The Nivkh and Itelmen are so fish-rich that dried roe is a basic food, which they call by special names, qʼomq *(qʼomq)* [35] and нэʼлнэʼл *(ŋəʼlŋəʼl)* [36] respectively. The Itelmen often eat it along with sapwood 'because the roe alone is so gluey it sticks to the teeth, and the bark is so dry it can't be swallowed alone'.[37]

Frozen fish

Wherever possible, fish is frozen in the same way as meat. In Russian this is known as *stroganina*, in the Ob Basin sometimes as патанка (*patanka*), from the Khanty and Mansi term *påtəm kūl*, elsewhere in Siberia occasionally by the Tungus word талака (*talaka*). When the fish is frozen less than rock-hard, it may be cut into chunks, rather than shaved in thin slices, a treatment the Russians call рубанина (*rubanina*).

Fermented (soured) fish

Fish is fermented in tubs, sacks or pits throughout northern Eurasia. The Lapps make a product much like the Swedish *surströmming*, and the Yakuts sour fish in pits and then freeze this product, called сыма (*sïma*), in 40-kilogram bundles.[38] The Itelmen rot fish in pits until the gristle dissolves – sometimes it rots to such a degree that it has to be removed from the pits with a sort of ladle. The resulting rancid flavor is highly esteemed.[39] This practice probably arose because the Itelmen don't have time during the great fish spawns to dry all the fish they land.[40] They also sour roe in pits. The Chukchi and Koryaks sour fish (and roe) in leather sacks.

Unique preservation methods

The Nanay (Goldi) of the Amur coast fry up a mess of fish with fish oil, making a sort of fish *confit* called *taksan*.[41] Their neighbors, the Negidal, make a preparation of honeysuckle, blueberries and red caviar boiled down to a thick paste which is eaten in winter with fish oil.[42]

245

Note on transliteration from the Cyrillic alphabet:

For Russian words I follow the Library of Congress system (i is either a vowel or consonant, depending on position, y represents a narrow mid back vowel halfway between the sounds of 'bit' and 'but,' an apostrophe indicates either a palatized consonant or, before a vowel, a syllable boundary, and kh is a guttural fricative). The languages of Central Asia and Siberia have been recorded by a number of idiosyncratic systems, sometimes several for the same language. For clarity, I have rendered Siberian words within parentheses using the following broad transcription: y is a consonant, the mid back vowel is represented by ï, ə is the vowel of 'but,' ŋ is the guttural nasal (ng), q is a voiceless uvular stop, an apostrophe indicates either palatization or (in Chukchi and Itelmen) a glottal stop, and an opening quote mark indicates aspiration in Nivkh.

Notes

1. Bogoras, W, 1904–1909, 'The Chukchee,' *Memoirs of the American Museum of Natural History*. Leiden: E.J. Brill, and New York: G.E. Stechert, p. 197. Priklonski, V. L., et al., *Yakut Ethnographic Sketches*. New Haven: Human Relations Area Files, 1953, p. 26.
2. Bogoras, op. cit.; p. 198: 'It is considered dangerous, however, to take all the roots from the nests, because the owner might retaliate by magic. Moreover, the Chukchee believe that some of the roots and herbs found in the storehouses of mice are poisonous, and are gathered by the mice partly for the purpose of poisoning the robbers....'.
3. Savel'eva, V.N. and Taksami, Ch. M. *Nivkhsko-Russkii Slovar'*, Moscow: Sovetskaia Entsiklopediia, 1970, p. 345.
4. Lytkin, V.I. *Komi-Russkii Slovar'*, Moscow: Gosudarstvennoe Izdatel'stvo Inostrannykh i Natsional'nykh Iazykov, 1966, p. 700.
5. Terziev, N., Boutelje, K. and Larsson, K. 'Seasonal Fluctuations of Low-Molecular Weight Sugars, Starch and Nitrogen in Sapwood of *Pinus Sylvestris* L.,' *Scandinavian Journal of Forest Research, 12*, Oslo: Scandinavian University Press, 1997, pp. 216–224.
6. Rheen, S. (1671), *Relation about the Life, Customs and Superstitions of the Lapps*, quoted in Collinder, B., *The Lapps*. Princeton University, 1949, pp. 78–79.
7. Bogoras, ibid.
8. Levin, M.G. and Potapov, L. P. (eds.) *The Peoples of Siberia*. University of Chicago, 1964, p. 414.
9. Norman, J. *A Concise Manchu-English Lexicon*. Seattle: University of Washington, 1978, p. 182.
10. Hangin, G. *A Modern Mongolian-English Dictionary*. Indiana University, 1986, p. 100.
11. Levin and Potapov, op. cit., p. 230.
12. Tsydynzhapov, G. and Badueva, E. *Buriatskaia Kukhnia*. Ulan-Ude: Buriatskoe Knizhnoe Izdatel'stvo, 1991, p. 10.
13. Norman, op cit, p. 19.
14. Valeev, F. T. and Tomilov, N. A. *Tatary Zapadnoi Sibiri*. Novosibirsk: Nauk, 1996, p.105 .
15. Azarovym, V. *Kazakhskaia Kukhnia*. Alma-Ata: Kainar, 1981, p. 100, эчегей (*echegey*). Butanaev, V. Ia., *Khoorai As-Tamakhtary/Natsional'nye Bliuda Khakasov*. Abakan, 1994, p. 9, эчигей (*echigey*). Weeks, M. E. *The New Kyrgyz-English Culinary Dictionary*. Northampton, Mass.: Martha's Samizdat, 2001 p. 89, эжигей (*ejigey*).
16. Norman, op. cit., p. 72.

17. Priklonski, op cit., p. 24.
18. Kulonen, U.-M., *Saami: A Cultural Encyclopedia*. Helsinki: Suomalainen Kirjalainen Seura, 2005.
19. Rheen, quoted in Collinder, op cit., p. 77.
20. Bogoras, op. cit., p. 195.
21. Collinder, op. cit., p. 80.
22,. Saval'eva and Taksami, op. cit., p. 156.
23. Azarovym, op. cit., p. 95.
24. Hajdú, P. *The Samoyed Peoples and Languages*. Bloomington: University of Indiana/The Hague: Mouton & Co.,1962, p. 20.
25. Bogoras, op. cit., p. 195.
26. Butanaev, op cit., pp. 3 and 6.
27. Levin and Potapov, op. cit., p. 813.
28. Post by Kotcheshkov, a coastal Koryak, at http://www.indigenous.ru/fotki/bull_eng/e_14.htm
29. Levin and Potapov, op. cit., p. 813. This preparation is also mentioned in Strogoff, M., Brochet, P-C. and Auzias, D. *Guidebook Chukotka*. Moscow: Avant-Garde, 2006. As the title indicates, this is not a scholarly work but a guide for visitors to the region. It thanks a large number of informants, many with Chukchi surnames, but I have no way of verifying the information it contains. Nevertheless, for their interest I will include here some of the Chukchi food preparations mentioned in this book. *Vilk'ityn*: Fermented reindeer. 'Meat from the summer slaughter is tightly packed in leather sacks and kept in a cool dry place. It is ready by the first frosts, and is eaten raw (*stroganina*) [that is, frozen and then shaved into edible pieces] or boiled.' *Villyegyt*: fermented seal flippers. 'They are wrapped in grass and packed in a tightly closed leather sack. In summer the dish is ready in three or four days. It is considered a great delicacy.' *Vilmullymud*: 'Reindeer hooves, horns and lips are fried [that is, roasted] on a naked flame. Then they are cleared of ash and put into cold water for three or four days to get rid of the bitter taste. Then they are simmered until soft, put into a leather sack together with fresh reindeer liver, kidneys and blood, and tightly fastened. After several months the dish is ready to eat.'
30. Seroshevskii, V.L. (1896), *Iakuty: Opyt Etnograficheskovo Issledovaniia*. Moscow: Rossiiskaia Politicheskaia Entsiklopediia, reprint 1993, p. 309. 'In the north, the Yakuts' consumption and preservation of fish is distinguished from that of the Russians only in this, that the Yakuts never salt fish, but rather smoke, dry or sour it.'
31. Ziker, J.P. *Peoples of the Tundra*. Prospect Heights, Ohio: Weyland Press, 2002, p. 58. This book records the practices of the Dolgans.
32. Hajdú, op. cit., p. 24.
33. Gemuev, I.N., et al. *Narody Zapadnoi Sibiri*. Moscow, Nauk, 2008, p. 683.
34. Butanaev, op. cit., p. 3. However, this word refers to meat, rather than fish.
35. Saval'eva and Taksami, op. cit., p. 150.
36. Dürr, M., Kasten, E., and Khaloimova, K. *Itelmen Language and Culture*. Munster: Waxman, 2001, p. 68.
37. Steller, G.W. *Steller's History of Kamchatka*. Trans. Engel, M. and Williams, K. Fairbanks: University of Alaska, 2003, p. 226.
38. Seroshevskii, op. cit., p. 311.
39. Steller, op. cit., p. 226.
40. Jochelson, W. *The Kamchadals*. Unpublished early twentieth-century MS; online typescript at www.faculty.uaf.edu/ffdck, p. 5.
41. Levin and Potapov, op.cit., p. 708.
42. Levin and Potapov, op. cit., p. 689.

Unlovely Images: Preserved and Cured Fish in Art

Gillian Riley

This paper will complement more detailed papers on salt cod, stockfish, and the varieties of salt and pickled herrings. It deals with visual information, and the things we might reasonably conclude from this.

Preserved and cured fish have been a staple food throughout history, but evidence of what they were like is hard to find. Printed and manuscript sources do not dwell on what were staple foods, and recipe books often ignore them. Some foodstuffs are visually appealing and so look good in paintings, but cured fish is not like a luscious peach, or a fine cooked ham, or loaf of crusty bread, and there has to be quite a strong agenda for it to be included in a still life or kitchen scene. Living or just recently dead fish are visually attractive, and have been celebrated in still lifes and kitchen and market scenes and seascapes, from Aertsen to Chardin, but shrivelled, darkened, wizened cured fish are not things of beauty. A still life from the 1660s by Bartolomeo Arbotori shows a whole range of preserved fish, but even his warm tones and skilful lighting cannot glamorize them. In the centre of the composition hang some salt cod or stockfish, flanked by candles and some supple and shining smoked fish, possibly haddock. Beneath are two rigid dried salt fish on a wooden board, and underneath them a shallow bowl with uncertain contents, maybe pickled small fish or anchovies. To the right is a deeper bowl with the protruding handle of a long spoon or ladle. The table on which they sit also has a group of fish, perhaps herring, their floppiness denoting a lighter cure. Central to the composition is a bitter orange, a welcome touch of brightness, and a welcome seasoning for almost all of the fishes represented.

Back in Renaissance Italy in the late fourteenth century the *Tacuinum Sanitatis*, a medieval Arab health handbook translated into Latin, circulated in manuscript, illustrated scenes from everyday life in northern Italy. One illustration shows a shop selling whole salt cod, and various kinds of fish packed in barrels and tubs of salt, and another establishment purveys fish in vinegar.

Anchovies and certain noble fish, tunny and salmon, were one of those fish whose qualities are enhanced by preservation, and so are greatly esteemed. On the other hand there are those which survive the process to become a staple with little to recommend them as fine food, like salt or pickled herrings or smoked fish, treated to survive heat, cold and shipwreck. Some from both categories appear in fine art, and are worth seeking out in work from the Low Countries, Italy and Spain.

A fish market of 1568 by Joachim Beuckelaer shows the arrival of the fishing fleet, the unloading and the sale of fish, ostensibly illustrating the bible story of the 'miraculous catch' set against the then modern port of Antwerp. In the bottom right-hand corner sits a young woman offering salt or smoked herring in bread rolls, *brodjes*, welcome street snacks today as then. The painting contrasts the fresh with the cured, the ephemeral with provisions for long voyages. Many fish-market scenes by Beuckelaer or his studio show as well as the day's catch, freshwater fish in tubs, and cured and smoked fish in wooden platters or barrels, and sometimes what might be a lump of salt cod, or stockfish. It is significant that the basic preserved fish are so frequently included in visual celebrations of the fresh catch of the day.

A still life of 1656 by Joseph de Bray in praise of the pickled herring is in the form of a memorial tablet draped in vine leaves with a garland of peeled onions at its base. From the scrolled head hang two kinds of salted and smoked herrings, and beneath the inscribed cartouche at its base is a linen-draped table with bowls of cheese, butter, some slices of bread, and a plate with the star item, a sliced, gutted lightly pickled herring, surrounded by a selection of the renowned Dutch beer, essential accompaniment. The inscribed tablet shows the text of a poem by the preacher and poet Jacob Westerbaen, extolling the visual and gastronomic delights of the herring, and some fairly coarse observations of its insalubrious gastric effects.

This delicious cheap fatherland food, displayed alongside the bread and beer that traditionally nourished the down-to-earth citizens of this proud maritime nation, is symbolic of the virtues that made the Netherlands great and invincible. So the sliced salt herring, onion, bread and beer, can be read as a patriotic snack, popular Lenten fare, or a symbol of the Eucharist. Both Catholic and Protestant painters and their clients depicted herrings in contexts where religion and national pride reinforced each other. *249*

In an *Ontbijtje* by Pieter Claesz, the bread, beer and herring speak for themselves. The herring is usually shown on the bone, with head and tail attached, cut into bite-sized pieces, usually accompanied by the bread and onion it is still served with today. Hard to tell if it is the *groene haring* (lightly salted overnight and eaten at once, for the enzymes and bacteria that, in conjunction with the gall bladder, create an ephemeral burst of flavour, do not give it everlasting life), or a pickled herring treated with a longer pickling and keeping time.

Herrings figure in works by Georg Flegel and Gotthardt Wedig. They occur in contrasting pairs of paintings – the *Poor Man's Meal*, and the *Rich Man's Meal*, by Hieronymus Francken the Younger and a generation later Clara Peeters, where the tasty food of the poor is presented as palatable if not visually exciting, in contrast with the sweetmeats and cookies, fine wines and expensive silver plate of the rich. Sébastien Stoskopf included a carp and a few pickled herrings, with a mysterious light filtering through a squat bottle of eau-de-vie in one of his still and numinous paintings. *Pronk,* or Posh Snacks, show lobsters, oysters, whose expensive freshness is a status symbol, along with hothouse fruit, musical instruments and fine wines. Humble salt fish sits on earthenware dishes, alongside ceramic beer jars and sturdy glass. This moral and gastronomic dichotomy was to be shattered by Willem van Aelst in the 1660s with his disturbingly Mannerist combination of a disembowelled freshly cured herring, cut up and ready to eat, the prized roe slurping over the edge of a silver platter, resting on sumptuous red silken velvet, with fine wines in priceless goblets, and an absurdly ornate salt cellar. Over-the-top luxury and a reminder of the austere simplicities of the founders of the Republic displayed together to point a moral – that commercial acumen and frugality is rewarded with worldly goods of great price.

Popular engravings contrasting the miseries of the Lenten or lean cuisine and the fleshpots of the fat, show preserved fish in a poor light, but give some idea of what was available and eaten by everybody during Lent. In an engraving by Pieter van der Heyden after Breugel of the lean cuisine, an emaciated figure is seen bashing a lump of stockfish with a mallet, the first stage in the preparation of this hard wind-dried fish. Chardin painted a pair of still lifes – *Menu de gras*, and *Menu de maigre*, where herrings, along with eggs and spring onions, are the components of a lean meal.

In eighteenth-century Madrid, Meléndez allows us one glimpse of salt cod, in the context of a recipe which includes cauliflower and eggs, and he also shows two meals which include salt fish. These are worth investigating for Meléndez always had a well-defined theme to his still lifes, and salt fish as part of an impromptu meal might explain some of the tubs and barrels on his paintings. They could have contained olives, but we can guess at anchovies and preserved fish. What looks like salt herrings are part of a meal, including spring onions and bread, with what might be a jug of gazpacho.

The salt cod is almost lost behind a resplendent cauliflower which glows with pale gold freshness and dominates the composition, and represents the ingredients of a typical Lenten dish, traditionally prepared on Christmas Eve. This unlikely combination is in fact delicious, made with respectful attention to what Meléndez is telling us in the painting, for both he and his patron, the Prince of Asturias, heir to the Spanish throne, would have known this dish and what went into it. Much garlic and plenty of olive oil are indicated. The little packets of spices probably contained pepper and cinnamon or cloves, while today many versions of the recipe use paprika or chilli which do not seem to have been available in eighteenth-century Madrid. Two other paintings attributed to Meléndez have the same combination of cauliflower and salt cod, so it is possible to surmise that this dish had some special significance for his wealthy clients, perhaps regional or religious loyalties.

The glimpses of preserved fish in the paintings discussed here tell us more than seemed likely about their gastronomic potential and visual appeal, and their importance as subsistence food and in more sophisticated recipes as well as their religious symbolism.

Unidentified Fermented Objects: the Secret Food Department of the National Museum of Ethnology

Linda Roodenburg

Animals transform into meat, plants into vegetables and fruits into vitamin C. Becoming food is the final stage of living matter. Some are privileged to a delay of the foreshadowed end. They gain years of life by being preserved. But a chosen few turn into objects and will never be crunched between the teeth of any other living being. They live anonymous, comatose lives in the hidden food department of a museum.

Museums collect and preserve objects that are valuable, beautiful and interesting for scientific research. In the last decades food museums have sprung up like mushrooms. Single-subject food museums (chocolate, foie gras, mustard, ramen, cheese, Coca Cola), agricultural and seafood museums: they all focus on food from different points of view. But none of them preserve food. They don't have food collections. *The Most Beautiful Oyster* is not a real oyster, but an oyster immortalized in paint by Pieter Claesz in 1630. And a preserved pig in a museum collection is no *confit de porc*, but a Damian Hirst, worth $8,000,000.

A few years ago the National Museum of Ethnology in Leiden invited me to curate an exhibition about 'food and culture'. This was a remarkable invitation, because it meant a break with the traditional display of Japanese paintings, Indonesian batiks, Mexican pottery and other typical ethnographic objects. An alarming decrease of visitors forced the newly renovated museum to change its policy and an exhibition about 'food' would hopefully attract a new public.

Objects in European ethnological museums are strongly connected to the colonial and scientific exploration of the non-Western world in the eighteenth and nineteenth centuries, an era with an unappeasable hunger for exotic objects. 'Ethnology' was a general term for what we consider now as separate disciplines. Palaeontologists, physicians, linguists, historians and ethnographers all made contributions to the study of exotic peoples and the development of mankind. A great variety of objects and material, organic and non-organic, was collected and shipped to Europe. The first museum in Western Europe for the storage and study of ethnological objects was founded in 1864 in Leiden.

At the turn of the twentieth century this generalistic view changed. Ethnology disengaged itself from natural sciences and evolved into a new discipline. Modern anthropology took shape, concentrating on analysing and interpreting social structures of primitive societies and functional connections between people. The measuring and classifying of the human race gave way to the study of cultures in the world. With this change certain objects in Dutch ethnological collections – human remains and all other organic objects – became irrelevant for new anthropological research. They moved to anatomical and natural history collections. But some survived.

I accepted the invitation and started my research. The images and object descriptions in the museum database gave a first insight into the collection. It was interesting to see that from a culinary perspective the majority of about 250,000 objects – bowls, pots, tools and even paintings – were more or less related to food. Masterpieces like a complete kitchen inventory for traditional cooking from Baltistan (northern Pakistan), a nineteenth-century wooden copy of a Wedgwood dinner set from west Africa, an amazingly detailed model of a traditional Japanese kitchen with all the miniature knives, bowls, pots and pans made from the real materials passed before my eyes, and were included in a first selection for the exhibition. But there was one problem. How could I make an exhibition about food without food? Displaying real food together with museum objects was out of the question, impossible. Organic material attracts insects which destroy vulnerable masterpieces.

When I visited the museum depots – safely hidden in Second World War bunkers in the dunes near The Hague – to look at the objects which I had selected, I discovered that I had missed an interesting part of the collection. Standing hidden in dark corners there were pots, jars, bottles and boxes covered with dust, with hardly visible and unidentified contents (see figure 1). A glass jar was filled with a black sludge, labeled 'Siam'; another one contained moldy, brown balls from 'Persia'. On an old cigar box someone had written: *shark fins*.

Nobody had looked after these objects for ages. They formed part of the museum's secret food department. Once collected as valuable objects for scientific research, but in the course of years downgraded as irrelevant, and for which the ultimate date of consumption had passed more than a century ago. Apparently no other museum had ever shown any interest in them. That is how they survived. Without any meddling from museum conservators, the contents fermented, dried, molded or evaporated; a process of slow museum preservation that is still going on. Although the conservation department muttered objections – the objects were not described properly, which could cause logistical problems – I added them to my list. They belonged to the museum collection, so they were not governed by the rule of not displaying organic material.

Including them in the exhibition also meant identifying the contents of the jars and boxes, where they came from, who collected them and why. Old inventory numbers, hand-written on the objects, seemed to be the key to their stories. They referred to more or less famous scientists and explorers or donations from other institutions. In old registration systems and books, carefully kept in the museum library, I found the data I was looking for.

Philipp Franz von Siebold food collection

In the eighteenth and nineteenth centuries the Dutch were the only foreigners with

Figure 1 (above). Delicacies from Siam, 1883: peas, sea cucumber and glutinous rice.
Figure 2 (left). Seaweed collected by von Siebold, 1826.

253

254   *Figure 3 (above). Delicacies from the Dutch Indies, 1883. First row: dried fish, turtle, squid and* emping melindjo.
Figure 4 (below). Chinese delicacies, 1883.

permission to stay in Japan. Commissioned by the Dutch East Indian government, the German scientist Philipp von Siebold (1796–1866) collected material for the study of Japanese nature and culture. From 1823 till 1829 he lived in the Dutch settlement of Deshima, a small, artificial island in the Bay of Nagasaki. He was not allowed to leave the island. He could only visit the nearby city of Nagasaki under the surveillance of Japanese warders. However, there was one possibility of seeing more of this unknown country. Every four years the Dutch at Deshima were obliged to visit the Shogun in Edo (Tokyo). Von Siebold made this five-month journey in 1826 and took advantage of the possibility of collecting as many objects and as much information as possible. He was interested in all aspects of Japanese flora, fauna and culture, including food. In Kokeno he reported about *shobakiri*, noodles made of buckwheat, eaten with soy sauce, mustard, onion and red pepper. In Koyanose he sent his assistants to the market to buy as many delicacies as they could get. Among them they bought a Japanese crane. The bird seemed to be not only a favorite in Japanese paintings, but also an expensive delicacy. Von Siebold reported that Europeans didn't like the cooked poultry, served in a soup. His Japanese informants admitted that no one save the Shogun was permitted to hunt cranes, but that they broke this law regularly. When von Siebold arrived in Edo, he wondered how people fed themselves without having butchers' meat, bread or potatoes. He obtained a list of all food products that were available in Edo at that moment (May 1826). The list reports a diversity of products we can only dream of nowadays: 100 varieties of vegetables, 8 kinds of sprouted beans and roots (*mojasi*), 25 kinds of dried and fresh mushrooms, 20 seaweed varieties, a choice of 70 kinds of fish, lobster, crab and shell-fish, 26 varieties of mussels, 30 sorts of poultry and game, 28 kinds of fruit and 12 varieties of grains. Rice is the staple. There was a daily supply of two million kilograms. Much of this was destined for the court of the Shogun, where each grain was carefully examined before being considered good enough for his daily meal.

255

On his journey to Edo, von Siebold collected seaweed (see figure 2), beans, rice and other grains. He bought different qualities of sake, soy sauce and mustard, together with shiitake mushrooms, sansho pepper and dried sepia (cuttlefish). He also collected a great variety of green teas of different qualities. Seeds of tea plants were shipped to Java. By packing them in a special way he protected the seeds from drying out during the long journey. The Japanese seeds were planted in Javanese soil, they sprouted, rooted and Dutch East Indian tea cultivation became a success.

In 1829 the Japanese government suspected von Siebold of spying for the Russians. They found out that he had bought topographic maps from Japanese scientists. Subsequently von Siebold was urged to leave the country. Just in time he shipped all his collected material to the Netherlands. Back in Leiden, he started to organize his collected objects and to analyse his notes and observations. Between 1832 and 1858 he published *Nippon. Archiv zur Beschreibung von Japan* (Archive of the description of Japan), a *Fauna Japonica* and a *Flora Japonica*. Almost his entire collection was bought by the Dutch state. The ethnographic objects became the founding collection of the

National Museum of Ethnology in Leiden. Among them were the food samples, carefully packed in cardboard boxes, glass jars and original Japanese porcelain bottles, or wrapped in paper.

Food products of the International Colonial and Export Trade Exhibition in Amsterdam 1883.

In a museum register dated 1880–1901 is written (in Dutch):

> 1884: Donated by H.M. King of Siam, a large collection objects and materials from the Siamese department at the International Colonial Export Trade Exhibition.

This refers to the Nineteenth World Exhibition that took place in Amsterdam from May to November 1883. In the main building, countries and trading companies presented their newest inventions and export products. In the colonial section, the host country exhibited thousands of objects and products from its most important dependency, the Dutch East Indies.

A few months after the opening, a catalogue in French was published that turned out to be full of errors. The subsequent Dutch version showed some improvements, but a complete catalogue of the exhibits of all the participating countries does not exist. A separate catalogue dealing with objects from the Dutch colonies gives insight in the diversity of agricultural products in the Indonesian archipelago at that time. It mentions 104 varieties of rice, 10 varieties of vegetable oils, 40 varieties of flour, 12 bottles of arrowroot from successive years, dried meat ('*deng deng*') from different animals, tropical fruits ('*nam-nam*', '*madoe*', '*salak*' and '*blimbing*'), 'Turkish wheat' (which is probably the same as *bulghur*), dried shrimp for preparing '*kroepoek*' and dried *melindjo* nuts (*Gnetum gnemon*) for making the crispy chips or crackers called *emping melindjo*. As special delicacies are mentioned: '*pasiran*' (sea turtle), '*mimi*' (a kind of lobster), '*troeboek*' (shad) and other ingredients you'll never find in a Dutch-Indonesian *rijsttafel*. To be sure, this variety of products never reached the European market. And meanwhile most of them have probably disappeared from local markets as well (see figure 3).

In the catalogue tuna fish is described as not suitable for the European palate because 'the meat, although tasty and healthy, doesn't taste like fish'. Special attention is given to Chinese delicacies: dried shark fins, bird's nests, '*ebbi*' (crayfish) and '*trepang*' (sea cucumber). It doesn't omit to mention that the Chinese are willing to pay a lot for an amorphous mollusk that crawls over the ocean floor (see figure 4).

The *Staatscourant* (official gazette) of 10 November (1883) announced that His Excellency Li Fong Pau, envoy extraordinary and plenipotentiary minister of the Emperor of China has donated objects from the Exhibition to the National Museum of Ethnology. The donation existed of the products Li Fong Pau did not think worth shipping back to China. Among them were glass jars, labeled in Chinese with French translations, of delicacies such as '*Radis doux*' (*mi luobu*, soft radish), '*Olive chinois*' (*gan*

256

lan, Chinese olives), *'lee-chee où guoué-yen'* (*gui yuan,* dried longan fruit) and *'comcombre rouge'* (red cucumber). There are also green glass bottles filled with wines like *Bai hua* ('Hundred Flowers'), *Huiquan, Shaoxing, Jingzhuang 1ˢᵗ quality* ('Capital Manor') and *Fuzhen* ('Lucky Treasure') (see figure 5).

The conservation of the generous Chinese donation has been somewhat lax. The sealing wax on two bottles was broken, causing the evaporation of flower essence and rice wine. The paper sealing of the glass jars was broken as well, causing fermented radish and moldy Chinese olives. And a bottle with rose essence was 'thrown away because of deterioration by frost'.

In a small corner of the main building of the Exposition the public could look at products from Siam. King Rama V had shipped ethnographic objects, materials (cobra skin, buffalo horn), minerals and an interesting variety of exotic edible products and delicacies. The *Staatscourant* (official gazette) of 22 November (1883) announced that King Rama V donated this collection to the Netherlands. The ethnographic objects and the edible products would be added to the national ethnological collection. But not all of them reached the museum. Some were thrown away because they were rotten, tainted, decayed or contaminated during the time they were exhibited. Forty-one edible objects remained and were registered in 1884. Now, 126 years later, a bottle with 'best quality cardamom', a salted fish, a special kind of lard and a box with seeds are missing, but 37 objects are still to be found in the museum depot. Among them the black sludge which can be identified as glutinous black rice, as well as dried shrimps and mussels, different kinds of peas and beans, lotus seed, fish oil, salt, betel-nuts, pistachio nuts, 'bastard cardamom' and long pepper. The Siamese shipment also contained delicacies for the Chinese market: sea cucumber, abalone, fish bladder, shark fins and birds' nests. A diligent museum worker repacked some products in wooden cigar boxes marked *'Trobo Royal, Licht en Geurig'* (Trobo Royal, Light and Fragrant), *'Emir'* and *'Corona/ La Accepta'*. In the exhibition catalogue all products are named, but the identities of *'lukrabas'* and *'duai'* seeds will probably remain a mystery for ever (see figure 6).

An intriguing object from the World Exhibition bears the inventory number 503–333, a reference to the collection of the Dutch entrepreneur Albert P.H. Hotz (1855–1930). At the age of nineteen he was sent to Persia by his father, who had founded the Perzische Handelsvereeniging (Persian Trading Association) in Teheran in 1874. Persia had opened its borders for international trade and the Hotz family started projects in mining, agriculture, banking, tapestry and the opium trade. This company was one of the first to drill for oil on Persian territory. Like von Siebold, Hotz was much interested in local culture. His bequest consists of a library of more than 10,000 books about Persian and neighbouring cultures and a collection of high-quality photographs. The Persian government invited him to select Persian products for the Exhibition in Amsterdam. Among them were food samples that the museum bought after the Exhibition was closed. A glass jar with 'melk' (milk), is mentioned in the exhibition catalogue as *kechk,* which we can identify now as *kashk* or sun-dried buttermilk or yoghurt formed into

257

balls, which are reconstituted in water (see figure 7). They are still common in Iran where they make a sour drink or are used as a binder in sauces, soups and stews. Iranian *kashk* is comparable to *quroot* in Afghanistan and Turkish *kurut* and *keş*. Hotz's choice of Persian culinary products was rather inscrutable. Number 503–333 seems to be a glass jar filled with the 'stomach of a lamb'. Why he selected this organ, together with bitter almonds, chickpeas, riceflour and 'mixed seeds', rather than the stand-out ingredients of Iranian cuisine such as rice, sheeptail fat, caviar, saffron, dried fruits, dates, pistachio nuts and essences from fruits and flowers, is a question that probably will never be answered.

Gottlob Krause's West African food collection

As an opponent of colonialism and slave trading, the German linguist Gottlob Krause (1850–1938) became opponent of his own country's governments as they joined the Western drive to secure colonies in Africa. In the 1870s he was sent to an area of west Africa that was still 'free' for foreign domination. When he found out that his linguistic and ethnological research was used as a screen to mask preparations for German colonization, he immediately refused all co-operation and started publishing articles about the colonial intentions and the misbehavior of the Germans in Africa. In 1888 he returned to Africa, this time as representative of an ivory trading company in Stuttgart, as well as studying languages and collecting ethnographic objects in Togo for his own sake. Needless to say, he did not offer his collection to a German museum. In 1889 the museum in Leiden bought his collection consisting of 1700 objects. Krause had bought many of his objects at the market in Salaga (Ghana). The edible part of the collection consists of twenty glass bottles filled with a variety of dried beans, rice, vegetables, fruits and flour (see figure 8). The non-preserved, perishable African fruits and vegetables have been transformed over time into moldy and unidentifiable food objects.

Unfortunately there is little information left about Krause's food collection. After his death in 1938 nobody was interested in his notes and archive. They ended on a scrap heap in Zürich, the city where he passed his last years.

Dr A.G. Vorderman's edible earth collection

Geophagy is the word for eating earth or clay. In 1891 Dr A.G. Vorderman, health inspector in the Dutch East Indies, donated a collection of edible earth to the museum (see figure 9). In his manual of comparative ethnology of the Dutch East Indies, Dr G.A. Wilken writes about eating clay: 'Many wild and semi-civilized Asian tribes, Negro tribes in Africa, American Indians and even people in Southern Europe eat clay'. The Javanese distinguished different kinds of *ampo*, which they prepared with great care. First they washed the clay and removed sand and stones. After soaking it an overnight in water, the clay was kneaded into flat cookies or small round bars. Then they were salted and finally roasted. Wilken writes that people eat clay, not only when they are very hungry, but also because it contains healthy minerals. If it is darkish red, it is full of

Figure 5 (above). Chinese wines, 1883.
Figure 6 (below). Shark fins, birds' nests and long pepper. Siam, 1883.

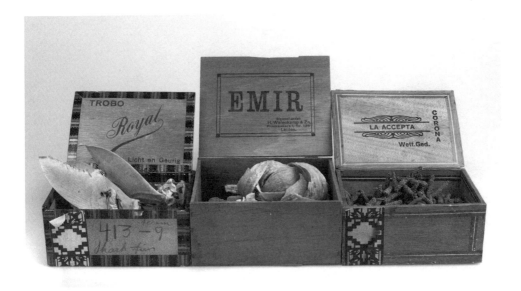

Figure 7 (above). Jar with Persian kashk, *1883.*
Figure 8 (below). Gottlob Krause's food objects. West Africa, 1888.

Figure 9. Clay cookies and raw edible clay, Dutch East Indies, ca. 1890.

iron, and specific kinds of clay contain salt, calcium and magnesium. Pregnant women all over the world eat clay. In Java, women told Wilken that it helps against sickness in the first months of pregnancy. He also discovered that the miners of the Oranje-Nassau Mine on Borneo replaced their opium addiction with an addiction to clay containing 28 per cent bitumen: '…their faces are pale and swollen; their eyelids are inflamed. They are lethargic, constipated and because of that melancholic as well.'

261

G.A. Vorderman collected 40 samples of raw and cooked clay from different parts of the Dutch East Indies. The raw clay samples are still wrapped in the original brown paper; the roasted clay cookies are kept in glass jars. All of them still have the original handwritten labels with the location where the clay was found.

Preserved as pixels
All the food objects described above were on display in the Food & Culture exhibition at the National Museum of Ethnology in Leiden in 2007/2008. Unfortunately I could not stop the conservation department from cleaning the jars and boxes, so they lost part of their inherent charm. The edible clay, the jars with fermented sludge and a set of mysterious vegetable oils from Indonesia were the exhibits that most caught the eye, together with dried insects imported from Mexico that people could taste and buy at the museum shop. The new visitors the museum hoped to attract did indeed turn up, but the museum's long-standing, regular supporters stayed at home, so that in the event the total visitor numbers did not increase that much.

Now the food objects have been put back in the museum store. For the time being nobody will bother them again. Recently, a few of them were accorded a proper place on the museum database, but the majority returned to their anonymous and comatose existence.

Their lives as museum objects are once more in danger. The National Museum of Ethnology is tidying up her overflowing stores by 'de-selecting' objects that are not worth preservation or restoration. Sooner or later the food objects will be noticed again. Modern curators are not interested in matured soy sauce, whether or not fermented over the ages. Nor in the flavors of different qualities of 200-year-old Japanese green tea, let alone in the smell of a sea cucumber that has been locked up in a jar for 127 years. Even museums don't preserve for eternity.

But before their lives as food objects end definitively, without ever being tasted or smelled by a human being, I will preserve them as digital photo pixels, with a history.

References
von Siebold, P.F. *Nippon. Archiv zur Beschreibung von Japan.* Leiden, 1832–1858.
Catalogus der afdeeling Nederlandsche kolonien van de Internationale Koloniale- en Uitvoerhandel tentoonstelling te Amsterdam. Leiden, Brill, 1883.
Wilken, A.G. *Handleiding voor de vergelijkende volkenkunde van Nederlandsch-Indië.* Leiden, 1883.
www.volkenkunde.nl

Acknowledgement
Thanks to Fuchsia Dunlop for identifying Chinese delicacies and wines.

Fermented Nagaland: a Culinary Adventure

Caroline Rowe

Conversation one evening at the symposium last year centred around potential fermented products to cover for the 2010 gathering. While India, my adopted home, has a cornucopia of fermented products ranging from *lassi* to *dosa*, I wanted to find something out of the ordinary. When Madhur Jaffrey mentioned a certain little-known fermented tea drink found in the wild hills of Nagaland in the far north-east of India, the product fitted the fermented bill, but little did I know what an adventure it would become.

Initial findings revealed a dearth of information on cuisines and beverages of the region. My searches from New Delhi revealed few examples of north-eastern cuisine beyond the Sikkimese *momos* and *thupka*. 'North-eastern' cuisine seemed to be lumped, from the mountainous Himalaya to the tropical plains of Assam, into one messy 'cuisine'.

However, as I spoke to food experts and writers on the north-east, as well as representatives from the Nagaland government, there was evidence for a multitude of fermented drinks in India's north-east and, beyond that, fermented foods also, purportedly over 150 different varieties in the region as a whole. Certainly some foods and beverages existed in Nagaland, although the tea specifically was not recorded. Due to the lack of information, there was no real choice but to head to the hills myself to find the mystical beverage. I settled on April for the trip and began asking every food writer I knew for their views on fermentation Naga-style. I soon realized that the actual story was not the tea, but the fermentation. The major tribes of the Naga hills, all fifteen of them,[1] have a host of sticky, stinky, and apparently unpalatable fermented foods ranging from fish to meat to cucumber. Should I not find the tea, I would at least come back with something worthwhile.

Background

When I wrote to Madhur Jaffrey for clarification on the tea, she sent an extract from William K. Ukers, *All About Tea*:

> The native Indian population of British India seems to have known about tea from time immemorial. They knew it first as a vegetable food in the form of miang, letpet or pickled tea. Later they made an infusion of it, a kind of soup, very like the butter tea of Tibet.

She then listed the Singpho hill tribe as the originators of tea cultivation and suggested I may want to learn more about them.

Indeed further investigation revealed more about the origins of tea in India's north-east. *The Ramayana*, compiled between 750–500 BC, documents its use. Later, during the first century AD, both Gan Lu and Bodhidharma chronicle the use of tea. It was only in the 1820s that the British East India Company introduced from China the way of cultivating and drinking tea that we now recognize. During this process, the fresh picked leaves are allowed to oxidize, turning brown to create the black, or oolong tea, we drink today. Ironically enough this process is often mis-named in early literature as being 'fermented', a mistake that could potentially spell disaster for my quest.

North-east India

The north-east of India is an area of great fascination and, more importantly, cultural and culinary isolation. Separated from the rest of India by a tiny strip of land just 21 km across at its narrowest point, it has a culture and cuisine quite apart from the rest of the subcontinent. The 'seven sisters' of the north-east: Assam, Mizoram, Nagaland, Arunachal Pradesh, Manipur, Meghalaya and Tripura, and the more recently added eighth sister, Sikkim, are largely untouched tribal areas, cut off from the central government of India by the protective geography of the Himalayas and the political geography of Bangladesh. As such, they have a variety of tribal dishes, passed down through generations, little known to the outside world. Adding to the culinary excitement is the fact that the north-east region is a meeting point of peoples from south, south-east, and east Asia. The cuisines of Burma (Myanmar), Bangladesh, Nepal, Tibet, Thailand, Bhutan and China are all in evidence here.

264

Nagaland itself is perhaps the most remote of the seven sisters and, along with Arunachal Pradesh, is the least studied of the north-eastern states.

Laphet and *miang*

We tend to be familiar with tea only as a leaf to be brewed in an infusion and drunk as a beverage. However, in the places where it is indigenous it is used in a variety of lesser-known manners. In Myanmar and northern Thailand, tea leaves are pickled. *Laphet* is regarded as a national delicacy of Myanmar and is prepared by steaming the leaves and then packing them into bamboo vats and placing into pits with heavy weights pressed on top of them. It is generally served with sesame oil and a variety of accompanying condiments such as fried garlic, dried peanuts and peas, coconut, preserved ginger and fried coconut. It is also widely available in Burmese restaurants around the world as a salad.

Miang is a tea chewed like tobacco throughout northern Thailand and exported in small amounts to Myanmar.[2] It uses *Camellia sinensis* var. *assamica* which is native to Indochina, south China and India.[3] One study in the PMO village, Mae Na Sub district, Chiang Mai Province, tells us that traditionally, wild tea bushes were utilized, but these are now under cultivation. Although the plant used for drinking-tea and chewing-tea is the same, the methods of preparation differ greatly, with drinking-tea being harvested six times a year, pruned every three months, and kept to a height of 50–70 cm. *Miang*

Figure 1: A selection of dried fermented products in a Kohima morning market.

Figure 2. Equipment for pounding sticky rice.

Figure 3. An octagarian artisan holding the tools of her trade.

266

Figure 4. A yeast cake.

trees, however, are allowed to grow up to two metres high, and pruned every two years. *Miang* is harvested quarterly and leaves are painstakingly steamed over wood fires, as opposed to drinking-tea leaves which are simply left out to dry in the sun.[4]

Kombucha

One 'fermented tea' which can be found in existence across Asia is *kombucha*. It is a tea which uses a starter of various yeast and bacteria to initiate fermentation, reputedly offering such medicinal benefits that health-food experts in California and Australia are attempting to spread its popularity throughout the globe. It was first studied in Russia and from there was taken to Australian and the United States. However, it has evidently been in use in Japan, China and Korea for many years. I headed off to Nagaland with this as potential evidence for such an alternative use of tea.

The journey to Nagaland

Heading to Nagaland in search of tea seemed at first glance to be a fun and mildly unusual thing to do. However, an almost total absence of maps and guidebooks to Nagaland, very little by way of online information, and the fact that I apparently would not legally be allowed to visit due to the fact that a Protected Areas Permit is required for all foreign visitors (and a Restricted Areas Permit for all domestic visitors) made the task seem rather more daunting. Add to this the fact that the PAP is only available to married couples or tour groups of four, and valid only on a few tourist routes and that permissions take a minimum of two months.

However, luck was very much on my side as I met the Public Relations Officer for Nagaland, Lisapila Anar, who by an extreme stroke of luck introduced me to Additional Chief Secretary, and one of the most powerful men in Nagaland, Alemtemshi Jamir, who just happened to be passing by Nagaland House in New Delhi. After explaining my rather bizarre quest for a little-known tea, Sir Alem, as he is affectionately known in Nagaland, invited me as a guest of the State, seeing an opportunity to uncover a hitherto under-discovered aspect of Naga culture. The PAP was rushed through in fifteen minutes, and arrangements were made for me to be looked after in Nagaland by Assistant Director of Women's Development, R. Khrienuo Tachü. In Delhi anything is possible if you only meet the right person.

The next challenge was to reach Nagaland. Dimapur, on the Nagaland Assam border, has an airport, but indirect flights from Calcutta are irregular and didn't suit my dates. The next best thing was to fly to Guwahati, the state capital of Assam, and drive to my destination in Nagaland, wherever that might turn out to be. Alemtemshi agreed to send a government car to take me to the Nagaland border.

The distance on the map between Guwahati and the interior of Nagaland couldn't possibly be more misleading. After arriving at eight a.m. following a three-hour flight at an ungodly hour from New Delhi, I began the drive along the long, flat, sub-tropical flood plains of the Bramaputra river. The land seemed exotic, but also entirely accessible.

I've been to Assam before and to me it is no big deal, hardly the stuff that adventure stories are made of, a land so accessible it surely holds no secrets.

We drove via Kaziranga National Park, home to the rare one-horned rhino, to Dimapur, the border town into Nagaland. Along the way, the population thinned a little, the tour buses of Kaziranga no longer plied the roads and the frequency of our car taking evasive action against dogs, goats, and cows on the road increased. Towards the border, we entered a thickly wooded and slightly hilly expanse which took us the better part of an hour to cross by car. Finally it felt as though the beaten track was being left behind. However, as we reached Dimapur and crossed the border into Nagaland, the landscape still seemed flat, and a cursory glance revealed the goods in the market to be not dissimilar to those in Delhi. Only the people had changed, as the vast majority of people were now Mongoloid in origin, and surprisingly, saris and shalwar kameez had given way to jeans and t-shirts.

After nine hours driving, the sun was low in the sky and, after transferring to a jeep, Kavito from the Women's Department picked me up for the three-hour drive to Kohima, the state capital of Nagaland.

Directly out of Dimapur the jeep wound its way up steep and somewhat uneven roads into the Naga Hills. Here the climate instantly changed, as did the flora of the surroundings. Pristine wooded slopes were to be seen at every turn and quiet prevailed, but for the hum of the traffic. I could well imagine how utterly inaccessible the region must have been even a few years ago, and marvelled at how the brush strokes of God looked to be so untouched by the human hand.

Early the next morning, before locals would arrive to help me along the way, I headed just after dawn to the local markets. Awaiting me was the most astonishing array of freshly collected produce, some brought from small kitchen gardens or fields, and some gathered fresh and wild from the jungle. In season were small pink caterpillars, at least twenty types of green leaf vegetables, river crabs, a deer, frogs, fresh and dried long-horned beetle larvae, fresh-picked wild mushrooms and an armadillo, ready to slaughter and smoke, a steal at 3,500 Rs (US$ 85). Aside from this, and of great interest to me, were a number of fermented products. A gentleman happened to stop and talk to me and, speaking perfect English, he helped me to pick up a selection: fermented soybeans hidden in packages of banana leaves and sold in bundles of three; fermented fish; fermented bamboo shoots in a variety of sizes and shapes, both dried and in juice. To my surprise, he bought them all as a gift; an early sense of Naga hospitality. Over the next few days, I was to discover an amazing depth of information, and to see each of these products being prepared in traditional homes.

Fermented food and drinks of Nagaland

I encountered a great many and varied fermented foods and beverages during my visit to Nagaland. A few are described below in as much detail as I have been able to gather from the limited amount of written research available, but mainly through the knowledge of

Figure 5 (above). Sticky rice and local rice.
Figure 6 (right). Aged akhuni.

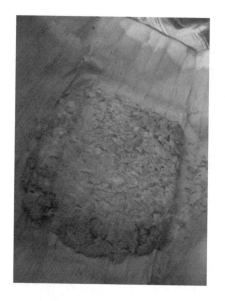

270

Figure 7 (above, left). Morning-market-fresh akhuni.
Figure 8 (above, right). Dried fermented bamboo shoots.
Figure 9 (left). A traditional Konyak kitchen.

the womenfolk of seven tribes with whom I was able to interact.[5] Primary amongst these was Rovi Chasie, trainer for the Green Village Project, an initiative seeking to bring back the traditional culinary arts, and author of one of the very few Naga cookbooks to exist in English.

Rice beer

My first real experience of the Naga kitchen came on Sunday evening when Ms Khrienuo came to pick me up and whisk me in the dark down tiny alleys deep into Kohima village. As we crossed the threshold into what felt like medieval times, my eyes settled on an elderly lady, Kitoshi, giggling in the corner and hiding behind her apron. The lady was in her eighties and had been making rice beer in the same way since she was a teenager. She sells only to those of the highest repute; government people and those with high standing in the community, and she doesn't let people drink on the premises.

The process begins with expensive, high-quality sticky rice being dried and then placed in a welled container and pounded with a giant wooden mallet (figure 2). The rice is then placed into what can only be described as a cauldron, and placed over the traditional Naga hearth to bring to the boil, stirring all the while. The mixture is then taken off the fire and stirred as it cools. It is left to cool overnight and, when fully ready, yeast is pounded and added, two handfuls to a potful. The mixture is then moved to another part of the hut to ferment and in a matter of two days is ready to drink.

This first experience, followed of course with hearty sampling, snacks and a gift of the only thing the elderly lady had available to give – dried soybeans – was a picture of a true artisan. Over the next day we went from hut to hut seeing increasingly large-scale production units for rice beer. At each hut the rice wine got stronger and our party got merrier and the people involved made their rice beer less for art and more for profit. After our first experience, every other production facility mixed expensive sticky rice with cheaper local rice (figure 5) and used yeast cakes bought in bulk from Dimapur (figure 4). Rice was not pounded before use and left spread out to cool. Industrial-sized batches were left to ferment. The final place we ended up at had a couple of rooms put aside as a makeshift bar.

Akhuni

Variously known as *akhuni*, *Dzacie*,[6] *aakhone* or *axone*, mainly due to the fact that Naga dialects are almost entirely spoken and not written, and have no common font of their own, *akhuni* is perhaps the most commonly used of all the fermented products of Nagaland. It is prepared year-round from soybeans (*Glycine max* (L.) Merrill) by people of all tribes, but most notably those of the Sema tribe of southern Nagaland. Soybeans grow up to an elevation of 1,500 m and in rainy conditions,[7] making it well suited to the Naga Hills. It is also a protein-rich legume in an otherwise traditionally protein-sparse diet.

Akhuni is prepared by picking and cleaning the soybeans well in fresh water, and then boiling them until they are soft, but still whole. The excess water is drained and

271

the soybeans are placed into a pot or *degchi* and put either outside in the sunshine, or next to the fire to warm and ferment. The ladies report that it takes three to four days to ferment in summer, and around one week in winter. As with the majority of fermented products in Nagaland, it is judged to be ready when it 'smells right'. The soybeans are then placed in a wooden pestle and smashed with a mortar. They are not mashed completely, but instead smashed as you would with garlic. A handful is then scooped up and placed in the center of a banana leaf, and the edges closed to make a parcel. The package is sold at market or stored next to the fire and can be used immediately or kept for some weeks, darkening in colour each day.

During the process proteolysis of soya protein to amino acids results in a distinctive umami taste.[8] The *akhuni* is then used in a huge variety of dishes. An example of just two are fire-smoked pork and *akhuni*, and *nula*, snails with *akhuni*. The bacteria isolated from samples is *Bacillus subtilis* and *Bacillus sp.*[9]

Similar preparations of soybeans are found across east Asia, from *natto* in Japan, to *thua nao* in northern Thailand, to *pe poke* in Myanmar and *chungkukjang* in Korea.[10] It is also available throughout north-eastern India, in Sikkim (*kinema*), Manipur (*hawaijar*), Meghalaya (*tungrymbai*), Mizoram (*bekang*) and Arunachal Pradesh (*peruyyan*).

Bamboo shoots

The most ever-present fermented product after soybeans is the family of fermented bamboo shoots. Like *akhuni*, the bamboo shoots undergo natural bacterial fermentation without any help from a starter. Three main types of fermented product result: wet fermented bamboo shoots; bamboo shoots which are fermented and then dried; and the fermented bamboo shoot juice.

For the initial basic preparation whole bamboo shoots are washed well and prepared, with the tendermost ends being put aside in medium-sized pieces and the tougher ends being shredded. A conical basket, made itself generally from bamboo, is then prepared by lining with plastic sheeting. Previously, banana leaves would have been used for this purpose. The bamboo shoots are then placed into the container, holes pierced in the bottom, the top covered with plastic or leaves, and stones placed to cause the juices to be squeezed out of the holes and collected for further use. It is said that once the majority of the juice is squeezed out, the shoots must be ready to use, a process which takes around two weeks, depending on the weather. Generally, the shoots are then separated and the shredded parts may be dried in the sun so that they keep longer. The juice is used to add to sauces, or to store meats with an effect close to vinegar in terms of preservation. Unlike *akhuni*, if the shoots turn brown, it means they have spoiled.

Anishi

Anishi, or fermented yam leaves, is far more complicated and time-consuming to make, and is a distinct speciality of the Ao tribe of Mokukchung. While Rovi and Ms Khrienuo could easily tell me about the production of *akhuni* and bamboo shoots, a friend of Ms

Khrienuo's schoolmistress sister, Purchila, had to be brought in specially to explain the *anishi*-making process to me. Mrs Keviseno John told me that to make *anishi* cakes, yam leaves, or the *Colocasia* species,[II] are picked, carefully cleaned, and kept for six to seven days wrapped in banana leaves until they start to yellow. They are then well crushed in a wooden pestle and mortar and again wrapped in banana leaves. The packages are then covered in rice husks, then ash, and finally charcoal, and put in the embers at the edge of a fire. Mrs John was sure to tell me that the art can only be learnt with experience, for if the leaves under the layer of ash and charcoal burnt, the entire package would be ruined, but at the same time, if the package remained uncooked, the *anishi* would make your mouth itch terribly when you tried to eat it. After two to three hours, when the package is deemed ready, the mixture is left to cool slightly, and the contents picked off in small balls and formed into cakes with clean hands. The hand and fingerprints of the maker can be seen on every finished cake. The cakes are then dried in a rice dryer, a bamboo container which is hung close to the fireplace overnight. It must not burn, nor dry out too much. During this period the cakes are turned frequently. After this, the cakes can be stored next to the fire, a sort of natural Naga preservation technique akin to our use of airtight containers and refrigerators, which keep the bugs away. *Anishi* cakes can be used in a wide variety of curries, providing an intense flavour. Although they can be used dry, it is it recommended that the cakes are soaked in hot water, and then placed next to the fire again to refresh the flavour and improve the texture before use. Favourite finished dishes are chutneys, and a curry made with tomato, potato, and dried, smoked meat.

273

Khocie

Khocie, a product of fermented fish, is one of the few which is clearly not embarked upon for its preservative qualities, the resultant dish lasting no more than one month. The dish, favoured by the Lotha tribe, uses small fish, or pieces of large fish, placed inside the hollow node of a bamboo trunk and left next to the fire for a matter of days. *Khocie* is then used in hot chutneys and vegetable curries.

Tsütuo ti

Perhaps one of the most repellent-smelling of the fermented products of the Naga Hills is this grey-green fermented cucumber liquid. Who could have imagined that the humble cucumber, normally so innocuous, would produce a liquid so foul-smelling that even Rovi, on showing me a fairly fresh sample, would exclaim that she couldn't stand it. Mercifully, the sample that Bano gave me, and I brought back to Delhi, was around a year old, and the smell had faded sufficiently for it to become at least tolerable for a brave few.

The method of preparation for *tsütuo ti* is as simple as the smell is complex. Cucumbers are washed, the skin discarded if it is too tough, cut or sliced, and placed in an airtight container. At times, pumpkin or cucumber leaf may be crushed and added to give a green colour. They are then left for fifteen to twenty days until bacterial fermentation takes place, after which the product is ready to use. It can be stored for up to three years, and is used in sauces, pickles, and a wonderful bright green dish called *galho*. It is also lauded for its medicinal properties, and is said to cure stomach upsets. The preparation is a specialty of the Angami tribe. *Lactobacillus plantarum*, *L. brevis* and *Leuconostoc* have been found in lab. samples.[12]

Gakrie ki

Fermented mustard leaves are another fairly time-consuming product. Leaves are picked and left to dry in the sun, although retaining a small amount of moisture, after which they are left in a basket to turn yellow. They are then washed and put into a pot and covered with water. The pot remains in situ for one to two weeks, allowing the leaves to soften. They are then removed from the liquid and squeezed dry. The liquid can then be heated and thickened as an optional step, and the leaves dipped back into the liquid before the final step of drying in the sun. Both the leaves and the liquid are used. The liquid is generally boiled so as to be close to a paste.

Other fermented foods

There is a vast wealth of other fermented products available across the villages of the Naga Hills, but I choose not to mention them here as I have not had a chance to directly sample them myself. Of interest amongst these are fermented crab prepared from various crabs, but most frequently a hard-shelled black, river crab, which is cleaned, entrails removed, mixed with black *till* (sesame seeds), wrapped in banana and kept over a fire for a week. This dish is a favourite of the Lotha, Mao and Angami tribes.[13] Animal fats are also fermented in remote villages,[14] as is *khovie*, or Naga *piaz*, a type of small indigenous leek, after which it is dried and kept for times when there are no vegetables to be found.

The fermented tea of the Konyak tribe

Despite the wealth of fermented foods and beverage I had been lucky enough to taste, see and make, I was still of course looking for the fermented tea of the Singpho tribe. Somewhat disturbingly, the name 'Singpho' didn't seem to be in current use amongst the fourteen tribes of Nagaland. However, I continued to ask people about the tea, and located on a map that the Singpho tribe would be found, broadly speaking, along the Nagaland/Myanmar/Arunachal Pradesh border in the state of Mon. This area was described as being inhabited by people of the Konyak tribe, who another informant stated were people inherently linked to the gathering of wild tea. In addition, Kavito sketched in to me the production of a tea which seemed to be fermented, and in roughly the same area. This came as something of a relief as even on my arrival in Nagaland, I had still not managed to locate a single solid written reference to the tea, and had heard nothing but murmurs that it might exist. It did at one point occur to me that this was a very long way to go for an imaginary tea.

However, with the help of somewhat approximate descriptions of what I thought I might be looking for and a fortunately deep understanding of the process of fermentation from every Naga I spoke to, a picture was gradually composed of what I was looking for. Ms Khrienuo's sister was contacted, as she was used to teaching Konyak students, and questions were asked and answered. As my time in Nagaland was drawing to a close, after many mugs of rice beer shared by the warmth of a hearth in a traditional bamboo hut, I was driven high up into the hills of Nagaland. After we had eaten some *phsusoshe* (a sort of tiny red plum, the colour of a ripe tomato) preserved in syrup, some members of the Konyak tribe were seated next to me. While it was not the right time of year to prepare a fresh tea, they described to me in great detail the creation of 'konyak tea', the fermented tea I had been searching for.

The konyak tea is made from small and medium-sized leaves plucked from cultivated trees (no longer from wild ones, although this used to be the tradition). Leaves are left for one hour in the sun, or until a little dried, and then gently rolled between the palms. Hard stalks and foreign objects are then removed and the leaves squeezed until any excess water is wrung out. That liquid is used medicinally, rubbed on wounds to promote healing. The leaves are then packed tight into the hollow nodes of bamboo trunks and hung close to the fireplace. They are left for three to four days in summer, and around one week in winter, until the tea is fermented and ready to use. It is then placed on bamboo mat right above the fire and dried for storage.

As we were talking, a small cup was placed in front of me on the table. As I took a sip it became clear I had found what I was looking for: a smokiness that would put the best *lapsang souchong* to shame, and an intensity like I have never before tasted in a tea lent astonishing complexity to the preparation. It was explained that my tea had been prepared in a similar way to our everyday tea, and so was light enough to drink easily. Indeed it had a freshness that I found entirely surprising. The traditional way to take the tea was to keep it heated on the side of the fireplace until the liquid had become almost black in colour. In this manner it aids digestion, gives energy, and is even said to cure cancer.

275

As is the tradition with people across Nagaland, they would not let me leave without a gift and, despite its rarity, the Konyak people handed me a bag of the precious tea to take back with me to Delhi.

Conclusion

My journey to Nagaland revealed far more about the cuisine of the region than just a rare tea. It revealed a huge wealth of knowledge passed down from generation to generation, and across tribal boundaries, of the qualities and benefits of fermented goods. What was most striking about this exploration was that although the Naga tribes use the lower pH of a fermented good as a method of preservation, storing seasonally produced goods for the longer term, this is most certainly not the only reason for their favouring of this method.

While there are undoubtedly nutritional benefits to fermenting food, which I'm sure others will cover in detail in their papers, the primary reason for modern Nagas to retain the techniques of fermentation seems to be one of taste.

This led me to go back to the paper I had presented at the Symposium last year, on the meaning of pepper. I came to a conclusion in that paper that while there were health and, in fact, preservation benefits to the use of various peppers around the world, the underlying reason that people used pepper was in fact as something that would add a quality to food beyond nutrition, beyond even the basic taste of a product. I argued that all cultures and cuisines around the world had their own version of a 'pepper'; something that gave heat; something that gave one an 'experience' of food above and beyond biological requirements. When I looked at Naga cuisine, I found that intense heat, in the form of capsaicin, would have been absent more than a few hundred years ago (although Nagaland has since caught up with the *bhut jolokia* measuring up to 1,000,000 Scoville units, the hottest-known chilli in the world). Nor do the remote, cold, and wet Naga Hills bode as well for growing spices as does peninsular India. Using the same argument, salt, the universal taste-enhancer, is exceedingly rare in the Naga Hills, there being but two or three salt-water wells held by the Zeliang tribe in the Peren district. Here salt is produced in a laborious eighteen-step process, and to this day is exceedingly expensive in the area; almost no traditional Naga recipes call for the use of salt. So then, in a diet of rice, vegetables, and the odd tiny piece of meat or fish, how can flavour be delivered? How can the palate be tempted and teased, and brought to life? How can the monotony of having to fuel the body add to the desire to feed the soul? The answer comes, it seems, in the intense umami tastes of the fermented products of Nagaland, givers of health, substance, and most importantly, the joy of flavour.

Notes

1. The fifteen major tribes of Nagaland are; Ao, Sema, Lotha, Rengma, Chakhesang, Sangtam, Konyak, Phom, Chang, Yimchuger, Khiamugan, Zeliang, Kuki, Kachari and Pochury.
2. Ayako Sasaki, Shinya Takeda, Pornchai Preechapanya, Mamoru Kanzaki, Seichi Ohta, *Social Dynamics, land use changes, and socioeconomic factors in a miang (Chewing tea) village in Northern Thailand from 1970–2002*.
3. Weatherstone, J. 'Historical introduction', in Willson, K.C. and M.N.Clifford (eds). *Tea: Cultivation to consumption*. Chapman & Hall: London, 1992.
4. Ayako Sasaki, Shinya Takeda, Pornchai Preechapanya, Mamoru Kanzaki, Seichi Ohta, *Social Dynamics, land use changes, and socioeconomic factors in a miang (Chewing tea) village in Northern Thailand from 1970–2002*.
5. I am indebted to R. Khrienuo Tachü of the Angami tribe for organizing my culinary guides; Bano (Angami tribe), Tune (Chakhesang tribe), Vikheni (Sema tribe), Avilo (Sema tribe), Amenla (Ao tribe), Lonele (Zeliang tribe), Naro (Khemuliam tribe), Robert (Mao tribe), Rovi Chasie (Angami tribe) and Kavito (Sema tribe).
6. Rovi Chasie, *Naga Cuisine: Ethnic Flavours*. Rovi Chasie, 2003.
7. Jyoti Prakash Tamang, Rajan Chettri & Rudra Mani Sharma, 'Indigenous knowledge of Northeastern women on production of ethnic fermented soybean foods', *Indian Journal of Traditional Knowledge* Vol. 8 (1), 2009.
8. Ibid.
9. Jyoti Prakast Tamang & Rajen Chettri (unpublished).
10. Alan Davidson, *The Oxford Companion to Food*, 2nd edn. Tom Jaine (ed.), 2006.
11. Ashiho A. Mao & N. Odyou, 'Traditional fermented foods of the Naga tribes of Northeastern India', *Indian Journal of Traditional Knowledge* Vol. 6 (1), 2007.
12. B. Tamang & J.P. Tamang, 'In situ fermentation dynamics during production of gundruk and khalpi, ethnic fermented vegetable products of the Himalayas', *Indian Journal of Microbiology*, 2009a.
13. ibid
14. ibid

Keata Kule Lorien: Finding the Ideal Balance Within the Smoke-Cured Fresh and Fermented Milk of Northern Kenya's Samburu

William Rubel, Jane Levi and Elly Loldepe

This paper is based on extensive field research amongst the Samburu in northern Kenya, working with a network of Samburu friends built up by William Rubel over nearly two decades of repeated visits to the district, and more recently with the assistance of local Samburu anthropologist Elly Loldepe. It offers a first description of a complex cuisine of fresh and fermented milk products produced by storing milk in calabashes – wooden or gourd containers – previously charred and smoked with burning aromatic woods. While both the cooking implements and raw ingredients are apparently simple, the palate the typical Samburu brings to milk is as refined as that of a wine connoisseur. The woman who prepares the calabash for milk with burning sticks strives to create milk that expresses a fundamental balance between bitter and sweet: she is seeking *keata kule lorien,* a milk-centred analogue for finding a perfect balance in the world at large *(keata nkop lorien).* Young girls, to suggest the intimacy and sweetness they feel for their best friend say *kule-enkutuk,* literally, mouth-milk. While this paper focuses on the complexity of the Samburu milk cuisine and offers a first glimpse of the techniques of smoke-curing milk and the Samburu's culinary aesthetic system, our talk will attempt to convey a broader picture of milk in the context of Maa-speaking Samburu culture.[1] We will supplement our talk with milk related songs, prayers, photographs and artefacts.

Background

The smoke-cured fresh and fermented milk of the Samburu, a tribe of nomadic pastoralists living in northern Kenya, has long been recognized by anthropologists as being one of their staple foods, alongside blood and meat. However, Samburu milk is unlike most other culinary staples: as a beverage it offers the additional dimension of aroma to the consumer. More importantly, while outsiders have tended not to recognize the sophisticated complexity of its preparation, it is in fact one of the world's most manipulated staples in terms of taste and, in some sense, texture: in many ways it makes more sense to see Samburu milk as a staple *ingredient* than as a staple food. This paper is the first look at Samburu milk as a cuisine or an ingredient within a more complex process and, we hope, breaks new ground in the study of tribal foodways. It asks questions that anthropologists tend not to ask, such as, what does this milk taste like to the Samburu, and what do they think of the taste? In demonstrating that there is actually a complex philosophy of taste within east African pastoralist foodways where a general observer might notice none, this research challenged us to think more deeply about cuisines of the past, and in particular, about cuisines of poverty.

While the Samburu do seem to be on the cusp of a radical break with the past and are now likely to assimilate rapidly into mainstream Kenyan culture, Samburu District is still a place where the vast majority of people live far away from modern urban culture. The Samburu live by nomadic pastoralism: they move their *manyattas* (villages) every few years, and even now most live outside modern life, existing largely without money, with few personal possessions besides dairy animals, and a minimum of household effects. They have still not entirely adopted Western dress. Within Kenya, beaded and painted young Samburu warriors symbolize cultural integrity, while for the industrialized world they stand for the last representatives of a people living before the age of steel (their steel knives, spears, Kalashnikovs, and veterinary medicine notwithstanding).

Experiencing Samburu milk

When we asked Haile Leselassie Leseeto, a Samburu Rastafarian friend, what the Samburu do first when taking a cup of milk he replied, 'We take the cup in our right hand, smell, and then drink, like you do with whisky or wine.' Smell, then taste. This is essential to keep in mind when considering the Samburu milk cuisine, as our own cultural bias is in favor of milk's taste, not its smell. We tend not to find the smell of milk particularly enticing, and consciously smell it usually only to see whether it has gone bad, but the Samburu always smell first. As Ali Lekudere explained, 'when the Samburu smell milk they want more and more of it because the smell is like an appetizer.' An English friend of ours who grew up on a farm in England remembers from her childhood the taste of the milk when the cows were eating wild garlic. A Samburu would explain the memory in terms of the milk *smelling* of garlic.

Samburu smoke-cured milk has three layers of complexity: one pertains to the tastes, smells and triggered memories of the milk itself; one pertains to the tastes and smells infused into the milk through the smoking of the calabash; and one pertains to the tastes and textures introduced by the degree to which the milk is fermented. All three layers are part of what a Samburu experiences as the taste of the milk. Additionally, though outside the scope of this paper, are many aspects of culinary culture pertaining to service and the social aspects of milk consumption.

Types of milk

When, in early 2010, we met with a group of college-educated Samburu in the town of Maralal to ask about milk, one member of the group began by telling us that one could not just speak about 'milk'. There is milk from cows, goats, sheep, and camels, and each milk's taste changes during the lactation period and so must be divided into three parts: colostrum (*manang*); milk up to about the fifth month of lactation; and milk towards the end of the lactation period. He suggested we draw a matrix showing these twelve types of milk. When we subsequently tried out this formulation, everyone agreed. While of course Samburu have a general word for milk, *kule,* they taste in specifics. They taste goat milk from a goat during the last months of lactation, not 'milk' in the abstract. This, we think, is one of the ways in which the language of outside observers simplified their observations. They conceptualized all milk as essentially fungible, while to the Samburu there are literally dozens of different milks that they can recognize at a whiff and a sip in the same way as a wine connoisseur recognizes wines.

To further suggest how complex the milk inputs are there is a seasonal component to the quality of milk. Seasonal changes affect both the taste and viscosity of the milk, which has a bearing on mouthfeel, an aspect of taste that is important to qualitative judgments. Thick and fatty (*keirusha*) is always better than thin and watery (*kebebek*) and is one basis for the hierarchy of milks with camel always on the bottom and cow and sheep vying for top place. The Samburu District is subject to two rainy seasons, a short rain in the late fall and a longer rain in the spring. In between, the pasture dries up. There is a Maa expression, *kemelok ana kule enkolong,* 'as sweet as the milk of the dry season'. Dry-season milk is fatter than rainy-season milk, and thus thicker, just as the milk from European cows used to be noticeably fatter during the winter than in the spring or summer. As the wine-taster assesses mouthfeel with each different wine, so the Samburu assess mouthfeel with each calabash of milk.

Another layer, one that further enriches for the Samburu the pleasure of a sip of milk, is that they know their herds, they know the land, and they can smell through to the forage the animals are eating. Thus, milk itself offers a narrative of the state of the herd, the owner's economic condition and, if a distinctively flavored forage plant is detected, it can even trigger a memory of place. For the Samburu, all of these perceptions are then merged into a far more complex evaluation of the aesthetics of the milk once it is smoke-cured and fermenting.

The dynamics of milk preparation

Samburu only drink milk that is stored in calabashes that were previously prepared by women for this purpose.[2] There is no refrigeration and limited water resources, so the wooden containers are made sterile between uses with burning sticks. These burning sticks leave a residue of resins that serve the practical function of curing the milk – of significantly slowing down fermentation – and of imparting desirable tastes and aromas. The Samburu do not like to drink milk straight from animals – it 'smells like cow' a friend told us – which is also their way of saying, in the academic dichotomy between the raw and the cooked, that they don't drink raw milk.

Manipulation of the milk's taste is achieved through the woods used, their degree of curing, the length of time taken to smoke and burn the calabash interior, and the material, time, and pressure employed in wiping the sides and lid of the smoked calabash. Once the milk is in the calabash there is no further manipulation by the preparer. This is the point where an infusion of compounds put down through smoking enters the milk and where the chemistry of the milk is shifted by the natural process of lactic fermentation.

Samburu readily differentiate between taste and aroma and so the calabash preparer is working to blend them to achieve an optimum balance, given the woods available to her and the type and condition of the milk. The mechanics of the smoke-curing and fermentation processes dynamically blends taste – sweet, salty, sour, and bitter – with aroma. The burnt aromatic woods introduce bitterness; the place of the lactating animal in its lactation cycle introduces saltiness; the extent of fermentation increases the perception of saltiness and introduces sourness; while sweetness in the sense of sugar is tied to the milk itself and the activity of lactic fermentation. There are concepts of ideal flavour defining the perfect cup of milk that entail balancing the opposites of sweet and bitter and sweet and sour; of finding the bitter within the sweet.

Maa provides a far richer vocabulary of taste and smell than we have at our disposal in English, and many words can only be translated descriptively. When discussing milk Samburu distinguish between *kemelok* or a sweet taste (like honey, sugar or good meat) and *koropili* or a pleasingly sweet aroma (like the smell of grass, frying onions or a well-prepared calabash). When they discuss sour or bitter flavours and smells, the concept works by degrees, beginning with *keisukut* (salty) as the milk first turns, progressing through *keisuicho* (slightly bitter) at the stage of very light fermentation, to *kedua* (bitter) when the milk is completely soured. Compound words describe well-balanced milk: *kemeloknodua* when it is both sweet and bitter; *kemeloknesuicho* when it is both sweet and salty. All of these are positive words for stages of milk that are appreciated for their aroma and flavour. Once the milk becomes *kedukulan* (salty with a taste of urine) it is beginning to go too far. As it deteriorates further it might be described as *kongu* (having a bad odour), *keisamis* (a very bad smell) or *kongu* (really stinky). The concept of *kedukalan* can also describe a particular mouthfeel, beyond the desirable *keirucha* (thick) stage. Milk that is light or watery has a mouthfeel that is *kebebek* (light) and *kekare* (like water) and a taste that is *memeloknomodua*, neither sweet or bitter. Milk that is *nkarer* is dilute, while *kemaga* is sticky. In blessings, the idea of *naishiokule* or honey and milk describes the sweet and happy life the conferrer of the blessing hopes you will lead.[3]

It is worth noting that while strangers to the Samburu tradition first taste or smell smoke within the milk, the Samburu never mention smoke or smokiness as a quality the milk possesses. Rather, they taste (smell) through to the underlying wood used to prepare the calabash in the same way that in our culinary tradition we say Laphroaig whisky tastes of peat, although the Samburu palate distinguishes between dozens of different woods, not simply 'wood'. Mouthfeel, which is both animal and season dependent, as well as affected by the degree of fermentation that has taken place in the calabash, also influences taste perceptions.

The way in which the woman has prepared the calabash determines the quality of the milk as it ferments in the calabash. A thorough preparation deposits fresh resins deep into the pores of the calabash offering a more complex taste and aroma profile in the finished product. The way in which the calabash was wiped clean after the smoking also affects tonal range. The milk of a woman who has scrubbed the calabash interior for a long time with a plastic scrubber produces a flatter end-product than a woman who has been more gentle with less abrasive materials like a cow tail brush or a fine cloth. Further research is necessary to associate cleaning styles with a heightening or lessening of the finished milk's underlying taste structure.

Collecting wood

The preparation of the calabash begins with the selection of the wood. Wamba, where much of our research took place, is geographically transitional between the Samburu lowlands and highlands and so wood from the mountains as well as lowlands are available to women there. Of course the wider district covers a wide range of habitats so what is used varies according to where one lives. Women rarely go out to collect wood alone, but seem to use wood-collecting trips as opportunities to spend time with friends. In this sense, they are luxuries. For some, wood-collecting and singing sexually explicit songs goes together. The *kakisha* is one such song. It can only be sung away from the *manyatta,* out of earshot of children and men. Collecting aromatic wood seems to be an activity in which play and work are combined.

Woods are roughly divided between bitter and sweet with the sweet woods generally being considered the best. But generalizations must be tempered with the caveat that personal taste is at work within the broader cultural tastes. *Sarai* is always categorized as a bitter wood (every wood is described as either bitter or sweet) but although we were often told that it is the worst as it is both bitter and may give the milk a greenish color, others told us it is the best wood. We tasted milk made from *sarai* and found it delicious. We suspect that as with experienced tasters of any beverage – tea, coffee, wine, whisky – the connoisseurs have more refined palates and can perceive fine gradations of taste and aroma that outsiders cannot. Those who consider *sarai* best may love the taste of bitter. It is our sense that within the aesthetic framework of Samburu smoke-cured and fermented milk that there are ideal combinations of taste (sweet, sour, salty, bitter) and aroma. Since our palates are not refined enough to taste what our hosts tasted we were not able really to understand subtleties of their system.

The wood consistently rated the best is *lngeriyoi*. As one woman, Noolpulsi Leparlero, put it, it makes milk taste sweet, like sugar, and makes a pleasant-smelling (sweet) smoke. As the women are often enveloped in a cloud of smoke when they smoke the calabash the smell of the smoke must be well known and important to them. Our first taste of *lngeriyoi*-infused milk reminded us of vanilla ice-cream. From a utilitarian standpoint *lngeriyoi* also preserves milk longer than most other woods – up to four days without refrigeration at average temperatures in the range of 22–33°C. *Sarai* and other bitter woods reduced butter production thus the use of bitter woods would then presumably be more common during times of milk scarcity since butter production is only associated with surplus.

The aromatic woods are harvested as branches of at least a few centimeters in diameter and often are thick enough that they must be split to be used. The wood is aged but used before being fully seasoned since one is looking for a smoky burn. Around Wamba we encountered a range of woods, by no means an exhaustive list, some sweet and some bitter:

Maa name	Botanical Name[4]	Quality
ldumei	*Maerua crassifolia*	sweet
lgilai	*Teclea nobilus*	sweet (medium)
lgilai orok	*Teclea simplicifolia*	
lkukulai	*Rhamnus staddo*	sweet (less than *masei* or *lngeriyoi*)
lmasei	*Tarenna graveolens*	bitter (the most bitter)
lngeriyoi	*Olea africana/europaea*	sweet
loisu(g)i	*Zanthoxylum usambarence*	sweet
sarai	*Balanites orbicularis*	bitter
serishoi	*Boscia coriacea*	sweet

Preparing the calabash

Samburu culture is highly structured and rule-bound. As calabashes are at the center of the most important Samburu food and as food is at the center of so many rules it is important to mention that there are many differently shaped milk containers each of which serves a specific function, or is designated for individuals of a particular sex who are at recognized, named stages of life. Thus, for example, there is the *nkilip* for boys, the *naitu* for older men, the *njonkor* for young girls, the *lkantir* for older women, etc. Calabash shape is a complex area deserving an entirely separate paper.

We did our best to clarify the English used to describe the preparation of the calabash. The Maa expression *airr mala* translates as preparing the calabash. Some referred to it in English as *cleaning* the calabash. As cleaning is a central function of the smoking and heating it is a reasonable word to use to describe at least part of what is being done. We feel that the distance between cleaning and preparing is a fruitful one for further research: it is in what is done beyond what is strictly necessary to sterilize the calabash and cure the milk that one finds both the personality of the preparer being expressed as well as the expression of larger cultural aesthetic preferences. Since the only person we found who had traveled outside the Samburu Disrict to visit other neighboring pastoralists was co-author Loldepe we found it difficult to get a sense as to what degree the preparation processes that we describe reflect Samburu aesthetic values as opposed to values more widely shared by pastoralists in the region. However, Loldepe's experience with the Kipsigis, a sub-tribe within the larger Kalenjin community, is suggestive. The milk served by his Kipsigis hosts was speckled with ash and included grit from small pieces of embers. Samburu milk is never ashy or gritty. A clear white color is highly prized, as is a smooth mouthfeel.

All Samburu fresh and fermented milk products are infused with the aroma of smoke from aromatic woods. Thus, when 'fresh' calabash milk is added to tea the rich tonalities of its smokiness blend with the tea and sugar to create an unusually warm and satisfying drink. The extent of curing and quality and degree of flavoring introduced through smoking is determined by how the calabash is prepared. There are women who have reputations as good preparers and some who are known as bad preparers, and a woman's personality is deemed to be reflected in the quality of her calabash preparation – there are the careful, the lazy, the gifted and the mediocre. The preparation of the calabash determines whether the milk stored in it might smell sweet and taste sublime or will quickly smell stinky, a condition of rottenness with such negative connotations that a woman who consistently produces stinky milk does so at great social risk.

Calabashes tend to be in constant use. They are rinsed with water after the milk within them is consumed, and are then cleaned within a few hours. A very small amount of water is deliberately left in the container when it is rinsed. When the woman is ready to clean the containers, those needing cleaning are assembled by the household fire along with a selection of sticks of aromatic woods. Most women use sticks all of one variety, but some women, (co-author Loldepe's wife, Lina Nterini Loldepe, for example), may combine sticks from two different trees in order to achieve a desirable taste profile. Burning sticks are usually small enough to fit entirely within larger calabashes. The tips of one or two sticks are placed in the fire until they are burning strongly. They are then popped into the calabash, the lid is replaced, and the calabash is shaken for a minute or so. The lid is then removed, the stick tipped out, the lid replaced and the sticks replaced in the fire to reach the desired heat again, and the action repeated many times until the preparer judges the calabash to have been sufficiently smoked and heated, a process that may take as much as twenty minutes. Cues to it being ready include the sounds given off by the heating water, by the production of steam building pressure under the lid, and by the temperature of the outside of the calabash. In addition to placing burning sticks into the container and closing it, longer burning sticks are also ground around the open belly, sides, and calabash cap. This grinding breaks embers off inside the calabash so that, as the preparation progresses, the sounds of the shaking of the calabash includes not just the sticks, but also these pieces of embers.

The final processing steps once the calabash has cooled are to pour out onto the ground any loose embers – these are mostly sand-sized but for larger calabashes include pebble-sized pieces. The calabash interior is then wiped. We observed three methods. The interior is wiped with a cow tail (the traditional system) or a clump of white plastic threads unwoven from a plastic sack (the most recent innovation) tied to the end of a stick, or with a piece of fine fabric. Several women told us that they felt the plastic threads led to over-scrubbing of the calabash and thus the removal of material that one had so carefully placed there through smoking and burning the interior. Several minutes can be spent wiping out the interior of the calabash leading us to believe that this is a process which marks the care of the preparer and stamps her particular aesthetic on the final milk product. Once the interior of the calabash (and the lid) are wiped and put back together, they are then again ready for milk. Animals are milked directly into a calabash held in one hand (usually the left), and calabashes have leather straps that facilitate holding the calabash firmly while milking. It is common practice to allow the baby animals the use of half the available teats, leaving the remaining half for human use.[5]

Milk products

As we have said, milk is rarely drunk straight from an animal. A minimum of several hours is allotted for the milk to absorb flavor and aroma from the prepared calabash. When there is a surplus, milk is churned into *ngorno* (butter) which is processed into *lkisiich* (ghee). Children drink the *kamanang* (buttermilk) and milk and blood are also sometimes mixed as a food for them. The historically unprecedented widespread shortage of milk means that today, even now there is no drought, most milk is consumed within a few hours of milking diluted with water in hot sugared tea.

Smoke-cured fermented milk

Until recent widespread milk shortages, most milk was consumed fermented. Fresh milk, *kule naairewua*, is left to ferment in the calabash. Flavors and aromas from the smoking soon leach into the milk and after approximately four hours one begins to smell and taste a well-balanced product.[6] Four to twelve hours is the stage when milk from a well-prepared calabash gives the most satisfaction when used to make tea or drunk fresh. The Samburu recognize distinct stages within the fermentation process and they experience fermented milk as a continuum from fresh to spoiled, consuming it at every point in between. Samburu milk is unpasteurized and bacteriologically alive. It is also never refrigerated. It is thus always changing. From *kule naairewua*, fresh milk, it begins to ferment and as it does the whole palate of aromas, tastes, and textures shift and realign themselves. The first shift in taste is to *kule naisukutan*, where the milk loses its freshness and turns salty. Cream rises to the top and although it is not yet sour, if boiled, the curds separate from the whey. This is not an esteemed state because, as one friend put it, 'it just tastes salty.' As the milk begins to ferment further it enters a stage called *aairiro* which is recognizable because the milk has thickened slightly. It is neither fresh nor fully fermented. This state lasts for at most half a day and is referred to as *kule naisukutan naairiirete*. At this point the taste changes, it loses some saltiness but is also not sweet.

Kule naawoto, fermented milk, divides between the sweet and sour. The initial stage is *kule naawoto leleru*. This is the state the milk is in after approximately one day in the calabash. Saltiness has receded. It is the most esteemed stage for milk. It is white and has an exceedingly soft curd, much softer than for yoghurt. There is a small amount of yellowish whey and a smooth sweet taste with no obvious sourness. For the Samburu this is the stage of perfection in milk where saltiness has receded and another element of sweetness with a distant background 'of sweet salt' is recognizable.

As fermenting bacteria continue to consume the lactose in the milk the taste shifts to sour and the milk becomes *kule nawoto naaisichete*. The longer the milk ferments the more sour it becomes until one reaches the stage where it has gone bad, *kule naawoto naataroitie (torrok?)*. At this end stage the milk is *kongu* or *keisamis*, stinky. Milk in this kind of state separates into the liquid part called *taar* (whey) which is very sour and the solid part called *nganayioi* (curds) which is sweet. *Taar* is usually colorless, like water, but depending on the time spent in the calabash might have a greenish tint. In this final state no amount of shaking will make the milk drinkable.

Conclusion

Our preliminary look at the smoke-cured fresh and fermented milk of the Samburu demonstrates a sophisticated but heretofore unrecognized culinary culture within what amounts to an elision in the anthropological literature. This has significant implications for culinary historical research of all kinds, in particular study of groups and civilizations who utilized what have usually been described as primitive tools with a limited range of culinary inputs. We feel that the Samburu milk offers possible insights into sophisticated foodways going back to the earliest periods of pastoralism.

Much more research needs to be done with the Samburu, and quickly, as their pastoralist system is in crisis. Women who are known to produce the best milk need interviewing, as do the elders most noted for their ability to correlate the taste of milk with the health of the herd and foraging locations. A Maa lexicon of taste, texture, and smells pertaining to milk processing could form the core of a Maa culinary dictionary.

Maa is likely to survive as a language longer than the smoke-cured milk that we describe in this paper. With thoughts of the electric pylons being installed a few miles from where we were talking, we asked the mother of a friend whether she would continue to prepare milk in the calabash if she could preserve fresh milk in a box made cold with electricity for two weeks. She did not hesitate: no. In her case, the question was already moot since all of her cows had died in the drought and she is now living mostly by trading in cornmeal. While ultra-pasteurized milk in boxes was widely thought to taste bad and be impure (Samburu seemed to interpret the lower butterfat-content and flattened taste as being adulteration with chemicals), the cartons are now sold in all shops. Samburu smoke-cured and fermented milk will soon be lost to the world. We believe that the world's cultures will benefit from a detailed record of this cuisine but, more importantly, we think that as the Samburu move into a new phase they may find that their smoke-cured fermented milk can provide them a long-lasting touchstone that will help them to maintain their own cultural identity while integrated into mainstream Kenyan life. But before the tradition can be reinterpreted in the light of what is likely to be a mostly urban lifestyle it must first be written down.

Notes

1. Maa is the language of the Samburu and their related tribe, the Maasai. A draft dictionary can be found at: http://darkwing.uoregon.edu/~dlpayne/Maa%20Lexicon/index-english/main.htm
2. Our study focused on milk preparation in *manyattas*. The *murran* (warriors) live segregated lives and their milk preparation practices may differ from those described in this paper.
3. Most of the flavour and aroma words are used exclusively for milk. *Kemelok* and *kedua* (sweet and bitter) are used in other food contexts. Only women singing about their smallest children and *murrans* singing about their sweethearts use *kemelok* in a non-food context.
4. Botanical names provided by Elly Loldepe.
5. Cows and camels have four nipples. Goats and sheep two.
6. Within the first hour that milk is in the calabash its flavor is perceived as flat. Taste and mouthfeel begin to develop after three to four hours.

Bibliography

Holtzman, Jon. *Uncertain Tastes : Memory, Ambivalence, and the Politics of Eating in Samburu, Northern Kenya*. Berkeley: University of California Press, 2009.

Mather, Amasa Stone. *Extracts from the Letters, Diary and Note Books of Amasa Stone Mather, June 1907 to December 1908. [with Plates, Including Portraits.]*. Vol. 2: A. H. Clark Co.: Cleveland, Ohio, 1910.

Spencer, Paul. *The Samburu; a Study of Gerontocracy in a Nomadic Tribe*. Berkeley: Univ. of California Press, 1965.

'Salty as Sailors Boots'; Salt-Cured Meat, the Blessing and Bane of the Soldier and the Archaeologist

Alexy Simmons

Salted meat was a staple food of armies from the time meat and fish were cured with salt and men marched to war. Prior to the widespread use of canned food, British army and navy messes relied on salt meat. Salted meat is also associated with historic whaling stations, mining settlements, logging camps, and ship voyages: places where the primary activity was not food acquisition.

The British Army Commissariat supplied salted or salt-brined beef and pork to British and colonial troops during the New Zealand War campaigns against various North Island Maori tribes from 1845–1872. Soldiers' diaries and newspaper correspondence refer to salted beef and pork rations. The archaeological reports about the campaign sites tell a different story, one devoid of salted meats.

The New Zealand War and the Waikato campaign

The soldiers, officers, Commissariat Corps and archaeological sites associated with the New Zealand War of 1845–1872 are the focus of this paper on salt-cured meat. The war involved British and colonial forces in 13 major conflicts against North Island Maori tribes. The war was as significant in New Zealand's history as were the English and US Civil Wars.[1] Commissariat records indicate salted meat was part of the food supply that was purchased, stored, and transported to the front during the Waikato Campaign of the war and afterwards to the army of occupation in the Waikato.

The New Zealand War was primarily a conflict fought for land ownership. The underlying cause was a demand for land by British immigrants. The Waikato River valley, south of Auckland, the major city of the time, was fertile and desirable. The Waikato valley was being cultivated by Maori using European methods learned from missionaries at stations throughout the region. The Waikato Maori raised most of Auckland's food, as well as shipping to Sydney. Pressure was exerted on Waikato Maori to sell their land. Tribal opposition to sale resulted in unification of the tribes under the rule of a Maori king in 1858. The Colonial Government interpreted the election of King Potatau I as a challenge to the sovereignty of Queen Victoria and the Crown. Maori recognition of her sovereignty had been embodied in the 1840 Treaty of Waitangi.

On 11 July 1863 Governor Grey issued a virtual declaration of war. He accused the Waikato chiefs of threatening peace and gave notice of military posts to be constructed in the Waikato. The Waikato campaign followed.

Ensuring the food supply; the role of the Commissariat Corps

During the Maori wars the army commissariat's mandate was to ensure the troops were battle-ready. The British force was manned by officers who were veterans of the Crimean campaigns and knew the cost of supply mistakes. The Commissariat Corps' duty was to ensure the soldiers had their allowed rations, no matter where they were based. The scale of allowances stipulated as being an ordinary field ration were: '1 lb fresh or salted meat, 1 ½ lb bread or 1 lb biscuit, and 1 gill of rum'.[2]

Prime mess beef and Irish pork, as well as generic salt pork and beef, were purchased. J. Leslie Robertson, Deputy Assistant Commissary General, noted in his August 1864 narrative of the campaign in the Waikato country: the beef cured in New South Wales was obtained at about 3*d.* (three pence) a pound for the 1863–1864 campaign, although the troops apparently preferred salt pork. Salt pork averaged 6*d.* (six pence) a pound and was obtained through a local contractor who supplied American, English and New Zealand brands.[3]

Salted meat contracts were advertised in the Auckland newspaper. The following advertisement appeared on 31 January 1862:

> Salted Beef at per ton of 2000 lbs
> Salted Pork at per ton of 2000 lbs …
> The salt beef and pork to be of the best quality. Each cask to be opened and re-packed at the expense of the contractor, and only the best pieces taken. Casks not to be charged for.[4]

Salt-cured meat; dry or wet curing

Meat is conserved with salt (sodium chloride), saltpetre, sugar, and sometimes spices, to preserve it during storage and render the meat safe for consumption.[5] The salted meat purchased by the Commissariat may have been cured using either a dry-salt or wet-salt (brining) process. In dry-salting the meat was rubbed with a dry salt and in some recipes a small amount of sugar and saltpetre. The process is repeated a number of times to ensure a good coating and penetration of the salt. No curing action takes place until the solid salt or sugar has dissolved in the fluid exuding from the meat.[6] The moisture (brine) that is drawn out is drained away, eventually producing what British sailors called 'junk' beef. If the brine that drains during the dry-salting process is retained and additional brine or pickling solution is added the result is wet-salted meat.[7] Brining without first dry-salting involves soaking the raw meat in a strong salt solution and rearranging the meat cuts to ensure coverage.

The 1853 British Naval Victualling Office instructions for butchering and salting oxen and hogs at Deptford document a wet-salting process. The Army Commissariat orders that required the pickle be monitored suggest a wet-salted meat was purchased. The regulations noted:

427. For the preservation of salt provisions, some pickle should be kept ready prepared and of full strength, in two open casks, so that whenever a cask of provisions is discovered not to be full of pickle, the storekeeper may always be prepared to fill it.[8]

Factors that preserve meat and affect preservation

Food decomposes due to the uncontrolled actions of micro-organisms and enzymes.[9] To conserve food, enzymes and micro-organisms (i.e. yeast, moulds and bacteria) must be inhibited to prevent spoilage or, in the case of some foods, used to transform foods chemically.[10]

Four environmental factors can be manipulated to manage spoilage:

1. The amount of free (unbound) water molecules in the food, i.e. the degree of dryness;
2. The temperature;
3. The pH, i.e. the degree of acidity/alkalinity;
4. The aerobic or anaerobic environment, i.e. the amount of oxygen present.[11]

Salt-curing preserves meat because the salts bind water molecules and have the same affect as drying. The salts draw moisture from the cells of both the meat and microbes by osmosis. This drying action inhibits the growth of *Clostridium botulinum* bacteria and permits the growth of salt-tolerant bacteria. If the food is weighted down and/or compressed, the salt diffusion into the meat and moisture drainage is accelerated.[12]

The addition of brining or pickling to wet-salted meat creates an anaerobic environment through immersion of the meat in the curing solution. Concentrations of salt up to 20 per cent are required to kill most species of unwanted bacteria.

The curing process continues until there is equalization of density between the pickle outside and the water or natural moisture inside the meat.[13] The pH of the meat is altered by the chemical changes that occur in the curing vat or barrel in both dry- and wet-salting.

The rate of penetration of the cure is affected by the size of the meat cut, type of meat, amount of skin on the surface of the meat and the ration of fat to lean meat.[14] The cleanliness of the meat packer and packing environment and the temperature during killing and curing processes can offset the beneficial effects of friendly microbes and cause putrefactive changes in the meat.[15]

Feeding an army on the move

As the battle front moved south, water transport and road access improved and fresh meat replaced the salted meat. Deputy Commissariat Robertson reported in December 1863: 'Live cattle were driven in sufficient numbers to the front, reducing the issue of salt meat, and relieving to some extent the pressure on the transport.'[16]

290

The army continued to move southward and by 1864 the force in the Waikato occupied a string of remote redoubts, many accessible only by pack-horse train. Consequently the weight of the salted meat containers was reduced to 100-lb kegs:

Salt pork, per lb, salt beef per lb. In ordinary packages or, if required, packed in kegs, the gross weight of which shall not exceed 100 lbs.[17]

In mid-February 1864, during the taking of Maori villages near Te Awamutu, Lieutenant-General Cameron, commander of the British and Colonial forces, required the Commissariat supply five days' provisions for the entire force of approximately 2,144 men, three days' forage for animals, and hospital appliances.[18] This would have required the provision of 10,720 lb of salted beef or pork, or approximately 107 barrels containing approximately 100 lb of salted meat each.

In late April 1865 the Commissariat Corps was ordered to stockpile salted meat:

although there appears to be a considerable quantity of good cattle in the country, the Lieutenant-General prohibits parties from going out to drive them in, and has now given orders that one month's consumption of salt meat for the whole force is to be provided at once. I anticipate a very considerable loss of this meat, as it is quite impossible to take sufficient care of it in the field.[19]

Supply and management of one month's ration of salted meat at Ngaruawahia, where on 1 July 1865 there were 332 regular forces, would involve monitoring 103 100-lb barrels, or 10,292 lb of salted meat.

291

The army commissariat and the soldiers

The army commissariat and soldiers were of two views on salted meat. The commissariat's records describe an army that literally moved on its stomach, sustained by a stockpile of salted meat. The views expressed by both enlisted men and officer suggest that grumbling stomachs were also part of moving the army.

8 August 1863 – The men confined last night [some of No. 5 Company had been put in the guard-tent from grumbling at their meat] were all let off with a reprimand.[20]

Salted meat was served out to both the officers and the men. Andrew Carberry, Assistant Surgeon, 18th Royal Irish Regiment, noted in his diary:

Since we came to this place Mauku we have been treated very badly by the Commissariat – nothing but salt pork and biscuit in the shape of rations the daily recurrence [sic] of which is nauseating – but fortunately I am not entirely independend [sic] on salt meat, and there is a small store near the stockade a couple of miles off where we can purchase flour and bad groceries. Parties go out pig hunting in the bush occasionally and bring in some fresh pork which is considered a great luxury.[21]

While the diaries of the men on the front line don't mention salted meat extensively, they do document the fact that salt meat was issued and consumed. Corporal George Brier of the 68th Regiment observed in 1866:

Once a week we had eather [sic] 12 ounces of salted beef or salted pork. The day we got salted meat we got 1 ounce of lime juice and 2 ounces of brown sugar. … We had to drink the lime juice to prevent us from having scurvy.[22]

Salted meat evidence at the Waikato campaign sites
While the bane of the soldier was consuming salted meat, the bane of the archaeologist is finding salted meat at the Waikato campaign sites. Remains of salted meat, in the form of bones and barrels, have not been identified at the ten sites that have been the focus of excavations. This raises the question of why bones and barrels aren't being found. The following text explores the problems associated with recovery of both types of remains.

Salt meat barrels
The barrels, casks or other commissariat packaging were not to be sold or traded.[23] Storage of other food items in salt meat barrels was probably limited due to salt-brine residue but the barrels could have been used as furniture and building material. Other historic sites contain barrels that have been reused for well-liners and privy cisterns.[24] The wooden barrels might have found use as fuel for cook and camp fires, leaving metal hoops.[25] A few metal hoops have been found in the Waikato campaign sites, but many things were packed in barrels, including the men's rum ration. Iron hoops, salt pork and salt beef were being auctioned by the commissariat at their post in Auckland from 1863 through 1866, along with other goods. No empty barrels were detailed in the auction notices.[26] Hardware such as bread-baking equipment was offered for sale locally so there is a potential that empty barrels were also sold locally by the commissariat.

Bones or no bones
There has been very little bone recovered from excavations at the ten or more campaign sites that have been investigated, except at Alexandra East Redoubt and Alexandra AC Redoubt. Some archaeologists have suggested salt meat is an invisible food because salt meat had no bones. Zooarchaeologist Elizabeth Reitz wrote in a 1987 paper, 'the presence of bones would enhance spoilage, if only because the piece of meat was too thick for adequate penetration of brine through muscle and bone'.[27] She noted the problem was solved in recent times because brine is forced into the meat.

An argument for the removal of bone from cuts that are being salted was also noted in Barbara West's 'Case of the Missing Victuals' (1995).[28] West carried out a detailed analysis of the faunal remains recovered from three periods of use of the former Royal Navy Victualling Yard from 1560 to 1726. The faunal remains were analysed in detail and revealed bone, antler, and tortoiseshell working during the middle period (1635–1726). What the bones did not reveal was evidence of a slaughter yard or victuals activities in the victualling yard. The lack of bones was considered unusual since beef and pork were salted and pickled at the victualling yards at a rate of 40 oxen a day, i.e. 880 kg of cattle bones. Although the inclusion of the bones in casked salt meat would have removed many of the bones from the site and explained the lack of bones, West argued that bones would not have been retained in salted meat cuts because inclusion of bone add extra weight. She suggested the bones were probably sold to glue-makers. The explanation does not taken into account the amount of ballast sailing-ships carried. The added weight from bones in salted meat would have had no effect, except on the sailors that loaded the vessels.

Reitz and West's observations about boned salt meat are refuted by historical records and the recovery of salted beef and pork bones from salt meat casks found in shipwrecks. Historical evidence that indicates bones were included in salted meat include The New York Agriculture Society (1853) report on an experiment carried out in May 1813 to assess waste in salted meat. In the experiment 100 lb of prime mess beef were cooked and 9 lb 10 oz of bones were recovered. A 56-lb keg of captain's beef was also cooked and yielded 5 lb 6 oz of bones.[29] This experiment suggests that a commissariat salt beef store of 100 casks weighing 100 lb each could potentially produce approximately 1000 lb of beef bone at a Waikato campaign site.

Canadian regulations, 1839

Canadian regulations in 1839 for salted meat cuts require no bone removal. The meat was cut into segments that were as near square as possible to facilitate tight packing to prevent bruising or other damage during transport. The salted beef cuts were to weigh no more than eight and no less than four pounds and pork no more than six and no less than four pounds, to assist in the penetration of salt into heart of the meat cut.[30] Boning the meat would have increased the handling and potential for spoilage, as well increasing production costs because of the additional labour time.

Instructions of the British Naval Victual Office at Deptford, 1838 and 1853

The instructions provided in 1838 and 1853 for the butchers at the British Naval Victual Office at Deptford for butchering beef and pork for salting allow for the inclusion of bone in most meat cuts. The naval butchering and processing instructions were very prescriptive. The cow was quartered and each quarter weighed. 'The marrow bones are to be taken out as clear of meat as possible, and the legs and shins cut off at the joint, or proper place, for which 16 lbs in each are to be allowed'.[31] The meat was then divided into 12 pieces of approximately 8 lb each. The specifications allowed for 'cutting the prime pieces a little under 8 lb, thereby allowing the other, agreeably to their coarseness and quantity of bone, to be over that weight'.[32] The kidney suet, head of the cow, legs, shins, marrow-bones, and waste scraps of meat produced in butchering are disposed of or delivered back to the contractor. The butchering of pork was similar. Every 200 lb of pork was to be divided in the same even manner as the beef. The hog was to be cut into 55 pieces of 4 lb each.

The weight of the cuts differed significantly in the two butchery instructions. Creating smaller meat units would have resulted in more cuts to the bone unless the meat was deboned, which appears to not have been the case. The larger meat cuts could have resulted in more secondary division in the field when meat rations were served out to the soldiers, depending on the size of their mess groups.

Grades of salted meat

Salted meat was graded according to the age of the animal and weight of the carcass at the time of slaughter, and the selection of cuts. Mess beef was the highest grade of meat and consisted of the brisket, thick flank, ribs, rump and sirloin from well-fattened and properly aged animals.[33] Prime beef and cargo beef were lower grades and contained less desirable joints. Pork was advertised in four grades: mess pork, prime mess pork, prime pork, cargo pork and clear pork. There was variation between countries in the nomenclature for grading, as well as use of other identifiers, i.e. Irish Pork. The best grades were mess pork and prime mess pork, the lower grades like the beef included less favored cuts.

The commissariat purchased prime mess beef, prime mess pork, and generic salt pork and beef. The beef was obtained from Australia and the pork included American, English, and New Zealand brands. Bones were part of the salted meat purchased and distributed, but which bones and how were the cuts divided?

The archaeology of salted meat

To understand the potential differences between salted meat cuts and fresh meat cuts I reviewed the findings from shipwreck sites and the Hoff Store site. The Hoff Store contained an inventory of salted meat when it was destroyed in the Great San Francisco Fire of 1851.[34] Similarly, comestibles in the holds of many wrecked vessels included salt meat. Two shipwrecks were identified that included reports that discussed the salted meat found; the *William Salthouse* and the *Earl of Abergavenny*.

Hoff Store site

The W.C. Hoff Store in San Francisco supplied mining communities and outward-bound ships from its waterfront location near Howison's Pier. On the night of 3 May 1851 the Hoff Store buildings caught fire. The Hoff Store deposits were preserved because the blazing structures plunged into the waters of the Bay and the Bay mud encased the

294

remains in a stable anaerobic environment that was later capped by fill. Archaeological excavation in 1986 exposed food remains, including salted pork. There were 257 pork bones and bone fragments from 3 barrels of prime pork, the lowest grade of US pork.[35] The pig bone assemblage included three heads and six jaws and a few foot bones. The animals were identified as young animals and the meat cuts were the less desirable pork shoulder, rib, and loin as might be expected.[36] But surprisingly, the more desirable roast of ham was found to be well represented, as was the shoulder cut. The researchers noted the meat cuts needed to be understood with reference to the animals being processed. 'Desirable cuts from a lean, packing pig might *not* be as highly valued as less desirable cuts from an extra heavy, well-fatted hog.'[37] The only distinctive butchering method noted was the division of the pig innominate bone. The ilium was sawn diagonally separating the ilial wing from the reminder of the innominate.

William Salthouse

The *William Salthouse*, a brig that traded between Canada and the settlement of Port Phillip in Australia, sank with a cargo of tierces and barrels of salt beef and pork in 1841.[38] The cargo included seven barrels of prime mess beef, a half-barrel lid branded with ribs, rumps, and briskets, nine barrels of prime mess pork, and four barrels of prime pork. Samples of both pork and beef were recovered and analysed in the 1990s by A.J. English.[39] The samples available from the cargo were not complete barrels and many of the bones were affected by taphonomic processes, in this case scouring and disturbance by recreational divers that degraded the information available. The salted meat 'contained a significant number of bones and a wide variety of skeletal parts.'[40] The pork skeletal sample was too small and fragmentary to draw conclusions from, but 'the treatment of the beef fore and hind limbs produced butchering marks not found on any terrestrial site studied.'[41]

English noted: 'the cuts are square in accordance with the legislation, and derived from sawing the bone through at the shaft, disarticulating the joints.'[42] The division of the long bones near the ends left the mid-shaft, thus separating the leg from the loin and rump, and breaking the leg into smaller meat units. This was not a standard butchering practice at the time. The forelimbs were divided in a similar way. The remaining beef elements were butchered in ways that made them indistinguishable from common butchering practices, although the meat cuts produced were still square cuts suitable for packing. For example 'the vertebrae column had been sawn in half down the sagittal plane, and then again transversely at a number of points, to produce square cut sections of articulated ribs and vertebrae.'[43]

Earl of Abergavenny

The *Earl of Abergavenny*, one of the largest vessels of the British East India Company, sank in 1805 near Weymouth, England on her outward-bound voyage. The faunal analysis of her cargo indicated there was a high proportional representation of square-cut portions of cattle ribs.[44] Two grades of salted pork were suggested by the analysis of the wreck. The barrelled pork in the stern included meatier cuts than that found in the bow. In the bow area pig bones included heads, jowls, and feet, or the lowest grade of salted pork.

Terrestrial sites

The information provided by shipwrecks and sites like the Hoff Store informs the identification of salt meat, but does not address the fragmentary skeletal remains and taphonomic effects on remains found at terrestrial sites. Sites that were identified where salted meat has been found included whaling sites and slave compounds. The context of the whaling stations and some slave compounds included isolation and a focus on activities other than food acquisition.

Smeerenburg at Spitsbergen

The Dutch whaling settlement Smeerenburg at Spitsbergen was dependent on barrelled beef in the seventeenth century, because domestic herbivores could not survive in the arctic circumstances of Spitsbergen.[45] Historical sources indicate that beef was transported from the Netherlands as salted meat packed in barrels. 'The zooarchaeological analysis of the cattle bone assemblage from Smeerenburg provided evidence for the selective introduction of skeletal parts to the site.'[46] The most noticeable indicators were the total absence of skulls, mandible, metapodia and phalanges of cattle coupled with a high frequency of fragmented ribs and parts of the sternum.[47] Long bones and vertebrae were also represented in the assemblage. In Chomel's 1743 *Household Dictionary* he mentions that for the salting of beef rib-pieces, the sirloin and those pieces that have a lot of bone should be selected.[48] The faunal remains recovered conform to Chomel's recommendation. The evidence from Smeerenburg indicates that skull, mandible, metapodia and phalanges were removed prior to salting, and that the cattle carcasses were chopped into standardized 25 cm portions.[49]

Tasmania

The Adventure Bay and Lagoon Bay whaling stations in Tasmania contained the remains of pork, beef and mutton. Historical records indicated the stations were supplied with barrelled beef along with live sheep and cattle. Because of the similarities in butchering techniques used for fresh and salt meat and the general variability in butchering patterns, element analysis was used.[50] The analysis found pig cranial and lower limb bones were absent and suggested a preference for meatier cuts being brought to the site. A similar pattern was evident for the cattle bone. It was concluded that some salt beef may have been used at the sites. The findings were less conclusive than for Smeerenburg because of the use of fresh meat as well as salted.

Brimstone Hill, St Kitts
At Brimstone Hill sugar plantation in the West Indies, along with other domestic mammalian remains, high meat-utility cattle bones (vertebrae, ribs, scapulae, pelves and upper limb bones) were found in association with an area occupied by slaves.[51] Not an association that would be expected but one possibly explained by an archival note that suggests expired salt meat stores should be fed to the slaves.[52]

This unexpected association of high meat-utility beef bones with a slave compound resulted in the analysis of the faunal material using stable carbon isotopes. The analysis was used to assess the cattle's diet and determine if the beef was imported rather than being butchered elsewhere on St Kitts and brought to the site as meat cuts. The stable carbon isotopes confirmed that beef skeletal remains recovered from the area occupied by slaves at Brimstone Hill, St Kitts were from salted meat remains.[53] It was concluded the salted meat probably represented a poor-quality product or expired stores.

Summary of archaeological evidence
One of the primary factors that resulted in the identification of salted meat at the whaling stations and Brimstone Hill slave compound was the context of the archaeological finds. The comparative findings from the sites are summarized in table 1. Indicators of salted meat include high-utility cuts paired with the lack of beef heads and feet. Some bone divisions might also indicate salted beef because of packing requirements. Salted pork bones based on the grades of meat and the high number of bones retained is virtually indistinct from fresh meat since bones that indicated higher-utility cuts are found in low-grade salt pork. Ultimately I found there were few characteristics of butchering or body-part frequency that make the bones from salt-cured meat distinct.

All the archaeological sites discussed were affected by taphonomic processes. Taphonomic processes at terrestrial archaeological sites include man-made and natural effects as well as intrusion by creatures such as dogs, rats, and birds.

Bones were also recycled by processing with bone mills to produce fertilizer, or modified by mechanical processes to manufacture buttons, spoons, sewing tools, and ornaments. Sanitary disposal was also part of the military system and ensured the proper disposal of food waste. At Alexandra AC Redoubt the skeletal remains of domestic animals were recovered from kitchen garbage pits.

Waikato campaign sites: skeletal evidence
The Waikato campaign sites generally contain very few bones or, if they do, the bone fragments are in very poor condition, perhaps for some of the reasons noted above. The AC and Alexandra East Redoubts are exceptions, but analysis shows no evidence of salted meat. There was very little pork, less than on homesteads from this period, and the pig bones included low-utility cuts and pigs' heads. The cattle, which were the dominant species, represented wholesale units rather than carcasses and included both high and low meat-utility cuts. Sheep were also represented in reasonable numbers.

297

The historical records indicate salted meat rations were purchased and available for the soldiers during the campaign. Why has no evidence been found of salted meat in the ten campaign sites excavated? The comparison of three sets of information about the campaign, i.e. the commissariat record, the soldiers diaries, and the archaeological evidence indicated an anomaly.

Salt meat Evidence	Sites
Beef cuts were divided into square segments/cuts of specific weights	*William Salthouse*
Beef – Better grades of beef included higher meat-utility meat cuts (i.e. vertebrae, ribs, scapulae, pelves and upper leg bones)	Smeerenburg, Tasmania, *William Salthouse, Earl of Abergavenny,* & Brimstone Hill
Beef – Better grades of beef *excluded* low meat-utility cuts (i.e. heads, lower leg bones, and feet)	Smeerenburg, Tasmania, *William Salthouse, Earl of Abergavenny* & Brimstone Hill
Pork – Better grades of salt pork included higher meat-utility meat cuts	*Earl of Abergavenny*
Pork – Lower grades of salt pork could include low meat-utility cuts (i.e. skulls, jaws/mandibles, lower leg bones, and feet)	*Earl of Abergavenny* & Hoff Store
Pork – Lower grades of salt pork could include high meat-utility cuts	Hoff Store

Table 1. Summary of salt meat evidence

Researching the anomaly

I found the commissariat records indicate salted meat was purchased as the battle front moved south in 1864, but a new meat contract was also effective on 1 February 1864.

> To ensure regularity in supply [of fresh meat to the front] a main depot for cattle was formed by the contractors in the vicinity of Otahuhu, and field depots were fixed at Pokeno, Paitai, and Whatawhata. An unfailing supply of fresh meat was thus insured at every post, no matter how remote or how difficult to access.[54]

A field depot for cattle was established in the lower Waikato valley at Whatawhata. If live cattle were delivered by an outside contractor directly to the posts the commissariat would only have been required to maintain a stockpile of salted meat at depots for emergencies, reducing the quantity of salt meat distributed and used and the potential for finding evidence of salted meat. This possible explanation was reinforced by two statements in Robinson's report in late August 1864:

> Little [needs] be said on the subject of salt meat, large quantities of which must of a necessity be available, if not for very frequent consumption yet as a reserve, in case of failure in the supply of fresh meat, or to be used on unexpected movements of troops.[55]

> Fortunately fresh meat has been regularly supplied [so] that the consumption of lime juice has not been great.[56]

Summary

The problem associated with the archaeological evidence of salted beef and pork is not the lack of bones, but too many bones and the similarities between fresh meat and salted meat cuts. The identification of salted meat is based on context, skeletal remains represented, taphonomic processes, and disposal practices. The latter may have had a major effect on bones associated with the campaign sites. While bones from salted meat have yet to be found at the Waikato campaign sites, as more sites are excavated or other areas in sites are sampled, salt meat may be identified.

What is recovered archaeologically at the campaign sites and is not documented in commissariat records and soldiers' diaries are the ingredients necessary to make the meat palatable, whether salted or fresh. Lea and Perrins' Worcestershire Sauce, curry powder, and pickle bottles are all found. The other kind of sauce that is also recovered in very large numbers is alcohol bottles.

299

Notes

1. James Belich, *The New Zealand Wars*. Auckland: Penguin Books, 1988, p. 15.
2. War Office, 'Scale of Allowance for Field Service', Appendix 4, Instructions to Commissariat Officers and Others for Field Service in New Zealand. London: Public Records War Office 33/17A, 1864, pp. 74–77 (p. 75).
3. J. Leslie Robinson, 23 August 1864, Continuation of Narrative of the Campaign in the Waikato Country, Auckland New Zealand 1863–1864, Inclosure 1 no. 18. London: Public Records War Office 33/17A, 1864, pp. 59–73 (p. 65).
4. *Daily Southern Cross*, Advertisements, 31 January 1862, p. 1 column 4.
5. Frank Gerrard, *Sausage and Small Goods Production*. London: Leonard Hill Limited, 1951, p. 82.
6. Ibid., p. 82.
7. John Frayler, 'Pickled Fish and Salted Provisions', *Historical Musings From Salem Maritime National Historic Site*, 6 (2004), pp. 1–8 (p.4).
8. War Office op. cit., Appendix 4, p. 74.
9. Astri Riddervold, 'On The Documentation of Food Conservation', in *Food Conservation Ethnological Studies,* ed. Astri Riddervold and Andreas Ropeid. London: Prospect Books, 1988, p. 211.
10. Ibid., p. 211.

11. Ibid., p. 212.

12. Ibid., p. 213.

13. D.A. Greenwood, H.V. Griffin and W. Lee Lewis, 'The Chemistry of Curing Meat', *Journal of Animal Science*, 1 (1939) http://jas.fass.org/cgi/reprint/1939/1/439.pdf [accessed 26 April 2010] (pp. 439–440).

14. Ibid., pp. 440–441.

15. Ibid., p. 445.

16. Robinson, op. cit., p. 61.

17. *Daily Southern Cross*, Army contracts, Commissariat, New Zealand, Auckland 14 January 1864, Advertisements, 19 January 1864, p. 1 column 4.

18. D.J. Gamble, Journals of the Deputy Quartermaster General in New Zealand: From the 24th December 1861 to the 7th September 1864. London: Printed at the War Office, 1864, p. 95.

19. H Stanley Jones, Commissary-General, Report of 26 April 1865, No. 15. London: Public Records War Office 33/17A, 1865, p. 35.

20. Private James Stichbury, 1st Battalion of the Auckland Militia, 'Diary 1863–64', *The New Zealand Wars, Volume 1*, James Cowan. Wellington: Government Printer, 1983, pp. 461–464 (p. 462).

21. Andrew Carberry, Assistant Surgeon 18th Royal Irish Regiment, *Journal November 18, 1863; Flying Column*. Hamilton: Public Library Archive SMS 0148, copied from original in possession of Mrs Andrea Shand, Christchurch, 1958, pp. 5–6.

22. Corporal George Brier, My Travels in New Zealand as a Soldier January 1865–March 1866. Wellington: Alexander Turnbull Library MS-0259, 1866, pp. 6–23, (p. 17–18).

23. 'Regulation 447. Neither the commissariat officer nor any person serving under him is to derive the smallest advantage from barrels, casks, bags, or other packages'. London: Public Records War Office 33/17A, 1864, Appendix 4 (p. 75).

24. Examples of the re-use of barrels are noted in Jill Hamel, *Nineteenth Century Town Life in Alexandra, Report to New Zealand Historic Places Trust* (2003) and Maria Butcher and Ian Smith, 'Talking Trash: Classifying Rubbish-bearing Deposits from Colonial New Zealand Sites', *Journal of Pacific Archaeology*, 1:1 (2010).

25. 'Regulation 431. During the summer months, the salt meat casks are liable to burst by the expansion of their contents from the heat … the oozing of the liquid may be so gradual as not to be perceived, whilst the strong saline liquid quickly corrodes or weakens the hoops on other casks, which in their turn burst or yield, and thus the evil is multiplied'. London: Public Records War Office 33/17A, 186, Appendix 4 (p. 75).

26. 'Auctioned condemned commissariat stores: 15,344 lbs biscuits, in 137 bags, 700 lbs salt pork, in 7 casks, 25 lbs oatmeal, in 1 bag, 900 lbs oats, in 5 bags, 200 lbs bran, in 2 bags, 2,850 sacks, 4,800 iron hoops. Together with other condemned articles. The whole to be removed from the stores the day after the sale. Terms: – Cash.' *Daily Southern Cross*, Advertisements, 19 November (1863), (p. 2 column 2). 'Auction 600 Barrels prime mess pork, 200 half Barrels prime mess pork, For quality unsurpassed, having been imported expressly for HM Commissariat. Also a quantity of Prime Mess Beef.' *Daily Southern Cross*, Advertisements, 27 April, 1864, (p. 5 column 5).

27. Elizabeth J Reitz, 'Urban/Rural contrasts in Vertebrate Fauna from the Southern Atlantic Coastal Plain', *Historical Archaeology*, 20 (2), 1987, pp. 47–58 (p. 53).

28. Barbara West, 'The Case of the Missing Victuals', *Historical Archaeology*, 29 (2), 1995, pp. 20–42.

29. Other waste from the experiment is also noted in: 'Beef and Pork Curing', *Transactions of the New York State Agriculture Society, Proceedings of the Annual Meeting*, 12, 1853, pp. 257–295. http://books.google.co.nz/books?id=Ma_NAAAAMAAJ&pg=PA287&lpg=PA287&dq=Mode+of+curing+oxen+and+hogs+1853&source=bl&ots=ftyHYmsvB9&sig=0VhqAFFXqwyuOCPzC [accessed 22 April 2010] (pp. 263–264)

30. A.J. English, 'Salted Meats From the Wreck of the *William Salthouse*: Archaeological Analysis of Nineteenth Century Butchering Patterns', *Australian Historical Archaeology*, 8, 1990, p. 65.

31. Thomas Grant, 'Mode of Curing Oxen and Hogs Slaughtered at the Establishment at Deptford',

Transactions of the New York State Agriculture Society, Proceedings of the Annual Meeting, 12, 1853, pp. 287–291. http://www.weymouthdiving.co.uk/research.htm#Section1 [accessed 22 April 2010] (p. 287)

32. Grant, op. cit., p. 288.

33. English, op. cit., p. 64.

34. Eugene M. Hattori and Jerre L. Kosta, 'The Hoff Store Site And Gold Rush Merchandise From San Francisco, California', *Society for Historical Archaeology Special Publication Series*, 7. Ann Arbor: Braun-Brumfield Inc., 1990, pp. 82–113.

35. US Prime pork – $10 barrel (used by slave owners on antebellum southern plantations to feed their slaves): lowest grade of packed pork. Made form light packing hogs, deficient in shape, quality, and finish (Dawson 1911). Among the potential cuts shoulders, jowls, and sides. . .pig crania and mandibles are not unusual cuts for the lowest grade of packed pork, in Hattori & Kosta, ibid., p. 86.

36. Ibid., p. 86.

37. Ibid., p. 86.

38 For information on the wreck see Mark Staniforth, 'Early Trade between Canada and Australia and the Wreck of the *William Salthouse* (1841)', *Urban History Review*, 28:2, 2000, pp. 19–31

39. English, op. cit., pp. 63–69.

40. Ibid., p. 66.

41. Ibid., p. 66.

42. Ibid., p. 66.

43. Ibid., p. 66.

44. Philip Armitage, 'The Study of Six Artefact Categories From the Wreck Site of the *Earl of Abergavenny*', (Section 1, pp. 1–12). http://www.weymouthdiving.co.uk/research.htm#Section1 [accessed 1 June 2010]

45. L. H. Van Wyngaarden-Bakker, 'Faunal Analysis and historical record: meat preservation and the faunal remains at Smeerenburg, Spitsbergen', *Animals and Archaeology, 4: Husbandry in Europe*, C. Grigson & J. Clutton-Brock, eds., London: BAR International Series 227, 1984, pp. 195–204, (p. 199).

46. L. H. Van Wyngaarden-Bakker, 'Zooarchaeological Research at Smeerenburg', *Smeerenburg Seminar: Report from A Symposium Presenting Results from Research into Seventeenth-Century Whaling in Spitsbergen*, C. Grigson & J. Clutton-Brock, eds., Oslo: Norsk Polarinstitutt, 1987, pp. 55–66, (p. 57).

47. Ibid., pp. 57 & 59.

48. Ibid., p. 57.

49. Van Wyngaarden-Bakker, op. cit., 1984, p. 201.

50. Susan Lawrence and Catherine Tucker, 'Sources of Meat in Colonial Diet: Faunal Evidence from Two Nineteenth Century Tasmanian Whaling Stations', *Environmental Archaeology* 7, 2002, pp. 23–34, (p. 32).

51. W.E. Klippel, 'Sugar Monoculture, Bovid Skeletal Part Frequencies, and Stable Carbon Isotopes: Interpreting Enslaved African Diet at Brimstone Hill, St Kitts, West Indies', *Journal of Archaeological Science*, 28, 2001, pp. 1191–1198 (p. 1193).

52. W.E. Klippel, 'Provisioning Enslaved Africans in the British West Indies: The Animal Bones from Brimstone Hill Fortress, St Kitts', *Brimstone Hill Archaeological Project Report No.21*, Brimstone Hill Fortress National Park Society, St Kitts, West Indies, 2002, pp. 1–13, (p. 4).

53. Ibid., p. 10.

54. Robinson, op. cit., Inclosure 1 No 18, p. 65.

55. Ibid., p. 65.

56. Commissariat directive and Robinson's report comment: 'lime juice should be issued on all days when salt meat is issued for more than one day, i.e. on the second day of salt meat, and on every other day till there is a break in issue. Fortunately fresh meat has been regularly supplied that the consumption of lime juice has not been great'. Ibid., p. 67.

Drying and Fermenting in the Arctic: Dictating Women's Roles in Alaska's Inupiat Culture

Zona Spray Starks

Food processing, particularly drying and fermenting techniques, affected Arctic Inupiat Eskimo[1] women's lives by channeling women into a manufacturing role: processing the family's food, producing clothing and shelter materials, and stockpiling trade commodities. To ensure a continuous manufacturing cycle, behavioural patterns were established to regulate women's lives because their activities were thought to influence food supplies. Eventually alcohol entered the trade system, wreaking havoc on a culture that had lived in sync with Alaska's Arctic for more than six hundred generations.

The time-period covered is from the late 1700s to *c.* 1920, unless stated otherwise.

Arctic residency

Drying and fermenting played a significant role in populating the New World's Arctic.[2] The earliest residents settled along Alaska's coast, moving north and south as the climate warmed and cooled (Dumond 1987: 47). Before permanent Arctic residency could be established, Inupiat ancestors needed three basic requirements, plus hunting tools, to live in a harsh climate: (1) storage facilities for food; (2) skin production for protective clothing and shelter; and (3) an extensive trade system. All three demanded indigenous foods, and all three demanded drying and fermenting. They also required a work-force to process food sources into byproducts for family use and trade. That work-force was women.

When Inupiat ancestors employed holes in the permafrost to keep food frozen for long periods, they solved the first barrier to permanent Arctic residency. Over the years, the holes grew to resemble straight-sided rooms called *si ġluaq*. Some were two storeys high, with a platform mid-way to expedite loading and unloading. Others were four-feet-square. Since women processed or manufactured nearly all *si ġluaq* contents, they were responsible for the cellar's organization, the inventory, its distribution and amassing enough stock for trade.

The second long-term residency requirement, skin production for clothing and shelter, was solved when seamstresses utilized animal furs according to their insulating qualities. The hairs of caribou were hollow, providing the greatest warmth during winter's possible minus-80°F temperatures. Rabbit fur worked admirably for bedding but lacked the warmth and durability needed for clothing. Eider drake skins, with feathers attached, shed water. When hunters donned two eider-skin parkas, one with feathers next to the body and the other with feathers to the elements, the insulating qualities successfully braced bodies against freezing temperatures (Bourdon 1990). Women also turned layers of bird, walrus and fish skins into suits of armor, which were especially effective when strapped to walrus ribs with leather thongs (Beechey 1831: 340, Ray 1975: 54). Wives fashioned *ugruk* (bearded seal, *Erignathus barbatus*) skins into *mukluk* (boot) soles and many large animal skins eventually became housing materials. During the worst of times, skins sufficed as food. Though they lacked nourishment, they were stored in every woman's *si ğluaq*, ready to boil and eat when starvation seemed imminent. Not well known but telling for the woman's story, drying and fermenting techniques were essential for manufacturing skins for clothing and housing materials – and drying and fermenting were indispensable for manufacturing trade goods (Brown 2005: 14; Okakok 1981: 175; Bockstoce 1968: 539).

The manufacturing cycle

To maintain adequate *si ğluaq* inventories and ensure a constant cycle of manufacturing food and byproducts, residents established committed working relationships. Marriage was one of them and functioned as a business in a world where food was the basic economy. Parents traditionally arranged marriages between families from similar environments; lives depended upon skilfully processing a particular area's food sources (Bourdon 1990). Cutting tons of fish had little to do with flensing a 400-pound *ugruk*, or drying and sometimes fermenting the skins of each for clothing. To ensure that a young girl understand her manufacturing role, she moved into her future husband's home when eleven to fifteen years old. Living in near-servitude, she butchered animals, processed food, cooked, prepared skins, and sewed. If her work failed expectations, the husband's family sent her home (Bourdon 1990; Murdoch 1988: xcvi). Though no longer traditionally arranged, parents in the 1930s continued to guide their children into either coastal or interior marriages (Bourdon 1990).

Monogamous marriages were customary, though an extra worker was often an economic necessity when successful hunters killed more game than their wives could process or manufacture into byproducts. For reprieve, a wife sometimes asked her husband to take another spouse. Or the husband might suggest taking another wife. Though the first wife always held rank over the newcomer, the second wife was frequently younger and more sexually attractive: a painful reminder for an older wife who shared the connubial bed, watching the copulating couple (Bockstoce 1968: 209; Cook 1910: 11).

Though working relationships frequently demanded sexual activity, sex in the committed co-marriage was not mandatory. The relationship was formed between two unrelated families in separate territories, providing safety when hunting husbands traveled in hostile areas. Usually arranged during trade fairs, the bond was instigated by husbands, but needed both wives' approval. Offspring were considered siblings; inter-marrying was taboo. Co-marriage lasted for generations, enabling hunters to travel long distances to procure skins for drying and fermenting. It also guaranteed trade

303

opportunities between the families at fairs and, in case of famine, a co-family offered escape from starvation. When far from home, co-marriage assured a weary traveler rest and warmth, food, a woman to dry and repair his clothing, and sex, if the woman agreed (Bodfish 1991: 271; Burch 1970: 31).

Partner-trading and wife-lending were other working relationships, probably devised by men, possibly with sexual overtones, but definitely for economic reasons. Unlike marriage and co-marriage relationships, partner-trading and wife-lending relationships were temporary. They usually involved travel, i.e., hunting trips, trips to trade fairs or short social trips (Birket-Smith 1971: 158; Chance 1966: 5). In partner-trading, husbands exchanged wives between their working partners, i.e., between two hunting partners. The trade cemented the men's working relationship and also increased the family's economic wealth. Inland, men typically left heavy, bulky meat behind while hunting in the mountains, packing home valuable skins and what little meat they could carry. But when accompanied by a woman, she dried the meat, put it on her back and hauled the heavy loads home. Once the trip was over, husbands and wives resumed a monogamous commitment to their married partners. If a pregnant or sick wife was unable to travel, her husband might borrow a friend's wife to cook and mend his clothes while on a trip. Women were not consulted in these exchanges, but sexual activity was expected (Spencer 1976: 83). Rasmussen noted that one woman refused, saying she wanted sex only with her husband. He beat her, contending that her resistance damaged his hunting partner-relationship, which limited the family's food supply and restricted marketable food and skins (1908: 64).

Limiting population was another means of managing the food cycle; a burden that weighed heaviest on women's hearts. Without contraception, infanticide was expected during food shortages. Because hunters were deemed more important than manufacturers, baby girls were apt to be discarded. Mothers stuffed snow into a newborn's mouth and left her under the snow or under a tuft of sod (Birket-Smith 1971: 159). When fathers died, the family faced inevitable food shortages. Unless someone adopted the children, or the mother married immediately, mothers were expected to kill little ones less than three years old (Oswalt 1967: 193). It was an act considered more humane than starvation. Though outsiders mistakenly believe that elders were sacrificed to reduce food consumption, in most cases elders decided when and how their life would end. Women usually outlived their spouse, typically leaving suicide for women. It was considered beneficial to the group, an act of good-will. My mother befriended an elder no longer able to dry and ferment food or work skins. Feeling she was unable to contribute to the family, she said her good-byes, sat down in a freezing blizzard and died peacefully.

Taboos and rituals were a means to control the hunted and alleviate starvation. They also controlled lives, and varied by region, sometimes by families. Most were probably established by men because the rules burdened women's lives more than those of men or children. However, no one was exempt. Taboos and rituals dictated when and where

304

women could process animals and store provisions, engage in skin manufacturing, when and with whom to have sex, and where to give birth. Directly or indirectly, nearly all female activities touched indigenous food sources, giving their work role social and economic power, though not always overtly acknowledged.

Successful whaling relied upon rituals, plus women's influence. Showing a whale respect was paramount. Greeting the whale in new white clothing and a clean white *umiak* (seal- or walrus-skin-covered open boat) was an act of respect. So all through the dark winter months women worked feverishly sewing the crew's seal- and caribou-skin clothing. They fermented skins, scraped them clean, dried them outdoors in freezing temperatures until bleached perfectly white, then stretched and worked them for hours until soft and supple. It was a formidable task: a race against sun's appearance at springtime, for once hunting sea animals began, sewing land animal skins was forbidden. The boats also required either a thorough cleaning or new covers each year: a task delegated to elderly women, since taboos forbade menstruating women to work on crew equipment, or to set foot on the ice. Each *umiak* required seven *ugruk* skins, previously fermented by burying them in the snow until the hair easily slipped off. Inside a tiny sod house, the aging women sewed for weeks, stitching water-proof seams with ivory needles and sinew as the bulky, rank-smelling skins weighed heavy on their laps. Too pressed for time to go to bed, when exhausted, the women slept sitting up (Brower 1942: 138; Foote: 132).

Beauty and experience also played a part in rituals. Residents believed that women charmed whales, which eagerly offered their lives to harpooners who had recently had sex with a woman. To increase hunting success, the *umialik* (whaling captain) offered his prettiest and youngest wife to join the harpooner for a tryst in the *umiak* the night before the crew set sail (Birket-Smith 1971: 107; Brower 1943: 49; Rasmussen 1952: 25). Similarly, Brewster tells of an excellent whale hunter trading wives with a poor hunter, thinking that a whale would prefer its body cooked by an experienced woman. After the ineffective hunter killed a whale, the wives returned to their respective husbands (1998: 202). Respectfully transitioning the whale's soul to land was accomplished by the *umialik's* wife pouring fresh water over a whale's head before butchering. And before whaling began, women meticulously cleaned a *si ǵluaq* (cellar) reserved only for whale meat. The rituals exemplified the whale's importance. So did *Nalukataaq,* the whaling festival, when the *umialik's* wife made *mikigak* by layering whale meat, blubber, tongue and blood, then putting it in a warm room for a few days to ferment. She was obligated to make enough to feed hundreds of people (Brower 1942: 16; Brewster 1998: 191).

Taboos also prevented women from eating land animals or preparing their skins while men hunted on the sea. The opposite was also true. Though women accompanied hunting husbands on the ice to cook and mend their caribou clothes, wives carried the clothes for repair, sometimes for miles, beyond sight of the sea (Ray 1885: lxxxix). As noted, menstruating women on the ice was an age-old taboo. When one woman's menses began, she refused to go ashore. Her husband beat her to death. Another man killed his wife for urinating on the ice, believing that urine drove seals away (Brower 1942: 149; Bockstoce 1968: 352).

Fish camp

Along the Arctic Circle in the Kobuk River area, taboos and rituals dominated women's lives less than in coastal areas. But up-river, hunting food was largely woman's work. Fish were a major food source and summer harvesting happened at fish camp. It was the domain of women, for lore taught that fish flew into women's nets when men were absent (Giddings 1967: 302). Perhaps it was true, for up-river women frequently harvested more food calories than men. In 2002 at Shungnak, my childhood village, women harvested 23,000 lb more fish than men killed land mammals (Magdanz 2004: 32). At the time, women were using fish nets designed like their ancestor's willow-bark nets. Men employed modern-day guns. The difference in total calories harvested would have been greater generations earlier, when men hunted with bows and arrows. So while men hunted in the mountains, women worked night and day seining for fish. Boys hauled them ashore for grandmothers to gut and fillet and young girls hung them to dry. By fall, their catch would hopefully last through winter, with enough for trade.

Between fish runs, women scraped partially fermented and dried caribou skins, and rubbed them until soft. Cranberries and blueberries were picked and dried, or picked and stored in oil-filled pokes to retard fermentation, then buried to keep cool. The oil didn't always work: the sweeter the berry, the more difficult to preserve. 'Blueberries were the worst', Lola Avessuk said, 'they cook', recalling when her aunt's berry-filled poke burst (1983). Young girls learned to identify young greens and were directed not to come home until their sacks were full. Half-smiling, Esther Bourdon said, 'They were sooo heavy, sooo big. I was only nine. I had to clean and mix them with seal oil. My mother put them in a seal *puuk* (seal-skin container). She opened it now and then to keep bubbles away before it froze' (1993). Grasses had to be gathered and dried to weave into floor mats, containers, mittens and *mukluk* (boot) liners. There were medicinal plants to harvest and hang until dried, such as dried Labrador Tea (*Ledum palustre*) for stomach-aches and constipation. My aunt explained how she dried and soaked willow bark in a *puuk* filled with water, chewing on it to ease her pain during childbirth – which she endured alone because of taboos (Schuerch 1993). Dried highbush cranberry (*Viburnum edule*) was another useful painkiller, though less effective than the willow bark containing salicylic acid, an ingredient found in aspirin.

Toward fall, cutting fish became nearly impossible when freezing temperatures wracked hands with pain. Not wanting to waste a catch, women piled fish by the river bank to ferment and freeze. The mound was large. While the exterior froze, the center fermented, offering a range of tastes from mild to strong, with soft to icy textures (Jones 2006: 278). By the sea in the 1920s, my mother helped pour fish into large holes lined with gunny sacks and covered them with leaves and sod. There they stayed: from two weeks to four months. King salmon heads were traditionally fermented in the same way, but in small holes lined with acidic leaves and grasses to create the classic *aurruq,* which outsiders call stink-heads. Sometimes the roe and livers were added (Boyer 1950).

Drying and fermenting fish was an artful science. For quick drying and minimum spoilage, each species demanded specific cutting techniques: and there were many. To utilize nature's cool, dry breezes effectively, women cut fish according to their fat-content and size, if eggs were present, whether the fish were for family or dog consumption, or intended for trade. Then, too, temperature and humidity had to be considered, and how to prevent flies from laying eggs on the newly cut flesh. During early salmon runs, the fatty fish were often cut into separate skin-covered fillets attached at the tail. The flesh was incised crosswise to facilitate drying, hung with tails pointing to the sky, and turned daily. Later in the spawning season, women cut salmon from the rib section toward the back, leaving the fillets connected by their back skin. After pulling the fillets from the backbone, the uncut egg-filled belly remained clinging to the backbone, protecting the eggs from incessant flies. Because tomcod flesh was lean, women cut one side of the whole fish open to resemble a door on a hinge, revealing the belly-contents. They removed the gills, guts and fatty liver, then hung the fish to dry, eggs pulled forward, peeking out of the cavity (Jones 2006: 79, 34, 70). Fall male salmon were cut similarly, but with the milt pulled forward to encourage drying (Anderson 1976: 182). When salmon eggs were hung to dry, their interior frequently fermented, changing flavors daily. Not to waste anything, women cooked the tomcod livers with a little water until thick enough to coat a stick, like testing *crème anglaise* with a spoon. It was set aside to ferment a few days and used as a dipping sauce for fish or meat (Bourdon 1993). Depending upon drying times, fish could be frozen, pickled in berries, stored in oil and frozen, or simply pulled into shreds and eaten with oil (Jones 2006: 305). Thoroughly dried fish were durable, easy to transport, making them a valuable trade item, especially when stored in seal oil.

307

In fish camps at coastal Shishmaref, women hung *ugruk* (bearded seal) meat on drying racks rather than fish. Wrestling a 75 lb, or heavier, *ugruk* skin with blubber attached took strength and stamina to flense, especially for a young mother carrying a baby on her back. The chore, however, was not an option, nor was hanging the thirty-pound-plus breasts on drying racks and turning them twice daily. During misty rains, dried skins covered the meat. To facilitate drying, elder women butterflied breast meat until they resembled lace. Nothing was wasted, including the yards and yards of intestines. After washing in the sea, they were hung to dry next to the bright red lungs, ready to enrich a soup. When women blew air into the intestines, dried and cut them into long narrow sheets, they were sewn into water-repellent rain gear or see-through containers, sometimes decorated with tiny black bird feathers. The dried intestines functioned as windows in sod houses, and the featherlight sheets were used for barter. Grandmothers unable to flense heavy seal, but who could help render blubber, took their work-share in seal oil, filling dried lungs or bladders and trading them for needles and sinew. Dried walrus and seal stomach were used for the same purpose, offering poor families a low price-point and grandmothers some financial independence (Fienup-Riordan 1988: 12).

Trade

Trade routes stretched from Siberia to Greenland, furnishing coastal areas with interior products, and vice versa. Most trade items were food: *puuks* filled with seal oil or with oil and meat, tons of dried fish, plus dried caribou and tallow. Sea and land animal skins were another major trade item (Burch 1975: 4). The time necessary to manufacture them entailed many waking hours. A good hunter could kill 168 seals in a year. Processing skins, from beginning to end, could take five weeks each, though only about five days' actual work time. Filling a *puuk* with oil could take three weeks: about two days' actual work time. Though rendering seal oil does not entail drying or fermenting, manufacturing skins and creating a *puuk* did. Women produced them by cutting the seal skin – intact – from the carcass, turning the skin inside out, tying-off the head area, filling the skin with oil, tying-off the anus, smearing the outside with blood and allowing it to dry (Bourdon 1993). Seal oil, the basic Arctic flavoring, was in great demand, though better prices came from *puuks* holding dried caribou, fish, seal, berries or plants. The highest prices, however, came from skins (Zagoskin 1967: 188).

Clothing depended upon skins from the sea and the land. Caribou skins produced the warmest leggings and parkas. The wide sunshine-ruff on women's parkas came from fox skins. Wolverine, an ice-resistant fur, was essential for lining ruffs. Squirrel skins created beautiful parkas but provided little warmth. Eider-skin parkas shed water; fish-skin *mukluks* and mittens were waterproof and historically, duck- and fish-skin armor was arrow-resistant. Coastal women prepared walrus hides and *ugruk* skins for drum and *umiak* covers, seal and walrus intestines for waterproof clothing, and *ugruk* hides for *mukluk* soles (Zagoskin 1967: 189; Apateki 1982). In 1830 when the Russian American Co. and The Hudson's Bay Co. vied for the native fur trade, Inupiats loaded their umiaks with 664 land animal skins – nothing more – and raced to meet the boats. In trade, residents received 167 items: mostly knives and hunting gear, 14 iron pots and kettles, beads, and 110 lb of tobacco (Bockstoce 2005: 26). If twenty women dried and scraped the skins, each would have labored four months – with little sleep.

Manufacturing trade commodities was no less rigorous than transporting them to fairs. That, too, was largely women's work, especially for interior women accompanying an *atturak* (a middleman). Women rowed the *umiaks*, unloaded their 12,000 lb cargo each night and dried the boat covers, mended them when necessary, reloaded the boat, plus portaging it and its six-ton contents to another river, sometimes fifty miles distant. The return trip was equally difficult: the boat now carried traded goods, and home was up-river (Anderson 1976: 242). According to Burch, fairs enticed 8000 people and 2000 metric tons (3,628,000 lb/1,649,091 kg) to five fairs annually each summer, with families traveling 400–500 km (240–300 miles) during July and August (1975: 8). On an average, 1500 people attended each major trade fair, uniting biological and co-married families,

308

and unifying people from Siberia to Canada. Fairs sometimes lasted six weeks while people bartered, harvested fish and game, and plants and berries, and socialized – non-stop.

The success of fairs was a nod to the lifestyle shared across the Arctic. Women living 600 miles apart gathered together for conversation (Burch 2006: 331). Surely they exchanged cooking techniques, drying and fermenting information. Families arranged marriages and co-marriages. Half-naked men challenged each other in games of strength, and unmarried girls donned their best fur garments, hoping to catch the eye of a handsome winner. Everyone danced through the sunlit nights, and they celebrated life by eating. The amount of food eaten in 1887 during a winter Kuskokwim River Feast for the Dead hints at the food consumed at trade fairs. In six days, 700 participants ate '2800 pounds of frozen fish, plus an undetermined amount of dried fish, lots of seal oil, and fourteen huge dishes of *akutuq*' (Eskimo ice-cream) (Langdon 1981: 71). Sled dogs surely ate their fair portion. But since major trade fairs were summer activities, attendees probably consumed more dried foods than eaten at smaller winter festivals. Six-week-long trade fairs also allowed women to gather greens and dry and ferment fish and eggs. Then there were cooking contests: husbands cheered-on their wives to create inventive *akutuq* dishes as they stirred and whipped seal oil and caribou fat into massive white puffs resembling whipped cream, seasoned with fresh or dried berries, plants, dried meats or fish, fermented livers or any number of food combinations (Zagoskin 1967: 118).

Trade fairs, like fish camp, offered a semblance of power and freedom from work for Inupiat women. During trade negotiations, men frequently referred to an elder woman's nod, designating if a trade was fair or not. But when back at home, manufacturing controlled their days again. After World War II, women discovered that arming themselves with high school and college degrees was an avenue for escaping a life of hard labor. But the freedom grew slowly, emerging from a cultural onslaught of alcohol – ironically, a fermented product.

The St Lawrence famine of 1879–1880 clearly depicts alcohol's destructiveness. It resulted from trading women's manufactured skins for whiskey, leaving hunters in a drunken stupor during the fall walrus migration. Over 1000 residents – two-thirds of the population – died of starvation. When a whaling vessel appeared the following spring, the survivors wanted only whiskey. In July 1881, the same ship's hands saw only one dog on the island. All the others had been eaten as starvation food, along with hides and skin clothing. The two largest villages were depopulated (Nelson 1983: 269). In 1894 at Kotzebue Sound, Brower met Inupiats loaded down with furs. They had traveled for a year, heading to a trade fair. Brower was in the fur business and eager for trade, but the Inupiats demanded whiskey. Brower refused. Fifteen years later he visited an old Inupiat chief close to Point Hope. He was drunk; his wealth and prestige gone. The village was run down, and many residents were making whiskey from sugar, flour, molasses, water and raisins (1943: 166, 142; Brewster 1998: 42).

Today many women boast master's degrees and PhDs. On summer weekends, they head for fish camp to help elders catch and dry fish, though fermenting food is not so popular. Whaling is still a festive occasion, including celebrating with fermented *mikigak*. But whalers now include women, and some are *umeliaks* (whaling captains). However, rarely do you find a young woman flensing seal or drying and fermenting skins for clothing. Instead, many are nurses, educators, village managers, town mayors, and school principals. They seem to draw upon their ancestral strengths, continuing the role of major contributors within an economic system more than six hundred generations old. It is a role history has long overlooked.

Notes

1. Inupiat Eskimos share a common lifestyle along coastal areas from Alaska's Norton Sound and across Arctic North America. Eskimo denotes early north-western Alaska residents. Inuit designates Canadian Arctic residents

2. Traditional drying in the Arctic occurs naturally, relying upon cool breezes to eliminate moisture. Though drying seems simple, each of Alaska's two-hundred-plus food sources demand specific handling. Consideration is paid to species, temperature, humidity, sun exposure and the presence of flies. Fermentation is a metabolic process that releases energy from a sugar or other organic molecule, either anaerobically or aerobically. Drying extended the storage life of food. Fermenting foods did the same, plus expanding flavor ranges. Since nearly all foods were stored in sizeable quantities, the interior typically fermented to some degree before being thoroughly frozen.

Bibliography

Anderson, Douglas B., and Wanni W. Anderson *Kuuvanmiut Subsistence: Traditional Eskimo Life in the Latter Twentieth Century.* National Park Service and Northwest Alaska Native Assoc., 1976.

Apateki, Thelma. Oral Interview. Ennis Apateki, trans. GAM.011, Eskimo Heritage Program: Nome, AK, 1982.

Avessuk, Lola. Oral Interview. Georgianna Agupuk-Merrill, trans. SHH.036, Eskimo Heritage Program: Nome, AK, 1983.

Beechey, Capt. F.W. *Narrative of a Voyage to the Pacific and Beering's Strait*, 2 vols. Samuel Bentley: London, 1831.

Birket-Smith, Dr. Kaj. *Eskimos.* New York: Crown Publishers, 1971.

Bockstoce, John, ed. *The Journal of Rochfort Maquire 1852–1854*, Vol. I. London: The Hakluyt Society, 1968.

_____ . 'The Opening of the Maritime Fur Trade at Bering Strait', *Transactions of the American Philosophical Society,* New Series Vol 95 (1), American Philosophical Society, 2005.

Bodfish, Waldo, Sr. *Kusiq, An Eskimo Life History from the Coast of Alaska.* Anchorage: University of Alaska Press, 1991.

Bourdon, Esther. Personal Interview. March, Nome, AK, 1990.

_____. Personal Interview. February, Nome, AK, 1993.

Boyer, Teresa. Personal Interview. Willamina, Ore, 1950.

Brewster, Karen. 'An Umialik's Life: Conversations with Harry Brower, Sr.' (unpublishedMaster's thesis, University of Alaska Fairbanks, 1998).

Brown, William E. *The History of the Central Brooks Range.* Fairbanks, AK: University of Alaska, 2005.

Brower, Charles. *Fifty Years Below Zero.* New York: Dodd, Mead & Co., 1942.

Burch, Ernest S. Jr. *The Eskimo Trading Partnership in North Alaska*. Anthropological Papers of the University of Alaska. 15 (1): 1970, 49–78.

_____. *Inter-Regional Transportation in Traditional Northwest Alaska*. Anthropological Papers of University of Alaska 17 (2): 1975, 1–9

_____. *Social Life in Northwest Alaska*. Fairbanks: University of Alaska Press, 2006.

Case, Christine. Internet correspondence, January 10, 17, 23, 2010.

Chance, Norman. *The Eskimo of North Alaska*. New York: Holt, Rinehart & Winston, 1966.

Cook, Dr Frederick A. *Autobiography, rough draft*. Ch. 7, p. 11, Box 9, fol 41. Columbus: Ohio State University, 1910.

Dumond, Don, E. *The Eskimos and the Aleuts*. [1977]. London: Thames and Hudson Ltd, 1987.

Fienup-Riordan, Ann, ed. *Yup'ik Eskimo as Described in Travel Journal of Ethnographic Accounts of John and Edith Kilbuck 1885–1900*. Kingston, Ont.: Limestone Press, 1988.

Foote, Beret Arnestad. *The Tigara Eskimos and Their Environment*. Point Hope, AK: North Slope Borough Commission on Inupiat History, Language and Culture, 1992.

Giddings, J. Louis. *Ancient Men of the Arctic*. New York: Alfred A. Knopf, 1967.

Jones, Anore. *Iqaluich Niġiñaqtuat, Fish That We Eat*. United States Fish and Wildlife Service, Office of Subsistence Management, Fisheries Resource Monitoring Program, Final Report No. 1, FIS02-023, Anchorage, Alaska, 2006.

Langdon, Steve and Rosita Worl. *Distribution and Exchange of Subsistence Resources in Alaska*, Technical paper No. 55. Juneau, AK: Dept. of Fish and Game, 1981.

Mackie, Richard. 'Strategies of Monopoly: The Hudson's Bay Company on the Pacific, 1821–1843', in *Trade and Commerce in Alaska's Past*. Anchorage: Alaska Historical Society), 1994.

Okakok, Kisautaq-Leona. *Puiquitkaat, The 1978 Elder's Conference*. Barrow, AK: North Slope Borough, 1981.

Oswalt, Wendell H. *Alaskan Eskimos*. New York: Chandler Publishing Co., 1967.

Magdanz, James S., R. J. Walker & Ronald R. Paciorek. *The Subsistence Harvests of Wild Foods by Residents of Shungnak, Alaska, 2002*, Technical Paper 279. Juneau, AK: Alaska Department of Fish and Game, 2004.

Murdoch, John. *Ethnological Results of the Point Barrow Expedition*. Washington, DC: Smithsonian Institution Press, 1988.

Nelson, William Edward. *The Eskimo About Bering Strait*. Washington DC: Smithsonian Institution Press, 1983.

Rasmussen, Knud. *The People of the Polar North*. Philadelphia, Pa: J. B. Lippincott, 1908.

_____. *The Alaskan Eskimos: Posthumous Notes of Dr. Knud Rasmusse*, ed. H. Ostermann. Nordisk Forlag, Copen: Gyldendalske Boghandel, 1952.

Ray, Dorothy Jean. *The Eskimos of Bering Strait, 1650–1898*. Seattle: University of Washington Press, 1975.

Ray, Lieutenant P. H. *Report of the International Polar Expedition to Pt. Barrow, Alaska*. Washington: Government Printing Office, 1885.

Schuerch, Pauline. Personal Interview. Kiana, AK., 1993.

Spencer, Robert F. *The North Alaskan Eskimo*. New York: Dover Publications, 1976.

Zagoskin, L.A. 'Lieutenant Zagoskin's Travels in Russian America, 1842–44', ed. Henry N. Michael, *Arctic Institute of the North*, 7. Toronto: University of Toronto Press, 1967.

The Stories of *Bacalao*: Myth, Legend and History

David C. Sutton

When my friend Jeanne Allard wrote a brief culinary history of the tomato, she was surprised to find herself embroiled in the sharply contested rival Mexican and Peruvian claims to primacy in the origins of the *tomatl* berry. I have encountered similar rivalries throughout my research on salt cod and the fishing of the northern seas (for cod is a cold-water fish, never found in southern seas such as the Mediterranean). There is often limited resemblance between the Norwegian, Portuguese, Breton, Gascon and Basque accounts of our story,[1] and even choosing to use '*bacalao*' in the title might be seen as contentious – although few would deny its Iberian primacy in the twenty-first century.

My first myth concerns Iberia and, like all the best myths, is still widely believed. It holds that the Spanish language has no word for fresh cod. The myth implies that the Spanish are so devoted to salted cod that no other form of cod is linguistically possible. It is a delightful idea, but it is a myth, because the Spanish word for fresh cod is ... *bacalao*. It is true that in Spanish culinary tradition, cod is so often dried and salted that the full term *bacalao seco y salado* is often shortened to just *bacalao*; but *bacalao* is cod.[2]

Etymologically *bacalao* is the same as the French word for cod, *cabillaud*. There has been a transference of the first two consonants. Most linguists believe that the original word is the Basque *bakailao* (shifting its consonants as it was absorbed into French); a few have seen a consonantal shift the other way: from the Gascon word *cabilhau* to the northern Spanish *bacalao*.

The northern European words for salt cod are linguistically cognate in a similar way. The English word *haberdine*, first recorded in Henry VII's naval accounts of 1496, and sometimes mistakenly linked with the port of Aberdeen, is in fact a variant of the word *laberdan*, which (in various spellings) is the word for salt cod in Dutch, German and Russian. The etymological origin of this cluster of words is Le Labourd, a Basque viscountcy whose capital was Bayonne. The *Oxford English Dictionary* (in its definition of *haberdine*) is clear. It is 'from *le Labourd* or from *Lapurdum* ancient name of Bayonne; the Basques having been the first to engage in cod-fishery' (an *OED* statement, of Victorian certainty, very pleasing no doubt to Basque readers).

***

And so we come to my second myth. This is also widely believed, and new versions appear regularly on the Internet. The myth says that the Basque cod-fishermen were moored in vast numbers in the mouth of the Saint Lawrence River when Jacques

Cartier first came upon the waterway in 1534. Here is the original version of the story, from Mark Kurlansky's popular book called *Cod*:

> In June [1497], after only thirty-five days at sea, Cabot found land, though it wasn't Asia. It was a vast rocky coastline that was ideal for salting and drying fish, by a sea that was teeming with cod. Cabot reported on the cod as evidence of the wealth of this new land, New Found Land, which he claimed for England. Thirty-seven years later, Jacques Cartier arrived, was credited with 'discovering' the mouth of the St Lawrence, planted a cross on the Gaspé Peninsula, and claimed it all for France. He also noted the presence of 1,000 Basque fishing vessels. But the Basques, wanting to keep a good secret, had never claimed it for anyone.[3]

This striking story is repeated on well over a hundred English and Spanish websites. Sadly, however, Jacques Cartier's charming accounts of his three voyages to Canada include no sighting of any Basque ships, let alone a thousand of them. The nearest incident is the sighting of 17 fishing boats in the harbour of Saint John on a fourth voyage, in 1542, by Cartier and the Sieur de Roberval. My edition of Jacques Cartier adds a note to say that these were probably Basque or Portuguese.[4]

By the time he came to write his equally popular book, *Salt*, Kurlansky was more circumspect about the early Basque presence in the North American cod-fisheries:

> Did the Basques reach North America before John Cabot's 1497 voyage and the age of exploration? During the fifteenth century, most Atlantic fishing communities believed that they had. But without physical proof, many historians are skeptical, just as they were for many years about the stories of Viking travels to North America. Then in 1961, the remains of eight Viking-built turf houses dating from AD 1000 were found in Newfoundland in a place called L'Anse aux Meadows. In 1976, the ruins of a Basque whaling station were discovered on the coast of Labrador. But they dated back only to 1530. Like Marco Polo's journey to China, a pre-Columbian Basque presence in North America seems likely, but it has never been proved.[5]

313

The myth of the thousand Basque boats is unfortunate because it tends to discredit what is probably the true story of cod-fishing and cod-preservation in the North American fisheries. It is likely that long before the voyages of Cartier and Cabot, Basque, Breton and Portuguese[6] sailors had all visited the cod-banks off Newfoundland and had begun to use salting as a way of preserving their copious catches.

A more credible recent account[7] estimates that in the sixteenth century there were over 200 fishing boats and over 6000 fishermen operating out of the Spanish Basque ports (Bermeo, Lequeitio, Bilbao, Santander, San Sebastián and others), and they were fishing Canadian rather than Icelandic waters, in competition with French and Portuguese boats. A sixteenth-century commentator, Anthony Parkhurst, estimated the total number of European cod-fishing boats at between 350 and 380, of which about 150 were French (including French Basques).[8] Fernand Braudel estimated that by the eighteenth century, with the growth of the Dutch and North American fleets in particular, the global figure for cod-fishing boats may have risen to around 1500.[9]

Some sources indicate puzzlement that the Basques and Portuguese were so rarely seen catching cod off Iceland. There is a Nordic fallacy, a navigational myth, within this puzzlement. The Viking discovery of North America was based on a process of 'going beyond' – on to Iceland, on to Greenland, on to Labrador. A look at a globe, however, easily indicates why the Basques and the Portuguese gravitated towards Newfoundland. Certainly for the Portuguese, it is nearer.

Because these intrepid early fishermen kept no records, we will never know the full story of their pre-Columbian travels across the Atlantic. It is plausibly claimed that the North American cod-banks are shown on Pizzigano's navigational chart of 1424 (produced in Portugal); certainly Andrea Bianco's atlas of 1436, designating the zone to the west of the Atlantic as 'stoc fis', shows them[10].

When the first chartered explorers, beginning with Giovanni Caboto (John Cabot) in 1497, arrived at the cod-banks, they all reported evidence of systematic fishing and cod-drying. They also noted the extraordinary abundance of the cod, and Sebastian Cabot famously reported that the fish were so densely packed in the sea that they impeded the progress of the ships.

One compelling piece of secondary evidence is that John Cabot chose to give the name *Baccallaos* to the lands surrounding the cod-banks, describing it as the name used by the local Native Americans. This reported adoption by the natives of a word derived from the Basque language hints at a long secret history.[11] Neither the Cabots nor the Corte Real brothers (in their first voyage of 1501) were able to identify the fishermen seen drying their fish on the shore. They were not from a registered Portuguese fleet, as the first such fleet arrived in 1502, in response, in fact, to the Corte Real reports. They were probably Basque; possibly Breton or Norwegian.

In order to get the fish back to Europe in an edible state, from the Icelandic seas or from Newfoundland, preservation skills were essential. The Vikings, from the earliest years of their maritime dominance, used the art of drying to create stockfish – rock-hard chunks of dried fish, often compared to planks of wood, from which pieces could be torn and (endlessly) chewed. According to the Norwegian Seafood Export Council, the earliest documents for the export of stockfish date back to the year 875.[12]

Stockfish (*stoccafisso*) remains a popular food in the Nordic countries and in Italy, but the usual assessment, both in culinary terms and according to the market, is that it is markedly inferior to salted cod. We know that in 1471, for example, the price of stockfish in Bristol was £5 for a last (12 barrels), whereas the price of salt cod was about double that.[13]

This was the great distinction amongst the early long-distance fishermen. The Spanish, the Portuguese and the French had salt. Salt made possible the fishing 'revolution' of 1500 and the exploitation of the Newfoundland banks for a foodstuff which was not only cheap and nutritious but also very popular. Most of the catch was dried and salted, leaving good time to find a market, but the really prized part of the catch was the so-called *morue verte*, cod which was salted but moist (not dried) and which regularly found its way onto the tables of the kings of France.[14]

The northern seafarers had either to do deals with the southern salters (deals sometimes described as Protestant fishermen in pursuit of Catholic salt) or to content themselves with stockfish. We have accounts of Norwegian and Danish fishermen sailing to Sanlucar de Barrameda to load up with salt before crossing to the Newfoundland banks. The payment for the salt was a proportion of the salt cod catch.[15] Ibiza was another major destination for sea-salt.

There was also inland salt in countries including England (notably many towns whose names end in –wich in Cheshire and Worcestershire), Austria (hence the name of Salzburg) and Poland. The extracting of salt from inland brine dated back to Roman times and is mentioned in the Domesday Book entries for Droitwich, Nantwich, Middlewich and Northwich. (The suffix –wich, however, means a settlement and does not always indicate salt; there are no salt traditions in Norwich, Ipswich, Greenwich or Woolwich.)

It was not until 1670 that it was discovered that the inland brine-springs and brine-pools derive from mineable underground seams of rock-salt. Prior to the 1670s, for fish-salting, the English and Austrian inland salt was generally found to be both too fine and too expensive to transport to the fishing ports. Coarser Mediterranean sea-salt was preferred on grounds both of taste and of cost.

315

The Worshipful Company of Salters was licensed in 1394, but their history adds little to our story; first, because most of their records were destroyed in the Great Fire of London in 1666, and, secondly, because most of their business was in the import and export of sea-salt, not in trading English salt.[16] The commerce in salted food was far more extensive and profitable than any commerce in table-salt for sprinkling.

***

Several reasons have been proposed for the critical importance of the supply of fish, and salt cod in particular, in mediaeval Europe. We can identify three principal themes: (1) economic reasons; (2) reasons of taste and food-preference; and (3) religious reasons.

The economic reasons were primary. Fish was a comparatively cheap, but nonetheless profitable, source of what we now call proteins and vitamins at a time when for many the main rationale for eating food and for making meals was simply staying alive, as the Franco-Egyptian food historian Maurice Bensoussan has recently emphasized:

> Even the idea of a meal – in the sense of a moment where one stops the work-activity in order to eat – is reserved for festivals, because the partaking of food is divided up in the course of a day into several snacks, calculated more to sustain the exhausting workload than to offer any sort of pleasure.[17]

At this level of mere survival, fish had long been a vital component of the European diet. After 1501, once the discovery of the Newfoundland banks had been officialized by the Cabots and the Corte Reals, organized fishing fleets (often with royal imprimaturs) set out from the Basque, Breton and Portuguese ports to bring back large quantities of cod. It is possible, and even likely, that these new fleets were following routes secretly well known to the fishermen's grandfathers and great-grandfathers.

Prior to 1500, the principal fish caught and sold in western Europe had been herrings and (more locally) freshwater fish. Barrels of salted herrings from the Baltic Sea and the North Sea were transported all around Europe, and were notably popular in England; salted sardines or pilchards were more prevalent in the southern countries. From 1500, herrings and pilchards were substantially replaced by cod in the market, although not in popular culture and thought. The English in particular have dozens of proverbs about herring, and almost none about cod; even today, English people who have never eaten a herring moralize freely about red herrings and herrings in a barrel.[18] (References to red herrings abound in English sources from the *Liber Cure Cocorum* around 1430 to Samuel Pepys's breakfast in February 1660.)

The import of cod into western Europe was clearly very profitable. We find metaphors comparing cod to gold in various sources in the sixteenth century, and the fishermen themselves referred to cod as their bread. Asked why he put up with the dangers and the privations of the journeys to Newfoundland, a fisherman would reply 'There's bread over there'.[19]

The master-historian and source-finder Fernand Braudel discovered in the Bibliothèque Nationale de France a letter from the Chevalier de Razilly to Cardinal Richelieu maintaining that fishing for cod is the best commerce in Europe, with the lowest overheads and the highest profit: '*le meilleur trafic de l'Europe, c'est d'aller pêcher la molue*' [*molue*: an early form of *morue*].[20]

The economics of salt cod fishery made the fortunes of merchants especially in the commercial ports which did not themselves send out cod-fishing boats (Marseilles, Bristol, Sète), after economic and military power saw many of the original fleets forced off the cod-banks, first by licensed piracy (initiated by Sir Francis Drake), then by war and treaty. The Spanish, the Portuguese and the Basques were forced out by the great naval powers of Britain, Holland and France (although the Portuguese quietly returned in the nineteenth century), and the cod-banks were a major factor in the wars and treaties between Britain and France throughout the eighteenth century. The cod-fishing islands of St Pierre and Miquelon notably changed hands several times before being returned to France in 1783. As French commentators were quick to point out, however, there was a difference in attitude between the two principal great powers: to the French salt cod was a vital foodstuff; to the British the salt cod represented vital commerce.

***

Taste and food preferences represent the most subjective of our three themes, and we should be cautious of individual accounts. Our Portuguese sources, however, give so many examples of salted cod being described as a faithful friend (*fiel amigo*) that we can be confident in describing the generalized Portuguese affection for *bacalhau*. There are branches of the Academia do Bacalhau in several Portuguese cities (also amongst the Portuguese communities of Toronto, New Jersey and Paris) and the Lisbon academy has succeeded in collecting over one thousand *bacalhau* recipes.

Salt cod is unusual in that its recipes belong both to the popular and to the gastronomic tradition. In the context of this essay, it is especially pleasing to note that one of the '*recettes de grande cuisine*', featuring salt cod and artichoke bottoms, is known as '*morue Jacques Cartier*';[21] but above all it is the dish known as '*brandade de morue*' which bridges the traditions and which sits as comfortably on the pages of Escoffier as on the back-street café chalkboards of Paris or Nîmes.

Going beyond the universal *brandade*, *morue à la crème* was specifically conceived as a dish fit for a king. Invented by François Massialot in the late seventeenth century at the suggestion of Louis Béchameil (or Béchamel), *morue à la crème* found its way into all the great recipe books of the eighteenth century, and significantly into Menon's *Les soupers de la cour* (1755). *Morue à la crème* had pride of place in the great banquet served to Louis XV and Madame de Pompadour in August 1757 at Versailles. Béchameil himself was a financier and his principal interest was not gastronomy or creamy sauces, but his investment in the Newfoundland fisheries.[22]

The historian Alain Drouard has authoritatively listed the foods most associated with the poor of Western Europe around the sixteenth century; they include garlic, onions, leeks, dried pulses, cheese, beer and salted foods;[23] largely, we might say, the smelly foods. Salt fish (and from 1500 onwards this meant predominantly salt cod) was a staple food for the European poor, but in its finer forms (derived from *morue verte*) it remained a favourite of the richest, most aristocratic and most gastronomic members of society, and featured heavily in their cookbooks and recipe books.

In Spain *bacalao* has this same social range, from the everyday to the highly gastronomic. For her classic 1940 collection of aristocratic Spanish recipes, the Marquesa de Parabese includes a mixture of classic Spanish favourites (such as *bacalao a la vizcaina* or *bacalao en salsa verde*) and the great French recipes (*bacalao a la brandade*, naturally, and *bacalao con espinacas a la Nîmes*).[24] The Marquesa does, however, make a class distinction between aristocratic white *bacalao* and the plebeian (smellier) yellow variety.

As well as its cross-class popularity, *bacalao/morue* was known for its extraordinary versatility. A great variety of ingredients are found to mix perfectly with it. Taking a personal favourite first, restaurants in the Canary Islands offer several recipes for *bacalao* cooked in honey – both bee-honey and palm-honey.[24] Other intriguing combinations include *bacalao a la Ericeira* (with turnips, celery, eggs and tarragon); *bacalao Noël* (with almonds, pine nuts, breadcrumbs, chili and nutmeg); *bacalao Camagüeyana* (with

317

toasted hazelnuts, chili, garlic and vinegar); and *bacalao con chipirones y chocolate* (with baby cuttlefish in their ink and bitter chocolate).[26]

To conclude these thoughts on the dangerously subjective notions of taste and food-preference, we should look briefly at the even more treacherous area of national preferences. To generalize broadly, we could suggest that the delightfulness of salt cod has been most evident to the Portuguese and the Spanish; significantly so also to the French; somewhat to the Greeks, the Lebanese, the Maltese and the Egyptians; less so to Italians, who retained a preference for stockfish and also for salted pilchards (*salsache*); and very much less so to the northern Europeans and to the British, despite the fact that the British national dish is often described as being fried battered cod with salt and vinegar – the famous 'fish and chips', which in fact probably originated as late as 1870 (perhaps in Oldham).[27]

***

The third imperative driving the success of salt fish and especially salt cod was religious. In the fourteenth and fifteenth centuries an apogee was reached for the idea that there should be abstinence on certain days of the year (holy days), together with all of the forty-day pre-Easter period (the *Quadragesima*, known in English as Lent), and also every single Friday. Between about 1350 and 1550 there could be as many as 150 or even 180 days in a year when the consumption of meat and other fatty foods was forbidden by the Church. Both rich and poor needed to find appropriate foods for these holy days, and fish was both the most palatable and nutritious meat-substitute and the food most strongly approved by the Church. Fish was especially indicated because of the curious Christian belief that 'its cold nature prevented the unleashing of the fires of luxuriousness'.[28] Numerous religio-medical mediaeval sources emphasize this supposed cooling (anti-sexual) effect of fish.

In European languages the days of abstinence are often called 'thin days' (*jours maigres, días magros,* etc.); but in English, although the expression 'Banian days' is sometimes found, the most frequent usage is 'fish days'. Fish days and *jours maigres* remained an important part of European culture through the succeeding centuries, especially among the strongly Roman Catholic populations of Portugal, Spain and France. It is noteworthy, however, that from Elizabethan and Jacobean times, with England wholly established as a Protestant country, fish days nonetheless continued – not only by custom and practice but also through legislation. Queen Elizabeth I was especially alert to the need to sustain a thriving English fishing fleet. And the idea of 'fish on Fridays' continues to this day in England and other Protestant countries as well as in the Roman Catholic and Greek Orthodox Mediterranean.

The socio-religious emphasis on fish gave salt cod an additional importance. This was especially so in areas which were far from the sea and where there were limited supplies of freshwater fish. But reasons of economics, food-conservation and food-preference also promoted salt cod in parts of Portugal and Spain where fresh fish was fairly easily available.

Some Roman Catholic communities appear to have seen salt cod as the ultimate, most austere example of acceptable food on days specified by the Church as non-meat. In the Lebanese Christian community in Egypt in the 1920s and 1930s, for example, salt cod (known by its Greek name of *bakaliáros*) was eaten only on the Fridays of Lent and then Good Friday, the thinnest days of all.[29]

We can witness the combining of the reasons for the importance of salt cod (together with salted and pickled tuna, and preserved sardines) in the records for the mediaeval Maltese galleys, from the Archives of the Order of Malta. Here the economic theme and the religious theme entwine, when we learn that it cost 13 *scudi* to provision a Maltese galley on a fish day compared to 32 *scudi* on a meat day.[30] Preferred food or not, religious requirement or not, this was clearly good business.

***

By way of conclusion, let us return to food-preference and the place of *bacalao* in both the food of the rich and the food of the poor.

Food-historians are constantly aware of this critical distinction between rich and poor. The whole structure of Alain Drouard's recent book *Les Français à table*, cited above, is based on the two differing traditions. Often, during the period between the beginnings of gastronomy around 1400 and the development of international food transport around 1850, the meals of the rich and the meals (or fuelling) of the poor had virtually nothing in common.

319

We have records of mediaeval poorhouses and hospitals which show poor people with diets which were over 80 per cent cereals. Bread was the staple; soup or pottage provided the essential liquid when the bread became too hard to chew. Hard cheese was an occasional third component. The monotony was overwhelming, the quantities often inadequate; proteins were at a premium. By contrast, the tables of the rich could overflow in variety and quantity to an extent which now appears ludicrous. François Massialot, the first creator of *béchamel* sauce, proposed a grand dinner with 43 dishes in each of the three courses.[31] The finest meals of the rich featured exotic ingredients like *ortolan* and *becfigue* buntings; swans and larks; carp's tongues; monkfish liver; lobsters and pineapples, whose exoticism and remoteness from everyday life were a strong part of their appeal.

What is remarkable about the history of *bacalao*, especially in Portugal, Spain and France, is the way in which this great divide is bridged. The *brandade de morue* and the *morue à la crème*, as we have seen, feature in all the great recipe books from Menon to Escoffier to Ferran Adrià.[32] Yet they are also part of the everyday back-street café culture of Paris, Marseilles or Nîmes.

Generally speaking the rich would refrain from eating the food of the poor simply because it was the food of the poor. The poor ate leeks; therefore the rich did not eat leeks (asparagus had to be the leeks of the rich). The poor had no access to veal or lobster; turbot or sturgeon; oranges or pineapples; truffles or saffron. Their use was exclusive. We recall the savagery with which the poor were punished if they helped themselves to the forest-food of the rich, such as venison or pheasant. And yet both rich and poor had regular access to *bacalao*. The only possible explanation I can find for the appearance of *bacalao* so conclusively on both sides of the food divide is one of taste. For richer, for poorer; all were agreed … that *bacalao* is uniquely delicious.

Notes

1. Contrast e.g. Mário C. Moutinho: *História da pesca do bacalhau: por uma antropologia do 'fiel amigo'*. Lisbon: Editorial Estampa, 1985; J. Garcia Fortuny & J. Jofre Español: *Todo el bacalao a su alcance*. Barcelona: Editorial Alta Fulla, 1992; Nelson Cazeils: *Cinq siècles de pêche à la morue: Terre-Neuvas et islandais*. Rennes: Ouest-France, 1997; Odile Godard: *Petit traité savant de la morue*. Barbentane: Éditions Équinoxe, 2007.
2. Despite her self-congratulatory title, Odile Godard (op. cit., pp. 17 & 22) can assert that not only is there no word in Spanish for fresh cod, but also that *Melanogrammus aeglefinus* in English becomes 'haddock' only when it is smoked. The OECD's *Multilingual dictionary of fish and fish products* (5th edition, 2008) leaves no excuse for such errors. The primary source for the etymology of *bacalao / cabillaud / haberdine* is J. Corominas: *Diccionario crítico etimológico de la lengua castellana*. 4 vols. Berne: Editorial Francke, 1954–1957.
3. Mark Kurlansky: *Cod: a biography of the fish that changed the world*. New ed. London: Vintage, 1999, pp. 28–29.
4. Jacques Cartier: *Voyages au Canada; avec les relations des voyages en Amérique de Gonneville, Verrazono et Roberval*. Paris: Maspero, 1981, p. 264. See also H. P. Biggar: *A collection of documents relating to Jacques Cartier and the Sieur de Roberval*. Ottawa: Public Archives of Canada, 1930; and H. B. Stephens: *Jacques Cartier and his four voyages to Canada*. Montreal: Drysdale, 1890.
5. Mark Kurlansky: *Salt: a world history*. London: Cape, 2002, p. 119.
6. On the Portuguese discovery of Canada by the 1420s, see Armando Cortesão: *Pizzigano's chart of 1424*. Coimbra: Junta de Investigação do Ultramar, 1970, and papers by Manuel Luciano Da Silva on the 'Verdadeiras Antilhas na América do Norte'.
7. Carlos Azcoytia: *Un pez muy 'salao': el bacalao*, www.historiacocina.com/historia/articulos/*bacalao*.htm, citing J. Garcia Fortuny & J. Jofre Español: *op.cit.*
8. See Nelson Cazeils: op. cit., p. 13.
9. Fernand Braudel: *Civilisation matérielle, économie et capitalisme, XVe–XVIIIe siècle. Tome 1: Les structures du quotidian: le possible et l'impossible*. Paris: Armand Colin, 1979, p. 185.
10. See Nelson Cazeils: op. cit., p. 11.
11. See Miren Egaña Goya & Brad Loewen: *L'aventure maritime, du golfe de Gascogne à Terre-Neuve*. Paris: Éditions du CTHS, 1995.
12. Quoted, www.scancook.com.
13. See J. A. Williamson: *The voyages of the Cabots and the English discovery of North America under Henry VII and Henry VIII*. London: Argonaut Press, 1929, p. 9; and H. A. Innis: *The cod fisheries: the history of an international economy*. Rev. ed. Toronto: University of Toronto Press, 1954, pp. 11–12.
14. See Fernand Braudel: op. cit., p. 184, citing Jacques Savary: *Dictionnaire universel de commerce, d'histoire naturelle et des arts et metiers*, 5 vols, 1759–1765.

15. Fernand Braudel: loc. cit.
16. For the Worshipful Company of Salters see www.salters.co.uk. For English salt history, see the History pages of www.saltsense.co.uk, website of the Salt Manufacturers Association; and Andrew and Annelize Fielding: *The salt industry*. Princes Risborough: Shire Publications, 2006.
17. Maurice Bensoussan: *La pulsion alimentaire. Tome I: De la fin du Moyen-Âge à l'arrivée de Catherine de Médicis*. Chatou: L'Arganier, 2009, p. 20.
18. See David C. Sutton: 'The language of the food of the poor: studying proverbs with Jean-Louis Flandrin', in *Food and Language: Proceedings of the Oxford Symposium on Food and Cookery 2009*. Totnes: Prospect Books, 2010, especially pp. 334–335.
19. Nelson Cazeils: op. cit., p. 9.
20. Fernand Braudel: op. cit., p. 185.
21. *La morue: sa pêche, son traitement, ses qualités alimentaires, culinaires et économiques;* illustrations de R. Mélissent; selection de recettes par Jacqueline Gérard. Paris: Comité de Propagande pour la Consommation de la Morue, 1961, p. 59.
22. Odile Godard: op. cit., pp. 153–154.
23. Alain Drouard: *Les Français à table: alimentation, cuisine, gastronomie du Moyen Âge à nos jours*. Paris: Ellipses, 2005, p. 52.
24. María Mestayer de Echagüe (Marquesa de Parabere): *La cocina completa*. Madrid: Espasa Calpe, 1940, pp. 302 ff. On preferences for white or yellow *bacalao*, see Lorena Gallart Jornet, Morten Heide & Jens Østli: 'Market situation of Norwegian *bacalao* on the Mediterranean Spanish coast: Barcelona and Valencia as an example of different tastes for *bacalao.*' *Økonomisk fiskeriforskning*, Årgang 15 (2005), pp. 51–55.
25. E.g. *Bacalao a la miel con patata laminada* (El Aguila, Santa Cruz de Tenerife); *Ensalada templada de bacalao con vinegreta de miel de palma* (La Rebotica, Santa Cruz de Tenerife).
26. The first three recipes from *Las mejores recetas del bacalao dorado*; ilustraciones Penagos; [el recetario de 1936]. Reimp. Madrid: Aqualarga, 1999; the fourth is a recipe of Clara Sánchez de Ron: www.telva.com.
27. E. J. Hobsbawm: *Industry and empire*. New ed. Harmondsworth: Penguin, 1969, pp. 162–163.
28. Translated from the exhibition 'Manger en Chrétien' at the Bibliothèque Nationale de France: expositions.bnf.fr/gastro/arret_sur/chretien/index.htm.
29. Information from Mrs M. L. Jenkins, née Schemali, Reading.
30. Joseph Muscat: *Food and drink on Maltese galleys*. Pietà, Malta: Pubblikazzjonijiet Indipendenza, 2002, p. 21.
31. For the diet of the poor see Fernand Braudel: op. cit., pp. 81–152; for Massialot and the food of the rich see Anthony Rowley: *Une histoire mondiale de la table*. Paris: Odile Jacob, 2006, p. 206; other examples from Jean-François Revel: *Un festin en paroles*. Paris: Pauvert, 1979, and *Histoire de l'alimentation* sous la direction de Jean-Louis Flandrin et Massimo Montanari. Paris: Fayard, 1996, pp. 549–575 & 657–703.
32. See Ferran Adrià, Hervé This & Joan Roca: *Bacalao*. Barcelona: Montagud Editores, 2003.

321

Yoghurt in the Turkish Kitchen

Aylin Öney Tan

Yoghurt: vital food for nomadic Yörük Turks

The mighty Shah of Persia at last has a son after years of expectation. However, the young heir's health is quite fickle and frail. Doctor after doctor fails to determine the cause or find a cure for this worrisome situation. At last a doctor insists that he needs to talk to the Shah's wife alone. When his wish is granted, he asks: This shall remain a secret between you and me, but tell me, whose son is this boy? The woman resists and does not answer. At last, seeing that the boy is about the die and the doctor is about to take his leave, she reveals her secret. Then the doctor comes out of the room and orders the head chef of the palace to feed the heir with yoghurt, *tarhana*, and *tutmaç*. The doctor's advice works, and within a short time, the boy becomes a healthy young man. It turns out that the confession was as follows: 'The Shah was infertile so I entertained myself with a Turk and eventually gave birth to this boy!' On this information the doctor devised his cure, which is effectively a triple dose of yoghurt: 1. Yoghurt, 2. *Tarhana* (fermented and dried grain and yoghurt soup mix) and 3. *Tutmaç*, a yoghurt and noodle soup-like dish. When he is fed three doses of yoghurt three times a day, the heir recovered his health because yoghurt was engrained in his genetic codes.[1]

According to another story, anthropologist Ulla Johansen recounts how as a young researcher, she wanted to travel for six months with the semi-nomadic Yörüks. As she tries to convince the leader of the tribe Isa Emmi to allow this European city-girl to accompany them for six long months, her last recourse is to say that yoghurt is her favourite food. She is then admitted to the join the Yörük migration of the Sarıkeçililer tribe.[2] Although half-way through the migration, she regretted her words so much that she did not ever want to see another spoon of yoghurt, she had to abide by them.[3]

As these examples testify, yoghurt is a must-have item of food for Turks. The word has entered all world languages from Turkish. Although opinions vary as to the origin of the word and when and where it first began to be used, in the geography stretching from India to central Europe, and from the Caucasus to the Middle East, yoghurt is one of the primary food items for all the peoples and nationalities living in this vast region. Needless to say in Turkey and in Turkish cuisine, it holds an indispensable position.

Yoghurt variations

Yoghurt to Western culture is either plain or flavoured with fruit. Although in Turkish culinary culture yoghurt has been always plain, the diversity of plain yoghurt is enormous. Made from cow, sheep, goat or buffalo milk, the consistency can range from slightly watery to very thick.

The making of yoghurt
Milk type

Traditionally yoghurt is mainly made from sheep's milk, which is still widely available in rural areas but getting rarer in urban areas. Traditional native sheep breeds are Anatolian Ivessi (Awassi), Sakız (Chios), Gökçeada (İmroz), Kıvırcık (a variety found in eastern Thrace), Akkaraman (White Karaman), Mor Karaman (Red Karaman), Hemşin, Dağlıç, Karayaka, Herik and Tuj (Tushin). Modern industrial yoghurts are almost always produced from imported cow breeds. However some regions traditionally produce cow's milk yoghurt from milk of native breeds. Foremost native cattle breeds are Yerli kara (native black), Kilis, Yerli Güney sarısı (South Anatolian yellow native), Boz ırk (Turkish grey) and Doğu Anadolu Kırmızısı (East Anatolian red). One rapidly decreasing yoghurt variety is buffalo yoghurt made with the milk of Anadolu mandası (Anatolian water buffalo), also known by the local names *manda, camız, camış, kömüş* and *dombay*. As for goat's milk yoghurt, this is generally confined to mountainous terrains and almost always produced from Kara keçi or Kıl keçisi, the native Anatolian black hair goat. The almost-extinct Norduz goat can still be found around the eastern border town of Van and the Kilis goat only near the Syrian border.[4] It has to be noted that the diet of the animal greatly affects the flavour of yoghurt, such as in the case of the famous dairy products of the central Anatolian town of Afyon, where buffalos are fed on the residue of pressed poppy seeds.

Starter culture

Yoghurt is the love-child of two bacteria *Lactobacillus bulgaricus* and *Streptococcus thermophilus,* happily married in the homely medium of lukewarm milk. The starter for yoghurt is usually another spoonful of yoghurt, already containing the two essential bacteria for the making of the next batch. Yet there are other recorded starters ranging from fig sap to pine cones or acorns, or, even more strangely, from ant's eggs to morning dew collected from grass. In many cases milk can even be self-fermented, turning milk into yoghurt, a not-unusual phenomenon in a kitchen environment full of yoghurt starter-bacteria. The spring ritual of collecting morning dew to start a new batch of yoghurt is still practised on the morning of *Hıdrellez*, 6 May, and if the yoghurt sets successfully, it is a sign that every wish is to become real for the following year. One study led by microbiologist Professor Dr Kadir Halkman revealed that the renewal of last year's yoghurt culture with fresh spring rain is widely practised.[5] Starter culture is often called *damızlık*, a colloquial term meaning inseminator or stud.

Utensils

The utensils used in cooking the milk are generally tinned copper cauldrons, pots or kettles and, for setting the yoghurt, metal (traditional tinned copper containers or, lately, aluminium trays), enamel or earthen trays or pots can be used. The traditional tinned copper vessel to set the yoghurt is called *bakraç* or *yoğurt bakracı* and has a bucket-like handle for easy transport. Large wooden spoons, *çomçe*, are used to stir air into the evaporating milk during the cooking process. Wooden pots for setting yoghurt are sometimes used to impart an aromatic pine flavour to the yoghurt, such as *çingil*, a small wooden pot, or *çatı*, a barrel like container.

Density/consistency/texture

The quality of milk is directly reflected in the taste and texture of yoghurt. Thickness is one quality often desired. Some yoghurt types can literally be sliced, not because they are hard but they can perfectly hold their shape when cut, like a jelly. Furthermore, to achieve an even thicker or denser consistency and flavour, yoghurt can be drained, or even dried. Drained yoghurt no longer has this sliceable capacity but has a rather creamier texture like a spread.

Techniques

The basic recipe for making yoghurt at home is quite simple: the fresh milk is boiled (getting rid of all unwanted bacteria); left to cool to lukewarm (tested with elbow or back of fingers), approximately 40–45°C; a minute amount of starter yoghurt is diluted and added to the milk (the desired useful bacteria added at the right temperature); the pan, pot, container is wrapped to maintain the temperature or the pot placed in a warm place (like in warm oven); after a good beauty-sleep, the milk is turned into the refreshing, cooling lactic-acid heaven called yoghurt.

In another method, milk is boiled and allowed to cool down overnight. In the same pot the starter yoghurt is diluted and mixed into the yoghurt when the milk is cool. The milk is then reheated to lukewarm while being constantly stirred (40–45°C) and then transferred to earthen pots. Pots are covered with a plate and wrapped in cloths to maintain the heat. The starter can also be butter made by churning yoghurt (half a tablespoon of churned yoghurt butter will be sufficient for 2–3 litres of milk).

The basic method of making yoghurt is pretty much the same all over, but there are a few tricks that make the whole difference. Boiling down the milk to a condensed state is one way to achieve thicker yoghurt, constant stirring and incorporating air with a spoon quickens the process without burning the bottom. When transferring the milk to the setting vessels, pouring from a height forms a foamy froth which will eventually be turned to a thick, clotted yoghurt cream, a delicacy in itself. The skin or cream formed on the surface of yoghurt is called *kaymak* or *yoğurt kaymağı* and yoghurt with a skin or creamy crust is called *kaymaklı yoğurt*. The creamy crust is usually delicately removed from the surface of yoghurt and eaten with a drizzle of honey for breakfast.

Fresh yoghurts

Fresh yoghurts are yoghurts to be consumed fresh within days or, if drained, within a week or so. They can be named after the milk or pot variety; according to the preparation method; by referring to a particular characteristic or by referring to a locality. Famous localities include Silivri (a town in north-west Turkey), Silifke (a town on the eastern

Mediterranean coast), Kanlıca (a district on the Asian side of Istanbul). Traditional, artisanal fresh yoghurts are never sweetened or salted or flavoured by additional ingredients.

Yoghurts named according to milk type

In most cases traditional yoghurts are named according to the milk from which yoghurt is made. *Manda yoğurdu* (buffalo yoghurt) is probably one of the rarest and most praised, resulting in a dense and creamy flavourful yoghurt. However, it is getting very scarce, since the native buffalo population is everywhere diminishing. *Koyun yoğurdu* (ewe's milk yoghurt) is the most common traditional yoghurt, but this is also becoming less available commercially with the rise of cow's milk products. *Keçi yoğurdu* (goat's milk yoghurt) is a rural variety, usually associated with semi-nomadic Yörük tribes. Goat's milk results in a thinner consistency yoghurt with a distinctive goat flavour and so it is sometimes mixed with sheep's milk to improve the consistency and modify the taste. Finally, *inek yoğurdu* (cow's milk yoghurt) is nowadays the most common type, with the commercial industrial yoghurts almost always prepared from cow's milk.

Yoghurts named according to pot type

Yoghurts can also be named according to the pot in which they are made. *Tepsi Yoğurdu*, (tray yoghurt) refers to yoghurt set in large, deep circular metal trays; *Çömlek Yoğurdu* (earthern pot yoghurt) refers to yoghurt set in earthen pots either deep or shallow, large or individual.

325

Süzme yoğurt (strained yoghurt)

Drained or strained yoghurt can also be named according to the size and shape of the cheesecloth bag in which the straining takes place, i.e. either a sack (*torba yoğurdu)* or a pouch (*kese yoğurdu).*

Yanık yoğurt (burnt or smoky yoghurt)

The ultimate oddity must be the smoked or burnt yoghurt. It is a local speciality of the city of Denizli (inner south-west Turkey), a drained fresh creamy yoghurt spread having an intense aroma of burnt milk. The burnt flavour is achieved by a particular method. The copper cauldron is heated until very hot, the milk poured in suddenly achieves an aroma of burnt milk protein and milk sugar (lactose). It must be noted that a traditional wood fire adds to the smoky smell of the final yoghurt.[6] The set yoghurt is then transferred into cheesecloth bags to drain, a process which intensifies the burnt flavour.

Preserved yoghurts

Yoghurt has a rather short shelf-life. Whether prepared at home or ready-made, it needs to be consumed within a week. However, since yoghurt has such an essential role in the Turkish kitchen, many preservation methods have been developed to keep yoghurt for longer periods. Preserving yoghurt for later use, especially during the winter months, in condensed, salted, potted, cooked, baked or dried forms is a common practice in Turkey. Dried yoghurt seems like an oxymoron for a food that is perceived for its cool, refreshing and even thirst-quenching properties, but the cheesy, tangy taste of dried yoghurt is much sought-after. In some cases yoghurt is drained and dried to a cheese-like state, rolled into little balls and preserved in olive oil. Most preserved yoghurts can be reconstituted with the addition of water to form a liquid yoghurt known as *ayran,* which is then used as an ingredient for cooking yoghurt-based dishes. Some, especially condensed paste-like ones can be consumed as spreads, or harder ones can be crumbled, crushed or grated like cheese onto dishes.

Tulum yoğurdu (yoghurt strained/preserved in skin sacks)

This preserving technique results in a dense, almost cheesy strained yoghurt spread which can keep considerably longer then regular drained yoghurt. Goat skin is treated with an herbal wash, usually a solution of infused pine wood shavings. This process is called *boyamak,* virtually meaning to paint the skin. This treatment makes the skin porous and less prone to deterioration. A day's production of yoghurt (3–4 kg) is collected in skin sacks. Every 2–3 days approximately 100 g of salt is added. The sack is hung in a cool and airy place and wiped every day to keep the pores open and stimulate the draining process. The inner southern Aegean (provinces of Denizli and Burdur) and Mediterranean regions of Turkey, especially the Taurus mountain zone, specialize in this preservation method.[7]

Yoghurt cheeses

There are cases when preserved yoghurt can be called 'cheese', as the taste and texture of the end-product strongly resembles certain cheeses. The first stage is yoghurt but it is usually churned and the whey curdled by a method similar to the process of making some cheeses. Such yoghurt cheeses include *Tomas Peyniri* (also called *Serto*) or *Karın kaymağı* (cream of belly) of eastern Turkey. A mixture of goat and sheep milk is first turned into yoghurt; the yoghurt is churned; the separated buttermilk is curdled; the curd is collected, drained, salted and re-mixed with butter or cream derived from the churning; sometimes extra fresh yoghurt is added to the mixture; the mixture is pressed into treated goat-skin sacks and left to mature. After a maturation period of 1–3 months the yoghurt mixture is taken out, kneaded and refilled and pressed into skins. This type of preserved yoghurt is consumed as a cheese.[8]

Other similar eastern-region yoghurt cheeses are named by the name of the tribe, i.e. *Şavak çökeleği,* or locality, i.e. *Tunceli çökeleği.* Widely produced and consumed, curd cheese *çökelek* can also be made by churning yoghurt. The conical, bright red, salty curd cheese *Sürk* of Hatay province (eastern Mediterranean) is a spiced-up version flavoured with hot red pepper, fresh wild thyme, cumin, allspice, cloves, nutmeg and garlic. Another example in this category is named *Kırktokmak,* literally meaning 'beaten

Figure 1. Conical keş, *dried yoghurt, at Bolu market. Bolu is the administrative centre of Bolu province in north-west Turkey, mid-way between Istanbul and Ankara.*

Figure 2. Local keş *producers at Bolu market.*

327

Figure 3. Drained yoghurt.

Figure 4. Soap-bar-shaped keş, *dried yoghurt, at Bolu market.*

forty times', this time referring to the churning process, thus shaken forty times.[9] This yoghurt cheese is a specialty of the Aegean region and is spiced with nigella seeds. Other regional examples of similar produce include *akçakatık*, or *katık* of the inner Aegean region. The word *katık* actually means anything to accompany or relish bread, and often used to refer to cheese or olives eaten with bread; in this case it is used for a yoghurt product which can easily substitute cheese. The eastern Black Sea coast has its own varieties, called *minzi, minci, kurçi,* or *ayran kırması.*[10]

Pişmiş yoğurt, tuzlu yoğurt (cooked yoghurt, salted yoghurt)

These two names usually refer to the same product, which actually involves three preserving methods, cooking, salting and potting. The freshly prepared yoghurt is mixed into a creamy state, condensed to a paste-like consistency by constant stirring over a medium fire, cooled and salted, sometimes further strained in cloth sacks and finally potted in earthen jars and sealed with melted sheep tail fat, or other animal fat. The pots are kept in cool caverns, basement larders or in some cases even buried. Yoghurt preserved by this method will keep for several years but is best consumed within a year or two. Cooked, salted and potted yoghurt is mostly consumed as a delicacy rather than a staple ingredient. The eastern Mediterranean town of Antakya in Hatay is renowned for its *tuzlu yoğurt.* [11]

Other names given to preserved yoghurts in this category can be listed as *kış yoğurdu* (winter yoghurt), *güz yoğurdu* (autumn yoghurt), *tutma yoğurt* (kept yoghurt).[12] This method is widely used in central and eastern Anatolia.

Peskütan (condensed and dried yoghurt)

Peskütan (dialect variations: *pastikan, pestigen, pestüken, pesküten, pesgüden*) is a name given to an array of preserved yoghurt varieties which involve churning, cooking, straining and potting or drying. The yoghurt is sometimes used whole or in the form of buttermilk (*ayran*) following churning. These are cooked, usually with the addition of whole or crushed wheat berries. The cooked wheat berries provide starch to achieve a more homogeneous creamy mass of curd. The condensed buttermilk is strained and either potted and sealed with fat or pressed and flattened into disks and dried. *Peskütan* is mostly associated with the town of Sivas, where a hearty winter soup is made with reconstituted *peskütan*, wheat berries and lentils. Researcher of folk culture Müjgan Üçer records an amazing array of yoghurt- and *peskütan*-based soups and dishes in her book on Sivas cooking. It is almost always used diluted or reconstituted in soups and other dishes, or sometimes turned into a garlicky sauce.[13]

Keş (dried yoghurt curd)

Keş is sometimes defined as dried yoghurt or dried curd cheese, however, it is usually a salted and dried buttermilk curd. *Keş* is either made from churned strained yoghurt or full-fat strained yoghurt. In the most common method the yoghurt is churned; the yoghurt buttermilk (*ayran*) is either strained through a cheese-cloth sack or heated; the precipitated curd is strained again, wrapped in cheesecloth and pressed under pressure overnight; and the remaining mass is salted, kneaded and moulded or shaped by hand. The shape can be like bricks or bars of soap, cones or pyramids. In some regions yoghurt is not churned at all, but simply drained to a very dense consistency. *Keş* is considered to be a special product of northern-central Turkey, namely the towns of Bolu, Mengen, Giresun and Ordu. It is shaved or grated onto pasta dishes, the most famous being *keşli cevizli erişte*, home-made flat noodles with melted butter, walnuts and grated *keş*, toasted in butter. There is also an oven-dried baked variety, resulting in a reddish, brownish coloured product, mostly used crumbled in savoury *börek* fillings.[14] *Keş* can also be served at breakfast, crumbled and slightly browned in butter. One very unusual dish is *gızduma*, whole fried *keş*, dried yoghurt balls left for a day in water to soften, then fried in abundant butter.

Kurut (dried yoghurt)

(dialect variations: *Gurut, grut, gurt*)

Kurut is very similar to *keş*, sometimes both names are used interchangeably. The simplest way of making *kurut* is salting and drying drained yoghurt. There is also *kara kurut*. Although *kara* means black, this does not necessarily refer to a product

329

of darkish colour but of a lesser quality, usually the name is given to a product made from buttermilk produced by churning yoghurt. An exact opposite is *kremalı kurut*, a fatty version with extra cream added to yoghurt. Similarly, *ak kurut* is a name given to a white version, in this case, white meaning of higher quality, made from full-fat yoghurt. Similar to *keş*, all *kurut* types are dried to a very hard state, and used either grated, crushed or pounded to powder. *Kurut* is almost always spherical or conical in shape.[15] The Ottoman army is recorded as stocking up with *kurut* as a rich source of protein when on campaign.

Yoghurt in the kitchen

Yoghurt is an indispensable ingredient in the Turkish kitchen. Whether rich or poor, urban or rural, no Turkish kitchen can do without yoghurt. The ubiquitous *cacık*, a cucumber and yoghurt concoction; the salted diluted yoghurt drink *ayran*, the famous thirst-quencher; and *mantı*, meat-filled tiny dumplings with a garlicky yoghurt sauce, are probably the first dishes that come to mind. Yet there is a vast array of other yoghurt-based dishes in Turkish cuisine, ranging from soups to desserts. Hot yoghurt soups of many variations are made, the most famous one being *yayla çorbası*, literally 'highland soup', probably deriving its name from the mountain pastures of the Yörük nomads, who are great producers and consumers of yoghurt. In some cases potted yoghurt is the key ingredient to achieve the desired intense flavour, as in the case of *peskütan çorbası* (*peskütan* soup). Cold soups based on yoghurt and boiled wheat berry and chickpeas, sometimes with the addition of wild greens or herbs, are very popular in the summer months. Yoghurt has an affinity with certain dishes like the meat-stuffed vegetables or vine leaves, so a hot dish of *dolma* or *sarma* can never be served without a spoonful of yoghurt or better still with a garlic-yoghurt sauce. Garlic and yoghurt may have a love affair going on, giving life to dishes like *mantı*, meat dumplings, or in the case of lesser known *çılbır*, poached eggs with garlicky yoghurt. Some vegetable dishes like sautéed spinach or purslane, fresh fava bean pods cooked in olive oil and fried eggplants are unthinkable without yoghurt as a companion. Yoghurt-based *meze* dishes constitute a whole chapter of their own, the most famous being *haydari*, a creamy thick yoghurt spread perked up with dried herbs. Yoghurt-based salads such as purslane or char-broiled and mashed eggplants are often served as *meze* as well. Sometimes the use of yoghurt is more or less disguised. Whipped with eggs and baked over a succulent stew of lamb it turns into a wonderful sauce in *Elbasan tava*, a dish of Albanian origin. Meat kebabs can also be served with yoghurt as in the case of *yoğurtlu kebap* or the famous *döner kebap* dish, *İskender kebap*. The use of yoghurt in desserts is another rich topic, often symbolized by *yoğurt tatlısı*, a kind of syrupy yoghurt-based sponge cake. Sometimes the use of yoghurt is more obvious, as in the case of *karga beyni*, literally 'crow's brain', which consists of a bowl of yoghurt simply drizzled with molasses and scrambled with a fork to resemble a brain. One last, but not least, example is a dried fig dessert, not made with yoghurt but ending up being a kind of yoghurt, maybe the only fruit yoghurt existing in the Turkish kitchen. The one-night sleep of warmed milk and dried figs under a heavy blanket results in the most delicious fermented dessert of the Anatolian kitchen, hence the name *uyutma*, sleep-induced.

Notes

1. This story is taken from ancient Anatolian folk tales, '40 Vizier Stories'.
2. Ulla Johansen *50 Yıl Önce Türkiye'de Yörüklerin Yayla Hayatı*. Trans. by Poyraz, Mualla (Nomadic life of Yoruk's in Turkey 50 years ago). Ankara: Kültür ve Turizm Bakanlığı, 2005, p. 12.
3. Ulla Johansen, pp. 85–88.
4. Prof. Dr. İhsan Soysal. *Native Animal Genetic Resources of Türkiye*, Tekirdağ, Namık Kemal Universitesi, 2007, pp. 3–23, 45–55, 71–79.
5. Artun Ünsal. *'Silivrim Kaymak!' Türkiye'nin Yoğurtları*. İstanbul: YKY, 2007, pp. 199–200.
6. Artun Ünsal, pp. 142–147.
7. Metin Yıldırım, Zeliha Yıldırım. 'Traditional Yoghurts in Turkey', *1st International Symposium on 'Traditional Foods from Adriatic to Caucasus'*, Tekirdağ: Turkey, 2010, p. 75.
8. Hüsnü Gündüz. 'Tomas Cheese', *1st International Symposium on 'Traditional Foods from Adriatic to Caucasus'*, Tekirdağ: Turkey, 2010, pp. 68–69.
9. Sevda Kılıç. 'Kırk Tokmak Peyniri: Özellikleri ve Yapılışı', *Proceedings of 1st National Symposium of Traditional Foods*. Van, 23–24 Sept. 2004 (*Geleneksel Gıdalar Sempozyumu*). Univ. of 100. Yıl, Van, Turkey.
10. Artemis Alpsan; Oktay Yerlikaya; Özer Kınık; Necati Akbulut; 'The Traditional Çökelek Cheeses of Turkey', *Proceedings of 1st International Symposium on 'Traditional Foods from Adriatic to Caucasus'*. Tekirdağ: Turkey, 2010, pp. 159–161.
11. Artun Ünsal, pp. 167–171.
12. Metin Yıldırın, Zeliha Yıldırım, p. 75.
13. F. Törnük; O. Sağdıç; H. Yetim. 'Peskütan, A Traditional Condensed Yoghurt', *Proceedings of 1st International Symposium on 'Traditional Foods from Adriatic to Caucasus'*. Tekirdağ: Turkey, 2010, pp. 225–227.
14. Nuray Güzeler, Yeliz Parlak, 'Oven-dried Kesh', *1st International Symposium on 'Traditional Foods from Adriatic to Caucasus'*. Tekirdağ: Turkey, 2010, p.291.
15. Arzu Kavaz, İhsan Bakırcı. 'Geleneksel bir süt ürünü olan kurut üzerine bir inceleme', *Proceedings of 2nd National Symposium of Traditional Foods*. Van, 27–29 May 2009 (*Geleneksel Gıdalar Sempozyumu*). Univ. of 100. Yıl, Van, Turkey, pp. 697–701.

Bibliography
Abdalla, Michael. 'Milk and its Uses in Assyrian Folklore', in *Milk: Beyond the Dairy. Proceedings of the Oxford Symposium on Food and Cookery 1999*, Harlan Walker ed. Totnes: Prospect Books, 2000.

Alpsan, Artemis, Oktay Yerlikaya, Özer Kınık, Necati Akbulut. 'The Traditional Çökelek Cheeses of Turkey', *Proceedings of 1st International Symposium on 'Traditional Foods from Adriatic to Caucasus'*, 15–17 April, 2010. Univ of Namık Kemal, Tekirdağ: Turkey, 2010

Batmanglij, Najmieh. 'Milk and its By-products in Ancient Persia and Modern Iran', in *Milk: Beyond the Dairy. Proceedings of the Oxford Symposium on Food and Cookery 1999*, Harlan Walker ed. Totnes: Prospect Books, 2000.

Gündüz. Hüsnü. 'Tomas Cheese', *Proceedings of 1ˢᵗ International Symposium on 'Traditional Foods from Adriatic to Caucasus'*, 15–17 April, 2010. Univ. of Namık Kemal, Tekirdağ: Turkey, 2010.

Güzeler; Nuray, Yeliz Parlak. 'Oven-dried Kesh', *1ˢᵗ International Symposium on 'Traditional Foods from Adriatic to Caucasus'*, 15–17 April, 2010. Univ. of Namık Kemal, Tekirdağ: Turkey, 2010.

Haroutunian, Arto Der. *The Yoghurt Book*. England: Penguin Books, 1983.

Johansen, Ulla. *50 Yıl Önce Türkiye'de Yörüklerin Yayla Hayatı*. Trans. by Poyraz, Mualla (Nomadic life of Yoruk's in Turkey 50 years ago). Ankara: Kültür ve Turizm Bakanlığı, 2005.

Kavaz, Arzu; İhsan Bakırcı. 'Geleneksel bir süt ürünü olan kurut üzerine bir inceleme', *Proceedings of 2ⁿᵈ National Symposium of Traditional Foods*, Van, 27–29 May 2009 (*Geleneksel Gıdalar Sempozyumu*).Univ. of 100. Yıl, Van, Turkey.

Kılıç, Sevda. 'Kırk Tokmak Peyniri: Özellikleri ve Yapılışı', *Proceedings of 1ˢᵗ National Symposium of Traditional Foods*, Van, 23–24 Sept. 2004 (*Geleneksel Gıdalar Sempozyumu*). Univ. of 100. Yıl, Van, Turkey.

Orga, İrfan. *Cooking with Yoghurt*. New York: Andre Deutsch, 1956.

Shaida, Margaret. 'Yoghurt in Iran', in *Milk: Beyond the Dairy. Proceedings of the Oxford Symposium on Food and Cookery 1999*, Harlan Walker ed. Totnes: Prospect Books, 2000.

Soysal, İhsan. *Native Animal Genetic Resources of Türkiye*. Tekirdağ, Namık Kemal Universitesi, 2007.

Üçer, Müjgân. *Anamın Aşı Tandırın Başı-Sivas Mutfağı*, İstanbul: Kitabevi, 2006.

Ünsal, Artun. *'Silivrim Kaymak!' Türkiye'nin Yoğurtları*. İstanbul: YKY – Yapı Kredi Yayınları, 2007.

Törnük, F., O. Sağdıç, H. Yetim. 'Peskütan, A Traditional Condensed Yoghurt', *Proceedings of 1st International Symposium on 'Traditional Foods from Adriatic to Caucasus'*, 15–17 April, 2010. Univ. of Namık Kemal, Tekirdağ: Turkey, 2010.

Yıldırım, Metin, Zeliha Yıldırım. 'Traditional Yoghurts in Turkey', *1st International Symposium on 'Traditional Foods from Adriatic to Caucasus'*, 15–17 April, 2010. Univ. of Namık Kemal, Tekirdağ: Turkey, 2010.

Stinking Fish, Salt Fish, and Smokehouse Pork: Preserved Foods, Flavor Principles and the Birth of African American Foodways

Michael W. Twitty

To appreciate the scope of the global presence of African-based cuisines one must go to a place where the trail seems to end rather than where it began. In New York, the place art-historian Robert Farris Thompson dubbed, 'the secret African city,' the multiple histories of the African Atlantic converge. Communities built by descendants of New York's earliest Angolan-Dutch enslaved community mingle with migrants from the American South, Afro-Caribbeans, Afro-Latinos and African immigrants. In one household *mofongo* (fried plantain fufu and pork) and *bacalaitos* (salt cod fritters) cook up in Spanish Harlem, home to a large Puerto Rican community, a third of which has its roots in west and central Africa. At Sylvia's, Amy Ruth's or Charles' Southern Style Kitchen in Harlem, cabbage, collards, green beans and black-eyed peas 'wink back' with the unctuous stock of smoked shoulder or turkey wings. Nearby oil-can grills send off wisps of hickory-chip smoke impregnating barbecued pork, chicken and beef. On 116th Street in the storefronts of Little Senegal, refrigerated cases hold stores of odoriferous authentic *kong* (smoked catfish), *bonga* shad, herring and sardines, while on the shelves are rusty, pungent bags of dried or smoked shrimp. Along the streets of Crown Heights and Flatbush in Brooklyn, one can enjoy authentic plates of St Lucian plantains with salt fish or the national dishes of Jamaica, meat that has been 'jerked', or scrambled akee fruit with salt fish.

All of these traditions are tied together through the notes they leave on the tongue. Salted fish, smoked meat, fish or shellfish provide the sensations of saltiness and umami favored across Africa and her diaspora. One expects the mineral tang of sodium and the balance of meaty-fishy-smoky-mouthy flavors from these cuisines just as one expects syrupy sweets, acid flavors or the not-unpleasant bitterness of leafy greens. They echo back to pre-colonial Africa where animal flesh was a condiment to a largely vegetable and starch-driven diet, its essence being more important than its substance. Each recalls the cheap and almost careless way enslaved Africans were fed in captivity; and all speak to a certain culinary resilience and defiant celebration of the proletarian palate. These elements are markers of a larger, morphing culinary DNA.

Our task is to trace these traditional flavor principles back to their sources. To do so means to come to terms with the relationship that such enduring sensual legacies have had with the concurrent development of identities and histories built in the womb of the transatlantic slave trade and the plantation economies of the New World. Though the state of being enslaved meant living in frameworks whose origins lay in Western Europe, the genius of enslaved blacks in New World societies was the melding of parallel customs and lifeways from African, European and Native American cultures so seamlessly that the exotic felt familiar and the seemingly foreign was reborn in an indigenous lens. Just as saints were reinterpreted as African divinities and African rhythms were coaxed from European violins and snare drums, the foodscape was likewise translated through what Charles Joyner coined 'an African culinary grammar' (Joyner, 244). As with no other community of enslaved people in the history of the world, a food creolization occurred that would enslave the tastebuds of the master class. They would make the herring and cod of the north Atlantic into reminders of Africa in the New World and make the northern European ham in such a way that many throughout the South echoed the feelings of the wife of one of the former governors of Virginia when she said in 1911, 'It takes a big, fat Negro mammy with a round shiny face to cook a ham, and the secret she can never impart. It is a sort of magic ... and when you get some of that kind of dainty [a sliver of cured Virginia ham] you are eating indeed' (Mitchell).

Stinking fish, salted fish and smoked fish: west and central Africa

No part of tropical Africa lacked challenges to long-term storage of food; along the Nile River valley in ancient times, fish were split, gutted, preserved with the red salts of Memphis and left in the sun to dry. True to later patterns, these fish were an important export (Bober, 48). Along the 3,500-mile coast from which the majority of enslaved Africans were drawn to meet the ravenous needs of plantation economies, most of the landscape is unforgivingly humid, sparsely forested, and teeming with an enormous biomass of bacteria and insects that inhibit the long-term storage of meat or fish. Some ethnic groups like the Hausa and Fulani were able to take advantage of the hot-dry climate of the Sahel, raising ruminants as their key livestock since they lived beyond the latitudes of the dreaded tsetse fly. These groups could dry meat and smoke it with some of the precious wood of their sparse savanna environment. For those living in arid plains with little water, fish traded from the Niger, Gambia, Senegal and other rivers was invaluable. Others in the tropical forest zone, the Asante, BaKongo and Igbo for example, could only raise a limited number of resistant stock and outside of the cooler dry season lived in a humid climate where mold, insects and vermin made keeping fresh fish, meat and shellfish difficult.

As early as 1154, Arab geographer al-Idrisi recorded the observations of travelers and traders in west Africa who witnessed the salting of fish to preserve it for trade throughout the western Sudan. Early centers for the salting and drying of fish were coastal and riverain Senegal and the region around Lake Chad (Lewicki, 101). The observations of Reisen Barth and Natchigal of nineteeenth-century Bornu (located in present-day Chad) hint at the use of these dried fish in the Middle Ages. Dried, pounded fish was dissolved into a mixture that was used as a relish with which to eat other foods (quoted in Lewicki, 207). The diet of west and central Africa, then as now, centered around a starch of some sort – rice, millet, sorghum, yams or other tubers – pounded or left whole, to be eaten with a savory sauce, soup or stew used to vary and flavor the 'daily bread'. Those regions of the interior that did not have access to a large body of water with sufficient fish stocks to meet everyday cooking needs would barter grains or other commodities for the essential protein tidbits that fish or game provided. In the medieval African interior, gargantuan Nile perch (*Lates niloticus*), catfish (order Siluriformes), and tilapia (*Oreochromis niloticus)* along with much smaller fry met the demand for ingredients used in the nightly sauce. Although smoking is not mentioned in early Arab sources, it seems likely that it was practised alongside salting and drying as a method of preservation.

These earliest recorded sources seem dim and distant compared to the rich and opinionated sources of the early slave trade. Traders and travelers during this period served as merchants and naturalists reporting back to European companies on their findings, often detailing fishing, fishing methods, hunting, livestock and the methods of preservation. Chief among the sensory memories recorded in this early period are mentions of 'stinking fish'. Divorced from their roots in Roman-era peasantry, these chroniclers had stumbled upon the west African answer to *garum*; stinking fish was indeed their own trans-ethnic 'national' condiment.

The earliest visitors to coastal Senegal during the late 1500s noted that the Wolof and other ethnic groups there preferred 'eating fish when it is rotten or dried in smoke' (Hair, 1:110). Dutch chronicler Pieter de Marees noted in 1602, 'They also eat of the old stinking Fish, dried in the Sun' (de Marees, 41). Jean Barbot, writing to the Compagnie du Senegal describing his voyages in 1678–1679 and 1681–1682, commented:

> since they are too lazy to go fishing often, they preserve a large number of these sardines in the sand along the shore, claiming that the sand is as effective as salt. After leaving them there for several days, they expose them to the sun which dries them, and they then make use of them as they need. One can see whole buildings full of them, and the shore at Rio-Fresca is covered with these sardines....The sight of so many little fish, half rotten and scattered everywhere on the sands makes one quite queasy...
>
> (Hair, 1:100–101)

In another statement, Barbot seems to foreshadow the diet of enslaved people in the New World, 'the peasants and poor people make do with another kind of cooked millet called sanglet. It is hardly more than millet bran, cooked either in plain water, or sometimes together with stale meat or stinking fish. This is what they normally feed their slaves on' (Hair, 1:123). He may be referring to *chere*, a Wolof/Serer staple often enhanced in its savory form with smoked or dried fish, or *dabere,* another millet dish served with a sauce including dried fish (Gamble, 37). In 1705, Willem Bosman described the daily meal of the people of the Gold Coast as 'a pot full of millet boiled to the consistence of bread, or instead of that jambs [sic] and potatoes; over which they pour a little Palm-Oyl [sic], with a few boiled Herbs, to which they add a stinking Fish. This they esteem a nice dish…' The dish described by Bosman echoes the contemporary preparation of a dish popular among the Twi-speakers of central and southern Ghana – *kontomire* ('African spinach' or *morongo*) eaten with *abom* – a sauce made from salted fish with other condiments.

Olaudah Equiano described the Aro traders among the Igbo bringing dried fish in exchange for fragrant woods and wood-ash salt. Of the fish he noted, 'the last we esteemed a great rarity, as our waters were only brooks and springs' (Equiano, 45). Equiano's memories are reinforced by later writings by Basden which describe the Igbo man as:

> …not an epicure. For his stock-pot, he has not many opportunities to exercise a preference; he has chiefly to rely on smoked fish and not much of that in interior districts. There is the consolation that a little of this goes a long way! It has distinct and pungent properties!

> (Basden, 157)

Just as in Senegal, Ghana and Angola, fishing huts built for the construction of smoking fish could be found throughout the landscape. Located on beaches, in mangrove swamps or along river banks, the fish were slowly smoked until well dried or charred. On his first voyage to Senegal, Barbot sketched fish-smoking frames constructed on the shore. Some shrimp, prawns, fish, oysters and mussels were slowly dried on nearly smokeless fires using special vessels, while others were placed in special baskets anchored above the cooking fire to slowly smoke them during the course of the day as well as to keep off insects. Catfish, sardines, mullet, mudfish (often sold curled on itself in a circle), eels, *bonga* 'shad' or *bonga* 'herring,' and in Angola, the *pungo* and *savelha* (*Clupea sagax*) were caught, split, dried and smoked. According to Monteiro the marketplaces of Luanda were full of dried and salted fish and another fish that was 'roasted like a herring.' (183) In nearby Kongo, which together with Angola constituted 40 per cent of the trade to North America, fish that were allowed to go bad were 'placed in leaves with salt and pepper and roasted' (Laman, 59).

Salt herring, shad and a little meat: the colonial- and federal-era South

The bridge between plantation slavery in the New World and slavery as known in west Africa was eased by certain similarities between the subsistence strategies employed to feed the workforce. It is clear that Europeans keenly observed indigenous forms of enslavement and adapted what they knew to the management of enslaved Africans in the New World. Barbot's earlier quoted statement about millet porridge and 'stinking fish' being the common food of the enslaved was remarkably parallel to the foodways of enslaved people in the Chesapeake, many of whom were brought from Senegambia where Barbot made his observations. Long before the settlement of British North America, slavery in the Caribbean took similar contours, taking many cues from African life in the cultural 'seasoning' process. In the French colonies the *Code Noir* (Black Code) recommended two pounds of salt beef or three pounds of salt fish (Harms, 357). In the British West Indies the diet was composed of garden produce from provision grounds, ground and boiled Indian corn, 'a few herrings, or other salt fish, is what is given for their support' (Benezet, 76). Influenced by the customs of the islands, American planters took their cues from early provisioning systems in the Caribbean and Latin America. In Virginia and Maryland, Thomas Anburey noted, 'their meals consist of hominy and salt, and if their master is a man of humanity … he allows them … rusty bacon, or salt herring to relish this miserable and scanty fare' (Anburey, 2:331).

Much of the protein found in early enslaved communities was either fish or game. Fresh meat from livestock came from the enslaved person's poultry yard; larger animals were usually only killed when injured, sick or superannuated. As Philip Morgan noted in *Slave Counterpoint*, enslaved people on the larger plantations of the Chesapeake received a preserved meat or fish ration of half a pound, while those in the Lowcountry seldom knew the luxury. The inadequate meat rations are attested in colonial documents, from leniency on laws for hog-stealing (owing to the fact that many enslaved people stole hogs because they hadn't had any meat in a year), to planter Landon Carter's use of meat as an incentive for good work or as a reward for catching six or more crows that could ruin the corn crop (Morgan, 136). Wealthy planters were able to supply the needs of their workforce in this way, but many enslaved people during this time went completely without. Some were expected to raise almost all of their own food in provision grounds, others were allowed to trap, hunt and fish to supplement their grain and salt fish rations. Others worked for other slaveholders on their 'off times' to procure meat. Most telling are store records researched by Barbara Heath in the Piedmont counties of Virginia where enslaved people used barter to purchase salt herring, shad and bacon to supplement their rations (Heath, 1997).

Despite the annual winter cull, only so much of this salted and/or smoked meat actually went to enslaved individuals. Most of the fresh but 'less desirable' cuts – the heads, spinal column, ribs, feet, tails and entrails – went to the enslaved community. Part of this tradition goes back to similar slaughtering-time customs begun in medieval times between lords and serfs. In the other guise, this custom had definite connections to west and central African foodways where all virtually all parts of the animal were considered desirable; and much of the 'offal' had spiritual and ceremonial significance. In at least one narrative from the slave-trade era, Captain Hugh Crow noted that on the occasion that at Bonny, a cow was slaughtered, King Pepple made it a condition that the 'head and offal' be sent ashore for his own use (Crow, 168).

The planters may have been working on the precedent established by their plantation community's earliest enslaved residents. For newly arrived enslaved Africans, the foods

337

and customs of their European captors were still too alien to be easily assimilated. Some Africans were practising Muslims with *halal* dietary restrictions. Observant Muslims like a man named Nero from along the Cooper River in Lowcountry South Carolina, took their rations in fish and beef rather than pork. This was particularly important for communities dominated by Senegambians like that Ayuba Ibn Sulayman was enslaved in on the eastern shore of Maryland where his interviewer noted that he would not touch pork but has 'no scruple about fish' (Diouf, 88). That many Africans viewed meat and fish as a condiment or dressing rather than as a common entrée also would have helped curtail the adoption of meat as a standard ration. The growing acculturation and move to a majority American-born population after the 1750s probably shifted the tastes of many from fish to pork.

Anadromous fish such as the alewife (*Alosa psuedoharengu*), gizzard shad (*Dorosoma cepedianum*), hickory shad (*Alosa mediocris*), American shad (*Alosa sapidissima*), blueback herring (*Alosa aestivalis*) and Atlantic herring (*Clupea harengus*) have been solidly documented in the zooarchaeological record confirming the species sourced in plantation fisheries. These fish provided a regular and reliable source of free protein that could be culled from the banks of the rivers where most large plantations were located for the purposes of shipping their cash crop. Northern Europeans had for centuries relied upon the Atlantic herring, cod and other pickled or stock fish, especially the poor and peasant classes and during the Lenten season. Add to this the enslaved Africans and their reliance on salted, dried or smoked 'stinking fish,' and an abundant native supply of spawning fish along the very tidal creeks and rivers slaveholders relied upon for access to marine shipping, and the customs of all groups were safely reinforced. George Washington had a six-week fishery in which he harvested millions of herring and shad each year, putting much of it up to 'secure a sufficiency of fish for the use of my own people' (quoted in Thompson, 25). In 1798, a Polish visitor to Mount Vernon, Julian Niemcewisz, called herring 'the best nourishment for the Negroes' (Thompson, 103).

The fish were processed by gangs of enslaved workers who were temporarily exempted from the preparation of the spring crop. 'We had an abundance of fish in the spring, and as long as the fishing season continued. After that, in addition to his allowance of corn, one salt herring a day,' said Charles Ball, himself a formerly enslaved fisherman and veteran of plantations in Maryland, South Carolina and Georgia. George Washington's description of eighteenth-century preservation methods used at Mount Vernon with its predominantly Senegambian population is relevant: 'I mean to make a brine and after cutting off the head and bellys [sic] dipping them in the brine for a short time, then hang them up and cure them by smoke, or dry them in the sun; for our people being so long accustomed to have fish whenever they wanted' (Thompson, 28). Amanda Nelson, the granddaughter of enslaved people from St Mary's County, Maryland, remembered brined herring being soaked, scaled and stuck on sticks to dry in the sun (McDaniel, 118). Salt fish was added to soups and stews, fried in cornmeal, cooked with domesticated and wild greens, or soaked and roasted

338

on its own by the fire. In urban settings, slave codes had to be passed that restricted the sale of 'spoiled fish, crabs and stale vegetables' which were key in the underground market of enslaved urbanites (Tyler-McGraw, 31).

The rise of smokehouse pork: late colonial to antebellum South

As the world of the Southern plantation pushed westward towards Missouri and Texas, lands that were formerly frontier became vast settled landscapes as white settlers, slaveholders and their 'animals of empire,' made complete the displacement and removal of the First Nations. The forced migration of hundreds of thousands of enslaved Blacks into what would become the Southern heartland marked another rupture in their lives. The enslaved people of the colonial South blazed the path to the rapid construction of what would become The Old South. Although plantations were never completely self-reliant, the antebellum age saw cotton, rice and sugar profits sufficient to order quantities of salted and smoked pork being raised in the central part of the country to supply a plantation's workforce for months on end.

In addition to these factors, plantations now had virgin ground on which to raise larger numbers of hogs and the nineteenth century saw a dramatic improvement in the breeding and husbandry of pigs. Pork production went up as worn-out land was diversified through grain production and livestock husbandry. The vast oak-hickory forest of the central United States submitted to the axe and thousands of hogs would be raised for slaughter, curing and shipment throughout the growing south and west. The people of the southern Midwest and middle South were largely from the Chesapeake *339* where the making of Southern country ham first developed on American soil. The fact that the center of the black population shifted from the tidal rivers of the seaboard to the central cotton belt where the fish species relied upon were unknown, meant that new sources of protein became necessary. Simultaneously, an entire knowledge-base built around the proper maintenance and management of enslaved blacks developed in the literature of plantation aristocracy (see McKee 1988).

Long before the plantation period there were hints that the traditions of eating vegetables cooked in meat stock had old roots in west Africa and early engagement with the European slave traders. Given the Portuguese presence at Elmina and other settlements along the Gold Coast, it seems conceivable that indigenous recipes (based on stews and soups with small amounts of protein and spiced leafy greens) were early merged with European ones like *caldo verde* (made of greens cooked with *linguica* and like cured pork) since kale, cabbage and coleworts (known as *couve* in Portuguese) were planted in European settlement kitchen gardens. We return to Barbot as he describes this exchange in process: 'The rich often have the meat of pigs, goats, harts and cows as well as of a large number of fowls, *from which they even make (stock for) cabbage soup, and several other stews which they have learned from the whites and passed on from one to another.* Malaguetta (pepper) is always prevalent in all their stews' (Hair, 2:513; emphasis mine). In America, enslaved men and women would build on this, taking salted, peppered and smoked pork and using it to create relishes for their hoe cake, hominy, or rice-based diets. The necessary and customary one-pot meals of west Africa and slavery meant that rations or garden truck – often potatoes, beans, cowpeas, greens and the like – would be boiled with hot pepper and a piece of meat to lend the vegetables the savor and fat that spread throughout the dish. According to a formerly enslaved Virginia man, Levi Pollard:

> Meat from de smokehouse was gived usen every four week. Us get twelve pounds and dat had ter last on us ain't get no more. What kind was hit? Side and shoulder of de hog. 'Twas cured and put down in plenty er salt. Sometimes us get plenty lean in hit. Us always had dat fer dinner. Cuts it up in square pieces and let hit boil, den put in yur salad or cabbages, or beans and dey was some kind 'er good. Dat was good and greasy when dere was much meat.
>
> (Perdue, 227)

Another formerly enslaved Virginian, Mrs Sarah Wooden Johnson, described the making of cush, a cornbread hash. 'Your mammy would crumble dis bread in dat good and greasy liquor, put a lot of pepper in hit and let her steam a little while in dat ole big skillet. Honey dat stuff is good!' (Perdue, 164). The palm oil and oily fish of their great-grandparents from Africa had been replaced by hog lard. Mrs May Satterfield declared that 'black eyed peas and hog jowl on New Year's Day' guaranteed money all the year (Perdue, 248). For all the bacon, side meat, ham rinds and cured hog jowl distributed throughout the sixteen slave-holding states on the eve of the Civil War, in some communities the stinking fish still reigned supreme. Mr Horace Muse recalled, 'In dem days de only thing we got to eat was a ash cake an half a herrin' and water. Ole woman brung us out our dinner to de fiel'. She brought bread and fish in a big basket' (Perdue, 216).

Conclusion

When enslaved Africans from Senegambia, the Rice Coast, the Gold Coast, south-eastern Nigeria and Kongo-Angola first came to the colonial South they shared numerous culinary commonalities that would ensure a fairly even base from which to draw in the re-creation of their foodways in North America. Their diets were based on the consumption of starches with soups, stews and relishes made with a bit of preserved protein well spiced in an oily sauce. With the transport of African plants to the New World and the substitution of American and European crops, animals and wild game for those lost in the transition to a new land and climate, they set about re-inventing the food and themselves, ingredient by ingredient. Denied by distance of their *bonga* shad, native 'herrings' and sardines, the generations that seeded African american culture made the critical choice to respond flexibly to foods and circumstances provided them, though living lives of seasonal want in rural peasantry had prepared them well. Africans used their rations to sustain themselves and probably retained old recipes using greens, cowpeas and tubers and grain mush with the 'stinking fish' they were provided.

Time moved forward and carried these traditions through economic, geographic and industrial shifts going on in the world around them. From 1750 onward the African american community was majority native-born, with the exception of those parts of the Lowcountry and Lower Mississippi Valley where the slave trade persisted. This proto-Dixie – not fully African, European or Native American – was the mixing-bowl for parallel traditions and customs that melded into something called 'Southern'. The grandchildren of these men and women raised in a Western milieu, and accustomed and acculturated to European American and Native American food and folkways, came to expect meat as a staple of their diet. From the rare slow-smoked barbecue only enjoyed at the 'big times', to the rusty, ripe rinds of bacon and side-meat came dishes of renown that still tempt the modern-day palate and define Southern foodways. From bits of salted fish and smoked pork, to collards and lamb's quarters, okra soup, and beans cooked with potatoes, the story of shift in culture and identity can be told as much by what was put in the pots as by the precious narratives we have of the people who stirred them. This history, redolent with the pungency of stinking and salt fish, zesty with the sharpness of hickory ash and red pepper, speaks to the power of these survivors who used preserved flesh in exile to preserve ancient connections to the land of their origins.

341

Bibliography

Anburey, Thomas. *Travels Through the Interior Parts of America*; In a Series of Letters, 2 volumes. London: William Lane, 1789.

Ball, Charles. *Fifty Years a Slave*. Mineola: Dover Press. (Originally published by John S. Taylor in New York, 1837), 2003.

Basden, George Thomas. *Among the Igbos of Nigeria*. London: Cass, 1966.

Benezet, Anthony. *Some Historical Account of Guinea*. London: J. Phillips, 1788.

Bober, Phyllis Pray. *Art, Culture and Cuisine: Ancient and Medieval Gastronomy*. Chicago: University of Chicago Press, 1999.

Crow, Hugh. *The Memoirs of Captain Hugh Crow: The Life and Times of A Slave Trade Captain*. Oxford: Bodelian Press, 2007.

de Marees, Pieter. *Description and Historical Account of the Gold Kingdom of Guinea (1602), Translated from the Dutch and edited by Albert Van Dantzig and Adam Jones*. Oxford: Published by the British Academy by Oxford University Press, 1987.

Diouf, Sylvaine. *Servants of Allah: African Muslims Enslaved in the Americas*. New York: New York University Press, 1998.

Equiano, Olaudah. 'The Interesting Narrative of the Life of Olaudah Equiano, Or Gustavus Vassa, the African', in *I Was Born a Slave: An Anthology of Classic Slave Narratives, 1770-1849*. Ed. Yuval Taylor. Chicago: Lawrence Hill Books, 1999.

Gamble, David P. *The Wolof of Senegambia*. London: International African Institute, 1957.

Hair, P.E.H. *Barbot on Guinea: The Writings of John Barbot on West Africa 1678–1712*. London: Haklyut Society, 1992.

Harms, Robert. *The Diligent: A Voyage through the Worlds of the Slave Trade.* New York: Basic Books, 2002.

Heath, Barbara. 'Slavery and Consumerism: A Case Study from Central Virginia.' *African-American Archaeology: Newsletter of the African-American Archaeology Network.* Number 19, Early Winter 1997. (2 March 2010).

Charles Joyner. *Down by the Riverside: A South Carolina Slave Community.* Chicago: University of Illinois Press, 1984

Laman, Karl. *The Kongo.* Upsala, 1953.

Lewicki, Tadeusz with Marion Johnson. *West African Food in the Middle Ages: According to Arabic Sources.* London: Cambridge University Press, 1974.

McDaniel, George W. *Hearth and Home: Preserving a People's Culture.* Philadelphia: Temple University Press, 1982.

McKee, Larry. 'Food Supply and the Plantation Order: An Archeological Perspective.' in *I Too Am America, Archaeological Studies of African American Life,* edited by Theresa Singleton. Charlottesville: University of Virginia Press, 1999.

Mitchell, Patricia. *The African Influence on Southern Cuisine.* http://www.foodhistory.com/foodnotes/leftovers/african/infl/01 (2 March 2010).

Monteiro, Joachim John. *Angola and the River Congo.* New York: Macmillan and Company, 1876.

Morgan, Phillip. *Slave Counterpoint.* Chapel Hill: University of North Carolina Press, 1998.

Perdue, Charles L. *Weevils in the Wheat.* Charlottesville: University of Virginia Press, 1992.

Thompson, Mary. 'Better…Fed than Negroes Generally Are'?: Diet of the Mount Vernon Slaves,' in *They Work Only From Sun to Sun; Slave Life and George Washington's Mount Vernon,* publication pending.

Tyler-McGraw. *Slavery and the Underground Railroad at the Eppes Plantations.* National Park Service: Northeast Region, 2005. http://www.nps.gov/history/history/online_books/pete/ugrr.pdf

342

A Preserve Gone Bad or Just Another Beloved Delicacy?
Surströmming and Gravlax

Renée Valeri

In the modern world, we demand that methods of preservation should not change the taste and the aspect of foods – perhaps a consequence of freezing becoming more common than other techniques. On the other hand, there are instances where it might be precisely the changes in taste which have contributed to keeping certain preserving methods in existence.

For some foods such as fish, however, postponing consumption is considerably more difficult than for others. All over northern Europe, herring from the North Sea has long been a staple for survival and, for many, the salted version was indeed the epitome of everyday food. However, in the northern part of Sweden, drying and salting were less suitable than they were further south – the former technique for climatic reasons, the latter for financial ones, as salt had to be bought from far away.

In the area of the northern Baltic, using only a small amount of salt, thereby producing fermentation of the fish, has long been a common technique for preserving fish, especially herring, which prepared in this way is called *surströmming* (literal translation: sour, fermented Baltic herring). As in many fermented foods, the result is a long shelf-life and a complex taste. An important side-effect of this fermentation is the strong smell, which many will associate with a food gone bad or one that is rotting.

Another fish that was in great supply in this area in the past was salmon, which gave rise to another rather special preparation, *gravlax* (literal translation: pit salmon). This is to most people a more accessible food, close to raw fish, a quickly made preserve pickled with some salt, sugar, and dill, often eaten with a sauce made with oil, vinegar, mustard and dill.

The first technique (*surströmming*) is interesting for several reasons, one being that fish is an unusual object for preservation other than in its dried, salted and/or smoked state. Even more intriguing, however, is the fact that in research on taste it is striking how most of the food literature has been concerned with what is good and delicious food – and how few examples one will find in the field of food history of writing about 'bad' taste. Today's vast food literature is brimming with suggestions for delicious foods, but few or no examples are given of what is perceived as disgusting – and why.

Still, with the growing interest in the different foods and techniques of preparation typical of other countries or cultures, finding comments and opinions on food from early travellers in this area – as well as more recent ones – could shed some light on the boundaries of taste in different societies or periods of time. Fish is a good subject for a food-mapping of Sweden, since both the surrounding seas and the many lakes and rivers have supplied the population with everyday foods, as well as more recherché ones, throughout history. This paper will focus on just one in each category.

As for the herring, which was historically a most common everyday food all over northern Europe, there is a clear difference between the herring species found in the Atlantic and in the Baltic (Davidson 1989: 26, 29). The latter (called *strömming*) is smaller and less fat than the one from Sweden's west and south coast (*sill*). Whereas there are many local ways of preserving the herring catch (salting, smoking, pickling, drying, etc.), *surströmming* has been the preferred one in the northern Baltic.

Several factors have contributed to the different food habits and preservation techniques in the northern part of the country. Until quite recently, this area was sparsely populated. The long and severe winters accentuated the great distances between villages and towns, especially away from the coast, affecting both trading patterns and other interactions. The original Sami population inland, moving with their herds of reindeer, and the Swedish settlers who lived mostly along the coast, have coexisted there for centuries, but with very different lifestyles.

In spite of good supplies of game, the early descriptions of the life in this area stress that fish was a mainstay of the diet, both fish from the Baltic and freshwater varieties from the numerous rivers and lakes. However, the distances between home and fishing waters, combined with long periods of snow, ice, lack of daylight, and the fact that roads were often not passable during the long spring thaws, necessitated methods of preserving the catch away from home for later retrieval and consumption. Wrapping it in birch bark and burying it in the ground with a little salt was a theory put forward by earlier researchers (Berg 1962: 49ff.) to explain names like *gravlax* ('*grav*' meaning a place dug in the ground) and the older and more general name for fish preserved like the *surströmming*, i.e. *gravfisk*. The oldest mention is from the province of Jämtland in 1348, where a man called Olafur Graflax changes a fishing allotment.

Another name for this same type of preserved fish was *lundsfisk*, a term used by Carl von Linné during his travels in Dalarna, where he encountered it on August 4, 1737 in the village of Lima: 'They also have lundsfisk here, put in birch bark or other bark, kept in ravines and cold holes, smelled bad, was red by the bones, and said to be delicious for those who liked it' (C. von Linné 1889/1984).

In his sixteenth-century work on many different aspects of the life of Nordic people, the Swedish Archbishop Olaus Magnus points out that salt was not easy to obtain for his Swedish contemporaries (O. Magnus 1555/1976, book 13: 43, on difficulties of importing salt into Nordic countries). This might have been the origin and *raison d'être* of *surströmming*. After the catch in the spawning season in May–June, and as a consequence of only a light salting, the fish starts to ferment in the summer, changing the taste – and adding the smell.

344

More recently, the *strömming* was put (and sold) in small wooden barrels, and for the last 100 years it has been preserved in metal cans. The prevailing technique is still in two stages: a preliminary light salting, starting the fermentation, followed by a transfer to a second, saltier brine, where the fish is kept for a longer period, ranging from a couple of months to over a year.

The sealed tin cans with today's *surströmming* will not reveal the state of their contents by the smell (as did the wooden kegs), but perhaps by bulging, as long as they are not opened. However, when pierced and opened, the smell of the contents will invariably provoke powerful spontaneous reactions from people nearby, ranging from 'this makes me hungry!' (a 22-year-old student who grew up in the north), to 'this is smell terrorism!' (a 40-year-old woman who had grown up in the south, passing by a *surströmming* dinner).

Although fermentation is fairly widespread as a method of preserving in various parts of the world (*choucroute*, pickles, etc.), not all of them share the contradictory characteristics of offensive smell and good taste. What is interesting in such foods (e.g. the French cheese Époisses, the Roman sauce *garum*, a similar present-day paste called *belatjan* in south-east Asia, and the fruit in the latter area named durian) is that if one is able to overcome the initial adverse reaction to the smell and try them, the taste is quite different – and beloved by its fans. Today, most of the population along the northern Baltic, as well as many *surströmming* converts in the rest of Sweden, celebrate the start of its season in late August with a *surströmming* party or feast.

A threat to the continued enjoyment of this speciality is a ban coming from the EU, caused by today's dioxin-content of Baltic fish. The current exemption ends in 2011, a great concern for many fans. Not surprisingly though, the paradox between smell and taste in *surströmming*, and concern about its health consequences, was actually studied (and put to rest) as early as the late nineteenth century by Carl Th. Mörner, a medical doctor in Uppsala, who in 1895 published a very serious article about *surströmming*. He began by saying that:

345

> In certain parts of Northern Sweden, there is an odd custom of preserving fish, preparing so-called *surfisk* (sour fish), a collective name covering products prepared from different species of fish and by methods that vary in detail.
>
> Characteristic of all kinds of sour fish is, however, that they are only lightly salted and that the final product has an intense smell, which causes a person unfamiliar with it to involuntarily pull back. The smell of this sour fish is, however, not in a strict sense sour or acidulous, nor does its taste have this quality ... but it is probably in the meaning of slightly putrid that it has become synonymous with sour fish and related names, such as *surströmming*, *sursik* [*sik* means whitefish]. Practically unknown south of the river Dalälven (i.e. 60° N), sour fish has a not-insignificant place in the food of the lower classes, and this has probably been the case for a very long time.

The *surströmming* is usually eaten either raw or pan-fried, together with potatoes or bread, and Mörner comments: 'Concerning a food with such an exquisite smell-taste like *surströmming*, it is natural that the subjective opinion regarding its taste or palatability goes in two opposite directions; many individuals – and in the regions where *surströmming* is not a common food, these represent the greater number – look on *surströmming* with disgust, whereas others see it as a great delicacy, although it must be admitted, that they usually have come to this conclusion through a shorter or longer period of training.'

Mörner realized, of course, that the reason for the very particular character of *surströmming* is to be found in a chemical alteration of the fresh fish and the impact of certain bacteria, but its nature was not known at the time, since it had not at that point been subjected to scientific enquiry. Naturally, the first question was what exactly gave the *surströmming* its notorious smell and Mörner's research provided an answer. The mixture of gases that emanate when you open a keg of *surströmming* is sufficient to noticeably 'perfume' an entire room in a couple of seconds. Apart from carbon dioxide and hydrogen sulphide (the latter being well-known for its unpleasant smell), another substance, methyl mercaptan (CH_3SH), is a 'primus inter pares' in affecting our olfactory organ, its smell being comparable to rotten cabbage (which incidentally is a comparison also used by the Dutch botanist Rumphius in 1747 when describing the experience of another of the foods mentioned earlier, the south-east Asian fruit durian, *Durio zibethinus*). Since the latter gas is very volatile, and although it is quite noticeable if the *surströmming* is raw, it will almost completely disappear when *surströmming* is grilled, leaving room for other transient smells, such as butyric acid.

So, should *surströmming* be considered a putrid product or not? Mörner's answer is no, basically because of the two-stage process of light salting followed by immersion in a saline solution, which excludes all air. In the first stage, the putrefactive bacteria are modified and, in the second, completely annihilated. In short, there is nothing to indicate that *surströmming* is a foodstuff which is harmful or unsuitable from a health point of view (Mörner 1895–96). Considering that for several centuries it has been eaten by large numbers of people in northern Sweden and Finland, this is reassuring. Whether, however, this also goes for other fermented fish preserves in the Nordic countries, which are more properly defined as 'buried fish' (cf. *gravlax*, above), is difficult to say. They include: shark on Iceland (buried in the gravel just by the water on the shore and eaten raw); the *rakörret* (salmon trout) made sour in Norway; and the tallow buried in the Faeroe Islands that was first allowed to rot slightly, then finely chopped and kneaded into big chunks, which were buried in damp ground and left there for a long period, until it ended up by smelling like old cheese (Bergius, 1780/1960, p. 64).

As mentioned above, the method still in use to produce *surströmming* was earlier used for several kinds of fish, both from the Baltic's brackish water and from inland lakes – the point being not which variety of fish was at hand, but the fact that a surplus catch needed to be preserved in order to serve as a food supply during the winter months.

A Preserve Gone Bad or Just Another Beloved Delicacy?

To illustrate this, I provide translations of a couple of answers to a list of questions on *surfisk*, *gravfisk*, pickled fish, *lutfisk* and similar preparations sent out by the Uppsala Institute for Dialectology and Folklore Research in 1956.

Twenty-seven answers were received from eleven Swedish provinces, mostly north of Stockholm:

For a period, *surströmming* fell into disuse; people did not want to eat 'rotten fish'. Some people 'spoiled' it by making *surströmming au gratin* with breadcrumbs on top. But, after a while, it came back in use again. Now, eating *surströmming* is almost one of the year's rituals. Many want to have a real *surströmming* feast, some eat it with the family – but often they want to have a party and invite some friends – naturally other *surströmming* consumers. Offering them *surströmming au gratin* would be considered cheating, and opening the tins outside would not be acceptable to 'real' *surströmming* consumers. The hosts would provide the *tunnbröd* (thin, flat, unleavened, soft bread) and schnapps. The guests sit down, full of expectation, the tin is opened, the smell spreads and the guests help themselves directly out of the tin. After having eaten a couple directly from the tin, the guests help themselves to *mandelpotatis* (a small kind of almond-shaped potato grown in northern Sweden), and roll the *surströmming* into the *tunnbröd*, accompanied by schnapps (and/or beer). They say real *surströmming* lovers eat up to twenty in one evening.

Both *strömming* and salmon were pickled raw. Preparing such fish was (and still is) considered a great art. Fish was, to a great extent, a poor man's food, except for herring, which was considered good for you and healthy.

(ULMA 219, Gästrikland 29063, 1973)

347

In the north-western province of Dalarna it was mostly freshwater fish such as roach (*mört*), ide (*id*) and bleak (*löja*) which were preserved with salt as *surfisk* (or *gamtfisk*). Spawning fish were preferred and could be caught in larger quantities. The roe of *mört* and *id* was eaten in different ways, for instance, spread on *tunnbröd*. The bones were removed from larger fish, after which the remainder could more easily be spread on the bread.

The *surfisk* can be saved for years as long as it is kept in a cool place after fermentation is completed, if it is well covered by the brine, and the stone weight is heavy enough to press out all the brine. As such, it is a good complement to potatoes and bread. The blood by the backbone is left, as it colours the brine and thus the fish.

The spawning fish caught from mid-May until around midsummer was not ready for consumption as *surfisk* until the end of September. Had it been kept in a warm place, however, it would be ready much earlier, although it should not be in large containers. This type of preparation still exists.

> There is a big difference in taste between *surfisk* and *surströmming*. To us the preparation of *surströmming* is a secret. The fish prepared in one of the ways above is called *surfisk* or *gamtfisk*.
>
> The *surfisk* was poor man's food, but even the rich liked it. Spring or autumn fish is the tastiest. Properly cooked and prepared fish is considered healthy.
>
> To 25–30 kg fish one should use a little more than 1 kg crushed coarse-grained salt (fish salt). After salting, the container should be left untouched for three days, so the salt will dissolve, and the brine cover the fish. The temperature during this time should be 15°C, after which a weight (of no more than 10 kg) is placed on the fish to ensure that the brine covers it. The same temperature should be maintained afterwards, if possible. After a month, or at most six weeks, the fish will be ready as *surfisk*, and one can start consuming it – but when some has been taken out, the stones must be replaced. (ULMA 23669, Dalarna, 1957)

Early Swedish sources rarely go into detail on everyday food preparation among the common people. However, even at that time there was obviously a difference between those who were offered *gravlax* and those who would encounter the fermented *surströmming*. Messire Aubéry du Maurier, visiting the Swedish Chancellor Axel Oxenstierna at the Swedish court in 1637, says in his *Mémoires* that he often ate there and one of the dishes offered was 'sundried salmon, in Sweden called *Lacs*, with a sauce made of oil, vinegar and pepper; and he told me one day that he found this *Lacs* better than he did the Bisques that had been served to him by the Cardinal de Richelieu & to confirm this, he cut a slice of this dried salmon, and ate it, after having dipped it in the sauce, with the best appetite in the world.'

In the seventeenth and eighteenth centuries, a number of foreign travellers came to visit Sweden and wrote accounts of their experiences in what was then quite an exotic country – partly since those who actually went beyond the court in Stockholm often made for Lapland and the Sami people in the far north. Since the latter lived a very different life from the settlers on the coast, food descriptions would naturally focus on reindeer products, and occasionally on venison, berries, etc., depending on the season (and they did not use salt, nor consume *surströmming*). However, some travellers also provided interesting descriptions of huge salmon traps in the rivers (Acerbi 1802).

In the same period, we find a surge of topographical sources, a number of which mention the existence of *surströmming* (sometimes under local names) as well as *gravlax*. Carl von Linné, on his early travels to investigate Sweden's economy, makes passing notes about it in the province of Dalarna and some years later in his travel account of Lapland – although that was on his return through Finland (at that time part of Sweden, not becoming independent until 1809).

In the early nineteenth century, a new type of traveller appeared, more like the travel journalists or tourists of today. One example is the Scotsman Samuel Laing (1839), who described the *strömming* fishery in Hudiksvall:

348

The stromming is about the size of a sprat, but is a much more delicate fish. They are cured like herrings; and a barrel of salted stromming is as necessary in every household on this side of the peninsula, as the barrel of herrings on the other. They are also used extensively over all Finland and the north of Russia. In these countries, salt is a scarce commodity in the interior. The sea affords none, and all that is used must come from Spain, France, or England. Salted fish seems to be the cheapest form in which salt can be carried into the interior; and from some natural craving of the constitution for salt as a condiment, people here relish, in a way we who are abundantly supplied with salt cannot understand, a dish once or twice a week of salted herrings. A herring or stromming raw out of the pickle, and bread with soup of milk or beer, make a favourite repast even in families of condition.

Laing also comments on salmon, a fish which was very common indeed in Swedish rivers in the past, and therefore a likely object for preservation. There are examples of work contracts from the west coast of Sweden, stipulating that the employees would not have to eat salmon more than a couple of days each week. With the expansion of various Swedish riverside industries in modern times, the quantity of domestic salmon has been reduced, and most of what is consumed today is the imported and cultivated variety, prepared in a very different way. Today's *gravlax* is a short-term preserve, closer to raw fish: the fleshy side of two equally sized pieces of fish are rubbed with salt, sugar and crushed pepper, liberally strewn with chopped fresh dill, and put together in the form of a sandwich. They are chilled for a couple of days with a heavy weight on top. The fish is eaten in thin slices, preferably with a dill-mustard sauce and has a very delicate taste. This version has been exported to restaurant menus in various countries – a fate which will hardly befall *surströmming*.

349

Laing also experienced eating *gravlax* (in Umeå):

There is nothing of Lapland here, except perhaps in the food. I had seen graf lax ... raw salmon, on the carte of a restaurateur in Stockholm; and seeing other people eat it with relish, I called for a portion too, but could not bring myself to swallow a slice of raw fish. Here it was put down for breakfast along with slices of smoked salmon, and slices of smoked reindeer flesh, but none of these articles had ever been on the fire. The two German shipmasters breakfasted at the same time, but could make nothing of these raw materials. I determined to try, since such is the food of the country – and I must live like the people of the country, to know how they live – and with oil, vinegar, and pimento, which is used here instead of black pepper, I found graf lax not a bad thing. The meat, however, of these fresh-water salmon (...) is of a finer texture, and is not oily or stringy; which I suspect a raw slice of a Tweed salmon would be.

Another traveller, Friedrich Wilhelm von Schubert, professor of theology in Greifswald, who travelled in Sweden in 1817, describes the fishing of salmon in a river much further south, near Gävle, and comments that,

> the salmon is here prepared in the same way as in the north of Sweden, i.e. it is salted like in other areas, boiled, fried, smoked, but it is also prepared as so-called Gravlax, and this is mostly the habit in Norrland, but it is also supposedly common in Scotland. To prepare gravlax, the fresh raw salmon is cut in pieces, which are strewn with salt and some sugar, and left so covered for a shorter or longer period of time, preferably two or three days. This way the salmon keeps for a rather long time, mostly so if it is salted twice, which is the custom in some places. With oil, vinegar, and sugar the gravlax is a tastier preparation than boiled or smoked. A necessary condition for this preparation is that it takes place as soon as possible after the catch. Only fifteen minutes later the salmon is edible, but the taste is still better if it has been in the salt for a couple of hours or for a day. … Gravlax is quite different from the salmon which has been salted in the usual stronger way. The latter will keep for several years, whereas the smoked one soon will be tough and be of no use, a reason why salmon smoking is in use in few places in Norrland, where the salmon fishery is such an important industry. By adding flour or grain people also make salmon soup, called salmon gruel.

Admittedly, *gravlax*, in spite of its unusual seasoning (salt, sugar, pepper and dill) and the fact that some people will hesitate because of its close relation to raw fish, is much easier to accept as food than its 'cousin' *surströmming*. The latter is indeed an odd preserve, which to newcomers invariably raises the question of why it was ever invented.

One answer is the history of salt in the north. Unlike Norway, Sweden had no natural salt deposits. Many attempts to extract salt on the west (North Sea) coast failed, and earlier the Swedes had no need to do so, since they bought their salt from the Dutch and German ships coming from Spanish, French and British ports who sold it at a reasonable price (O. Magnus). The weak point in this trade was, of course, that in wartime, such as during the sixteenth century, the salt trade becomes a political issue, affecting the Swedish national economy. Shrinking supplies of salt affected the food stores of settlers and fishermen in northern Sweden, already dependent on barter for their subsistence (O. Magnus 1555/1976, Book 13, chapter 43–44; for a more detailed account of salt in Sweden, see Bonge-Bergengren, 1989).

Nature was generous in supplying fish for subsistence, but in order to store the catch of spawning herring (or other fish) for winter needs, salt was necessary. The different techniques used traditionally have been well described in the answers to questionnaires above, sent out by the Swedish institutes of ethnology. Comparing these answers, stretching back to the mid-eighteenth century, with descriptions and comments in printed and archival sources of the past, we find that the technique of *surströmming* has been an acquired taste in the north. But looking at the contemporary situation, with comments on the internet and interviews with *surströmming*-converts in the very south of Sweden (born and raised with very different food and taste habits), the acceptance of this food is no longer learned, but a matter of personal choice.

Dr Mörner's research, quoted in the beginning of this article, was no doubt a relief to many *surströmming* consumers at the time, although a large number of them had come to similar results through personal empirical research. At his time (the end of the nineteenth century), an 'export' of *surströmming* was already taking place to people in the area north of Stockholm. Indeed, the consumption is still spreading to parts of the country well beyond the northern regions. Today *surströmming* is sold to, and consumed by people originating from the very south of the country, albeit on a smaller scale than in the north. There is even a health-food based on it …

It is probably no coincidence that Mörner's research was published about the same time as an interest in culinary matters, of French origin, became noticeable in Sweden. Another man combining a medical profession with a great interest in and knowledge of the art of cooking was Charles Emil Hagdahl, author of *Kok-Konsten som vetenskap och konst* (The Art of Cookery, as a Science and an Art), the 'Swedish Brillat-Savarin', clearly also inspired by A. Dumas. He describes *surströmming* in the following manner:

> *Surströmming* is an old preparation, which nature itself has always taken care of ever since the creation of the world. Our first parents caught the scent of it just outside the gates of Paradise, and it was a well-known smell from earliest times, beside all the *kjökkenmöddingar* (kitchen middens) and the *pålhyddor* (pile-huts), as well as for the Greeks and Romans, for everyone knew what rotten fish meant; but the taste for it was not yet as developed as it is now – people did not yet know *haut goût*. *Surströmming* is eaten only by the initiated, *au naturel*, without any other sauce than that the mouth waters. They consider it a delicacy of the most sublime kind; but it will never become a festive food, unless the host prefers to eat alone, or maybe chooses guests who have no nose.

Although Hagdahl has been proved wrong in predicting the *surströmming*'s role today, the question might now be more one of why the new adepts (addicts?) have adopted a dish which has such a bad reputation, and which is socially exclusive in shared housing situations. For today's mobile population, one answer might lie in our desire to expand the boundaries of taste – be they geographical or physical, or both. The closely related preserve *gravlax* has had a less controversial history. Made in a couple of days, it is eaten practically raw, although this to some people can also be repugnant. Here the boundary is maybe more one of nature/culture, which can be difficult for some civilized individuals.

Thus, in the final analysis, both preparations mentioned are interesting through their place on the outer margins of food habits. *Surströmming* questions our sense of smell, which since ancestral times is supposed to have been basic for selecting what is safe to eat or what should be avoided. *Gravlax* challenges our idea of defining ourselves as civilized persons, who should eat cooked meat or fish (cf. Lévi-Strauss, *Le Cru et le cuit*), a concept which has been loosened through travel and food-custom exchanges (cf. sushi) in recent years. One young woman travelling to the north and trying *surströmming* for the first time with some trepidation, commented that just after the meal she thought that it was fun to try, but once was enough. But thinking back, a few weeks later, she would definitely sit down for some more – just as she had with sushi. Maybe that is how taste is acquired.

Bibliography

Andersson, Sten. *Matens roller.* Almqvist & Wiksell Förlag AB, 1980.

Acerbi, Joseph, *Travels through Sweden, Finland and Lapland, in the years 1798–1799.* London, 1802.

Aubéry du Maurier, Louis, *Memoires de Hambourg, de Lubeck et de Holstein, de Dannemarck, de Suede et de Pologne.* Amsterdam, 1736.

Berg, Gösta, 'Gravlax och surströmming', in *Gastronomisk Kalender.* Stockholm, 1962.

Bergius, Bengt, Tal om läckerheter både i sig själva sådana och för sådana ansedda genom Folkslags bruk och inbillning [Speech at the meeting of the Royal Academy of Sciences on May 3, 1780: About delicacies, both those being so in themselves and those considered as such through people's usage and imagination]. Printed by Victor Pettersons Bokindustri AB, Stockholm, 1960.

Bonge-Bergengren, Inge, *Den nödvändiga sältan.* Fataburen, 1989, pp. 123–141.

Bonnefon, Paul. *Mémoires de Louis-Henri de Loménie Comte de Brienne*, dit Le Jeune Brienne, Paris, 1916.

Consett, Matthew, *A tour through Sweden, Swedish Lapland, Finland and Denmark…* London, 1789.

Davidson, Alan, *North Atlantic Seafood.* New York: Harper & Row (Perennial Library edn), 1989.

——, *The Oxford Companion to Food.* Oxford: Oxford University Press, 1999.

——, *Sea Food: a connoisseur's guide and cookbook.* London: Mitchell Beazley, 1989.

Hagdahl, Charles Emil: *Kok-konsten som vetenskap och konst* (The art of cookery as science and art), 2nd revised edn. Stockholm, 1896.

Hogguer, Daniel von. *Reise nach Lappland und dem nördlichen Schweden.* G. Reimer: Berlin, 1841.

Keyland, Nils, *Svensk Allmogekost.* Carlsson Bokförlag in co-operation with the Inst. f. Folklivsforskning och Nordiska Muséet, 1989.

Linnaeus, Carl, *Dalaresan/Iter Dalecarlia, Natur och Kultur* 1889/1984.

——, *Lappländska resan/Iter Lapponicum 1732*, edited by Magnus von Platen & Carl-Otto von Sydow. Wahlström och Widstrand, 1957.

Mat i Västerbotten, Västerbottens Museum och Två Förläggare Bokförlag, Umeå 1985.

Mörner, Carl Th. 'Meddelande om surströmming', in *Uppsala läkareförenings "Förhandlingar"* 1895–96, pp. 365–373.

Olaus Magnus, *Historia om de Nordiska Folken*, Roma 1555 (1976, second edition, together with Inst. för folklivsforskning vid Nordiska muséet. Kommentar av prof. John Granlund).

Outhier, Reginaud. *Journal d'un voyage au Nord en 1736 & 1737.* Paris, 1744.

Scheller, Johann Gerhard. *Reisebeschreibung nach Lappland und Bothnien.* Jena, 1713.

Schubert, Friedrich Wilhelm von. *Reise durch Schweden, Norwegen, Lappland, Finnland und Ingermanland in den Jahren 1817, 1818 und 1820.* Bd 1–3. Leipzig 1823–24.

Seigneur A de la. *Motrayes resor 1711–1725* (facsimile edition by Rediviva 1988, from the 1912 edition).

Talve, Ilmar. *Folkligt kosthåll i Finland, en översikt.* Gleerup, 1977.

Archival sources:

DAUM: Institute of Language and Folklore research in Umeå

ULMA: Uppsala Institute for Dialectology and Folklore Research

Nordiska Muséet: Collection of excerpts by Prof. Gösta Berg concerning surströmming and gravlax.

From *Poi* to *Fufu*: the Fermentation of Taro

Karin Vaneker

When rice and wheat were just weeds

Taro, or aroids, are common names for plants belonging to the Araceae family, whose main centers of origin and diversity are tropical Asia and tropical America, and include edible members such as L. *Colocasia*, *Alocasia*, *Cyrtosperma* and *Xanthosoma* taro. The beginnings of taro are put in the Cretaceous when primitive taro formed colonies in swampy areas of tropical regions. Ever since the Cretaceous, which started around 140 million years ago and lasted 65 million years, it has remained a tropical rainforest plant with a liking for moisture and shelter (Bown 2000, 49–50). According to ethnobotanists and archaeologists, taro is the oldest cultivated crop, its domestication and cultivation in terraced paddies occurred when rice and wheat were just weeds (Matthews 1995, Bown 2000, Ivancic & Lebot, 2003).

The history of Asian taro

Colocasia, *Alocasia* and *Cyrtosperma* taro are believed to originate in Asia, in the area between Myanmar and Bangladesh. From here, also known as the Indomalaya ecozone, *Colocasia* taro in particular spread eastwards to other regions with homogeneous equatorial climates. From south-east and east Asia and the Pacific Islands, it probably diffused westwards to Madagascar and Africa, from where it expanded to the Mediterranean, the Caribbean and the Americas (Candolle 1885, Seidensticker 1999, Ivancic & Lebot 2003). Archeological evidence from stone mortars and pestles from the Solomon Islands suggests that *Colocasia* taro was already in use around 28,000 years ago. The first European navigators observed cultivated taro in places as far distant as Japan and New Zealand, and written records indicate that Captain Cook and his companions noticed taro in Maori plantations in 1769 (Candolle 1885, Matthews 1995). Taro remains a popular ingredient even today and especially in traditional dishes of the Pacific Islands. Furthermore, research into the linguistic relationship between the English word 'taro' and Proto-Oceanic term *'talo'* is believed to support the origin and dispersal of taro throughout Asia and the Pacific region (Bellwood 1995, 52).

In several areas of ancient China taro was an important staple crop, its cultivation is dated back to 8,000 BC or before. Apart from being a staple for the common people, records from the Han and T'ang periods[1] list taro among the foodstuffs acceptable for persons of noble and imperial standing. In later times taro became a less important staple crop and food than rice and cereals (Simoons 1991, 104–105).

Around the Mediterranean

> Colocasia (*Ḳulḳàs*). *Colocasia esculenta*, the very large-leaved species the tuber of
> which is extensively eaten by the natives of Egypt and neighbouring countries.
> Roland L.N. Michell, 1900 [2]

Several records indicate that the cultivation of tubers and roots in ancient Egypt predate
the domestication of cereals such as barley, millet and wheat.[3] The agriculture of the
fertile Nile delta was highly sophisticated, and the ancient Egyptians developed irrigation
techniques to produce wetland crops, e.g. papyrus, lotus and taro.

Roots and tubers of wetland crops were important foods that were consumed as
(cooked) vegetables and used for the production of flour. Their use in ancient Egypt is
referred to in various ancient treatises. As these employ different definitions and do not
provide pictures,[4] and also due to the extinction of plants, the identification of ancient
plants and plant-names is complicated. As a result several plants and plant-names got
confused. Also because botanical descriptions by the Greeks and Romans were not
necessarily based on first-hand observation, the identity of many plants mentioned in old
literature remains obscure and has to be inferred from an analysis of existing literature or
scientifically, for instance through archaeological evidence (Seidensticker 1999).

Herodotus (*c.* 484–*c.* 426 BC), Theophrastus (*c.* 327–*c.* 288 BC), Dioscorides (*c.* 40–*c.*
90 BC), and Pliny the Elder (23–79 CE) probably all referred to taro in their writings, but
used different definitions, e.g. the Egyptian bean and lotus (Candolle 1885, Seidensticker
1999). In the course of history these descriptions resulted in and added to confusion.
Even today, a number of botanists and scientists doubt whether taro was cultivated
in Egypt. A recurrent confusion in the ongoing discourse dates back to Herodotus,
probably the earliest author to describe taro; in his work he mentions the features of two
Egyptian plants, e.g. lotus and *Faba aegyptiaca*.[5] Theophrastus, Dioscorides and Pliny
the Elder based their taro descriptions on Herodotus or on each other (Seidensticker
1999, 88–92). The sixteenth-century herbal the 'Wiener Dioskurides' (Constantinople
c. 1512) includes a drawing showing *Colocasia* taro which is mistaken for lotus. As in
later centuries someone probably tried to correct this mistake by adding the Arab
words *handaquq* and *qulqas* (Seidensticker 1997, 88). Pliny the Elder referred to taro as
the arum of the Egyptians, and as Pliny did not see the plant himself, his description
is probably based on the works of Theophrastus and Dioscorides (Candolle 1885, 74;
Seidensticker 1999, Grocock & Grainger 2006, 338). Regardless of its names, since
ancient times the Mediterranean region has been familiar with the arum, *aron*, *qulkas*
or *kolkasia*. As well as in Egypt, the plant was cultivated and consumed in Palestine,
Greece, Cyprus [6] and Italy (Candolle 1885, Burkill 1938). The oldest collection of Roman
recipes, Apicius, lists taro as an ingredient, a vegetable. The recipes in Apicius reflect
the cuisine of a wider group of urban cosmopolitans, thus indicating that the Romans
were familiar with taro and considered it suitable for the palate of many financially
secure Romans (Flower & Rosenbaum 1958; Grocock & Grainger 2006, 8, 338).

Arum officinarum? Aro di Egitto? Colocasia esculenta var. *antiquorum?*

Since ancient times taro has been referred to by a great variety of names. During the Middle Ages the definition *Arum officinarum* became popular.[7] In the centuries that followed, naturalists, e.g. Pierre Belon (1517–1564), Prosper Alpin (1553–1617), and Charles de L'Ecluse (1526–1609), better known as Carolus Clusius, start to observe plants in their natural habitat. The nineteenth-century French-Swiss botanist Alphonse de Candolle (*Origin of Cultivated Plants*, 73–75) was the first to start documenting the geographic origins of cultivated plants. Candolle made an inventory of the existing taro descriptions by the ancients, and notes that the sixteenth-century Venetian physician and botanist Prosper Alpin actually saw taro and speaks of it at length as *culcas*. In the same century the Flemish doctor and botanist Clusius observed the cultivation of taro in Portugal; according to Clusius it was called *alcoleaz* and was an introduction from Africa. The eighteenth-century French botanist Alire Raffeneau Delile (1778–1850) refers to taro as *qolkas* and *koulkas*, and the Italian botanist Filippo Parlatore (1816–1877) writes that the *aro di Egitto* has become naturalized in several parts of southern Italy (Candolle 1885, 74, Raffeneau Delile 1803). Since Candolle the nomenclature for aroids or taro genera and species has become less obscure.[8] In general taro, as used in antiquity and Apicius, is referred to as L. *Colocasia esculenta* var. *antiquorum*.

The origin of New World taro

New World taro (L. *Xanthosoma* spp.) originates in tropical America, where the bulk of the diet of many (Pre-Columbian) Amerindian cultures consisted of starchy roots and tubers such as cassava, sweet potato and taro. Starchy root crops leave traces of pollen sparingly, and as the edible portions of the plant are soft these are rarely preserved in (sub)tropical arid climates. Even so archaeological records indicate that the Amerindians domesticated and cultivated New World taro around 5,000 BC (Bray 2000, Piperno & Holst 2004). Within the archaeological context, the exact cradle of origin of New World taro remains obscure, but its domestication and dispersal throughout the Americas took place long before Columbus arrived.

At the time of the Columbian Exchange New World taro was among the most important crop plants, cultivated from Brazil to southern Mexico, in Bolivia and the greater Caribbean. Indigenous farming communities commonly planted root crops in a *conuco*. Depending on its size and locality, this home garden was located in or at the edges of tropical forests. Apart from vegetables such as peppers, beans and corn, the *conuco* provided for starchy root crops such as sweet potatoes, cassava and New World taro (Esquivel & Hammer 1992, Buerkert A. 2009, Vaneker 2007).

The first eyewitness account of roots and tubers in the Amerindian diet is from Michel de Cuneo. In 1492 the aristocratic shipmate of Columbus writes of 'roots like turnips, very big and in many shapes, absolutely white, of which they make bread… This root is their main food, they eat it raw and cooked.' De Cuneo indicates that the local diet consisted of several roots and tubers, and because of the comparison with bread (an important colonial food), these were a staple food in the greater Caribbean region (Parry 1979, 71, 271). In the Old World roots and tubers like turnips were part of the staple diet of the commoner. When the Americas were discovered, the European élite considered these to be inferior foods as a staple of the diet; the explorers were accustomed to eat wheat (Vaneker 2009, 217–218).

Como himoconas

The explorers were neither familiar with, nor particularly interested in tropical roots and tubers. Nevertheless after the discovery of the Americas, both in the Caribbean basin and on the South American continent, several eyewitness accounts refer to the cultivation and consumption of New World taro. Fernández de Oviedo (1478–1557) notes that it is cultivated in Santo Domingo (Hispaniola), in his chronicles *Historia general y natural de las Indias*. The Spaniard describes 'Yautía, by others called diahutía, is one of the most common plants Amerindians cultivate with great care and diligence'[9] (Moscoso 1999). In *Historia de Cartagena* the Spanish chronicler Juan de Castellanos (1522–1606) describes a 1534 expedition in Colombia and how two explorers observe the 'very large yucca tillage and other estimable roots, like potato, pepper and "himoconas"'[10] (Calderón 1999, 10).

As well as Oviedo and De Castellanos, writers such as Bartolomé de las Casas (1484–1566), Georg Marcgrave (1610–1648) and Henri François Pittier (1857–1950) refer to New World taro.[11] Overall historical accounts from many parts of the New World use different names for the plant and its parts, e.g. *ymocona* (Puerto Rico), *yautia* (Hispaniola), *ocumo* (Venezuela), *taioba* (Brasil), *quisquisque* (Costa Rica), *macal* (Guatamala), *oto* (Panama) and *rascadera* (Colombia). The great variety of words in indigenous languages and dialects indicates that taro was widely spread in the New World.[12] Several indigenous Amerindian communities use(d) the same terms for different plants. The Maya, for instance, commonly employed the word *macal* both for true yam (L. *Dioscorea*) and New World taro (Bronson 1966). In the nineteenth century the Austrian botanist Heinrich Wilhelm Schott (1794–1865) classified around 900 New World taro species. Since the 1950s the research efforts of botanists have resulted in the identification of around 104 genera and some 3500 species within the family *Araceae*.[13] Therefore the botanical nomenclature (in Latin) is consistent, but at present both in the Southern and Western Hemispheres a great variety of common and uncommon names in various languages and dialects are used to describe New World taro. As a result, and in contrast to major staples such as wheat, rice and potatoes, for which overlapping names exist, the nomenclature for taro still tends to be confusing.[14] Although at present widely dispersed throughout the Americas, and a staple for millions, so far taro and its multiple uses have received scant research attention (Reyes Castro 2006, Vaneker 2009).

Tuber migration

In the aftermath of the discovery of the Americas a vast array of indigenous American vegetables and fruits spread across the globe. In the Old World the arrival and acceptance of the New World potato, maize and tomato were of great economical and nutritional significance. In the same period, and as a result of the colonization of Latin America and the African diaspora, both Asian and New World taro migrated unnoticed from the Americas to (west) Africa and vice versa (Sokolov 1972). In the following centuries and today, New World taro is successfully cultivated in countries such as Cameroon, Ghana, Kenya, Nigeria and the USA. Both *Colocasia* and *Xanthosoma* taro became prominent staples in the diets of numerous indigenous African communities that use starchy tubers and roots – alone or in combination – for the preparation of traditional dishes such as *fufu*, a porridge or pudding (Osseo-Asare 2002). In many parts of western and central Africa New World taro, better known as (new) cocoyam is meanwhile perceived as a traditional food.[15] At present both types of taro are cultivated in approximately 70 (sub-) tropical countries, and consumed by around 400–600 million people in and from the tropics (Vaneker 2009).

In the second part of the twentieth century de-colonization and the growing demand for low-skilled labour resulted in a massive global migration from the South to the North. Migrants are known to have a strong appetite for the foods, ingredients and dishes familiar to them from their countries and cultures of origin (Van Otterloo 1990, Kloosterman & Rath 2003). Together with the migrants from Africa, Latin America and the greater Caribbean basin (and previously unnoticed), taro arrived in the Western world, where nowadays it is available in so-called ethnic stores and on tropical markets, where it is sold fresh, frozen and as flour (Vaneker 2007).[16]

357

Propagation and cultivation

Once taro is cultivated the plant does not naturally produce viable seeds. It is therefore predominantly vegetatively propagated (Bown 2000, 248). The introduction of taro into areas such as the Pacific, Africa, Hawaii and Europe required human intervention. As well as cassava and (sweet) potatoes, today taro remains an important food and crop for people in and from (sub)tropical regions where the tuberous root frequently has special cultural significance and economic value. Although commercially cultivated in fields, most taro cultivars are from very old species, and crop varieties are traditionally and mainly cultivated by small farmers (Bown 2000, Matthews 2004).

'… really, why the hell is anyone eating this thing?'[17]

In Western societies (sub)tropical roots and tubers, for example taro, potato and sweet potato, are staples that are usually eaten cooked, not raw. If uncooked, these roots are hard to digest and sometimes even toxic. All parts of New World taro are edible, indeed, the starchy tuber provides carbohydrates and other valuable nutrients. But raw, these are hard to digest. Taro contains oxalic acid, and the acridity of the leaves and corms is known to cause irritation of the skin and mouth. High levels or prolonged consumption of oxalic acid can produce physical side-effects (Bown 2000, Matthews 2004). However, the control of fire enabled humans to cook plant foods so that carbohydrates and proteins were better digested. The incorporation of cooked tubers into the diet allowed humans to expand activities and proliferate further. Human control of fire is considered a turning point in history. It is widely accepted that cooking is around 250,000 years old. New evidence indicates that the human control of fire might have occurred 1.8 million years ago (Wrangham and Conklin-Brittain 2003).

Common and ancient techniques to make roots and tubers digestible and denature toxins are, cooking (e.g. baking, roasting and boiling), drying and fermentation. Fermentation (digestion via enzymes formerly known as ferments) occurs in and outside the human body. Especially in (sub)tropical areas and forests, temperature and (relative) humidity increase the natural fermentation of plants. Since ancient times natural fermentation is known to make fruits and other plant foods suitable for consumption.

Humans employ numerous fermentation techniques to make foods sufficiently digestible or more palatable. With and without the intervention of humans, and similar to cooking, fermentation is known to break down physical barriers such as thick skins. Ferments burst cells open and make the cell content more easily available for digestion and absorption. When ferments modify the physical structure of molecules, such as protein and starches, these become more accessible for enzymatic digestion (fermentation in the body). Similar to cooking, fermentation denatures toxins and/ or digestion-reducing compounds in roots and tubers. Like cooking, most types of fermentation tend to increase the digestibility of starch. Cooking and fermenting softens plant foods and makes them easier to bite and chew They are known to increase the taste, texture or shelf-life of foods. Research also indicates that fermentation might increase the nutrient value of roots and tubers (Sahlin 1999, Wrangham and Conklin-Brittain 2003, Groenewold).[18]

Human evolution and survival are closely connected to yeast and bacteria, and depending on the conditions, fermentation occurs naturally in foods. Fermentation is known to be one of the oldest forms of food preparation and preservation applied by humans. Many existing fermentation techniques predate modern science and the recognition of the existence of micro-organisms e.g. yeast and bacteria. Also nowadays the diets of numerous societies depend on the fermentation of staple foods e.g. rice (wine), wheat (bread and beer) and roots and tubers (*chuño*, *fufu*, *poi*).[19] Indigenous culinary knowledge about fermented roots and tubers foremost is transmitted orally, and only sometimes put into numbers, data, and statistics by scientists (Sahlin 1999, Woolfe 1987, Beuchat 2008, Scott 2008). Unlike Western societies where fermentation is an industrialized and regulated process, many indigenous communities practise fermentation out of necessity and as a household art. Traditional and indigenous knowledge about the fermentation of roots and tubers is scattered and a neglected area of research. Facts can only be inferred from an inventory of existing literature or first-hand observations (Sahlin, 1999, Beuchat 1987, 2008).

	Type	**Ingredient**	**Geography**	**Use(s)**
Burukutu	Liquid	Cassava	Nigeria	Beverage
Casareep, Casripo or Cassiri	Liquid	Cassava	Guyana, Surinam	Cooking Liquid
Chicha	Liquid	Cassava	Guyana	Beverage
Parakari	Liquid	Cassava	Guyana	Beverage
Sarawau	Liquid	Cassava	Guyana	Beverage
Attiéké	Cake	Cassava	Ivory Coast	Staple
Banku	Dough	Cassava	Ghana	Staple
Chichwangue	Paste	Cassava	Congo	Staple
Gari	Wet paste Granules	Cassava	West Africa	Staple
Lafun	Paste, Powder	Cassava	West Africa, Nigeria	Staple
Tapé or Tapé ketala	Soft solid	Cassava	Indonesia	Staple
Chuño blanco	Dry	Potato	Andes, South America	Staple
Tongosh, or Tokosh	Dry	Potato	Andes South America	Staple
Fufu	Paste (porridge) Flour	Yam, Cassava, Taro,(both *Colocasia esculenta, Xanthosoma* spp.)	Central and West Africa	Staple
Sapal		Taro	Papua New Guinea	
Poi	Semi solid, Paste	Taro	Hawaii	Staple and side-dish
Poe Poe, Popoi,	Paste (pudding)	Taro	Tahiti, Rapa, Tonga	

Table 1. Overview of Indigenous Fermented Roots and Tubers.[20]

359

Fufu, foo-foo, foufou, foutou, fu fu

The above overview indicates that, apart from its domestication and cultivation, and despite its acridity, humans have figured out how to ferment taro. West and central Africans commonly use non-indigenous varieties of taro, alone or in combination with yam (L. *Dioscoreaceae*), cassava (L. *Manihot esculenta*) and plantain (L. *Musa x paradisiaca*) for the preparation of *fufu*.[21] Traditionally the preparation of *fufu* involved the pounding and fermenting of tubers and roots, but nowadays the staple food is also prepared from flour, and as such is available throughout the world.

Taro, dalo, kalo, talo, tato

From the Indo-Malaysian Peninsula, the accepted region of taro's origin, the plant was probably taken further into the Pacific around 1600 to 1200 BC, when the invention of a new type of canoe permitted long-distance voyages. From western Polynesia (Samoa and Tonga) taro migrated into eastern Polynesia (the Cook, Society, and Marquesas Islands) around 800 to 900 AD (Cho et al. 2007). After Captain Cook observed cultivated taro in Maori plantations in 1769, several eyewitness accounts start making mention of the cultivation and preparation of taro.

> My talo that I planted with my hands,
> Who could guess that it would grow
> To be taken as oil for the anointing?
> My talo from beyond the horizon.
> I shall name it eight points.
> My talo from beyond the horizon.
>
> Edward Tregear 1900[22]

Since 1769, Polynesians are on record cultivating taro and fermenting pounded taro in large pits in the ground. In various Polynesian cultures fermented taro pastes and 'puddings' are recorded to be of great cultural and ceremonial significance (Leach 2008). According to Leach, Polynesian 'puddings' were served to chiefs and important guests, and were an integral part of Polynesian feasts. In west Polynesia grating taro was the technique commonly applied for the preparation of the starchy 'pudding'. For eastern Polynesians the prevalent practice was to pound the taro. In Polynesia there is no generic term for taro, which is also known as *dalo*, *kalo* and *talo*, also no overlapping name exists for the fermented paste or 'pudding' locally also known as *fakakai*, *fai'ai*, *feikai*, *fekei*, *loloi*, *poke*, *po'e*, *poi*, *popoi*, *roroi*, *sua*, *susua*, *tukituki*, *taufolo*, and *vaihalo* (Leach 2008).[23]

All over the region, and as an integral part of Polynesian life, taro is cultivated and fermented. Taro pastes or 'puddings' are not only widespread but of great cultural significance (Leach 2008, Cho et al. 2007). Best known for its love of taro and fermented taro 'pudding' is Hawaii, where the plant and *poi* are 'sacred' and indigenous people believe that taro, locally better known as *kalo*, contains the greatest life-force of all foods. According to Hawaiian mythology *kalo* is also linked with creation. The legend is that taro grew from Hāloa-naka, the first stillborn son of Wākea (Father sky) and Papa (Mother earth). After the burial of Hāloa-naka, and from this union a second child, Hāloa (Everlasting breath) was born. Hawaiians believe themselves to be descendants from Hāloa, and by eating *poi*, not only people are brought together, but also *ohana* (family) relationships are supported and the *aumakua* (ancestors) are appreciated (Krauss 1993, Cho et al. 2007). Ever since Cook established the first contacts, a wealth of alternative and industrialized (Western) foods have arrived in Hawaii. And although science is far from knowing all there is to know about taro and its fermentation, according to many Hawaiians the plant that managed to survive and evolve since the Cretaceous period is superior to man himself.[24]

Acknowledgements

I wish to thank John Cho and Jan Groenewold, Helen Saberi, and Harlan Walker for their insightful comments.

Notes

1   The Han period 206 BC–AD 220; the T'ang period AD 618–907; as in Frederic J. Simoons (1991) *Food in China: a cultural and historical inquiry*. Simoons notes that the Han can be characterized as a period of culinary innovation and the T'ang period by its agricultural innovation.

2. From: An Egyptian Calendar for the Koptic Year 1617 (AD 1900–1901) Corresponding with the Mohammedan Years 1318–1319. http://ia341324.us.archive.org/0/items/cu31924029742693/cu31924029742693.pdf (accessed 23 April 2010). According to the Almanac (first published Egypt 1877) Egyptians traditionally harvest Colocasia taro in January (see p. 15).

3. Indigenous grasses and cereals were domesticated early by the Egyptians, http://www.reshafim.org.il/ad/egypt/botany/cereals.htm (accessed 25 April 2010).

4. Early treatises on plants by Theophrastus and Dioscorides were in part medical studies which articulated folklore combined with observations of the physical plants. http://en.wikipedia.org/wiki/History_of_plant_systematics (accessed 21 April 2010).

5. According to Seidensticker, Herodotus describes two plants growing along the Nile. One Seidensticker describes as having a round root, and identifies as *Colocasia* taro, while the other plant produces something like olive cores in a capsule (Seidensticker 1999, 90: 'Herodot, der früheste Author, führt zwei Pflanzen auf, die am Nil wachsen, deren eine eine runde Wurzel habe und bei der es sich un die *Colocasia* handle, während eine andere in einder Kapsel so etwas wie Olivenkerne hervorbringe').

6. In *The Deipnosophists* Athenaeus notes that in Sikyon there is a temple of Athena Kolokasia (http://www.archive.org/stream/sicyonarchaeologooskal/sicyonarchaeologooskal_djvu.txt, accessed 22 April 2010). The Greek goddess Athena was nicknamed Kolokasia. Shrines to Athena Kolokasia have been excavated in Greece and Cyprus, where at present taro is served as a Cypriot speciality root vegetable.

7. http://www.flowersinisrael.com/Arumpalaestinum_page.htm (accessed 21 April 2010).

8. Most taro research is carried out by botanists. Bown (2000, 24) estimates that annually more than 50 million aroids are sold as houseplants.

9. 'Sobre la yautía, Fernández de Oviedo señaló: 'Yautía, por otros llamada diahutía, es una planta de las más ordinarias que los indios cultivan con mucha diligencia ó especial cuydado.' Translated by the author from *Sociedad y Economia de los taínos*.

10. 'Grandisimas labranzas de yucales y otras raices de ellos estimadas, como batata, ajies, himoconas' translated by the author from http://www.lablaa.org/blaavirtual/historia/putiles2/putil1a.htm (accessed 25 April 2010). *Himoconas* is probably the first written record of a local Latin American name for *Xanthosoma* taro.

11. http://www.lablaa.org/blaavirtual/historia/putiles2/putil1a.htm (accessed 26 April 2010).

12. For an inventory of various ancient Amerindian names in historic accounts for *Xanthosoma spp* in the post-Columbian period see: http://www.lablaa.org/blaavirtual/historia/putiles2/putil1a.htm

13. Botanists refer to taro as *Araceae*, *arum* and *aroids:* http://www.aroid.org/literature/croat/history/efforts_after_1950.php (accessed 28 April 2010).

14. The lack of an overlapping name for taro, amongst others, can be attributed to the fact that taro is mostly consumed where its grown and rarely exported (Bown 2000, 24).

15. Amongst others among the Bakweri people in south-west Cameroon.

16. Based on personal communication and interviews with end-users, and through first-hand observations at markets and in ethnic stores in the Netherlands, Costa Rica and the UK (London) conducted since 2004.

17. Quoted from: 'Toxicity in Humans by Ingestion of *Colocasia esculenta* (Elephant Ear)', a Powerpoint made by Audrey Medina, Barry Sandall and Loucia Jose from the University of New Mexico (Biology 445, May 04, 2007). '*Colocasia esculenta* (Elephant Ear, taro) can cause many toxic effects in humans with potential for serious damge or death. … Taro must be the most delicious dish in the world. Because, really, why the hell is anyone eating this thing? Yummy!' (biology.unm.edu/toolson/biotox/colocasia_esculenta_toxicity.ppt; accessed 28 April 2010).

18. Based on personal communication Feb/March 2010. Jan Groenewold is a physical chemist at Utrecht University (NL) and, as a part of the Cook & Chemist, specialized in the science behind the cooking process.

19. Which are actually corms or cormels, that are also known as modified underground stems.

20. Compiled from Beuchat (2008, Coulin (2006), Gubag (1996), Sahlin (1999), Steinkraus (1995), Woolfe (1987), http://www.airtahiti.aero/news.php?id=264 and http://www.unu.edu/unupress/food/V184e/ch3.htm (accessed April 2010).

21. Osseo-Asare 2002.

22. From Edward Tregear: A song of Savage Islands (Niue) (1900 *JSP*. Volume 9 (No. 4): 234–235. Polynesian Songs and Chants: http:starling.rinet.ru/kozmin/polynesia/niue.php (accessed April 2010).

23. According to Leach (2008) the terms might relate to the processing (to poke, to mix, to pound), to the processing tools or to the preserved (fermented) pastes, such as *poi*.

24. http://www.thepoicompany.com/artman/publish/article_4.php (accessed 30 April 2010).

Bibliography

Bellwood, Peter et al. (eds.) *The Austronasians: Historical and Comparative Perspectives*. Australia, Canberra: ANU E Press, 1995.

Beuchat, Larry R. (ed.) *Food and Beverage Mycology* (second edition). New York: Van Nostrand Reinhold, 1987.

———. 'Indigenous Fermented Foods', in *Biotechnology* (eds. Rehm and Reed), Volume 9 (Second Edition), 2008, 505–559.

Bown, Deni. *Aroids: Plants of the Arum Family* (second edition). Portland, OR: Timber Press, 2000.

Bray, Warwick. 'Ancient Food for Thought', *Nature*. Vol. 406, (20 July 2000), 145–146.

Bronson, B. 'Roots and the Subsistence of the Ancient Maya', *Southwestern Journal of Anthropology* 22, 1966, 251–79.

Buerkert A. and Gebauer J. (eds.) *Agrobiodiversity and genetic erosion. Contributions in Honor of Prof. Dr. Karl Hammer*. Journal of Agriculture and Rural Development in the Tropics and Subtropics, Supplement 92, 2009.

Burkill, I.H. 'The contact of the Portuguese with African food plants which gave words such as 'yam' to European languages', *Proc. Linn. Soc. Bot. London*. 150(2), 1938, 84–95.

Calderón, Jorge Conde. *Espacio, sociedad y conflictos sociales en la Provincia de Cartagena 1740–1815* (Space, society and conflict in the Province of Cartagena 1740–1815). Colombia: Universidad del Atlántico, 1999.

Candolle, Alphonse de. *Origin of Cultivated Plants*. The International Scientific Series. New York: D. Appleton and Company, 1885.

Cho, John, Roy A.Yamakawa and James Hollyer. 'Hawaiian Kalo, Past and Future', *Sustainable Agriculture*, (February 2007), 1–8. (Electronic Document: http://www.ctahr.hawaii.edu/oc/freepubs/pdf/SA-1.pdf retrieved April 2010)

Coulin P, et al. 'Characterisation of the microflora of attiéké, a fermented cassava product, during traditional small-scale preparation', *Int J Food Microbiol*. 106(2), 2006, 131–136.

Esquivel, M. & Hammer, K. 'The Cuban Homegarden 'conuco': a perspective environment for evolution and in situ conservation of plant genetic resources', *Genet. Resour. Crop Evol.*, 39, 1992, 9–22.

Flower, Barbara and Elisabeth Rosenbaum. *The Roman Cookery Book: a critical translation of The art of Cooking by Apicius: for use in the study and kitchen*. London: George G. Harrap & Co. Ltd., 1958.

Grocock, Christopher & Sally Grainger. *Apicius: A Critical Edition with an Introduction and an English Translation of the Latin Recipe Text Apicius*. Totnes, Devon: Prospect Books, 2006.

Gubag R. et al. 'Sapal: a traditional fermented taro [*Colocasia esculenta* (L.) Schott] corm and coconut cream mixture from Papua New Guinea', *Int J Food Microbiol* 28(3), 1996, 361–367.

Henkel, Terry W. 'Parakari, an indigenous fermented beverage using amylolytic *Rhizopus* in Guyana', *Mycologia*. 97(1) 2005, 1–11.

Ivancic, Anton & Vincent Lebot. *The genetics and breeding of taro*. France: Cirad, 2003.

Kloosterman, Robert and Jan Rath (eds.) *Immigration Entrepreneurs: Venturing Abroad in the Age of Globalization*. Oxford/New York: Berg Publishers, 2003.

Krauss, Beatrice. *Plants in Hawaiian Culture*. Honolulu: University of Hawaii Press, 1993.

Leach, Helen. 'Translating the 18th century pudding', in Clark, Geoffrey et al. (eds.) *Islands of Inquiry: Colonisation, Seafaring and the Archaeology of Maritime Landscapes. Papers in Honour of Atholl Anderson*. Terra Australis No. 29. Canberra: ANU E Press, 2008, 381–396. (Electronic Document, Retrieved April 2010: http://epress.anu.edu.au/terra_australis/ta29/pdf/whole_book.pdf)

Matthews, Peter. 'Aroids and the Austronesians', *Tropics*. Vol. 4 (2), issued February 1995, 105–126.

———. 'Genetic Diversity in Taro, and the Preservation of Culinary Knowledge', *Ethnobotany Research & Applications*. 2, 2004, 55–71.

Michell, Roland L.N. *An Egyptian calendar for the Koptic year 1617 (1900–1901 AD) corresponding with the Mohammedan years 1318–1319*. London: Luzac and Co., 1900.

Moscoso, Francisco. *Sociedad y economía de los Taínos* (Society and economy of the Taínos). Puerto Rico,

363

Rio Piedras: Editorial Edil, Inc., 1999.

Osseo-Asare, Fran. '"We Eat First With Our Eyes": On Ghanaian Cuisine', *Gastronomica.* Vol. 2 (1), Winter 2002, 49–57.

Otterloo Van, Anneke H. *Eten en eetlust in Nederland [1840–1990]: een historisch-sociologische studie* (Food and appetite in The Netherlands [1814–1990]: a historical-sociological study). The Netherlands, Amsterdam: Uitgeverij Bert Bakker, 1990.

Piperno, Dolores R. & Irene Holst. 'Crop domestication in the American tropics: Starch grain analyses' in *Encyclopedia of Plant & Crop Science*, ed. by Robert Goodman New York: Marcel Dekker, Inc., 2004, pp. 330–332.

Raffeneau Delile, Alire. 'Observations on the Lotus of Egypt', *The Philosophical Magazine: comprehending the various branches of science, the liberal and fine arts, agriculture, manufactures and commerce.* (1803) Vol. XV: 257–265.

Reyes Castro, Guillermo. 'Studies on cocoyam (*Xanthosoma* spp.) in Nicaragua, with an emphasis on Dasheen Mosaic Virus.' Doctoral thesis. Uppsala: Swedish University of Agricultural Sciences, 2006.

Sahlin, Peter. 'Fermentation as a Method of Food Processing: production of organic acids, pH-development and microbial growth in fermenting cereals.' Licentiate thesis. Lund University: Lund Institute of Technology, 1999.

Scott, Christopher B. *A Primer for the Exercise and Nutrition Sciences: Thermodynamics: Thermodynamics, Bioenergetics, Metabolism.* New York: Humana Press, 2008.

Seidensticker, Peter. *Die Seltsamen Namen all: Studien zur Überlieferung der Planzennamen* (The Rare Names of All: Studies regarding the Transmission of Plantnames). Stuttgart: Franz Steiner Verlag, 1997.

——. *Pflanzennamen: Überlieferung – Forschungsprobleme – Studien* (Plant-names: Transmission – Research problems – Studies). Stuttgart: Franz Steiner Verlag, 1999.

Simoons, Frederick J. *Food in China: a cultural and historical inquiry.* Boca Boca, FL: CRC Press Inc., 1991.

Sokolov, Raymond. 'Monserrat's Secret Gardens', *Natural History Magazine*, April 1992, 72–75.

Steinkraus, Keith H. *Handbook of indigenous fermented foods* (2nd edition revised and expanded). New York: Marcel Dekker, Inc., 1995.

Sullivan, William C. 'Ecology of Fermented Foods', *Human Ecology Review*. Vol 15 (1), 2008, 25–31.

Vaneker, Karin. 'Cooking Pom', *Petits Propos Culinaires 83*. Devon, Totnes: Prospect Books, 2007, 30–48.

——. 'The Pomtajer', in *Vegetables. Proceedings of the Oxford Symposium on Food & Cookery 2008*. Susan R. Friedland, ed., Totnes, Devon: Prospect Books, 2009, 216–224.

Woolfe Jennifer A. *The Potato in the Human Diet.* Cambridge: Cambridge University Press, 1987.

Wrangham, Richard and NancyLou Conklin-Brittain. 'Cooking as a biological trait', *Comparative Biochemistry and Physiology – Part A: Molecular & Integrative Physiology*. Volume 136 (1), 2003, 35–46.

Ancient Jewish Sausages

Susan Weingarten

In this paper I shall be looking at a number of texts dealing with sausages and sausage-makers in antiquity.[1] Most of the texts come from the Jerusalem Talmud (henceforth JT), but one is an inscription from the city of Rome.[2]

Our first text, from late antique Palestine, sounds to a modern ear like the introduction to a funny story, in the incongruity of the setting of its sausage.

> A sausage was found in the synagogue of the city council... R Jeremiah said: Sausage-makers [*siqiyar*] should recognise their own product.[3]

Here in the tractate *Sheqalim* (=shekels), the JT is discussing the question of when finders can be keepers, and when they must make an effort to track down the original owner of the object they found. The rabbis discuss a number of cases, both real and theoretical.

The synagogue setting, incongruous as it might seem to us, may have been less so to an ancient audience, or may have been entirely theoretical. Unfortunately we have no way of knowing what a sausage might have been doing in an ancient Palestinian synagogue. It was forbidden to eat in a synagogue, but presumably this rule had to be made because people did sometimes eat there. It is possible, of course, that they ate in a side-room.[4] And what was the 'synagogue of the council?' The same R Jeremiah is associated with this synagogue in another place, where people are discussing where to pray for rain, but this does not enlighten us further.

The sausage itself, however, may be a little easier to get to grips with. The word used here is *noqaniqa/noqniqa/nuqaniqa* from which is derived the modern Hebrew *naqniq*. This would seem to be derived from the Latin *lucanica*, sausages which were named from the area of Lucania in Italy, and were supposedly brought to Rome by the army.[5] And in fact, one manuscript fragment of the Jerusalem Talmud does preserve the reading *luqaniqa*.[6] Johan Mathiesen, writing some years ago in *PPC*, tracked evidence for variants of this name in Greece, Bulgaria, France, the Basque country, Spain, Majorca, Portugal, the New World and the Philippines.[7] But he did not note the presence of *lucanica* in the ancient Near East around the fourth century CE.[8] We should not be too surprised to find it in Palestine, however, since the Greek form of this sausage, *loukanika*, also turns up in Antioch and Athribis, north and south of Palestine, in the accounts left by the fourth-century tax collector Theophanes who travelled from Egypt to Antioch via Palestine, and back again, and left detailed lists of his purchases.[9] Theophanes bought sausages on no less than six occasions, paying a relatively large sum of money for them, although it is impossible to know whether this was because they were expensive items, or because he simply bought a large quantity.[10]

What were these sausages made of? The talmudic sources, unfortunately, give us little information, nor does Varro add much when he notes that the *lucanica* of his day was made of stuffed intestine. However, there is a recipe in the collection attributed to Apicius:

2.4 Lucanicae

Lucanicae are made in a way similar to the above (ie stuffed into an *intestinum*). Pound pepper, cumin, savory, rue, bay-berry spice and *liquamen*. Add meat which has been thoroughly pounded so that it can then be blended well with the spice-mix. Stir in *liquamen*, whole peppercorns, plenty of fat and pine nuts. Put the meat in the *intestinum*, draw them quite thinly and hang them in the smoke.[11]

We note here the abundance of *liquamen*, which would have provided salt for preservation, and the ample fat, which would protect the pounded meat from bacteria. The well-pounded mixture is inserted into animal intestines and hung up to be smoked.

It is not easy to insert stuffing evenly into intestine cases: modern Internet sites sell machines for doing this for large sums of money.[12] Clearly it required a certain degree of expertise, and each sausage or string of sausages was liable to turn out differently. The ingredients must have varied too. Thus our talmudic source notes that an expert sausage-maker should be able to recognize his own work.

The talmudic sausage-maker is called *siqiyar,* clearly derived from the Latin *insiciarius*, presumably via Greek. *Insicia*, forcemeat or forcemeat balls, was not originally a word for a sausage, but a sausage filling. However, the archive of Theophanes which contains the first recorded occurrence of the Greek *loukanika* for a sausage, also mentions purchases of *eissikiaria*, sausages made by an *eisikiar*.[13] Matthews thinks these terms had become interchangeable, and this would seem to be confirmed by the talmudic source, where the *noqaniqa* is made by a *siqyar*.

The context of the talmudic passage is a list of found objects, with a rabbinical discussion on whether it is possible to identify them or not. Talmudic discussions often present topics in an associative series. The lost objects mentioned in the passage immediately before the sausage are wine-skins swept away by a stream, where the wine merchants are said to be able to recognize their property by their knots. It is possible that it was the association with filled skins which led to the insertion of the passage on the lost sausage here, or maybe the knots, for we shall see in the next source that the process of making sausages also includes tying thread between the sausages.

The work of the sausage-maker is described in more detail in another passage from JT Shabbat 10a. The context is a discussion of work on the Sabbath. Here actions carried out by different workers are identified with the 39 *avot melakhah*, i.e. the original types of work forbidden on the Sabbath, exemplified by activities carried out in the course of various everyday tasks. It may therefore be significant that the work of the sausage-maker as described here, immediately follows a description of preparing pounded garlic:

dividing the cloves, husking, pounding etc. The Apicius collection, aimed at the Roman upper classes, rarely uses garlic, and garlic is indeed absent from all its different varieties of forcemeat and sausages, although the whole of Apicius book 2 is devoted to these: 17 recipes, including the *lucanicae* above. This talmudic text, however, may give us a hint that garlic was a more common ingredient of sausages than Apicius would suggest, in ancient as in modern times. Its anti-bacterial qualities would also have contributed to the keeping qualities of the sausage.[14]

The section on sausage-making reads as follows:[15]

> As for the *siqiyar*:
> 1. when he [prepares] the skin coverings by pulling them out, this is 'sifting';
> 2. when he crushes with a *margezaiyah*, this is 'threshing';
> 3. when he pounds in a mortarium this is 'grinding';
> 4. when he adds liquid this is 'kneading;'
> 5. when he puts into the intestine [*enterin*] this is 'building;'
> 6. when he cuts up [the sausage string] with a fibre thread [*gome*], this is 'cutting';
> 7. when he finishes his work this is 'striking with a hammer.'

Let us examine all these actions one by one.

1. when he [prepares] the skin coverings by pulling them out, this is 'sifting';

The first action attributed to the sausage-maker, doing something to skin coverings by pulling them out is compared to the prototypical forbidden work, 'sifting,' an action which separates the wanted product from the unwanted. Our JT text here is clearly corrupt, as the verb describing this action is written as *mekahed*, 'destroys.' One editor has proposed substituting *mevaher*, 'chooses,' as in the parallel passage about the garlic crusher who precedes the sausage-maker.[16] However, I propose substituting *memaheh*, since *mihui* is the technical term used elsewhere, in the Mishnah, to describe the act of squeezing the entrails of the lamb sacrificed on Passover, to extract the unwanted contents.[17] This action separates out the unwanted contents from the wanted intestines, and is thus parallel to sifting. Racheline Seidelman from Alexandria tells me her mother used to do this using the back of a knife. Our sausage-maker, then, begins by squeezing out the dirt from the intestines he wants to fill.

2. when he crushes with a *margezaiya* [?cutting-tool], this is 'threshing';

The verb used here for threshing, beating grain to remove the husks, could also refer to the process of pounding grain until it broke up into grits, just as a cutting tool would cut or pound meat or fat into smaller pieces. The term used for the cutting- or crushing-tool here is interesting: *margezaiya* or *mergeziya*, and it appears nowhere else. The talmudic dictionaries suggest it should really be *megzariya*, from *gazar*, to cut, although it is difficult to see how the letters could have become so unusually mixed up.[18] However, the association of *margezaiya* and sausages raises a further question. Small spiced red sausages called *merguez* are popular today among Jews who come from Tunisia and Algeria, where they are still eaten by the locals under the name of *mirkas*. A recipe for *mirkas* is found in the thirteeenth-century 'Anonymous Andalusian Cookbook' translated by Charles Perry. I cite it here, in spite of the hundreds of years which separate it from the talmudic source, because of several very suggestive similarities, in the preparation methods as well as the name.

Recipe for Mirkâs (Merguez sausage)

It is as nutritious as meatballs (*banâdiq*) and quick to digest, since the pounding ripens it and makes it quick to digest, and it is good nutrition. First get some meat from the leg or shoulder of a lamb and pound it until it becomes like meatballs. Knead it in a bowl, mixing in some oil and some *murri naqî'*, pepper, coriander seed, lavender, and cinnamon. Then add three-quarters as much of fat, which should not be pounded, as it would melt while frying, but chopped up with a knife or beaten on a cutting board. Using the instrument made for stuffing, stuff it in the washed gut, tied with thread to make sausages, small or large. Then fry them with some fresh oil, and when it is done and browned, make a sauce of vinegar and oil and use it while hot... Some cook it in a pot with oil and vinegar, some make it *râhibi* with onion and lots of oil until it is fried and browned. It is good whichever of these methods you use.[19]

Mirkas or *mirqas* comes from a root r-k-z/s, which does not exist in Arabic, so the name must have come from some outside source.[20] Could these sausages be named after the ancient Palestinian sausage-making tool? Could they have come from Palestine with the Jews to al-Andalus, then returned with them, via north Africa, back again to Israel in the twentieth century?

3. when he pounds in a mortarium, this is 'grinding';

Having crushed or chopped with the *margezaiya*, our sausage-maker now pounds in a mortarium. This would appear to parallel the stages of chopping and pounding noted by the Apicius collection in making sausages (*farcimina*): *pulpa concisa et fricta*.[21] It is also interesting to note that the recipe from al-Andalus specifies that the meat is pounded, but the fat is 'chopped up with a knife or beaten on a cutting board.'

Other pounded ingredients would presumably have been spices. We do not know which spices were used in the sausages of ancient Palestine, but of those mentioned in the Apicius collection recipe, we note that talmudic texts mention pepper and cumin quite often in other contexts. Pepper, indeed, is mentioned in the Mishnah as having a special mill for grinding it.[22] It was, however, regarded as a luxury,[23] and we cannot be sure that it would have been included in every sort of sausage, as seems to have been the case in the Apicius collection.[24] Pepper is also mentioned in the recipe from al-Andalus, together with coriander seed (which appears elsewhere in the talmudic sources), and other spices.

4. when he adds liquid this is 'kneading';

We do not know what liquid our sausage-maker added here. However, we saw that the Apicius collection adds *liquamen* to sausage meat. *Liquamen* is the term used in this work for the salty fermented fish-sauce elsewhere called *garum*, and sometimes *muria*, which was an ingredient in so many dishes. The recipe from al-Andalus adds *murri naqi*, and oil. *Murri naqi* was a salty condiment very similar to the Graeco-Roman *liquamen*, but based on cereal, rather than fish.[25] *Muries* appears in the talmudic literature quite often as a very strong salty fish-sauce, and there is also *hilme*, 'made by an expert,' water with salt in a solution strong enough to float an egg.[26] Salt is necessary in fermented or smoked sausages to preserve them from harmful bacterial growth, so that it must have been added in some form. The recipes from Apicius and from al-Andalus would suggest that it may well have been here, as one of these strongly salty liquids.

The *lucanica* from the Apicius collection was hung up to dry out in smoke, which together with the high salt-content would have preserved it. The *mirkas* from al-Andalus, in contrast, even though it too contains salty *murri*, is a fresh sausage, cooked by frying or boiling in a pot. Both these versions of sausage appear to have existed in antiquity, as we see from Athenaeus in third century Graeco-Roman Egypt, contemporary with the Mishnah. Athenaeus talks of *chordai* and *koiliai*, sausages made of stuffed guts which were served in slices, and tripe. These are included by him under the heading of 'meat prepared with water' and he tells us they were sold in Alexandria at boiled meat shops, *hephthopoloi*.[27]

Hundreds of years earlier, in the *c.* 4th BCE, the hero of Aristophanes' play *Knights*, the sausage-seller, is depicted as selling both these *chordai* and *koiliai*, as well as his *allantes*, from *allas*, the general Greek word for sausage. It is possible that our *siqyar* made this sort of sausage too, but the sausage forgotten in the synagogue of our previous source, seems more likely to have been preserved, rather than fresh. There may indeed be a hint that the sausage of JT Shabbat was also a preserved one, since the following passage discusses the treatment of fish preserved in brine on the Sabbath.

5. when he stuffs the intestine [*enterin*] this is 'building';

In this stage our sausage-maker fills his sausage casings with the mixture he has made. Forcemeat could be cooked by itself, or with a fatty covering [*omentum*], but the most usual way was to fill an animal's intestines [Latin *intestinum*; Greek *enteron*], usually a pig's. In Jewish contexts, of course, it would be sheep or goat intestines, and the recipe for *mirkas* specifies lamb. The term *enteron* as a sausage-casing appears in Aristophanes' *Knights* (1183) as part of the equipment of the sausage-seller. It can therefore hardly be doubted that this is the source of the Aramaic *enterin*, used here for the intestines into which the sausage-maker stuffs his product, even though earlier scholars have

369

proposed a derivation of this term from the Greek *antron*, a cave, or (with considerable emendation of the text) from the Latin *farctum*, stuffed.[28] The process of stuffing the pulp into the floppy intestines, using a special instrument in the case of the al-Andalus *mirkas*, creates a new solid mass of sausage, such that the talmudic image here of 'building' seems quite appropriate.

> 6. when he cuts up [*meqate'a*] [the sausage string] with a fibre thread [*gome*], this is 'cutting' [*meḥatekh*];

My translation of this text is at odds with previous scholars of Talmud who show a lack of awareness of the process of sausage-making. The term *gome* has more than one meaning. It has been translated as a knife, presumably a sharpened reed.[29] There have also been attempts at complex textual emendations to turn 'with a reed' *ba-gome*, into *bargimina*, supposedly from the Latin *farcimina*, sausages.[30] I find these readings unconvincing. From the context, it must have something to do with the process of cutting off one sausage from the sausage before it, or from the rest of the intestine. In the recipe for *mirkas* from al-Andalus, after the forcemeat is stuffed into the intestines, the sausages are separated from each other by tying thread between them. And indeed there is another meaning for *gome*: 'a fibre thread.'[31] Thus the talmudic text must mean that each individual sausage is cut off from its neighbours by a tied thread, and the whole string is thus 'cut up' into sections.

370

> 7. when he finishes his work this is like 'striking with a hammer.'

Unfortunately we do not know what the finishing touch to sausage-making was considered to be. Chopping off the string of tied-up sausages from the rest of the intestine? Hanging up in the smoke, as in the Apicius recipe for *lucanicae*? The comparison with work forbidden on the Sabbath does not help here, for 'striking with a hammer' is the generic talmudic term for putting the finishing touches to any work.

The third passage about the sausage-maker from the Jerusalem Talmud is as follows:

> This shows that this sausage-maker [*siqiyar*] is forbidden to work on a festival because he cuts with a fibre thread [*ba-gome*]. [32]

Our previous passage dealt with work forbidden on the Sabbath. This passage deals with work forbidden on a festival, which was somewhat different from actions forbidden on the Sabbath. Once again we are told that cutting off with a thread is not allowed. We should note that the talmudic context here supports our interpretation of 'cutting up *ba-gome*' as 'cutting with a thread.' The passage immediately before our ruling about the sausage-maker deals with how to cut up a lamp wick on a festival, saying that while actual cutting is not allowed, burning it in two with a flame is permitted. The image of cutting a thread is now followed by cutting with a thread.

Finally we have a source which (as far as I know) has not previously been identified as having any connection to sausage-making:

> R. Za'ura asked Qalah from the South, the servant of R Yudan Nesiyah: Does he grind spices [*qonditon*] on a festival? He said to him: Yes, and all kinds of *siqariqon*. [33]

The rabbis disagreed as to whether grinding spices was allowed on a festival. Here we find a rabbi, Za'ura, who does not ask about this directly, but inquires from the servant of the patriarch, R Yudan, whether his master allows them to grind spices for spiced wine, *qonditon*, on a festival. He replies that he allows this, as well as all kinds of 'siqariqon.' The standard talmudic dictionaries do not know what this term means. I would suggest that it refers to the products of a *siqyar, siqarion*, i.e. forcemeat, *isicia* in the Apicius collection. When Theophanes, whom we met above, buys this food in Antioch he calls it *eissikiaria*, i.e. the products of a sausage-maker, *eissikiar*.[34] This minced meat was extremely carefully ground, and it is the question of grinding on a festival which is the rabbinical concern here. The extra letter *qof* [=q] was wrongly inserted into 'siqarion' here making it 'siqariqon,' which has a completely different meaning,[35] and is totally inappropriate in this context.

We turn now to our final Jewish source, quite unlike the talmudic sources, since it is a marble epitaph to a Jew called Alexander, found in the Vigna Randanini catacomb in Rome and now housed in the Ashmolean Museum.

The epitaph runs:

> Alexander,
> bu[t?]ularus de ma
> cello q vixit annis
> xxx anima bona om
> niorum amicus
> dormitio tua inter
> dicaeis
>   [engraved *menorah*]

which may be translated as:

> Alexander, *bu[t?]ularus*, at the Market, who lived for 30 years. A good soul and friend of all. May your sleep be among the righteous.

The inscription has been dated to the third or fourth century CE.[36] It is in mixed Latin and Greek, with weak grammar. The term *dikaioi* is that used in the LXX to translate the Hebrew *tsadiqim*, the righteous. This, together with the *menorah* (seven-branched candelabrum), and its site in a Jewish catacomb makes it clear that Alexander was Jewish.

The first word of the second line is unclear, and has been the subject of discussion. The first letter is almost certainly a 'b,' but the third is less clear. It has been proposed to restore this word as *bucularius*, a cow-herd, *bubularius*, a beef butcher or *butularius/ botularius*, a sausage-maker or hawker of *botuli*, blood puddings. It is unlikely that a mere cowherd would have been given a marble epitaph, so that *bucularius*, which looks most like the inscription as it has survived, is the least likely possibility.

Margaret Williams has discussed the other two possibilities at some length, opting finally for *bubularius*, which she translates as a beef butcher. The only literary reference we have to *bubularii* is in a fourth-century satirical document, the *Testamentum Porcelli*, where '*bubularii*' are to inherit the eponymous Piglet's innards [*intestina*].[37] Williams admits that this reference is problematic, and suggests that having beef butchers receive the intestine of a pig suggest that their products may not have always been what they purported to be. She then cites two inscriptions of clearly well-off *bublarii* [sic] from first-century Rome, and suggests that a *bublarius* may well have been a large-scale dealer in beef products. As for the possibility of *butularius*, she notes that this term appears only once in the literature in a letter of Seneca where it appears to refer to a low-class sausage-maker/huckster. It was most unlikely, she says, that a Jew would be a 'maker of blood puddings... the particular form of pork sausages that *botularii* specialized in making.' She thus concludes that Alexander could not have been a *botularius*, a sausage-maker but must have been a *bublarius*, 'a large-scale dealer in kosher beef,' and possibly also a Jewish ritual slaughterer.

There are problems with some of Williams' arguments. It is true that in the first century *bublarii* appear to have been well-off beef traders, but this may not have been the case by the fourth century. Williams' interpretation of the joke made by the *Testamentum Porcelli* about the beef *bublarii* receiving the pig intestines is somewhat forced. Indeed, her explanation would fit *botularii* sausage-makers, who were about to stuff the intestines, better than her *bublarii*/beef butchers.[38] And certainly in some parts of the empire by the fourth century, pork was more expensive than beef, as we see both from Diocletian's price edict and the accounts of Theophanes.[39] As for *butularii*, once again it is a first-century source which describes them as low hucksters. We do not have evidence for later times. Williams makes much of the original meaning of *botelli* as blood sausages, saying correctly that these would not have been considered kosher by Jews. However, this does not allow for names to have been transferred, but with changed ingredients. Most of the recipes for *isicia*, forcemeat, in the Apicius collection include non-kosher ingredients: squid, prawns, pork liver, etc., but we can presume that the *siqyar* in the Jerusalem Talmud did not use these ingredients. (We saw that in thirteenth-century Andalusia *mirkas* were made of lamb, but by 1505 we find *merkīs alhanzīr*, pork *mirqas* in Spanish sources.)

Nowadays, most modern versions of *lucanica* tend to be made of pork, according to Mathiesen, but Israeli Jewish *naqniqiot* are generally kosher.[40] It would seem most unlikely that the talmudic *nuqaniqa* was made of pork, or there would have been far more fuss about its being found in the synagogue.

In fact, *lucanica* today tend to be made of very good cuts of meat, rather than the gristly bits and sweepings off the butcher's floor that are popularly feared in sausages. Was this the case in antiquity? Certainly, as we have seen, the Apicius collection makes its forcemeat out of top-class ingredients, like oysters. There may well, then, have been meat sausages like this, *charcuterie*, rather than cheap sausages. We note that the *isiciarii* of the *Testamentum Porcelli* are to receive whole pig's legs, prime cuts of meat. Further support for the existence of high-quality sausages may be found in two papyri from late-antique Egypt, The first of these mentions a Christian father and son, Aurelius Petrus and Aurelius Paulus, each described as '*isikiomageiros*' a forcemeat chef or butcher. If the term *mageiros* has the meaning here of 'chef,' rather than 'butcher,' as it does in contemporaneous Jewish sources,[41] then we can assume that Peter and Paul were producing high-quality forcemeat. Further support for this may be found in another papyrus mentioning a guild of *isikiomageiroi*, putting up one of their members for office in Oxyrhynchos, again in Egypt.[42] Someone standing for office must have had a certain amount of property, and would certainly not belong to the low-class sausage hucksters decried by Seneca.

It is difficult to extrapolate from Egypt to Rome, and the relationship between *butularius* and *isikiomageiros* is unclear anywhere. But from the assembled evidence it would seem just possible that by the fourth century the Latin word for sausage-maker, *butularius*, could have been used for the makers of better quality sausages in Rome too. Thus this term may not be out of keeping with the marble plaque on which Alexander's epitaph was inscribed.

And perhaps a final piece of possible evidence tending towards *butularius*, a sausage-maker, rather than *bubularius*, a beef wholesaler, is that of the unusual nature of the plaque itself, albeit not interpreted as such by earlier scholars. If it were not a gravestone, we might even be forgiven for seeing it as part of the sausages and satire tradition, for Alexander's epitaph is inscribed on a round piece of pink marble, looking for all the world like a slice of sausage.

373

Notes

1. I am grateful to Professor Werner Eck, Dr Yuval Shahar, Dr Youval Rotman, Herr Georg Schaeffer and Adam Jackson for their help with this paper. This research was supported by a grant from the German-Israeli Foundation.
2. For an explanation of the talmudic sources, see my paper 'Nuts for the children' in *Nurture: Proceedings of the Oxford Symposium on Food and Cookery 2003*.Bristol, 2004, p 264.
3. JT Sheqalim 50c.
4. Tosefta Megillah ii, 18 and see M.J. Martin 'Communal meals in the late antique synagogue' in W. Mayer, S. Trzcionka *Feast, Fast or Famine, Food and Drink in Byzantium*. Brisbane, 2005, 135–146; A. Oppenheimer '*Havurot* in Jerusalem at the end of the Second Temple period' in id. *Between Rome and Babylon: studies in Jewish leadership and society*. Tübingen, 2005, 102–114.

5. Varro *On the Latin Language,* 5,111.

6. L. Ginzberg *Yerushalmi fragments from the Genizah.* NY, 1909, (repr. Hildesheim 1970) p. 138, l. 26. I am grateful to Aharon Oppenheimer for this reference.

7. J. Mathiesen 'The children of Lucanica', *PPC* 43. 1993, 62–3.

8. It is not noted by F. Frost 'Sausage and meat preservation in antiquity', *Greek Roman and Byzantine Studies* 40, 1999, 241–52 or A. Dalby *Food in the ancient world from A to Z.* London, 2003. Sausages made from small intestines called *maqāniq naqāniq* or *laqāniq* are found in the 9th-century Istanbul MS of al Warraq, ed. N. Nasrallah et al. Leiden, 2007, p. 8.

9. P. Rylands IV, and see Andrew Dalby *Siren Feasts: a history of food and gastronomy in Greece.* 2nd ed. London, 1997, 181; Frost n.4 above.

10. See J. Matthews *The Journey of Theophanes: travel business and daily life in the Roman East.* New Haven/ London, 2006, 149f.

11. Translation: S. Grainger, C. Grocock (eds and trs) *Apicius.* Totnes, 2006, 152–4.

12. http://www.sausagemaker.com/sausagestuffers.aspx accessed 1.12. 2009

13. Matthews (above n. 10) 149.

14. A. Davidson *The Oxford Companion to Food.* 2nd ed. T. Jaine, Oxford, 2006, sv garlic

15. I have inserted numbers for convenient reference.

16. Bar Ilan Responsa project ad loc.

17. MPesahim 6.1

18. Charles Perry writes to me: 'g-z-r > r-g-z is such a violent transposition that I seriously doubt it. G-z-r > g-r-z isn't impossible, but I can't see the r moving all the way to the head of the line.'

19. Cited from http://daviddfriedman.com/Medieval/Cookbooks/Andalusian/andalusian_footnotes. htm#fno accessed 15.12.2009.

20. Charles Perry writes that he has been unable to identify this root.

21. Chopped ground meat in *farcimina: Apicius* 2.5.2; cf. 2.1.5 (*isicia*): *teres diligenter;* 2.3.1(*bulbule esiciatae*): *pulpae bene tunsae et fricatae;* 2.4 (*lucanicae*):*pulpa bene tunsa*

22. M Beitzah 2.8; JT Shabbat 10b.

23. It is mentioned with luxuries from afar such as pheasants and silk in Midrash Ecclesiastes Rabbah 2.2.

24. Almost every forcemeat and sausage recipe in book 2 contains pepper, and the ones which do not can be presumed to have taken it for granted.

25. See on this D. Waines '*Murrī:* the tale of a condiment', *Al-Qanṭara,* vol. 12, 1991, pp. 371–388; S. Weingarten 'Mouldy Bread and Rotten Fish: Delicacies in the Ancient World', *Food and History* 3. 2005, 61–72 esp. n.3.

26. See on this my paper above.

27. Athenaeus *Deipnosophistai* 94c

28. *antron:* see Krauss *Lehnworter; farctum* Jastrow *Dictionary* sv *be-antrin,* which he proposes to read *bargeton = farctum.*

29. Neusner's translation has 'knife' here. I do not know what this is based on.

30. Jastrow *Dictionary* sv *ba-gome*

31. I am grateful to Dr Yuval Shahar for pointing this out to me.

32. JT Beitzah 62c

33. JT Beitzah 60d. Variants: *Übersetzung des Talmud Yerushalmi: Besa – Ei.* Ed. A. Lehnhardt, Tübingen 2001, 51.

34. Matthews (above n.10, p 149).

35. *Siqariqon* is a much-debated term, apparently referring to land sequestration.

36. D. Noy. *Jewish Inscriptions of Western Europe* II *The City of Rome.* Cambridge, 1995.

37. F. Buechler (ed) *Petronii saturae et liber priaporum: adiectae sunt varronis et senecae saturae similesque reliquiae.* Berlin, 1922, 6th ed., 269, gives *bubulariis* here, with a variant *botularius,* but it is not clear to me whether this is a variant manuscript reading or an emendation by Haupt, an early editor.

38. This is how it is taken by D. Daube, *Roman Law*. Edinburgh, 1968.
39. Matthews (above n. 10) 149.
40. K. Stow 'Life and society in the community of Rome in the sixteenth century' *Peamim* 37 (1988) 55–66 esp. 65–66 (in Hebrew) records that Jews in the ghetto in Rome ate *locaniche* (*salcicce*) in 16th–17th centuries (between 1536–1640), according to documents in the Archivio Storico Capitolino.
41. S. Weingarten '*Magiros, nahtom* and women at home: cooks in the Talmud', *Journal of Jewish Studies* 56. 2005, 285–297.
42. P Mich inv 3780; and see P. J. Sijpesteijn 'Five Byzantine papyri from the Michigan collection', *ZPE* 62 (1984) 133–137.

Remembering Lessons from the Past: Fermentation and the Restructuring of Our Food System

Mark Wiest and Bill Schindler

A deep history exists between humans and fermented foods. Our ancestral interaction with fermentation provides a platform from which to explore the lessons that fermentation can offer in the contemporary attempt to create a food system that is ecologically sustainable. The simple interaction between people, food, and the environment during prehistoric fermentation represents a human/environment interaction that is characterized by a simple, subtle, and sustainable manipulation of ecological processes for human benefit.

Prehistorically, these simple manipulations that promoted beneficial forms of microbial activity have played a crucial role in the human diet as a tool for detoxification, increasing nutrient bioavailability, preservation, and enhancement of taste and organoleptic qualities of food. This interaction between humans and fermented foods continued into historical times and has only recently been lost with the widespread industrialization of food and the proliferation of the Western diet. The connections between people and fermented foods clearly transcend time and space (see, for example, Campbell-Platt 1987) and the rediscovery of the early forms of human/environment interaction embodied in fermented foods have important implications as we seek to understand our own participation in the contemporary industrial food system.

In the most basic sense, fermentation represents a paradigm that works with environmental processes instead of against them. This is a valuable lesson in the contemporary movement to restructure an industrial food system that seeks to remove ecological processes from the food-producing environment through advances in technology and increased dependence on chemicals. Fermentation is just one of many culinary traditions rediscovered by modern cooks seeking to re-engage with their local food-producing environments and that cooking in general is a necessary, yet neglected, element that reinforces links between people and their foods that have been eroded with food industrialization.

Prehistoric roots

While much of human prehistory has been framed as a conflict in which human ancestors struggled to survive in hostile environments, a more accurate portrayal of the human/environmental relationship may be symbiotic whereby our ancestors utilized the simplest of technologies to modify their environments for mutually beneficial purposes. Fermentation, or the transformation of substances by bacteria, yeasts, and other micro-organisms, is an ecological process that occurs all around us, all the time and would have played a key role in the ancient relationship between our human ancestors and the environment. Some authors have argued that fermented foods have been a part of our diet since humans first appeared on earth (Steinkraus 1994: 259) and even go as far as to identify fermentation as the 'oldest form of biotechnology' (Cook 1994: 309). While direct evidence for a hominin/fermentation association is lacking from the Miocene and Pliocene epochs, our primate ancestors most certainly consumed foods that had fermented naturally. The drunken-monkey hypothesis (Stephens and Dudley 2004) suggests that mammals may actually intentionally 'seek out' fermented foods – a practice that clearly has very ancient roots and suggests a long-standing relationship between our ancestors and fermentation.

We may even imagine the earliest intentional fermentation technology beginning around 5 million years ago. Mitochondrial DNA evidence suggests that it is during this time that the ancestral line eventually resulting in modern-day humans broke away from that branch leading to modern-day chimpanzees. Shortly thereafter, a variety of Australopithecines appeared and recent paleodietary reconstruction suggests that they began to supplement their herbivorous and frugivorous diets with underground storage organs (hereafter USOs) (Wrangham 2009). It is thought that these energy-rich roots, tubers, and corms provided the extra nutrients and energy required to promote encephalization. However, many wild USOs worldwide require detoxification prior to consumption. Ethnographic, archaeological, and experimental evidence identify several methods to detoxify USOs, depending on the particular toxin, including slicing and dehydrating, cooking for extended periods of time, fermentation, and geophagic supplementation (Johns & Kubo 1988; Messner & Schindler 2010). The production of stone tools does not appear in the archaeological record until *Homo habilis* began crafting them 2.5 million years ago, prohibiting early mechanical detoxification methods such as slicing, grating, or grinding. The earliest date for controlled use of fire appears 2 million years ago, and although varying degrees of an association with fire may be much earlier, the ability to detoxify USOs through cooking was prohibited through much of early hominin history (Burton 2009). Animals and humans have been documented intentionally consuming 'earth' primarily in the forms of clay, a practice that acts to buffer and sometimes chemically bind with toxins allowing them to pass safely through the consumer's digestive tract (Johns 1986; Johns & Duquette 1991). While this practice is technologically simple and very easily could have been practised by Australopithecines millions of years ago, if USOs began to comprise a regular and large portion of the Australopithecine diet, and a significant percentage of the resource was toxic, then a more systematic and reliable system may have been implemented.

Intentional fermentation may have served this purpose. Fermentation has been known to detoxify a variety of plants (Steinkraus 1994: 266) destroying, reducing, and/

377

or deactivating phytates, tannins, cyanogenic glycosides, oxalates, saponins, lectins, and enzyme inhibitors (Reddy and Pierson 1994; Johns and Kubo 1988). Fermentation of USOs could certainly have been accomplished through the simplest of technologies including simply placing the extracted tubers in a reducing environment such as a marsh and extracting them weeks later. This practice has been documented for Huron maize-processing in New York. Tooker (1991: 69–70) reported that,

> To make *leindohy*, or stinking corn, the [Huron] women put a large number of ears of corn, not dry and ripe, into the mud of a pool of stagnant water for 2 or 3 months. Then it was taken out and cooked ... for important feasts. ... the Indians sucked it and licked their fingers as they handled these ears, as if it were sugarcane.

This was certainly less labor-intensive than other food-processing technologies such as nixtamalization, which utilizes lime to increase the bioavailability of nutrients. If a fermented USO on the Pliocene savanna smelled or tasted anything like fermented corn from Holocene marsh in New York, then the relationship between Australopithecines and their food-producing environment was transformed to permit a new foul-smelling item with a unique taste and texture to be included in the category of 'food'.

378

This simple process would have produced an entire new context within which these hominins viewed and interacted with their environment. Instead of opportunistically procuring food and consuming it relatively quickly, the relationship between the acquired food and the environment is extended. Fermentation extends the relationship between the food consumers and the food source for several days or weeks while microbes convert the toxic foods into a safe source of nutrition. The concept of externalization, or processing of food outside of the body for a net energetic gain, has important implications for evolutionary anthropologists exploring the interaction between diet, brain development, and social organization in early hominins (Henneberg 1994). This, potentially the first, example of extrasomatic processing of food could have provided important nutritional additions to our ancestor's diets as well as been a significant link between the microbial world and the more tangible world in which these hominins lived.

Over time this simple food-processing technology would expand to include other floral and faunal resources available to the hunter and gatherer, including fermentable vegetables, fish, and meat. Approximately 10,000 years ago the Neolithic revolution transformed the relationship between humans and their food. The domestication of plants and animals allowed humans to produce food instead of solely collecting, extracting and hunting for their nourishment. This revolution also introduced brand new fermentable foods into our diets in the form of grains and dairy (Prajapati and Nair 2003). Each dietary milestone in our past intensified the role of fermentation in our diets except the most recent – the move to the industrialized Western diet. For the first time in at least 10,000 years, and perhaps for as long as 5 million years, the modern food system has actually begun to remove nutritious, tasty, storable foods, produced through the simple act of fermentation, from our diets.

Co-operation in the kitchen

The art of fermentation is a contemporary representation of the significant bonds that have existed between fermenters and their environment since our prehistoric origins. As we continue to march farther into an industrialized food system many argue that these connections between people, the food they eat, and the environment from which it comes are being eroded and forgotten (Nabhan 2002), and this dissolution is blamed for a multitude of challenges currently faced by communities seeking to maintain human and ecological health (DeLind 2006).

In today's world, rediscovering the intimate relationship between production, preparation, and consumption inherent in traditional food systems is an important element that adds to the restructuring of our current food system with an eye toward long-term sustainability. Fermentation, along with a suite of other culinary traditions and skills, is being utilized by a growing number of cooks who are seeking to once again make food preparation an important element of daily life (Johnston and Baumann 2010). Fermentation is unique in its ability to connect cooks to their environments at the micro level. This level is encompassed within the traditional category of 'local' so often used in food discourse, but it applies a finer resolution that incorporates the microbial world (Katz 2003). While there is a constant interaction between people, food, and the microbes of local ecologies, this interaction is most often framed in terms of a struggle between people and microbes over what they both consider food (Campbell-Platt 1987). Participating in fermentation projects connects cooks to this microbial world, but instead of being framed as a conflict, this interaction is appreciated as carry-over of the ancient symbiosis explored in the previous section. These intimate connections between fermenters, bacteria, yeasts, and other micro-organisms have some important implications for both human and ecological health.

At their heart, these connections represent a dramatically different approach than the typical 'war on germs' most of us are currently waging in the US (Adler and Interlandi 2007). Instead of all out antibiotic war, home-fermenters engage powerful microbial allies to out-compete harmful bacteria and, in doing so, impart many of the distinctive qualities of our favorite foodstuffs that are often overlooked in discussions of 'local food.' This level of local is recognized by fermenters who are expanding the classic viticultural term *terroir* that encompasses the complete local environment, i.e., soil, climate, topography, of the region in which wine grape varietals are produced. Fermenters are expanding the concept of *terroir* by including local microbiology into the suite of environmental conditions giving rise to particular flavors. In particular, these micro-level connections are being built with foods such as cheese or bread that rely heavily upon the local microbiology of a single region, or even a single cave or corner of a baker's kitchen, to impart the characteristic flavors that distinguish one variety from another (Paxson 2008).

Home-fermenters utilizing wild micro-organisms to populate their food preparations develop an appreciation for this level of 'local' and only by allying themselves with their local microbes can they hope to successfully ferment foods. This method presents an important alternative for cooks in the contemporary US where 'clean' and 'sterile' are often used interchangeably to describe the state of one's home kitchen. In some projects, in which the home-fermenter wishes to inoculate the food with a specific strain of bacteria or yeast, sterility is arguably necessary, but in most cases the beneficial bacteria that ferment foods are hearty strains that will out-compete the other microbes that will inevitably be on the kitchen counter, the crock, or the Mason jar. In nearly all cases it is the remnants of household cleaners that will ruin a fermentation project before it even begins. The barrage of antibiotic soaps, cleaners, wipes, and washes used in the home kitchen represent a marked change in the evolution of human and microbe interaction, and are actually problematic for many fermentations because they kill off beneficial bacteria thereby inhibiting their ability to work for us (Katz 2003). While there have been innumerable benefits arising from the development of antibiotics Pasteur himself insisted, 'It's the microbes that will have the last word' (Katz 2003).

The 'war on germs' within the US is truly a 'Red Queen' phenomenon (Van Valen 1973) in which the evolution of more antibiotic-resistant microbes necessitates the development of more intense antibiotic agents. We are essentially forced to run as fast as we can just to stay in the same place in this relationship with bacteria. Instead, home-fermenters follow an ancestral heuristic by choosing to work in *clean* but not *sterile* kitchens. Reconnecting with beneficial microbes instead of attempting to fight them continues an interaction between humans and microbes that has existed since the time of our earliest ancestors who discovered the difference between the 'rotting' and the 'fermenting.'

Health and environment

The germ warfare that occurs in kitchens also occurs within people themselves. Although there is a growing movement that recognizes the importance of exposure to certain bacteria to promote long-term human health and strong immune systems (von Mutius 2001), the dominant paradigm in the US is still guided by principles that attempt to exclude anything that is not 'human' from our systems – a truly impossible task when confronted with the sheer number of bacteria living within our bodies (Stanton et al. 2003). In much the same fashion as the alliances described above that take place in kitchen, fermenters offer up a different paradigm that seeks to promote populations of beneficial bacteria by the consumption of fermented foods.

Introducing populations of certain bacteria to one's system is increasingly recognized as providing benefits ranging from bettering immunological health to improving digestive function (Farnworth 2003). Fermented foods can be seen to promote health, and more importantly, they act as a vehicle that connects people to the functioning of their own bodies. As the current nutrition transition (Caballero and Popkin 2002) continues to take hold in the US and the consumption of highly processed carbohydrates and fats steadily increases, fermentation's ability to connect people back to dietary and nutritional aspects of health promotion is a valuable asset. In an era of increased chronic disease and epidemic obesity, with dietary recommendations meant to stem all of these, consuming fermented foods is not just another diet fad – it is an interaction between people, their food, and microbial environments that has existed for thousands of years. The vast geographical and temporal range of fermented food speaks to the importance of this long-standing interaction between people and 'living' foods.

While fermented foods are still produced at the industrial level, these foods typically require pasteurization to ensure standard qualities and meet food-production safety requirements. Oftentimes, traditional fermented foods such as the ubiquitous pickle or traditional ketchups (see, for example, Smith 1996), have switched from a lacto-fermentation preservation process to one based on pasteurized vinegar or sugar. The industrial production of these foods is made easier by avoiding any manipulation of beneficial bacteria with an approach that destroys any and all living elements of the product. However, this focus on sterility and pasteurization also destroys the benefits for human health that are typically associated with live foods (Stanton et al. 2003). Fermentation at the household level is truly the only scale at which the quality control that is necessary to ensure successful fermentation can be synthesized with the benefits of living foods. This situation has some striking similarities to current issues in agriculture and the scaling-up and commoditization of organics. As the organic sector continues to grow and we see single corporations controlling production on 40,000 acres and shipping arugula packed into little plastic containers by migrant workers, we must begin to question the degree that these companies are still adhering to the commitments to human and ecological health on which the organic movement was founded (Salatin 2007, Pollan 2006, Guthman 2004).

The symbiosis represented in the fermenter's allegiance with certain microbes reflects a larger scale symbiosis that has existed between people and food production since people first began to manipulate their food-producing environments. The widespread disappearance of traditional agro-ecological practices from large and small farms alike is comparable to the continuation of the 'war on germs' within the US. The concepts embodied within agro-ecology, permaculture, and traditional cropping systems represent a symbiosis between farmers and their food-producing environments that has been tested by time. As farming becomes increasingly chemically dependent, traditional strategies such as natural soil amendments and crop rotation for pest control become less important. Although this chemical agriculture has certainly increased yields in the agricultural revolution of the past 50–60 years, farmers are beginning to take note of the disappearance of topsoil, the susceptibility of crops to different and stronger pests, not to mention the dramatic fluctuations in prices they are paid for their crops (Jackson 1985). Farmers in the US currently face another prime example of a 'Red Queen' phenomenon in which they need to work as hard as they can, develop stronger pesticides, apply more chemical fertilizers, and till more acres all to just barely get by on a year-to-year basis. This system cannot sustain itself forever. A solution, much like the discussion above about utilizing beneficial microbes for our own health, lies in rediscovering the symbiosis inherent in traditional human/environment interaction. We believe many of these lessons can be learned from fermentation.

Conclusion

The time-tested methods of fermentation teach many important lessons that will be necessary as we recreate a food system that utilizes ecological principles to our advantage instead of continuing a futile fight against them. Our current food system separates people's health, the food they eat, and the environment from which it comes into distinct categories. Fermentation offers up a different paradigm that stresses the interconnections between these categories, with food being an essential element that links people with the environment. The future strength of these connections depends not just on *consumers* but on *cooks* who understand and support their local ecologies by actively seeking out quality ingredients, abiding by seasonal availabilities as they plan meals, and who are willing to pay the true cost of unsubsidized products from producers who are willing to internalize costs that are typically externalized to the detriment of human and ecological health. The long-term viability of these types of producer-consumer interactions depends on a more direct and tangible relationship than what is currently being demonstrated with the wide scale commoditization of food (DeLind 2000).

The viability of the current food movement in the US relies on more than just health-conscious consumers who eat organic frozen chicken nuggets as they tune into the *Food Network*. Cooking needs to be more than entertainment that we tune into in the evening and food needs to be more than simply something to eat when we are hungry (Pollan 2009). Looking back to prehistory, it was not always as easy as running to the grocery store, and as the unsustainable nature of our current system is further revealed, it is apparent that it will not always be this easy. Fermentation reconnects people to a time-tested form of human-food interaction that can be used as a powerful form of resistance to the production, processing, marketing, and distribution of foodstuffs by a few multinational corporations, which continue to pose serious threats to agrobiodiversity, traditional agricultural livelihoods, and human and ecological health. Fermentation along with rediscovered interest in offal, wholegrains, 'nose-to-tail' eating, and other 'exotic' foodstuffs from around the world synthesizes local connectivity with a cosmopolitan appreciation of food (Johnston and Baumann 2010). Fermentation is a vehicle that permeates these local food systems and instills an appreciation of food that extends well beyond local food traditions. Instead of building walls around our communities it is much more productive to think about the ways in which we can use globalization to our benefit. As we acknowledge other cuisines we are participating in global communities, but at the same time rejecting the cultural commoditization of global food systems, relying instead on a synthesis of local ingredients with global recipes. In bridging these divides between the local and the global, the past and the present, fermenters are able to glean the benefits of global connectivity and use this knowledge to rebuild local food systems, which were themselves built on cultural exchange and environmental connections that have existed for millennia.

References

Adler, Jerry and Jeneen Interlandi. 'Caution: Killing Germs May Be Hazardous to Your Health', *Newsweek*, 27 October 2007: http://www.newsweek.com/id/57368/page/1, accessed April 1, 2010.

Burton, Frances. *Fire: The Spark that Ignited Human Evolution*. New Mexico: University of New Mexico Press, 2009.

Caballero, Benjamin and Barry Popkin, eds. *The Nutrition Transition: Diet and Disease in the Developing World*. Boston: Academic Press, 2002.

Campbell-Platt, Geoffrey. *Fermented Foods of the World: A Dictionary and Guide*. Boston: Butterworths, 1987.

Cook, P. E. 'Fermented foods as biotechnological resources', *Food Research International*, 27(3): 1994, 309–16.

DeLind, Laura B. 'Transforming Organic Agriculture into Industrial Organic Products: Reconsidering National Organic Standards', *Human Organization* 59(2), 2000, 198–208.

____. 'Of Bodies, Place, and Culture: Re-Situating Local Food', *Journal of Agricultural and Environmental Ethics* 19, 2006, 121–46.

Farnworth, Edward R, ed. *Handbook of Fermented Functional Foods*. New York: CRC Press, 2003.

Guthman, Julie. *Agrarian Dreams: The Paradox of Organic Farming in California*. Berkeley: University of California Press, 2004.

Henneberg, Maciej. Comment on 'The Expensive Tissue Hypothesis: The Brain and Digestive System in Human and Primate Evolution', Leslie C. Aiello and Peter Wheeler, *Current Anthropology* 36(2), 1994, 199–220.

Jackson, Wes. *New Roots for Agriculture*. Lincoln: University of Nebraska Press, 1985.

Johns, Timothy. 'Detoxification function of geophagy and domestication of the potato', *Journal of Chemical Ecology* 12(3), 1986, 635–46.

—— & Isao Kubo. 'A Survey of Traditional Methods Employed for the Detoxification of Plant Foods', *Journal of Ethnobiology* 8(1), 1988, 81–129.

—— & Martin Duquette. 'Detoxification and mineral supplementation as functions of geophagy', *American Journal of Clinical Nutrition* 53, 1991, 448–56.

Johnston, Josée and Shyon Baumann. *Foodies: Democracy and Distinction in the Gourmet Foodscape*. New York: Routledge, 2010.

Katz, Sandor Ellix. *Wild Fermentation: The Flavor, Nutrition, and Craft of Live-Culture Foods*. White River Junction, Vermont: Chelsea Green Publishing Company, 2003.

____. *The Revolution Will Not Be Microwaved: Inside America's Underground Food Movements*. White River Junction, Vermont: Chelsea Green Publishing Company, 2006.

Messner, Timothy C. & Bill Schindler. 'Plant Processing Strategies and their Effect Upon Starch Grain Survival in Rendering Arrow Arum (*Peltandra virginica*) (L.) Kunth, Araceae Edible', *Journal of Archaeological Science* 37(2), 2010, 328–36.

Nabhan, Gary. *Coming Home to Eat: The Pleasures and Politics of Local Foods*. New York: Norton, 2002.

Paxson, Heather. 'Post-Pasteurian Cultures: The Microbiopolitics of Raw-Milk Cheese in the United States', *Cultural Anthropology* 23(1), 2008, 15–47.

Pollan, Michael. *The Omnivore's Dilemma: A Natural History of Four Meals*. New York: Penguin Press, 2006.

——. 'Out of the Kitchen, Onto the Couch', *The New York Times Magazine*, 29 July 2009.

Prajapati, Jashbhai B. and Baboo M. Nair. 'The History of Fermented Foods', *Handbook of Fermented Functional Foods*, Edward R. Farnworth (ed.) New York: CRC Press, 2003, 1–27.

Reddy, N.R. and M.D. Pierson. 'Reduction in antinutritional and toxic components in plant foods by fermentation', *Food Research International* 27(3), 1994, 281–90.

Salatin, Joel. *Everything I Want to Do Is Illegal: War Stories from the Local Food Front*. Swoope, Virginia: Polyface Press, 2007.

Smith, Andrew F. *Pure Ketchup: A History of America's National Condiment With Recipes*. Columbia: University of South Carolina Press, 1996.

Stanton, Catherine, Colette Desmond, Mairead Coakley, J. Kevin Collins, Gerald Fitzgerald, and R. Paul Ross, 'Challenges Facing Development of Probiotic-Containing Functional Foods', *Handbook of Fermented Functional Foods*, Edward R. Farnworth (ed.) New York: CRC Press, 2003, 27–59.

Steinkraus, Keith. 'Nutritional Significance of Fermented Foods' *Food Research International* 27(3), 1994, 259–67.

Stephens, Dustin & Robert Dudley. 'The drunken monkey hypothesis: the study of fruit-eating animals could lead to an evolutionary understanding of human alcohol abuse', *Natural History*, December 2004.

Tooker, Elisabeth. *An Ethnography of the Huron Indians, 1615–1649*. New York: Syracuse University Press, 1991.

Van Valen, Leigh. 'A new evolutionary law', *Evolutionary Theory* 1, 1973, 1–30.

von Mutius, Erika. 'The Increase in Asthma Can Be Ascribed to Cleanliness', *American Journal of Respiratory and Critical Care Medicine* 164(7), 2001, 1106–07.

Wrangham, Richard. *Catching Fire: How Cooking Made Us Human*. New York: Basic Books, 2009.

Smoked and Mirrored in the Foods of Fantasyland

Shana Worthen

Smoked foods provide a useful means of insight into the assumptions made by modern fantasy novelists; this is because smoked foods are more likely to be used under more selective circumstances than almost any other category of food preparation in fantasy novels.[1] As a result, it is thus clear that authors use smoking by itself as a preservative technique, for example, when, pragmatically, it should be combined with another form of preservation to achieve the kind of implied edible longevity.

Fantasy literature from the mid-to-late twentieth century usually describes worlds which reflect our own in some way, whether accurately or otherwise. In discussions of food in particular, fantasy novels most clearly show their real-world sources of inspiration. For example, boiling, baking, grilling, simmering, and frying are all performed by all sizes of households and in a wide variety of cultures with fantasy worlds. In contrast, as will be argued, smoked foods tend to be primarily used as the sustenance of travelers; or of resourceful households, often of extremes of richness or poverty. Additionally, meat is almost always 'smoked meat' rather than a particular species or cut; authors are much more likely to mention species when referring to fish.

In the following discussion, I have focused on examples of smoked food found in alternate worlds, instead of food introduced to indicate a real-world specific place. Instead, I am interested in the way smoked food is used, the means by which it is used for world-building. World-building, the 'creation of an imaginary world...especially for use as a setting in science fiction or fantasy stories', evokes and labels a world which is not the one we know, even if it may be indebted to it.[2]

The default world-building for commercial fantasy novels is based on the medievalesque. The food within these novels is designed to sound plausible for that period, and historically distant enough to feel 'other' to the modern reader. As a consequence, bread is the most widely-eaten food in them, good for grand feasts and modest meals, whether the characters are traveling or have access to a full kitchen. Stew, rather than bread, is the best-known of the foods in fantasy novels, thanks to the way its overuse and culinary abuse was highlighted in Diana Wynne Jones' influential, satirical guidebook, *The Tough Guide to Fantasyland*. Its ubiquitous presence leads to such striking declarations as this piece of advice for would-be fantasy novelists: 'Life, even medieval life, does not consist of stew alone.'[3]

Medieval cuisine is not, however, the only one which has helped to shape uses of food in the genre. Most fantasy novels are not historically-researched ones with fantastical elements, so much as they are set in a pseudo-medieval world more shaped by previous genre novels than by a particular historical time and place. Indeed, contemporary culinary resources have played at least as much a rôle in shaping food in fantasy novels as has older historical food.

Consider, for example, how increasing mentions of smoked food maps on to rising interest in food as a subject in its own right more generally. There was a decline in household-help in the late nineteenth and early twentieth centuries in western Europe and North America, the world's hotbeds of speculative fiction.[4] This initially gradual decline was caused, in part, by the development of the iron stove. This, combined with rising literacy rates which increased the rate of cookbook use and publication, led to an increase in the number of people both cooking and able to write about aspects of food over the course of the twentieth century.

Another feature of food in fantasy literature is the way it may reflect how technological innovations have altered authors' understandings of foods. From a culinary perspective, refrigeration and the microwave have opened up new means for food efficiency for authors, particularly women, whose writing-time is infringed on by the tasks of daily life.[5] The recipe which prolific author Mercedes Lackey provided for a collection of recipes by science fiction and fantasy authors, entitled simply 'Food', begins with '1. Go to freezer', continues with '5. Put food in microwave' and concludes with '8. Eat'. (As she and her partner concisely note in their contribution's introduction, 'We don't cook much.')[6] Not all authors imply they are so culinarily illiterate, but, at the same time, an author whose primary food preparation technique is the microwave brings different default assumptions to their created world than do authors who love to cook. More specifically, their experience of cooking may not reflect that of the pseudo-historical period they are recreating, such as the cooking of the Middle Ages. Modern households are more likely to store smoked food in the refrigerator than hang it from the rafters.

Within the fictional worlds of fantasy novels, then, there are primarily two types of people who have or make use of smoked foods: travelers; and people who need large or regular supplies of preserved foods, whether because they live in an isolated location or because they run a large household whose preservation patterns are tied to seasonally dependent produce. These two categories are related, firstly because smoking is a preservative, and secondly because it is, by definition, an odiferous one. Homes which smoke foods are often implied to be frugal ones, or ones with inadequate access to regular supplies of meat.

In some cases, an author will describe the infrastructure necessary for large-scale smoking on a well-off estate. In *The Spirit Ring* (Lois McMaster Bujold), there is a smoke-house to provide smoked sausages flavored with apple wood for a large household.[7] Other authors, such as David Eddings in *The Pawn of Prophecy* and Barbara Hambly in *Dragonstar*, also use the presence of a smoke-house to indicate the large scale of a household.[8] Even more impressively, Philip Pullman includes an entire Smokemarket in *The Golden Compass*, the first volume of His Dark Materials series, a structure which, encountered at night in mist, is more the smell of oak-smoked fish than it is a visible building.[9]

As a plot device, smoked meats and fish are useful for hungry travelers in search of food in the dark of night as they can be sensed by means other than sight. It is the smell of smoked meat which lures the starving traveler across a stone storehouse she has broken into in the dark of night in Morgan Howell's *Clan Daughter*.[10] As with Pullman's Smokemarket, it is implied that the distinctive choices of woods with which the foods were smoked gives them olfactory labels, food identified by scent, and distinguished from other variants of objects which might be smoke-suffused.

The smells of homes and businesses are markers of cleanliness and status in fantasy worlds: a home small enough to smell of smoke is implicitly an inadequately-ventilated one. (Larger households can afford separate, dedicated smoke-houses and storage.) It does not matter if it smells of smoke because of a flue which is not drawing effectively, or if there is a collection of smoked, preserved meats. Consider, for example, the home of the three witches in Neil Gaiman's *Stardust*. With the exception of a magic mirror, everything in it is coated in an 'oily grime'. The smoke of the food is textually indistinguishable from the smoke of the fire: 'Smoked meat and sausages hung from the rafters, along with a wizened crocodile carcass. A peat fire burned smokily in the large fireplace against one wall, and the smoke trickled out of the chimney far above.'[11] Everything about the house, including its occupants, are smoke-covered, older than they look, but well preserved. The meats in this scene work as both comestibles and as symbols. Robin Hobbs makes similar use of descriptive interchangeability in *Assassin's Quest*: 'Inside the hut, a driftwood fire burned in the hearth. Most but not of the smoke was going up the chimney. ... Smoked hams and sides hung low from the rafters.'

387

Preservation, specifically, is the reason for travelers to consume and transport smoked foods, as in *The Wizard of Earthsea* (Ursula Le Guin), in which two sailors, at sea for far longer than expected, survive for much of it on 'a few scraps of smoked meat'.[12] In Tad Williams' novel, *The Dragonbone Chair*, a protagonist scrounging in desperation for food turns up 'smoked, dried meat wrapped in a rough cloth'.[13] Dried, smoked meat too is what one restless man chews 'half-heartedly, as if he were too tired to sit down and eat properly' in Marion Zimmer Bradley's Darkover novel, *Thendara House*.[14]

Meats and fish can be smoked for transportation as a bulk good in their own right. In Anne McCaffrey's *Dragonsong*, a sea-based smallholding sends 'their tithe of sea produce, salted, pickled, or smoked' to the community of dragons and their riders to which they are beholden.[15] The contrast between salting, pickling, and smoking, when the three are regularly combined to lengthen a food's longevity may be literary abbreviation – or it may encode the assumptions of an author who grew up with refrigeration, and thus assumes that smoking alone may be sufficient for preservation purposes.

In the modern world, smoking is used primarily as a flavoring agent, rather than as a preservative.[16] This is in part because wood smoke has carcinogenic elements, and in part because the diversification of preservation methods from the nineteenth century onwards, particularly the advent of refrigeration and flash-freezing, has reduced the need for this particular one. Yet the wide variety of ways in which all sorts of foods, from fruits to flour, can be smoked is hardly ever reflected in the mainstream default settings of fantasy. This weakness is often a generic literary one: if a creative dish, such as cod with smoked lettuce cream, sounds improbable to the author, it may sound inconceivable to the reader. As the saying goes, truth is stranger than fiction.[17]

Here is the extent of creative uses of smoking foods in fiction that I have found. In Tanith Lee's *Piratica*, shipboard officers are encountered, eating smoked cheese with their roast meat.[18] Their decadence is reinforced by a sideboard of cake; but the fact that this is a decadence is already alienating for the protagonists. The high-class strangers indulge in foods strange to the point-of-view characters. Status too is implied in the smoked goose on which guests dine on while aboard a lavish, brocade-curtained barge in *Swordspoint*, a more obscure meat as these texts go, designed to provoke mild surprise in the reader's imagination.[19] Smoked cheese, along with smoked meats, designed to feed a large household throughout the winter, also appears in *Dragonstar*; but these are, so far, the only two mentions of smoked cheese I have found.

Descriptions of food in fantasy novels are very rarely so specific as these which specify a meat in order to emphasize its relative rarity. More usually, authors will not say what kind of meat was smoked. This is a deliberate vagueness on the part of the author, the balance between the details of world-building and the distraction of too much information. Too many made-up words used to indicate otherness ('smoked smeerp'), and the text becomes unreadable.

Among scholars and fans of speculative fiction, the 'smeerp' is the classic example of an excess of neologisms. James Blish, author and critic, is credited with coining this word as a theoretical example, in order to mock authors who relabel familiar species without giving them any other form of otherness, such as calling a rabbit a smeerp.[20] The term is useful as a label for a common textual problem.

The major alternative, however, is to sketch out a world with words which sound as generic as possible. This has led, in English-language fantasy to a strong preference for food words from Old English such as 'meat', 'drink', and 'bread'; or which, like 'spice,' have been used in English for hundreds of years. These are the words which are least specific to the English reader because they encompass so many alternatives. Readers can evoke their own fantastical edibles by means of whatever associations they happen to have with these neutral nouns. It is the difference between describing an extruded carbohydrate paste as 'pasta' and calling it a 'noodle'. It might be both, but each word brings with it different cultural assumptions. In English, 'curry' is not a generic synonym for 'stew'; it is a subset or relative, associated with particular other countries.

As a result of this preference for non-committal but evocative English-language food preparations, fantastical food tends to be named in nouns, with adjectives and verbs remaining recognizably English. Thus McCaffrey's fictional packtails are smoked in preservation for later baking or boiling, while fishermen in Torvaldsland, on Gor (from the series of the same name by John Norman), trade away 'barrels of smoked, dried parsit fish'.[21] The reader does not need to know what the parsit's distinguishing features are in order to comprehend its function in the narrative. Like the packtail, it is a fish, locally abundant, and well-suited to preservation by smoking in combination with other preserving and later reconstituting techniques. Its role can be comprehended because the reader knows what the methods of preparation are, associating it with other things for which those methods are more familiarly used. It is a judicious way of evoking alienness with an unknown fish, while not needing to go into monotonous detail to explain how speciation or the barrels or choice of wood for smoking differs from those on our own planet. Such details, however fascinating to someone attempting to unpick the food history of fictional words, are sensibly sacrificed on the altar of readability.

That packtails and parsits are mentioned by species is more typical of fish – as they are – than it is of meats when it comes to smoked foods. Some fish are fantastical, such as the 'vast, silvery smoked fish' in a fairy-like land which proves, improbably, on asking, to be a minnow.[22] Mercedes Lackey refers to 'smoked sturgeon', while Hobbs, who mentions many generic smoked fish, uses smoked salmon in one book and, exotically, smoked candlefish in another.[23] Gaiman's *Neverwhere* includes smoked herring in the world beneath London, while Brian Jacques uses it as a feast for a tyrant in a castle under siege.[24] Pullman's Smokemarket encompasses 'smoked herring and mackerel and haddock' with their 'pleasant reek'.[25] The nineteenth-century English innovation, the kipper, also appears in fantasy literature, among other places in *Harry Potter and the Half-Blood Prince*, where it is typical of a broader diet of old-school British cuisine.[26] They are implicit too in the 'smoked fish' on the breakfast menu, along with the black pudding, in Pratchett's *Wyrd Sisters*.[27]

389

As for meat, generic descriptions of 'smoked meat' may usually be the order of the day, but occasionally authors are more specific. Smoked sausages are a popular casual snack in a number of fantasy works, including *Equal Rites* (Terry Pratchett), *Fool's Fate* (Robin Hobbs), and *Ptolemy's Gate* (Jonathan Stroud).[28] In another of Hobbs' works, they are journey foods, made from haragars, swine-like animals herded by nomads.[29]

It is worth noting where smoked foods are absent. There were none listed in at least half of the books and series I examined in the course of this project, unlike the far-more-frequent stew. They were notably absent too from the cookbooks designed as accompaniments to fictional series, such as *Nanny Ogg's Cookbook* or the recipes in *The Dragonlover's Companion to Pern*. These volumes, whose recipes are usually usable and tested, can provide useful context for how the author conceptualizes briefly-mentioned food within a popular series. This absence is not necessarily a particular prejudice against or ignorance of smoked foods among authors of speculative fiction, so much as it is a reflection of the conservative approach to food which is generally found in fiction, and the limited vocabulary usually used to describe it. Deep-frying and fermented foods are rarely mentioned either. As Brian Stableford, scholar of speculative fiction, observed of the historical advent of refrigeration, freeze-drying techniques, irradiation, and cling film, 'as with so many other life-transforming technologies, this sequence of development was almost invisible in history and literature'.[30]

Modern technological innovation may be only occasionally reflected in constructed fantasy worlds, but that does not mean that the food their authors write is not predicated on them. Few of the fictional smoked foods I have mentioned have been provided with an explicit method of preservation which would help them last beyond smoking's limited effects. This may be literary simplification, or it may reflect a lack of authorial experience of smoked foods. The lack of variety in the foods which are fictively smoked reflects not only the merits of smoking on fat in particular, but a disconnect between creative modern culinary experimentation and the conservatism of most fictional food. Regardless, it is certainly clear that most uses of smoked foods in fantasy literature are by travelers, whether desperate or well-provisioned; or are for showing off the resourcefulness and organizational planning of a household, whether out of smoke-suffused poverty or neglect, or out of planning for large, well-off estates.

Smoked food, like any other, is a tool for an author, an element of world-building and characterization. It is not clear if it is realistic to generalize beyond the usual uses I have documented, part of accrued genre conventions, to understand how the process is conceptualized by larger segments of the societies in which they live. Yet, through smoked food's cumulative uses across a wide variety of authorial choices, patterns in their collective assumptions about it become clear. Smoking is above all thought of as a method of preservation, specifically for meat and fish (often named by species), and only secondarily as a flavoring agent.

Notes

1. My thanks to Kristina Buhrman, Debbie Gascoyne, Liz Gloyn, Gill Othen, Gillian Polack, Jakob Whitfield and the attendees of the Oxford Symposium on Food and Cookery 2010 for their feedback on this paper.
2. 'world-building' in Prucher, *Brave New Words*, 270.
3. Acker, 'Medieval Food', 130. While Jones identified an element of lazy food writing on the part of mainstream fantasy novelists, the attention paid to her observation has, if anything, exasperated the problem as satirists, including Jones herself, now consciously use stew in their characters' diets.
4. See, for example, Levenstein, *Revolution at the Table*, chapters 1, 2, and 5. There are mythic and fantastical traditions of literature from all over the world, but modern fantasy as a commercial genre in English is centered on these two regions. Most of these texts draw, as Tolkien put it, from the same 'cauldron of story'. Tolkien, *On Fairy-stories*, 44–45.
5. See the recipes written by speculative fiction authors in Anne McCaffrey's two recipe collections, *Serve it Forth* and *Cooking out of this World*.
6. Lackey, 'Food', 106.
7. Bujold, *The Spirit Ring*, 81.
8. Eddings, *Pawn of Prophecy*, 52; Hambly, *Dragonstar*, 30.
9. Pullman, *The Golden Compass [Northern Lights]*, 116.
10. Howell, *Clan Daughter*, 24.
11. Gaiman, *Stardust*, 51.
12. LeGuin, *A Wizard of Earthsea*, 200.
13. Williams, *The Dragonbone Chair*, 254.
14. Bradley, *Thendara House*, 555.
15. McCaffrey, *Dragonsong*, 28.
16. Davidson, 'Smoking foods', 728–9.
17. From the menu at Wild Honey, London.
18. Lee, *Piratica*, 161.
19. Kushner, *Swordspoint*, 54.
20. Blish, *The Issue at Hand*, 92. See also 'Call a Rabbit a Smeerp'.
21. McCaffrey, *Dragonsong*, 43; Norman, *Marauders of Gor*, 29.
22. McKinley, 'The Frogskin Slippers', 190.
23. Lackey, *Fortune's Fool*, 36; Hobbs, *Assassin's Quest*, 124; Hobbs, *Fool's Fate*, 245.
24. Gaiman, *Neverwhere*, 119; Jacques, *Martin the Warrior*, 342.
25. Pullman, *The Golden Compass*, 116.
26. Davidson, 'Smoking foods', 729; Rowling, *Harry Potter and the Half-Blood Prince*, 285.
27. Pratchett, *Wyrd Sisters*, 16.
28. Pratchett, *Equal Rites*, 29; Hobbs, *Fool's Fate*, 779.
29. Hobbs, *Assassin's Quest*, 141.
30. Stableford, 'Food Science', 185.

Bibliography

Acker, Michele. 'Medieval Food' in *The Complete Guide to Writing Fantasy*. Darin Park and Tom Dullemond, eds. Dragon Moon Press, 2002.

Blish, James. *The Issue at Hand: Studies in Contemporary Science Fiction*. Chicago: Advent Publishers, 1964.

Bradley, Marion Zimmer. *Thendara House*. Compiled in The Saga of the Renunciates. New York: Daw Books, 2002 [1983].

Bujold, Lois McMaster. *The Spirit Ring*. Riverdale, NY: Baen Books, 1992.

'Call a Rabbit a Smeerp' on *T.V. Tropes & Idioms*. [Wiki] http://tvtropes.org/pmwiki/pmwiki.php/Main/CallARabbitASmeerp. 25 Apr 2010. Last viewed 30 Apr 2010.

Davidson, Alan. 'Smoking Food' in *The Oxford Companion to Food*. Oxford: Oxford University Press, 1999.

Eddings, David. *Pawn of Prophecy*. New York: Del Rey, 1982.

Gaiman, Neil. *Neverwhere*. New York: HarperCollins, 2003 [1996].

——. *Stardust*. London: Headline Book Publishing, 1999.

Hambly, Barbara. *Dragonstar*. New York: Del Rey, 2002.

Hobbs, Robin. *Assassin's Quest*. New York: Bantam Spectra, 1998 [1997].

——. *Fool's Fate*. New York: Bantam Spectra, 2004.

Howell, Morgan. *Clan Daughter*. New York: Del Rey, 2007.

Jacques, Brian. *Martin the Warrior*. New York: Penguin, 1993.

Jones, Diana Wynne. *The Tough Guide to Fantasyland*. London: Vista, 1996.

Kushner, Ellen. *Swordspoint*. New York: Bantam Spectra, 2003 [1989].

Lackey, Mercedes. 'Food' in *Serve it Forth: Cooking with Anne McCaffrey*. Anne McCaffrey and John Gregory Betancourt, eds. Holicong, PA: The Wildside Press, 1996.

——. *Fortune's Fool*. Luna, 2008.

Lee, Tanith. *Piratica*. London: Hodder Children's Books, 2004 [2003].

Le Guin, Ursula. *A Wizard of Earthsea*. London: Puffin Books, 1971 [1968].

Levenstein, Harvey A. *Revolution at the Table: The Transformation of the American Diet*. Oxford: Oxford University Press, 1988.

McCaffrey, Anne. *Dragonsong*. New York: Aladdin Paperbacks, 2003 [1976].

——, ed. *Cooking out of this World*. Newark, NJ: The Wildside Press, 1992.

McCaffrey, Anne and John Gregory Betancourt, eds. *Serve it Forth: Cooking with Anne McCaffrey*. PA: Wildside Press, 1996.

Mendlesohn, Farah and Edward James. *A Short History of Fantasy*. London: Middlesex University Press, 2009.

Norman, John. *Marauders of Gor*. Tandem, 1978.

Nye, Jody Lynn and Anne McCaffrey. *The Dragonlover's Guide to Pern*. 2nd ed. New York: Del Rey, 1997.

Pierce, Meredith Ann. 'The Frogskin Slippers', in *Waters Luminous and Deep*. New York: Viking, 2004. pp. 179–218.

Pratchett, Terry. *Equal Rites*. London: Gollancz, 1995 [1987].

——. *Wyrd Sisters*. New York: HarperCollins, 2001(a) [1980].

——, Stephen Briggs, Tina Hannan, and Paul Kidby. *Nanny Ogg's Cookbook*. London: Corgi, 2001(b) [1999].

Prucher, Jeff, ed. *Brave New Words: The Oxford Dictionary of Science Fiction*. Oxford: Oxford University Press, 2007.

Pullman, Philip. *The Golden Compass*. Compiled in His Dark Materials. New York: Borzoi, 1995. [Originally published as *Northern Lights*.]

Rowling, J. K. *Harry Potter and the Half-Blood Prince*. Waterville, Maine: Thorndike Press, 2005.

Stableford, Brian. 'Food Science' in *Science Fact and Science Fiction*. New York: Routledge, 2006, pp. 184–7.

Sterling, Bruce. 'Turkey City Lexicon – A Primer for SF Workshops'. 2nd ed. http://www.sfwa.org/2009/06/turkey-city-lexicon-a-primer-for-sf-workshops/. 18 June 2009. Last viewed: 28 Apr 2010.

Tolkien, J.R.R. *On Fairy-stories*. Verlyn Flieger and Douglas A. Anderson, eds. London: HarperCollins, 2008.

Williams, Tad. *The Dragonbone Chair*. New York: Daw Books, 1988.